lonely planet

Egypt

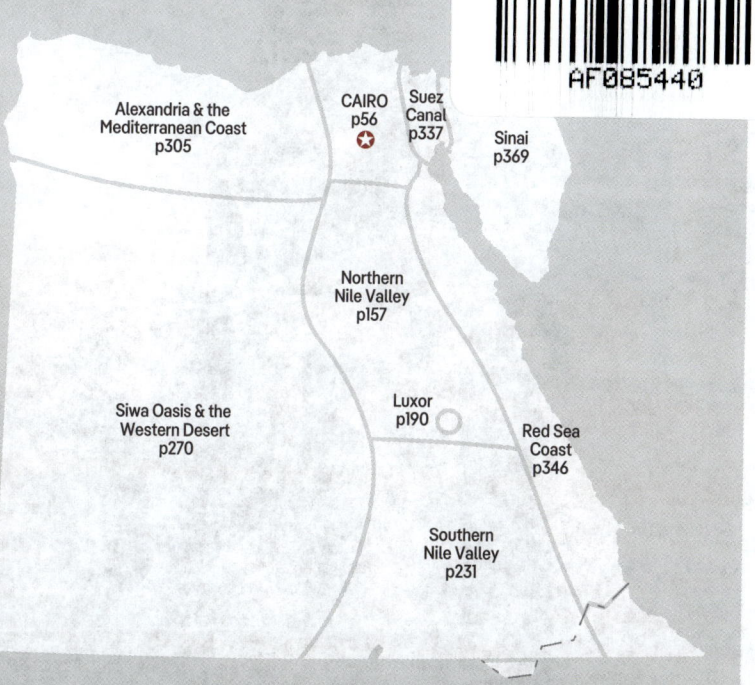

Alexandria & the Mediterranean Coast p305

CAIRO p56

Suez Canal p337

Sinai p369

Northern Nile Valley p157

Siwa Oasis & the Western Desert p270

Luxor p190

Red Sea Coast p346

Southern Nile Valley p231

Sanad Tabbaa, Jessica Buxbaum, Mary Fitzpatrick, Paula Hardy, Anthon Jackson, Lauren Keith, Lama Obeid, Dr Jenny Walker, Nada El Sawy, Shoroq Galal

Statue of Ramses II, Luxor Temple (p202)

CONTENTS

Plan Your Trip

The Journey Begins Here 4
Egypt Map 8
Our Picks 10
Regions & Cities 24
Itineraries 26
When to Go 36
Get Prepared 38
Believe Like an Egyptian 40
The Food Scene 42
How to... Haggle 45
The Outdoors 46
How to...
Dive Responsibly 48
How to... Ride a Camel 49
Action Areas 50
Road Tripping 52

The Guide

Cairo 56
Giza 62
Downtown Cairo 77
Islamic Cairo
& the Citadel 93
Coptic Cairo,
Fustat & Maadi 119
Zamalek & Dokki 125
Garden City
& Roda Island 134
Heliopolis
& New Cairo 139
Beyond Cairo 143

Northern Nile Valley 157
Al Fayoum 162
Minya 168
Beyond Minya 172
Asyut 176
Sohag 179
Beyond Sohag 182
Qena 185

Luxor 190
East Bank 198
Gezira 207
The Valley
of the Kings 211
The Valley
of the Queens 217
West Bank Temples 221
The Wider
Necropolis 225

Southern Nile Valley 231
Luxor to Aswan 236
Aswan 247
Beyond Aswan 258
Lower Nubia
& Lake Nasser 261

**Siwa Oasis
& the Western Desert** 270
Siwa Oasis 278
Beyond
Siwa Oasis 283
Bahariya Oasis 285
Beyond
Bahariya Oasis 288
Farafra Oasis 291
Dakhla Oasis 295
Al Kharga Oasis 300

**Alexandria &
the Mediterranean Coast** 305
Alexandria 310
El Alamein 328
Marsa Matruh 332

Suez Canal 337
Port Said 340
Ismailia 342
Suez 344

Red Sea Coast 346
Hurghada 352
Beyond Hurghada 358
Marsa Alam 361
Beyond Marsa Alam 364

Sinai 369
Sharm El Sheikh 374
Beyond Sharm
El Sheikh 380
Dahab 386
Beyond Dahab 392

Egyptian Museum (p78)

Toolkit

Arriving 406
Getting Around 407
Bus & Train Travel 408
Nile Cruising 410
Money 411
Accommodation 412
Family Travel 413
Health & Safe Travel 414
Food, Drink & Nightlife 416
Responsible Travel 418
Accessible Travel 420
Women Travellers 421
Nuts & Bolts 422
Visas, Embassies
& Tour Guides 423
Language 424
Pharaonic Glossary 426

Storybook

A History of Egypt
in 15 Places 432
Meet the Egyptians 436
The Gastronomy
of Egypt 438
Understanding Egypt
with Adel Emam 440
The People of the Nile 442
Egypt's Environmental
Challenges 446

Diving Sharm El Sheikh (p376)

EGYPT
THE JOURNEY BEGINS HERE

Nowhere else on Earth is quite like **El Horreya** (p87) in Cairo. With ridiculously high ceilings, vintage style and a pervasive smell of cigarette smoke and beer, it has an atmosphere so thick you can taste it. An ever-present roar of conversation from the tables around you crawls into your brain and wreaks havoc on your limbic system. In that way, it's a microcosm of Egypt. Simply put, Egypt has an intense *feel* to it, and that intensity can make a person reevaluate themselves. It's the weight of understanding that some things are simply bigger than you are. Who are you, standing in the hot desert sun and staring at the Great Pyramid, which has outlasted every human civilisation and will almost certainly outlast you? Who will you be afterwards? Egypt will help you find out.

Sanad Tabbaa

sanadtab.net

Sanad is a short story and travel writer specialising in the odd and off-kilter. He wrote the Our Picks, Regions & Cities, Itineraries, When to Go, Get Prepared, Road Tripping, How to Haggle, How to Dive Responsibly, The Outdoors and Action Areas chapters, and several Storybook essays.

My favourite experience is scuba diving the **Tower** (p377) in Sharm El Sheikh. Slowly descending into a sheer canyon pockmarked with coral as lionfish flit about is simply awe-inspiring.

WHO GOES WHERE

Our writers choose the places that, for them, define Egypt.

Dahab (p386) is a wonderland of colourful cafes, bold murals and eccentric wanderers. The moment the waves curled over my toes, I felt tension release. Holidays are usually jam-packed for me, but in Dahab I felt the pull to slow down and recharge.

Jessica Buxbaum
@jess_buxbaum

Jessica is a political journalist covering the Middle East. She wrote the Sinai chapter.

Experiencing **Abu Simbel** (p265) at dawn is unforgettable. Ramses II gazes over the water, swallows swoop through the air and the unparalleled skill of Abu Simbel's builders stands as tribute to a mighty past and hope for the future.

Mary Fitzpatrick
@MaryFitzTravel

Mary is an Africa-based writer who lived for five years in Egypt and returns at every opportunity. She wrote How to Ride a Camel, Southern Nile Valley and Toolkit.

Alexandria (p310) is an endlessly surprising city. Come for a day, or dig in to get to the good stuff, such as Orthodox Easter celebrations, ballet at the Opera House (pictured) or chatting to nostalgic émigrés at the Greek Club.

Paula Hardy
@paulahardy

Paula is a travel journalist who's been reporting from the Maghreb for over 25 years. She wrote Alexandria & the Mediterranean Coast and contributed to the Toolkit and the Pharaonic Glossary.

Only a few hours from Cairo, the unspoilt swathe of the Nile at **Minya** (pictured; p168) feels much more removed. After having its ancient churches, quarries, temples and tombs to yourself all day, rejoin the crowds in town to stroll Minya's pleasant corniche.

Anthon Jackson
@anthonjackson_

Anthon is a Utah-born, Denmark-based writer and photographer and a longtime student of the Middle East. He wrote Northern Nile Valley and Suez Canal.

Halaka Fish Market (p354) embodies the soul of Hurghada, which began as a fishing village in 1905 and developed into a Red Sea resort in the 1980s. The market brings the city's story together: local fishers thrive on the large number of visitors and the visitors depend on the fishers to enjoy the bounty of the sea.

Lama Obeid
@Lama_writes4u

Lama Obeid is a Palestinian writer focusing on gastronomy, travel, culture and politics. She wrote Red Sea Coast and Gastronomy of Egypt.

Descending into **Luxor's west-bank tombs** (p207) near sunset, there's a particular scent of crushed herbs in the air. The outstretched hand of a goddess or a king appears to reach across the divide and pull you under a canopy of stars. Velvet blackness, unknown magic.

Dr Jenny Walker
@jennywalkertravel

Jenny is a higher education consultant and has contributed to over 50 Lonely Planet titles since 2002. She wrote Luxor and Siwa Oasis & the Western Desert.

Near the Great Pyramid of Khufu, my guide, Mosheira, and I followed the site guardian into the **Tomb of Meresankh III** (p65; pictured). Its north wall has a feature not found in any other tomb, a carved row of 10 women, and we two women stood admiring their beauty 4500 years later.

Lauren Keith
@noplacelike_it

Lauren is a travel writer often found somewhere between the Midwest and the Middle East. She wrote the Cairo chapter.

With its large white chalk rock formations protruding from a sea of dunes, the **White Desert** (p293) is a surreal and peaceful place to camp. Watching the sunset and seeing the stars light up the sky is magical.

Nada El Sawy
@Nada_El_Sawy

Nada is an Egyptian-American freelance journalist who writes about travel, arts and culture, and human interest. She has lived in Cairo since July 2020. She updated the Food Scene chapter.

Old Cairo (p119), even if it's not the oldest place in Egypt (or Cairo), is certainly the most magical. There I allow the narrow, winding streets to guide me to places I would never find with a map. I ask the first older person I encounter to tell me a story – any story. And they always do.

Shoroq Galal
@astoryfromhere

Shoroq shares stories about authentic Egypt and Egyptians. She wrote Believe Like an Egyptian and Meet the Egyptians.

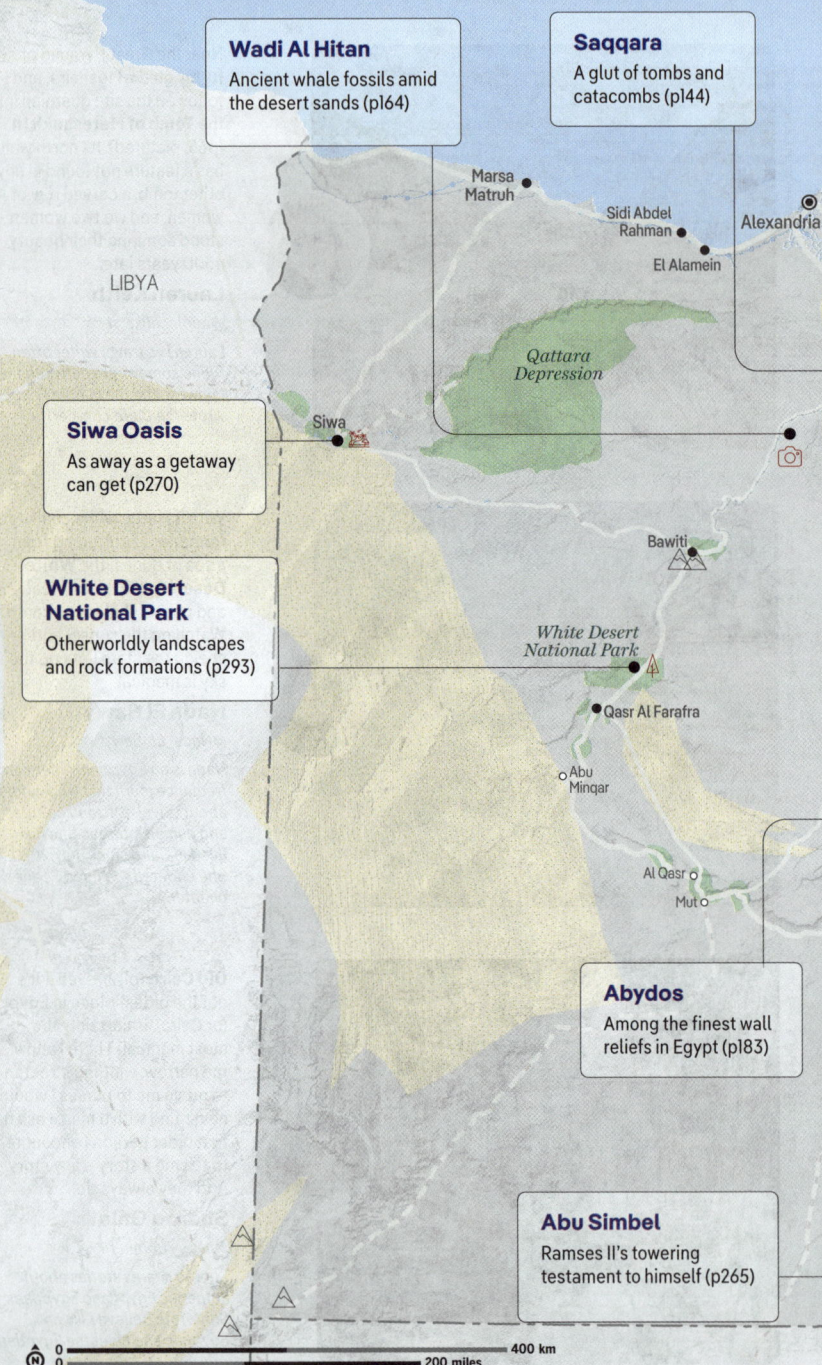

TOMB ARTISTRY

The carved and painted tombs of Egypt's Pharaonic era are one of Egypt's greatest artistic treasures. Within them you are standing amid a gallery of vivid, lustrous colours and intricately detailed scenes that display the mastery of ancient Egypt's artists. Luxor's west bank and Saqqara are home to the country's most fêted tombs, but also seek out sites along the Nile Valley and out in the Western Desert for a more rounded understanding of Pharaonic artistry.

Visiting Times

Major sites get crowded in peak season. Visit in the early morning (Luxor's west bank sites open at 6am) to have them all to yourself.

Baksheesh

Site guardians supplement dire wages with baksheesh (tips) for unlocking tombs and pointing out features. Hoard smaller notes to have them handy when you visit.

Tomb Access

To attend to restoration and preservation, tombs open for public viewing are rotated every few years.

Mortuary Temple of Hatshepsut (p221), Luxor

BEST TOMB ART EXPERIENCES

Experience Old Kingdom artistry at its finest amid the dazzling cache of tombs at ❶ **Saqqara** (p144).

Clamber into the tombs of the ❷ **Valley of the Kings** (p211) in Luxor to marvel at the famed resting places of the New Kingdom pharaohs.

Take in the celebrated wrestler scenes and depictions of daily life inside the tombs of local governors at ❸ **Beni Hasan** (p170).

Admire the most colourful, inventive wall paintings in Egypt in the tombs of the pharaohs' artists at ❹ **Deir Al Medina** (p219) on Luxor's west bank.

Head to the tombs of ❺ **Qarat Al Muzawwaqa** (p297) in Dakhla Oasis for their peculiar meld of Pharaonic and Graeco-Roman styles.

BELOW THE SURFACE

The Red Sea is one of the top dive destinations in the world, so for fans of underwater exploration a trip to Egypt is all about the sights below the surface. Head offshore to venture into an ethereal realm of shipwrecks, shallow reefs studded with coral pinnacles and swarms of colourful, flitting fish.

BEST DIVE EXPERIENCES

Explore the WWII wreck of the ❶ *Thistlegorm* (p385), voted one of the world's top 10 wreck dives.

Plunge into the endless sinkhole known as the ❷ **Blue Hole** (p389), Dahab's most famous dive site.

Dive the multiple sites of ❸ **Ras Mohammed National Park** (p382) in Sinai, home to one of the world's most stunning coral-reef ecosystems.

Spot hammerheads and manta rays at the ❹ **Elphinstone** (p363) site off the Red Sea coast in Egypt's Deep South.

Head out from Sharm to dive the ❺ **Straits of Tiran** (p377) and experience the kaleidoscope of the soft corals on the reefs.

Peak Diving Conditions

Experienced divers often brave summer's scorching on-land heat so they can enjoy the superior underwater visibility and calm seas on offer from July to September.

Dugong Sightings

The dive sites of the Red Sea coast's far south offer the best chances of spotting a member of the region's elusive dugong population.

Accessible Diving

Camel Dive Club in Sharm El Sheikh offers fully accessible dive holidays, with both boats and all areas of the resort fitted for wheelchair users.

Red Monastery (p179)

COPTIC HERITAGE

Tap into the rich history and vibrant modern-day culture of Egyptian Coptic Christianity amid its ancient churches and the remote desert sites where Christian monasticism began. Many of the traditions carried on today by Egypt's native Christians have direct links to the Pharaonic era.

BEST COPTIC MONUMENTS

Gaze at the frescoes and geometric designs that cover the altar of the ❶ **Red Monastery** (p179).

Tour ❷ **St Anthony's Monastery** (p359), where Christianity's monastic traditions began.

Trace the artistic legacy of Coptic Christianity in Egypt in Cairo's ❸ **Coptic Museum** (p120).

Take a monk-led tour of the fortified monasteries of ❹ **Wadi Natrun** (p151).

Visit the ❺ **Church of St Sergius & Bacchus** (p122) in Cairo, believed to be built over a site where the Holy Family sheltered.

Visiting Coptic Sites

Historic churches and monasteries in Egypt are all free to enter (donations are welcome). They are normally open from approximately 7am to sunset.

Appropriate Dress

Shoulders and knees should be covered when entering Coptic churches and monasteries, so refrain from wearing items such as singlets, shorts or short skirts.

DESERT LANDSCAPES

Despite the focus on the fertile ribbon of the Nile Valley, Egypt is mostly desert, and it's here you'll experience the country's most raw and cinematic scenery. The Western Desert's dunes and rock outcrops romp across two thirds of the country, the mountainous spine of the Eastern Desert swaths the interior of the Red Sea coast, and the Sinai Peninsula is a wilderness of craggy peaks that backgrounds the beaches of the South Sinai resorts.

Winter in the Desert

First-time desert visitors may be surprised by how cold it gets on winter nights. Temperatures drop substantially after dark. Bring thermals and decent outer layers.

Desert Logistics

Travelling in the Western Desert requires an experienced local guide and a permit obtained via an Egyptian travel agency at least 21 days before entry.

Diving & Desert Activities

To avoid decompression sickness, you must wait 48 hours after diving before heading into the mountainous desert interiors of the Red Sea coast and Sinai.

White Desert National Park (p293)

PLAN YOUR TRIP

OUR PICKS

BEST DESERT EXPERIENCES

Venture into ❶ **White Desert National Park** (p293) to experience the weirdest arid landscapes Egypt can offer.

Bag the peak of ❷ **Mt Sinai** (Gebel Musa; p399). This is Egypt's most popular hike, and the carpet of peaks that rolls out below you from the summit is worth the sweat to get there.

Take in the dunescape on the edge of ❸ **Siwa Oasis** (p278), then head out to the lonely terrain of craggy cliffs in **El Arag Oasis** (p283).

Dig deeper into the desert mountain area of the ❹ **St Katherine Protectorate** (p399), hiking to the summits of Gebel Katarina and Gebel Abbas Basha.

Explore remnants of Roman emerald mines in the desert basin of ❺ **Wadi Gimal** (p366), surrounded by an amphitheatre of rugged mountains in Egypt's Deep South.

ANCIENT SANCTUARIES

If you want to experience a glimmer of how the ancient Egyptians revered their pantheon of gods, stand amid the mammoth pylons, re-erected obelisks and statuary, and gargantuan forests of columns inside their preserved temples. More than anywhere else in Egypt, these still-mighty buildings, believed to be home to their gods, reveal the pomp and circumstance that lay at the heart of Pharaonic culture and allowed the pharaohs to wield absolute power over their domain.

Photography Tickets

Phone photography is free at temples and most archaeological sites, but if you want to take camera photos you usually have to buy an extra photography ticket.

Best Times to Visit

To see open-air temple complexes such as Karnak in the best light conditions, come in the late afternoon and linger inside until closing time.

Family Savings

Kids under six years old enter free at temples and other historic and archaeological sites in Egypt, and student tickets are half-price.

FROM LEFT: KAMIL MACNIAK/SHUTTERSTOCK, XANNESJACKB4/SHUTTERSTOCK, ANTHON JACKSON/LONELY PLANET

Temple of Seti I, Abydos (p183)

BEST TEMPLE EXPERIENCES

Stroll between the looming giant statues and the Great Hypostyle Hall's colossal columns within the ❶ **Karnak Temple Complex** (p200) on Luxor's east bank.

Witness Pharaonic temple art at its most vibrant and lively amid the restored interior of Dendara's ❷ **Temple of Hathor** (p186) in Qena.

Stand in awe in front of Ramses II's hulking tribute to himself at the ❸ **Temples of Abu Simbel** (p265) on the shore of Lake Nasser, in Egypt's Deep South.

Admire the finest, most delicately carved artistry of the New Kingdom across the walls inside the ❹ **Temple of Seti I** (p183) at Abydos.

Crane your neck to view the battle reliefs adorning the walls of ❺ **Medinat Habu** (p224) on Luxor's west bank.

Siwa Oasis (p278)

RURAL IDYLLS

This is the Egypt the tour-coach crowds don't reach. Watch egrets roosting amid the fronds of date palms along the banks of the Nile, soak up the scenery of patchwork quilts of fields and stroll around mud-brick villages where donkey carts still provide transport. Egypt's rural areas offer a gentler experience of the country.

Retreats amid Tourist Hot Spots

Enjoy a more relaxed atmosphere by staying on the west bank in Luxor and on Elephantine Island in Aswan rather than in the city centres.

Budget Travel

Rural stays don't have to break the bank. Many of Egypt's best tranquil destinations have plenty of budget-friendly and locally run guesthouse options.

BEST RURAL RETREAT EXPERIENCES

Soak up the far-from-anywhere vibes in Egypt's Western Desert outpost of ❶ **Siwa Oasis** (p278).

Enjoy beach life at one of the Bedouin-run camps on the ❷ **Nuweiba–Taba highway** (p392).

Learn about Nubian culture on a walking tour of the mud-brick villages of ❸ **Elephantine Island** (p250).

Take a break from city life in ❹ **Al Fayoum** (p162), with pottery shopping and trips to Wadi Al Hitan.

Chill out with tranquil Nile views at a Nubian-run guesthouse on ❺ **Heissa Island** (p258).

PHARAONIC TREASURES

Trust us: scrambling, bent double, into the corridor network of the pyramids' interiors will be the highlight of your visit to Egypt's fields of monuments. Don't miss brushing up on Pharaonic history in Egypt's premier museums either. Even if you're not a museum person, there are at least two you should make time for.

Kids & Pyramids

For active children who enjoy adventurous activities, clambering within the more difficult interiors at Dahshur (pictured) and Meidum brings Pharaonic history alive.

An Easier Interior

If you're claustrophobic or have mobility issues, the southern entrance to Saqqara's Step Pyramid (pictured) only has one short open-air staircase descent and one wide, walkable tunnel.

Clothing

Pyramid interiors aren't flip-flops and sandals territory. Wear decent shoes, and clothes you can easily move in and don't mind getting dusty.

BEST PYRAMID & MUSEUM EXPERIENCES

Take on the ultimate pyramid challenge by clambering down and then up, up, up inside Dahshur's ❶ **Bent Pyramid** (p143).

Head to Al Fayoum to scramble within the pyramids of ❷ **Meidum** (p167) and ❷ **Al Lahun** (p167).

Take in the galleries devoted to Egypt's Pharaonic history in Giza's dazzling new ❸ **Grand Egyptian Museum** (p72).

Navigate the internal corridor shafts of the most famous pyramid in the world inside Giza's ❹ **Great Pyramid** (p64).

Few museums rival Cairo's ❺ **Egyptian Museum** (p78) for character, wayfinding difficulty or pure coolness.

SLOW JOURNEYS

Egypt may have a mind-boggling array of world-class historic sites, but you don't have to try to see everything on one trip. It's a completely impossible task anyway. Choose to delve deeper into one region instead and you'll experience more of Egypt than any bucket-list tour whizzing between the country's checklist of highlights ever could. Slow the pace right down and journey in more traditional ways for a truly distinctive Egyptian adventure.

Felucca Sailings

Multiday felucca (Egyptian sailing boat; pictured) trips usually begin in Aswan so that you're sailing with the aid of the Nile's strong northward currents.

On Foot

Sinai has some great, quite contained hikes, especially around Nuweiba (pictured), that allow you to enjoy Egypt one step at a time.

Nile Journey Timings

Sandstorms caused by the seasonal *khamsin* wind can ground feluccas from March to May. Have a few days spare in your itinerary to counter any issues.

Feluccas on the Nile at Luxor (p204)

BEST SLOW JOURNEY EXPERIENCES

Experience Nile scenery up close when you cast off from ❶ **Aswan** and set sail on an overnight felucca trip (p242). Or for oodles of old-fashioned style and personalised service, choose a dahabiya (houseboat; p241).

Take the time to explore beyond the Western Desert's famed White Desert highlight and head to Dakhla to discover oasis heritage in ❷ **Al Qasr** (p298).

Journey across Lake Nasser to see the ❸ **Temples of Abu Simbel** (p265) from the water for the most dramatic introduction to the ruins.

Take a felucca trip through ❹ **Luxor** (p204) to experience the city and the surrounding ruins in classic style.

ISLAMIC ARCHITECTURE

The mosques, madrasas (theological colleges) and mausoleums contained in Cairo's core and across Egypt are some of the world's greatest collections of historic Islamic architecture. Just as much of a highlight as Egypt's Pharaonic monuments, the grand buildings of the Islamic empires represent some of the most inspired surviving architecture of the medieval age.

BEST ARCHITECTURE EXPERIENCES

Be inspired by the interior of the ❶ **Mausoleum & Madrasa of Qalawun** (p97), prototype for the grand Mamluk public buildings.

Tour the ❷ **Khanqah & Mausoleum of Farag Ibn Barquq** (p111) in Cairo, and climb the minaret for city vistas.

Marvel at the harmony of design inside the iwans (vaulted halls) of the ❸ **Mosque & Madrasa of Sultan Hassan** (p112).

Admire the restored dome of the ❹ **Mausoleum of Imam Al Shafi'i** (p124), one of Cairo's essential pilgrimage sites.

Head up onto the vast roof of the ❺ **Mosque of Ibn Tulun** (p114), the only surviving remnant of the Tulunid dynasty.

Ar Rashid Merchant Houses

On the Mediterranean coast, the old centre of Ar Rashid (Rosetta), with its Ottoman-era merchant houses harks back to the town's role as a prominent trading port.

Al Quseir's Vernacular Architecture

The Red Sea's historic port of Al Quseir is a squiggle of lanes rimmed with traditional coral-block architecture overlooked by an Ottoman fort (pictured).

Site-Guardian Tours

Many site guardians of historic mosque complexes will offer a tour showing you areas of the complex you would otherwise miss. Please be sure to tip.

Khan El Khalili (p95)

BEST CITY EXPERIENCES

Encounter downtown Cairo's food scene on the ❶ **Bellies En-Route food tour** (p83).

Delve into Cairo's live music scene in ❷ **Zamalek** (p131), a fun activity most visitors miss.

Explore ❸ **Bibliotheca Alexandrina** (p325); a contemporary take on the ancient world's most famous library.

Sneak some shopping in amid the skinny lanes of Cairo's ❹ **Khan El Khalili** (p95).

Stroll through Luxor's ❺ **Avenue of Sphinxes** (p198) or Corniche for a different view of the city.

CITY CULTURE

Dive full tilt into Egypt at its most intense, surprising and chaotic. Whether you like music, art, cafe culture, museums or simply strolls taking in historic architecture, cities such as Cairo and Alexandria are where you take the pulse of Egyptian life. They're rarely easy-going, but could never be considered boring.

Best Time for City Walks

City streets are usually quietest before 11am. Head out for walks early so you don't have to battle to cross the roads.

Smaller Kids

Pavements can be nonexistent or littered with obstacles; challenging for young visitors. The attention they'll likely receive from locals can be too much for shyer children.

REGIONS & CITIES

Find the places that tick all your boxes.

Alexandria & the Mediterranean Coast

A COSMOPOLITAN CITY AND A STUNNING COAST

Alexandria is more ambience than activities. Experience fresh sea breezes along the Corniche and soak up the city's atmosphere of decaying glory. To the east is Ar Rashid (Rosetta) with its well-preserved Ottoman-era old town, while the western coast hosts the beach resorts of Cairo's upper classes and the WWII memorials of El Alamein.

Alexandria & the Mediterranean Coast
p305

Siwa Oasis & the Western Desert

EGYPT'S DESERT HEART

The raw, brutal Western Desert is simply majestic, with towering crescent dunes and otherworldly landscapes. In stark defiance of the barren beauty that surrounds them are date-palm-speckled oases such as Siwa. They abound with water and life in the midst of parched sands, a sight that cannot be described, only experienced.

Siwa Oasis & the Western Desert
p270

Southern Nile Valley

TEMPLES, TRADITIONS AND RIVER LIFE

This is Egypt at its most languid and lush, centred on the sinuous Nile and backdropped by golden dunes. Aswan, the region's only city, is your base for setting off on felucca (sailing boat) trips, exploring Nubian culture and visiting the dramatically located temples of Philae and Abu Simbel.

Luxor

WHERE THE LIVING HONOUR THE DEAD

At this unrivalled open-air museum displaying the glories of ancient Egypt, you can gawp at the rich colours inside the painted tombs of the pharaohs and then stand in awe amid the giant columns and statues of Karnak. Few other places in the world can compete for bringing the ancient world so alive.

Cairo

MOTHER OF THE WORLD

Cairo is where modern Egypt, in all its crowded chaos, collides with the architectural kaleidoscope of successive sets of caliphs and conquerors. The city is bisected by the Nile, with Cairo proper on the east bank. Giza on the west bank hosts the final surviving Ancient Wonder of the World, the Great Pyramid.

Suez Canal

WATERFRONT, GARDEN CITIES AND NATIONAL HERITAGE

An area of no small national pride, the Suez Canal and the cities around it are more than a monument to Egyptian sovereignty. There's much to explore, from the university town of Ismailia with its getaway character and sublime seafood spots to the ancient-yet-new city of Suez to Port Said, christened in conflict and reborn through resilience.

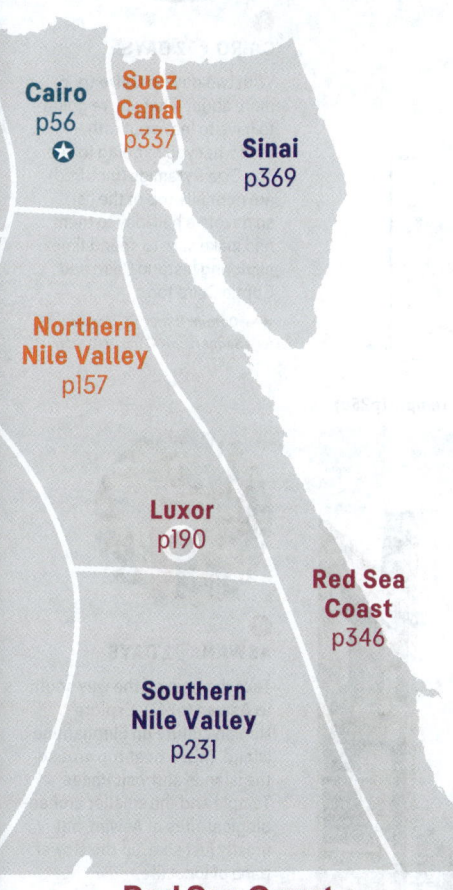

Sinai

SUN, SAND AND A BEDOUIN SOUL

The Sinai Peninsula's mountain core is Egypt's hiking capital, while its coastline, rimmed by some of the world's most famous coral reefs, draws both divers and sun and sand seekers. Dive the sites of Ras Mohammed National Park or head into the heartland centred on Mt Sinai to experience the peninsula's rugged beauty.

Northern Nile Valley

EGYPT'S UNDISCOVERED SWEEP OF THE NILE

Home to both Abydos and Dendara – two of ancient Egypt's best-preserved temples – Middle Egypt brims with Pharaonic-era tombs, historical sites and Coptic monasteries that most visitors miss. Close by, Al Fayoum offers desert experiences on the doorstep of Cairo – fun without the fuss of deep desert travel.

Red Sea Coast

UNDERWATER MAGIC BEYOND THE DESERT FRINGE

More than just a beach-resort hub and winter-sun escape, the Red Sea coast is a major activity centre for families and solo travellers alike. Dive the Deep South sites from Marsa Alam, kitesurf in El Gouna and Hamata, or get way out of the water and explore the Eastern Desert.

ITINERARIES

Classic Nile Journey

Allow: 9 days
Distance: 1130km

This itinerary takes you to big-hitter Nile Valley sights with its most famous tombs, temples and treasures, but it's not all rushing about. You're going to be doing your Southern Nile Valley sightseeing the old-fashioned, back-to-basics way with a felucca (Egyptian sailing boat) adventure.

Philae Temple (p258)

❶ CAIRO ⏱ 2 DAYS

With two days in **Cairo** (p56) it's more about what you're going to have to leave out rather than what you're going to see. The Giza Pyramids (pictured) are normally top of the list, so devote a half-day to them and make sure to spend time exploring historic Cairo and Coptic Cairo too.

🐪 *Detour:* If you can, reserve time for a **Saqqara** (p144) trip. Half a day.

❷ ASWAN ⏱ 2 DAYS

Take the train all the way south to **Aswan** (p247). Explore Nubian culture on Elephantine Island, take a boat trip around the islands and visit Philae Temple and the smaller archaeological sites of Aswan, but mostly just soak up the slower pace of local life.

🐪 *Detour:* Head out on a day trip to **Abu Simbel** (p265) in the Deep South to marvel at Ramses II's triumphant temples. 1 day.

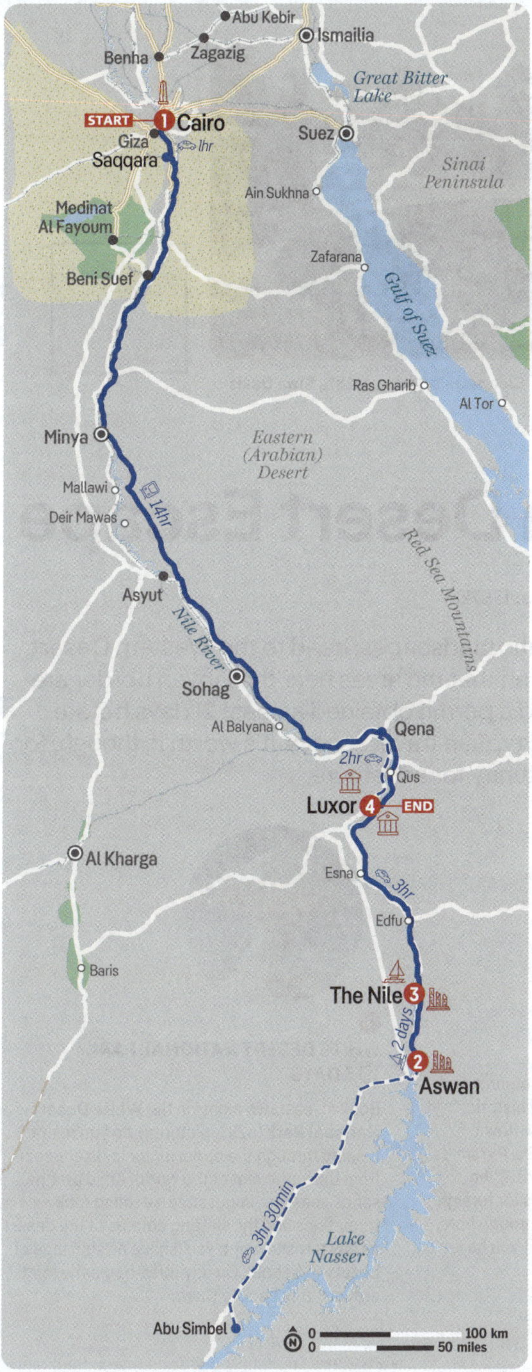

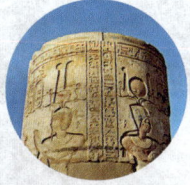

3 THE NILE ⏱ 2 DAYS

Board a felucca and sail north from **Aswan** (p242) on a one-night tour up to **Kom Ombo Temple** (p243; pictured). This is Nile sightseeing at its most slow paced and close up. All felucca trips are customisable, so stop off at a few villages along the way. After visiting Kom Ombo Temple at the end of the trip, transfer to Luxor by car, making a stop at Edfu Temple.

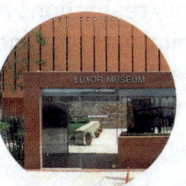

4 LUXOR ⏱ 3 DAYS

With Karnak, Luxor Temple and Luxor Museum (pictured) on one bank of the Nile and the fabled Valley of the Kings on the other, there's much to see in **Luxor** (p190). To avoid overcrowding your brain and to make the most of your trip, budget at least three days.

***Detour:** Hire a private driver for the journey to **Dendara temple** (p186) in Qena. Half a day.*

TOP-BOTTOM: LENSFIELD/SHUTTERSTOCK, D-VISIONS/SHUTTERSTOCK

Cleopatra's Spring (p281), Siwa Oasis

ITINERARIES

Western Desert Escape

Allow: 10 days   **Distance:** 1357km

For Egypt's most dramatic landscapes, head to the Western Desert. Security restrictions mean that the areas near the Libyan border are off limits, and you'll need a permit obtained at least 21 days before entry submitted by an Egyptian travel agency. It's worth it, though, for the unparalleled opportunity for adventure.

① CAIRO ⏱ 2 DAYS

Stroll between the mosques, mausoleums and madrasas (theological colleges) of historic **Cairo** (p56), take a food tour of downtown Cairo and allow a full day for the Giza Pyramids and the Egyptian Museum (pictured). If the Bahariya–Siwa road is still off limits for foreign travellers, you'll be backtracking through here, so add an extra Cairo day mid-trip if you haven't seen everything you want to see.

② WHITE DESERT NATIONAL PARK ⏱ 3 DAYS

Book at least two nights in the **White Desert National Park** (p293; pictured), so you're not rushing through the opportunity to disconnect from the entire rest of the world. Amid orange sands, massive, impossible-seeming rock formations and the shifting colours of the desert as day turns to night, you'll have no shortage of beauty to behold. On day three begin the long, arduous trek back to Cairo.

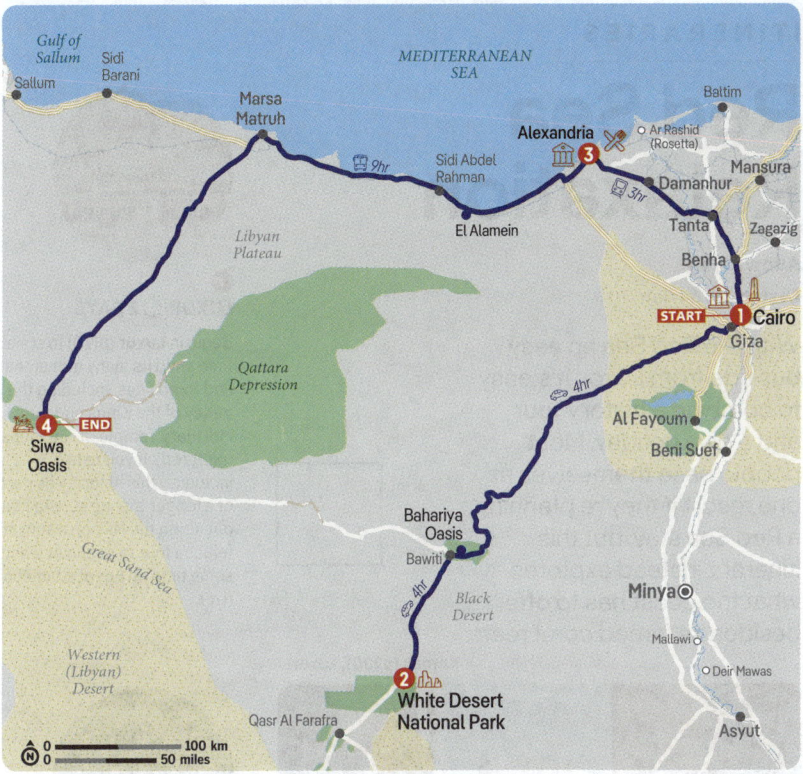

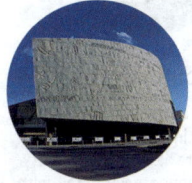

3

ALEXANDRIA 2 DAYS

After you rediscover the concept of a shower, catch the morning train from Cairo to **Alexandria** (p310; three hours). Check out the opulent former palaces of the Mohammed Ali dynasty, stroll across the Corniche and explore the street eats of Anfushi on an Alexandria food tour. If you're feeling literary, check out the Bibliotheca Alexandrina (pictured) too.

Detour: *Take a trip to the WWII memorials at* ***El Alamein*** *(p328). Half a day.*

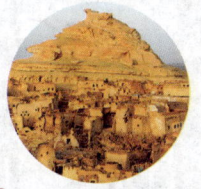

4

SIWA OASIS 3 DAYS

Time slips past easily in **Siwa Oasis** (p278) and many people find it hard to leave. If you have limited time, though, plan to at least stroll up to the top of Siwa town's Fortress of Shali (pictured), visit Aghurmi's sights and go for a dip in Cleopatra's Spring before heading out to the desert that skims the oasis edge to spend an afternoon amid the dunes.

FROM LEFT: SURONIN/SHUTTERSTOCK, NICKOLAYV/SHUTTERSTOCK

ITINERARIES

Red Sea Relaxation

Allow: 7 days
Distance: 647km

With the Red Sea an easy bus ride from Luxor, it's easy to combine a history tour and a dive holiday. Most people base themselves at one resort if they're planning a Red Sea stay, but this itinerary instead explores what the coast has to offer besides its famed coral reefs.

Karnak (p200), Luxor

① LUXOR ⏱ 2 DAYS

Begin in **Luxor** (p190) to spend time amid its many monuments and tomb sites, including the Valley of the Kings and the Mortuary Temple of Hatshepsut (pictured). If you're not including this itinerary as part of a longer trip, be sure to head out along the Nile on a sunset felucca tour to spend at least some time on Egypt's famous river.

② EL GOUNA ⏱ 2 DAYS

It's all about sun, sand and diving in **El Gouna** (p358). If you're a diver, this activity will dominate your stay, with the Straits of Gubal, just to the north, and sites around Hurghada, just to the south, all accessible by boat trip. Other visitors will be happy to take a day off for some beach time.

⤳ *Detour: Add some history with a trip up the coast to **St Anthony's Monastery** (p359). 1 day.*

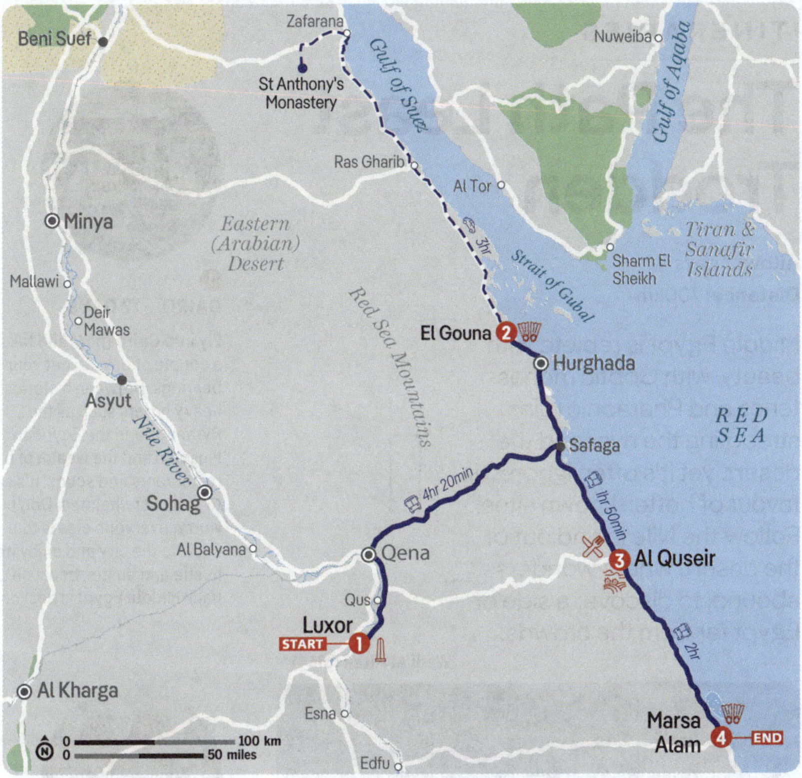

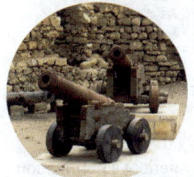

3

AL QUSEIR ⏱ 1 DAY

To see a different side of the coast, turn south to **Al Quseir** (p364) to stroll the old-town lanes of this ancient port that has preserved its coral-block architecture. Explore the little Ottoman-era fort and then eat fresh fish on the waterfront. There are dive sites offshore as well, though Al Quseir is better known as one of the only heritage-focused towns along the coast.

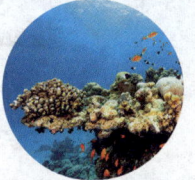

4

MARSA ALAM ⏱ 2 DAYS

Egypt's Deep South hosts a treasure trove of dive sites, less known and therefore less crowded than those to the north and unmissable for scuba enthusiasts. For those who prefer their adventures drier and unhindered by an oxygen tank, **Marsa Alam** (p361) is the access point for the wild desert landscapes of Wadi Gimal in Egypt's Eastern Desert.

TOP-BOTTOM: FEDOR SELIVANOV/SHUTTERSTOCK, JAG_CZ/SHUTTERSTOCK

ITINERARIES

The Path Least Trodden

Allow: 7 days
Distance: 700km

Middle Egypt is replete with beauty, with Coptic monasteries and Pharaonic ruins straddling the river and the desert, yet it's often ignored in favour of better-known sites. Follow the Nile in and out of the desert, where wonders abound, to discover a side of Egypt far from the crowds.

① CAIRO ⏱ 2 DAYS

Fly into **Cairo** (p56) and take a couple of days to get your bearings. Between historical heavy hitters such as the Pyramids and the Egyptian Museum and the wealth of bars, restaurants and souqs, it's easy to feel overwhelmed. Don't worry: everyone else is too. Explore the city and enjoy its hustle and bustle, because laid-back Middle Egypt is beckoning.

② AL FAYOUM ⏱ 2 DAYS

Drive down to **Al Fayoum** (p162), the geographical equivalent of a purification ritual to purge yourself of Cairo's chaos. Make your way to Tunis village, a hub for local handcrafts, particularly pottery (pictured). Use this as your base to discover the fossilised whales at Wadi Al Hitan and the temples at Medinat Madi.

Detour: Consider hiring a 4WD to explore the Qarun Protected Area, home of an ancient **lake** (p165) with a maximum elevation of 46m below sea level. Half a day.

Wadi Al Hitan (p164)

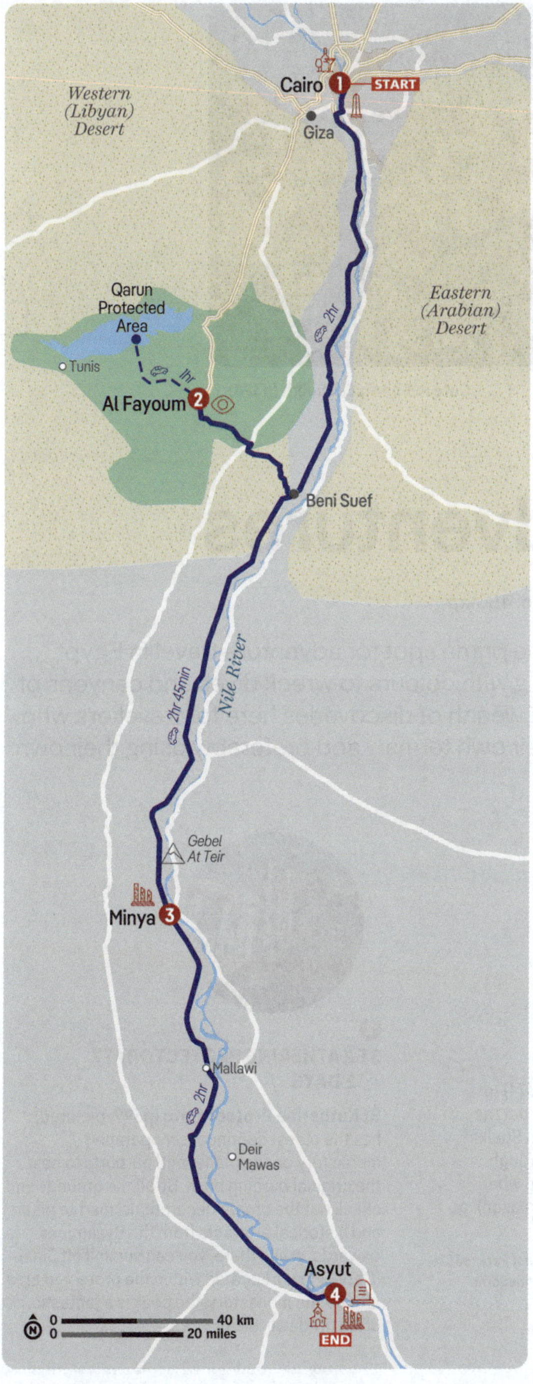

③ MINYA ⏱ 1 DAY

From **Minya** (p168) onwards, intermittent police escorts may be required. Don't be discouraged or afraid: this is a bureaucratic precaution and these laws are both old and born of an excess of caution. Besides, Minya is the perfect base for visits to Gebel At Teir, a Coptic complex nestled on a mountain named for its winged wildlife, and the vast necropolis of Tuna Al Gebel (pictured).

④ ASYUT ⏱ 2 DAYS

Asyut (p176) is the Coptic capital of Egypt, with the sites to prove it. The Holy Family are said to have stayed here for about six months, and this has resulted in no small number of shrines, churches and monasteries in the area, located among Pharaonic ruins such as Deir Dirunka (pictured), Deir Al Muharraq and the ominously named Tombs of Mir.

TOP-BOTTOM: SAMIR_MUSTAFA/SHUTTERSTOCK, LUIS DAFOS/GETTY IMAGES

Cafe in Sharm El Sheikh (p374)

ITINERARIES

Sinai Adventures

Allow: 8 days **Distance:** 450km

The Sinai Peninsula is the prime spot for adventure travel in Egypt. From coral reefs bursting with colours to wreck dives and canyons of muted pastels, there's a wealth of discoveries here for travellers who enjoy exploration on their own terms – and preferably using their own two feet.

1 SHARM EL SHEIKH ⏱ 2 DAYS

Fly directly to **Sharm El Sheikh** (p374) to start your Sinai adventures. Check out the mummified animals at the Sharm El Sheikh Museum or chill out with a jaunt through Sharm's Old Town. Alternatively, do what everyone else does (and for good reason): go snorkelling or scuba diving.

Detour: Visit **Ras Mohammed National Park** (p382) for serious scuba sites including the SS Thistlegorm.

2 ST KATHERINE PROTECTORATE ⏱ 2 DAYS

St Katherine Protectorate (p399; pictured) has the oldest continuously operating monastery on the planet and purports to host the original burning bush. Stroll the grounds and check out the ornate decorations, marble pillars and historical artefacts from the Byzantines onwards. While there, you can summit Mt Sinai (Gebel Musa). Located within the protected area around the monastery, the peak is a fantastic, often predawn, hike.

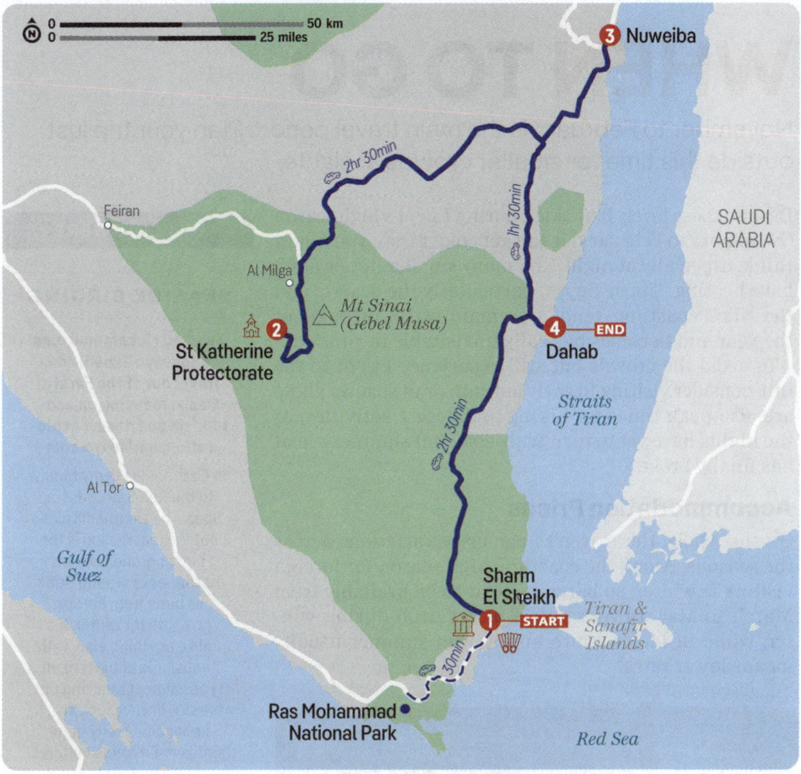

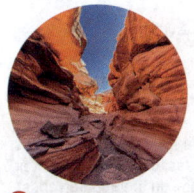

3

NUWEIBA 2 DAYS

Since the closure of the Sinai and Red Sea Mountain Trails, **Nuweiba** (p397) is your best bet for some proper technical hiking. Factor in a couple of days for canyon hopping, with appealing trails on offer including Ain Khudra Oasis and Canyon Salama (pictured). For safety, you will always need a guide.

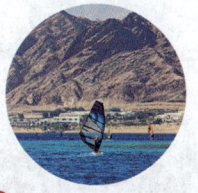

4

DAHAB 2 DAYS

Make your way to **Dahab** (p386) for some dedicated relaxation after your adventures around Sinai – or, if you've still got it in you, learn to windsurf at the Blue Lagoon (pictured). There are also a few great dives here, some of which are accessible from the shore, such as the Eel Garden. Alternatively, have a drink at one of the beach cafes and lie in the sun.

FROM LEFT: PAOPANO/SHUTTERSTOCK, SUN_SHINE/SHUTTERSTOCK

WHEN TO GO

November to February is the main travel period. Plan your trip just outside this time for smaller crowds at sights.

Despite those lovely blue skies, during Egypt's high season (November to February) it can get colder than you might think, especially at night, and many smaller hotels don't have heating. Upper Egypt, particularly the deserts and the Nile's coastline, tends to remain warm throughout the year and becomes basically unvisitable in summer.

To avoid the crowds but still experience Egypt to the full, consider visiting in early autumn or in spring. These are also peak times for hiking and desert activities, as the nights have yet to turn truly cold, but summer's heat has finally broken.

Accommodation Prices

On the whole, there aren't huge price variations across the seasons. Along the coastline high season for foreign visitors is winter, so bargains tend to be available from March to May. In Alexandria prices drop during winter, while in Luxor, Cairo and Aswan summer usually means lower rates.

> ### I LIVE HERE
>
> **SEASIDE BIRDING**
>
> **Saad Ali Mohammad** runs Badawiya Expedition Travel out of the Farafra Oasis, focusing on ecotourism and desert exploration; *badawiya.com*
>
> In October I take my family to the Red Sea coast or Suez. The weather is nice, but the real reason is the bird migration, which bottlenecks around Suez as birds from Europe go south for winter. It's unlike anything else, with thousands of birds of all types almost blocking out the sky. If we're lucky we'll spot some really huge herons or Egyptian vultures.

> ### DIVING
>
> Diving is year-round in Egypt, but during winter rough seas sometimes prevent access to further-flung sites. In Marsa Alam, on the Red Sea coast, April and May are best avoided due to a plankton bloom that reduces visibility for a few weeks.

Sandstorm in Cairo

Weather through the Year: Cairo

JANUARY	FEBRUARY	MARCH	APRIL	MAY	JUNE
Avg. daytime max: **19°C**	Avg. daytime max: **20.5°C**	Avg. daytime max: **23.5°C**	Avg. daytime max: **28°C**	Avg. daytime max: **32°C**	Avg. daytime max: **34°C**
Days of rainfall: 3	Days of rainfall: 2	Days of rainfall: 2	Days of rainfall: 1	Days of rainfall: 0	Days of rainfall: 0

THE KHAMSIN

The *khamsin* is a hot, southerly, sand-laden current that blows from March to May, causing periodic, intense sandstorms lasting a few hours that can ground flights, prevent feluccas from sailing and make sightseeing at outdoor sites functionally impossible.

Ramadan & Eid Al Adha

Ramadan (p40), the ninth month of the Islamic calendar, is dedicated to fasting by day and feasting by night. Tourist sites, shops and businesses close early (around mid-afternoon) and many restaurants shut during daylight hours. Visiting night owls, particularly in Cairo, will enjoy the late-night revelry. After dark, restaurants lay out a lavish fast-breaking feast called *iftar*. The goal is to stay up – or catnap and get up again – for the *sohour*, another big meal just before dawn.

Eid Al Adha is a four-day religious and national holiday commemorating Ibrahim's (Abraham's) sacrifice. Every family who can afford it sacrifices a sheep or goat. There's literally blood in the streets and the air smells of roasting meat.

Islamic holiday dates change annually, as the Islamic calendar is based on the lunar year.

> ### ⓘ I LIVE HERE
>
> ### ALEXANDRIAN GETAWAY
>
> **Jeneen Ezzat**, a self-professed *bint balad* ('hardcore Egyptian woman'), has lived in Cairo for almost 50 years.
>
> In November I like to gather my friends for a day trip to Farag Fish restaurant (p312) in Alexandria. The view from the windows on the long car or train journey can't be beat. As a bonus, it's the season for an amazing caviar salad they serve as part of the mezze. Afterwards, it's obligatory to go for mastic ice cream.

Local Festivals

People flock to Abu Simbel to watch the sun penetrate the inner sanctuary of the **Temples of Abu Simbel** (p265) and illuminate the statues of gods on 22 February (Ascension of Ramses II) and 22 October (Birth of Ramses II).
🌣 **February** 🌣 **October**

The **Sham An Nessim** festival is celebrated by Egyptians of all creeds and heralds the start of spring on the 13th. 🌣 **April**

The year's date harvest is celebrated in Siwa during the **Siyaha Festival** (p280), which occurs during the month's full moon. 🌣 **October**

D-CAF (p91; Downtown Contemporary Arts Festival) hosts art exhibitions and theatre and dance performances at venues across Cairo's downtown for three weeks. 🌣 **October**

In Al Fayoum you can watch sunlight strike the temple sanctuary of **Qasr Qarun** (p167) in perfect alignment at sunrise on the 21st. 🌣 **December**

Corniche, Alexandria (p310)

THE NORTHERN WINTER SEA

Along the Mediterranean coast, November to February are more damp than the rest of Egypt. December is the wettest month in Alexandria, with an average 53mm of rain. Pack an umbrella.

JULY	AUGUST	SEPTEMBER	OCTOBER	NOVEMBER	DECEMBER
Avg. daytime max: 34°C	Avg. daytime max: 34°C	Avg. daytime max: 32.5°C	Avg. daytime max: 29°C	Avg. daytime max: 25°C	Avg. daytime max: 20°C
Days of rainfall: 0	Days of rainfall: 0	Days of rainfall: 0	Days of rainfall: 0	Days of rainfall: 1	Days of rainfall: 2

Khan El Khalili (p95), Cairo

GET PREPARED FOR EGYPT

Useful things to load in your bag, your ears and your brain

Clothes

Long-sleeved tops and long trousers: Outside the beach resorts modest attire is recommended. Egypt is a conservative country, and nothing screams 'freshly arrived tourist' louder than wandering around dressed in a singlet and shorts. Dressing modestly will help you blend in, and guard against sunburns and scams in equal measure. T-shirts are fine, as are three-quarter trousers and midi skirts. Consider bringing something long-sleeved and a pair of long trousers or a long skirt for religious sites.

Closed shoes: Once you've seen the state of your feet after walking around Cairo or Alexandria in flip-flops, you'll discover why locals favour closed shoes.

Scarf: Women travellers should pack a scarf to cover their head with before entering mosques.

Manners

Remove shoes before entering a mosque.

During **Ramadan**, when Muslims fast from sunrise to sunset, it's considered disrespectful for non-Muslims to eat, drink or smoke in public during the daytime.

It's considered rude to point the **soles of your feet** at someone.

Kissing and **public displays of affection** are not socially acceptable.

📖 READ

The Cairo Trilogy (Naguib Mahfouz; 1956–57) Nobel winner's novels spanning the era of British rule are a masterwork of Egyptian literature.

The Days (Taha Hussein; 1926–1967) Hussein's autobiography tackles his increasing blindness and shows Egypt changing in real time.

The Yacoubian Building (Alaa Al Aswany; 2002) Portrays Egyptian society in the 1990s through characters in Downtown Cairo.

Taxi (Khaled Al Khamissi; 2011) The hardscrabble life of Cairo's taxi drivers in 58 fictional monologues.

Words

Ahlan is 'hello' in Arabic. You'll also hear **ahlan wa sahlan**, which means 'welcome'. You can reply with **ahlan beek** if addressing a male or **ahlan beeki** for a female. You'll also be greeted with **as-salaam alaykum** (literally 'peace be upon you'), to which you reply with **wa alaykum as-salaam**. **Sabah il-khayr** is 'good morning'. Reply with **sabah in-noor**. You may also hear **sabah il-asal** ('morning of honey') or **sabah il-full** ('morning of jasmine'), among many other delightful variations.
Shukran (gazeelan) is how to say 'thank you (very much)'. You'll hear **afwan** ('you're welcome') in reply. To introduce yourself, say **ismee** ('my name is') followed by your name. To ask 'what is your name?', say **ismak ay?** to ask a male or **ismik ay?** for females.
Aywa is 'yes' in the Egyptian Arabic dialect. **Na'am** is the more formal, standard Arabic 'yes'. **La** means 'no'.
Shwaya shwaya is a colloquial term used to tell someone to slow down. It's an easy phrase to pull out if your taxi driver gets a touch speedy. Conversely, **yallah** means 'let's go'.
Inshallah is a word you'll hear everyone use. Literally, it means 'God willing', but it's used freely to answer queries and as a general expression of hope. Another phrase you'll hear often is **ilhamdulillah**. It's used as an expression of thanks when something good has happened; it literally translates as 'praise be to God'.

▶ WATCH

Terrorism & Kebab (Sherif Arafa; 1992) Black-comedy classic starring Adel Emam (p440).

The Square (Jehane Noujaim; 2013) Award-winning doco about the 2011 revolution and its political consequences.

Secret of the Nile (Mohamed Shaker; 2016) Originally titled *Grand Hotel,* this 30-episode period drama, with lush sets and costuming, is set in Aswan's Old Cataract Hotel (pictured).

Photocopy (Tamer Ashri; 2017) An older gentleman in Cairo rediscovers life and love after retirement.

🎧 LISTEN

Kalthoumiat (Umm Kulthum; 2015) Compilation of eight beloved Umm Kulthum hits. You'll hear them everywhere you go in Egypt.

Mahraganat Hassan Shakosh (Hassan Shakosh; 2019) Good introduction to the *mahraganat* (Egyptian street music) scene from one of its biggest names.

Ya Ana Ya La (Amr Diab; 2020) Earworm bangers from the undisputed king of modern Egyptian pop.

Cairokee Studio Sessions (Cairokee; 2020) Acoustic versions of this Cairene rock-ish band's greatest hits, alongside a few newer melancholy numbers.

Ramadan in Cairo

TRIP PLANNER

BELIEVE LIKE AN EGYPTIAN

Egypt has seen many foreign conquests over the years, but one thing has always stood firm: its faith. Egyptians' stock response to new cultures and religions is to adapt and make them their own. To get under the skin of Egypt, you need to understand the locals' belief in belief.

Ramadan

As it is a majority Sunni Muslim country, Egypt observes the holy month of Ramadan as its most significant religious occasion. Ramadan follows the lunar calendar and lasts 29 to 30 days. It will fall during winter for the next five years or so, making the challenge (very) slightly less arduous for adherents.

THE FAST

Fasting during the month of Ramadan involves refraining from food and drink from *fagr* (dawn) prayer until *maghreb* (sunset). More broadly, the fast also means avoiding swearing, smoking, arguing and any other kind of negative behaviour. The hope is that adherents will go on to maintain these good habits year-round. Think of the Ramadan fast as a kind of whetstone for willpower: a detox for the body and a habit-building program for the mind.

If your trip to Egypt coincides with Ramadan, be prepared to adjust your mealtimes and avoid eating, drinking and smoking in public during the day. Also be ready to join in the communal festivities – most Egyptians break their fast in (large) groups.

It's also a good idea to double-check the opening hours for museums and events, as these often change during Ramadan.

💡 TIPS FOR VISITORS

You'll be warmly welcomed no matter when you visit, but by respecting local customs, culture and religions you'll earn an enduring place in Egyptians' hearts. Here are some pointers to bear in mind:

- Respect for all faiths, but especially the Abrahamic religions, is paramount. Atheism is generally frowned upon or considered deviant.
- Respect Egypt's holy sites as you would respect the Egyptian sun: cover up. For men this means exposing only those parts of the body below the elbows and knees. Women might consider bringing a scarf to cover their hair.
- Regardless of your dietary preferences, if you visit during Eid Al Adha remember that ritual sacrifice is central to the holiday's celebration. There will be blood.
- Try not to visit popular tourist spots or beaches during Eid Al Fitr, Eid Al Adha and Sham An Nessim (the ancient Egyptian celebration of spring that always falls on Easter Monday), as these are peak travel times for domestic tourists.
- Around Sham An Nessim, visit a farm for a traditional hearty meal of *fiteer* (a sweet or savoury flaky pastry) with molasses and cheese. This is known as the breakfast of the *falahin* (peasants) and will fuel you with enough energy to build a pyramid or three. A farm visit at this time of year is a truly unforgettable experience.

SUHOOR

Each fasting day revolves around two main meals. *Suhoor* is the pre-dawn meal and resembles a traditional Egyptian breakfast. Typically, it will include *fuul* (fava-bean paste) and *ta'amiyya* (falafel made from fava beans), accompanied by cucumber, lettuce and yogurt. It's all washed down with of water, juice, tea and coffee. You'll see *fuul* carts and restaurants doing a roaring trade in the small hours. While the streets of Egypt never truly sleep, during Ramadan they become positively insomniac.

An *iftar* meal

IFTAR

The meal that breaks the fast, *iftar* was historically heralded by the firing of a canon from atop Cairo's Citadel. For Egyptians it tends to involve daily invitations among family, friends and colleagues. Make sure you reserve restaurants in advance or head out (very) early to avoid the pre-*iftar* rush.

Suhoor

ENDURING UNITY IN BELIEF

Around 1353 BCE, Pharaoh Akhenaten laid down that all Egyptians should worship just one deity: Aten, the god of the sun. This decision is regarded as the first instance of monotheism in history.

Over 3000 years later (a few polytheistic blips notwithstanding), modern-day Egyptians remain overwhelmingly united in their faith in a single god. The ancient Egyptian temples are testament to this preoccupation with matters of the spirit and the hereafter, and religion continues to be a central pillar of Egyptian identity. Unlike the Sphinx's nose, it has not been eroded by time.

Frying falafel

THE FOOD SCENE

Underrated and overlooked, Egyptian cuisine is rustic, honest home-style cooking bursting with flavours.

Egyptian food's lack of frills has meant it has flown under the radar in comparison to the big-hitter regional cuisines of Lebanon, Türkiye and Iran. Its reputation isn't helped either by the number of restaurants offering same-same menus of kebabs and koftas. However, that's starting to change. Egyptian chefs such as Khufu's Mostafa Seif offer a fresh take on the cuisine that's packed with simple, fresh and honest flavours.

Pulses, particularly *fuul* (fava beans), play a large part in the diet. *Fuul* is the main ingredient of *ta'amiyya* (an Egyptian variant of falafel) and in Egypt's cumin-spiked breakfast stew, also called *fuul*. Carbohydrates dominate because they're filling and cheap. *A'aish* (bread) is the country's most important staple, while vegetables come stuffed (*mahshi*; usually with rice), in stews (called *tagens*; often with a tomato base), as simple salads and pickled (*torshi*).

Local specialities include pigeon stuffed with spiced rice and fried or roasted, and the love-it-or-hate-it jute-leaf soup *molokhiyya,* which can be texturally challenging for first-timers.

Egyptian Breakfasting

Egypt has distinctive and delicious breakfast fare, but you likely won't find a large selection as part of the buffet spread at many hotels. Instead, head to one of the hole-in-the-wall breakfast canteens or food carts. Here you can feast on a selection of traditional dishes such as *ta'amiyya, fuul, mish* (a pungent fermented cheese), *beid bel bas-*

Best Egyptian Dishes	HAMAM MAHSHI	KEBDA ISKANDARANI	KUSHARI	MAHSHI KURUMB
	Roast pigeon, stuffed with *fireek* (green wheat) and spiced rice.	Cumin-, chilli- and coriander-marinated liver, fried and packed into a sandwich.	Noodles, rice, brown lentils, chickpeas and fried onions smothered with tomato sauce.	Rice- and meat-stuffed cabbage leaves, doused with *samna* (clarified butter).

turma (eggs with dried beef) and *betengan mekhalel* (pickled aubergines). If that all sounds too heavy to start the day, you can grab a *ta'amiyya* or *fuul* sandwich loaded with salad, tahini and chips.

Street Food

Most travellers will be familiar with shawarma. The Egyptian version uses chicken or lamb sliced from a spit and sizzled on a hot plate with chopped tomatoes and garnish before it's stuffed into bread and drizzled with tahini. Along with *ta'amiyya* sandwiches, this is Egypt's most ubiquitous street food.

There's a lot more to Egyptian fast food, though. *Kushari* is a dish of macaroni, rice, brown lentils, chickpeas and fried onions smothered with a tangy tomato sauce. It's normally served at dedicated *kushari* restaurants. *Fiteer* is a flaky layered pastry (often called Egyptian pizza) that's served plain or stuffed with a variety of savoury or sweet fillings, and *hawashi* is a sandwich filled with spiced ground beef and then baked.

Vegetarian & Vegan

Observant Copts eat a mostly vegan diet during their many fasting periods throughout the year, so it's no surprise that vegan-friendly foods such as *kushari*,

Kushari

ta'amiyya and *fuul* are so readily available. At restaurants, vegetables often play a bit part rather than the main role, but there are usually oven-baked *tagens* of okra and aubergine, lots of soups, and mezze options such as *bessara* (cold fava-bean dip), *baba ganoush* (grilled-aubergine dip) and *sambousek* (samosa-like pastries stuffed with cheese) to put together and make into a meal. Be aware that some soups, including *molokhiyya*, may have a chicken-broth base.

Ask restaurants for *seyami* (fasting-friendly food) to tell them you're vegan.

Stella beer

EGYPTIAN ALCOHOL

● Alcohol in Egypt is available in bars, at most upper-end restaurants and at the many restaurants that cater to foreign visitors in tourist areas. In major cities, shops Drinkies and Cheers sell beer, wine and spirits.

● Egypt's two beers, Stella and Sakkara, are both refreshing Pilsners. They won't win any awards for complexity, but they go down just fine at the end of a hot day.

● Egyptian wines are improving. Beausoleil is one of the better labels and produces a full-bodied white from Egypt's banatti grapes and a selection of reds.

● Alcohol should only be consumed on-site (in the restaurant or bar where you bought it) or in private.

MOLOKHIYYA	OMM ALI	RUZ BI LABAN	TA'AMIYYA
Garlicky, coriander-spiked stew-soup made from jute leaves.	Baked pudding of milk, cream and flaky pastry loaded with raisins and nuts.	Rice pudding; the best versions are enhanced by nutmeg, allspice and cinnamon.	Fava-bean falafel with a fluffy, herb-flecked and cumin-spiced interior.

Local Specialities

Soups, Stews & Vegetables

Bamya Okra (and often meat) cooked in a garlic- and coriander-flavoured tomato sauce.
Shurbat ads Lentil soup.
Shurbat lesan el asfour Literally 'bird's tongue soup', though the soup is orzo pasta (the 'bird's tongues') in chicken broth.
Tagen Any vegetable or vegetable-and-meat variation cooked in a clay pot.
Wara ainab Vine leaves stuffed with herby rice and often meat and cooked in a broth.

Meat

Daood basha Meatballs in tomato sauce and topped with pine nuts.
Kebab and kofta Kebab is lamb, beef or chicken grilled on a skewer; kofta is spiced meatballs grilled on skewers.
Makaroneh beshamel Also called *makaroneh bi lahm*; pasta bake with mincemeat and béchamel sauce.
Mombar Sausages made from a herb-and-spice-loaded rice and minced-meat filling, encased in sheep intestines.

Basbousa

Shish tawooq Ubiquitous kebab option. Cubes of marinated chicken grilled on skewers.

Sweet Treats

Basbousa Syrup-drenched semolina cake.
Zalabiyya Fried dough balls dunked in honey or syrup (also called *luqmat el qadi*).
Kunafa Middle Eastern dessert staple; the Egyptian version normally wraps layers of syrup-soaked shredded *kataifi* (filo pastry) around a cream or sweet-cheese filling.
Mahallabiya Milk custard topped with nuts and cinnamon.

MEALS OF A LIFETIME

Downtown Food Tour (p83) Sample Egypt's favourite snacks, street food, canteen flavours and sweet treats on a four- to five-hour wander through the heart of Downtown Cairo with Bellies En-Route.

Khufu's (p71) Egyptian food gets the fine-dining treatment, served on a terrace with a million-dollar view of Giza's Pyramids.

Terrace (p255) Watch the Nile flow by while you enjoy old-school English high tea at Aswan's Old Cataract Hotel.

White & Blue (p317) Feast on seafood and take in the view of Alexandria's Mediterranean bay from this perch at the Greek Nautical Club.

THE YEAR IN FOOD

SPRING
For many Egyptian Copts, Coptic Easter and Sham An Nessim (a spring celebration) means *fesikh* (pictured), a sun-dried, salted and fermented grey mullet. The flavour is an acquired taste.

SUMMER
Mango trees were imported to Egypt from India during the 1800s and the fruit is now a summer staple. Beat the heat with a glass of *karkadai* (pictured), a drink made from hibiscus sepals.

AUTUMN
Egypt's endemic *zaghloul* (red) dates are harvested when semi-ripe in late summer and early autumn and reach maturity in late October. Look for their distinctive red-wine-coloured skins at markets and shops.

WINTER
Vendors sell sweet potatoes baked in a tin oven on top of *batata* (potato) carts. This is the season for *sahlab* (pictured), a milky drink thickened by starch from the orchid tuber and sprinkled with chopped nuts.

Khan El Kalili (p95), Cairo

HOW TO... Haggle

For thousands of years the curious and adventurous of the world have made their way to Egypt to be dazzled by the awe-inspiring monuments of the Pharaonic civilisation. That means the inhabitants of this beautiful country have had millennia to discover exactly how much tourists are willing to pay for anything and everything. To attempt to mitigate the damage that this will inflict on your wallet, and potentially your sanity, keep these helpful tips in mind as you shop.

Weigh Up Recommendations

Rethink visiting places that have been recommended by Uber drivers, taxi drivers, tour guides or hotel staff. There is often a finder's fee attached to the price, along with an exorbitant tourist tax.

Know When to Haggle

If the price is verbally quoted, it's fair game to be haggled over. If the price is clearly displayed, exercise your judgment – some vendors will negotiate while others may be insulted. That said, it never hurts to ask, 'Will you let it go for a lower price?'.

The Basic Strategy

Start negotiations by refusing the first price and asking if the vendor will sell the item for a specific lower price. Always quote a figure that's less than the amount you're actually willing to pay. If the vendor responds with another price lower than the first, the haggle has begun. The rest of the process is simply finding a place in between the two prices that you both agree on. Cajolery, accusations and guilt-tripping are common. Keep in mind that nobody will ever sell you anything at a loss. If a vendor refuses your offered price outright without caveats, you have pitched the price too low and may have insulted them.

Keep It Civil

Haggling doesn't have to be a stressful or combative process. If you approach people pleasantly and respectfully, they tend to reciprocate. Minding your manners will invariably make the whole process more enjoyable for everybody and achieve the same result. Be direct, but don't be rude or unkind.

TWO FUNDAMENTAL THINGS

Be prepared to say no. If you don't want the item, don't buy it, regardless of what the vendor says. If you're interested but the price is too high, say so. Virtually nothing is unique, and you will almost certainly find whatever you're looking for elsewhere and probably more cheaply. There's nothing wrong with simply saying thank you and walking away.

Don't expect local prices. If you're not Egyptian you won't be offered the local price, even if you speak Arabic. Coming to terms with this in advance will save you quite a bit of grief.

White Desert National Park (p293)

THE OUTDOORS

Less archaeologically inclined and more adrenaline inspired? Egypt's mountain ranges, desert wildernesses and marine marvels may be more your style.

While many think that visiting Egypt is an exercise in roasting yourself on the beach, roasting yourself in the desert looking at artefacts or roasting yourself on the Nile, the Egyptian outdoors has far more to offer than a sunburn. Diving is the main Red Sea activity, but in recent years reliable offshore winds have piqued the interest of windsurfers and kitesurfers. And Egypt's desert landscapes are among the world's lesser-tapped hiking and camping destinations.

Diving

The Red Sea's coral reefs can easily go head to head with the Pyramids as one of the world's wonders. Their fantasia of coloured corals and flitting sea life pulls diving enthusiasts to Egypt in their thousands. Off the Sinai Peninsula the dive sites of Ras Mohammed National Park and the Straits of Tiran are what first put Sharm El Sheikh on the tourism map, while the Straits of Gubal, between Sinai and the Red Sea coast, are home to the *Thistlegorm,* one of the world's premier wreck dives.

For good-value PADI courses and long-stay diving vacations with plenty of budget accommodation, Dahab is a popular base, but for experienced divers Marsa Alam may be Egypt's best destination.

The Red Sea can be dived year-round, but from July to September conditions

---

Sea, Sand, Sky & More

FELUCCA TRIPS
Have a close encounter of the Nile kind with a felucca trip from Aswan to **Kom Ombo Temple** (p242).

CYCLING
Explore **Luxor's west bank** at a more leisurely pace by biking between the temples (p209).

FRESHWATER FISHING
Head out on **Lake Nasser** to try your hand at catching a monster-sized Nile perch (p262).

FAMILY ADVENTURES

An early-morning bird-watching boat trip in Aswan (p241) offers families with older kids a chance to take in the river's natural beauty.

Sneak in some science education on a trip to Wadi Al Hitan (p164) in Al Fayoum to see the skeletons of ancient whales amid the sands.

In Siwa, teenagers will enjoy **taking a plunge** in Bir Wahed (p283) hot pool and then heading out to sandboard on the nearby dunes.

For a **short camel ride** that won't be too much for little ones, ride from the Tombs of the Nobles (p255) to the Monastery of St Simeon (p256) on Aswan's west bank.

In St Katherine Protectorate, more active kids can tackle Mt Sinai (p399), and **hikes to mountain gardens** are opportunities to learn about Bedouin culture.

---

are at their peak, with calm seas, water temperatures averaging 26°C and excellent visibility.

Hiking & Trekking

First things first: you need a guide to hike in Egypt. With no waymarked trails and a remote environment it would be dangerous to venture into the desert by yourself.

For guided desert and mountain trekking, the Sinai Peninsula is hard to beat. St Katherine Protectorate in South Sinai's interior is the prime base, with Mt Sinai (Gebel Musa) and Gebel Katarina (Mt Katherine) right on the doorstep, day hikes through nearby wadis (valleys) and up to hidden mountain gardens, and multiday treks easily arranged with Bedouin operators in Al Milga (Katreen; the village 3.5km from St Katherine's Monastery). While the Sinai and Red Sea Mountain Trails have temporarily shut down due to recent events to the north and increased governmental restrictions, nearby Nuweiba offers fantastic hikes such as the Malha and Wishwashi valleys and Canyon Salama.

The hiking season runs from approximately September to May, as it's too hot to hike in summer. Go from mid-February to mid-March or mid-October to November for optimal conditions.

Gebel Katarina (p402)

Desert Adventures

To enter the Western Desert you'll need a permit, which must be submitted by an Egyptian travel agency at least 21 days before you arrive. The forward planning is well worth it because the region can't be beat for surreal, otherworldly landscapes. Both the Bahariya and Farafra Oases are ideal launchpads for camping trips in the White Desert National Park. Further west, Siwa has rolling dunes right at the edge of its oasis. You can also experience a desert taster in Al Fayoum, just a short hop from Cairo, or head to the east for 4WD trips into the Wadi Gimal Protectorate near Marsa Alam.

KITESURFING	HORSE RIDING	HOT-AIR BALLOONING	SNORKELLING
Learn to ride the offshore currents at prime windsurfing spots **El Gouna** (p358), **Hamata** (p365) or **Dahab** (p386).	See the Pyramids from another angle on a desert trot between **Giza** and **Abu Sir** (p67).	Marvel at the Theban mountains glowing dusky orange as the sun rises over the Nile's west bank on a balloon ride from **Luxor** (p210).	Test the waters off **Dahab** (p382) or **Sharm El Sheikh** (p376), both of which have plenty of snorkelling opportunities.

SS *Thistlegorm* (p385)

HOW TO... Dive Responsibly

Egypt's Red Sea coastline boasts some of the best and most accessible dive sites on the planet, from the wreck of the SS *Thistlegorm* to the Tower and many, many more. As you enjoy the region's breathtaking marine beauty, stunning underwater visibility and balmy seas, it's important to keep a few things in mind to protect the crystalline depths.

Keep It Clean

Unfortunately, many people, especially on longer boat dives, harm the marine environment by littering, whether by tossing rubbish into the sea or being careless with packaging and other litter. Leave no trace of your presence after your dive.

Hands Off

The corals are gorgeous and the fish are incredible – but be sure to look and not touch. This is not only for the protection of the reef but for your own safety as well. Far too many people have attempted to pick up an apparently dead branch of fire coral only to learn, with excruciating vividness, exactly why it is so named. Then there's the multitude of potentially venomous fish, which will generally leave you alone as long as you extend them the same courtesy.

Fin Etiquette

Fins are very useful tools but, simply by virtue of being rather far behind you and difficult to see, can wreak no small havoc on the ecosystem if you're not careful with them. Egypt's dive destinations have a consistent current, so you'll probably be using your fins quite a bit. From kicking up sand to disturbing wildlife to breaking off bits of coral, fins can be far more destructive than they might appear. Practise careful buoyancy control and keep as much distance as you can between you and the marine landscape.

Don't Feed the Fish

It's impossible for a wild fish to naturally encounter a Ritz cracker, and it's best that everybody keeps it that way. Though some fish may have become accustomed to little gifts from humans, human food is simply bad for their health. Despite how appealing they may be, don't feed the fish.

CHOOSING YOUR DIVE CENTRE

Not all dive centres are created equal. Sadly, some outfits are rather unscrupulous both in their business practices and in their adherence to safety guidelines and overall standards of responsibility. Do your research before you visit and pay close attention to such considerations as nitrox surcharges and lunch fees.

You may well find that the difference in price between a well-regarded and highly professional dive centre and its slightly seedier neighbour is much smaller than it seems at first glance. Look for smaller group sizes, official accreditation and well-maintained rental equipment. Dive safe!

HOW TO... Ride a Camel

Riding a camel is great fun and part of the Egypt experience. Done right, it can also be a chance to learn more about these incredible creatures, gain insights into the realities of life for camel owners and contribute towards improved conditions for camels and local communities.

Staying in the Saddle

To begin your ride, approach your camel slowly from the side while it is sitting, maybe with a few calm words of introduction or a gentle pat, and climb aboard. As the camel gets up (it will raise its hind legs first), lean slightly back and then (as it unfolds its front legs) slightly forward. Reverse this when it's time for the dismount.

Keeping Comfortable

Camels pace – that is, they move the two legs on the same side of their body simultaneously. Keep your own body flexible and relaxed and try to feel yourself into their movement, keeping a bit of sway in your position. Many Bedouin ride with one leg crossed, which is often more comfortable than sitting in a straddle. If you'll be riding for lengthy periods, consider breaking up your camel ride with intervals of walking.

Riding Essentials

Wear long trousers, ideally with a zip pocket, and long socks to guard against chafing. For protection against heat and sun, be sure to bring a hat, sunscreen and drinking water.

Up Close & Personal

Riding a camel is a chance to observe one of nature's most remarkable creatures up close. Camels' wide, flat feet keep them from sinking into the sand, their long lashes keep sand out of their eyes, their nostrils can squeeze closed (also against sand) and their flexible lips allow them to dine on cacti and other tough desert scrub. During rest breaks you'll get to hear plenty of camel talk as these ships of the desert grunt, gurgle and harrumph.

CAMEL WELFARE

Egypt's National Programme for the Care and Protection of Horses, Camels and Pets at Archaeological Sites, launched in late 2024, aims to improve animal treatment countrywide with regular veterinary care and vaccinations, and educational initiatives for camel owners.

You can help by avoiding riding on unwell or listless-looking camels and not negotiating with drivers who are beating or yelling at their animals. Politely letting drivers know your concerns can be a force for change. Don't overload your camel (one adult maximum) and don't try to haggle the price down to the last penny, for the sake of both owner and camel.

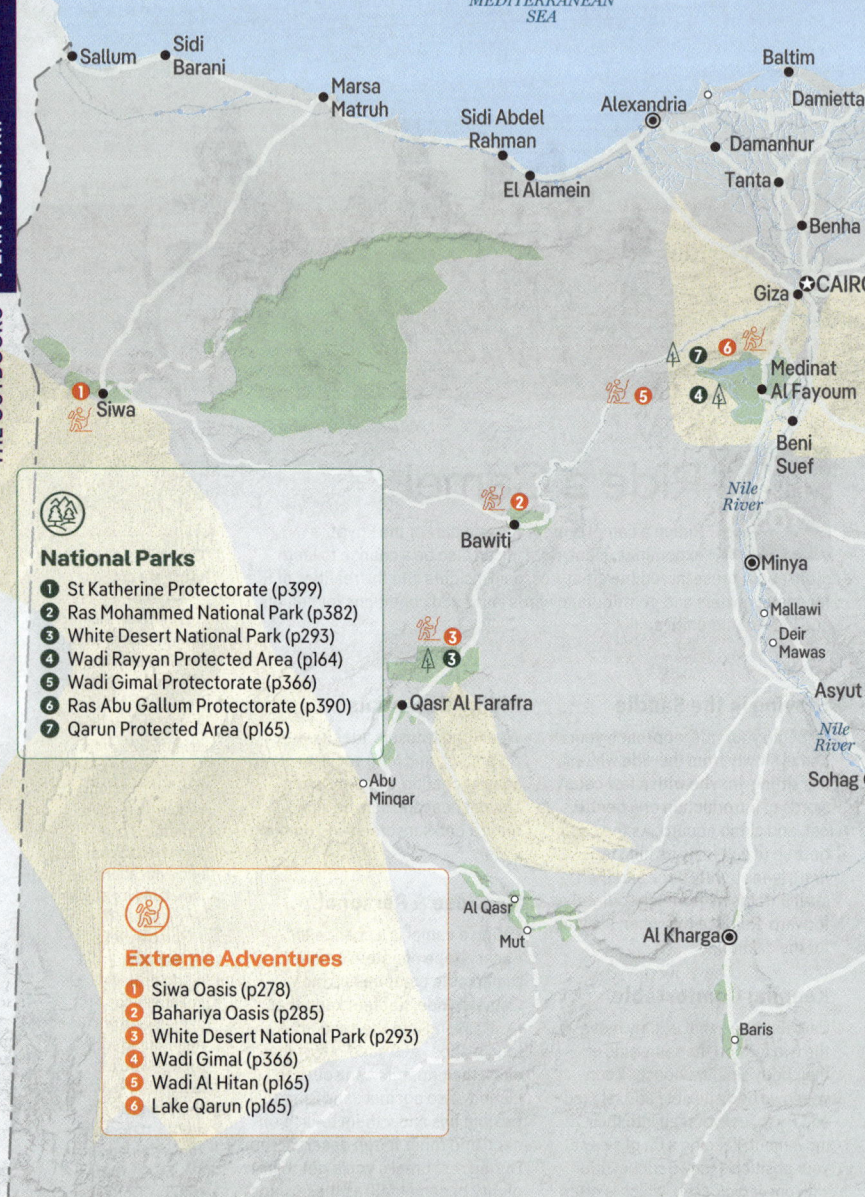

Natural spring, Farafra Oasis (p291)

TRIP PLANNER

ROAD TRIPPING

If you're looking to get off the beaten path and explore Egypt on your own terms, there's no better way than by renting a car. Though a road trip here isn't as straightforward as in other places, adventurous travellers will be rewarded with a far more personal relationship with this beautiful country.

Planning Your Drive

WHERE TO START

It's best to begin your journey from a major urban centre such as Cairo or Alexandria. It's also a good idea to get a local to contact the rental agency for you. Though the bureaucracy won't change, the prices almost certainly will. If you leave from Cairo, keep in mind that driving in the capital can be exceedingly chaotic. Consider renting a car only after you've finished exploring the city. Driving in Alexandria and elsewhere is somewhat more laid-back.

WHAT TO KEEP IN MIND

Egypt used to have a convoy system in place where only certain roads were available to foreign vehicles, and then only with a police escort. That isn't the case any more, but vestiges of the system remain. Police escorts are still required in some places, especially the Northern Nile Valley. Additionally, the Western Desert is not accessible by rental vehicle. Entry for foreigners is restricted and people looking to explore such stunning areas as Farafra Oasis must request permission from the government by way of an Egyptian travel agency at least 21 days before entry. These regulations are prone to change without much notice, and it's prudent to check with a local travel agency right before you intend to start your road trip.

The border area between Egypt and Libya in the Western Desert is forbidden to all civilians, Egyptians included. At the

🚙 HIRING A DRIVER

● A good way to have the adventure of independent travel but avoid the hassles and risks of going it alone is to hire a car and driver. This is a popular way of touring the country and one that will smooth out many of the kinks of driving in Egypt.

● A variety of car-and-driver packages with preplanned itineraries are available, often through local travel and tourism agencies, and they're the best way to visit the Western Desert in particular. If you choose to go off the beaten path and hire a driver to follow your own itinerary, that can come at an extra cost, though it can be well worth it.

● Most drivers are affable and pleasant, but bear in mind that they will expect a generous tip at the end of the journey, which can drive up the total cost. That said, the removal of the stress of checkpoints, wayfinding and possible government restrictions can make the whole experience much more straightforward while still covering the sights you want to see.

● When choosing a driver, get some form of written verification of the agreed total price before setting out. Be specific, direct and firm. Try to meet the driver ahead of time as well – you'll be together for a while. Happy travels!

---

time of writing, the Siwa–Bahariya road was also inaccessible.

PACKING SUPPLIES

Having made up your mind to explore Egypt according to your own schedule and without the organisational support of a tour company, you'll need to get yourself ready. Before you leave your urban-centre departure point, be sure to pack plenty of water and sunscreen and stock up on any creature comforts you may require for the journey. The highways in the country have absolutely stunning scenery, but opportunities to replenish your supplies are few and far between. Plan accordingly so that practical considerations don't spoil your enjoyment of the trip.

Police checkpoint

Western Desert (p270)

CHECKPOINTS

Egyptian highways are punctuated by checkpoints staffed by police officers. Although it's rarer now than it used to be, there's still a possibility that officers at the checkpoint will ask you for an unregulated fee. This is unfortunate, but it's by no means exclusive to foreigners. It's usually best to be polite to the officer and simply pay the fee, though playing dumb may get you out of it.

The fee should never be more than US$50; if it's more than that, say you will contact your embassy to complain, or simply turn back. Don't use the threat to contact your embassy lightly.

THE GUIDE

EGYPT
THE GUIDE

Alexandria & the
Mediterranean Coast
p305

CAIRO
p56

Suez
Canal
p337

Sinai
p369

Northern
Nile Valley
p157

Siwa Oasis & the
Western Desert
p270

Luxor
p190

Red Sea
Coast
p346

Southern
Nile Valley
p231

Chapters in this section are organised by hubs and their surrounding areas. We see the hub as your base in the destination, where you'll find unique experiences, local insights, insider tips and expert recommendations. It's also your gateway to the surrounding area, where you'll see what and how much you can do from there.

Hot air ballooons over Luxor's West Bank (p210)
DELPIXEL/SHUTTERSTOCK

Researched by
Lauren Keith

Cairo

MOTHER OF THE WORLD

Magnificent, infuriating, nerve-jangling and beautiful; Cairo's dazzling chaos is a full-frontal assault on your senses.

In the 14th century, Arab historian Ibn Khaldun wrote that Cairo surpassed anything one could imagine, and that's as true today as it was then. You can't believe Cairo's frenetic energy until you've walked Downtown, its overworked air-con units on the faded facades of once grand buildings dripping water on your head while car horns battle with the *muezzins'* calls to prayer from duelling mosques. You might think Egypt's capital can't possibly be functional.

Although the 22 million inhabitants of Greater Cairo may be crushing the city's ragged infrastructure, they also lift its spirits with their resourcefulness and humour.

Cairo isn't a Pharaonic city. When the Pyramids of Giza were built, the capital of ancient Egypt was Memphis, 20km southeast of the Giza Plateau, though the religious centre of Iunu (which the Greeks called Heliopolis) lies under northeastern Cairo. The Romans built a fortress on the Nile's east bank, and when Mecca-born army commander Amr ibn al-As conquered Egypt in 641 CE, he established his new capital of Fustat at the same location. The grand walled medieval city of Al Qahira ('the Victorious', which Europeans later corrupted into 'Cairo') didn't get its start until the Fatimid caliphate arrived in 969.

Some of Cairo's problems seem insurmountable. Government modernisation programs – including roads that have bulldozed through heritage areas and the destruction of low-income districts to make way for 'development' – are controversial. In the desert east of the city, the government is busy constructing an as-yet-unnamed New Administrative Capital, perhaps to ease Cairo's overcrowding or maybe to stifle protests and create an enclave where the upper class can seal themselves off from the city.

Many travellers are understandably overwhelmed on their first encounter with Cairo, but this city rewards as much as it befuddles, with the splendour of its medieval Islamic architecture and ancient churches and the buzz of its street life and late-night crowds. Spend time here and you'll understand why Egyptians call their country – especially its capital – *umm al dunya*, the mother of the world.

THE MAIN AREAS

GIZA
The world's only surviving ancient wonder. **p62**

DOWNTOWN CAIRO
Buzzing streets below belle époque architecture. **p77**

ISLAMIC CAIRO & THE CITADEL
Medieval markets, mosques and monuments. **p93**

COPTIC CAIRO, FUSTAT & MAADI
Religious history, royal mummies and chill cafes. **p119**

For places to stay in Cairo, see p154

THE GUIDE

CAIRO

From left: Muhammad Ali Mosque (p109); Khan El Khalili (p95)

ZAMALEK & DOKKI
Where the capital gets creative.
p125

GARDEN CITY & RODA ISLAND
An extravagant palace and musical culture. **p134**

HELIOPOLIS & NEW CAIRO
Dining hot spot and Cairo's most bizarre building. **p139**

Find Your Way

Greater Cairo is the largest urban area in the Middle East and Africa, and it can take time to get around. The Nile separates Cairo (on the east side of the river) from Giza (on the west). Downtown Cairo sits at the heart of the action, about 20km from the Pyramids.

FROM THE AIRPORT
Cairo International Airport is where major airlines from around the world arrive. Opened in 2022, **Sphinx International Airport** serves budget airlines from Europe and the Middle East. Book a transfer through your accommodation instead of dealing with ride-hailing apps or the scrum of taxi drivers (p95).

METRO
Cairo Metro runs frequent services on clean trains, but the stations aren't as densely concentrated as in other major world cities, so it can be a long walk to reach your destination. Tickets are some of the cheapest in the world (LE8 for up to nine stops).

Sphinx Airport (24km)

Zamalek & Dokki
p125

Giza Train Station

Nile River

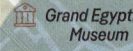
Grand Egyptian Museum

Giza

p62

Pyramids of Giza

Saqqara (15km)

Nile River

Heliopolis & New Cairo
p139

✈ Cairo International Airport (7km)

THE GUIDE

CAIRO

Downtown Cairo
p77

🚉 Ramses Train Station

🏛 Egyptian Museum

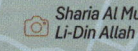
Sharia Al Muizz Li-Din Allah

Islamic Cairo & the Citadel
p93

🏛 Darb Al Ahmar

 Citadel

Garden City & Roda Island
p134

Coptic Cairo, Fustat & Maadi
p119

WALK
It may not look like it at first glance, but apart from the problem of crossing busier streets, much of Cairo is walkable. Within neighbourhoods it's the quickest way to get around. Wear sturdy shoes and be mindful of the traffic.

TAXI & RIDE-HAILING APPS
Taxis are ubiquitous, but few cars have working meters. Do not expect to get local prices. Ride-hailing apps like Uber and Careem offer the relief of fixed fares and are the best way to cover medium or longer distances. You can pay by card or cash.

N | 0 — 5 km
0 — 2.5 miles

Plan Your Days

Cairo's sights are spread throughout the city, so if you're spending more than a few days here, it makes sense to devote each day to a different area to save transport time.

Tomb of Kagemni (p148)

Day 1

Morning
● Set an early alarm and head to the **Pyramids of Giza** (p64) for an 8am start. Pinch yourself – you're really here. Explore Egypt's most famous necropolis: climb inside the Great Pyramid, survey the scene from a panoramic viewpoint and dine on elevated Egyptian dishes with an unforgettable backdrop at **Khufu's** (p71).

Afternoon
● The world-class **Grand Egyptian Museum** (p72) is just a few kilometres away from the Pyramids and houses the country's most spectacular ancient treasures, including the golden grave goods of Tutankhamun.

Evening
● After a big day out, feast on a heaping bowl of *kushari* from **Koshary Abou Tarek** (p83) in Downtown Cairo.

YOU'LL ALSO WANT TO...

Pack in more of Cairo's historic architecture, soak up city views and head out of town for pyramids even older than those at Giza.

DAY TRIP TO SAQQARA
Head to Cairo's outskirts to take in the Pharaonic necropolis of **Saqqara** (p102) with its Step Pyramid and tombs. Add a visit to **Memphis** (p151), ancient Egypt's first capital, and **Dahshur** (p143) for more pyramids.

MARVEL AT MOSQUES
Cairo has mosques that span the centuries, including the **Mosque of Ibn Tulun** (p114), the oldest in the city; the **Mosque of Sultan Hassan** (p112), a Mamluk masterpiece; and the Ottoman **Muhammad Ali Mosque** (p109).

SEE CAIRO FROM ON HIGH
Climb atop **Bab Zuwayla** (p107) or **Bab Al Futuh** (p100), two surviving gates of Cairo's city wall. In Zamalek, zip to the top of **Cairo Tower** (p132) or grab a cocktail at rooftop **Crimson Bar & Grill** (p128).

Day 2

Morning
- Though some of its best pieces were crated up and transported west to new museums, the historic **Egyptian Museum** (p78) on Midan Tahrir is an iconic institution and still has plenty to see.

Afternoon
- Book the Downtown Cairo Food Tour with **Bellies En-Route** (p83). This walk delves into the neighbourhood's heritage and modern culture as well as its vibrant street-food scene.

Evening
- You probably won't want to move too far (or eat anything) after the food tour, so soak up Downtown's nightlife by chilling out with a shisha at **Zahrat Al Bustan** (p87) or grabbing a beer at **El Horreya** (p87).

Day 3

Morning
- Explore Coptic Cairo's **churches** (p120) and the **Coptic Museum** (p120) before moving on to the **National Museum of Egyptian Civilization** (p119) to take in 5000 years of Egyptian history and a cache of royal mummies.

Afternoon
- Get lost in Islamic Cairo. Shop amid the medieval maze of alleys in **Khan El Khalili** (p95) and have mint tea at **El Fishawy** (p96). Emerge from the chaos to check out the stunning Islamic monuments along **Sharia Al Muizz Li-Din Allah** (p97).

Evening
- Sample home-cooked flavours at **Fasahet Somaya** (p84) and then take a short boat trip on the Nile from **Mamsha Ahl Misr** (p87) or **Dok Dok Landing Stage** (p137).

CATCH A CULTURAL PERFORMANCE

Hear traditional music from Egypt and the wider region at **Makan** (p136) and **El Dammah Theatre** (p90), or you can watch the Al Tannoura Egyptian Heritage Dance Troupe at the **Mausoleum of Al Ghouri** (p105).

ADMIRE ORNATE PALACES

Drool over **Manial Palace** (p134), which blends Ottoman, Persian and European rococo styles, and wonder at **Baron Empain Palace** (p139), known as the 'Hindu Palace' for the elephants and serpents on its facade.

SHOP FOR LOCAL SOUVENIRS

The Zamalek neighbourhood is home to boutiques by Egypt-based creatives selling beautiful ceramics, textiles, homewares and fashion. **Caravanserai** (p128) and **Madu Cairo** (p128) are two of many worth popping into.

VISIT COPTIC MONASTERIES

Witness Coptic Christianity's modern culture and ancient soul amid the monasteries of **Wadi Natrun** (p151) on a day trip from Cairo. Free tours led by resident monks dive into history, architecture and their lives of daily devotion.

Giza

THE WORLD'S ONLY SURVIVING ANCIENT WONDER

☑ TOP TIP
Buying tickets online before you visit the Pyramids of Giza can save you time at the often-crowded entrance (*egymonuments.com*; search 'Giza Plateau').

GETTING AROUND
Most people visit the Pyramids of Giza on an organised tour with a guide, the best and most hassle-free option. Every hotel, guesthouse and hostel arranges tours (of varying quality), but for a guaranteed good guide, book with **Magic Carpet Travel** (*magiccarpetegypt.com*).

To coincide with the full opening of the Grand Egyptian Museum in late 2025, the Giza Plateau has also undergone a logistical makeover. The entrance point to visit the Pyramids has shifted from near Mena House and the Great Pyramid to Al Fayoum Rd.

Technically, all of Cairo on the west bank of the Nile is Giza, but the name is inextricably linked with the Pyramids, 8.5km from the river. The Giza Plateau is Egypt's most famous site, and it can be a sensory overload. The roads are a rolling parade of horse-drawn carriages, camels, massive tour buses, and ever-persistent touts trying to sell you scarves and pyramid-shaped key chains.

This area is undergoing perhaps the biggest changes it's seen since the Great Pyramid was constructed 4500 years ago, with the opening of the long-awaited Grand Egyptian Museum, new rules and regulations on horse and camel drivers, modern cafes and toilet facilities, and upscale restaurants dishing up plates of Egyptian food alongside unbelievable pyramid views.

Truly time-strapped sightseers could conceivably stay in Giza and bypass Cairo entirely, but that's missing a lot of the fun. More realistically, you'll visit Giza on a day outing.

Watch the Weavers at Wissa Wassef
Makers of masterpieces

The two dozen artists at **Ramses Wissa Wassef Art Center** (*wissawassef.com*) are known for their distinctive tapestries depicting nature and scenes of rural Egypt. Crude imitations are standard in souvenir shops, but the ones for sale and on display in the gallery here are in a completely different class, like museum-worthy paintings in wool. Stop by for a free guided tour around the workshops and then admire the finished works in the museum.

Feast with a View
The ultimate in atmospheric dining

Exploring Giza can be hungry work. If you have a little more time in the area, head to **Khufu's** (*9am-4pm*). One of Cairo's

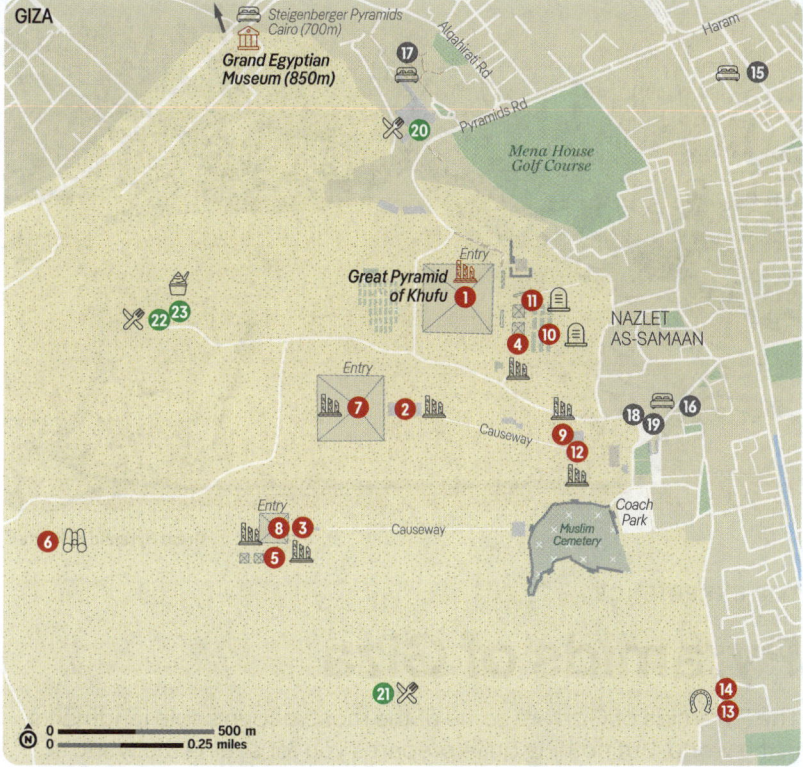

HIGHLIGHTS
1. Great Pyramid of Khufu

SIGHTS
2. Funerary Temple of Khafre
3. Funerary Temple of Menkaure
4. Khufu Queens' Pyramids
5. Menkaure Queens' Pyramids
6. Panoramic Viewpoint
7. Pyramid of Khafre
8. Pyramid of Menkaure
9. Sphinx
10. Tomb of Meresankh III
11. Tombs of Qar & Idu
12. Valley Temple of Khafre

ACTIVITIES
13. FB Stables
14. NB Stables

SLEEPING
15. Khan Duidar Inn
16. Mamlouk Pyramids Hotel
17. Mena House Hotel
18. Pyramids Overlook Inn
19. Pyramids Valley Boutique Hotel

EATING
20. 139 Pavilion
21. 9 Pyramids Lounge
22. Khufu's
23. Ladurée

best dining experiences sets the scene with pyramid views and wows with modern takes on Egyptian dishes. For something more casual, all-day **139 Pavilion** *(24hr)* at Mena House has an international menu and huge windows opening onto the pyramids.

Andrea El Mariouteya *(noon-11pm)* is famous for its spit-roasted chicken and tasty mezze dishes – eat in the garden while overlooking the city sprawl. For an elegant night out, make a reservation at **Barranco** *(6pm-1am)* at the **Hyatt Regency**. It lacks the showstopping views, but dishes up Japanese-Peruvian fusion plates you won't find anywhere else in the city.

Great Pyramid of Khufu

TOP EXPERIENCE

Pyramids of Giza

The Pyramids of Giza are some of the most recognisable landmarks in the world, but nothing quite prepares you for seeing the world's last standing ancient wonder up close. It's not all about the Sphinx and the three massive pyramids, though. The entire Giza Plateau is a necropolis dedicated to ancient Egypt's 4th dynasty, and it's worth exploring beyond the major monuments.

DON'T MISS

Great Pyramid of Khufu

Great Pyramid interior

Pyramid of Menkaure

Pyramid of Khafre

Tomb of Meresankh III

Khufu's

Sphinx

Great Pyramid of Khufu

Built as a tomb for the 4th-dynasty Pharaoh Khufu (reigned c 2589–2566 BCE), the **Great Pyramid** is the oldest on the Giza Plateau and the largest in Egypt, standing 146.5m high when it was completed around 2570 BCE. It was the tallest structure in the world for nearly four millennia, but after 46 windy centuries and the loss of its limestone casing, its height has been reduced by 9m. Get close up to check out the mammoth stone blocks, each weighing 2.5 tonnes.

PRACTICALITIES
- egymonuments.com; search 'Giza Plateau'
- Giza Plateau LE700
- 7am-4pm (last entry)

Going Inside the Great Pyramid

Although there's not much to see, for most visitors, just being able to explore inside such an ancient monument is an unforgettable experience despite the high ticket price *(LE1500 in addition to Giza Plateau entry)*. However, if you suffer from claustrophobia or have mobility issues, give it a miss. The wait to get inside can be hours long when it's busy, and it's a sweaty endeavour of climbing, crouching and squeezing through steep, narrow passageways.

When you pause in the Great Gallery to catch your breath, look up and notice how precisely the blocks in the ceiling fit together, an impressive feat of ancient engineering. Keep climbing; your reward at the end of the journey is the dank, dark King's Chamber, with walls of red granite blocks. Khufu's empty sarcophagus stands at one end.

Queens' Pyramids

The three small, weathered **pyramids** on the Great Pyramid's eastern side were built as tombs for Khufu's mother, wife and possibly his daughter. Today, they look more like large piles of rubble, but they once stood about 30m high. In the past, the interiors had been open to visit, but they have been closed for several years.

Eastern Cemetery

East of the Queens' Pyramids is the Eastern Cemetery, filled with rectangular tombs called mastabas (the Arabic word for 'bench' and so called because of their shape). Members of the royal family and high-ranking nobles were buried here, and unlike the unadorned interior of the Great Pyramid, these tombs have beautifully detailed decorations.

Which tombs are open depends on the Egyptian government's mysterious restoration schedule, the mood of the site guardians and the persuasiveness of the guide you've hired. The **Tomb of Meresankh III** *(LE200 in addition to Giza Plateau entry)*, burial place of the granddaughter of Khufu, is generally open and has some of the best in-situ wall paintings from this era, depicting fishing, farming and baking, plus endless offerings to set her up well in the afterlife. On the right side of the tomb is a row of 10 statues of women half carved from the wall, a feature not found anywhere else. They are believed to depict Meresankh's mother and daughters, as well as Meresankh herself.

The nearby **Tombs of Qar and Idu**, two high officials, have been closed but are expected to reopen soon.

Visiting this area without a guide or being able to speak Arabic can be tricky. The tombs are kept locked, so finding the entrance and the keeper of the keys is difficult on your own – check at the Tombs of Qar and Idu for the site guardian. Even though you've paid for a ticket, the guardians expect baksheesh (a tip) for opening the door.

Pyramid of Khafre

From certain angles, the **Pyramid of Khafre**, the only pyramid still capped with its original polished-limestone casing,

---

> **COPING WITH THE PYRAMID HUSTLE**
>
> Usually crammed with tour buses and camel and horse touts, the Giza Plateau is an intense tourist scene, and many visitors find it the most gruelling part of their trip. The site is undergoing extensive changes that could completely transform a visit here, but until it's properly managed and the people in the village by the pyramids have other income besides selling horse and camel rides, it's impossible to avoid the sales pressure and scam attempts. Most vendors and touts are just trying to make a living, but be wary of anyone offering 'advice' or telling you that certain places are closed.

looks taller than the Great Pyramid. But it's an illusion: it stands on higher ground.

Khufu's son Khafre (reigned c 2558–2532 BCE) was the fourth pharaoh of the 4th dynasty. The interior might be open to visit – the inside of the Great Pyramid is always open, but access to the inner architecture of the pyramids of Khafre and Menkaure alternates every couple of years. Inside, you descend the claustrophobic shaft to a passageway and then across to the burial chamber, which still contains Khafre's large granite sarcophagus.

Funerary Temple of Khafre

On the east side of the Pyramid of Khafre are the substantial remains of his **funerary temple**, where the pharaoh was worshipped after his death, with daily rounds of offerings to sustain his soul.

From the temple, a rock-paved causeway once provided access from the Nile to the tomb, and you can still walk it down to the Sphinx (but not yet because there's still another pyramid to see!).

Pyramid of Menkaure

At 62m (originally 66.5m), the **Pyramid of Menkaure** is the smallest of the trio, only about one-tenth of the bulk of the Great Pyramid. Menkaure (reigned c 2532–2503 BCE) died before the structure was finished, and if you look around the bottom of the pyramid, you can spot several pieces of granite that were never properly smoothed.

Sphinx

If this pyramid interior is open *(LE280 in addition to Giza Plateau entry)*, you'll descend into three distinct levels – the lowest surprisingly large – and you can peer into the main tomb.

Menkaure's Funerary Temple sits on the eastern side of his pyramid, and to the south is a set of **Queens' Pyramids**.

Sphinx

Down the plateau from the pyramids, the famous **Sphinx** is accessed through the **Valley Temple of Khafre**, filled with pink-granite columns. If you look in the corners, you can see how the stones aren't rectangular blocks but curve past the corner, making them less susceptible to earthquakes because they fit together like a jigsaw puzzle.

Look for the rectangular recesses in the floor. The temple originally had 23 statues of Khafre that were illuminated with the ancient version of mood lighting: through slits between the top of the wall and the flat roof.

The temple exit brings you onto the pavement that runs along the southern side of the sunken pit that holds the Sphinx. While everyone is snapping the obligatory Sphinx headshot, walk to the end of the platform so you can view its brickwork paws and haunches.

The ancient Greeks dubbed this sculpture the Sphinx because it resembled their mythical winged monster that set riddles and killed anyone unable to answer them. In Arabic, it's known as *Abu Al Hol* (Father of Terror). Although no one knows which pharaoh it's supposed to portray, geological surveys have confirmed that it was most likely chiselled out from the bedrock during the reign of Khafre.

Between the Sphinx' Paws

An increasing number of Egypt's ancient sites have 'private tour' options that get you up close with exclusive access – for a price (upwards of US$500). At the Giza Plateau, some tour companies get permission from the Ministry of Antiquities to offer the opportunity to stand between the paws of the Sphinx and see the Dream Stele, erected by Thutmose IV in 1401 BCE. The granite stone tells how Thutmose, as a young prince, fell asleep near the Sphinx, by that point a 1000-year-old relic that was nearly buried in sand. A god appeared to Thutmose to say that if he cleared away the sand, he would become king.

Less expensive but newly offered is a visit to the mud-brick tombs of the workers who built the pyramids, discovered between 1990 and 2010. You can book the tickets online *(egymonuments.com)*, but you must pay for a minimum of five people (LE3500).

Horse & Camel Rides at the Pyramids

If you're going to ride a camel anywhere in the world, Giza is a good choice, plodding out into the sand to get those famed panoramas of three pyramids surrounded by a sweep of desert. In the same vein, horse rides in the desert with the pyramids as your backdrop can be one of the highlights of a visit. The Giza

continues on p70

FOREVER IS NOW

For three weeks in October and November, part of the Giza Plateau is transformed into an outdoor sculpture park. 'Forever is Now' is an exhibition put on by **Art d'Egypte** *(artdegypte.org)*, an arts-promotion organisation. Since 2021, about a dozen international and Egyptian artists have created large-scale, site-specific works in response to the Pyramids of Giza that rise in the background.

The results are fascinating and surreal. *Horizon* by Greek sculptor Costas Varotsos placed eight metal-ringed glass circles half-filled with water on the sand, and from the right angle, it looked like the pyramids were once again sitting on the banks of the Nile. Dutch artist Sabine Marcelis created *Ra*, a vertical ombre glass sundial that stored sunlight by day and emitted the rays by night.

After the exhibition, the art is removed and the desert returns to its natural state.

The Giza Pyramids

❶ Great Pyramid of Khufu (Cheops)
Clamber inside the corridors to marvel at the precision engineering of the seamless stone blocks, each weighing 2.5 tonnes. Pause to consider the full weight of 2.3 million of them.

❷ Pyramid of Khafre
Khafre's pyramid still holds onto its limestone cap. Over the centuries this casing was stripped from the pyramids and carted off to be used in Cairo's palaces and mosques, exposing the softer inner-core stones to the elements.

Khafre's Valley Temple

Eastern Cemetery

❼ Sphinx
It's clear from the accounts of early Arab travellers that the Sphinx's nose was hammered off sometime between the 11th- and 15th-centuries. Part of the fallen beard was carted off by 19th-century adventurers and is now on display in the British Museum.

❻ Tombs of Qar & Idu
These two adjoining tombs for Qar and his son Idu date from the reign of 6th-dynasty pharaoh Pepi I, showing how use of this necropolis remained continuous throughout the Old Kingdom.

❸ Pyramid of Menkaure (Mycerinus)

This pyramid opens alternately with the Pyramid of Khafre. The gash in the exterior is the folly of Sultan Al Aziz Uthman, who tried to dismantle the pyramid in 1196.

❺ Tomb of Meresankh III

Make sure to note the alcoves holding finely cut seated-scribe statues on the southern wall and the reliefs depicting farming and craftspeople. The Giza Plateau is dotted with tombs like this one but opening schedules vary each year.

❽ Ticket Booth & Entrance

Decide what you want to see before you visit – tickets for pyramid interiors and tombs can be bought only from the entrance gates or online (egymonuments.com). You can also buy parking passes online. Tickets bought online are sent to your email as PDFs with QR codes.

❹ Queens' Pyramids

These smaller piles are in bad shape, but some show the original limestone casing at the base – feel how smoothly the stones are fitted.

PARAMOTOR OVER THE PYRAMIDS

If you thought seeing the pyramids from your EgyptAir flight into Cairo was cool, you can fly even closer to these ancient wonders on a paramotoring trip. These tours are often called paragliding, but the term 'paramotoring' is more accurate: you and an instructor sit in a contraption that looks like a tandem bicycle with a motor at the back and a parachute overhead. Operators offer these trips in the winter months and usually only on the weekends (Fridays, Saturdays and Sundays). The 30-minute experience (15 minutes of a safety briefing and 15 minutes of flying) costs about US$200, which includes pick-up and drop-off at your hotel. You also need to buy the Giza Plateau entry ticket (LE700).

For more high-adrenaline activities that keep you closer to Earth, operators also offer one- or two-hour quad-biking trips that race around the sands. Inspect the vehicles before you set off and pay at the end of the tour.

9 Pyramids Lounge

continued from p67

Plateau certainly has no shortage of camel and horse drivers who want to help make your desert panorama dreams come true, but organising it can be a hassle (and a prolonged haggle).

Inside the pyramids complex, camel, horse and horse-carriage touts hang out around the Great Pyramid and at the **panoramic viewpoint** west of the Pyramid of Menkaure. While there's technically an official government-set rate for rides, in practice, bargaining is the name of the game, and most touts charge at least US$20 for a 30-minute ride. Do not get on the animal until you've agreed on a price.

It is up to you to make sure your horse or camel looks healthy and well fed before hopping on. Do not choose an operator who uses whips. Outside the site, two stables with good reputations for well-cared-for animals are **NB Stables** (*facebook.com/NasserBreeshStables*) and **FB Stables** (*fbstablesgiza.co.uk*). The only hassle-free way to arrange your riding experience is to book with them.

Dining with Pyramid Views

After all that trudging around the plateau – clambering down shafts into tomb chambers, feeling bamboozled by the sheer weight of history right in front of you, and dealing with vendors and touts – it's nice to simply kick back and soak up the pyramid views from afar. Before 2020, there was nowhere to eat within the pyramids complex, but that's now changed with the opening of two upscale eateries, plus a selection of cafes, including French macaron marvel **Ladurée** *(laduree. eg)*, dotted around the site.

At **Khufu's** *(khufus.com)*, chef Mostafa Seif offers feasts of traditional Egyptian dishes that have been given the fine-dining treatment with fresh, contemporary twists. Egypt's street-food classic *kushari* (a mix of noodles, rice, brown lentils, fried onions and tomato sauce) is flipped and turned into a salad. Ingredients such as date molasses and ginger spike up normally humble home-style dishes, and roasted pigeons are stuffed with spiced freekeh. You dine on a chic desert-neutral outdoor terrace shaded by sails and with a view of the pyramids emerging from the desert directly in front of you.

Get even better views (though a less impressive menu) at **9 Pyramids Lounge** *(instagram.com/9pyramidslounge)*, far from the bustle down an unpaved road on the south side of the plateau. The traditional cushioned seats on the ground are the perfect spot to soak up the scene over an Egyptian breakfast or grilled meats. Reservations are required for both restaurants, and you must have the LE700 entry ticket to the Giza Plateau to access them, so plan to eat here while touring the site instead of on a different day.

TOP TIPS

● The complex opens at 7am (in reality, around 7.15am), and the first tour buses turn up just after 8am, so early birds can get the pyramids all to themselves for about an hour. The problem with this is the plateau's wild dogs, which are docile once the area gets busier but can be aggressive when it's just you. A start time of 8am works better.

● New public toilets have been installed around the plateau, but they are pay-to-pee (LE10).

● If you're on a tour or have a taxi driver taking you around the complex, ask whether you need to pay for their parking (car/microbus/bus LE25/50/100).

Khufu's

TOP EXPERIENCE

Grand Egyptian Museum

Perhaps the world's most anticipated cultural opening, the Grand Egyptian Museum (GEM) is one of the largest archaeological museums, as well as the largest such institution dedicated to a single civilisation. A project 20 years in the making, the museum is set to open its final galleries in late 2025.

DON'T MISS

- Ramses II colossus (Grand Hall)
- Grand Staircase
- Funerary furniture (Gallery 2)
- Troop Models (Gallery 4)
- Statue of Queen Hatshepsut (Gallery 8)

Museum Grounds & Grand Hall

The pyramid is a common design motif throughout the Grand Egyptian Museum – no surprise as the museum was built to complement these stunning ancient structures that stand just a couple of kilometres away. The museum grounds are still works in progress, and a boardwalk that links the museum to the Pyramids of Giza is one of the features yet to come. Before heading inside, don't miss the **hanging obelisk**, so called because it sits up on a platform separated from its base.

PRACTICALITIES
- with/without guided tour LE1700/1200
- 9am-3pm (last entry)
- Scan this QR code for more information

A cartouche containing the name of Ramses II was chiselled onto the obelisk's underside, now visible for the first time in thousands of years.

Fronted by an alabaster and glass pyramid covered in cartouches and hieroglyphs from pharaohs of many dynasties, the museum astonishes as soon as you step inside. In the Grand Hall, visitors are greeted by a colossal 11m-tall **statue of Ramses II**. The high-ceilinged Grand Hall is not enclosed (and therefore not air-conditioned) and can be warm.

If you paid for the more expensive ticket that includes a guided tour, you'll meet your guide and group near the information desk on the left side, but first, pick up an audio headset from the windows on the far left. You're required to leave your passport in exchange.

Grand Staircase

Ascend the Grand Staircase by foot or escalator – on foot is better because the stairs are dotted with artefacts. The first section near the bottom of the Grand Staircase covers the **Royal Image**, explaining how pharaohs liked themselves to be depicted. Middle Kingdom rulers often had oversized ears and serious faces to show that they were listening to the concerns of the Egyptian people, while pharaohs of the New Kingdom were carved with slight smiles. The **Divine Houses** section moves on to temple architecture for worshipping the gods, as shown through columns, lintels and naos, small shrines that housed statues of the deities. Further up, **Kings and Gods** tells how the pharaohs linked themselves to the ancient pantheon of deities by close association in statuary and representations of divine birth. Finally, **Journey to Eternity** presents the evolution of funerary architecture.

This section flows gracefully into a wall of floor-to-ceiling windows at the top of the Grand Staircase, with showstopping **views of the Pyramids of Giza**, themselves considered symbols of eternity by the ancients.

Main Galleries

The Main Galleries are split into four time periods, from 700,000 BCE to 394 CE, across three themes: society, kingship and beliefs. The beautifully lit displays of statues, tomb furniture and painted reliefs have descriptions, but it's hard to fit centuries of stories into a single printed paragraph, so it's worth signing up for the **90-minute guided tour**, which runs through the highlights with a knowledgeable English-speaking guide, and then venturing around afterwards on your own.

If you're short on time, look at fixtures hanging from the ceiling and dark-blue information panels, which indicates a highlight of the collection.

Galleries 1–3: Prehistory to the First Intermediate Period

The entrance and exit point for the Main Galleries is in Gallery 1, which covers society from 700,000 to 2034 BCE, before and after the time of the Old Kingdom. Many of the Old Kingdom artefacts come from the nearby Pyramids of

> **TAKE A BREAK**
>
> The museum has taken an upscale approach to its food offerings, which include several coffee shops (Starbucks, 30 North), ice cream and pastry places (Dolato Gelateria, Ladurée), and two full-service restaurants: Zööba (the beloved Cairo chain) and Bittersweet, serving pizza, pasta and Egyptian dishes. These outlets are at the bottom of the Grand Staircase, making it easy to look through the exhibits until you're hungry and then return when you're full.
>
> The gift shop features Egyptian-made products and is a good place to pick up some souvenirs. High-end shops include famous jeweller **Azza Fahmy** (p128), as well as luxe leather bags from **Okhtein** *(okhtein.com)*.

MUSEUM ACCESSIBILITY

The GEM is one of the most accessible museums in Egypt, good news for travellers with disabilities in a city – and country – otherwise poorly equipped. Some galleries have Braille signage and tactile models of the displays. Lifts, escalators and ramps help visitors with mobility needs to move around.

Giza and the Step Pyramid in Saqqara, including miraculously surviving wooden statues of priests, scribes and other elites. Notice how the women are often the same height as the men. The painted limestone **statue of Scribe Nefer**, who sits cross-legged with a papyrus scroll on his lap and has a look of concentration on his face, is particularly remarkable. If you haven't visited Saqqara yet, the vibrant **tomb paintings from Dahshur** on the back wall show you just what a treat you're in for. Many blocks show agricultural scenes, but look for the monkey, a favourite pet of the rich, under the table in the banquet panel.

As you head towards Gallery 2, stop at the large **Royal Tomb Development panel**, which shows how the styles of tombs changed from small bench-shaped burial chambers called mastabas to stacked mastabas that later gave way to smooth-sided pyramids. The highlights in this gallery are the gold-foil-covered **grave goods of Queen Hetepheres**, the mother of Khufu, the builder of Giza's Great Pyramid. The glittering funerary furniture includes an armchair decorated with tied papyrus flowers and a gilded bed with a headrest that would have been covered with a feathered pillow.

Galleries 4–6: Middle Kingdom & Second Intermediate Period

Gallery 4 contains beautifully decorated coffins and mummy beds of governors and nobles. Many of them have eyes painted or are inlaid with stone on one side of the coffin to allow the deceased to 'see' out of the coffin and follow the rising sun, symbolising rebirth. The **Outer Coffin of Mesehti**, a provincial governor in the 11th dynasty, is particularly

Solar Boat of Khufu (p76)

striking, with eyes made from black volcanic glass on an unpainted case of imported cedar wood. Nearby, look for the **Troop Models**, long lines of miniature figures of Egyptian military men holding spears and Nubians carrying archery bows. The ancient Egyptians believed that the figures would be animated in the afterlife to protect their master.

In Gallery 5, statues of Middle Kingdom pharaohs were carved in much larger proportions compared with the Old Kingdom, to show off their power through their strong bodies and big ears for listening to their people.

The papyrus documents in Gallery 6 show the inner workings of the royal residence, and one scroll records the names of workers and financial transactions in the palace in Thebes (modern-day Luxor).

Galleries 7–9: New Kingdom

The New Kingdom was a high point in the timeline of ancient Egypt, and many of the best-known pharaohs are from this period. Ancient Egypt's influence and borders expanded, and it was a golden era of art and architecture. In Gallery 8, you can't miss the **kneeling statue of Queen Hatshepsut**. This larger-than-life sculpture shows the female pharaoh presenting two offering pots to Amun-Ra, the king of the gods. This gallery also dives into the story of Akhenaten, thought to be the world's first monotheist, for which he was branded the 'heretic' pharaoh for changing ancient Egypt's state religion. Look out for the digital depiction of the 'Great Hymn of the Aten', a poem dedicated to Akhenaten's god that's represented as a solar disc with outstretched hands at the end of the sun rays. The hymn has many parallels with Psalm 104 in the Bible.

The granite **Restoration Stela** in Gallery 9 shows what happened after Akhenaten's death. During the reign of his son Tutankhamun, the state religion reverted to the former belief system.

Galleries 10–12: Third Intermediate Period to the Graeco-Romans

Ancient Egypt's fortunes were starting to fade by the time of the Third Intermediate Period, and the Ptolemaic era was marked by political unrest. Despite this, the strong tradition of art and temple-building carried on. In Gallery 10, the **Dendera Treasure Hoard** contains seriously stunning finds, including a large winged scarab. Its body is carved from lapis lazuli, and its wings are made of gold and silver and inlaid with semi-precious stones. Next to it is a golden statue of Horus, the falcon-headed god, that's hollow inside to store a mummified bird. Further display cases have specimens of mummified animals, including ibises and a huge Nile crocodile. Human mummification continued through the Roman period – look for the mummy of a woman whose hands and jewellery are moulded in 3D to display her wealth.

GEM CHILDREN'S MUSEUM

Kids have long been fascinated by all things ancient Egypt, but endless exhibits in museums can be a tough place to keep their attention. To balance learning and interactive fun, the GEM has opened a dedicated Children's Museum, accessed partway up the Grand Staircase. Suitable for kids ages six to 12, the interactive displays put a playful spin on Pharaonic history. You can visit at your own pace or have your kid tag along with an Egyptologist docent on a 45-minute tour. Experiences include an archaeological 'dig' using magnets and sitting on a replica of Tutankhamun's throne. A ticket is required to access the **Children's Museum** *(LE750)*, and an adult chaperone has to stay with those aged six to nine years.

You can also sign up for the GEM **Discovery Challenge** *(LE125)*, a smartphone-based game in which you solve puzzles using information in the galleries. It's offered daily at noon and 2pm, and winners take home a special souvenir.

Tutankhamun & Khufu's Solar Boats

TOP TIPS

- The Grand Egyptian Museum is huge, so give yourself at least half a day to visit, but ideally longer.

- Bring your passport if you've signed up for a guided tour. You leave it with the staff for the audio device.

- Arriving by public transport is a challenge, and the closest metro station is a 16km drive away. Get an Uber or a taxi.

Has any other museum in the world been this long in the making? Touted for nearly a decade, the final two – and most highly anticipated – galleries of the Grand Egyptian Museum are set to open in late 2025 and will display the complete collection of golden grave goods of Tutankhamun, the famous boy king, and the funerary boat of Khufu, the builder of Giza's Great Pyramid.

Tutankhamun Collection

Tutankhamun ruled for only nine years (c 1336–1327 BCE), but the treasures found in his tomb have made him Egypt's most famous pharaoh.

Before you go to see Tutankhamun's death mask, take in the larger items from his tomb. Don't miss the two life-size wooden and bitumen-coated **statues of Tutankhamun**, found in the tomb's antechamber. Their black skin suggests an identification with Osiris and the rich, black river silt, symbolising fertility and rebirth. Admire the **canopic jars** with their stoppers shaped like Tutankhamun's head. Inside these jars, four miniature coffins held Tutankhamun's internal organs.

Eventually, you'll come face to face with **Tutankhamun's death mask**, which weighs 11kg and is made of solid gold, as well as his two golden inner coffins. Also included in the collection are displays of the tombs' smaller treasures, including delicately detailed falcon-headed golden jewellery.

Tutankhamun's death mask

Downtown Cairo

BUZZING STREETS BELOW BELLE ÉPOQUE ARCHITECTURE

For many visitors, Downtown Cairo (*Wust Al Balad* in Arabic) is simply the base from where they launch out to explore the rest of the city. Although the only big-hitter sight here is the powder-pink puffball of a building that is the Egyptian Museum, Downtown is the soul of the city: a whirlwind of traffic-clogged roads, strolling crowds and *ahwas* (coffeehouses) that spill out onto the street.

The golden rule Downtown is don't forget to look up – though not to the extent that you forget to look where you're going because potholes and random obstacles are rampant here. Soaring above are the ornate facades of Egypt's belle-époque period, which began in the 1860s when Khedive Ismail set about transforming Cairo into a duplicate of Paris. Time has wearied Downtown's now dust-caked architecture, but formerly dilapidated facades are increasingly being revamped, and cafes are multiplying, infusing the central city with an upbeat, youthful buzz.

Stand in Midan Tahrir
The core of the city

MAP P88

Midan Tahrir has been a focal point of Downtown Cairo for more than 150 years, long before it gained international name recognition when tens of thousands of Egyptians converged here to oust then-President Hosni Mubarak during the 2011 Arab Spring uprisings. On a regular day, it's just your average giant traffic circle, where half a dozen major arteries converge. Laid out in the 1860s at the same time as the building of the Suez Canal, it was originally called Midan Ismailia and was renamed *tahrir* (liberation) after the Revolution of 1952. A Ramses II obelisk from Tanis in the Nile Delta crowns the roundabout, and the surrounding ram-headed sphinxes come from Karnak.

The main reason you'll pass through Midan Tahrir is to visit the dusty pink bulk of the Egyptian Museum (p78).

continued on p82

☑ TOP TIP

Friday morning is the best time to wander around Downtown Cairo, as the neighbourhood snoozes until midday prayers. Many shops and restaurants don't open until later in the day – or not at all.

GETTING AROUND

Most streets have walkable pavements. Midan Tahrir, in front of the Egyptian Museum, and Midan Talaat Harb are easy-to-find landmarks and focal points of the neighbourhood.

This area has five metro stations to connect you to Greater Cairo, and Ramses Station has trains to Giza and Alexandria. From late 2024, trains to the southern Nile Valley no longer depart from Ramses but now leave from Upper Egypt Train Station (also called Bashtil) near the Giza neighbourhood of Mohandiseen.

Coffin of Akhenaten

TOP EXPERIENCE

Egyptian Museum

The oldest museum in the Middle East, the Egyptian Museum opened in 1902 and still takes pride of place in Downtown Cairo. Many of its treasures have been crated up and sent to the Grand Egyptian Museum (p72) in Giza, but this vast pink building remains home to one of the world's most important collections of ancient artefacts.

DON'T MISS

- Narmer Palette
- Statue of Djoser
- Statue of Khafre
- Statue of Ka-aper
- Death masks of Yuya and Thuya
- Silver coffin of Psusennes I

Ground Floor

The ground-floor galleries are set up so that you sweep through 700,000 years of ancient Egyptian history in chronological order by turning left from the entrance and going clockwise. Look for the gallery numbers high on the walls.

Pre- & Early-Dynastic Egypt

Walk straight ahead from the entrance to enter Gallery 43 and look for the **Narmer Palette** taking centre stage. Examine

PRACTICALITIES
- LE550
- 9am–4pm (last entry)
- Scan this QR code for more information

both sides. Pharaoh Narmer of Egypt's 1st dynasty (c 3100–2890 BCE) is depicted wearing the crown of Upper Egypt on one side and Lower Egypt on the other, suggesting his reign was the first time the country was united, marking the foundation of 3000 years of Pharaonic history.

Old Kingdom

The ground-floor Old Kingdom section treats Egypt's mighty pyramid builders with the respect they deserve, and it's a good one to visit shortly before or after the Pyramids of Giza and Saqqara. In Gallery 46, you're greeted by a limestone **statue of Djoser** backed by a wall of blue faience tiles taken from the interior of his Step Pyramid at Saqqara.

Don't miss the **panel of Meidum geese** in Gallery 41. The geese were painted on the wall of a mud-brick mastaba (rectangular tomb) around 2500 BCE in Meidum, near Al Fayoum.

In Gallery 42, groups tend to cluster around the ivory **statue of Khufu** – just 7.5cm tall and the only surviving representation of the builder of Giza's Great Pyramid – as well as the dramatic black diorite **statue of Khafre**.

Surrounding the pharaohs are small figures of workers (look for the female beer brewer) and sculptures of members of the royal court. In Gallery 37 you'll find the astonishing sycamore-wood **statue of Ka-aper**, a chief priest with a protruding belly and lifelike eyes. It is one of the masterworks of the Old Kingdom.

New Kingdom

In the middle of Gallery 11, you'll find the spot-lit painted limestone **head of Hatshepsut** and, in a neighbouring cabinet, her **sphinx**. Both once graced her mortuary temple at Deir Al Bahri.

The vaulted sandstone **chapel of Tuthmosis III**, with its painted walls and a life-size cow statue, all in a remarkable state of preservation, is in Gallery 12. Inside, you can see scenes of the pharaoh, his wife and two princesses making offerings to Hathor.

Gallery 3 is dedicated to the Amarna Period under the rule of Akhenaten (reigned c 1353–1336 BCE), the 'heretic' pharaoh. Notice the statues' different artistic style, with elongated faces and bulbous bellies, compared with the hard-edged sculptures in the previous galleries. Look closely at the **coffin of Akhenaten**. Nearly all of the face is missing, and his cartouche has been removed so that his soul can't find its way back to his body.

Upper Floor

On the upper floor, the galleries are arranged by theme and finds from specific tombs.

Yuya & Thuya

The east galleries on the upper floor are dedicated to the funerary goods from the tomb of Yuya and Thuya (Queen Tiye's parents and Tutankhamun's great-grandparents). Before Tut-mania in the 1920s, the treasures found inside this

---

TOP TIPS

● In the peak-season winter months (December to February), it's difficult to avoid huge crowds of tour groups. Try beginning around noon when the morning buses are finishing and other coach groups are still at lunch.

● If the amount of history gets to be too much (this museum has a *lot* to see), head to the cafes and small eateries on the west side of the building.

● A guide can be helpful if you want to dive into the details of specific pharaohs or artefacts. Some exhibits have excellent labels, while others have none at all. Some old typewriter-written labels are still displayed.

ANOTHER ROSETTA STONE

The Rosetta Stone is one of Egypt's most famous artefacts and has long been located in the British Museum in London. But it wasn't the only block that was inscribed in hieroglyphs, Demotic and Greek. On the right side of the Egyptian Museum's entry hall, look for the **Canopus Decree**, a large limestone slab that records a meeting of priests in 238 BCE.

Egyptian Museum

First Floor

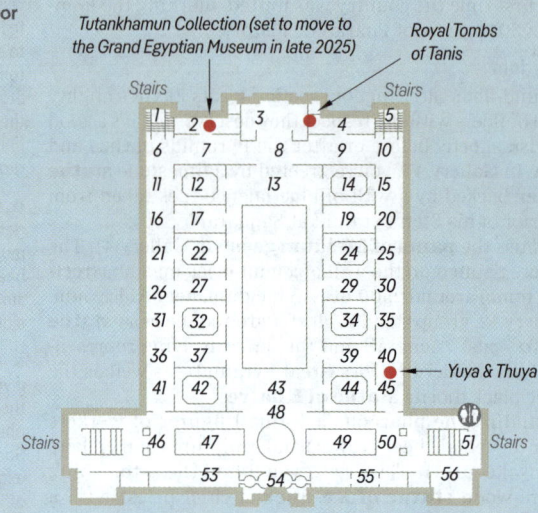

Ground Floor

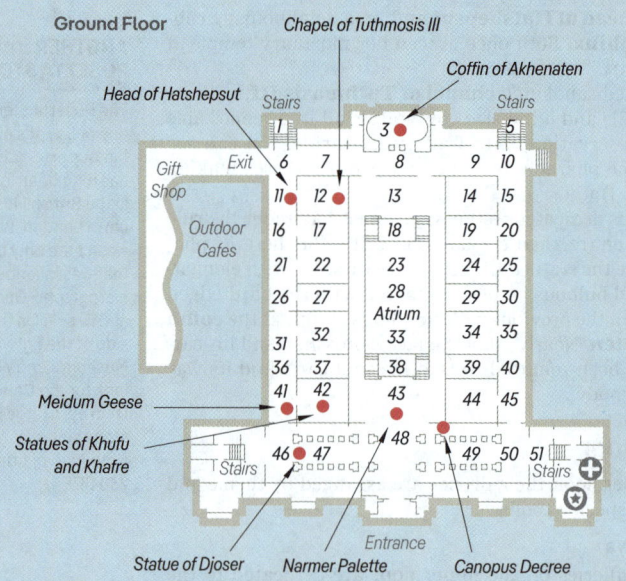

Narmer Palette (p78)

virtually intact tomb in the Valley of the Kings in 1905 were Egyptology's most spectacular find.

As well as the gilded, bead-trimmed **death masks of Yuya and Thuya** and their **golden coffins**, with their well-preserved mummies encased inside, the grave goods on display include an entire haul of furniture, from Yuya's gilded wood and leather chariot to Thuya's blue faience inlaid jewel casket. Make sure to also see the less glittery items, such as Yuya and Thuya's reed sandals, placed in the tomb so that they'd have shoes to wear in the afterlife.

Running for nearly 20m along the wall is the **Papyrus of Yuya**, the most complete ever found.

Royal Tombs of Tanis

You might not have heard of **Tanis** (p153), but the treasures unearthed from six intact 21st- and 22nd-dynasty tombs discovered at this Delta site in 1939 rival the riches of Tutankhamun.

In Gallery 4, check out Amenemope's tiny **baboon-headed heart amulet** and the display of golden **finger and toe stalls**, which were placed over the mummy's fingers and toes to make sure they could still use them in the afterlife.

In Gallery 3, the gold **death mask of Psusennes I** (c 1047–996 BCE) and his gleaming, highly detailed **silver coffin** steal the show, but make sure to also take in the display of his glittery jewellery, including a chunky oversized gold and lapis lazuli necklace that wouldn't be out of place at the Met Gala.

WHAT'S NEXT FOR THE EGYPTIAN MUSEUM?

It was feared that when the Grand Egyptian Museum opened, the old Egyptian Museum might be shuttered for good, but an ongoing revitalisation campaign has actually improved it despite the heavy machinery and number of packed-up crates on the ground floor. Even though it's lost some of its substantial artefacts, including the royal mummies to the **National Museum of Egyptian Civilization** (p119) in 2021 and the prized Tutankhamun collection to the **Grand Egyptian Museum** (p72), the 'old' Egyptian Museum's galleries are still stuffed with unmissable treasures, some of which are now better lit and labelled, including in Braille.

DOWNTOWN CAIRO

SIGHTS
1. Abdeen Palace Museum
2. Egyptian Postal Museum
3. Egyptian Railway Museum
4. Mamsha Ahl Misr
5. Royal Carriages Museum

ACTIVITIES
6. Imkan Boats

SLEEPING
7. St Regis Cairo

EATING
8. Abdel Rahim Koueider
9. El Tabei El Domiaty
10. Groppi Garden
11. Koshary Goha
12. Latif Wassily
13. Zaza Cuisine by the Nile

DRINKING & NIGHTLIFE
14. Carlton Hotel Roof Garden

ENTERTAINMENT
15. Zawya Cinema

TRANSPORT
16. Ramses Station

continued from p77

The brutalist concrete building taking up most of the southern side of the square is the **Mogamma**, known to Cairenes simply as the 'Complex'. Famous for its sprawling rabbit warren where you could lose days trying to get a piece of paper stamped, this once notorious heart of Egypt's infernal bureaucracy was the star of the classic 1992 Egyptian comedy film *Irhab Wal Kabab* (*Terrorism and Kebab*), in which the frustrated main character played by Adel Emam holds everyone in the building hostage. In 2021, the government offices departed for the New Administrative Capital, and the building is being redeveloped into a 500-room Marriott Autograph luxury hotel with shops, restaurants and a rooftop pool.

Fuel Up on *Kushari* at Abou Tarek

MAP P88

Egypt's favourite fast food

The king of Egyptian street food is *kushari*, a carb-heavy mix of noodles, rice, brown lentils and chickpeas, topped with crispy fried onions that you smother in tomato sauce, douse with garlicky vinegar and dab with hot sauce. Cheap, filling and tasty, *kushari* is the fuel that keeps Egypt going, and many Egyptians regard it as their national dish.

For your first experience, head to **Koshary Abou Tarek** (instagram.com/koshariabotarek). This temple of *kushari* on Champollion St has been in business for 70 years and continues to hold on to Cairo's unofficial 'best *kushari*' title. Head upstairs to eat amid the restaurant's retro-glam canteen decor that includes chandeliers, random blue up-lighting fitted in the ceiling, tropical fish tanks, a fountain in the middle of the room and a massive portrait of Abou Tarek keeping a fatherly eye on his happy diners.

It's open from 7am to midnight and is packed with diners for most of that time. The friendly staff are used to foreign visitors, and the menu has only two items anyway (*kushari* and lentil soup in a bread bowl). When your *kushari* arrives, mix the tomato sauce into the macaroni-rice-lentil-chickpea-onion combo and then grab the metal bottles on your table to splash vinegar and spicy sauce on top. The staff often offer to do it for you, and they put on a good show. Give your dish a good stir to make sure everything's mixed through and dig in.

Eat Your Way Through Cairo on a Walking Tour

Dig into Downtown's best dishes

Put comfy walking shoes on. Don't wear skinny jeans. Avoid eating lunch beforehand. If you want to get the lowdown on Downtown's food scene, tours run by the local Cairo foodie guides of **Bellies En-Route** (belliesenroute.com) are packed with insider know-how on the classic dishes and street-food favourites that keep Downtown Cairo running. Better yet, local culture takes centre stage as you munch your way between family-run canteens, a famed old-school coffee roaster, traditional patisserie, and hole-in-the-wall stands selling *ta'amiyya* (Egyptian falafel) and *fiteer* (sweet or savoury flaky pastry).

SAY HELLO TO EGYPTIAN FOOD

Laila Hassaballa is a co-founder of Bellies En-Route. @belliesenroute

We use food as a medium to showcase a different side of the country and act as a starting point to talk about Egypt and Egyptian culture. We want to show a different side of Egypt that gives visitors the opportunity to enter into a dialogue and helps them have a more meaningful experience.

As well as that, we've set out to create a tourism model that both protects and supports the local businesses we use, paying them fairly and making sure that our tour visits are a help to them rather than a hassle.

 EATING DOWNTOWN: ESSENTIAL EGYPTIAN EATS — MAPS P82, P88

Felfela: A Downtown institution since 1959, this restaurant serves endless plates of Egyptian classics below colourful glass ceiling panels. *11am-midnight* $$	**El Gomhoureya Restaurant:** Grilled pigeon is the star of the show, dished up alongside salad and mugs of peppery, lemony broth. *noon-midnight* $$	**Al Hamra Street:** Grab a takeaway shawarma from the spits on street level or head upstairs to scoff a sandwich at a sit-down table. *8am-3.30am* $	**Koshary Goha:** As the name implies, the *kushari* is excellent, but instead, go for *makaroneh bi lahm*, the Egyptian version of a pasta bake. *10am-midnight* $

Koshary Abou Tarek (p83)

CROSSING THE STREET

Cairo's roads might prove to be the biggest challenge of your trip. In parts of Downtown, improvements have been made, including working traffic lights and more traffic police controlling intersections, but crossing many streets can still seem impossible.

If you see operational traffic lights or an on-duty officer, it's best to wait – the flow of traffic will stop eventually. Elsewhere, watch how Cairenes cross. They don't hesitate or turn back, and they keep eye contact with drivers coming towards them. If you're nervous, wait for a Cairene to cross and follow in their wake. They might even help you across with some tongue-in-cheek advice for next time: 'Close your eyes and open your heart to God'.

Their **Downtown Cairo Food Tour** is the polar opposite of Egypt's many cookie-cutter tours: infused with local knowledge and providing both first-timers and return visitors with deeper insights into modern Egypt and Downtown's heritage. The tours have a no-food-waste policy (leftovers are packed up and given away) and support community restaurants that wouldn't normally get tourists through the door by providing a new income stream.

The tour runs from Saturday to Thursday and covers eight to 10 stops over four to five hours. The small-group tour costs US$72 per person and must be booked in advance. Private tours are also available, including the **Women of Egypt Food and Shopping Tour**, where you'll meet local women from various backgrounds crafting unique dishes flavoured with their own stories.

If you want to get hands on, sign up for the **Egyptian Cooking Class and Market Tour**, where you'll shop for ingredients at a Downtown market and then make falafel, moussaka, or *kabab halla* (beef stew) and *mahshi* (rice-stuffed vegetables).

 EATING DOWNTOWN: ELEVATED FARE — MAPS P82, P88

Fasahet Somaya: A highly recommended taste of Egyptian home cooking, with unusual ingredients on a small daily-changing menu. *5pm-7pm Sun-Fri* $$

Fish & Chips: Egyptian-style seafood dishes served in a cute, colourful restaurant. Unsurprisingly, it's also adored by local cats. *11.30am-11.30pm* $$

CaiRoma: A little slice of Italy in the Egyptian capital with excellent pizza, vegetarian options and off-street courtyard seating. *3pm-12.30am* $$

Le Bistro: Tucked away below street level, Le Bistro offers European plates for an Egyptian palette. *Steak frites* can make a nice change from kebab. *6pm-3am* $$

Downtown Rising
A new life for the neighbourhood

MAPS P82, P88

Some of Downtown Cairo's beautiful buildings are getting a glow-up thanks to heritage-focused property developer Al Ismaelia (see *downtowncairo.com*). Much of the focus has been around **Cinema Radio** *(instagram.com/cinemaradio.eg)*, built in 1932 and set to become a mainstay of Cairo's cultural scene once again. The updated arcade leading to the building from Sharia Talaat Harb is lined with excellent restaurants, cafes and shops in refurbished quarters, including a branch of the beloved bookshop **Diwan** *(diwanegypt.com)* and **Markaz** *(markazstore.com)*, which sells Egyptian homewares with contemporary twists, including embroidered cushions, glassware and ceramics.

For ethically-minded shopping in revamped premises, head through artsy Radio Lane on the left side of Cinema Radio to find several cute boutiques. **Up-Fuse** *(up-fuse.com)* repurposes plastic bags, bottles and car tyres into clothing, wallets and laptop sleeves. **Saqhoute** *(saqhoute.com)* is a zero-waste 'slow fashion' brand, while **La Boga** *(shoplaboga.com)* produces beautiful leather bags. These shops sit across from the sadly dilapidated Said Halim Pasha Palace, built in 1899 for Mohammed Ali's grandson, who went on to become the Grand Vizier of the Ottoman Empire. The beautiful building is just begging for its turn to be restored to its former glory.

The latest opening is **Mazeej Balad** (p154), an elegant five-room boutique hotel with a **rooftop restaurant** (p86) that joined the ranks in January 2025. It has taken over part of the restored La Viennoise building, constructed by an English architect in 1896. The restaurant is on the 4th floor, but the feeling of sitting in the mid-rise canopy of Downtown Cairo's concrete jungle, among the taller buildings pockmarked with satellite dishes and strings of laundry fluttering in the wind, only serves to emphasise the sense of place.

CAIRO JAZZ FESTIVAL

For just over a week in October and November, the capital grooves to smooth beats during the **Cairo Jazz Festival** *(cairojazzfestival.com)*, which has taken place for around two decades. The 2024 lineup included musicians from 15 countries, including Egypt, Switzerland and the UK, and artists put on 20 concerts, plus workshops, talks, film screenings and events for kids over nine days.

The venue isn't always the same from year to year, but in 2024 it took place at the American University in Cairo (AUC) near Midan Tahrir. Check online (the festival's website or *instagram.com/cairojazzfestival*) for the latest dates and other announcements.

Abdeen Palace: Downtown's Royal Residence

MAP P82

Mansion turned museum

The centrepiece of Khedive Ismail's Europe-like new Downtown district was **Abdeen Palace** *(LE150)*, built in neoclassical style. When its construction was finished in 1874,

 EATING & DRINKING DOWNTOWN: BREAKFAST & COFFEE — MAPS P82, P88

Eish + Malh: Great flat whites, brunch and Italian dishes in a high-ceilinged cafe. A favoured hangout for cool, young Cairenes. *7am-midnight* $$

Oldish: Cute courtyard cafe with Middle Eastern and European breakfast options, plus flavoured lattes and fresh juices. *8am-midnight* $$

Cilantro: This coffee shop is Egypt's answer to Starbucks and a favourite of AUC students coming from campus across the street. *7am-midnight*

La Poire: This cafe is locally known for its European-style patisserie, and it's also a popular spot for coffee and smoothies. *7.30am-midnight*

AROUND MIDAN TALAAT HARB

Downtown's two main streets, Talaat Harb and Qasr El Nil, intersect at the roundabout of **Midan Talaat Harb**, a short walk from the **Egyptian Museum** (p78). Many of Downtown's best restaurants and hotels radiate off this roundabout, making it a useful landmark. Cars whizz around a statue of tarboosh-sporting Harb, an economist who co-founded Banque Misr (Bank of Egypt).

Sharia Talaat Harb was originally named after Suleiman Pasha, a French-born Egyptian military commander, but Gamal Abdel Nasser, Egypt's second president, renamed it in 1954 in a purge of reminders of the Mohammed Ali dynasty.

Qasr El Nil St boasts some particularly fine architecture, best seen on a DIY walking tour (p92).

Ismail promptly upped sticks and moved here from the **Citadel** (p109), breaking with 700 years of tradition that had seen every Egyptian ruler preside over their domain from the heights of the hilltop fortress since Salah ad-Din (Saladin), the founder of the Ayyubid dynasty. It remained the royal household's official address right up until the Revolution of 1952.

Today, a small portion of the 500 salons of Abdeen Palace houses a hodgepodge of museums, including several galleries dedicated to antique weapons, glass, silverware and ceramics. Unless you have a particular interest in regal chinaware or antique daggers, you're here to gawp at the unintentionally funny **Presidency Gifts Museum**, packed with a baffling array of useless sparkly stuff that world leaders and other notables gift each other. Where else are you going to store your multiple clock towers from Mecca or your collection of Russian machine guns? Don't miss the portrait of Egyptian President Sisi that's made entirely of pushpins.

The ticket office is located on the eastern side of the complex, and the museum entrance is across the road through a large gate. An extra fee is charged for taking photos, even on your phone (at least LE20, depending on the type of camera you have).

EATING & DRINKING DOWNTOWN: NEAR CINEMA RADIO — MAPS P82, P88

Almería: Presents the best flavours from all corners of the Med (pomegranate, yoghurt, honey, aubergine) in a mod-retro space. *11am-11pm Mon-Sat* $$$

Mazeej Balad Rooftop: Atop a boutique hotel, Downtown's best rooftop offers Egyptian-European fusion, such as *kushari arancini*. *8am-1am* $$$

Jade Pizza: Traditional and speciality pizzas made with creative ingredients (figs, sumac onions) delivered with a side of karaoke on select nights. *3pm-1am* $$

Sip: Small, hip coffee shop with minimalist millennial vibes (dusty pink accent wall, on-table succulents) in the redeveloped Cinema Radio arcade. *8am-11pm*

Abdeen Palace (p85)

Stroll Mamsha Ahl Misr

MAP P82

Walk along the Nile

Cairo can be a challenge to walk around, but **Mamsha Ahl Misr** *(Walkway of the Egyptian People; instagram.com/mamshaahlmisr)* takes the hassle out of finding a spot to stroll, particularly for families, women and solo travellers. This Nile-front promenade has two levels, and the **lower section** *(LE20)* sits just above the river, providing a pedestrian-only space removed from the street-level car-horn-honking chaos on the Corniche road above. Cafes and restaurants line the walkway and are popular spots in the evenings for dinner, coffee and shisha.

The promenade also has docks for motorboats heading out onto the Nile. **Imkan Boats** *(instagram.com/imkan_boats; per person LE50)* is an inexpensive option for getting on the water if you're travelling alone or don't want to rent out a whole vessel. Squeeze onto the side seats and enjoy a short loop along the river as Egyptian pop music blares from the speakers.

Mamsha Ahl Misr currently stretches from a few hundred metres north of the 26th of July Bridge to **Zaza Cuisine by the Nile** *(zazacuisine.com)*, near the steel arcs of Imbaba Bridge, built in the 1920s. This restaurant is one of the best spots for waterfront relaxing in town, with plenty of riverside and over-water seating, a fine selection of mocktails, shisha,

continued on p90

TOP SHOPS IN DOWNTOWN CAIRO

Oum El Dounia:
High-quality crafts, including ceramics from Fayoum, Bedouin needlework from Sinai and homewares from across Egypt. It's on the 1st floor of 3 Sharia Talaat Harb *(instagram.com/oumeldounia)*; look for the sign at street level.

AUC Bookstore:
Cairo's best selection of English-language books about Egyptian history, heritage and modern politics, plus Arabic literature in translation. It's inside the American University in Cairo campus but has its own entrance on Sharia Sheikh Rihan *(aucpress.com)*. Bring your passport for entry.

Lehnert & Landrock:
Old maps, books about Cairo and Egypt (some secondhand), great vintage postcards and reprints of wonderful old photographs.

 DRINKING DOWNTOWN: BEST BARS & NIGHTLIFE — MAPS P82, P88

Zahrat Al Bustan: Do as the Cairenes do: pull up a plastic chair on the street, smoke shisha, drink tea and watch the world go by. *9am–1am*

Carlton Hotel Roof Garden: Have a beer or a shisha with a view of the city lights from the 8th floor of the 1930s Carlton Hotel. *5pm–2am*

Carol Bar & Restaurant: A lively crowd packs into the narrow space below the bottles of alcohol curving up the bar wall. *5pm–2am*

El Horreya: Downtown's most famous *baladi* (local) bar, with cheap beer and an interior of high ceilings, mirrors and vintage drinks signs. *2pm–2am*

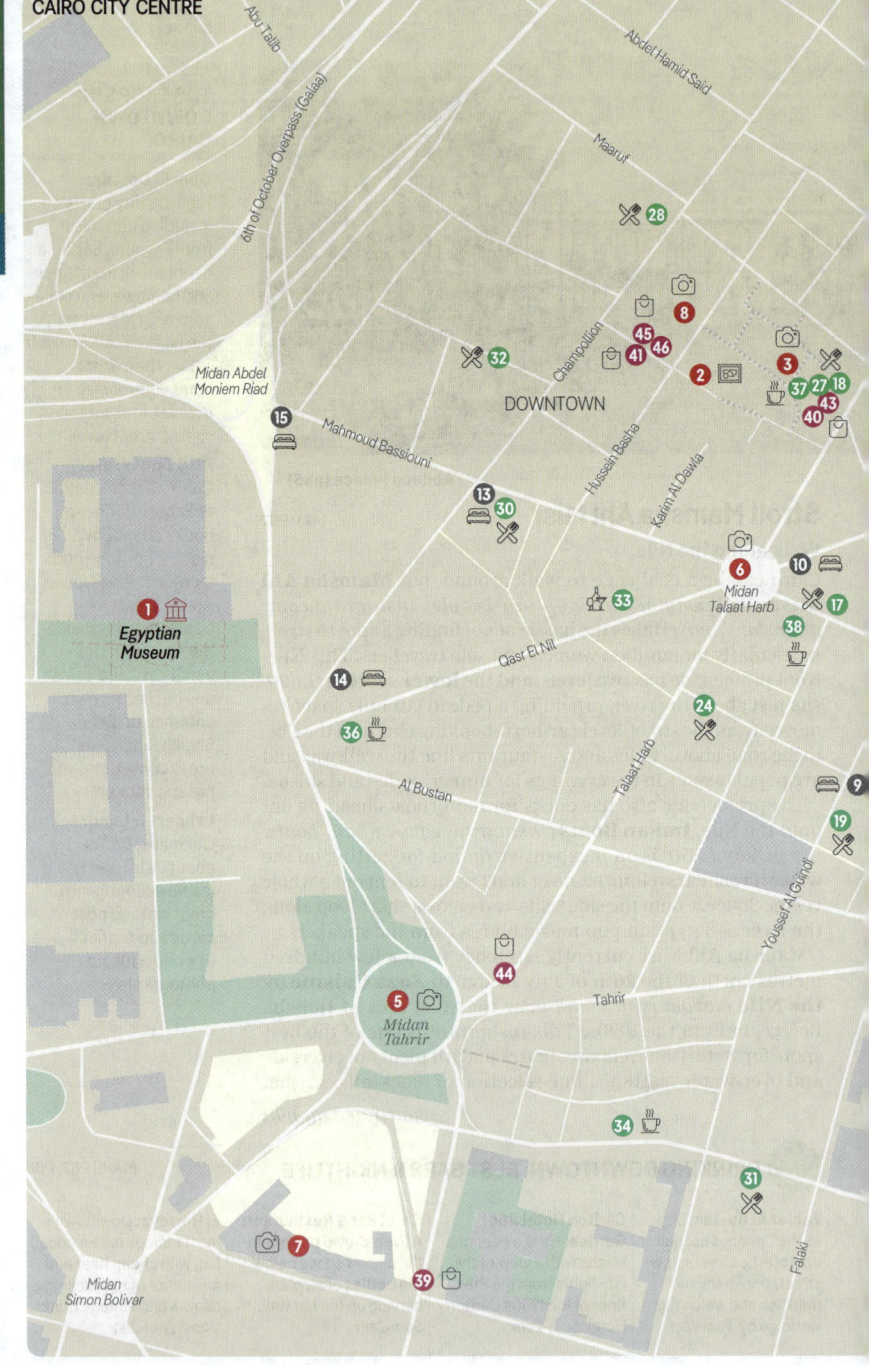

⭐ HIGHLIGHTS
1 Egyptian Museum

● SIGHTS
2 Access Art Space
3 Cinema Radio
4 El Dammah Theatre
5 Midan Tahrir
6 Midan Talaat Harb
7 Mogamma
8 Rawabet Art Space

● SLEEPING
9 Eileen Hotel
10 Hathor House
11 Holy Sheet Hostel
12 Immobilia
13 Mazeej Balad
14 Steigenberger Hotel El Tahrir
15 Tahrir Plaza Suites

● EATING
16 Akher Saa
17 Al Hamra Street
18 Almería
19 CaiRoma
20 Eish + Malh
21 El Abd
22 El Gomhoureya Restaurant
23 Fasahet Somaya
24 Felfela
25 Fish & Chips
26 Gad
27 Jade Pizza
28 Koshary Abou Tarek
29 Le Bistro
30 Mazeej Balad Rooftop
31 Oldish
32 Saad Al Haramy

● DRINKING & NIGHTLIFE
33 Carol Bar & Restaurant
34 Cilantro
35 El Horreya
36 La Poire
37 Sip
38 Zahrat Al Bustan

● SHOPPING
39 AUC Bookstore
40 Diwan
41 La Boga
42 Lehnert & Landrock
43 Markaz
44 Oum El Dounia
45 Saqhoute
46 Up-Fuse

THE GUIDE · CAIRO DOWNTOWN CAIRO

continued from p87

and a menu that runs from Middle Eastern classics to pasta. (Stick with the Egyptian and Lebanese dishes rather than the European options.) Ticket booths to enter Mamsha Ahl Misr's lower level are dotted all along the walkway at street level. The walkway is set to be extended south along the river, with more restaurants starting to set up shop.

ANTIQUE ELEVATORS

If you're staying in historic digs Downtown, you'll almost certainly encounter a lift of the likes you might not have seen before. Egypt is full of ancient artefacts, and some of its lifts might also qualify for that title: the kind with exposed cables, detailed metal doors, gleaming wooden cabs and patinaed mirrors. They are relics of the bygone belle-époque era, and like the buildings' exteriors, these gems have somehow held on. Though the lifts are generally safe, be careful when using them. It's easy to pinch fingers in the heavy and finicky doors, especially when you have a suitcase. If you don't trust them, you can always walk the well-worn marble staircases instead.

Enjoy Egypt's Musical Heritage at El Dammah Theatre

MAP P88

Keeping traditions alive

To delve into traditional Egyptian music, catch a performance by the **El Mastaba Center for Egyptian Folk Music** *(face book.com/mastabafolk)* bands at **El Dammah Theatre** *(el-mastaba.org; LE100)*. El Mastaba represents nearly a dozen groups, covering the breadth of distinct folk music traditions across Egypt, from the trancy Sudanese folk of Rango to El Tanbura's *simsimiyya*, a style from the Suez Canal region.

Performances take place most Thursdays at 8pm (doors open at 7pm). Check whether there's a show and who's playing online.

Other Sides of Egyptian History

MAP P82

Off-the-beaten-track museums

Cairo's major museums are understandably focused on Pharaonic history, but those looking to dive deeper into other aspects of Egypt's past should check out these lesser-visited but still fascinating spots.

Near Maspero metro station, the **Royal Carriages Museum** *(egymonuments.com, search 'Royal Chariots Museum'; LE300)* houses a collection of horse-drawn vehicles used by Egypt's royalty from Khedive Ismail (r 1863–79) to King Farouk (r 1935–52) in the former royal stables. Many of the carriages were made in England and France and were used to receive foreign dignitaries, go to mosque on Fridays, train horses or just for the royal littles to ride around the palace gardens of Montaza in Alexandria. One of the most impressive is the carriage gifted from Napoleon III and his wife Empress Eugénie to Khedive Ismail for the inauguration of the Suez Canal in 1869. Don't miss the saddles used on Shetland ponies for the young princes and the saddle for a donkey, which King Fouad I (r 1922–36) preferred to ride over horses. Also on display are royal relics, including massive portraits, glittering jewellery and over-the-top office

EATING IN DOWNTOWN: SWEET TREATS

MAPS P82, P88

Abdel Rahim Koueider: Our vote for the best mango ice cream in the city. Other local flavours include mastic and pistachio. *11am-midnight* $

El Abd: Cairo's most famous bakery is always packed with customers jostling for cookies, cakes and ice cream every hour that it's open. *9am-midnight* $

Groppi Garden: Started by a Swiss national in the 1890s, Groppi is still a favourite for pastries and fondant-covered cakes. *9am-midnight* $

Latif Wassily: Old-school counter-service-only bakery that's been in business for more than a century, selling bread and pastries. *8am-11pm* $

Royal Carriages Museum

furniture. Farouk's desk, made of galaxy granite, weighs 1 tonne and is carved with his name in hieroglyphic script in a cartouche.

At the eastern end of Ramses Station, the **Egyptian Railway Museum** *(LE100, photo permit LE10)* is heaven for railway geeks and model-train hobbyists. The highlights of the collection are the original 1862 train built by British engineer Robert Stephenson, the first train to run in Egypt, and the locomotive built for Empress Eugénie on the occasion of the opening of the Suez Canal. The museum as a whole traces the long history of transport in Egypt from the Pharaonic era to the modern age, using a series of models, replicas, documents and old photos, though labels don't provide much detail.

The **Egyptian Postal Museum** *(LE50)* might sound a bit dull, but its expansive exhibits on the 2nd floor of the historic Central Post Office building are an interesting peek into history. The museum traces the history of mail back to the Old Kingdom, but the most absorbing of the 10 rooms houses a collection of more modern commemorative stamps, which mark historic events such as the laying of the first stone at the relocated temples of Abu Simbel, the 100th anniversary of the Suez Canal opening and solidarity with Palestinians in the wake of the 1967 Arab-Israeli War.

DOWNTOWN'S ART SCENE

Rawabet Art Space: A packed calendar of performing arts ranging from stand-up comedy and theatre to music concerts. Upcoming events are announced online *(facebook.com/RawabetArtSpace)*.

Access Art Space: Cool showcases of work by modern Egyptian artists. Check online *(instagram.com/accessartspace)* to see what's on before you visit. It's tricky to find; look for 10 Sharia Al Nabrawi and go up to the 1st floor.

D-CAF: If you're in Cairo in October, don't miss this big annual arts festival *(d-caf.org)*, which brings a three-week program of cutting-edge visual art exhibitions, installations, theatre and other performing arts to venues across the neighbourhood.

 EATING IN DOWNTOWN: QUICK & CHEAP — MAPS P82, P88

Akher Saa: This busy *fuul* (fava-bean paste) and shawarma takeaway joint off Sharia Talaat Harb has a limited menu, but its food is fresh and good. 24hr $

El Tabei El Domiaty: Does a roaring trade in shawarma and *ta'amiyya* (Egyptian falafel). Look for the red sign with white Arabic lettering. 7am–1am $

Gad: This branch of the Cairo-wide shawarma chain is near local beer bar El Horreya, and you can take your food to eat there. 24hr $

Saad Al Haramy: Basic canteen on a quieter Downtown side street serving *fuul*, *ta'amiyya* and *mish* (fermented cheese). 6am–11pm $

UNCOVERING VINTAGE CAIRO

Inspired by Parisian architecture, Khedive Ismail used European architects to make over the Egyptian capital starting in the 1870s.

START	END	LENGTH
Cinema Radio	Shaar HaShamayim Synagogue	1km; 45 minutes

A focal point of Downtown, ❶ **Cinema Radio** (p85), built in 1932, once had regular performances by Egypt's famed singer Umm Kulthum. The wall on the right side gives histories of other iconic Downtown buildings. Head south towards Qasr El Nil, looking up as you stroll through ❷ **Baehler Passage**, an Art Deco shopping arcade.

Cross Qasr El Nil and go one street east. Walk down palm-tree-lined Sharia Al Qadi Al Fadel to admire the 1928 Art Nouveau entrance of the ❸ **Cosmopolitan Hotel**. Return to Qasr El Nil and head northeast, stopping to see the 1911 neo-Islamic ❹ **Assicurazioni Generali di Trieste Building**, constructed for an Italian insurance company. Don't miss the company name in Italian and Arabic in green and gold mosaics. Further northeast, the ❺ **Immobilia Building**, built in 1940, is credited as Egypt's first skyscraper.

Turn left (north) on Mohammed Farid, spotting the neoclassical Shorbagui Building. Poke your head into ❻ **Stephenson's Pharmacy**, a time-warp chemist in business since 1905 with preserved vintage advertising and original display cases. Walk west for 20m and duck through Kodak Passage (named because Kodak opened its first Middle East shop here) to Sharia Adly. Across the road is ❼ **Shaar HaShamayim Synagogue** with its Art-Nouveau-meets-ancient-Egypt facade.

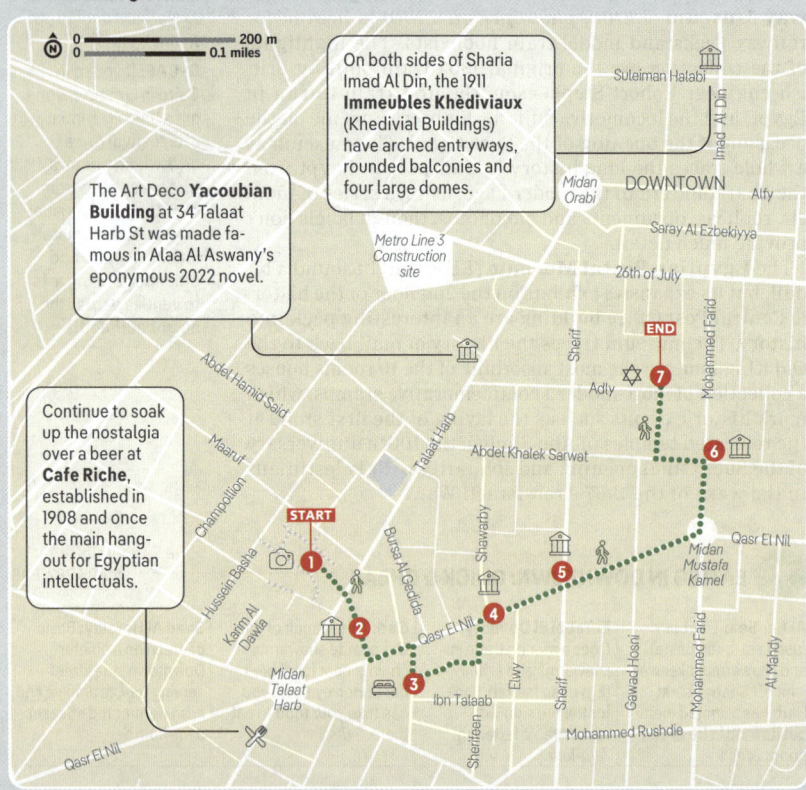

Islamic Cairo & the Citadel

MEDIEVAL MARKETS, MOSQUES AND MONUMENTS

Despite the number of minarets on the skyline in this part of the city, 'Islamic' Cairo is a bit of a misnomer, as this area is not significantly more religious than other districts. But for many centuries, it was the power centre of successive Islamic empires, and its monuments are some of the most significant architecture inspired by Islam.

Today, Islamic Cairo remains a more traditional part of town, where men wearing *galabeyas* (full-length robes) still outnumber those in jeans, buildings and crowds press closer, and the din comes less from car horns and more from the cries of street vendors and the clang of hammer on metal in small workshops. The streets are a warren of blind alleys, and it's easy to lose not only a sense of direction but also a sense of time.

Crowning a cliff overlooking the neighbourhood, the Citadel was home to Egypt's rulers for 700 years.

Discover Centuries of Craftsmanship at the Museum of Islamic Art

MAP P102

Creativity that spans continents

On the western edge of Islamic Cairo, the **Museum of Islamic Art** *(miaegypt.org; LE340)* houses one of the world's finest collections of Islamic art and is one of the most beautifully curated museums in Egypt – and the entire Middle East. What's on display is only a sliver of the 80,000 objects the museum owns, but the selected items are stunning.

Head right as you enter for chronologically arranged exhibits from the Abbasid era to the Ottoman period, including frescoes, inlaid wood, ceramics and carved plaster so fine that it looks like lace. In the Fatimid section, note the lustreware ceramics decorated with musicians, horse riders and duellers.

To the left of the entrance, pieces are grouped by function or medium. The astrolabes and the Safavid robe covered in Quranic verses in the science gallery are highlights.

☑ TOP TIP

Many shops close Friday mornings and all day Sunday. Visit then to admire architecture without the crowds – but the neighbourhood is also missing part of its chaotic personality.

GETTING AROUND

Walking or taking a tuk-tuk is the only way to get around many of these narrow streets. The alleys through the squished-together market stalls in and around Khan El Khalili can be claustrophobic at busy times. Taxi drop-offs and pick-ups around the market are easiest on the major roads outside of Al Azhar Mosque and Bab Al Futuh.

The Citadel sits at the top of a hill, so start explorations there, heading downhill to venture onwards.

The nearest metro station is Bab El Shaariya (Line 3), northwest of the medieval city.

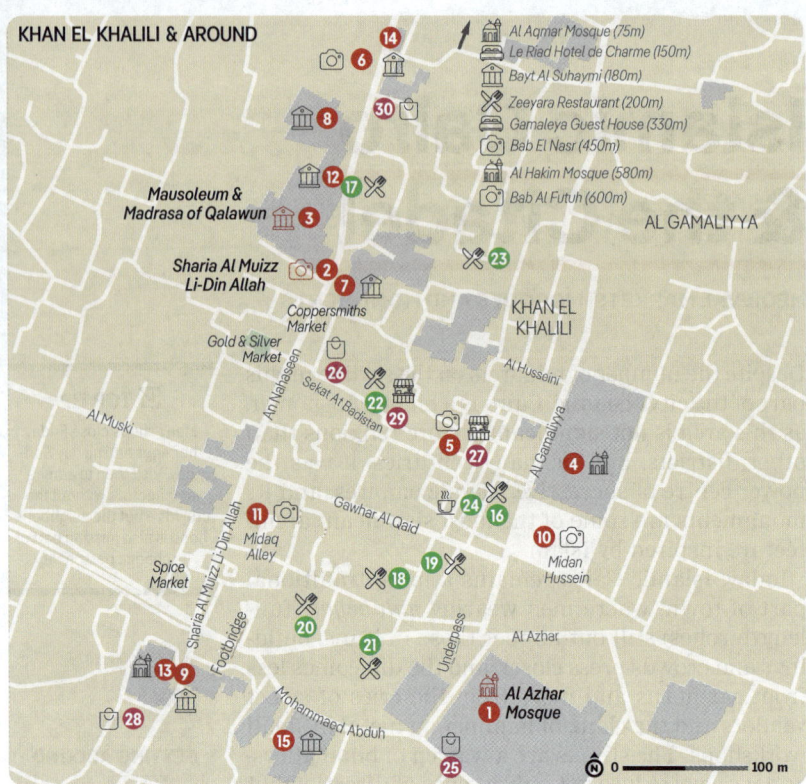

KHAN EL KHALILI & AROUND

★ HIGHLIGHTS
1. Al Azhar Mosque
3. Mausoleum & Madrasa of Qalawun
2. Sharia Al Muizz Li-Din Allah

● SIGHTS
4. Al Hussein Mosque
5. Bab Al Ghuri
6. Hammam Inal
7. Madrasa & Mausoleum of Al Saleh Najm Al Din Ayyub
8. Madrasa & Mausoleum of Sultan Al Zahir Barquq
9. Mausoleum & Sabil-Kuttab of Al Ghouri
10. Midan Hussein
11. Midaq Alley
12. Mosque & Madrasa of Al Nasir Muhammad Ibn Qalawun
13. Mosque & Madrasa of Sultan Al Ghuri
14. Sabil-Kuttab of Abdel Rahman Katkhuda
15. Wikala of Al Ghouri

● EATING
16. Al Hussein Rooftop Restaurant
17. Bayt Al Qadi
18. Egyptian Pancakes
19. El Halwagy
20. Farahat
21. Gad
22. Khan El Khalili Restaurant & Naguib Mahfouz Cafe
23. Maq'ad of Mamay Al Sayfi

● DRINKING & NIGHTLIFE
24. El Fishawy

● SHOPPING
25. Abdelzaher Book Binding
26. Atlas
27. Khan El Khalili
28. Nasser Abdel Baset's Tarboosh Workshop
29. Sekat At Badistan
30. Yehia El Khawanky & Sons

Lose Yourself in the Chaos of Khan El Khalili

MAP P94

A medieval shopping mall

Khan El Khalili, Cairo's medieval market, is a warren of skinny lanes and hidden courtyards where merchants have been plying their trades since the 14th century. You can buy pretty much anything here, from handcrafted copper crescent moon finials that top mosque domes to plastic pyramid keyrings.

Thread your way along the narrow alley of **Sekat At Badistan**, which runs between **Midan Hussein** (p104) and **Sharia Al Muizz Li-Din Allah** (p97), to experience its commercial heart. The shops here and in the surrounding tiny passageways sell handcrafted products such as metal lampshades, engraved mirror frames, Bedouin rugs and inlaid woodwork. Don't miss the high-quality handcrafted jewellery at **Atlas**, in business since 1948, with designs inspired by Islamic art and the Pharaonic era. Although you're probably here primarily to do some souvenir shopping, make sure to look up and note the elaborately carved medieval gate of **Bab Al Ghuri** as you walk through.

Shops and stalls generally open from 10am to late at night, except on Fridays and Sundays when many shops don't open until after noon (or not at all).

Dine in a Prince's Palace

MAP P94

Eating among opulent architecture

Built in 1496 as a reception hall for a Mamluk prince, the **Maq'ad of Mamay Al Sayfi** (*instagram.com/mamai_ _restaurant ; reservations WhatsApp +20 120-666-3325; LE200, plus minimum spend LE300*) has been transformed into a restaurant and performance space that opened in March 2025. Diners sit at tables filled with plates of Egyptian food in the open-air courtyard or on the elevated arched platform while watching whirling dervishes, live music or *tanoura* dancers. Like most other restaurants in Islamic Cairo, the food leaves something to be desired, but the setting is one of a kind.

Prince Mamay Al Sayfi served as *gamadar* (responsible for the sultan's wardrobe) under Qaitbay (r 1467–95) and his son Al Nasir Muhammad (r 1495–97), whose mosques, mausoleums and madrasas are nearby on Sharia Al Muizz. Sayfi was later promoted to royal cupbearer. In the Ottoman area, the building was used by the courts of law, so it's sometimes known as the Maq'ad of the Judges' House.

After a 2018 restoration, the space was used only for one-off exhibitions and events, so this iteration is opening the doors of the *maq'ad* more widely and consistently for the first time in years. The *maq'ad* is the only surviving part of the palace, which must have been seriously grand given the size of this reception hall. Its wooden ceiling is gilded and painted and has a frieze of inscriptions of Sayfi's titles.

SURVIVING ARRIVING IN CAIRO

Getting hassled is part and parcel of travelling in Egypt, but the barrage of taxi drivers at Cairo's airports might make you feel as if you've entered another level of hell. Do not rely on Uber or other ride-hailing apps to get you into the city, even if they claim to be available. Uber drivers often sit outside the airport gates and send a message to demand a higher fare to be paid in cash, leaving you stranded and wasting your time.

Another airport pain point is getting through immigration; queues can be horrendously long. Skip a step of the process by applying online for an eVisa *(visa2egypt.gov.eg)* before departure; otherwise, it'll be another airport queue you'll have to wait in.

TRADITIONAL CRAFTWORK TO TAKE HOME

Metalwork: Pierced copper and silver lampshades in a variety of shapes and sizes.

Muski glass: Hand-blown glassware with a distinctive bubble finish, made from recycled glass.

Bedouin rugs: Flatweave rugs from Sinai, usually decorated with simple geometric designs in muted colour shades.

Inlaid wood: All sizes of boxes, backgammon boards and larger pieces are inlaid with intricate mother-of-pearl designs.

Shisha pipes: The highly decorative bowls of some shisha pipes make for great ornaments even if you're not going to use them back home.

Yehia El Khawanky & Sons *(instagram.com/yehiaelkhawankysons)*, opened in 1891, is a good place to look.

Khan El Khalili (p95)

Grab a Drink at El Fishawy

MAP P94

Cairo's oldest coffeehouse

After navigating your way through **Khan El Khalili** (p95), there's no better place to rest your weary feet than **El Fishawy**, found down a narrow passage off Sekat At Badistan.

In business since 1773, Fishawy is reputed to be the oldest *ahwa* (coffeehouse) in Cairo. Relax with a shisha and cold *karkadai* (hibiscus drink) while you admire the interior's clouded mirrors, copper tables and dusty chandeliers, and chat with the vendors trying to convince you to henna your hands or buy a scarf. Although a favourite stop on any Islamic Cairo itinerary, Fishawy is also a regular *ahwa*, serving up a caffeine fix to as many stall holders as wide-eyed tourists.

Watching Artisans at Work

MAP P94

Modern continuations of traditional crafts

Because of mechanisation, many artisan professions that **Khan El Khalili** (p95) was once famous for have disappeared, but the ones that are still hanging on are worth a visit.

Ahmed Shawky runs the only workshop of Quranic embroiderers left in Khan El Khalili. Egypt's embroiderers were considered so skilful that they traditionally sent the *kiswa* cloth that covers the Kaaba to Mecca every year. Ahmed's grandfather was one of the 10 hand embroiderers who made the *kiswa* in 1932, 1934 and 1936. As well as Quranic embroidery, Ahmed creates made-to-order pieces of hand embroidery and brocade, which can take from a few days to 40 days to complete, depending on the size. To see the workshop and discuss commissions, message him on WhatsApp at +20 122-256-3215. He's usually in his

continued on p101

Al Hakim Mosque from Bab Al Futuh (p100)

TOP EXPERIENCE

Sharia Al Muizz Li-Din Allah

Named after the Fatimid caliph who conquered Cairo in 969 CE, Sharia Al Muizz Li-Din Allah was once Cairo's grand thoroughfare reserved for the elites. The part of Sharia Al Muizz north of Khan El Khalili's gold district is known as Bayn Al Qasrayn (Palace Walk). Today, the street's Mamluk complexes provide the most impressive assembly of medieval Islamic architecture anywhere in the world.

DON'T MISS

Mausoleum & Madrasa of Qalawun

Madrasa & Mausoleum of Al Saleh Najm Al Din Ayyub

Hammam Inal

Climbing Bab Al Futuh

Mausoleum & Madrasa of Qalawun

If you have time to see only one Mamluk monument around Khan El Khalili, make it the **Mausoleum & Madrasa of Qalawun**. This soaring religious complex of Sultan Qalawun, who founded the Mamluk dynasty in 1279, is one of the finest examples of the Mamluks' exuberant eye for ornamentation and combines a mausoleum, a madrasa (theological college) and *bimaristan* (hospital).

PRACTICALITIES

- egymonuments.com, search 'El Moez Street'
- multisite ticket LE220
- 9am–5pm

CAIRO'S MOST IMPORTANT STREET

Sharia Al Muizz is one of the oldest roads in Cairo, running about 1km between **Bab Zuwayla** (p107) and **Bab Al Futuh** (p100). In the Fatimid era (973–1171), only the ruler, state officials and palace workers were allowed inside the city walls.

Salah ad-Din (Saladin) came to power next and opened Cairo to all. Eager to erase the monuments of the Fatimids, who were Shiite, the Sunni Ayyubid and Mamluk dynasties tore down and rebuilt their own structures along Sharia Al Muizz. The 20th-century construction of Sharia Al Azhar sliced through the soul of the neighbourhood and is an annoyance to cross.

Madrasa & Mausoleum of Sultan Al Zahir Barquq

From the narrow passage entrance, turn right into the mausoleum with its near-giddy profusion of artistry: stained glass, stone inlay, carved stucco archways, marble panelling and the finely restored coffered ceiling with intricate, painted designs. Note the columns – stolen from a Ptolemaic-era temple – and the mihrab, which is the earliest example of what would become a typical Mamluk style of decoration, using coloured marble panels.

A doorway in the back wall leads into the madrasa with its courtyard and then into the *bimaristan* with its high-arched iwans. It was once one of the most impressive medical facilities of its era. Qalawun added it to the design of the building after he was treated for colic in a similar facility in Damascus.

Madrasa & Mausoleum of Al Saleh Najm Al Din Ayyub

Hop directly across the road from the Mausoleum & Madrasa of Qalawun to enter this **complex** and notice its austere interior, a direct contrast to Qalawun's exuberant decoration. That's because this school and mausoleum is an earlier structure, erected in 1244, for the last Ayyubid sultan of Egypt, Al Saleh Najm Al Din Ayyub, grandson of Saladin. He died defending Egypt against the Crusader attack led by Louis IX of France.

This building is important because it's the first example of a joint mausoleum and madrasa, so it is a trendsetter for the Mamluk building works that followed.

Mosque & Madrasa of Al Nasir Muhammad Ibn Qalawun

Snug next door to Qalawun's complex is the **mosque and madrasa of his son**, Sultan Al Nasir ('the Victor'), who ended Crusader domination in Acre (Akko in modern-day Israel). He was both despotic and exceedingly accomplished. The madrasa was built in 1304 with a Gothic doorway he carted off from Acre's Crusader church. Buried in the mausoleum (on the right as you enter; you might need to ask the site guardian to unlock the door) are Al Nasir's mother and his favourite son. The sultan himself is buried next door in the mausoleum of his father.

Madrasa & Mausoleum of Sultan Al Zahir Barquq

Enter this complex through the bold black and white marble portal and walk along a narrow lamp-lit passageway with a colourful inlaid marble floor. It leads into a courtyard paved with the same marble pattern. Check out the iwan on your right-hand side. Its lavish blue and gold ceiling is supported by four porphyry Pharaonic columns.

Sultan Barquq seized power in 1382 when Egypt was reeling from plague and famine, and his Sufi school was completed four years later. Barquq's daughter is buried in the splendid domed tomb chamber, while the sultan preferred to rest in the **Northern Cemetery** (p111), surrounded by Sufi sheikhs.

Hammam Inal

Hammam Inal, built in 1456, is one of Cairo's only restored examples of hammam (bathhouse) architecture. Inside the marble-clad central room, crane your neck up at the domed ceiling, studded with tiny coloured-glass windows to allow in shafts of light.

Sabil-Kuttab of Abdel Rahman Katkhuda

This *sabil* and *kuttab*, built in 1744, sits in the middle of the road and is one of Islamic Cairo's most iconic buildings, featured in many paintings and lithographs. The multisite ticket isn't required to visit, but it makes an interesting stop en route.

Building this fountain-school combo was an atonement for sins, as it provided two things commended by the Prophet Muhammad: water for the thirsty and enlightenment for the ignorant. The ground floor now houses a souvenir shop, to whose walls still cling some original Ottoman tilework. Outside, look south back up the road for a vista of minarets and domes.

TOP TIPS

- If you have time, devote a whole day to exploring this street and the surrounding neighbourhood. Beyond the ticketed monuments are plenty of free-to-enter mosques.

- The main attractions on Sharia Al Muizz should be open as advertised, but some of the smaller sites might close temporarily with no notice. On our visit, the Mosque and Sabil-Kuttab of Sulayman Agha Al Silahdar was shut.

- Bring a headscarf, dress modestly and wear shoes that are easy to slip off.

- Would-be guides might follow you around and start giving you a tour. They expect baksheesh. If you're not interested, say no and be firm from the beginning.

COMBINATION TICKET FOR SHARIA AL MUIZZ

To visit all the ticketed monuments on Sharia Al Muizz Li-Din Allah, you must pay for a multisite ticket. You can buy it online or at the ticket window across the street from the Mausoleum & Madrasa of Qalawun. Start your visit here.

The mosques along the street are generally free to enter, though the guardians expect baksheesh if you leave your shoes.

Bab Al Futuh

Bab Al Futuh

The only two remaining gates of Cairo's northern city wall are the rounded **Bab Al Futuh** (Gate of Conquest), with its delicate carved stone arch, and the square-towered **Bab El Nasr** (Gate of Victory), built in 1087. Look for the site guardian on the western side of the inner wall to show your ticket and then climb the tower's internal stairs to the top of the gate and walk along the city wall.

Keep an eye out for the inscriptions left by Napoleon's troops as well as carved animals and Pharaonic figures on the stones scavenged from the ruins of ancient Memphis. To the east, you can walk around the ceiling of **Al Hakim Mosque** (p104), looking down into the gleaming white courtyard below. Notice that the mosque's minarets have been left in their original state, while the building's interior is a modern update.

If you're short on time, Bab Al Futuh is our top pick on Sharia Al Muizz after the Mausoleum & Madrasa of Qalawun, particularly if you didn't climb **Bab Zuwayla** (p107), the southern city gate. It recently reopened to visitors after restoration, so you might be the only one taking in the views from on high.

MONUMENTAL WORDS TO KNOW

Madrasa Theological secondary school or university.

Sabil Public fountain used for drinking.

Kuttab School for children, often situated above a *sabil*.

Mihrab Niche indicating the direction of Mecca; sometimes the most beautifully decorated part of a mausoleum or mosque.

Minbar Pulpit in a mosque where an imam delivers sermons.

Muqarnas Stone carving used to decorate domes, vaulted ceilings and entrance portals. Sometimes called honeycomb vaulting.

continued from p96

workshop from 2pm to late daily, and he'll collect you from **El Fishawy** (p96). His workshop is steps away, but because it's upstairs, it's difficult to find on your own.

More traditional crafts are made by hand at **Gamaleya** *(gamaleya.com)*. Visitors are welcome to wander in and watch the artists, both masters and students, working their magic in copper, delicate silver filigree, inlaid wood and wool in the small, open-plan workshops. You can see copperwork artisans hammering geometric designs onto vases, plates and pots, or woodworkers shaping wood inlaid with mother-of-pearl or semi-precious stones. It's a good opportunity to understand how much effort goes into making handcrafted pieces and, if you're looking to buy, to support artisans directly by purchasing at their source. Stop by in the afternoons from Saturday to Thursday for a chance to catch most artisans in action. The shop also runs a **guesthouse** (p154) upstairs.

Nasser Abdel Baset, Cairo's last tarboosh (fez) maker, still shapes the red felt hats using traditional techniques on Sharia Al Muizz Li-Din Allah, about 50m south of the **Mosque and Madrasa of Sultan Al Ghuri** (p105). A favourite fashion accessory of the Ottoman Empire, the tarboosh was worn by every top official and *effendi* (gentleman), but President Gamal Abdel Nasser banned the hats after the Revolution of 1952 that ousted the royal family, as they were a symbol of the former rulers. Tarbooshes are now mostly bought by religious students at Al Azhar University and costume designers working on TV shows. The workshop is open from 10am to 6pm on Monday to Thursday and Saturday.

Near **Al Azhar Mosque** (p104) is **Abdelzaher Book Binding** *(abdelzahers.com)*, Cairo's last working bookbinder. As well as selling notebooks, journals, diaries and photo albums, Abdelzaher can also make leather and oil paperbound blank books, and bind your old books. Gold monogramming is included in the price. Find the shop on Sharia Mohammed Abduh, which runs along the mosque's southern wall.

HOW MANY WAYS TO SPELL A WORD?

As you're looking up information about Cairo, you might notice that the spelling of places, historic sites and people's names varies from source to source, including Google Maps, this book and even Egyptian government ministries. For example, Google Maps calls the Mamluk sultan 'Ghoury', the Ministry of Antiquities says 'Ghuri', the government's ticket-selling website says 'Guri', while other online sources use 'Ghouri'. What's the deal?

Many options exist for romanising Arabic words, but a single standard hasn't been agreed upon, and there's no single government entity for the entire Arabic-speaking world to enforce it (unlike, say, pinyin for romanising Chinese).

EATING IN ISLAMIC CAIRO: OUR PICKS — MAPS P94, P102

Zeeyara Restaurant: Drool over contemporary Egyptian cooking at this restaurant on the rooftop of Le Riad Hotel de Charme. *8am-1am $$$*

Bayt Al Qadi: Friendly service at this spot that's good for a coffee or cold drink while sightseeing along Sharia Al Muizz. *10am-midnight $*

El Halwagy: This place has been serving up plates of *ta'amiyya* and other local favourites for nearly a century. *9am-1am $*

Khan El Khalili Restaurant & Naguib Mahfouz Cafe: Staff in tarboosh hats ferry dishes around the Moorish-style interior. *11am-midnight $$*

Farahat: Locally famed haunt for anyone looking to eat pigeon stuffed with spiced rice or grilled. *noon-4am $*

Egyptian Pancakes: Does what it says on the tin: *fiteer* (sweet or savoury flaky pastry) plus pizza. Double-check your bill. *24hr $*

Al Hussein Rooftop Restaurant: Hotel restaurant heavy on grilled meat. You're here for the view over Midan Hussein. *10am-2am $$*

Gad: When you need to fuel up on shawarma or *fuul* after exploring Khan El Khalili, head to this busy branch on Sharia Al Azhar. *10am-2am $*

ISLAMIC CAIRO & THE CITADEL (SOUTH)

★ HIGHLIGHTS
1. Bab Zuwayla
2. Citadel
3. Mosque & Madrasa of Sultan Hassan
4. Mosque of Qaitbey
5. Museum of Islamic Art

● SIGHTS
6. Al Azhar Park
7. Al Rifa'i Mosque
8. Al Tanbugha Al Maridani Mosque
9. Amir Khayrbak Funerary Complex
10. Aqsunqur Mosque
11. Bait Al Razzaz
12. Beit Zeinab Al Khatoun
13. Church of St Simon the Tanner
14. Craftastic
15. Gayer-Anderson Museum
16. House of Al Harawy
17. House of Egyptian Architecture
18. Khanqah & Mausoleum of Farag Ibn Barquq
19. Maq'ad of Sultan Qaitbey
20. Mawlawiyya Takiyya
21. Mosque of Ibn Tulun

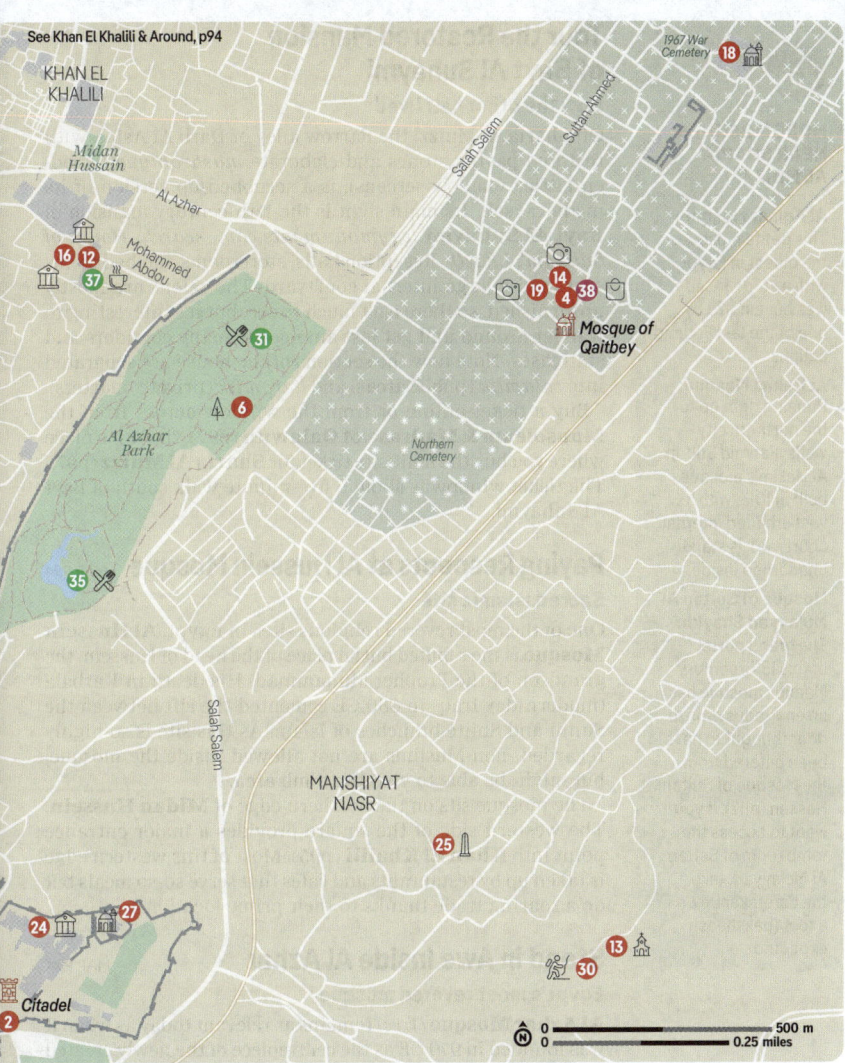

22 Mosque of Sultan Al Mu'ayyad Shaykh	**27** Suleiman Pasha Mosque
23 Muhammad Ali Mosque	**28** Sultan Al Nasir Muhammad Mosque
24 National Military Museum	**29** Umm Al Sultan Shaa'ban Mosque & Madrasa
25 Perception Mural	**see 16** Wasila Historical House
26 Police Museum	

● **ACTIVITIES**
30 Mario High Ropes

● **EATING**
31 Citadel View Restaurant
32 El Gahsh
33 Fathy Kebda
34 Ibn Hamido
35 Lakeside Restaurant
36 Muhammed El Rafaei Kebab Restaurant

● **DRINKING & NIGHTLIFE**
37 Tekiyt Khan Khatun

● **SHOPPING**
38 Mishka
39 Street of the Tentmakers

Tour the Restored Mansion of Bayt Al Suhaymi

MAP P94

How the other half lived

Off Sharia Al Muizz, the narrow alley of Darb Al Asfar, with restored paving stones and elaborate *mashrabiyya* (wooden lattice window screens), is a scrubbed-up version of its medieval self. Its main sight is the 17th-century mansion of **Bayt Al Suhaymi** *(egymonuments.com, search 'House of Suhaym'; LE220)*. Reception halls, storerooms and bedrooms surround a large internal courtyard. The salons are mostly unfurnished, so there isn't much to see, but it's interesting to wander around and get lost among the many corridors and staircases. Note how the sections of the house are separated into *salamlik* (public areas) and *haramlik* (private quarters).

Buy a ticket online or from the window across from the **Mausoleum & Madrasa of Qalawun** (p97), the same place where you buy the multisite ticket for **Sharia Al Muizz** (p97). The ticket window is about a five-minute walk south of Bayt Al Suhaymi.

Paying Respects at Al Hussein Mosque

MAP P94

Sacred Islamic site

One of the most revered religious sites in Egypt, **Al Hussein Mosque** is the reputed burial place of the head of Hussein, the grandson of the Prophet Muhammad. His death in Karbala (modern-day Iraq) in 680 CE cemented the rift between the Sunni and Shiite branches of Islam. As this site is so highly regarded, non-Muslims are not allowed inside the mosque, but might be able to visit the tomb area.

The mosque sits on the northern edge of **Midan Hussein**. The western side of the square provides a major entrance point into **Khan El Khalili** (p95). Most of this western edge is taken up by restaurants and cafes that serve so-so meals but do a roaring trade thanks to their prime location.

Stand in Awe Inside Al Azhar

MAP P94

Egypt's most revered mosque

Al Azhar Mosque *(free)* remains as relevant today as when it was founded in 970 CE as the centrepiece of the newly created Fatimid city of Al Qahira. A madrasa (theological college) was established here in 988 CE, growing into a university that is the world's second oldest. Today, Al Azhar's modern campus to the east is still the most prestigious place to study Sunni theology in the world, and the mosque's grand imam is considered the highest religious authority for Egyptian Muslims.

The mosque is a blend of architectural styles, the result of numerous enlargements over more than 1000 years. Visitors can enter on the western or northern sides of the mosque. The Ottoman-era prayer-hall extension alongside the northern corridor was built by janissary commander and architectural patron Abdel Rahman Katkhuda, and his tomb chamber sits against the southern wall.

MORE MOSQUES NEAR SHARIA AL MUIZZ

Al Aqmar Mosque: This petite mosque, the oldest in Egypt with a stone facade, was built in 1125 by one of the last Fatimid caliphs.

Al Hakim Mosque: Running right up to the northern city walls, Fatimid Sultan Al Hakim's mosque, built in 1013, with its vast arcaded internal courtyard, is starkly unadorned inside.

Mosque of Sultan Al Mu'ayyad Shaykh: The grand portal of this 15th-century Mamluk mosque has an enormous bronze door thought to have been pilfered from the Mosque of Sultan Hassan (p112). If you want to access the tomb room of Sultan Al Mu'ayyad, take the caretaker up on a tour (baksheesh expected).

Bayt Al Suhaymi

Both entrances open into Al Azhar's vast courtyard of blinding-white marble. Take in the mirror effect of the flooring, so shiny that it reflects the arched aisles wrapping around it and the minarets above. From the aisles, you can access the prayer hall. If you've already visited some of Cairo's Mamluk mosques, you might find Al Azhar rather austere.

If you entered from the northern side, make sure to walk through the mosque's western Bab Al Muzayanin (Gate of the Barbers), faced by Mamluk-era madrasas. You can also take good photos of the minarets from here.

Spy an Architectural Wonder at the Al Ghouri Complex

MAP P94

Magical Mamluk buildings

This complex, built by the penultimate Mamluk Sultan Al Ghouri in 1504, straddles both sides of Sharia Al Muizz Li-Din Allah at its intersection with Sharia Al Azhar.

On the western side of Sharia Al Muizz is the **Mosque & Madrasa of Sultan Al Ghuri** *(free)*, with four iwans (vaulted halls) surrounding a sunken courtyard, all richly decorated with painted wood panelling and intricate geometric paving. The caretaker offers tours (baksheesh expected) that take you up to the 2nd-floor balcony of the iwan (so you can get a closer view of the exuberantly detailed cedar-wood ceiling), out onto the roof and up the minaret for bird's-eye views of Cairo.

The **Mausoleum & Sabil-Kuttab of Al Ghouri** *(egymonuments.com, search 'Al-Guri Dome'; LE150)* is on the eastern side of the street. Walk around the building to its Sharia Al Azhar side and go down the stairs to enter. At the age of 78, Al Ghouri was beheaded in Syria, and his body was never recovered. The elegant domed mausoleum contains the body of Tuman Bay II, his successor, who was hanged at nearby **Bab Zuwayla** (p107) by the Ottomans in 1517, ending the Mamluk dynasty.

VISITING AL AZHAR AS A TOURIST

Women must wear a long skirt or dress: Female visitors have to wear a long skirt or a dress that reaches the floor – trousers aren't allowed. Don't fret if you don't have the right attire. After entering, the female attendants will lend you one, as well as a headscarf if needed.

Dress modestly: All visitors must wear modest clothing or borrow cover-ups from the attendants.

Take off your shoes: After you've removed your shoes at the door, leave them in the shoe-deposit cupboards or carry them with you while inside. (Bringing a tote bag is useful for this.)

SHOES OFF

You cannot wear shoes inside mosques. As you enter, take your shoes off and leave them with the caretaker at the counter. When you collect your shoes, it is polite to tip the caretaker a small amount (LE5 to LE10).

If you don't want to leave your shoes behind, you could put them in a tote bag to carry with you. However, some caretakers will insist you leave your shoes with them, and it's not worth your time to argue. If you don't have small enough bills for baksheesh, it's OK to ask for change back.

Muhammad Ali Mosque (p109) in the Citadel and the **Mosque of Ibn Tulun** (p114) provide plastic covers to put over your shoes instead of asking you to take them off.

Al Azhar Mosque (p104)

Back on street level outside the entrance, walk a few paces west until you see stairs leading up to the Sabil-Kuttab. The caretaker can point out interesting features of the former public fountain *(sabil)* and will open the shutters in the *kuttab* (school for children) to give you great views over Sharia Al Muizz from the upper storey.

Admire the Architecture of Wikala of Al Ghouri

MAP P94

Centuries-old caravanserai

Constructed at the same time as his mosque and madrasa, the **Wikala of Al Ghouri** *(egymonuments.com, search 'Wikalet Al-Guri'; LE100)* was built as an inn for traders following the caravan routes stopping to sell their wares in the city. Though it's one of the best-kept examples of a caravanserai surviving in Cairo, the higher-than-expected ticket price doesn't quite justify a visit unless you're particularly interested in architecture. Up until a few years ago, artists' ateliers had taken over the upper rooms, and the former stables were used as craft shops, but these stalls are now locked up and inaccessible, though you're free to roam the dark, abandoned corridors.

Domestic Architecture Around Al Khatoun Square

MAP P102

Have historic houses all to yourself

On a small square southeast of **Al Azhar Mosque** (p104) is a clutch of historic mansions that see few visitors. The tickets are overpriced compared to other attractions in Cairo, but a visit is rewarding if you enjoy history and architecture.

Built in 1664, **Wasila Historical House** *(egymonuments. com; LE100)* is a lovely example of Ottoman residential architecture. The 1st floor has some beautiful fresco maps of Mecca,

Medina and the Hejaz region of Saudi Arabia painted high on the walls. Crane your neck further to look at the partially gilded ceiling swirled with floral decorations. Many of the windows are covered with *mashrabiyya*, intricate wooden lattice screens that allow people inside to see out but not vice versa. This historic home is the headquarters of the House of Arab Poetry, so cultural events sometimes take place here, particularly around Ramadan.

Next door, the **House of Al Harawy** *(egymonuments.com; LE100)* is another fine 18th-century mansion, but its sparse interior means that paying an entry fee feels disappointing. The building is home to the Arabic Oud House, a music school, which sometimes puts on concerts.

Beit Zeinab Al Khatoun, under renovation on our visit but expected to reopen, is a small Ottoman-era house with a rooftop affording superb views of the surrounding minaret-studded skyline.

Because these buildings rarely receive visitors, the site guardian is likely to force you to join him on a tour, though this isn't necessarily a bad idea considering that it's easy to get lost in the maze of rooms and darkened, dusty corridors. Afterwards, take a break from sightseeing at **Tekiyt Khan Khatun** *(facebook.com/zeinabkhatun)*, which has outdoor seating, shisha and traditional Egyptian dishes and drinks.

Get Outside at Al Azhar Park
MAP P102
Green lungs of Cairo

For a dose of greenery and skyline views, head to the blooming gardens and the grand promenade lined with Cuban royal palms of **Al Azhar Park** *(azharpark.com; Thu-Sat/Sun-Wed LE50/40)*. The main reason to visit is the view overlooking Cairo to the west. You can soak it up from the viewpoints, the **Lakeside Restaurant** or the even more elevated **Citadel View Restaurant** – you're here for the view more than the food, so stick to the mezze if you decide to order. If you're travelling with little ones, this park is one of the few places in Cairo where kids can run wild. Its northern section has a children's playground.

The park, the largest green space in central Cairo, was transformed from a mountain of medieval garbage with funding from the Aga Khan Trust. During landscaping, Saladin's Ayyubid-era walls at the bottom of the hill, long lost under the rubbish, were rediscovered and have been restored.

The main gate is on Sharia Salah Salem. Another gate, on the northern side, is within walking distance of **Al Azhar Mosque** (p104). Walk east along Sharia Al Azhar until Al Hussein Hospital. Cross the road and take the car park entrance signposted for the park.

Climb Bab Zuwayla
MAP P102
Minaret-studded gate with views over the neighbourhood

Built in 1092, **Bab Zuwayla** *(egymonuments.com; LE100)* is the gate that lower-class workers would file out of at the end

WATCH A SUFI SPECTACLE

Every Wednesday and Saturday at 7pm, the **Mausoleum of Al Ghouri** (p105) plays host to a performance of the **Al Tannoura Egyptian Heritage Dance Troupe**, Egypt's only group of Sufi dancers. You may have seen the better-known Mevlevi dervishes of Türkiye's sedate, swirling ritual before, but this performance is a more raucous and colourful spectacle of spinning, whirling dervish devotion.

First-come, first-served tickets are sold at the door (LE90) from 6pm, and the show begins at 7pm. It's a great opportunity to see this medieval space in use. Arrive early to secure a seat, as performances often sell out.

WHY I LOVE CAIRO

Lauren Keith, Lonely Planet writer

They say opposites attract, and my love affair with Cairo constitutes perfect evidence. I'm an introvert and a planner, but as soon as my flight lands in Egypt's chaotic capital, I realise that all notions of who I think I am have parachuted out the window somewhere over the Mediterranean. The way I operate elsewhere won't work here.

Cairo can be a tough place to love. It pushes your buttons and gets under your skin. You can resist and get dragged under or take some notes from the Nile and simply go with the flow. The more I learn about this place, the more I find out about myself as well.

of each day, leaving the palace district of Al Qahira to their Fatimid rulers. Today, it is the only remaining southern gate of the medieval city. As you walk through, flanked by the gate's two towers, remember that the street level has risen about 2m since it was built. The loggia above the entrance was where the Mamluk sultan sat to watch the annual hajj caravan exit the city en route to Mecca. During the Mamluk period, the gate was also used for public executions. The gateway's eastern door is said to be home to the spirit of a holy man, and believers used to hang offerings on the doors to ask for healing.

Inside are a few exhibits about the gate's history. Up on the roof, you can savour panoramic vistas that stretch to the Citadel. If you have a head for heights, wind your way even further up the twisty minaret stairs to the balcony at the top.

Shop on the Street of the Tentmakers MAP P102
Cairo's top stop for textile fans

Running south from Bab Zuwayla is the **Street of the Tentmakers** (Sharia Al Khayamiyya), one of the only remaining medieval speciality quarters. The street takes its name from the artisans who produce the bright fabrics used for the ceremonial tents at wakes, weddings and feasts. They also make intricate applique wall hangings, cushion covers and bedspreads by hand. The highest concentration of artisan shops is within the covered bazaar and in the courtyard of the Maq'ad of Radwan Bey, about 10m south.

The tentmakers' bazaar has plenty of stores, but two shops in particular stand out. Ashraf Hashem *(WhatsApp +20 100-568-7206)* handmakes applique pieces portraying Egyptian rural scenes at **Egyptian Patchwork**. Arabic calligraphy designs feature in Hany Abd El Kader's *(WhatsApp +20 100-306-1198)* fine-detailed applique at **Suosan**.

Inside the Mosque of Qaitbey MAP P102
The resting place of a Mamluk sultan

One of the longest-ruling sultans of the Mamluk era, Al Ashraf Qaitbey (r 1468–96) was something of an aesthete. He was a prolific builder, and with some 80 structures in his name, he truly refined the Mamluk style. In the Northern Cemetery, the **Mosque of Qaitbey** *(free)*, completed in 1474 as part of a larger funerary complex, marks a high point of Islamic architecture in Cairo. Before you head inside, notice the exteriors of the domes, carved with fine, intricate floral designs.

The mosque's central courtyard is flanked by lantern-hung iwans, but the truly impressive feature is the mausoleum, which you need to ask the caretaker to unlock. The soaring, domed tomb chamber of Sultan Qaitbey is lit by shafts of light from its multiple stained-glass windows.

When you've finished in that room, ask the caretaker to let you up the stairs and onto the roof so you can see the exterior of the tomb chamber's dome up close. Baksheesh is expected.

Main prayer hall, Muhammad Ali Mosque

TOP EXPERIENCE

Citadel

Standing high on a limestone spur on the city's eastern edge, the Citadel, started by Saladin in 1176 as a fortification against the Crusaders, was home to Egypt's rulers for 700 years. Their legacy is a collection of three very different mosques, several palaces that house some underwhelming museums and a couple of terraces with superb city views.

DID YOU KNOW?

Mohammed Ali (r 1805–48) is considered a moderniser of Egypt, and he didn't care much for history. At the Citadel, he demolished a Mamluk-era palace to make way for his mosque.

Muhammad Ali Mosque

Modelled on classic Ottoman lines, with domes upon domes upon domes and pencil-thin minarets, the alabaster-white **Muhammad Ali Mosque** took 18 years to build (1830–48). Its interior is all twinkling chandeliers and striped stone, and the main dome is a rich emerald green. Mohammed Ali, who was the de facto ruler of Egypt from 1805 to 1848, lies in the tomb on the right as you enter.

PRACTICALITIES

- *egymonuments.com*
- *LE550*
- *8am–4pm*

> **BUILDING THE CITADEL**
>
> Because the Citadel has been restructured so often, it's difficult to get a handle on its original form. In general, the northern enclosure (where the National Military Museum and Suleiman Pasha Mosque sit today) is the oldest section, built by Saladin between 1176 and 1182. This area became a military barracks when later Ayyubid rulers began constructing the southern enclosure as a royal residence.

> **TOP TIPS**
>
> ● Unless you're coming to pray, avoid visiting on Fridays. The mosques are still in use and close to non-worshippers for midday prayers. Friday afternoons are busy.
>
> ● It's possible to walk between the Citadel and the Mosque of Sultan Hassan (1.6km, about 25 minutes). The route is along busy roads, but the pavement runs alongside for most of the way. It's uphill to the Citadel, so it's a better idea to start here.
>
> ● Find snack stands near the ticket office and in front of the National Military Museum.
>
> ● During winter, morning haze often obscures the view of the distant Pyramids of Giza.

The glitzy clock in the entrance courtyard was a gift in the 1840s from King Louis Philippe of France in return for the obelisk that stands in the Place de la Concorde in Paris, but the clock arrived damaged. Many repair attempts were made throughout the decades, and Egypt's first public ticking clock was finally fixed in 2021.

Plastic covers to put over your shoes are available before entering the courtyard if you'd rather not take them off. Female visitors are generally not required to wear headscarves in the mosque.

Sultan Al Nasir Muhammad Mosque

Dwarfed by the Muhammad Ali Mosque to the southwest, the more subdued **Sultan Al Nasir Muhammad Mosque**, built in 1318, is the only Mamluk work that Mohammed Ali didn't demolish – instead, he used it as a stable. Before that, Ottoman Sultan Selim I stripped its interior of much of its adornment, but the intricate woodwork on the ceiling (restored in the left-side arcade) and the bold black and white marble mihrab show up nicely. The twisted tops of the minarets are interesting for their covering of glazed mosaics, a feature rarely seen in Egypt.

Police Museum & Grand Terrace

Head through Bab Al Alam (Gate of the Flag) north of the Sultan Al Nasir Muhammad Mosque and make a quick detour to the right to find the Citadel's former **prison**, which has some open cells with startling figures inside.

At the far end of this area is the large **terrace** that Mohammed Ali built, and from here, you can see why Cairo's nickname is 'the city of a thousand minarets'. The **Police Museum** is on the right side of the terrace. It's worth a quick peek to see the odd exhibits of weapons and dioramas of famous political assassinations.

National Military Museum

The former harem palace of Mohammed Ali is now the **National Military Museum**, which documents – in more detail than most people need – great moments in Egypt's military history, from Pharaonic times to the 20th century. Cast your eyes up from the display cases and kitschy dioramas to gaze at the painted-stucco and frescoed ceilings of the halls.

Suleiman Pasha Mosque

Few visitors make their way to the **Suleiman Pasha Mosque**, about a 10-minute walk along the road from outside the gate of the National Military Museum. Built in 1528, this mosque has detailed marble panels and a colourful floral motif on the interior dome. It was built by Suleyman Pasha, who rose from eunuch in the court of Suleyman the Magnificent to be Ottoman governor of Egypt between 1524 and 1534.

The site guardian might allow you to climb the minaret for baksheesh.

Mosque of Qaitbey

The Second Life of the Maq'ad of Sultan Qaitbey   MAP P102
Culture and crafts

A short walk west of the **Mosque of Qaitbey** (p108) is the restored **Maq'ad of Sultan Qaitbey**, which has been reborn as **Multicultural & Artistic Spaces at Qaitbey's** *(instagram.com/masq.hub)*, a cultural centre that puts on a huge range of events, including market days, walking tours of the Northern Cemetery, live music and history talks. Art exhibitions and **craft workshops** *(instagram.com/mishka .handcrafts; LE1200)* with local glass-blowers, inlaid-wood artisans and copper-jewellery makers often take place at nearby **Craftastic** *(instagram.com/craftastic.hub)*. Check what's on before you visit, as there's not much to see in the buildings otherwise.

Nearby, the **Mishka** boutique sells jewellery, homewares, art and accessories inspired by designs found in the Mosque of Qaitbey, and much of it is made by women who live in this low-income neighbourhood.

The Double Domes of Ibn Barquq   MAP P102
Intricate interiors and city views

Built by a son of Sultan Barquq, whose great madrasa and mausoleum stand on Sharia Al Muizz, the **Khanqah & Mausoleum of Farag Ibn Barquq** *(free)* was completed in 1411 in this location in the Northern Cemetery because Barquq wished to be buried near some illustrious Sufi sheikhs. The *khanqah* (Sufi monastery) is a fortress-like building with high, sheer facades and twin minarets and domes, the largest masonry domes in Cairo.

After entering through a dimly lit passageway, you arrive in a large outdoor courtyard. The site caretaker will most

IMPORTANT ERAS OF ISLAMIC CAIRO

Fatimid (973–1171): Conquered Egypt in 969 and established the new capital, Al Qahira, centred around grand palaces along Sharia Al Muizz.

Ayyubid (1171–1250): Started with Salah ad-Din (Saladin). He constructed the Citadel, changing Cairo from a city of the elite to one open to all.

Mamluk (1250–1517): Former enslaved people turned soldiers who rose to power during the Crusades and ushered in a golden era of grand Islamic architecture.

Ottoman (1517–1882): Selim I defeated the Mamluks, though many remained powerful. Napoleon briefly invaded from 1798 to 1801, and then Mohammed Ali Pasha, an Ottoman army officer, took control, making Egypt a nominally independent state.

VISITING THE 'CITY OF THE DEAD'

The large Northern Cemetery (Qarafa in Arabic), where domed Mamluk tombs rub shoulders with squat apartment blocks and neighbourhood shops, is sometimes referred to by the dramatic moniker the 'City of the Dead'. But people have lived within Cairo's cemetery areas pretty much since they were initially laid out. There's nothing spooky or eerie about it, so don't let the nickname put you off visiting. However, be aware that it's a lower-income area that doesn't often see visitors, so dress modestly and expect to get long stares. The area is sliced in half by busy Sharia Salah Salem. Many of the roads are too narrow for taxis, but it's a short walk to and between the main sights.

likely find you here and offer to open the tomb chambers and guide you onto the roof and up the minaret (baksheesh expected). The tomb chambers on either side of the prayer hall have two of Cairo's most beautifully decorated, patterned dome interiors.

On another side of the courtyard, up some steep sets of chunky stairs to the roof, you're rewarded with vistas over the whole building and the neighbourhood beyond, speckled with stone domes. If you take the twisty, narrow stairs up the minaret, you'll get a panoramic view of Cairo with the high-rises of Downtown and the **Cairo Tower** (p132) poking up in the far distance.

From Mamluk to More Modern

MAP P102

Two mosques for one entry ticket

Most mosques in Cairo are free to enter; these two structures charge a fee, but they shouldn't be missed. The entrance to Al Rifa'i Mosque is first after the ticket booth, but walk past it to visit the bigger and oldest mosque first.

Massive and elegant, the grand **Mosque & Madrasa of Sultan Hassan** (egymonuments.com; LE220) is regarded as the finest piece of early Mamluk architecture in Cairo. It was built between 1356 and 1363 by Sultan Hassan, a grandson of Sultan Qalawun. He took the throne at the age of 13 and was deposed and reinstated no fewer than three times. He was then assassinated shortly before the mosque was completed.

From the portal studded with *muqarnas* (stalactite-type stone carvings), a dimly lit passageway provides an element of dramatic anticipation as it leads to the central open-air courtyard. The courtyard, with its inlaid red, black and white marble paving and ornate fountain (an Ottoman-era addition), is surrounded by four soaring iwans, each dominated

Mosque of Ibn Tulun (p114)

by a curtain of low-hanging glass lamps. The iwans were dedicated to teaching the four main schools of Sunni Islam. Between them, doors lead into what were originally student living quarters. The eastern iwan was also the prayer hall, and at its rear is a colourful marble-panelled mihrab (niche indicating the direction of Mecca). To the right of the mihrab, a bronze door leads into Sultan Hassan's mausoleum. Plan your visit for the morning when sunlight penetrates the iwans.

Although much younger than the Mosque & Madrasa of Sultan Hassan – work started in 1869 but wasn't finished until 1912 – **Al Rifa'i Mosque** *(egymonuments.com; both sites LE220)* stylistically complements its venerable neighbour. It's only when you enter that the differences become striking. The massive prayer hall cherry-picks inspiration from Cairo's grand mosques. Take in the panelled walls that use 19 types of marble, the domes rimmed with *muqarnas*, and lace-like stuccowork on the towering archways.

The tomb of Sufi Sheikh Al Rifa'i is directly in front of the mosque entrance. The tombs of King Fuad, King Farouk and the last shah of Iran are in the room to the north.

For a higher view of the mosques, head to the nearby **House of Egyptian Architecture** *(LE100)*. This 18th-century home was built by a merchant, and its typical Ottoman floor plan, with salons centred on a courtyard, has been carefully preserved. The building was later home to acclaimed Egyptian architect Hasan Fathy (1900–89) and is now a museum focused on architecture, though the labels are in Arabic only. On the top floor, Hasan Fathy's workrooms have been preserved (check out the curvaceous fireplaces, typical of his designs). Head up onto the roof to see the mosques of Sultan Hassan, Al Rifa'i and Amir Akhur slap-bang in front of you.

RAZING THE NORTHERN CEMETERY

In Cairo's quest for 'modernisation', some lower-income neighbourhoods have fallen prey to the government's fast-moving bulldozers, and the Northern Cemetery – home to the mausoleums of rulers, notable officials and everyday Egyptians, as well as actual homes – is one such victim.

As part of a development plan called Cairo Vision 2050, the Egyptian government is set on redistributing the city's population and improving traffic flows in the car-clogged capital, constructing new highways and flyover bridges and demolishing parts of this UNESCO-listed area. This destruction represents an erasure of history but also means further marginalisation of poor Cairenes, some of whom have lived in the 'City of the Dead' for generations.

Living History at the Mosque of Ibn Tulun

MAP P102

Cairo's oldest intact mosque

The city's most historic, still-functioning Islamic monument, the **Mosque of Ibn Tulun** *(free)* is easily identified by its high walls topped with neat crenellations that resemble a string of paper dolls. It was built between 876 and 879 CE by Ibn Tulun, who was sent to rule the outpost of Fustat in the 9th century by the Abbasid caliph of Baghdad. Its geometric simplicity is part of its beauty and is best appreciated from the top of the minaret. Its colossal footprint spans 2.5 hectares.

The mosque is the only surviving remnant of Egypt's short-lived Tulunid dynasty. In 868, as Abbasid centralised rule declined, Egypt's governor Ahmed Ibn Tulun grabbed his chance to reign independently from his Baghdad masters. He began his own capital, Al Qatai, north of Fustat, built this mosque and extended his reach into Syria. In 905, everything except the mosque was razed to the ground as Baghdad wrested back control.

To climb the spiral minaret, leave the central courtyard and walk between the massive walls to the northwestern side of the mosque. As you climb up the external staircase of the minaret, you can see how Ibn Tulun drew inspiration for the mosque's design from his homeland, particularly the ancient Mosque of Samarra in modern-day Iraq, on which the spiral minaret is modelled, as well as the use of brick. He also added innovations of his own; according to architectural historians, the Mosque of Ibn Tulun was the first structure to use the pointed arch, a good 200 years before the European Gothic arch.

Mansion Turned Museum

MAP P102

Treasures collected by a 20th-century British traveller

After visiting the **Mosque of Ibn Tulun**, walk southeast along its walls to find the **Gayer-Anderson Museum** *(egy monuments.com; LE100)*. This quirky museum gets its name from John Gayer-Anderson, a British major and army doctor who restored the two adjoining 16th-century houses between 1935 and 1942, filling them with lovely furniture, artworks and other souvenirs acquired on his travels across Egypt, the Middle East and Asia. The house was also used as a location in the James Bond film *The Spy Who Loved Me*. On his death in 1945, Gayer-Anderson bequeathed the lot to Egypt.

The puzzle of rooms is decorated in a variety of styles. The Persian Room has exquisite tiling, the Damascus Room is covered in lacquer and gold, and the Queen Anne Room displays ornate furniture and a silver tea set. The enchanting gallery of *mashrabiyya* looks down onto a magnificent *qa'a* (reception room), which has a marble fountain, decorated ceiling beams and carpet-covered alcoves. The rooftop terrace has been restored, with more *mashrabiyya* and views of the mosque.

CAIRO WITH KIDS

Cairo can be exhausting for kids, but there is much they will enjoy. Be aware that the pavements and traffic can be a nightmare for parents with little ones, so backpack-style child carriers are a much better idea for toddlers than pushchairs.

Children of all ages will like an excursion on a Nile felucca (p137), gawking at Tut's treasures in the **Grand Egyptian Museum** (p72) and investigating the **Pyramids of Giza** (p64). For evening entertainment, most kids will be mesmerised by a colourful performance of the Al Tannoura Egyptian Heritage Dance Troupe (p107).

Parents with smaller children should head to **Al Azhar Park** (p107) on a Friday or Saturday when local families flock here for picnics.

Find Forgotten Sufi Stories at Mawlawiyya Takiyya   MAP P102
A hidden dervish hall

This jewel box of a *sama khane* (ritual hall) is one of the area's most charming buildings, but **Mawlawiyya Takiyya** *(LE100)* is rarely visited. Go against the grain and seek it out; it's on Sharia Suyufiyya, a five-minute walk northwest of the **Mosque & Madrasa of Sultan Hassan** (p112), accessed through a door with a sign for the 'Italian-Egyptian Centre for Restoration and Archaeology'.

The Ottoman-era wooden structure, with its intricate painted decorations rimming the domed ceiling, is where Mevlevi dervishes would hold their *sama* (ritual whirling performance). Entering feels like discovering a secret treasure. Downstairs are the remains of a 14th-century madrasa that forms the building's foundations and contains mostly empty museum display cases.

See the Cave Church & Ride a Zip Line in 'Garbage City'   MAP P102
Exploring Manshiyat Nasr

Looking around some parts of Cairo, you might think garbage is never collected – but it certainly is, by some 65,000 people of the Coptic Christian Zaraeeb community. Known (derogatorily) to most Cairenes as Zabbaleen ('garbage people'), this community makes a living by collecting rubbish from Cairene homes, sorting and recycling the salvaged materials, and feeding the organic waste to their pigs. The Zaraeeb live in the district of Manshiyat Nasr (also known as 'Garbage City') east of the Citadel.

Above Manshiyat Nasr on a ridge of the Mokattam Hills is one of the most surprising churches in the country. Built in the 1970s, the **Church of St Simon the Tanner** *(samaan church.com; free)* is one of the largest churches in the Middle East. It's nicknamed the 'Cave Church' because it's built straight into the escarpment with a rock overhang used as the ceiling. Its official name comes from a 10th-century ascetic who prayed to make Mokattam move at the behest of Fatimid Caliph Al Muizz Li-Din Allah (r 953–75). Today, the church is a major site of Coptic pilgrimage. Crowds throng here on Fridays and Sundays when Mass takes place. For a quieter experience, avoid visiting on these days.

COLLECTING CAIRO'S RUBBISH

The Zaraeeb recycle about 80% of the waste they collect, and their methods have been recognised as among the most efficient in the world. Despite this, in 2004 under President Mubarak, Cairo's waste collection was handed out to multinational corporations, threatening the Zaraeebs' livelihood. In 2014, after the failure of the official waste collection system, the government partially reversed the policy, reinstating the community's role and registering around 60 Zaraeeb companies to take charge of waste disposal in part of the city.

Densely populated Manshiyat Nasr is where it all gets sorted. Apartment-block roofs are piled high with discarded materials, and huge bags are sifted through in the neighbourhood's narrow alleys.

 EATING NEAR THE MOSQUE OF IBN TULUN: OUR PICKS — MAPS P94, P102

Fathy Kebda: Local favourite for liver. From the Mosque of Taghribirdi on Sharia Al Saliba, walk north and take the first left. *10am-2am* $	**El Gahsh:** All-day breakfast canteen serving *ta'amiyya* and *fuul*, 500m west of the Mosque of Ibn Tulun on Sharia Al Saliba. *24hr* $	**Ibn Hamido:** Dig into a massive seafood feast on Sharia Port Said, a 750m walk north of the Mosque of Ibn Tulun. *9am-2am* $$	**Muhammed El Rafaei Kebab Restaurant:** Devour plates of grilled meat across from the Mosque of Sayyida Zainab. *4.30pm-2am* $

> **CONSERVING ISLAMIC CAIRO**
>
>
>
> **Omniya Abdel Barr** is an architect and historian working with the Egyptian Heritage Rescue Foundation on restoring Bait Al Razzaz (p118). @ehrf.eg
>
> This palace, built in the 15th century, is located in Darb Al Ahmar, a vibrant neighbourhood with an exciting urban fabric holding vestiges of Cairo's traditional architecture. Its proximity to Al Azhar Park encouraged the Aga Khan Trust for Culture to invest in restoring Mamluk-era buildings. Cairenes – and also adventurous travellers – visit this neighbourhood to experience the real life of the medieval city. The narrow alleys and streets are full of activity, and traffic can be intense, but you can watch craftspeople working in traditional forms, such as woodwork, textiles and leather.

A fun but incongruous addition to the neighbourhood is a small adventure park with a zip line, ropes course, a giant swing and a rock-climbing wall. It's run by **Mario High Ropes** (instagram.com/mario.high.ropes.team; activities per person from LE190; closed Sun), founded by the namesake Polish artist who carved some of the religious scenes in the Cave Church. For an additional LE100, you can hold a GoPro attached to a selfie stick and laugh at the footage later, sent to you on WhatsApp.

In 2016, French-Tunisian street artist eL Seed created one of the most astonishing pieces of street art in the Middle East in Manshiyat Nasr. **Perception** covers 50 buildings in a mammoth, exuberant swirl of Arabic calligraphy that quotes St Athanasius, the 20th pope of the Coptic Church: 'Anyone who wants to see the sunlight clearly needs to wipe his eyes first'. The mural is a tribute to the community and a reminder to those who perceive the district – and people themselves – as dirty, and of the vital work this community does clearing the Cairo streets of rubbish. Since the mural's creation, new buildings have popped up in front, obscuring some of the script. Get a view of it from the 1st floor of the cafe across the street, from Cave Church or from the car park behind the cafe building.

The streets of Manshiyat Nasr are narrow and often clogged with traffic. Many taxis and Uber drivers will not take you right insider the neighbourhood because of this, and will drop you at the neighbourhood edge, from where it's a 1.5km walk to reach the church. To get a truly local insight, sign up for a tour with guide **Abanoub Melad** (WhatsApp +20 100-175-2498), who grew up in the neighbourhood and will take you to multiple churches, a mural viewpoint and up a rooftop pigeon tower.

Get a Dose of Culture at the Citadel Festival for Music and Singing

Exploring Manshiyat Nasr

Held at the height of summer in mid-August, the **Citadel Festival for Music & Singing** brings a dose of culture to stages around Cairo after the sun goes down. Some of the biggest names in classical Arab music, plus contemporary-music artists, perform more than 30 concerts across this two-week festival, which is organised by the **Cairo Opera House** (p131).

Performances take place within the **Citadel** (p109) but also at other venues around town. Two shows take place on each evening of the festival, one at 8pm and one at 10pm. In 2024 tickets cost LE60 and could be purchased on the same day of the concert from the ticket booth at the entrance of the Citadel.

Amir Khayrbak Funerary Complex

TOP EXPERIENCE

Darb Al Ahmar

Darb Al Ahmar (Red Road) was the main thoroughfare connecting Al Qahira from the walled city's southern gate at Bab Zuwayla to the Citadel during the medieval era. Thanks to funding and restoration work by the Aga Khan Trust for Culture and the European Union, the stunning monuments on this street are finally receiving the attention their history deserves.

DID YOU KNOW?

Mamluk-era elites were keen to build palaces and homes near the Citadel to be close to the ruling sultan, which fuelled the historic development of this area.

Amir Khayrbak Funerary Complex

This complex was built between 1502 and 1521 by Egypt's first Ottoman-era governor, its namesake traitorous Mamluk ruler. Khayrbak defected to the Ottoman side in 1516, which effectively ended Mamluk rule. He then became the governor of Egypt. Take in the view of the complex's surrounding minarets and domes from the internal courtyard. Soak up Khayrbak's high-ceilinged mosque and then visit the *sabil* (public fountain) with its delicately engraved stone panels.

PRACTICALITIES
- *multisite ticket LE120*
- *9am–5pm*
- *Scan this QR code for more information*

GUIDED TOURS

Darb Al Ahmar has a visitor centre in **Al Azhar Park** (p107) and runs 2½-hour guided tours of the street (LE2000 for four visitors) by electric golf-cart shuttles. You must also pay LE50 to enter Al Azhar Park to reach the visitor centre.

It's worth signing up to learn specific details about the sites. Book via WhatsApp (+20 109-377-1222) at least two days in advance.

TOP TIPS

● Visit Darb Al Ahmar in the morning before the narrow road gets chock-a-block with tuk-tuk traffic so you can appreciate the architectural details you might miss otherwise.

● The multisite ticket can be purchased only at the Amir Khayrbak Funerary Complex, so it makes sense to start there unless you're joining a guided tour.

● It's about a 10-minute walk from the Mosque & Madrasa of Sultan Hassan to the Amir Khayrbak Funerary Complex, but some of the neighbourhood's small streets aren't shown on navigation apps. Stick to the roads that look larger on the map to reach the site easily.

Aqsunqur Mosque

Aqsunqur Mosque is often called the Blue Mosque, and you'll see why as soon as you walk in. The prayer hall's qibla wall that shows the direction of Mecca is covered in floral Iznik tiles that were installed during an Ottoman-era restoration 300 years after the mosque was built in 1347. On the right side are the mausoleums of the mosque's founder, Shams Ad Din Aqsunqur, and its later restorer, Ibrahim Agha Al Mustahfizan. You might have to ask the site guardian to unlock the door.

Bait Al Razzaz & Umm Al Sultan Shaa'ban Mosque & Madrasa

Sometimes it's the little details that help you understand how a city's layers of historic fabric are stitched together. The entryway to the mansion of **Bait Al Razzaz** and the adjoining **Umm Al Sultan Shaa'ban Mosque & Madrasa** (built in 1369) is one of these places.

From street level, head down the entryway steps to the lowest level facing the mosque. You're now standing on the road level of the 14th century, when Sultan Shaa'ban built this complex for his mother. Above you, the large, wooden, loggia-like projecting window is where musicians played as the sultan's procession passed by. Directly below is a drinking trough.

Now look down at the flooring to see slices of relief-covered Pharaonic-era stones that were incorporated into the paving. Walk up the stairs to the doorway into Bait Al Razzaz, and you've just climbed up 500 years and are now in the 19th century when an extension to the mansion replaced an alleyway.

Stroll through Bait Al Razzaz' narrow passage entrance and into its internal courtyard, surrounded by walls studded with *mashrabiyya* windows and decorated with preserved scraps of painted decoration. Turn back and examine the arched portal you just walked through. The house may be named after a family of wealthy 18th-century Ottoman rice merchants, but the rondels on the doorway display the blazon of 15th-century Sultan Qaitbey. The **Egyptian Heritage Rescue Foundation** *(instagram.com/ehrf.eg)* is working to restore the building.

Next door, the entrance of Umm Al Sultan Shaa'ban Mosque & Madrasa is trimmed with *muqarnas*. Inside is the tomb chamber of Sultan Shaa'ban's mother.

Al Tanbugha Al Maridani Mosque

Built in 1339, **Al Tanbugha Al Maridani Mosque** is Darb Al Ahmar's earliest monument. This building incorporates architectural elements from several different periods. Eight granite columns were taken from a Pharaonic monument; the arches contain Roman, Christian and Islamic designs; and the Ottomans added a fountain. Trees in the courtyard, attractive *mashrabiyya* and a lack of visitors make this a peaceful place to stop.

Coptic Cairo, Fustat & Maadi

RELIGIOUS HISTORY, ROYAL MUMMIES AND CHILL CAFES

When the conquering Arab army rolled into Egypt in 641 CE, they snubbed Alexandria, founding their capital of Fustat beside a Roman fortress called Babylon and building the first mosque in Africa, which still stands. Even after the Fatimid conquest some 325 years later, Fustat continued to prosper as the neighbouring commercial hub to the new walled capital of Al Qahira. It has long been a centre of ceramics production, and pottery studios still cluster along a few of the district's streets.

Today, the wider area is known as Coptic Cairo or Old Cairo, home to the city's oldest church and oldest synagogue. It's a fascinating counterpoint to the rest of the capital. Nearby, the National Museum of Egyptian Civilization houses an unmissable collection of royal mummies.

Further south, the leafy, well-to-do neighbourhood of Maadi doesn't have any sights, but it's sprinkled with coffee shops and restaurants perfect for taking a break from Cairo's intensity.

Meet the Royal Mummies at the National Museum of Egyptian Civilization

Modern museum of ancient artefacts

Yes, Cairo has a lot of museums with Pharaonic artefacts, but the **National Museum of Egyptian Civilization** *(NMEC; nmec.gov.eg; LE550)* and its incredible collection of royal mummies, transferred here in a regal procession in 2021, is not to be missed. But this museum is more than its prized collection of pharaohs; it's an attempt to encompass the entire sweep of Egyptian heritage under one roof.

As you enter the main hall, ignore the walkway leading down to the subterranean Royal Mummies Hall and veer right to zigzag between exhibits covering prehistory through to the Pharaonic era. The exquisite pieces highlight different facets of ancient Egypt's culture from the finely detailed

☑ TOP TIP

Visitors must have their shoulders and knees covered to enter churches or mosques. Avoid visiting on Fridays and Sundays when churches celebrate Mass.

GETTING AROUND

Metro Line 1 provides easy access to Coptic Cairo and Maadi from Downtown. Coptic Cairo's sights are walkable, but you need a taxi to reach the National Museum of Egyptian Civilization.

The Coptic compound has four entrances. The main gate in the centre of Mar Girgis St (directly opposite the metro exit) is for the Coptic Museum. To the south, another doorway leads to the Hanging Church, while to the north is the entrance to the Church of St George. On the street outside, a staircase gives access to alleyways leading to the other churches and the synagogue.

TIPS FOR VISITING THE NMEC

Buy tickets online in advance: The museum's website sells tickets so you don't have to wait if there's a queue.

Sign up for a behind-the-scenes tour: Visit the artefact restoration labs and speak with conservators on a 45-minute tour (LE1000); these run between 10am and 4.30pm on Mondays, Wednesdays and Sundays. Book in advance.

Have a look at Sira Lake: The palm-fringed water rimmed with walking paths on the eastern side of the NMEC looks enticing, but it still wasn't open when we visited. For now, enjoy the scene from the viewing platform or the cafe.

Old Kingdom wooden statues of men grinding wheat to the Ptolemaic-era gilded-stucco coffin of the priest Nedjemankh.

Backtrack now to the Royal Mummies Hall entrance. Inside, the vault-like rooms are the final resting places for some of Egypt's most famous pharaohs and queens. Seti I's mummy, with his smooth black skin, is one of the most flawlessly preserved, and Ramses II, with his grey hair tinged with henna, is a close rival.

The exit transfers you back into the main hall. Exhibits on the left side speed through the last 2000 years of history. Don't miss the mosaic panels from Ablaq Palace in the **Citadel** (p109) and the huge *kiswa* cloth, which Egypt used to send annually to Mecca to cover the Kaaba.

Admire Religious Artistry at the Coptic Museum

A dazzling repository of Christian heritage

The **Coptic Museum** *(egymonuments.gov.eg; LE280)* contains one of the most important collections of Christian antiquities in the world. Inside, the colourful frescoed niches from the Monastery of St Jeremiah in Saqqara and the Monastery of St Apollo at Bawit are the highlights, but also take time to examine the friezes and column capitals from Ahnas with scenes from Greek mythology. These artefacts demonstrate how long it took Christianity to bed down and replace earlier traditions artistically. Upstairs, one room is devoted to the Nag Hammadi Library, the primary source for Gnosticism.

The ornate building was purpose-built by prominent Copt Marcus Simaika Pasha in 1910 to store Coptic artefacts salvaged from the dusty, neglected corners of Egypt's churches and desert monasteries. The museum's interior, with its elaborate wood-carved painted ceilings, is an attraction in itself. Set aside at least an hour to delve into the breadth of Coptic art, history and heritage in Egypt, which extends back to the earliest days of Christianity.

Wander into the Hanging Church

Cairo's most famous Christian site

The **Hanging Church** *(free)* is so old that its founding date isn't fully remembered. This 9th-century (some say 7th-century)

EATING & DRINKING IN MAADI: OUR PICKS

Carmel California: Cute indoor-outdoor space serving all-day brunch, plus pizza, pasta and fresh juices. *7am-midnight* $$	**Estro:** Cheers to *la dolce vita* with an aperitivo and Italian plates from this sleek 9th-floor rooftop. *9am-midnight* $$$	**Villa Belle Epoque:** Maadi locals worship Acacia, the Mediterranean-spanning restaurant at this 1920s boutique hotel. *7am-midnight* $$$	**Villa Sumatra Coffee:** Relax in the leafy back garden with a brew made with ethically sourced beans from Indonesia. *7am-11pm*

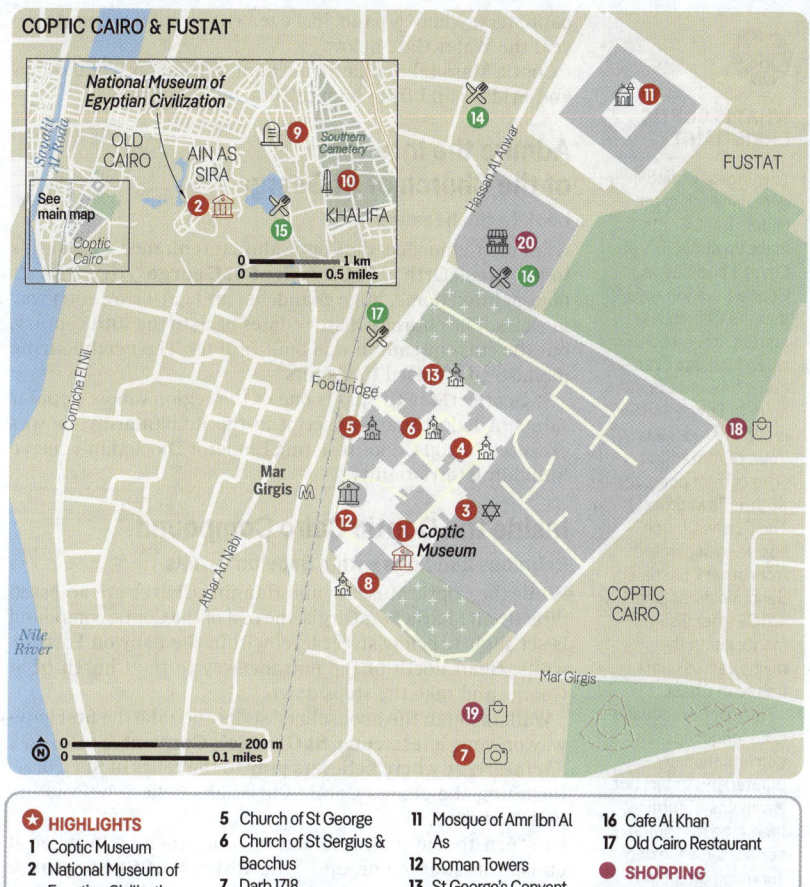

COPTIC CAIRO & FUSTAT

⭐ HIGHLIGHTS
1. Coptic Museum
2. National Museum of Egyptian Civilization

● SIGHTS
3. Ben Ezra Synagogue
4. Church of St Barbara
5. Church of St George
6. Church of St Sergius & Bacchus
7. Darb 1718
8. Hanging Church
9. Housh Al Basha
10. Mausoleum of Imam Al Shafi'i
11. Mosque of Amr Ibn Al As
12. Roman Towers
13. St George's Convent

● EATING
14. Abu Ahmed Couscous
15. Bayt Elmoazz
16. Cafe Al Khan
17. Old Cairo Restaurant

● SHOPPING
18. Foustat Traditional Craft Centre
19. Heba Helmi Pottery
20. Souq Al Fustat

church gets its curious name because it's suspended over the Water Gate of Roman Babylon. The courtyard entranceway is just south of the Roman Tower.

When you walk into the interior with its three barrel-vaulted, wood-roofed aisles resting on 13 pillars, it feels like entering an upturned ark. Take note of the inlaid ebony and ivory screens hiding the altar; their intricate geometric designs are distinguishable from Islamic patterns only by the tiny crosses worked into them. The aisle pillars represent Christ and his Apostles – the darker one is believed to represent Judas.

The church has 110 icons including an 8th-century painting of the Virgin Mary known as the 'Coptic Mona Lisa'. Walk through the door in the southeast corner to access the

WHAT IS COPTIC CHRISTIANITY?

The largest Christian denomination in the Middle East, Copts make up about 10% of Egypt's population. Coptic tradition says that the Church was started around 50 CE when Mark the Evangelist brought Christianity to Egypt, and he is considered the first Pope of Alexandria. (The current pope, the 118th, is Tawadros II.) The Coptic Church has been separated from other Christian denominations since 451 CE after disagreements about the divine versus human nature of Christ.

The Coptic language is no longer spoken conversationally, supplanted by Arabic, but it remains a liturgical language for church services. It's the only surviving direct language descendant of ancient Egyptian Demotic.

baptistery, where a panel has been cut out of the floor to reveal the Water Gate below.

Coptic Mass takes place from 8am to 11am on Wednesdays and Fridays and from 9am to 11am on Sundays.

Admire the Interior of the Church of St George
Look to the heavens

A few metres north of the Coptic Museum entrance, a gate leads to the Greek Orthodox **Church of St George** *(free)*, with its blue-painted dome, huge chandelier and glittering entryway mosaics. The church's history dates back to the 10th century, but the current church was built in 1909. The neighbouring monastery is closed to visitors.

St George (Mar Girgis) is one of the region's most popular saints. A Palestinian conscript in the Roman army, he was executed in 303 CE for resisting Emperor Diocletian's decree forbidding Christianity.

Inside the Coptic Cairo Compound
Religious buildings within Babylon's walls

While the Coptic Museum and Hanging Church are accessed directly off Sharia Mar Girgis, the rest of the Coptic compound is set slightly below street level within the Babylon Fortress walls. Head north of the entranceway to the Church of St George and take the steps down.

Walk through the booksellers' stalls and take the first gateway on your left to enter **St George's Convent** *(St George's Shrine; free)*, where believers pray to the relics of St George, including the chains Coptic Christians believe he was imprisoned with.

Return to the main passageway and turn right when it ends. You soon come upon the **Church of St Sergius & Bacchus** *(Abu Sarga; free)*, the oldest church site in Cairo. It dates from the 5th century, although the original structure was destroyed and the current church has been constantly restored over the centuries. The interior, with its stone walls rising to a wood-rafter ceiling, is imbued with a serene simplicity. Note the intricate ivory inlay and wood carvings of the templon (the screen separating the nave from the sanctuary).

The church is built over a cave where, according to Coptic tradition, the Holy Family are said to have taken shelter

EATING IN COPTIC CAIRO & FUSTAT: OUR PICKS

Old Cairo Restaurant: Filled with tourists because it's the closest food option to the churches; serves Egyptian staples. *9am-10pm* $$

Abu Ahmed Couscous: Famous joint dishing up *couscousy* (couscous with hot milk, powdered sugar and other sweet toppings). *9am-late* $

Bayt Elmoazz: Big portions of grilled meats, rice and salads across busy Sharia Fustat from the National Museum of Egyptian Civilization. *11am-midnight* $$

Cafe Al Khan: Decent Egyptian restaurant with reasonable prices in the Souq Al Fustat complex. *10am-1am* $$

Exterior of the Hanging Church (p120)

during their flight into Egypt to escape persecution from King Herod of Judea, who had embarked upon a 'massacre of the firstborn'. The cave of the Holy Family – now the crypt – is reached by a door to the left of the altar.

On the corner just past Abu Sarga, the **Church of St Barbara** *(free)* houses rare icons of its namesake saint, as well as of the Virgin Mary and Jesus Christ. St Barbara was an early Christian convert who was beaten to death by her pagan father for her beliefs.

Next, visit the 9th-century **Ben Ezra Synagogue** *(free)*, built inside the shell of a 4th-century church but no longer in use. According to tradition, this place is where the Prophet Jeremiah gathered the Jews after Nebuchadnezzar destroyed the temple in Jerusalem. The adjacent spring is supposedly where the pharaoh's daughter found baby Moses in the reeds. Photos are not allowed inside.

REMNANTS OF ROME

Emperor Diocletian built the Roman fortress of Babylon – no, not of the hanging gardens variety – in around 300 CE to guard a canal that once connected the Nile to the Red Sea. The name Babylon is likely a corruption of Per-hapi-en-on (Estate of the Nile God at On), a Pharaonic name for the area, and the fortress would have been right on the riverfront, with the Nile lapping against the walls

Today, the only recognisable features of the fort are two stone and brick **Roman Towers** that formed part of the western gate and now stand beside the entrance to the Coptic Museum.

Get Arty at Darb 1718
Culture and ceramics in Fustat

Darb 1718 *(darb1718.com; facebook.com/Darb1718)* is a cultural centre and creative space that puts on art exhibitions, runs craft workshops and has evening concerts that take place in the garden or on the roof, as well as movie screenings. Check what's on at its Facebook page before you visit.

The Site of Africa's First Mosque
Islam's first foothold in Egypt

The **Mosque of Amr Ibn Al As** *(free)* was the first in Egypt and Africa. A forest of columns, many repurposed from ancient sites, greets you inside the austere prayer hall.

COPTIC MONASTERIES NEAR CAIRO

To further explore the heritage and traditions of Egypt's Copts, visit the monasteries of **Wadi Natrun** (p151), which are within day-tripping distance of Cairo.

The original mosque, built in 632 CE, was made from palm trunks and thatched with leaves, and has been heavily remodelled over the centuries, so you're not standing in Cairo's oldest surviving original-form mosque, but, as the site where Islam first began in Egypt, it resonates with importance.

Exploring Al Qarafa

Visit Fustat's historic cemetery

The neighbourhood east of the NMEC is Al Qarafa, a historic cemetery founded to service the capital of Fustat. Today, residents still live beside the multi-domed tombs, shrines and mosques of important Islamic scholars, spiritual leaders and royalty from the Fatimid to Ottoman eras. Two of Cairo's most interesting and beautiful mausoleums are located within this area's wriggle of dusty, pot-holed lanes.

Because of the narrow streets, taxis drop you off on the larger outer roads, and tuk-tuk drivers might be around to offer to take you to the sites inside. Otherwise, you'll have to walk. Don't be intimidated by the area's obvious poverty. Friendly locals on the street will point you in the right direction if they see you wandering around looking like you're lost, and it's safe, though multiple residents kindly warned us against visiting as a solo female. Dress modestly as Al Qarafa is a pilgrimage destination for Muslims.

Al Qarafa's main highlight is the **Mausoleum of Imam Al Shafi'i** *(free)*, built in 1211 and one of Cairo's most important Islamic shrines. The mausoleum has been added to and beautified across the centuries by various rulers. Its most recent restoration finished in 2021 and was led by architect May Al Ibrashy, who has carefully highlighted the building's mesh of influences. Inside, the soaring red-patterned dome has beautiful *muqarnas* and is Egypt's only remaining wooden dome.

Imam Al Shafi'i (767–820 CE) created the principles of Islamic jurisprudence and founded the Shafi'i school of Sunni Islamic law, which is particularly dominant in East Africa, the Arabian Peninsula, Indonesia and Malaysia.

On the other side of the block, **Housh Al Basha** is a five-domed mausoleum of the Mohammed Ali dynasty, which ran Egypt through Ottoman and British rule. It was undergoing restoration when we visited, but when it reopens, you can walk through the chambers and between the large ornate tombstones topped by tarbooshes and turbans (men) or crowns (women). Some of the steles are intricately decorated with delicate floral designs. To reach it from the Mausoleum of Imam Al Shafi'i, turn left out of the main door, exiting the fenced area. Turn left at the next main road and then curve left at its end.

BEST CRAFT SHOPS IN COPTIC CAIRO

Fustat has been a centre for ceramics since the Fatimid era more than 1000 years ago, and it's a top spot to shop for vessels of all shapes, sizes and colours directly from the workshops.

Foustat Traditional Craft Centre: Ceramics, woodwork and silverwork craft complex where you can buy from local artisans or watch them at work.

Souq Al Fustat: Modern souq complex just north of the Coptic compound with some Egyptian handicrafts boutiques.

Heba Helmi Pottery: Modern ceramic pieces that use influences and elements of Islamic art in their designs. Located near Darb 1718 (p123).

MORE COPTIC CULTURE

If you want to see more Coptic art on your trip, visit the **Monastery of St Anthony** (p359) in the northern mountains of the Red Sea Coast and the **Red Monastery** (p179) near Sohag.

Zamalek & Dokki

WHERE THE CAPITAL GETS CREATIVE

The Nile cuts through the city, separating Cairo from Giza. An island in the middle of the river, aptly named Gezira (the Arabic word for island), is home to the affluent district of Zamalek (pronounced zeh-*meh*-lek). Its streets are leafy and quiet – for Cairo at least – and are lined with historic villas and dozens of embassies. West across the two bridges that connect Gezira to Giza, the district of Dokki spills down the riverside.

Before the mid-19th century, Gezira was uninhabited. In 1869, Khedive Ismail built Gezira Palace (now a Marriott hotel) and turned the island into a royal botanical garden. The elite air has remained ever since, and today, Zamalek is filled with boutiques of goodies made by Cairo-based designers, small art galleries and museums, and hip coffee shops. Most visitors short on time in Cairo skip this area, but it's an ideal option for seeing a more peaceful side of the capital.

Boutique Buys
Where to shop in Zamalek

Zamalek has become a hub for local designers to show off their wares, and the island's boutiques make excellent stops for made-in-Egypt souvenirs. Unlike in the markets, the shopping experience in Zamalek is no hassle, and the fixed prices are a breath of fresh air if you're tired of bargaining.

Some shops can be tricky to find. Not all have ground-level storefronts, so don't be afraid to duck into buildings, climb stairs and ring doorbells.

At **Fair Trade Egypt** *(instagram.com/fairtradeegypt)*, find crafts from across the country, including Bedouin rugs, ceramics from Fayoum and beaded jewellery from Aswan. Head up the stairs to the 1st floor at 27 Sharia Yehia Ibrahim. Old-school **Mamlouk** *(instagram.com/mamloukgallery)*, stacked with everything from furniture to Sphinx figurines, is like Khan El Khalili in miniature, but thankfully without the

continued on p128

☑ TOP TIP

Gezira has two metro stations. Opera (Line 2, red) is next to Cairo Opera House and is also handy for Cairo Tower and nearby art museums. Safaa Hegazy (Line 3, green) is close to the neighbourhood's cafes and shops.

GETTING AROUND

Cairo often feels actively hostile towards pedestrians, but Zamalek is one of the capital's most walkable areas. Most roads have pavements, though Cairenes still prefer walking on the street. On our visit, a Nile promenade on the east side of Zamalek was under construction and is sure to be a scenic stroll when it opens (p132).

Gezira measures about 4km from north to south and 1km from east to west. When your legs get tired, taxis are plentiful.

ZAMALEK & DOKKI CAIRO

THE GUIDE

SIGHTS
1. Aisha Fahmy Palace
2. Cairo Tower
3. El Sawy Culture Wheel
4. Mahmoud Mukhtar Museum
5. Mamsha Ahl Misr
6. Mohamed Mahmoud Khalil Museum
7. Museum of Islamic Ceramics
8. Museum of Modern Egyptian Art

ACTIVITIES
9. M/Y Christina

SLEEPING
10. Cairo Marriott Hotel
11. Hilton Cairo Zamalek Residences
12. Houseboat65
13. President Hotel
14. Sheraton Cairo
15. Sofitel El Gezirah

EATING
16. Abou El Sid
17. Batates & Zalabya
18. Cairo Kitchen
19. Crave
20. Crimson Bar & Grill
21. Dara's Ice Cream
22. Five Bells
23. Gelato Mio
24. Granita
see 15 Kebabgy
see 13 La Terrace
25. L'Aubergine
26. Le Tarbouche
27. Luuma
28. Maison Thomas
29. Mandarine Koueider
30. Nile Maxim
see 13 Olivo
31. O's Pasta
32. Sag & Shawarma
33. Sapori di Carlo
see 14 Sapporo
34. Saraya Gallery
35. Simonds
36. U Bistro & Bar
37. Zööba

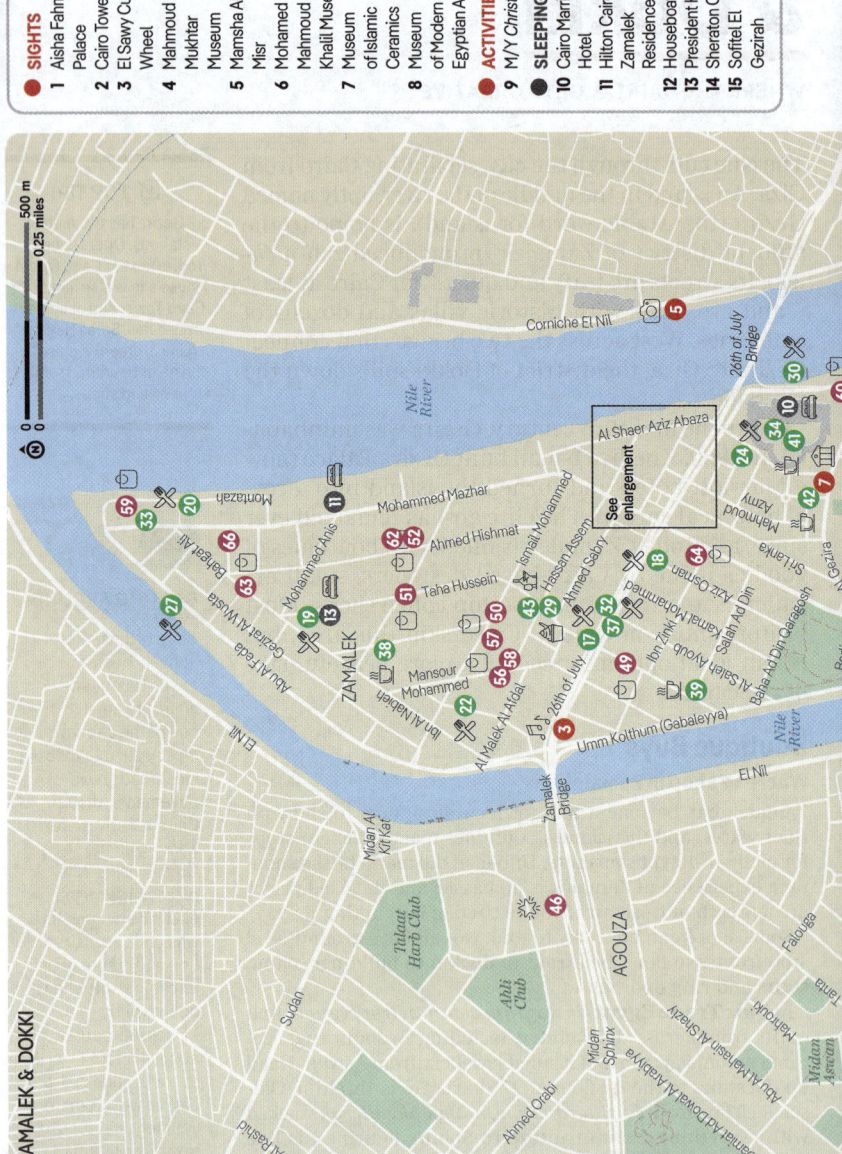

CAIRO ZAMALEK & DOKKI

THE GUIDE

DRINKING & NIGHTLIFE
- **38** 30 North
- **39** Amor Perfecto Specialty Coffee
- **40** Deals
- **41** Garden Promenade Cafe
- **42** Holm Cafe
- **43** Pub 28
- **44** Social Specialty Coffee
- **45** Sufi Cafe & Bookstore

ENTERTAINMENT
- **46** Cairo Jazz Club
- **47** Cairo Opera House

SHOPPING
- **48** Al Masar Gallery
- **49** Anut Cairo
- **50** Asfour El Nil
- **51** Azza Fahmy
- **52** Caravanserai
- **53** Diwan
- **54** Fair Trade Egypt
- **55** Loft Gallery
- **56** Madu Cairo
- **57** Maison 69
- **58** Mamlouk
- **59** Motion Art Gallery
- **60** Nomad Gallery
- **61** Safarkhan
- **62** Siwa Creations
- **63** Tintera
- **64** Ubuntu Art Gallery
- **65** Zamalek Art Gallery
- **66** Zawal

continued from p125

pressure to buy. There's no sign, so look for the faience blue shopfront tiles. **Loft Gallery** *(loftegypt.com)* is another excellent jumble of one-of-a-kind antiques and furniture in a historic former apartment.

Behind a bright green storefront (no English sign), **Asfour El Nil** *(instagram.com/asfourelnil)* has contemporary takes on ancient craft traditions with cute handbags and accessories, colourful homewares and cotton clothing. Don't be worried that you've gotten it wrong as you approach clothing boutique **Maison 69** *(instagram.com/maison69store)* down the street – the frontage looks like a flower shop, but head inside and turn left to find a Tardis-like store that expands into several rooms of fashion and homewares.

For a more monochromatic take on interior design, visit **Caravanserai** *(caravanserai-design.com)*, which blends beautiful Egyptian styles with minimalism in its bowls, lanterns and wall decor. **Zawal** *(instagram.com/zawal.eg)* sells artistic prints, homewares and accessories from the Middle Eastern artistic centres of Cairo, Beirut and Damascus.

For beautifully crafted high-end jewellery inspired by Islamic and Pharaonic designs, **Azza Fahmy** *(azzafahmy.com)* is a must-visit for catwalk-ready pieces. Fahmy was the first woman to work as an apprentice silversmith in Egypt and has been a world-renowned contemporary jeweller for decades.

Meaning 'people' in ancient Egyptian, **Madu Cairo** *(instagram.com/madu_cairo)* stocks gorgeous cotton bed linens, patterned textiles and more made by Malaika (p128). In 2024 one of Malaika's cofounders started **Anut Cairo** *(instagram.com/anut.cairo)*, named for the ancient Egyptian goddess of the sky and selling ceramics, glassware and linens. **Siwa Creations** *(instagram.com/siwa_creation_official)* is another excellent place to look for homewares, such as salt-block candleholders, and desert-inspired *galabeyas* and *abayas* (robes for men and women).

Nomad Gallery *(nomadgallery.net)* specialises in traditional Bedouin and Amazigh crafts, as well as high-quality silver jewellery. It's a bit tricky to find; it's in an apartment building next to the Tunisian embassy. Head up to the 1st floor and ring the doorbell.

Exploring Egypt's Art Scene
Little-visited museums around Gezira

If you need a break from Cairo's history, Gezira has a glut of art museums that can shift your focus back to the present.

EGYPTIAN BRANDS TO LOOK FOR

A growing number of Cairo designers are crafting modern, ethically made goods while using traditional materials and methods.

Malaika: 100% Egyptian cotton linens (bedsheets, tablecloths, accessory bags) hand embroidered or silk-screen printed by underprivileged women *(malaikalinens.com)*.

Up-Fuse: Employs Egyptian women to create trendy upcycled totes, wallets and accessories from discarded plastic bags and car tyres *(up-fuse.com)*.

Rasha Pasha: Boldly accented coats, cloaks, blazers and dresses that are sure to turn heads *(instagram.com/rashapashacairo)*.

Ramla: Beautiful babouche-style slip-on shoes with Pharaonic and desert motifs *(ramlastore.com)*.

EATING IN ZAMALEK: BEST ROOFTOPS & NILE VIEWS

Luuma: Spacious west-facing Nile-front terrace dining, with a menu that bounces from Egyptian to international. *8am-4am* $$

Crimson Bar & Grill: Enjoy elevated Nile views from the east-facing balcony over breakfast or for late-night cocktails. *8am-midnight* $$$

La Terrace: Hip, plant-filled 11th-floor rooftop above the President Hotel with an all-day international menu. *7am-11.30pm* $$$

Kebabgy: Fancy kebab restaurant with a waterfront terrace on the southern tip of the island. *noon-midnight* $$$

Bring ID, as security staff require you to write down your passport number at all of these places.

Across the Qasr El Nil Bridge from Downtown, head through the large gateway into the Gezira Exhibition Grounds to the **Museum of Modern Egyptian Art** (LE20). Its three floors filled with displays give you a solid grounding in Egypt's 20th- and 21st-century art scene. It's closed Mondays and Fridays. The **Palace of Arts** next door is sometimes open for temporary exhibitions.

About a 10-minute walk west on Sharia Tahrir (enter through the gate at Montazah Al Giza), the **Mahmoud Mukhtar Museum** (LE10; closed Tue & Fri) highlights the work of independent Egypt's sculptor laureate (1891–1934). This 1960s-built space contains about 80 pieces of Mukhtar's work, as well as his tomb. Temporary galleries showcasing today's Egyptian artists are set up in the basement and a modern building on the museum's east side.

Across the El Galaa Bridge in Dokki, the **Mohamed Mahmoud Khalil Museum** (LE100; closed Mon & Fri) is an art lover's treat. The walls of this neoclassical villa are hung with European Impressionist and Romantic art, including works by Gauguin, Renoir and Monet, and glass cases display ceramics from across Asia. You're required to leave your handbag and passport at reception to gain access. Although this museum might seem like a sedate oasis, it has been the victim of two notorious art heists...of the same painting (p130).

In the centre of Gezira, the **Museum of Islamic Ceramics** (free) is housed in a 1920s palace that's just about as beautiful as the porcelain and tiles on show. **Aisha Fahmy Palace** (free) is another art and architectural stunner, built in 1907 for an Egyptian aristocrat. Its sublime rococo interior boasts silk-clad and frescoed walls, carved wood fireplaces, painted lacquer work and a wonderful triple-arched stained-glass window overlooking the grand staircase, but you have to wait for a temporary exhibition to open its doors. The arts centre doesn't have a website, but the exhibitions are advertised on the fence outside.

PLUCKED POPPY FLOWERS

In 1977, Van Gogh's 1887 *Poppy Flowers* (worth about US$55 million) was stolen from the **Mohamed Mahmoud Khalil Museum** (p129) and eventually turned up a decade later in Kuwait.

The painting was put back on show, but in 2010, it vanished again. This time, the piece was cut from its frame and taken during the museum's visiting hours. Two Italian tourists were detained at Cairo International Airport, and Egypt's Minister of Culture announced that the painting had been recovered but later retracted the statement.

To this day, *Poppy Flowers* has yet to be found, and the case remains one of the world's greatest unsolved art crimes.

EATING IN ZAMALEK: BEST FOR EGYPTIAN FOOD

Zööba: Street food with modern twists, such as pickled lemon and spicy pepper *ta'amiyya* sandwiches. *8am-midnight* $	**Abou El Sid:** Classic Egyptian dishes, including stuffed pigeon and *molokhiyya* (jute leaf soup), served in retro-glitz salons. *1pm-1am* $$	**Cairo Kitchen:** The bright splashes of colour in the decor also appear in the heaping helpings of Egyptian favourites. *noon-midnight* $$	**Five Bells:** Garden restaurant offering traditional Egyptian mezze to a soundtrack of live piano in the evenings. *noon-2am* $$
Le Tarbouche: Named for the Ottoman red hat, this Egyptian restaurant on a moored Nile cruiser is styled like a pasha's palace. *noon-1am* $$$	**Nile Maxim:** Enjoy dinner and belly dancing, whirling dervishes and live music on Cairo's best river cruise. *8-10pm* $$$	**Sag & Shawarma:** Follow the crowds of students to Zamalek's most popular street-food stand. *8am-3am Sat-Thu, from 11am Fri* $	**Batates & Zalabya:** The fryers are hard at work at this street stall, pumping out sizzling fries and dough balls sprinkled with sugar. *9am-3am* $

CAIRO INTERNATIONAL FILM FESTIVAL

Egypt dominates the Middle Eastern film industry, producing about 75% of what appears on the silver screen in the Arab world, and Cairo is considered 'Hollywood on the Nile'. One of the longest-running cultural events in the region, the **Cairo International Film Festival** *(ciff.org.eg)* takes place every November at the **Cairo Opera House** (p131). It celebrates movies from across the world but has a particular focus on Arab and African contributions. As well as the festival competition and a glitzy award ceremony, plenty of films are shown – more than 100 in 2024.

Museum of Islamic Ceramics (p129)

Modern Galleries Worth a Look

Contemporary Egyptian art

In addition to the art museums, Zamalek is packed with smaller galleries for browsing and buying. Check exhibition information online before visiting, as some places close for weeks between shows.

Safarkhan *(safarkhan.com)* is a small two-level gallery that has been showcasing and supporting Egyptian artists since the 1960s. **Motion Art Gallery** *(instagram.com/motionartgallery)*, secreted away on the 3rd floor of a residential building at the northern tip of the island, displays whimsical works of painting, sculpture and furniture. **Tintera** *(tintera.art)* is also tough to track down, but it's worth the adventure to find Cairo's first gallery dedicated solely to photography. Find the building at 17 Bahgat Ali and then head to the 2nd floor, door 14.

Al Masar Gallery *(almasargallery.com)* has a roster of established artists who often work internationally. It's on the 1st floor of the Behler mansion off Sharia 26th of July. **Zamalek Art Gallery** *(zamalekartgallery.com)* is a stalwart of the scene and supplies luxury hotels like the Four Seasons with locally produced pieces.

 EATING IN ZAMALEK: BEST INTERNATIONAL CUISINE

Granita: Contemporary take on Cairo's old European-style cafes, inside the grounds of All Saints Cathedral. *7am-11pm* $$

Saraya Gallery: French-accented dishes below massive chandeliers and damask curtains in a former palace, now the Cairo Marriott. *noon-midnight* $$$

Sapporo: Inside the Sheraton, the first Japanese restaurant in Egypt has had a makeover but still serves fresh sushi and has teppanyaki tables. *6pm-midnight* $$$

Crave: This cool spot's globe-trotting plates travel from burgers and truffle potatoes to tikka masala and Thai chicken salad. *noon-midnight* $$

Ubuntu Art Gallery (*ubuntuartgallery.com*) helps young Egyptian artists working in all kinds of media break into the international scene. You can't miss the entrance, guarded by a life-size sculpture of a water buffalo.

Capital Culture
Best live music and performances

Built in the 1980s, **Cairo Opera House** (*cairoopera.org*) is home to both the Cairo Symphony Orchestra and the Cairo Opera, as well as many other music and dance companies. It's the city's premier cultural venue and regularly hosts concerts of classical, chamber and traditional Arab music, as well as ballet and other dance performances. The dress code is formal (jacket and tie required).

The program of concerts and performances, from up-and-coming local rock bands to traditional folk ensembles, makes **El Sawy Culture Wheel** (*culturewheel.com*) one of the best destinations in town if you want to dip your toe into Egypt's contemporary music scene. It's also home to the **El Sakia Puppet Theatre**, and the Umm Kulthum puppet concert brings the music of Egypt's most acclaimed and beloved singer back onstage on the first Thursday of every month.

Cairo Jazz Club (*cairojazzclub.com; from LE200*) is one of the capital's major live performance and nightlife venues and has been going for years. Check what's on and reserve a table via the website.

Zamalek Cafe Crawl
Chill out with a coffee

With a slightly slower speed and a more laid-back attitude than central Cairo, Zamalek is an ideal place to while away an afternoon at cool cafes and bookshops among the capital's literati.

Young Cairenes tap on their laptops while sipping coffee amid the creaky wood-floored rooms rimmed by shelves of old books at arty **Sufi Cafe & Bookstore** (*instagram.com/sufibookstoreandmore*). Nearby **Diwan** (*diwanegypt.com*) has a bigger focus on books, with a good selection of Arabic titles in translation, but also has a small cafe.

The friendly baristas at **Social Specialty Coffee** (*instagram.com/socialspecialtycoffee*) make some of the best flat whites in town. Find more top-notch brews at **30 North** (*30north.coffee*), which has an excellent outdoor courtyard.

PALACE INTRIGUE

Dazzling **Gezira Palace** was built in 1869 at the behest of Egypt's then-leader Khedive Ismail. Seeking to impress French Empress Eugénie, who was presiding over the inauguration ceremony of the Suez Canal, Ismail instructed the architect to make the structure look like the Palace of Versailles, and indeed its sumptuous architecture is a beautiful blend of European and Islamic.

Arrivals to the palace, now a **Marriott hotel** (p155), are still greeted by skinny orange-gold columns that hold horseshoe arches aloft. Inside, swooping chandeliers glitter from triple-height ceilings in the ballroom, and heavy damask curtains hang at the high windows of grand sitting rooms.

 EATING IN ZAMALEK: BEST FOR PIZZA & PASTA

| **Sapori di Carlo:** Run by Michelin-starred chef Carlo Adib, this Italian joint bakes perfect Neapolitan pizzas in its wood-fired oven. *11.30am-11.30pm* **$$** | **Maison Thomas:** A little slice of the Continent with loads of brass and mirrors, Maison Thomas has been serving up some of Cairo's best thin-crust pizza for decades. *24hr* **$$** | **O's Pasta:** Squeeze into this teeny pasta place for globe-spanning dishes that range from Italian fettuccine and spaghetti to pad thai and Red Sea calamari. *noon-1am* **$$** | **Olivo:** The ambience is friendly, the Egyptian beer is cold and the thin-crust wood-fired pizza is delicious. *1pm-1am* **$$** |

THE NILE IN ZAMALEK

The ancient Egyptians revered the life-giving Nile, but the modern country has turned its back on the river for many years. The Nile flows from south to north, so Cairo is close to the end of the line before the water empties into the Mediterranean near Alexandria, meaning that the river near the capital is very polluted after its 6650km journey. But new infrastructure projects are once again giving the Nile the attention that it deserves.

The riverside walkway of **Mamsha Ahl Misr** (p86) in Downtown opened to great fanfare in 2022, and a similar pedestrian promenade is coming soon to the eastern side of Zamalek. It hadn't yet opened during our visit, but work appeared to be nearly complete.

Amor Perfecto Specialty Coffee is a serious caffeine haunt that makes mean cortados, cold brews and iced Spanish lattes. Hip **Holm Cafe** *(holmcafe.com)* has seats for people-watching while sipping fresh-pressed juice and cappuccinos. For a drink in palatial surroundings, visit **Garden Promenade Cafe** *(marriott.com/caieg)* at the Cairo Marriott Hotel, originally a 19th-century khedive-built mansion.

Savour the View from Cairo Tower
Central city vistas

For 360-degree views across the central city with the Nile below, zoom up the 187m-high **Cairo Tower** *(LE350)*, built in 1961 and resembling a stylised lotus plant with its latticework casing.

For the clearest vistas, come in the late morning after the haze burns off or in the late afternoon when it's sometimes possible to spy the pyramids. Unfortunately, the experience is somewhat tarnished by touts at the top and security guards telling you that you have just five minutes to soak up the scene.

Close to sunset, there's usually a long wait for the lift (possibly up to several hours), but you can skip most of the queue by paying extra for a voucher to eat at Sky Window Cafe (LE250) or Al Dawar Restaurant (LE500) near the top of the tower. The food is overpriced and not great – you're paying for the view.

EATING & DRINKING IN ZAMALEK: BEST RESTO-BARS & NIGHTLIFE

U Bistro & Bar: This modern-Med restaurant morphs into a cocktail bar after dark and is a favourite with Zamalek's see-and-be-seen crowd. *noon-2am* **$$$**

L'Aubergine: Seamlessly transition from the downstairs restaurant to the friendly, unstuffy bar upstairs. *11am-2am* **$$**

Deals: This classic Zamalek hangout has an old-school-pub atmosphere but can get crammed and seriously smoke-filled late in the evening. *2pm-3am*

Pub 28: Small dark bar where the regulars are usually conferring in clouds of cigarette smoke. Decent pub grub. *noon-2am*

Cairo Opera House (p131)

On Board the M/Y *Christina*
Private Nile cruising

For a stylish, no-hassle, private Nile cruising experience, hop aboard **M/Y *Christina*** (mychristina.net; 1/3/5hr LE1775/5175/8475, cash only), a yacht that operates from its own dock in Dokki.

Book online in advance for a comfortable way to soak up Cairo's riverine life, relaxing on deck and watching the lateen-sailed feluccas glide past, backed by the city's high-rises in the distance. The yacht can hold up to 25 guests. You can bring along a picnic, and staff even provide ice to keep your drinks cold.

Kayak the Nile
Paddle part of the world's longest river

To get out on the water under your own steam, gliding below the towering luxury hotels on the riverbanks, get in touch with **Zamalek Kayak** (WhatsApp +20 122-911-7114; facebook.com/Zamalek.Kayak; per hr LE150), which offers single and tandem kayaks for outings from 8am to 3.30pm. Reserve via WhatsApp.

THINGS YOU MIGHT NOT THINK TO PACK FOR CAIRO

Slippers or thick socks: It might be hot outside, but the tile floors in your accommodation can be pretty cold, especially in winter.

Tote bag: Useful for carrying your shoes around at mosques.

Water bottle with a built-in filter: Cairo has a rubbish problem, particularly with single-use plastics. Look at straw options from LifeStraw (lifestraw.com).

Tissues and hand sanitiser: Toilet paper isn't always a given, nor are sinks with soap. Proper paper towels are a rarity.

Earplugs: The *fajr* call to prayer rings out before sunrise, which means you might start your morning bright and early.

 EATING IN ZAMALEK: BEST FOR A SWEET TOOTH

Mandarine Koueider: This ice-cream parlour is a hit with families taking the kids out for a treat. For a fruity kick, try the *zabadi bi tut* (yoghurt with blackberry). *9am-11pm* $

Dara's Ice Cream: These cones mix ice cream with even more sweet snacks, such as salted caramel crunch, honeycomb or fudge brownie. *9am-1am* $

Gelato Mio: Cool off with a scoop of gelato, with flavours from Italy (panna cotta) and Egypt (*karkadai*; dried hibiscus). *11am-11.30pm* $

Simonds: It's a Cairene tradition to sit on a rickety chair at this century-old cafe and enjoy a flaky pastry. *6.30am-10pm* $

Garden City & Roda Island

AN EXTRAVAGANT PALACE AND MUSICAL CULTURE

☑ TOP TIP

A rejuvenation project to create a new promenade is ongoing between the 26th of July Bridge and Garden City's Four Seasons hotel. It will link up with the **Mamsha Ahl Misr walkway** (p86) in Downtown.

GETTING AROUND

Walking is the best way to get around the small area encompassed by Garden City, but getting a taxi or using ride-hailing apps is your best bet for reaching the further stretches of Roda Island. The pedestrian Manasterly Bridge links the southern side of the island with the Nile Corniche west of Coptic Cairo, and you'll have better luck with taxi pick-ups and drop-offs here. The campus of Cairo University is north of Manial Palace, and traffic can be heavy throughout the day as students come and go.

Garden City was developed in the early 1900s along the lines of an English 'garden suburb' that sought to bring a taste of the countryside to the city. The neighbourhood's curving, tree-lined streets were designed for tranquillity, and even though it's on the doorstep of Downtown, its quieter, shaded roads, lined with low-rise apartment buildings and old European-style mansions, make it seem a world away. Today it's still considered one of the central city's premier addresses, with the UK and US embassies on its northern border and five-star hotels on its Nile-facing rim. Just before sunset, when the birds are swooping above, it's one of the most atmospheric corners of the city, and the air of faded romance is palpable.

Roda Island, just to the south, was first settled by Mamluk soldiers in the Ayyubid era and became a popular island hideaway for Cairo's elites during the Khedival era. It's home to a couple of historic sites and contemporary Nile-front cafe culture.

Marvel at Manial Palace

Sumptuous interiors and Throne Hall bling

Some of the most eclectic interiors in Cairo are hidden behind the high walls of the **Manial Palace complex** (*egymonuments.com*, search 'Prince Mohamed Aly Palace'; LE220), so if you're seeking some insight into the lifestyles of Cairo's 1-percenters in the early years of the 20th century, don't miss a visit here. It's pure eye candy.

Set amid a tranquil Nileside garden on Roda Island, just across Al Saraya Bridge from Garden City, Manial Palace was built between 1899 and 1929 by Prince Mohammed Ali, uncle to King Farouk and once heir apparent to the throne. The palace's grand salons are spread over several buildings within the grounds and reflect the prince's eye for the eclectic and his well-travelled lifestyle, blending Ottoman, Persian and neo-Moorish elements with European Art Nouveau and rococo flourishes.

HIGHLIGHTS
1 Manial Palace

SIGHTS
2 Makan

ACTIVITIES
3 Dok Dok Landing Stage

SLEEPING
4 Four Seasons at Nile Plaza
5 InterContinental Cairo Semiramis
6 Kempinski Nile

EATING
see 4 8 Restaurant
7 Birdcage
8 Escobar
9 Fuul Mahrous
10 Il Nilo
see 6 Osmanly
11 Sabaya by the Nile
12 Taboula
13 Tasha Restaurant

DRINKING & NIGHTLIFE
14 Falak
15 Room Art Space

SHOPPING
16 Cairopolitan

You enter the grounds through the **Reception Palace**, where guests would have been received under the lavishly carved and painted wood ceiling in the Ceremonial Hall. Upstairs features two more impressive halls, one decorated in Moroccan style, with colourful ceramic tiles on the walls, and the other in Syrian style, with stained-glass windows and wood panels painted with floral patterns and verses from the Quran.

The **Residential Palace** is where the prince lived and it has two floors with nearly a dozen rooms, each in a unique decorative style. Check out the Blue Salon with its battered leather sofas sitting against walls decorated with glorious blue faience tiles and oil paintings.

THE ALMOST KING

Born the second son of Khedive Tewfik, grandson of Khedive Ismail, **Prince Mohammed Ali** (1895–1955) seemed destined for the throne. He served as crown prince three times, but his relatives kept having male children, pushing him further down the list of succession.

The prince wasn't particularly interested in politics anyway and preferred to travel, as is evident by his wide-ranging decoration styles and the souvenirs on display in his palace. When Egypt became a republic after the Revolution of 1952, which put an end to the royal dynasties that had ruled the country for centuries, Mohammed Ali left for Switzerland, living in exile until he died three years later at age 79.

Afterwards, head to the **Throne Palace** for the Throne Hall's gaudy gold styling and, upstairs, the in-your-face rococo and baroque overload of the Aubusson Room.

Even Manial Palace's **mosque**, which is mostly Ottoman in style but has an over-the-top rococo-inspired ceiling, and **clock tower** (based on Moroccan Almohad-era minaret design), are a marvellous mesh of influences. The nearby **museum** houses a curious collection of dusty artefacts from Egypt's erstwhile royal family, including paintings, hunting trophies, rare Arabic manuscripts and carpets.

Listen in on History at Makan Cultural Centre
A hub for Egypt's musical heritage

If you want to dig deeper into Egypt's musical traditions, visit **Makan** *(Egyptian Centre for Culture and Art; WhatsApp +20 122-112-4980; egyptmusic.org; facebook .com/ECCAMakan; LE200)*, a performance venue determined to keep the country's distinctive musical heritage alive.

On most Wednesday and Sunday evenings, it hosts a zar performance by the Mazaher Ensemble, some of the last zar musicians left. Zar is a women-led healing and purifying ritual combining polyrhythmic drumming and chanting that was traditionally performed to drive out bad spirits. You have not heard music this hypnotic and spellbinding until you've witnessed a zar.

Makan also puts on semi-regular performances by folk-music groups that specialise in Nubian-style music and also stand-up comedy events by local comedians. The organisation keeps both its website and Facebook page up to date with all upcoming events.

The venue is small, so it's worth booking your spot ahead of time. Send a WhatsApp message at least one day in advance. There are usually shows at 8pm and 9.45pm on Wednesdays and 7pm and 8.45pm on Sundays. Tickets are also available at the door 15 minutes in advance if there are empty seats.

Shop at Cairopolitan
Browse contemporary Egyptian art

Egypt is so well known for its traditional handicrafts that it's easy to forget that this heritage also has a thoroughly contemporary side. Head to **Cairopolitan** *(cairopolitan.com)* in Garden City to discover local modern work by Cairo's artists. Whether you're looking for a print of a Cairo street scene rendered in 8-bit, a pencil pouch that looks like the ubiquitous

 EATING IN GARDEN CITY: EGYPTIAN & MIDDLE EASTERN

| **Tasha Restaurant:** Egyptian home-cooking dishes with *tagens* (stews), *mahshi* (stuffed vegetables) and a knock-out Alexandrian liver. *11am-midnight* **$** | **Taboula:** Long-running favourite for upmarket Lebanese mezze and shisha in a cosy, warm-toned basement. Alcohol served. *11am-1am* **$$** | **Osmanly:** Exceptional Turkish food at the luxe Kempinski Nile, starting with a selection of cold mezze and moving onto riffs on Ottoman palace cuisine. *1pm-1am* **$$$** | **Sabaya by the Nile:** Lebanese food in a sumptuous but relaxed atmosphere at the InterContinental, with equally delicious Nile views. *noon-midnight* **$$$** |

baladi bread or a wall shelf that resembles a Downtown Cairo balcony, this shop is one of the top places in town to support the work of the city's emerging creatives.

Another branch, called **Gizapolitan** *(instagram.com/gizapolitan)*, is set to open near the **Sphinx** (p67).

Felucca Rides on the River
Sailing on the Nile

Reserve time for heading out onto the Nile to see the city from a different angle. The most gentle and traditional way to do this is to hire a felucca (traditional sailing boat) for an hour or so.

Luxor and Aswan have multiple felucca docks strung out along their waterfronts, but Cairo has far fewer. **Dok Dok Landing Stage** is the best option in the central city, particularly because it's set on a broader spot of the river, on the Nile Corniche right in front of Garden City's Four Seasons hotel. Despite the Corniche undergoing renovations, Dok Dok is still accessible to felucca goers through a gap in the hoarding.

The best time to head out is in the late afternoon, about an hour before sunset. Bring along a picnic to have on the boat and (if you want) beer for a sundowner while you sail. Prices are subject to haggling, and captains expect an additional tip.

Get to Know Egypt's Greatest Diva at the Umm Kulthum Museum
Personal belongings of a superstar singer

The small **Umm Kulthum Museum** *(LE20)* is your introduction to Egypt's most famous singer. It's a shrine-like space where Umm Kulthum's signature rhinestone-trimmed glasses and bedazzled dresses are hung under spotlights, and you can watch a biographical film with English subtitles that traces her career. The documentary shows footage of her funeral when millions of mourners flooded Cairo's streets.

Like the **Nilometer** (p138), the museum is set in the gardens of Manasterly Palace.

Get Breakfast at Fuul Mahrous
A traditional morning feast

One of Cairo's best traditional breakfast spreads is found at the humble kiosk **Fuul Mahrous**, with roadside tables and chairs under the trees on Sharia Dr Mahmoud Fawzy in

CAIRO ENTERTAINMENT GUIDES

Want to know what's on at various performance venues such as Room Art Space while you're in Cairo? These online sources offer entertainment listings for the city.

Scene Now: An online magazine covering lifestyle, culture and art news both in Cairo and across Egypt. The calendar is the most thorough for listings of nightlife (from comedy to bands and DJ sets) and art and culture events in the city *(scenenow.com)*.

Cairo 360: A similar setup to Scene Now with lifestyle, culture and art news for the city, event and performance listings, and nightlife, restaurant and cafe reviews *(cairo360.com)*.

 EATING IN GARDEN CITY: TRAVEL YOUR TASTEBUDS

Escobar: Cracking city views, cocktails and a Tex-Mex menu. Morphs into a more club-like venue later in the evening. *5pm-2am Mon-Sat* $$$

Il Nilo: Scoff wood-fired pizza on a riverfront restaurant terrace right beside the Nile, across the Corniche road from the Four Seasons. *9am-2am* $$

8 Restaurant: Find Egypt's best Cantonese food at the Four Seasons at Nile Plaza. Don't miss the Friday dim sum feast. *6pm-1am Sat-Thu, from 7pm Fri* $$$

Birdcage: Authentic and beautifully presented Thai plates at this soothing, wood-panelled restaurant at the InterContinental. *noon-midnight* $$$

MANASTERLY PALACE

The Nilometer and Umm Kulthum Museum are on the grounds of **Manasterly Palace**, built in 1851 for Hassan Fouad Pasha Al Manasterly, the then-governor of Cairo. On our visit the palace was undergoing extensive renovations, but in the past it was open as the International Centre for Music, giving occasional concerts, though more recently it's been open only for events and official governmental functions. It's worth getting a peek inside if you can – the walls and ceilings in one of the halls are painted an exuberant green and gold.

Only the public halls of this one-storey building still stand; the private residence was torn down to build a water-treatment plant.

Nilometer

Garden City. Better yet, it's usually open all day so you can scoff *fuul* (fava-bean paste) for lunch or dinner.

The *fuul* here is a cut above what is served elsewhere and has an added spice kick. The normal spread includes salad, *torshi* (pickled vegetables), a cheesy tomato dip, chips, *fuul*, *ta'amiyya*, eggs and bread, though you can mix and match if that all sounds too much or you want to make it fully vegan.

Check Out the Nilometer
Measuring the water levels

At Roda Island's southern tip, the **Nilometer** *(egymonuments.com; LE120)* is one of Cairo's earliest Islamic monuments and dates from 861 CE. The pointed-roof building covering it is an Ottoman addition. Nilometers measured the rise and fall of the river and thus predicted the fortunes of the annual harvest. If the water rose to 16 cubits – a cubit is about the length of a forearm – the harvest was likely to be good.

Don't rely on navigation apps to get here. Instead, set your destination for the pedestrian-only Manasterly Bridge; the entrance gate to the Nilometer is a short walk south of the bridge's western side at the end of Sharia Al Malek As Salih. The site guard required us to purchase a ticket online instead of paying on-site.

 DRINKING IN GARDEN CITY & RODA ISLAND: BEST CAFES

Falak: This cafe, craft shop, book shop and gallery on the ground floor of a villa in Garden City is a good place for a quiet afternoon coffee. *9am-11.30pm*

Room Art Space: A cafe and performance venue hosting regular intimate concerts, open-mic nights and stand-up comedy. *11am-midnight*

Carpaccio Nile Lounge: Right on the river with terrace seating beside the Nile. A relaxing spot for shisha, coffee or a smoothie. *10am-3am*

River Hub: Chill vibes and a good selection of fresh juices. Come at golden hour to snag a seat in the west-facing outdoor area and watch the sunset. *9am-2am*

Heliopolis & New Cairo

DINING HOT SPOT AND CAIRO'S MOST BIZARRE BUILDING

Heliopolis is an upper-middle-class neighbourhood east of the central city, known for its restaurants, cafe life and wide boulevards lined by once-grand but now dust-covered apartment blocks and Art Deco villas. This area shows a different, more relaxed side of the city and is a nice antidote to central Cairo's tourist pressure. With all its trees and outdoor cafes, it's a pleasant place for an evening's wander. Many Egyptians think so too, as Heliopolis has become 'Downtown' for people living in dull satellite cities further east.

Belgian industrialist Édouard Empain laid out Heliopolis in the early 20th century as a 'garden city' for the colonial officials who ruled Egypt. Its whitewashed Moorish-style buildings with dark-wood balconies, grand arcades and terraces are the European vision of the 'Orient' set in stone. Baron Empain Palace is the neighbourhood's only real sight, but if you like oddball architecture, it's not to be missed.

Poke Around Baron Empain Palace
An architectural oddity

Nicknamed the 'Hindu Palace', this brilliantly bonkers building from 1911 was the home of Baron Édouard Empain, one half of Heliopolis' founders. **Baron Empain Palace** (*egymonuments.com; LE220*) is what happens when you take French beaux-arts style, squish it together with Indian and Khmer temple architecture and then throw the whole thing down on the vast tract of empty desert you've been tasked with turning into a new suburb.

Even before you've entered the manicured gardens, you can see how extraordinary the building is. Its front is crowned by a *shikhara* (rounded Hindu temple tower), and its facade is decorated with friezes and sculptures of elephants, serpents, and Hindu-style deities and dancing women. Once inside the grounds, make sure to circle the entire building to take in all the different sculptural elements.

☑ TOP TIP

To experience Heliopolis' social life at its best, come on a Friday or Saturday when the outdoor cafe terraces of the central area, called Korba, are packed.

GETTING AROUND

This area is close to Cairo International Airport, so if you stay in this part of the city you can get a taste of Cairo even if you're just on a pit stop before an early flight.

Most of the neighbourhood is walkable, but don't count on being able to cross the many, always busy lanes of Sharia Al Uruba. Baron Empain Palace and some hotels are on the southeast side, while the restaurants and cafes are on the northwest side, but no traffic lights are there to stop the flow. Don't feel bad about catching a taxi to reach the other side.

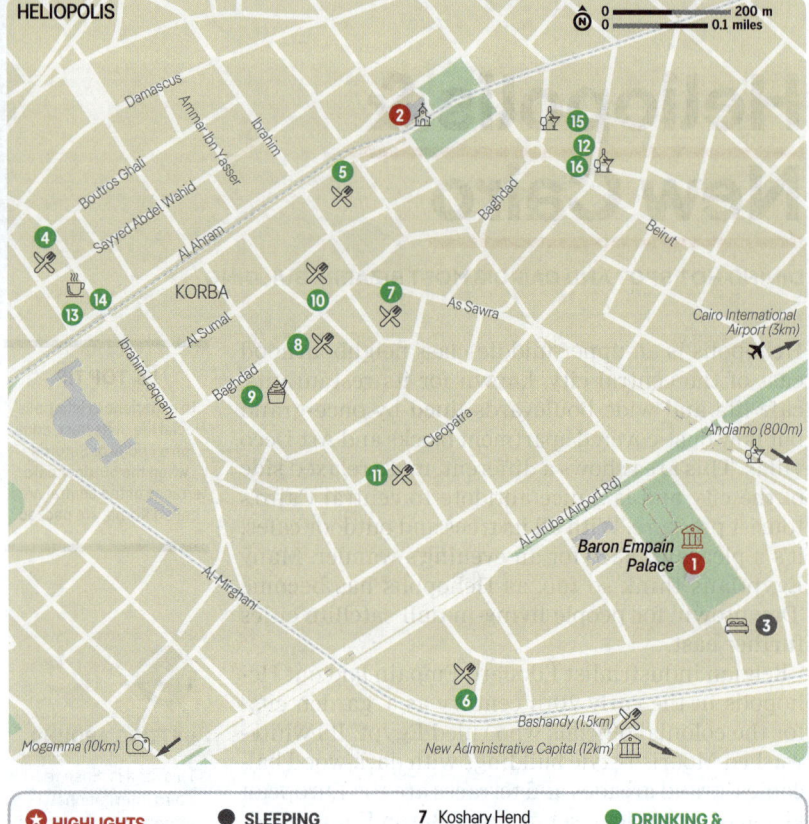

- **HIGHLIGHTS**
  1. Baron Empain Palace
- **SIGHTS**
  2. Basilique Notre Dame d'Heliopolis
- **SLEEPING**
  3. Baron Hotel
- **EATING**
  4. Abou Haidar
  5. Abu Ammar Al Souri
  6. Eldahan
  7. Koshary Hend
  8. Le Chantilly
  9. Mandarine Koueider
  10. Pepenero
  11. Sachi
- **DRINKING & NIGHTLIFE**
  12. Anzu Rooftop Lounge
  13. Groppi's
  14. L'Amphitryon
  15. Minglings
  16. Smokery

Inside, the bare salons are home to display panels that explain the history of both the building and Heliopolis, as well as the mansion's restoration process. You can also climb a wooden spiral staircase to the **roof terrace** (*extra LE120*) for a closer look at the tower and to admire the elaborately carved pavilion and the roof's lift entrance decorated with more elephants.

The entrance gate is along the property's eastern wall.

Baron Empain is buried in the **Basilique Notre Dame d'Heliopolis**, a neighbourhood landmark that's often described as a miniature version of Istanbul's Hagia Sophia because of its neo-Byzantine architectural style. It's closed to visitors but open for Roman Catholic Mass.

Foodie Finds in Heliopolis
Dining out for all budgets

If you want to rub shoulders with the city's fashionable set, **Sachi** *(sachirestaurant.com)* is a good introduction to Heliopolis' burgeoning reputation as Cairo's most vibrant upmarket dining destination. Inside the low-lit interior, with its plush cocktail-bar vibe, the see-and-be-seen sip on thyme gimlets and vodka sours spiked with orange-blossom essence while munching on a continent-spanning menu of sushi and sashimi, pasta and risotto, and hulking made-to-share meaty mains of steak and glazed short ribs. Like many popular upscale restaurants in Cairo, Sachi attempts to cater to all tastes and not all of it works; stick to the Japanese dishes. Dinnertime reservations are recommended.

But Heliopolis isn't all about expensive eats. The jury is out on whether this is the best shawarma in Cairo, but for the horde of devoted fans at **Abou Haidar** *(facebook.com/abouhaidarrestaurant)*, there is no competition. The beef shawarma meat, mixed with tomatoes, parsley and a tahini sauce that's been spiked with more than a dab of vinegar, is considered a cut above your average shawarma sandwich filling. Order it stuffed in a kaiser (a soft white-bread roll) for the true traditional Heliopolis experience.

A Night Out in Heliopolis & New Cairo
Vintage cafes to cocktail bars

On Fridays and Saturdays, Heliopolis is prime cafe territory, and its many terraces are crammed with people enjoying a lazy afternoon with friends over hot drinks and shisha, which inevitably morphs into a long evening.

For vintage vibes, stop for a drink or shisha on the raised terrace of the Heliopolis outpost of **Groppi's** *(groppi-eg.com)*. This old-timer is not fussed about following the latest trends. Nearby **L'Amphitryon** is another institution, once a favoured hangout for Allied soldiers during the world wars.

After dark, Heliopolis has a thriving bar scene (most places are resto-bars) that is big on cocktails, colourful mood lighting and thumping music. Find a clutch of popular bars within the walled compound around the **1920s Boutique Hotel** on Sharia Beirut, including **Minglings** *(instagram.com/minglings.eg)* and **Anzu Rooftop Lounge** *(instagram.com/anzu.eg)*. During the day, this compound is also a good spot for lunchtime restaurants and afternoon-into-evening coffee shops. You'll forget you're in the middle of the desert when you step into **Smokery** *(instagram.com/thesmokery)*, an upscale bar where giant, lush plants seem to be staging a jungle invasion. Join locals for colourful cocktails and salmon spires at this glam addition to the nightlife scene in Heliopolis.

For something more low-key and casual, head to **Andiamo** *(instagram.com/andiamocairo)*, with its garden bar and pizza restaurant outside of central Heliopolis.

Finding well-made cocktails in Cairo can be a chore, but Sachi also has an excellent cocktail menu.

A BUILDING BROUGHT BACK TO LIFE

For decades, Baron Empain Palace was just the weird, dirt-encrusted, derelict building you glimpsed from your taxi window on the way to or from Cairo International Airport. In the 1990s the dilapidated ruin even found itself at the centre of a moral panic when local rumours circulated that 'satanists' were holding rituals amid the abandoned rooms (though it turned out the so-called 'satanists' were just a bunch of upper-class teenage metalheads).

The palace opened to the public for the first time in 2020 after undergoing a three-year US$10.9 million restoration.

LOCAL EATS IN & AROUND HELIOPOLIS

Mia Nezar is co-founder of Bellies En-Route (p83), which runs private food tours in Heliopolis. @belliesenroute

Mandarine Koueider
On Sharia Baghdad, this is where you come for ice cream and Egyptian desserts in Heliopolis. It's known for its pistachio, yoghurt and berry, and mastic-flavoured ice cream.

Koshary Hend
On Sharia Abou Bakr El Sedeek, Koshary Hend is one of the best places to get *kushari* in the neighbourhood. It's where you'll see everyone of every class eating together, and it's open basically 24/7.

Bashandy
Bashandy, in Nasr City, south of Heliopolis, is famous for everything breakfast related, such as *fuul* and *ta'amiyya*. Try the *fuul bi zeit haar* (*fuul* with flaxseed oil).

Witness the Future of Egypt in the New Administrative Capital

Constructing a brand new city

In the not-so-distant future, Cairo will no longer be the capital of Egypt, and that honour will belong to a city rising in the desert 50km east of Downtown. The as-yet-unnamed New Administrative Capital (NAC) has been under construction since 2015, and some government offices, such as those that were previously housed in the infamous **Mogamma** (p82) building on Midan Tahrir, have already moved in, as have foreign universities and banks. The Egyptian government says 48,000 government workers now have offices in the NAC, and 10,000 families have moved in, but on our visit, it felt like a newly constructed ghost town.

Like most of the construction that happens in the Middle East, the adjectives tend towards the superlative. Not yet complete, the 400m-tall **Iconic Tower** will be the tallest building in Africa, rising 77 storeys. Opened in 2019 by President Sisi and Pope Tawadros II of Alexandria (the leader of the Coptic Church), the **Cathedral of the Nativity of Christ** *(free)* is the largest church in the Middle East, with a capacity of 8000 worshippers. Its design is shaped like Noah's Ark, and it has one of the largest hand-painted domes in the world.

The **Egypt Capitals Museum**, which has been open in previous years but was closed on our visit and was set to reopen 'soon', details how Egypt's seat of government has moved to different places over the years – six times, in fact, from Memphis to Thebes and later to Alexandria and Fustat before reaching Cairo.

 EATING IN HELIOPOLIS: BUDGET BITES

| **Eldahan:** This family-friendly, upmarket chain serves traditional grilled meat and *tagen* (stew) dishes. Look for the off-kilter gold doorway. *10.30am-2am* **$$** | **Pepenero:** Dine on pizza, pasta and other Italian favourites with views overlooking the central Korba area. *noon-midnight* **$$** | **Le Chantilly:** This old-school Swiss restaurant seems to have been beamed straight out of the 1980s and onto Sharia Baghdad. *7am-midnight* **$$** | **Abu Ammar Al Souri:** Syrian-style shawarma and other Middle Eastern fast-food favourites draw late-night crowds. *24hr* **$** |

Beyond Cairo

Find adventure in even older pyramids and sense a continuity with the past in Wadi Natrun's Coptic monasteries.

If Giza didn't provide enough pyramid action for you, don't fret. Even more pyramids, which predate those in Giza, pop up around the desert edge of Cairo within day-tripping distance. Egypt is home to at least 118 ancient pyramids, the majority of which are in the desert between Giza and the semi-oasis of Al Fayoum. By far the most popular day trip is to Saqqara: home to Djoser's Step Pyramid and Egypt's largest archaeological site, which still grabs headlines with its finds.

To experience the living traditions of Egypt's Coptic community, head north of Cairo to the monasteries of Wadi Natrun, a worthwhile side trip if you don't have time to visit the monasteries in the Eastern Desert.

Places
Dahshur p143
Saqqara p144
Memphis p150
Abu Sir p151
Wadi Natrun p151
Karanis p153
Tanis p153

Dahshur
TIME FROM CAIRO: 1½ HRS

Egypt's greatest pyramid interior scramble

If the interiors of the Pyramids of Giza seemed a bit tame, an adventure awaits at **Dahshur** *(egymonuments.com; LE200)*. This pyramid field, a 15km drive south of Saqqara, is where you get to clamber, bent double, sometimes on hands and knees, into the belly of a pyramid. It's usually visited in combination with Saqqara and Memphis instead of being its own dedicated trip because there's nothing to do unless you go inside the pyramids.

Dahshur was once home to 11 pyramids from the 4th and 12th dynasties, although only the two Old Kingdom ones, built by Pharaoh Sneferu (reigned c 2613–2589), father of Khufu, remain intact. Head to the easier **Red Pyramid** first. It is the world's oldest true pyramid, Sneferu's architects having learned from their experiences building the deformed Bent Pyramid and adjusted their angle to a gentler 43 degrees.

Walk up the 125 steps to the pyramid entrance and then crouch to head down the 63m-long shaft, which deposits you into two stunning 12m-high corbel-ceilinged antechambers before ascending a short flight of stairs into the 15m-high corbelled burial chamber. Check out the charcoal graffiti left by 19th-century British explorers along the way.

Ready for the **Bent Pyramid**? Your knees will wobble, and your thighs won't thank you the next day, but if you make

continued on p150

GETTING AROUND

Day-trip destinations around Cairo are best visited by joining a guided tour. Without a guide, you're unlikely to understand what you're seeing, as signage on the ground is minimal.

You could also go with a taxi or private driver. Agree on a price in advance. You're also expected to pay their parking fees (at least LE25 depending on the size of the vehicle) at each of the sites.

Step Pyramid of Djoser

TOP EXPERIENCE

Saqqara

Covering a 7km stretch of the Western Desert, Saqqara is the vast necropolis of Memphis, ancient Egypt's first capital. It was an active burial ground for pharaohs, their families and high-ranking officials for more than 3500 years and is Egypt's largest archaeological site, where huge discoveries are still unearthed. Its Step Pyramid and painted tombs make for Cairo's best day out.

DON'T MISS

- Step Pyramid of Djoser
- Pyramid of Unas
- Tomb of Maya
- Serapeum
- Tomb of Ty
- Tomb of Mereruka
- Tomb of Kagemni

Step Pyramid of Djoser

Around 2650 BCE, Pharaoh Djoser (reigned c 2667–2648 BCE) asked his chief architect Imhotep to build him a **Step Pyramid**. It is the world's earliest stone monument, and its significance cannot be overstated. Surrounding the 60m-high Step Pyramid is a vast funerary complex enclosed by a 1.6km-long panelled limestone wall, part of which survives.

Previously, temples were made of perishable materials, while royal tombs were usually underground rooms topped with a

PRACTICALITIES

- egymonuments.com
- LE600, all-inclusive ticket LE1000
- 8am-4pm

mud-brick mastaba (a structure in the shape of a bench). However, Imhotep developed a stacked mastaba that looks like a pyramid and built it in hewn stone. From this flowed Egypt's later architectural achievements.

Enter the complex at the southeastern corner via a collonaded corridor and broad hypostyle hall. Note the 40 'bundle columns' in the corridor, ribbed to resemble a bundle of palm or papyrus stems. As you pass through the half-open ka (spirit) door, check out the stone 'hinge' near the bottom, painted to resemble wood. These doors allowed the pharaoh's ka to come and go at will. The hypostyle hall leads into the Great South Court, flanking the pyramid's southern side.

Inside the Step Pyramid

You can go inside the Step Pyramid through an entrance on its southern side (for an extra LE280; not included in the all-inclusive ticket), where a wide, columned and atmospherically lit corridor tunnelled out during the 26th dynasty leads to a viewing platform that looks down into Djoser's vaulted granite burial chamber and onto the top of his mammoth sarcophagus. The northern entrance is open only for private visits, which must be arranged through a tour operator and the Ministry of Antiquities, allowing you to explore some of the pyramid's original maze of subterranean tunnels lined with blue faience tiles that run for nearly 6km through the rock.

Great South Court

The **Great South Court** is a huge open area flanking the south side of the pyramid. If you're short on time, you can skip this area and carry on to the nearby tombs.

Look on the southern wall to find a frieze of cobras. The cobra (uraeus) represented the goddess Wadjet, a fire-spitting protector of the pharaoh.

In the centre of the court are two D-shaped stone boundary markers, which delineated the ritual race the pharaoh had to run, a literal demonstration of his fitness to rule. The race was part of the Jubilee Festival (Heb-Sed), which usually occurred after 30 years of ruling and showed the pharaoh's symbolic rejuvenation and the recognition of his supremacy by officials from all over Egypt. The construction of the Heb-Sed within Djoser's funerary complex was intended to perpetuate his revitalisation for eternity.

The buildings on the eastern side of the pyramid are also connected with the royal jubilee and include the **Heb-Sed Court**. Buildings on the east side of the court represent the shrines of Lower Egypt, and those on the west represent Upper Egypt.

North of the Heb-Sed Court is the **House of the South Court**, which features one of the earliest examples of tourist graffiti. In the 47th year of Ramses II's reign, nearly 1500 years after Djoser's death, Hadnakhte, a treasury scribe, recorded his admiration for Djoser while 'on a pleasure trip west of Memphis' in about 1232 BCE. His hieratic script, written in black ink, is preserved behind perspex.

Back outside, walk around the Step Pyramid to its northern side. A stone serdab (a small room containing a statue of the

---

> **WHAT'S OPEN?**
>
> As with other large archaeological sites in Egypt, which tombs are open at Saqqara changes constantly and can depend on many factors, including the mood of the site guardians, how much money you're willing to tip and whether you've come with a guide. You can check online or at the ticket office to see which monuments are officially open, but some sites are also 'baksheesh open' (unlocked if you tip) or are actually closed (actively undergoing restoration or excavation).
>
> Even if you've paid for the all-inclusive ticket, the guardians of lesser-visited tombs expect baksheesh to unlock the tomb and show you around.

> **WHERE TO EAT**
>
> Pack a lunch and bring water before heading out on a day trip to Saqqara, as there is little in the way of recommendable places to eat in the area. You can stop at basic roadside *ahwas* (coffeehouses) on the road leading to Saqqara and directly opposite the entrance to Mit Rahina (p151).

deceased) sits in front of the northern entrance. Look through the holes in the serdab wall to come face to face with Djoser himself. The statue inside is a copy; the original is in the **Egyptian Museum** (p78).

Pyramid of Unas

Stroll west from Djoser's funerary complex to the **Pyramid of Unas** (Unas reigned c 2375–2345 BCE), today not much more than an unassuming pile of stone blocks but once 43m high. Its interior marks the beginning of a significant development in funerary practices. For the first time the royal burial chamber was decorated.

A short, easy descent shaft deposits you down into the antechamber and burial chamber, their white alabaster-lined walls inscribed with blue hieroglyphs and the ceiling adorned with stars. These hieroglyphs are some of the earliest examples of the funerary inscriptions now known as the Pyramid Texts (later compiled into the Book of the Dead), which were 'spells' to protect the soul of the deceased. Of the 283 separate phrases in Unas' tomb, most were prayers, hymns and lists of items, such as food and clothing, that the pharaoh would require in the afterlife.

Tombs Around the Causeway

As you walk along the 750m-long causeway running between the east side of the Pyramid of Unas and the sparse remnants of his valley temple, imagine the ceremonial walkway as it would have originally looked: roofed and decorated with painted reliefs.

On either side of the causeway are numerous tombs. More than 200 have been excavated. Those nearly always open for visits are the 5th- and 6th-dynasty **Tombs of Idut, Unasankh and Inerfert**, where you can spot finely detailed scenes of hunting, fishing and butchery on the walls, and the **Tomb of Mehu** (a 6th-dynasty vizier), where the walls are covered with depictions of daily life, from cooking geese to brewing beer. You might have to track down the site guardian with the keys; baksheesh is expected.

New Kingdom Tombs

Saqqara is best known as a cemetery for the greats of the Old Kingdom, but a 300m walk west from the Pyramid of Unas are the little-visited **New Kingdom Tombs** *(LE400, inc in all-inclusive ticket)*, the final resting places for high officials, with job titles such as director of the harem, royal butler and steward of the sun temple, who served Akhenaten, Tutankhamun and Ramses II. This area has 15 excavated tombs. The **Tomb of Maya** (Tutankhamun's treasurer), with its wall reliefs depicting Maya, his wife and the god Osiris, all painted with a dominant yellow pigment, is a highlight. The **Tomb of Horemheb** (Tutankhamun's general and later a pharaoh) has delicate reliefs of Horemheb interrogating foreign prisoners in the courtyard. Baksheesh is expected here, and the site guardian will likely offer to open other tombs for extra tips.

The New Kingdom Tombs are kept locked (the site guardian will likely approach you when he sees you wandering around nearby) and aren't well signposted, so it's a good idea to go with a guide.

Serapeum

A five-minute drive northwest of the Step Pyramid is the curious **Serapeum** *(LE340, inc in all-inclusive ticket)*. This subterranean warren of tombs was used for the burial of sacred animals that corresponded with ancient Egyptian deities, including cats (the goddess Bastet), jackals (Anubis) and particularly bulls called Apis, which were worshipped in Memphis. Walking through the tunnels past the enormous stone coffins, which weigh up to 80 tonnes each, it's impossible not to be impressed by the sheer effort put into it.

The first Apis burial took place during the reign of Amenhotep III (1390–1352 BCE), and the practice continued until 30 BCE, at the end of the Ptolemaic era.

On the walk from the car park to the Serapeum, you pass the **Hemicycle of the Greek Philosophers & Poets**, a sad-looking semicircle of ancient Greek statues. Ptolemy I (r 305–282 BCE) set up this as a wayside shrine as part of his patronage of learning.

TOP TIPS

● Saqqara is a huge site, covering 7 sq km, and there are no public transport options for getting here or getting around. Visit on a guided tour from Cairo, which often also includes Dahshur and Memphis.

● Good guides truly enhance a visit, as the tombs have no signage inside. Contact a tour operator like **Magic Carpet Travel** *(magiccarpetegypt.com)* to arrange one.

● If you've hired a taxi or a private driver you'll need to pay their parking fee (car/microbus LE25/50).

● Visit *egymonuments. com* to buy your ticket online to save time and also see which tombs are open.

Pyramid of Unas

TOMB OF AKHETHOTEP & PTAHHOTEP

On the way to the Serapeum, see if it's possible to stop by the **Tomb of Akhethotep and his son Ptahhotep**, which were was restoration on our visit but expected to re-open soon.

Akhethotep and his son, Ptahhotep, were senior royal officials during the reigns of Djedkare (c 2414–2375 BCE) and Unus at the end of the 5th dynasty. Akhethotep served as vizier, judge, supervisor of pyramid cities and supervisor of priests, and his titles were eventually inherited by Ptahhotep, along with his tomb.

You can see two burial chambers, two chapels and a pillared hall, but it's in Ptahhotep's section that you should linger. Note the detailed portrayal of a wide range of animals, from lions and hedgehogs to domesticated cattle and fowl, that were brought as offerings to the deceased. Ptahhotep is portrayed as resplendent in a panther-skin robe, inhaling perfume from a jar.

Tomb of Ty

Tomb of Ty

The **Tomb of Ty**, who was overseer of the Abu Sir pyramids and sun temple during the 5th dynasty, is not only the finest example of Old Kingdom art but also one of the main sources of knowledge about life in Old Kingdom Egypt. The detailed scenes of daily life covering the walls include people farming, preparing food, fishing, building boats, dancing, trading and avoiding crocodiles. Their images are accompanied by chattering hieroglyphic dialogue.

Tomb of Mereruka

A five-minute drive east from the Serapeum is another clutch of tombs. A maze of rooms greets you in the huge 6th-dynasty **Tomb of Mereruka** *(LE200, inc in all-inclusive ticket)*, vizier to King Teti. The tomb has more than 30 chambers, some of which are dedicated to his wife and son. Reliefs throughout are exquisitely detailed, but it's the columned burial chamber with its preserved painted reliefs, overlooked by a statue of Mereruka, that's the tomb's highlight.

Tomb of Kagemni

The **Tomb of Kagemni**, who was the chief justice under Teti, has splendid and lively friezes showing the riches of the land, including catfish and eels in the Nile, cows being milked and men feeding puppies. The most vivid scenes detail a crocodile and hippo fighting and a row of vigorous dancers and acrobats.

Pyramid of Teti

Today, the **Pyramid of Teti** (first pharaoh of the 6th dynasty, reigned c 2345–2323 BCE) looks more like a humble mound, but if you take the short descent shaft into the burial chamber, you can see portions of the hieroglyphic spells of the *Pyramid Texts*, as well as a shower of stars on the ceiling. Within the intact burial chamber, Teti's basalt sarcophagus is well preserved and represents the first example of a sarcophagus with inscriptions.

Imhotep Museum

It's near the entrance, but leave the small **Imhotep Museum** for the end of your visit. It displays finds from around the site, but the best pieces are in the museums in Cairo.

It's framed as a tribute to the architect Imhotep, who served King Djoser and is credited with creating ancient Egypt's first comprehensive vision of stone architecture. The installation of turquoise faience tiles from inside the Step Pyramid of Djoser and the mummy of Merenre I (the oldest complete royal mummy, of the fourth pharaoh of the 6th dynasty) from 2292 BCE are two of the most striking pieces.

Exploring South Saqqara

For most visitors, the multiple pyramids and tombs of the northern section of Saqqara are enough, but if you're a dedicated pyramid fan, a trip to the Old Kingdom tombs and collapsed pyramids of South Saqqara is a worthwhile add-on. At the time of research, visiting this area requires special permission from the Ministry of Antiquities and a high entry fee. Check with specialised, archaeology-focused tour operators for the latest information.

The **Mastaba of Al Faraun**, the unusual funerary complex of the short-lived 4th-dynasty Pharaoh Shepseskaf (reigned c 2503–2498 BCE), is the southernmost of the structures. Inside his rectangular tomb, head down the 21m-long passage to the vaulted burial chamber.

Of the four collapsed pyramids here, the 52m-high **Pyramid of Pepi II** is the most prominent. This 6th-dynasty pharaoh's 94-year reign (c 2278–2184 BCE) was probably the longest in Egyptian history.

> **HOW TO SPEND YOUR TIME AT SAQQARA**
>
> Count on spending at least half a day at Saqqara, though it's most often sold as a full-day tour from Cairo and includes visits to Dahshur and Memphis. Saqqara has a lot of burial chambers, and many of them look similar, so it's easy to get tomb fatigue – don't try to see them all unless you want to. The site is about an hour's drive from Downtown Cairo.
>
> **If you're short on time**
> Visit the Step Pyramid of Djoser and see the beautifully painted Tombs of Idut, Unasankh and Inerfert nearby.
>
> **With half a day**
> Check out the Step Pyramid and the Tombs of Idut, Unasankh and Inerfert before driving to the Serapeum and Tomb of Ty.
>
> **With a full day**
> Squeeze in as many Saqqara sights as you're interested in, climb inside the pyramids at Dahshur and visit the museum in Memphis.

FOR YOUR 'SECURITY'

At Wadi Natrun and lesser-visited archaeological sites outside of Cairo, the Egyptian police officers standing guard outside the monastery gates can be overzealous in their questioning and paperwork before allowing you through, and they might demand baksheesh for transporting you via convoy between the monasteries. You often don't have a choice in whether you want this 'service', and it's another reason why it's a good idea to travel with a guide, who can act as a translator and mediator.

The threat to Coptic Christians in Egypt is a legitimate concern, as several terrorist attacks claimed by the Islamic State have been directed against them; however, tourists' interactions with police at these places can feel like heightened security.

Deir Al Baramos (p153), Wadi Natrun

continued from p143

it all the way to the top burial chamber (many people turn back halfway through), you've completed what has to be the most thrilling pyramid experience of them all. Anyone with mobility issues, particularly knee problems or claustrophobia, should give the Bent Pyramid a miss.

This structure was Sneferu's first attempt to create a smooth-sided pyramid. His architects began with the steep angle and inward-leaning courses of stone they used to create step pyramids, and when this began to show signs of stress and instability around halfway up its eventual 105m height, they reduced the angle from 54 degrees to 43 degrees.

Climb up the metal staircase attached to the side of the pyramid to the entrance. If it's winter and you're wearing a jacket, sweater or scarf, leave it with the site guardians (you'll thank us later) and then bend yourself into the steep corridor shaft to descend 74m. Take time to catch your breath when you get to the bottom because now you're heading up – first up one narrow and steep flight of stairs into the 12m-high lower burial chamber and then up a sturdy scaffolding structure of metal staircases to near the top of the chamber.

Here comes the difficult part. At the top of the staircase is an entrance into a tunnel. If you're tall, it's easier to tackle this bit by admitting defeat and crawling through it on your hands and knees. Shorter people should be able to get through most of it in a crouched shuffle. Prepare to get dusty and sweaty.

Exiting the tunnel, you arrive in the Bent Pyramid's higher burial chamber, which retains its original ancient scaffolding of great cedar beams to counteract internal instability. It usually takes a few minutes after the elation of making it to the finish line for you to realise that the only way out is back the way you came.

Memphis
TIME FROM CAIRO: **1 HR 10 MINS**

Ancient Egypt's first capital
The only surviving remnant of **Memphis** is the small open-air museum of **Mit Rahina** *(egymonuments.com; LE200)*, a 6.5km drive southeast of Saqqara. The garden displays statuary and stone blocks unearthed from Egypt's original capital. It's built around a colossal fallen statue of Ramses II. Its twin is the colossus that stands guard in the entry hall of the **Grand Egyptian Museum**.

Given the museum's small size and badly eroded artefacts, the experience is a bit disappointing (30 minutes is enough to see it all). Visiting Memphis is best as an add-on to Saqqara, not as a dedicated trip.

Abu Sir
TIME FROM CAIRO: **55 MINS**

Ride horses around the Abu Sir Pyramids
The **Abu Sir Pyramids** have been closed to visitors for years, but an atmospheric way to experience the desert scenery is to sign up for a horse-riding trip with **KFB Stables** *(kfbstables.net)*, which also offers horse-riding adventures around Saqqara and all the way to Giza for experienced equestrians. This outfit is great with young visitors and nervous riders and matches steeds to your level of experience. Set out into the desert from the date-palm edge of the Nile's cultivation area in the late afternoon to approach the pyramids in the softer light.

Wadi Natrun
TIME FROM CAIRO: **1½ HRS**

Coptic Christian heartland
The Coptic monasteries of Wadi Natrun have roots 17 centuries deep, and it's where thousands of Christians escaped from Roman persecution in the 4th century. Of the 60 or so original compounds in the valley, only four remain. The impressive monastery buildings were fortified after years of Bedouin and Arab raids, although only scraps of fresco art are still in situ.

Most days at the monasteries are quiet, but visitors mob the churches on Christian and public holidays, yielding a glimpse into contemporary Coptic traditions. The monastic tradition is thriving, and the Coptic pope is still chosen from the Wadi Natrun monks.

Monks give free tours at each of the monasteries. Most monks speak excellent English, but you might have to wait for a bit until one is available to show you around.

Start at **Deir Abu Makar** *(Monastery of St Macarius; stmacariusmonastery.org)*, closest to Cairo and the best of the bunch, signposted from the motorway. It's famous as the monastery where most Coptic popes have hailed from, and many are buried here. Today, 127 monks live here and start their days at 4am with prayer. The tours visit the stark 18th-century monk cells, the 11th-century fortress, the former refectory with a room-spanning communal stone table and the main Church of St Macarius. In the nave, peer through a

CASH-FREE ARCHAEOLOGY
Starting in 2023, archaeological sites across Egypt that are run by the Ministry of Antiquities no longer accept cash, and visitors must buy tickets online *(egymonuments.com)* or pay by card in person. This is a major change and a boon in a country that doesn't often accept card payments elsewhere. In practice, some sites still accept cash, but others don't even have the equipment for on-site card payment so will make you order online at the entrance.

If you buy tickets online, a PDF is sent to you by email after payment. The PDF includes a QR code, which is scanned on-site.

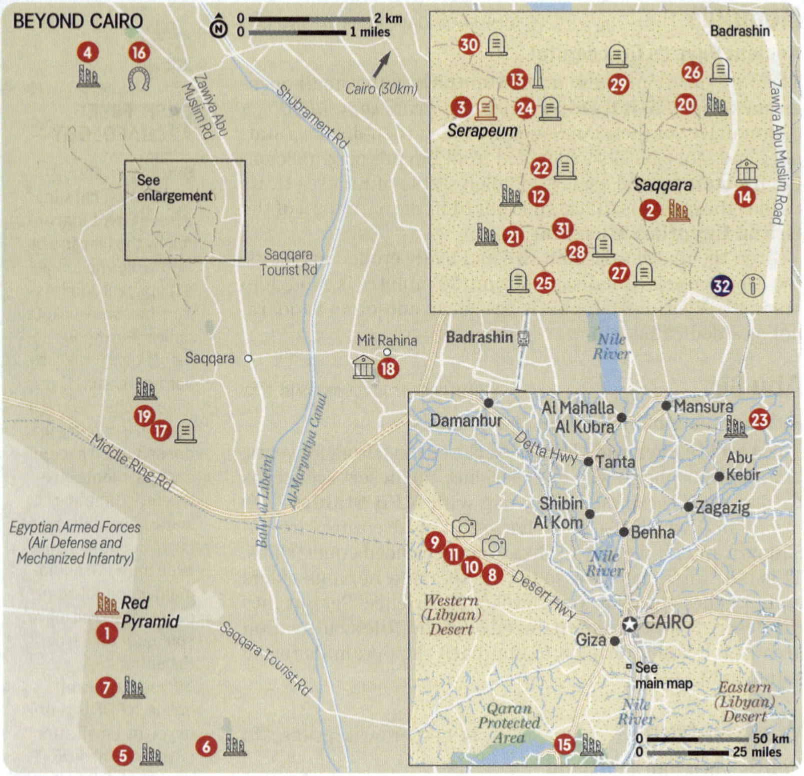

BEYOND CAIRO

HIGHLIGHTS
1. Red Pyramid
2. Saqqara
3. Serapeum

SIGHTS
4. Abu Sir Pyramids
5. Bent Pyramid
6. Black Pyramid
7. Dahshur
8. Deir Abu Makar
9. Deir Al Baramos
10. Deir Anba Bishoy
11. Deir El Sourian
12. Great South Court
13. Hemicycle of the Greek Philosophers & Poets
14. Imhotep Museum
15. Karanis
16. KFB Stables
17. Mastaba of Al Faraun
18. Memphis
19. Pyramid of Pepi II
20. Pyramid of Teti
21. Pyramid of Unas
22. Step Pyramid of Djoser
23. Tanis
24. Tomb of Akhethotep & Ptahhotep
25. Tomb of Horemheb
26. Tomb of Kagemni
27. Tomb of Maya
28. Tomb of Mehu
29. Tomb of Mereruka
30. Tomb of Ty
31. Tombs of Idut, Unasankh & Inerfert

INFORMATION
32. Saqqara Ticket Office

trapdoor into the crypt, discovered during restoration work, where the monks found relics claimed to be of St John the Baptist.

Next, drive about 45km (45 minutes) to **Deir Anba Bishoy** *(Monastery of St Bishoy)*, founded in 340 CE. Tours take in the refectory, the fortress (where the monks sheltered from Bedouin raids in the 9th century), the fortress roof with views over the monastery's palm-shaded gardens, and the old church with its faded fresco fragments.

About 600m west is **Deir El Sourian** *(Syrian Monastery)*, named after the wandering Syrian monks who bought the monastery from the Copts in the 8th century, though the Copts took it back in the 14th century. This monastery is the best to visit to see restored frescoes. White plaster used to cover many of the paintings, but renovations in the last few decades have uncovered the art and brought a vibrant splash of colour back to the sanctuary. The church was built around the 4th-century cave where St Bishoy lived and tied his hair to the ceiling to keep himself awake during prayers.

A 12km drive northwest, **Deir Al Baramos** (*Monastery of Baramos*) is the furthest from Cairo and has a serene feeling. Tours take in the well-cared-for garden and visit a restored millstone, the refectory and the monastery's Church of the Virgin Mary, which contains the remnants of 13th-century frescoes. The restored medieval fortress is not open to the public.

Karanis

TIME FROM CAIRO: 1 HR

Ptolemaic city remnants

If you're heading to Al Fayoum (p162) from Cairo and have time to spare, stop in at the archaeological site of **Karanis** *(LE150)* on the Giza–Fayoum road. This mud-brick city was founded by Ptolemy II's mercenaries in the 3rd century BCE. Today, little remains apart from half-buried crumbling walls and two Graeco-Roman temples. The larger temple is dedicated to the local crocodile gods, Pnepheros and Petesouchos.

At the site entrance, the **Kom Aushim Museum** *(extra LE100)* displays artefacts from Fayoum, including a couple of the famed Graeco-Roman Fayoum portraits. This site is little visited, and the guardians will insist on taking you around and, of course, expect baksheesh for this. It's helpful to go with a guide who can translate.

Tanis

TIME FROM CAIRO: 3 HRS

Pharaonic ruins far from the crowds

To ramble around ruins with not a tour bus in sight, head to **Tanis** *(egymonuments.com; LE120)* in the Nile Delta. A modern visitor centre with a museum welcomes you and does a decent job of explaining the site's history. Outside, the scattered columns, obelisks and statues from the reign of Psusennes I (r 1039–991 BCE), some re-erected, are surrounded by mighty mud-brick enclosure walls.

The mightiest era of Tanis – called Djanet by the ancient Egyptians – was during the Third Intermediate Period and Late Period. Psusennes I's royal tomb and five others from the 21st dynasty were unearthed in 1939, and the burial goods, now in the **Egyptian Museum** (p78), are one of the most spectacular treasure troves ever discovered in Egypt.

Unfortunately the experience of visiting Tanis is marred by the site guardians and security guards who accompany you around the site and are overzealous about baksheesh – they wouldn't let us leave without paying an additional LE500, an amount that's unheard of elsewhere. Another issue is that the site is a long drive from Cairo and not on the way to anywhere else.

BLACK PYRAMID

The crumbling Black Pyramid (closed to visitors) you can spy in the distance to the east of the Bent Pyramid and Red Pyramid was built by Middle Kingdom Pharaoh Amenemhat III (reigned c 1855–1808 BCE). It had a whole host of structural problems, hence its appearance. The ground it stands on is just 10m above sea level, and even during construction, water was seeping in. Unlike other pyramids built of stone, the mud-brick structure couldn't withstand the water, and over time, the pyramid sank into the ground, collapsing several of the chambers below it. The tombs had been robbed in antiquity, but in 1993 archaeologists discovered several funerary artefacts that had been left behind.

Places We Love to Stay

$ Budget $$ Midrange $$$ Top End

Giza
MAP p63

Pyramids Overlook Inn $
Rooms are dark and a bit basic but spick and span – you should spend most of your time on the view-tastic rooftop anyway.

Khan Duidar Inn $$
Comfortable contemporary rooms, many of which have views of the pyramids. (The hotel also has a communal terrace.) Free airport pick-up if you stay at least two nights.

Pyramids Valley Boutique Hotel $$ Great location and view. The smallish rooms offer touches of Egyptian character, a nice feature not found in most accommodation in Giza.

Steigenberger Pyramids Cairo $$ Slightly dated but decent rooms across the street from the Grand Egyptian Museum. Because of traffic, you need to take a taxi 1km to reach the entrance.

Mamlouk Pyramids Hotel $$ Solid midranger with small, clean rooms and a rooftop restaurant offering pyramid vistas.

Hyatt Centric Cairo West $$$ Opened in late 2024, Egypt's first 'art hotel' has dozens of playful site-specific installations dotted around the property. Shares amenities, including the relaxing spa and phenomenal Barranco restaurant, with the Hyatt Regency across the street.

Mena House Hotel $$$ Modern rooms with up-close pyramid views on the lush grounds of Khedive Ismail's former hunting lodge.

Downtown Cairo
MAPS p82, p88

Holy Sheet Hostel $ Reliable option for a soft, budget-friendly landing in Cairo. Friendly, social vibe in the well-designed dorms. Private rooms are also available.

Eileen Hotel $$ Lovely rooms on the 6th floor of a historic Downtown building. It's the HQ for Magic Carpet Travel and is on the doorstep of the neighbourhood's best restaurants.

Tahrir Plaza Suites $$ Six individually styled rooms, most with balconies, inside a heritage building steps from the Egyptian Museum.

Hathor House $$ Hip rooms carved out from a historic apartment block close to Midan Talaat Harb, which means good people-watching from the balconies but lots of street noise.

Immobilia $$$ Grit meets glamour when you rent one of the four luxe private apartments in the Art Deco Immobilia building. Rates include a personal driver, butler and cook. One of Cairo's best stays.

Mazeej Balad $$$ Opened in January 2025, this boutique hotel offers just five well-designed suites in an 1896 building. Gorgeous umbrella-covered rooftop restaurant and bar.

St Regis Cairo $$$ A phenomenal five-star stay in every aspect, from the beautiful interiors to the impeccable service, plus one of Cairo's best spas. First-timers often get auto-upgraded to Nile-view rooms.

Steigenberger Hotel El Tahrir $$$ A soothing oasis in the heart of the city. Some rooms overlook the Egyptian Museum and Midan Tahrir. Good value compared with other high-end options.

Islamic Cairo
MAPS p94, p102

Gamaleya Guest House $$ A welcome midrange option with a handful of rooms above the traditional crafts workshop of the same name. Rooms have a few nods to the artistry going on downstairs. Rates include breakfast and dinner.

Le Riad Hotel de Charme $$$ Large, colourful suites and superior service in the heart of Islamic Cairo. There's a great rooftop restaurant, but the rooms are extremely expensive given the limited amenities.

Maadi
p119

Villa Belle Epoque $$$ Egypt's first boutique hotel takes over two 1920s villas with a pool in leafy surrounds. It's far from the action, but that's the point – it's gloriously quiet.

Zamalek & Dokki
MAP p126

President Hotel $$ Mid-rise business-style hotel with a restaurant and minimalist-style rooms in taupe and cream. Don't miss La Terrace, the rooftop restaurant. New President, its slightly cheaper but still great sister hotel, is next door.

Sheraton Cairo $$$ Two tall towers, one with chic refurbished rooms. The cherry on top is the 26th-floor Club Lounge with wraparound floor-to-ceiling windows with views of the pyramids in the distance and the Nile at your feet.

Houseboat65 $$$ One of Cairo's most unique stays: a houseboat on the western side of Zamalek. Cosy decor and near-the-Nile balconies make it difficult to leave.

Cairo Marriott Hotel $$$ Towers of modern rooms flank the former 19th-century Gezira Palace, thick with historic atmosphere, where swooping chandeliers glitter from triple-height ceilings. Guests can join free guided tours with the on-staff historian.

Sofitel El Gezirah $$$ An unmistakable desert-pink cylinder rising from the southern tip of the island, this hotel has excellent restaurants and an infinity pool with Nile views.

Hilton Cairo Zamalek Residences $$$ The rooms are slightly dated with carpet and dark wood but it's a quiet place to crash, with balconies overlooking the city and a Nile-side pool.

Garden City & Roda Island   MAP p135

Four Seasons at Nile Plaza $$$ Book in to one of the premium floors, refurbed in 2022, with clean white decor accented with pottery from Fayoum. Flawless service plus thoughtful tech touches, like the lift auto-selecting your floor after tapping your key.

InterContinental Cairo Semiramis $$$ One of the older five-star hotels on the Nile wears its age gracefully. Great restaurants and a rooftop pool that watches over the river and Qasr El Nil Bridge.

Kempinski Nile $$$ An ideal Cairo combo: bright and modern rooms with skinny balconies, a pool with excellent Nile views and drool-worthy on-site restaurants so you don't have to venture far.

Heliopolis   MAP p140

Baron Hotel $$ Good-value option for staying close to Cairo International Airport but far enough away to get a taste of the city. Some rooms have views of the quirky Baron Empain Palace, as does the stunning rooftop bar.

Le Méridien Cairo Airport $$ Connected to Terminal 3 of Cairo International Airport; a wise choice for late-night or early-morning flights without having to battle traffic.

Waldorf Astoria Cairo Heliopolis $$$ Opened in 2024, this property is the first from the brand on the African continent. The impressive glassy lobby atrium is tall enough to fit full-sized palm trees.

Mena House Hotel, Giza

For places to stay in Northern Nile Valley, see p189

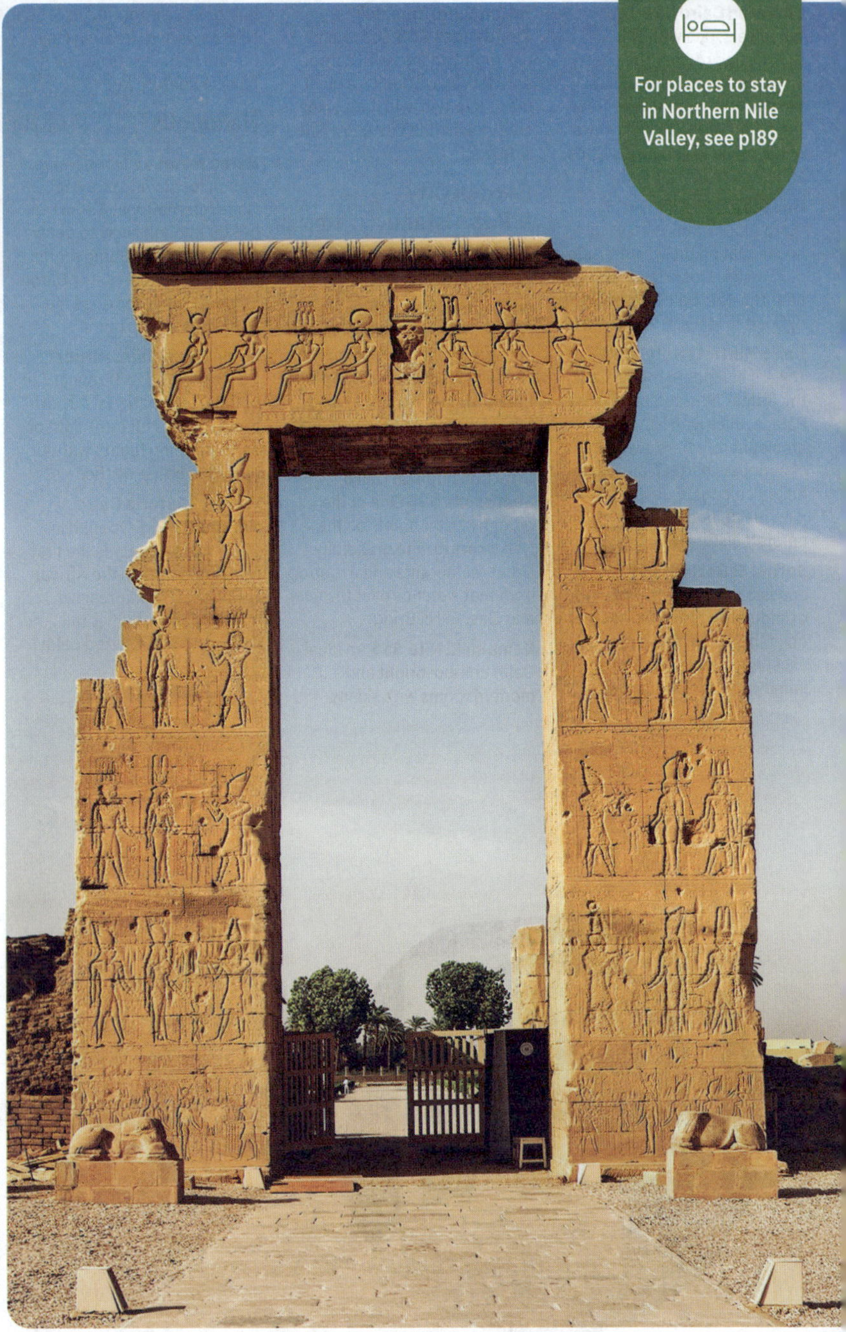

From left: Entrance to the Temple of Hathor, Dendara (p186); Wadi Al Hitan (p164)

Researched by
Anthon Jackson

Northern Nile Valley

EGYPT'S UNDISCOVERED SWEEP OF THE NILE

Take a slower pace and discover the Pharaonic riches and early Christian heritage in the stretch of Egypt most visitors entirely miss.

Luxor may steal all the thunder, but the northern Nile Valley rewards those who take their time heading south. As the vital link between Lower and Upper Egypt, the region's historical role has been fundamental. Two of the Pharaonic era's most fêted temple complexes are here, at Abydos and Dendara. Near Minya are the Middle Kingdom tombs of Beni Hasan and the remnants of Pharaoh Akhenaten's ill-fated city. Some of Coptic Christianity's most celebrated sites lie just outside Asyut and Sohag, while Fayoum's clutch of weathered pyramids appears sprightly next to the sand-swept Eocene boneyard of Wadi Al Hitan.

Despite straddling the country's geographical core, 'Middle Egypt' can feel relegated to its margins, long underserved when it comes to investments in education, development and tourism. Economic woes and opportunity shortages have contributed to a history of unrest, most notably an Islamist insurgency crushed in the 1990s and followed by sweeping crackdowns. Tensions still simmer to the surface, but the situation has markedly improved since the last major wave of turmoil here, that occurred in the wake of the 2011 revolution.

While it's open to tourism today, lingering security protocols make travel more challenging here than elsewhere. Bring your patience. But don't be deterred: the extra effort is amply rewarded. This is Egypt's ancient and abiding heartland, and – in our view – its best-kept secret by far.

THE MAIN AREAS

AL FAYOUM	**MINYA**	**ASYUT**	**SOHAG**	**QENA**
Prehistoric whales and village life. **p162**	Surrounded by Pharaonic-era riches. **p168**	Two key Coptic pilgrimage sites. **p176**	Ancient monasteries and sacred Abydos. **p179**	Base for Dendara's temple complex. **p185**

Find Your Way

Most visitors barely dip their toes into the northern Nile Valley (or 'Middle Egypt'), a 600km ribbon of green that traces the Nile between Luxor and Cairo, hemmed in on either desolate edge by rocky escarpments or walls of dunes.

CAR

For most travellers a private car or taxi, arranged through a travel agency or your hotel, is the preferred means of transport between Minya and Sohag. Where required, they'll relay your plans to police, thus minimising delays.

TRAIN

All major towns are linked by the railroad, though the going can be slow and prices relatively steep. Rates for foreigners are set in US dollars and online booking is unavailable to foreigners; arrive early to purchase at the ticket window. Check train schedules at *enr.gov.eg*.

BUS & MICROBUS

Buses mainly operate to towns outside rather than within the region (eg Minya to Cairo). Microbuses make up for this shortfall locally but foreigners aren't always permitted aboard. In any case, they're strongly discouraged here: if spotted and stopped by police (not unlikely), you won't be the only one delayed.

Al Fayoum, p162

The scene is centred around arty Tunis with ancient whale fossils, desert landscapes and slumping pyramids on its doorstep, all within easy reach of Cairo.

Minya, p168

Rarely seen wonders speckle the countryside in all directions from this city's breezy Corniche: lavishly painted tombs, clifftop churches and the vast, eery ruins of Tell Al Amarna.

THE GUIDE

NORTHERN NILE VALLEY

Qena, p185
A bustling market town lies on the east bank; the richly coloured reliefs and giant Hathor-headed-topped columns of Dendara's temple are on the west.

Asyut, p176
As deep as it gets in 'Middle Egypt', this city is ringed with a bevy of rock-hewn tombs as well as a pair of lively pilgrim-age centres: Dirunka and Al Muharraq.

Sohag, p179
Jumping-off point to discover the Coptic art of the Red and White Monasteries and Seti I's elaborately decorated temple in the Pharaonic cult centre of Abydos.

159

Plan Your Days

Independent travellers tend to concentrate on Minya and/or Fayoum (from Cairo) and Qena (from Luxor) rather than doing a sweep down the region, as security regulations are less of a hassle in these areas.

Pyramid of Hawara (p167)

Pressed for Time

● If you're fighting the clock, you can visit **Dendara** (p186) in Qena and the **Temple of Seti I at Abydos** (p183) all in a day from Luxor on a tour or with a private driver. You could even squeeze it all in via public transport, starting with an early train to Balyana (for Abydos).

● If you can only dip your toe in the region, another option is to concentrate on **Al Fayoum** (p162), just a two-hour drive from Cairo. With two nights in Tunis you could fit in the major sights, including the whale skeletons of **Wadi Al Hitan** (p165) and, with your own private transport, a sweep of the pyramids of **Meidum** (p167), **Hawara** (p167) and **Al Lahun** (p167) on the third day on the way back to Cairo.

SEASONAL HIGHLIGHTS

Avoid peak summer heat. Late May to August can be sweltering. Come between mid-October and April if you can.

FEBRUARY
The **Moulid of Abd Al Rahim Al Qenawi**, among Egypt's largest Sufi festivals, draws huge crowds to Qena on the 14th of the Islamic month of Sha'ban (early February until 2026; late January 2027).

APRIL
On Coptic Easter Monday, Egypt's ancient spring festival, **Sham An Nessim** ('smelling the breeze'), is held in style in Minya, Asyut, Sohag and Qena, featuring family picnics and pungent *fesikh* (salted, fermented fish).

JUNE
A week-long festival at **Deir Al Muharraq** (p176) to observe its consecration attracts tens of thousands of pilgrims, usually from the 21st to the 28th. Mid-morning on the 21st, sunlight illuminates the sanctuary of Hathor at **Dendara** (p186).

Historic Highlights in Four Days

● Start off in **Minya** (p168) and hire a driver to reach the ruins and tombs of **Tell Al Amarna** (p174). With an early start, add a stop at the west bank necropolis of **Tuna Al Gebel** (p172). Stick around the next day for the scenic road to **Gebel At Teir** (p168), **Zawiyyet Al Mayyiteen** (p170) and the **Tombs of Beni Hasan** (p170). Moving on to **Sohag** (p179), hike to the **Tombs of Al Hawawish** (p181), and visit the **Red and White Monasteries** (p179) and ancient **Athribis** (p181) en route to the sacred **Temple of Seti I at Abydos** (p183).

● On your last day, rise early for the train to reach **Dendara** (p186). If heading to Luxor afterwards, you'll have plenty of time to get into town by mid-afternoon.

A Week or More up the Nile

● Add a couple of days for the wild desertscapes surrounding **Al Fayoum** (p162), from **Wadi Rayyan** (p164) to the eerily desolate sweep to the north of **Lake Qarun** (p165).

● Alternatively, stretch out your stay in **Minya** (p168), granting time to relax along the Corniche. Reserve to **Tell Al Amarna** (p174) the full day it deserves, combining a separate visit to **Tuna Al Gebel** (p172) with a stop at ancient **Hermopolis** (p172); perhaps even add in an east-bank adventure to the churches and tombs of **Deir Al Barsha** (p173).

● Meanwhile, a night or two in **Asyut** (p176) will allow for visits to the dune-swept **Tombs of Mir** (p176), the hallowed monasteries of **Al Muharraq** (p176) and **Dirunka** (p177) and the far-flung **Tombs of Al Hammamiya** (p178).

THE GUIDE

NORTHERN NILE VALLEY

AUGUST
Enlivened old souqs are pervaded with sugary treats in celebration of **Moulid An Nabi** (the Prophet's Birthday). On the 22nd, pilgrims converge in their thousands on **Deir Dirunka** (p177), near Asyut, for the **Feast of the Assumption**.

OCTOBER
Along the Nile Valley, October's soft light makes this an optimal month to travel for keen photographers. Along with April, it offers an excellent balance between ideal temperatures and extended sunlight hours.

NOVEMBER
Fayoum's distinctive ceramics and other handicrafts are centre stage at the **Tunis Village Festival** (p164), usually held in late November or early December and drawing crowds from Cairo.

DECEMBER
At sunrise on the 21st, winter solstice, rays of light perfectly penetrate the holy of holies at Fayoum's **Qasr Qarun** (p167), where statues of Sobek, the crocodile god, once stood.

Al Fayoum

LONELY PYRAMIDS | DREAMY DESERTS | HERITAGE HANDICRAFTS

☑ TOP TIP

Tunis village, 47km west of Medinat Al Fayoum, is the best base for day trips in the area. Fayoum's several pyramids are best visited on the way in or out.

GETTING AROUND

Sights are scattered widely, and for many (such as Wadi Al Hitan), 4WD is required. With limited time, take a private tour or hire a driver. From Cairo, microbuses depart when full from under the Ring road north of El Monib metro station, connecting to Medinat Al Fayoum (LE50), the region's transport hub. For Tunis village, board the microbus for Ibshiway (LE50), alighting at the Lake road for the final 20km leg. Between Tunis and Medinat Al Fayoum, change microbuses in Ibshiway. A taxi for this trip costs LE400 to LE450. From Medinat Al Fayoum, three daily trains go to Cairo.

Fresh air, lush farmland, desert vistas; two hours' drive from Cairo, the Fayoum's backwater rhythms are guaranteed to lower your blood pressure. A favourite weekend haunt for Cairenes, it remains under the radar for foreigners.

South of Lake Qarun, this fertile basin unfurls in a farming plot patchwork of wheat, calendula and cabbages. Sunflowers sway in the breeze and water buffaloes lounge in the shade of date palms. Often called an oasis, the Fayoum isn't: it's watered not by springs but by the Nile via capillary canals, some dating all the way back to the Middle Kingdom. Studded with remnants from this ancient heyday, the region continues to be shaped by waterworks today, as seen in a series of human-made lakes that punctuate the deserts at its doorstep. Among castle-like bluffs and peculiar rock formations lies a landmark still stranger than the rest: a dune-swept graveyard of the carnivorous whales that roamed here in prehistoric times.

An Arty Rural Hideaway

Exploring the pottery village of Tunis

Think of **Tunis** village as your decompression chamber after time spent in Cairo. Bougainvillea tumbles over walls, narrow squiggles of alleys lead to boutique hotels in stone-cut villas, and pottery workshops displaying the wares of local artists are scattered along the main road, sprinkled with fanciful murals. Brushed-up in comparison to much of Egypt's agricultural heartland (and a favoured weekend-home destination for wealthy Cairenes with a bohemian streak), it could be considered rural-Egypt-lite, but that doesn't mean that while strolling about you won't have to manoeuvre around a cow munching clover on the side of the street or a tuk-tuk speeding full tilt down a dirt lane.

The village's relatively recent fame is owed to its distinctive ceramics, a modern trademark launched in the 1980s when

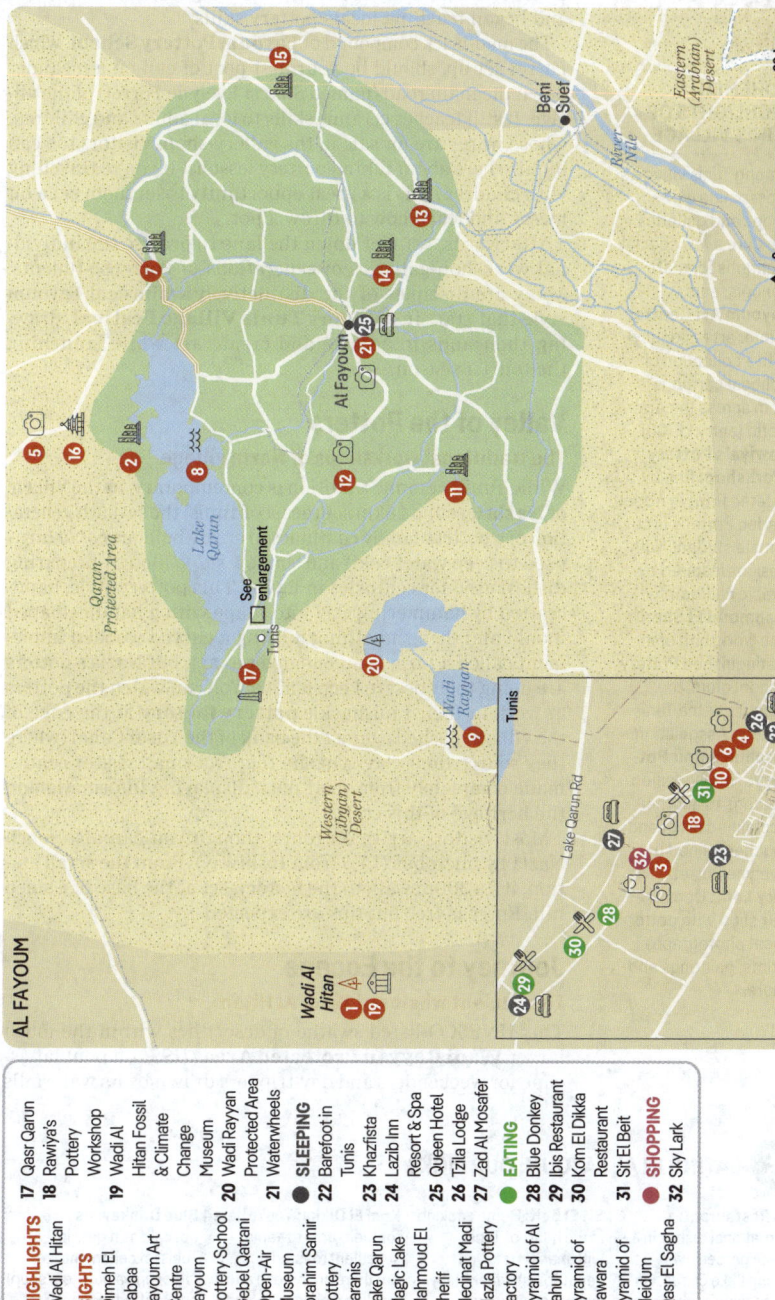

BOHEMIAN HIGHLIGHTS OF TUNIS VILLAGE

Among Tunis village's blossoming workshops and galleries, here are a few special mentions for craft connoisseurs.

Fayoum Art Centre: Winter art residency with a collection of political cartoons from across the Arab world (entry LE100).

Rawiya's Pottery Workshop: Run by veteran Rawiya Abdel Qader, Porret's first female student, with designs inspired by Arabic calligraphy.

Mahmoud El Sherif: The workshop of a distinguished Pottery School alum, the founder of the Tunis Potters Association.

Ibrahim Samir Pottery: This workshop belongs to another acclaimed artist and teacher trained by Evelyne Porret.

Sky Lark: Upmarket gift shop with pottery, local photography prints, paintings and more.

Swiss ceramist Evelyne Porret, who died in 2021, settled here and began teaching locals pottery skills.

The mud-brick compound of **Fayoum Pottery School**, which Porret set up, should be your first port of call on a meander down the main road (named Sharia Evelyne Porret) of the village. It still teaches ceramic skills to local adults and children, whose wares are for sale in the gallery-shop. Visitors too can inquire here about taking pottery lessons. If you're travelling with children, this is a great opportunity to let them get a bit messy and learn how to throw a pot.

Afterwards, wander down the lane to browse the individual workshop-galleries of generations of Porret's students. Many are disciples of the distinctively whimsical Fayoum style that stars in autumn's **Tunis Village Festival**, drawing thousands to admire and create art while launching the tourist season.

Valley of the Potters
The traditional workshops of Nazla village

While Tunis' ceramic tradition is contemporary, in the village of **Nazla** (around 28km southeast of Tunis) the seventh generation of a pottery family continues to create bulbous *bokla* (urns used to keep water cold) and shallow *sahfa* (dough-preparing dishes) used for centuries in Egypt. This pottery style, handcrafted by hammering clay into shape with a handle-shaped mould and then smoothing it using a curved wooden implement called a *tara,* is an endangered art, but Nazla's potters are doing their best to keep it alive. You can watch the potters at work in their ramshackle **pottery factory** at the edge of the village, pushed against the bank of the Yusuf Canal (where they source their clay). On site there's a small visitor centre, made completely from their pots, displaying information on the heritage of this craft.

Most visitors arrive on tours, though you can also reach Nazla by microbus (LE6 from Ibshiway). From the small station, it's a 300m walk to the factory, set at the base of a steep hill. Entry is free but tips are expected.

Journey to the Eocene
The ancient whales of Wadi Al Hitan

This UNESCO-listed swathe of desert lies within the much larger **Wadi Rayyan Protected Area** *(US$5),* a popular escape for weekenders and day-trippers drawn by its waterfalls

---

EATING IN AL FAYOUM: OUR PICKS

Ibis Restaurant: International dishes in a serene garden overlooking Lake Qarun. On-site cooking school has trained a generation of local chefs. *8am-9pm* **$$**

Sit El Beit: Home cooking in the heart of Tunis with *mahshi* (stuffed vegetables), *fiteer* (flaky, sweet and savoury pastries) and grilled pigeon. *8am-9pm* **$$**

Kom El Dikka: You're here for their farm-to-table succulent roasted duck, but there are pigeon and chicken dishes too – and save room for dessert. *9am-9pm* **$$**

Blue Donkey: As upscale as it gets in Tunis; excellent mezze, *molokhiyya* (jute leaf soup) and stuffed pigeon with lovely lake views. *7.30am-midnight* **$$$**

and scenic lakes. The entrance to the protected area is just 20 minutes south of Tunis village. From here, a desert track (4WD only) will land you inside the reserve of **Wadi Al Hitan** *(US$10)*, requiring roughly an hour's drive. Here, surrounded by low, tawny cliffs and punctuated by rock formations sculpted by water and wind, is one of the most important fossil sites in the world.

Walking the 3km trail, along which many fossils are displayed where they were found, is an experience in witnessing the mind-boggling numbers needed to understand deep time.

From the visitor centre, the **walking track** weaves between fossil sites dating from the Eocene epoch, which 40-odd million years ago would have been on the seabed of the shallow Tethys Sea. The world's best-preserved and largest number of *Archaeoceti* (primitive whales) have been found here. Among these are more than 400 skeletons of *Basilosaurus* and *Dorodon,* both rather fierce water predators (the former known to prey on the latter) with small, vestigial front and back legs, demonstrating the evolution of land-based mammals into sea-going ones.

The 17 fossils left in situ are largely intact and look bizarrely out of place with their curved backbones poking out of the sand. Walk up to the panoramic point at the furthest end of the trail for views across the entire expanse of Wadi Al Hitan.

Afterwards head back to the visitor centre to visit the **Fossil & Climate Change Museum**, which elucidates the geological history and nature of the area aided by a short documentary on an Arabic/English rotation. The crowning exhibit is the 18m-long complete skeleton of a *Basilosaurus isis* whale unearthed here.

Lonely Off-Road Ruins

Exploring the desert north of Qarun

The standard desert itinerary from Al Fayoum heads south to Wadi Rayyan's desert lakes and Wadi Al Hitan. Far quieter and no less desolate are the northern shores of **Lake Qarun**, officially the **Qarun Protected Area** *(US$5)*, which makes for a good day-long loop by 4WD. From Tunis village, you'll wrap around the northwest edge of the lake, a geological wonderland speckled with wind-whittled spires and, further east, a field of large concretions (spherical rocks).

Continuing along the shoreline you'll spot the solitary ruins of **Dimeh El Sabaa** long before you arrive, the jagged-teeth chunks of its mud-brick walls piercing the desert horizon. This is the Ptolemaic temple complex of Soknopaiou Nesos ('the island of Soknopaiou', the Hellenistic variant of the Egyptian crocodile god Sobek), built in the 3rd century BCE. Ongoing excavations, however, have found evidence of much earlier settlement. Rounding the enormous walls of the temple enclosure to the southward-facing gates, take a walk along the remarkably well-preserved processional way linking the lake (now some 2km away), keeping an eye at your feet to spot lustrous shards of turquoise faience.

WADI RAYYAN'S DESERT LAKES

The idea for a reservoir south of Al Fayoum traces back to the Muhammad Ali Pasha era, but it was a century later, beginning in the 1970s, that today's three artificial lakes took form, slowly inundated by a southward-cutting canal from the Fayoum.

The water, agricultural overspill, tumbles from the Upper Lake into the Lower Lake via a series of low cascades, creating Egypt's only waterfalls. If you've seen waterfalls before, you mightn't be particularly impressed, but they're a major draw for the day-tripping Cairene crowds.

Further along, the third, youngest and prettiest of the three is **Magic Lake**, ringed by low dunes beneath the rocky rise of Gebel Al Modawara, an especially busy spot just before sunset.

WATERWHEELS OF AL FAYOUM

Mahmoud Kamel is a researcher, Al Fayoum's only local specialist guide and founder of Explore Fayoum tours. *fayoumegypt.com, @explorefayoum*

Today, some 20 waterwheels remain out of the 200 once scattered across Al Fayoum to irrigate its farmlands. These water-driven wheels are similar to those that appeared in the Middle East during the Roman era. While the current design of Fayoum's waterwheels may have been developed during the time of Muhammad Ali, their origins likely date back to Roman times, much like the famous waterwheels of Hama, Syria.

In Medinat Al Fayoum, four **waterwheels** are now a tourist site. Another place to see them is at **Mandara** village, where three 6m-high waterwheels sit beside the main road.

Fossil & Climate Change Museum (p165)

Relatively hidden against the slopes a further 8km north of the lake, **Qasr El Sagha** once stood on the shoreline too. A small Middle Kingdom temple, it's comprised of oddly shaped blocks pieced together in jigsaw style. It's linked to the basalt quarries of Widan El Faras, mined from the Old Kingdom onwards (rocks from here can be seen on the eastern side of Giza's Great Pyramid), by scant but still visible remnants of the oldest paved road in the world, made of basalt and petrified wood.

Still further north along a windy sand track spreads **Gebel Qatrani Open-Air Museum**, a petrified-forest area. Here you can walk a short trail dotted with huge petrified tree trunks and small fossils of the animals that roamed here some 33 million years ago, during the Oligocene era, when the desert you are standing in was a tropical forest.

Ancient Al Fayoum

Middle Kingdom and Ptolemaic temples

There's a lot of desert scenery and deep-time history to absorb, but don't forget that Al Fayoum, with its fertile agricultural land, is rich in human heritage as well. During the Middle Kingdom's 12th dynasty, Al Fayoum had its heyday under Amenemhat III (reigned c 1855–1808 BCE), who built the city of Dja, now known as **Medinat Madi** (Arabic for 'City of the Past'). Its small **temple** *(LE120)* – which is one of the only Middle Kingdom temples to have survived in Egypt – was dedicated to the crocodile god Sobek and the cobra goddess Renenutet. You reach the temple via a later Ptolemaic-era processional avenue, flanked by rather friendly-looking lion statues and sphinxes. The lonely ruins, located on the southeast edge of the fertile basin, are a bit of a slog to get to, accessed either by a track heading east from the Wadi Rayyan lakes or by skinny roads, sided by farming plots and villages, running south from Tunis. Either way, you'll need a 4WD.

Amenemhat III was quite the inventive builder and a man before his time. As well as building some of Al Fayoum's irrigation canal network and the Pyramid of Hawara with its legendary, lost-to-history labyrinth, he seems to have also invented a type of sand windsurfing (check out the replica of his sailing cart in Medinat Madi's little museum).

For an easier-to-access temple, head to **Qasr Qarun** *(LE150)*, near the southwest shore of Lake Qarun, built in 4 BCE and all that remains of the Ptolemaic city of Dionysias. Climb to the temple's roof for panoramic views and to spot the site's only surviving relief of Sobek.

Al Fayoum's Pyramid Circuit
Egypt's less seen pyramids

Make sure you're wearing sturdy shoes. You're about to do some stair-clambering. Head to the Old Kingdom **Pyramid of Meidum** first, 45km northeast from Medinat Al Fayoum. It was commissioned by Pharaoh Huni (reigned c 2637–2613 BCE) but built by his son Pharaoh Sneferu, the great pyramid-building pioneer. It began as an eight-sided structure, with the steps later filled in to form the shell. Sometime after completion the pyramid's weight caused the sides to collapse and today only the core stands. Inside, clamber down the 75m-long corridor and then up a series of short, steep staircases to the empty burial chamber. Afterwards, the site guardian will guide you to the large mastaba tomb (mud-brick structure in the shape of a bench) of some of Sneferu's family just to the north.

From here, move 33km southwest to the lumpen remnant of the Middle Kingdom **Pyramid of Al Lahun**, built by Pharaoh Sesostris II (also known as Senusret II; reigned c 1880–1874 BCE). The extensive tunnels beneath the pyramid are the highlight here, leading you deep under the surface and wrapping around to reach the tomb chamber, bats flitting overhead. Back above ground, circle to the pyramid's north to admire a row of eight mastabas and a satellite pyramid believed to have been built for the royal women.

Another 16km west, back towards Medinat Al Fayoum, you arrive at the **Pyramid of Hawara**. The mud-brick core of this pyramid slumps over the north banks of the Bahr Yusuf (Yusuf Canal) that connects Al Fayoum to the Nile. It was the second pyramid built by Amenemhat III (the first having been at Dahshur) and once connected to a famed, long-gone temple Herodotus described as a 3000-room labyrinth.

Tickets for each pyramid are LE150 (students LE75). The easiest way to knock off all three pyramids in one swoop is to hire a driver for a half-day-or-so circuit. If you're travelling between Minya and Cairo with a private driver, these three make for good stops along the way.

THE CROCODILE GOD

The cult of Sobek, the god whose sweat was said to have birthed the Nile, particularly thrived across the Fayoum. In Ptolemaic times, the god's incarnations thrashed in untold temples here, pampered in sacred pools and embalmed as mummies to be worshipped after death, believed to bestow fertility – both to land and people.

Medinat Madi is the best-preserved cult site today, but fainter traces abound: at nearby Umm Al Borigat (Tebtunis), on the roof of **Qasr Qarun**, at **Dimeh El Sabaa** (p165) and at the ruins of **Karanis** (p153), where you'll also find what's left of Kiman Faris (Crocodilopolis in Greek); the rest is buried beneath the sprawl of Medinat Al Fayoum.

Minya

ANCIENT TOMBS | NILE DRIVES | COPTIC HERITAGE

☑ TOP TIP

Thanks to Minya's location, size, exceptional hotels and its relatively relaxed police protocols for foreigners (allowing you to wander around town unescorted), this is the best base for independent travellers visiting the sites between Beni Suef and Tell Al Amarna.

GETTING AROUND

Just a 10-minute walk (or LE10 taxi) links the train station to the Corniche. There are frequent departures north (to Cairo) and south (to Asyut, Sohag, Qena, Luxor etc). Buy tickets on the day (about an hour before the train). Microbuses are discouraged as your presence is likely to delay fellow passengers at checkpoints. The best option for trips out of town is hiring a car. Most taxi drivers are happy to be hired. You'll be joined by a police escort and, as far as you're able, always clarify your itinerary in advance.

Just three hours south of Cairo, this provincial capital, with its breezy Corniche and sugarcane fields, is a relaxed base for a swag of historic sites. The scatter of dilapidated early-20th-century buildings dotted around town harks back to a bygone era when Minya was the heart of Egypt's cotton industry.

Unfortunately, sporadic violence (targeting the Coptic minority) has left this so-called 'Bride of Upper Egypt' jilted by would-be visitors for decades. Epitomising its tragically untapped potential is the city's landmark Aten Museum, completed in 2010. Never opened, its pyramid-shaped outline appears as a mirage across the Nile from town.

As of writing, subtle signs do bode well, including a spate of new, excellent-value hotels. Security protocols have begun to loosen too, with police escorts no longer a given. Named 2025's Capital of Egyptian Culture, Minya yearns for its share of the spotlight – for the right reasons this time.

The Road to Gebel At Teir

A history-packed drive north of Minya

A scenic road hugs the base of the cliffs right at Minya's doorstep on the Nile's east bank, running north to the celebrated Coptic complex of Deir Al Adhra. The 22km route offers a wonderful snapshot of rural life, passing a patchwork of sugarcane and sunflower fields, while a handful of rarely seen wonders make it a more than worthwhile jaunt from Minya.

Approached in order of age, the road's highlights begin with the Old Kingdom **Fraser Tombs** *(LE100)*. Cut into the cliff face about 8km north of Minya, these were carved for high officials in the 4th and 5th dynasties. The best-preserved statues are in the Tomb of Nikaankh, where he has stood (and sat) hand-in-hand with his wife for roughly 4500 years.

Another 3km north at a rise in the ridge is the richly layered **Tihna Al Gebel** (officially closed; tip the custodian), a vast field of Graeco-Roman rubble next to the present-day town of the same

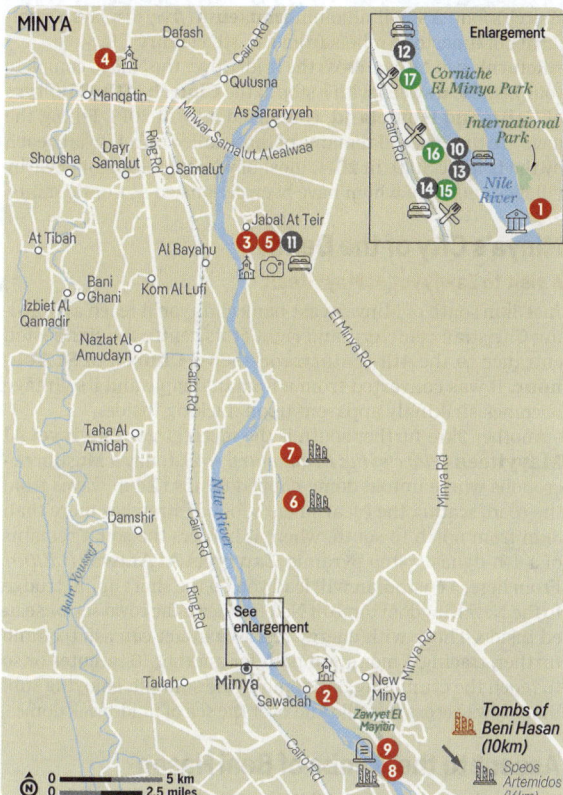

MINYA

● SIGHTS
1. Aten Museum
2. Church of St Abahour
3. Church of the Blessed Virginr
4. Church of the Martyrs of Faith and Homeland
5. Deir Al Adhra
6. Fraser Tombs
7. Tihna Al Gebel
8. Zawiyyet Al Amwat
9. Zawiyyet Al Mayyiteen

● SLEEPING
10. C-Boat
11. Holy Family Hotel
12. Horus Resort
13. Omar El-Khayam Hotel
14. Savoy

● EATING
15. Al Negma
16. Bondokah Restaurant
17. Orkeed

SECURITY PROTOCOLS

Come prepared to be halted for questioning at train stations, checkpoints and even stepping out of your hotel. Foreigners are generally assigned armed escorts for trips outside Minya, Asyut or Sohag and even within Sohag and Asyut. Expect delays for directional disputes, convoy swaps and general disarray, but remember that, however strict, these measures are there for your safety. Show only appreciation. To minimise hassle, arrange excursions with local tour companies or private drivers and, before setting out, be sure that your plans have been clearly conveyed to police.

---

name, guarding the mouth of a wadi at the foot of an imposing, pockmarked cliff. At its base you'll find the remaining pillars of a New Kingdom Temple of Amun. The crudely quarried rock face itself has also been chiselled with churches, pagan chapels and temples, the largest dedicated to Sobek. You can glimpse a few incarnations of the latter through a doorway off to the right: desiccated crocodiles caked in dust on frayed reed mats.

Continuing for another 10km north, the road passes beneath the escarpment of Gebel At Teir (Mountain of the Birds), atop which spreads **Deir Al Adhra** (Monastery of the Virgin). Left of the modern stairway to the top, look out for the old rock-hewn steps that once ascended from straight over the Nile, linked by rope and pulley. By road, you'll continue north to climb the escarpment, passing New Kingdom quarries and a pair of police checkpoints on the approach to the ancient **Church of the Blessed Virgin** *(free)*. Spruced up in 2022 in connection with the Holy Family Trail (p177), its fame among Copts derives from the tiny cave past the entrance to the right, believed to have sheltered Jesus, Mary and Joseph. The 4th-century basilica built around it is ascribed to Helena, mother of Emperor Constantine, the builders having taken wise advantage of an earlier Roman structure's hefty pillars. Entirely cut from one such pillar is the

RISE OF THE NOMARCHS

In ancient Egypt a province was called a nome and the governor of a nome was a nomarch. During the 5th dynasty the role of nomarch became hereditary and this rise of a provincial upper class was a factor in the collapse of centralised power that ended the Old Kingdom and ushered in the First Intermediate Period (c 2160–2025 BCE), where nomarchs may have still paid lip service to whoever had been proclaimed pharaoh, but in reality reigned over their nome autonomously.

The local sway of many nomarchs carried over into the Middle Kingdom and the Beni Hasan tombs of the 'Great Overlords of the Oryx Nome' are among the best surviving evidence of the power some governors wielded over their own fiefdoms.

church's font. A small, adjoining **museum** *(free)* displays a smattering of limestone reliefs from the 4th century CE.

Returning to Minya, cross the bridge over the Nile to complete your historical sweep with a stop at the **Church of the Martyrs of Faith and Homeland**, completed only in 2018. Filling the nave are the encased remains of those killed on a Libyan beach by the Islamic State in 2014, most of whom hailed from nearby villages and all of whom have been canonised as Coptic saints.

Minya's City of the Dead
A visit to Zawiyyet Al Mayyiteen

Just 3km south of Minya's east-bank cliffs you'll reach a sprawling Christian cemetery, and right at its centre the signposted entrance to the 4th-century, rock-hewn **Church of St Abahour**. It was converted from a Roman temple and its vintage becomes strikingly apparent upon ducking inside.

Another 3km further south is the much larger **Zawiyyet Al Mayyiteen** *(Place of the Dead; entry free),* today a Muslim necropolis where untold dome-capped tombs rise in waves from the road, scaling the escarpment's foot. It stretches more than 3km from north to south, where it borders the squat remains of a 4th-dynasty step pyramid **Zawiyyet Al Amwat** *(LE100).* From here, a custodian will lead you on the short uphill trudge to the New Kingdom tomb of Nefersekheru, the royal scribe seated inside. Those with energy reserves intact can ask to climb further, tracing a mountain path for another 10 minutes or so to reach the crumbling Sufi tomb at the summit, enjoying sublime views across the Nile and over the sea of mud-brick domes.

Ascent to the Tombs of Beni Hasan
The painted tombs of the Oryx nomarchs

For a different take on Egypt's tombs, don't miss the necropolis of **Beni Hasan** *(adult/student LE200/100),* where the Middle Kingdom governors of the Oryx nome had their tombs chiselled out of the cliffs. The decoration inside is more focused on day-to-day details than in Egypt's regal tombs, providing a contrast to Pharaonic pomp and bling and a glimpse of ancient provincial life (even if the tombs themselves still belong exclusively to elites).

From the site's basic rest house above the road, some 25km south of Minya, both the guardian entrusted with the keys and an armed escort will typically accompany you up the trail.

Of the 39 tombs that dot the limestone ridge, only four are open to the public, with these dating from the 11th and

EATING IN MINYA: OUR PICKS

Bondokah: Meaty favourites including good-value kofta and kebab plates plus *tagens* (clay-pot stews) and *molokhiyya*. *9am-2am, from noon Fri & Sat* $

C-Boat (p189): Highly affordable breakfast spreads and Western staples on a deck overlooking the Nile Corniche. *8am-midnight* $

Al Negma: Busy hole-in-the-wall near the railway station with top-rated *kushari* (noodles, rice, brown lentils, fried onions and tomato sauce) at rock-bottom prices. *7am-late* $

Orkeed: Nile views with traditional Egyptian meals including pigeon, *molokhiyya* and kebabs. *noon-2am* $$

Beni Hasan

12th dynasties (c 2135–1795 BCE). The first up the steps is the papyrus-columned **Tomb of Khety (No 17)**, belonging to the governor of the Oryx nome. Allow your eyes to adjust to admire the back (east) wall, decorated with 122 pairs of wrestlers. On the left-hand (north) wall are hunting scenes, female acrobats, weavers and board-game enthusiasts.

The next tomb along the ridge belongs to **Baqet III (No 15)**, possibly Khety's father. Again, the far (east) wall here is covered with wrestlers, with no less than 220 pairs. Further along, through the columned-portico entrance of the **Tomb of Khnumhotep (No 3)**, note the large wall painting of Khnumhotep spearing a fish along the back wall.

Finally, inside the **Tomb of Amenemhat (No 2)**, perhaps the most impressive of the bunch, you'll count farmers, potters, fishers and carpenters on the entrance (west) wall and more wrestling scenes on the back (east) wall.

Beni Hasan is easily combined into a day trip from Minya with **Tuna Al Gebel** (p172). If hoping to squeeze in **Tell Al Amarna** (p174), start early and take the Desert Rd.

Exploring Speos Artemidos
Lonely cave temples and quarries

Most tourists turn back towards Minya at Beni Hasan, but another cluster of entirely rock-cut tombs sits 3km south, then nearly a kilometre east into the desert, sprinkling the lip of a wadi. This is **Speos Artemidos** ('cave-shrine of Artemis' in Greek), known locally as Istabl Antar. Among the ravaged tombs here is a temple of the goddess Pakhet, adorned by the Pharaoh Hatshepsut herself.

You'll need to alert the custodian in charge of the keys in the nearby village (to save time, inquire at Beni Hasan). There's no entry fee or set hours, but as at Beni Hasan, a tip (to both the custodian and the security escort) is expected.

MIDDLE EGYPT'S LIMESTONE QUARRIES

Exploring the northern Nile Valley, you can hardly miss the chiselled lines striping its cliffs, among the oldest and most extensive ancient quarries anywhere on earth. Particularly burdened with sating the Pharaohs' need for limestone blocks was the stretch from Minya to Abydos. Here, roughly a hundred such quarries (in Arabic *mahaagir*, 'places of stone') dot the valley's margins. But they're more than cut rocks; they're heritage sites in their own right, excised over some 3500 years to the Roman era, using tools of stone, copper, bronze and iron. Today, modern quarries are abuzz with mechanised saws, kicking up clouds of white powder that blur the horizon east of Gebel At Teir.

Beyond Minya

Welcome to Middle Egypt's heart, its richest stretch for archaeological pickings!

Places

Mallawi to Tuna Al Gebel
p172

Deir Al Barsha & Beyond
p173

GETTING AROUND

Foreign travellers are generally forbidden (in any case, strongly discouraged) from using microbus transport here. As buses link only destinations outside Middle Egypt, the train is the only viable public transport option.

Expect police company when departing the stations of Minya and Mallawi (for Tell Al Amarna). Indeed, police will generally insist on providing a security escort for all excursions beyond Minya's boundaries. If driving, this often consists of one man riding along in your car rather than a separate police vehicle.

The Minya governorate's sweep of the Nile Valley is catnip for history lovers. Without doubt, the showpiece here is the lonely expanse of Tell Al Amarna, the ill-fated city of the revolutionary Pharaoh Akhenaten, ringed with grand tombs. Of the trickle of the region's passers-through, a majority limit their visit to here (often combined with Tombs of Beni Hasan; p170) – barely scratching the surface of the historical wealth between the valley's cliffs and dunes: the sprawl of ancient Hermopolis, the vast bird necropolis of Tuna Al Gebel, the smattering of ancient churches and tombs around Deir Al Barsha, to name just a few. At most of these, you'll likely be the sole visitor in sight.

Mallawi to Tuna Al Gebel

TIME FROM MINYA: **1 HR 20 MINS**

Visit a sprawling Graeco-Roman necropolis

The small **museum** *(adult/student LE120/60)* at the centre of **Mallawi**, an hour's drive south of Minya, provides welcome context for the wealth of archaeological sites strewn here. Don't miss Tell Al Amarna's Talatat blocks, engraved with scenes of cutting stone and crafting furniture. You'll also find a preview of several sarcophagi and mummified birds from Tuna Al Gebel. The west bank's richest archaeological cluster begins about 8km west of Mallawi, at **Hermopolis** (ancient Khemenu; capital of the 15th Upper Egyptian nome), now encircled by the scruffy, modern town of **Al Ashmunein**. The stars of the site's open-air **museum** *(adult/student LE50/25)* are two colossal baboons representing Thoth, god of magic and writing, while nearby are the still-standing columns of an imposingly large, 5th-century **basilica** *(free)*.

More impressive is Hermopolis' necropolis, **Tuna Al Gebel** *(adult/student LE200/100)*, a further 10km west at the desert's edge, hiding rambling catacombs of ibis and baboons and a pair of free-standing tombs. The **Tomb of Petosiris** (a high priest of Thoth) is a mashup of Greek, Persian and ancient Egyptian tomb art styles. Just behind it stands the smaller and simpler **Tomb of Isadora**, containing the mummy of a wealthy woman who drowned in the Nile during the reign of Antoninus Pius (138–161 CE).

Tuna Al Gebel

The site's policeman will walk you to the entrance of the subterranean galleries; tread carefully on the stairs. In the first chamber, come face to face with a mummified, robed baboon. If you descend the ladder steps to the catacomb's lowest level, you can see the sarcophagus of the only human to be buried here.

Deir Al Barsha & Beyond

TIME FROM MINYA: **1 HR 30 MINS**

Off-path ancient churches and ruins

The bumpy road north of the bridge opposite Mallawi offers a rarely seen sprinkling of sites – Pharaonic, Roman and Coptic. About 4km along is the early-5th-century complex of **Deir Al Barsha**. A steward will happily lead you from the lower to the upper **Church of St Bishoi**, once employed as a keep, its ceilings adorned with patterned frescoes. In the chiselled cliffs immediately east of the village spreads the archaeological site also called Deir Al Barsha (officially closed), its Old and Middle Kingdom tombs embellished with Coptic-era graffiti. A further 4km north is the ancient, basilica-style **Church of St John the Short** in **Deir Abu Hinnis**, another staunchly Christian hamlet similarly bounded by rock-cut, hermitage caves.

The town's exit to the north comes abruptly in the form of a vast, desolate rise of rubble: **Kom Maria**, revered as a resting place for Mary on her flight from Judea.
The ruins run for 4km to the next village, **Al Sheikh Ibada**, abutting the still visible outline of **Antinopolis**, built by the Roman Emperor Hadrian in 130 CE. Almost nothing remains of his signature triumphal arch, picked apart by Muhammad Ali. Rather, the most eye-catching monument is much older, the sandstone pillars of its hypostyle hall standing just east of the village: a New Kingdom temple of Thoth built by Ramses II.

If headed back to Minya, there's no need to backtrack to Mallawi: hop aboard the Nile ferry from Al Sheikh Ibada.

MINYA'S MOLASSES

The Agricultural road north and south of Minya is slow going but memorably varied (unlike the fast, bland Desert road), alternatively bisecting dozens of towns then slicing through fields of vivid greens: wheat, corn, cotton and sugarcane. It's the latter for which Minya – the country's top producer – is particularly famed. Introduced well over a thousand years ago, it's harvested from here to Aswan. Travelling along the Agricultural road, it's sugarcane that accounts for the puffs of black smoke on the horizon, rising from twin sooty chimneys of small-scale factories: the by-product of brewing its juice *(asab)* into the beloved, viscous molasses *(asal eswad,* 'black honey'), an Egyptian kitchen staple and, here, a point of pride.

Tomb of Ay (No 25)

TOP EXPERIENCE

Tell Al Amarna

Oh Akhenaten! Misfit monotheist who just wanted everyone to worship the sun? Or megalomaniac cult leader on a major power trip? The jury may still be out on this 18th-dynasty New Kingdom pharaoh, but you can visit the tombs (and scant city remains) of the short-lived city he created to learn how he shook ancient Egypt's culture and beliefs to their core as no other pharaoh ever dared.

DID YOU KNOW?

Akhetaten ('Horizon of the Sun'; now Tell Al Amarna), the city of Akhenaten (reigned c 1352–1336 BCE), was capital of Egypt for less than 15 years and abandoned around a decade after the pharaoh's death.

Northern Group Tombs

This group of tombs, built for elite members of Akhenaten's city, is cut high into a cliff ridge. After climbing up the stairs, head to the **Tomb of Ahmose (No 3)**, belonging to the holder of the lofty title of 'True Scribe of the King; Fan-Bearer on the King's Right Hand'. A lot of the interior was left unfinished, which allows you to see the different artistic stages.

Next on the ridge is the **Tomb of Meryre I (No 4)**, belonging to the High Priest of the Aten. Look on the left-hand wall

PRACTICALITIES
- Northern & Southern Tombs adult/student LE200/100
- Royal Tombs adult/student LE120/60
- 8am–5pm, last entry 4pm
- Scan to purchase tickets

of the chamber to see a procession carrying Meryre to see the royal couple, and then the right-hand wall, where Akhenaten and his wife Nefertiti are depicted on their way to the Great Temple of Aten.

The nearby **Tomb of Penthu (No 5)** holds simpler decorations, but on the left-hand wall, check out the scene of the royal family at the Great Temple of Aten. Penthu was the chief physician and a royal scribe.

Afterwards, one of the site's policemen will escort you across the ridge to the **Tomb of Panehsy (No 6)**, where you can spot Nefertiti driving her chariot and, if you look on the left wall of the passage between the chambers, Panehsy himself is depicted as a fat, old man.

Southern Group Tombs

A low cliff about 8km south is home to the Southern Group tombs where you can see well-preserved scenes of the day-to-day duties of Akhenaten's chief of police inside the **Tomb of Mahu (No 9)**. You can spot Mahu escorting prisoners and going to the Great Temple of Aten. In the otherwise bare **Tomb of Apy (No 10)**, the royal couple is beautifully depicted worshipping the Aten.

Only half-completed, the ambitious **Tomb of Ay (No 25)** is regarded as Tell Al Amarna's best. Ay was the pharaoh's vizier and Tiye, his wife, was Nefertiti's wet nurse. (After Akhenaten's son Tutankhamun died, Ay went on to rule as pharaoh himself.) Take in the wall reliefs of Ay receiving rewards from Akhenaten, and Ay and Tiye worshipping the sun.

Royal Tomb of Akhenaten

Drive the dramatic, cliff-rimmed road into the Royal Valley (Wadi Darb Al Malek) to visit the **Royal Tomb of Akhenaten**. This valley was where Akhenaten's royal city saw the sun rise each day and where he planned to be buried. If you've bought the separate ticket to visit this tomb, you'll probably pick up the site guardian on the road along the way and he'll need your driver to stop just before the site so he can start up the tomb's generator.

The tomb warren here is huge, with passages leading to separate chambers, but little remains of the wall reliefs, as they were painted on plaster and much has fallen off, so it's probably only worth visiting if you're seriously into the Amarna period. In the large right-hand burial chamber, note the rectangular outline on the floor. This once held the chamber's sarcophagus, which is now in Cairo's Egyptian Museum (having been repatriated from Germany).

CENTRAL CITY RUINS

If you're really into the history of Akhenaten's reign, stop at the Central City Ruins, which hold the (very scant) remnants of the palace and the **Great Temple of Aten** complex that contained a sanctuary and a 190m Long Temple divided into six courts. Most Tell Al Amarna visitors don't stop here though, so make sure to tell your driver you want to visit them.

TOP TIPS

● Nasser, at the site entrance rest house (which serves tea and has cold drinks for sale), is a fount of information on the site and can be hired as a guide for the less visited city ruins.

● Even if the security situation allowed for it, getting to Tell Al Amarna by public transport would be tricky and the site is extensive, which means it's impossible to tackle on foot. The easiest way to visit is with a taxi/private driver from Minya.

● Be sure to specify which areas you want to visit or your driver may refuse to go to the more far-flung sites.

Asyut

ANCIENT MONASTERIES | MOUNTAINSIDE TOMBS | OFF-PATH EXPLORATION

☑ TOP TIP

Some tours attempt to race through Asyut's attractions on long day trips from Minya, but you're better off spending at least a night here, for time to visit some of the area's less seen sites.

GETTING AROUND

As in Minya, security protocols make the train the only practicable public transport option to connect other regional hubs, with frequent connections north (to Minya and Cairo) and south (to Sohag, Qena and Luxor). Asyut's station marks the centre of town, between the souq and the Corniche. Each hop costs LE10–15 by taxi. Tourist police will insist on knowing your every move, even within town, but may or may not join your walks (it helps to appear to know where you're going). The same applies for excursions beyond town: count on a police escort tagging along.

The guardian *(sioot)* of the border between Upper and Lower Egypt, Asyut is the region's largest city and Egypt's Coptic heartland. Proportionally speaking, more Christians live here than anywhere else in the country, so it's no surprise that it hides some heavyweight Coptic pilgrimage sites. On its desolate margins are rarely seen Old and Middle Kingdom tombs, making Asyut a worthy base for day trips.

Few linger in the city, though traces of its storied past abound, particularly up the spine of Al Qaysaria, the old souq, which was once the terminus of the infamous Darb Al Arba'een (see p300). Its covered stretch is speckled with urban caravanserai *(wakalat)*, venerable mosques and baths. Downtown by the Nile, you'll glimpse (through locked gates) a bevy of elegant colonial villas, further fuelling the feeling that Asyut's potential for tourism has scarcely been tapped.

Old & Middle Kingdom Colours
The sand-swept Tombs of Mir

Though within sight of the Nile Valley, there's a desolate feel to the escarpment holding the **Tombs of Mir** *(LE100)*, 62km northwest of Asyut, which the Old and Middle Kingdom nomarchs of Cusae chose for their necropolis. The nine tombs here comprise a fascinating counterpart to other tomb sites.

Among the first cluster of tombs that you'll reach up the steps, all belonging to 12th-dynasty nomarchs, the impressive Tomb 4 was never finished, as attested by the original, uncoloured grids of its hunting and agricultural scenes. The 6th-dynasty tombs north and south both require a further trudge along the ridge. The much shorter walk to the north is more worthwhile, as its tombs, half-buried by dunes, are the most colourful of the lot.

Pilgrimage to Deir Al Muharraq
The Coptic 'second Bethlehem'

Just 8km southeast of the nomarchs' tombs, you'll encounter the fortress-like gates of **Deir Al Muharraq** (The Burnt Monastery;

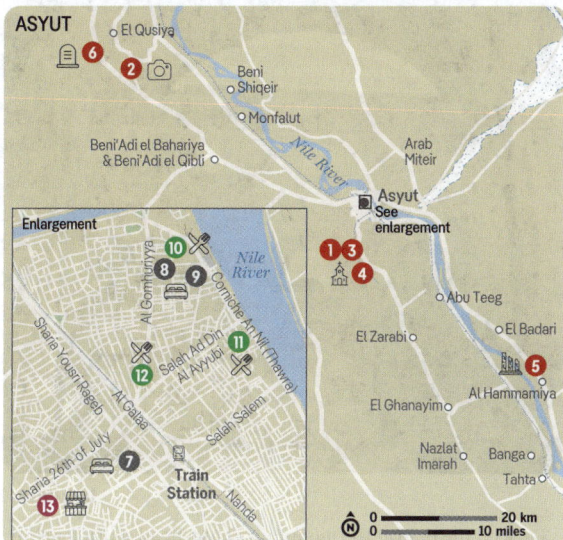

free), a hive of monastic activity since the 4th century CE. What most sets Al Muharraq apart is its role, according to the Coptic tradition, in hosting the Holy Family for six months and 10 days (making it the longest sojourn during their flight into Egypt). Attesting to its holiness is the constant flow of pilgrims from across the length of the Nile. One of the 50 or so monks and nuns who live here usually offers to show you around.

Past the third set of massive walls that guard the approach, turn right to follow the signs to the 'ancient church'. Remove your shoes before entering the sanctuary. Dividing the altar from the sanctuary inside are two iconostases (wooden screens). The first (on your left) belonged to an Ethiopian church that stood on the roof until 1936, while the second, from the 16th century, has inlaid ivory crosses and fish representing the Gospels.

Deir Dirunka & Deir Rifeh

Coptic monasteries and cave churches

South of Asyut, a 10km drive will land you at the base of **Deir Dirunka** (Convent of the Holy Virgin), another monastic complex entered through an enormous set of gates. The ascent is dominated by a 22m-tall statue of the Virgin Mary, built in 2023. It commemorates the most recent of several miraculous apparitions believed to have manifested here.

The end of the road brings you close to the heart of the complex, the cavernous **Church of the Virgin Mary**, cutting deep into the mountain with a pair of gated caves at the far end, left of the entrance. According to the faithful, these were the southernmost lodgings of the Holy Family on their celebrated journey. Removed to the right, another chapel enclosed by the mountain is dedicated to Anba Mikhail (1920–2014), the late, larger-than-life bishop who's credited for cementing Dirunka's prominence on the Coptic map.

HOLY FAMILY TRAIL

In the early 5th century, the Coptic Pope Theophilus reported a vision at Deir Al Muharraq. In this, the Virgin Mary recounted her flight from King Herod's wrath into Egypt, Joseph and the infant Jesus in tow. It was a zigzagging route, since developed into a pilgrimage path now known as the **Holy Family Trail**, stretching from the Delta southward, deep into Upper Egypt. According to Theophilus' vision, it was at Al Muharraq that an angel informed the Holy Family of Herod's death: the coast was clear for their return. And so, according to the monks at Al Muharraq, they did. A rival claim at Deir Dirunka, however, places their journey's end 50km further south.

ASYUT'S WESTERN MOUNTAIN

Asyut's tourism potential is most glaring in the tomb-studded mountain abutting its southwestern border: **Gebel Asyut Al Gharbi**. It's home to some 300 tombs, among them the largest of any nomarch in Middle Egypt (the Tomb of Djefaihapi I). Archaeological efforts, though (long having consisted of shipping its unplundered treasures to the museums of Cairo, Paris, London and Turin), are only recently catching up. The area was cordoned off as a military zone in the 1960s, and it wasn't until 2003 that access was granted to a German-Egyptian team that continues to turn up undisturbed burial chambers, coffins and stores of canopic jars. For now, though, tourists must settle for admiring the mountain from afar.

Deir Rifeh

Back on the road at the mountain's base, head south for a further 5km to the town of **Deir Rifeh**, above which appears an unmissable cluster of Middle Kingdom tombs, some repurposed by early Christian monks. Before heading up, call in at the town proper's Church of the Amir Tadros to alert the custodian. If they haven't joined yet, the police will tag along for your visit. From the mountain roadside, a modern stairway leads to the largest church, dedicated to Tadros, a 4th-century martyr, commander and dragon-slayer to boot. Up another stairway to the left, the smaller Church of the Virgin Mary is no less evocative.

Exploring Asyut's Eastern Tombs

The Tombs of Al Hammamiya

Some 50km south of Asyut is the village of **Al Hammamiya**. The area is the hub of the pre-dynastic Badari culture, preceding by over a thousand years the far more visible Pharaonic traces in the cliffs north of town. Here, a modern stairway climbs over the Muslim cemetery to connect with a trio of **decorated tombs** *(LE100; 2 open to visitors)* of the 5th-dynasty governors of Upper Egypt's 10th nome. The second is especially impressive and well preserved, adorned with reliefs and statues of its owner, Kai-khent, and his wife, Iufy, a priestess of Hathor. Able hikers can continue climbing in a bit of a scramble to a giant, chiselled cave above the tombs, known to locals as the *mahkama* (court).

 EATING AND DRINKING IN ASYUT: OUR PICKS

Abou Shakra: Friendly service in a sparkling setting with classic grilled-meat plates (kebab, kofta and *shish tawooq*) plus *tagens* and desserts. *10am-1am* $$

Al Hamd Sea Food: Asyut's first port of call for fresh fish: great soups and starters and your pick of tilapia, perch and bass on ice. *noon-11pm* $$

Domiati: Take-away only breakfast favourite on Sharia Al Gomhoreya, cranking out delicious street food staples: *fuul*, *'egga* (Egyptian omelette) and *ta'amiyya*. *6am-2am* $

Assiutel Hotel: The unpretentious, 10th-storey bar of this Nile-side hotel is about the only place in town where you can find a cold Stella. *noon-2am*

Sohag

COPTIC MARVELS | FORGOTTEN TEMPLES | PHARAONIC RELICS

The Nile-side sprawl of Sohag, a modern, provincial capital descended from the east bank's ancient city of Akhmim, can resemble an overgrown village. Even close to its centre, agricultural plots break up sprouts of mid-rise apartment blocks and the too-narrow roads are forever traffic-jammed by rumbling produce trucks, zippy tuk-tuks and clopping horses and carts.

Nevertheless, to base here is to place yourself within easy reach of quite the enviable line-up of cultural, historical and architectural delights, not least the heavyweight temple complex of Abydos (p183), an hour-and-a-half-drive to the south. Right on the city's own doorstep awaits a pair of venerable Coptic churches, pressed against the desert in their walled monastic compounds. The Red Monastery is particularly stunning, its sanctuary's frescoes a true medieval marvel to behold. Among other ruins scattered nearby are the Ptolemaic temples of Athribis and, high on the opposite end of the valley, the rock-hewn Tombs of Al Hawawish.

A Masterclass in Coptic Art
The Red and White Monasteries

Prepare to be dazzled when you step into the **Red Monastery** (Deir Al Ahmar), one of late antiquity's most remarkable surviving buildings. Inside the monastery's **Sanctuary of St Bishoi & St Bigol** you come face to face with a frenzy of design. The triple apses surrounding the altar are crowned with frescoed semi-domes and the ornamented stonework below, with its multiple niches and columns, is completely covered with colourful, decorative patterns and paintings of monks, bishops and saints.

The sanctuary dates from 500 CE and most of the paintings date from the 6th and 7th centuries. Outside the sanctuary, the column-aisled, open-air courtyard was once the church's nave. The walls here offer a strange and beautiful jumble of large, ornate crosses and decorative roundels that were painted during the medieval era.

> **TOP TIP**
>
> Most of Sohag's accommodation is on the Nile Corniche Rd or around Sohag train station. Sohag's museum (the only central sight) is on the eastern bank, just north of Akhmim Bridge. The Red and White Monasteries are 11km and 8km east of the centre, respectively.

> **GETTING AROUND**
>
> Sohag enjoys Middle Egypt's strictest security protocols; the train is the only viable public transport option. At the station you'll be met by police, whose company you can expect for even short hops across town. Expect the same when sightseeing and expect it to be disorganised. Most Sohag taxi drivers are willing to be hired for day trips around the Sohag area. To minimise delays, give your itinerary in advance to the policeman stationed outside your hotel and, fingers crossed, he'll relay that to his boss.

⭐ HIGHLIGHTS
1. Red Monastery

🔴 SIGHTS
2. Akhmim
3. Athribis
4. Basuna Mosque
5. Monastery of the Martyrs of Akhmim
6. Sohag National Museum
7. Tombs of Al Hawawish
8. White Monastery

🔵 SLEEPING
9. Al Amir Palace Hotel
10. Diamond Azur Hotel
11. Grand Hotel Abo El-Wafa

🟢 EATING
12. Abo Sleem
13. Abu Salah
14. Koshary Goha
15. Pesca

MARTYRS OF AKHMIM

Overshadowed by Sohag's pair of monasteries to the west is its eastern cluster on the valley's opposite margins: eight monasteries, each very much alive with devotion. Each of them draws on the resolute faith of the 4th-century Coptic community of Akhmim, who bravely endured an especially bloodthirsty bout of persecution here. Roman governor Arianus, a sadistic hunter of Christians under Emperor Diocletian, is said to have overseen the killing of 8140 local Christians. Recently exhumed, supposed relics are encased in glass at many of these monasteries, the lion's share on display at the **Monastery of the Martyrs of Akhmim**.

The astonishing state of preservation, particularly in the sanctuary, is thanks first to a brick wall, which from the 18th century covered the apse area to prevent its collapse and inadvertently protected the paintings up to its removal in 1909, and second to painstaking restoration works finally completed in 2018.

The **White Monastery**, 3km south along the road back to Sohag, is also known as the Church of St Shenoute, after a hermit who founded the monastery in roughly 400 CE. Its other name refers to the limestone used in its construction, scavenged from Pharaonic sites such as nearby Athribis. Inside its 13m-high walls, speckled with upside-down hieroglyphs, its sanctuary is plainer than that of the Red Monastery, though adorned with ancient columns, shell-capped niches and 12th-century frescoes.

Entry is free to both monasteries and they're open from approximately 7am to dusk. Take your shoes off before entering.

Side Trip for Modern Architecture Fans
An award-winning contemporary mosque

At the centre of Basuna village, 18km north of Sohag, stands the innovative **Basuna Mosque**, built in 2019 to synthesise sustainable architecture with Islamic principles.

Inside, the prayer hall's tranquillity is preserved by the near-absence of windows, cocooning the interior from noise, dust and heat while the roof provides natural light and ventilation. Echoed in the dome's pattern is the 'cube-on-cube' design of the mihrab, representing the 99 names of Allah. Visit between 9am and 11am or 1pm and 3pm to avoid prayer times.

Sohag's Pharaonic Collection
National museum and colossi of Akhmim

It won't take you more than 20 minutes to circle the two floors of the **Sohag National Museum** *(adult/student LE200/100)* on the east bank of the Nile. But its carefully chosen pieces offer a rounded approach to exploring Egypt's past, with plenty of context on day-to-day life in ancient Egypt and the enduring reach of Pharaonic rituals and traditions. It's open 9am to 2.30pm.

Just 5km east of Sohag, its satellite town of **Akhmim** sits on the site of ancient Ipu (Panopolis during Graeco-Roman times), dedicated to the fertility god Min and a major weaving centre during antiquity. Right in the centre of town, an **excavation pit** *(adult/student LE100/50)* hosts two colossal, 11m-high statues, discovered in 1981. Beside Ramses II stands Meret Amun, the Pharaoh's daughter, priestess of the Temple of Min. It's the largest statue of this queen found anywhere in Egypt.

Sohag's Old Kingdom Tombs
Touring the Tombs of Al Hawawish

Head 15km east from Sohag to the craggy escarpment home to the **Tombs of Al Hawawish** *(adult/student LE150/75; LE10 for parking)*, opened to the public in 2021. Get here early to beat the heat (it's open 7am to 4pm) and be prepared for some serious stairs. This was ancient Akhmim's necropolis and there are over 800 tombs dating from the Old Kingdom and First Intermediate Period, chiselled high up into the cliff face here. Of the five open tombs (95, 22, 43, 24 and 26), the paintings in Tomb 26 are the most rewarding for the uphill trudge. Illustrating the life of 'Ka Hep', its walls are decked with scenes of acrobats, dancing, fishing and a still-vivid coloured wheat-harvesting panel.

Alone at Ancient Athribis
Ptolemaic temple ruins and reliefs

Curled at the foot of a mountain honeycombed with quarries some 4km south of the White Monastery is **Athribis** *(adult/student LE150/75)*, a city whose temple complex was devoted to the lion-headed goddess Repit. Construction here spanned two centuries, from late Ptolemaic to Roman times, after which the great bulk of its blocks was repurposed (particularly for the monasteries nearby), but you'll still find a wealth of reliefs, with over a thousand inscriptions filling several dozen rooms.

The German team here since 2003 has placed QR-linked panels to guide you around the temple. In 2024, excavations unearthed a separate temple at the mountain's base. Indeed, a majority of the archaeological area remains to be uncovered.

BEHIND THE BASUNA MOSQUE

Waleed Arafa is the architect of the Basuna Mosque and founder of Dar Arafa Architecture. *@dar_arafa_architecture*

In creating the mosque, I wanted the design to provide a connection with the few remaining examples of Basuna's traditional architecture and restore pride in this heritage.

I also wanted to re-establish the original purpose of a mosque in the community, not used only as a place for prayer but functioning inclusively, where everyone, no matter their gender or religion, feels welcome. The multi-purpose hall introduces a community centre space, which can be used for vocational and education classes and medical clinics, benefiting all rather than the mosque being used only for a few hours each day.

🍴 EATING IN SOHAG: OUR PICKS

Abo Sleem Restaurant: On the Corniche, this family restaurant specialises in kofta, *sambousek* (parcels of meat and cheese) and soups. *10am-midnight* **$$**

Koshary Goha: Sohag's best *kushari;* separate seating for women and families. Order a small to leave room for *ruz bi laban* (rice pudding). *7am-midnight* **$**

Pesca: There's no English menu at this bright, airy juice bar, but you'll find helpful staff and pictures of the colourful cocktails and inventive desserts. *9am-1am* **$**

Abu Salah: Chain beloved for its succulent chicken shish kebabs and mixed grills plus *molokhiyya*. Find one just southwest of the station. *10am-2am* **$$**

Beyond Sohag

Home to Abydos and the enchanting Temple of Seti I, one of ancient Egypt's most venerated sites.

GETTING AROUND

The most common, straightforward way to visit is via private transfer from Luxor (often visiting Dendara too). On your own, your best bet is the train, alighting at the town of Balyana (roughly 10km east of Abydos). From the station you'll easily hail an onward ride to Abydos (tuk-tuk LE75; taxi LE150). For trips to the south of Balyana, foreigners are also welcome on microbuses from the *maw'af* (stop). From Qena, head first to Nag Hammadi (LE20, 1½ hours) to connect to Balyana (LE15, 45 minutes).

The swathe of Middle Egypt between Sohag and Qena, where the Nile Valley swerves to the east, sees more foreign travellers than anywhere else in the region thanks to the allure of ancient Abydos.

The centre of the cult of Osiris throughout the Pharaonic era, Abydos' Temple of Seti I is a breathtaking wonder, the walls of its pillared halls delicately etched with beautifully preserved reliefs. The expansive complex here was used as a necropolis from the pre-dynastic era right through to the Christian period (c 4000 BCE to 600 CE). Most visitors are whisked in and out on day tours, but it's worth sticking around a bit longer to soak up the ambience at your own pace.

Abydos

TIME FROM SOHAG: **1 HR 30 MINS**

Primordial monuments of the pharaohs

Less than a kilometre north of the splendid **Abydos** temple complex of Seti I and Ramses II, exemplars of an artistic style at its apex, stands the funerary enclosure of **Shunet El Zebib** *(adult/student LE100/50)*, one of Egypt's earliest Pharaonic sites. Approaching by road, you'll spot the hulking, fortresslike rectangle off to the left, ringed with gargantuan mud-brick walls rising 12m tall and embellished with pilasters and niches. It was built for the 2nd-dynasty Pharaoh Khasekhemwy, whose actual tomb (along with those of the very first pharaohs) is nearby at Umm Al Qaab ('Mother of Shards'; closed), about 1.5km south towards the ridge. Stretched to the right of the approach, the other enormous, ancient mud-brick wall is what remains of **Kom El Sultan** *(entry included),* the original temple complex for the worship of Osiris.

Note that the ticket for Shunet El Zebib and Kom El Sultan is separate from the Abydos temple complex and includes neither transport nor tips. Though it's an easy walk from the temples, police require that tourists arrive by car, taxi or tuk-tuk, accompanied by a local inspector.

KHALED DESOUKI/AFP VIA GETTY IMAGES

TOP EXPERIENCE

Temple of Seti I at Abydos

This limestone masterpiece is the work of Seti I (reigned c 1294–1279 BCE) and his son Ramses II (reigned c 1279–1213 BCE). The painted carvings adorning the walls in the older (Seti I) section of the temple are among the finest, highest quality and best preserved you will see in Egypt. It's a magnificent spectacle of New Kingdom artistry that never fails to impress.

DID YOU KNOW?

Built less than 50 years after the Amarna 'heresy' (when Pharaoh Akhenaten broke with tradition by creating a new religion and artistic style), this temple attempts to revive the old ways.

Temple of Seti I Entrance

As you walk from the visitor centre, across and up the open courtyards built by Ramses II, the broad, columned **portico** of the **Temple of Seti I** rises up before you. This portico was the work of Ramses II, seen on the reliefs here worshipping Osiris and slaughtering Hittites at the Battle of Kadesh, a clash that is among the most celebrated stalemates in all of history. Enter the temple through the portico's central doorway, just one of the seven doorways that originally led to the First Hypostyle Hall.

PRACTICALITIES
- adult/student LE260/130
- 7am–5pm, last entry 4pm
- Scan to purchase tickets

PLACE OF PILGRIMAGE

As early as 4500 years ago, Osiris' myth made Abydos a place of pilgrimage, a role that's recently seen some revival with a stream of seekers detecting an energy here. Pioneering this trend was London-born Dorothy Eady, who died here in 1981. Known as Omm Seti ('Mother of Seti'), her work drew on 'memories' of a life as a temple priestess and concubine of the pharaoh.

TOP TIPS

● Consider staying the night in Abydos village (also called Al Araba Al Madfuna) to boost your odds of solitude at the sites. The bulk of the big tour coaches tend to visit between 10am and 3pm. Accommodation options include the **Flower of Life Guesthouse** (p189), near the exit to the Temple of Ramses II, and the upscale **House of Life** (p189), along the main road to the entrance.

● If hoping to visit Shunet El Zebib independently, minimise delay by arranging transport in advance (for yourself and an inspector) from the main temple entrance. Arrival on foot is not allowed.

Hypostyle Halls

In the **First Hypostyle Hall** you're still in the younger part of the temple, added by Ramses II. It's studded with 12 pairs of bulbous, relief-inscribed columns, its walls adorned with further images of the pharaoh.

Another set of seven gates leads into the **Second Hypostyle Hall**, which was the last temple section to be decorated by Seti I, who died before its completion. The finely detailed, colourful reliefs in this older temple are regarded as some of the New Kingdom's greatest artistic achievements. On the rear right-hand wall you'll spot Seti I standing in front of a shrine to Osiris, upon which sits the god himself. Standing before him are the goddesses Maat, Renpet, Isis, Nephthys and Amentet, just over a frieze of the Nile god Hapi.

Sanctuaries

At the rear of the Second Hypostyle Hall are the seven **sanctuaries** of the temple's gods (from right to left: Horus, Isis, Osiris, Amun-Ra, Ra-Horakhty, Ptah and a deified Seti I himself). The colours of Amun-Ra's shrine, restored in 2022, are particularly dazzling.

Turn left from the sanctuaries to enter a series of rooms carved with reliefs depicting the mysteries of Osiris, including a scene with Isis as a bird, hovering above a mummified Osiris.

Gallery of the Kings

Head left from the Second Hypostyle Hall into the temple's famous **Gallery of the Kings**, where the walls show Seti I, his eldest son (the future Ramses II) and a list of the pharaohs who preceded them. Midway along, head right to climb the stairs leading out to the Osireion.

Osireion

Directly behind the Temple of Seti I is the **Osireion**, a unique structure that continues to baffle Egyptologists. It's usually interpreted as a cenotaph or dummy tomb to Seti I as Osiris. Unfortunately, entry is closed to the general public (special permission required from the Ministry of Antiquities), but visitors can peer from above into the mysterious complex and its central hall of unadorned granite, ringed with water channels to simulate an island.

Temple of Ramses II

Only a few minutes' walk to the north, the smaller **Temple of Ramses II** sees only a trickle arriving along the desert trail as little remains of its humbler pair of hypostyle halls. But the reliefs are impressive in the sunlight, many again depicting the glories of Kadesh, while the inner sanctum at the back still houses a massive granite statue of (left to right) Ramses II, Horus, Osiris, Isis and Seti I, though all but the last two are defaced.

Qena

ANCIENT COLOURS | HYPOSTYLE HALLS | ISLAMIC SHRINES

This provincial capital of mid-rise concrete blocks sits on a huge bend of the Nile. It doesn't look like much at first, but it's got one big trick up its sleeve. Across the river is the temple complex at Dendara, one of Egypt's most astonishing sites.

As it remains largely intact, there are few better places to experience how entering a temple in ancient times might have felt: under its great stone roof, gazing up at its massive Hathor-headed columns, entering its shadowy chambers, all carved with coloured hieroglyphs.

With Dendara checked off, most visitors make a beeline for nearby Luxor or the Red Sea. But linger in town to find one of the Nile's friendliest cities, home to a buzzing old souq and famed for its Mosque of Sidi Abd Al Rahim Al Qenawi, the focal point of one of Egypt's greatest Sufi festivals.

The Mosque of Sheikh Al Qenawi
Qena's Sidi Abd Al Rahim Al Qenawi Mosque

Just north of the canal , a slender white minaret marks the city's landmark **mosque**, dedicated to its patron saint Abd Al Rahim Al Qenawi. A beloved Sufi teacher from Morocco, Sheikh Al Qenawi is believed to have died in Qena at the end of the 12th century. His *moulid* (birthday celebration), culminating on the 14th of the Islamic month of Sha'ban, fills the city with pilgrims. Beyond prayerful solemnity, the festival summons uniquely Upper Egyptian traditions, including equestrian spectacles and *tahteeb,* an ancient martial art featuring long wooden poles. Such events can also be glimpsed around Qena during Moulid An Nabi (the Prophet's Birthday).

Throughout the rest of the year, it's relatively straightforward to visit the saint's gilded **shrine** *(free)*. Removing your shoes at the mosque entrance, you'll find the tomb set immediately under the main dome. The northwest entrance (around the corner to the left) serves female visitors, required to cover their heads with a scarf.

☑ TOP TIP

Most visitors to Dendara arrive on tours from Luxor or Hurghada. This means that if you overnight in Qena you can beat the day-trippers and have the temple pretty much to yourself.

GETTING AROUND

Qena's train station is set at the eastern end of Sharia Al Gomhoreya, the city's main street. Long-distance bus companies operate nearby. A taxi across town (from the train station to the Nile, for example) shouldn't charge more than LE30; for Dendara's temple no more than LE100. When visiting the temple, there's no need to have your taxi wait. The tourist police here will call one for you. The sprawling *maw'af* for microbuses is north of the centre by the Nile, linking Luxor (1½ hours) and Balyana (for Abydos; 2½ hours) via Nag Hammadi.

TOP EXPERIENCE

Dendara

The multiyear (still-ongoing) restoration of the walls, ceilings and columns inside the Temple of Hathor at Dendara allows you to see Pharaonic temple decoration as it would have originally looked – vivaciously coloured and crackling with energy. Don't miss a visit here. At the moment, there is nowhere else in the country where ancient Egypt's artistry feels so alive.

DON'T MISS

Ceiling paintings of sky goddess Nut

Western stairway reliefs

Osiris and Isis scenes on the roof

Chapel of the New Year

Crypt reliefs

Cleopatra and Caesarion relief

Dendara's Front Enclosure

You enter the complex's courtyard through the towering gateway standing among the remnants of Dendara's mud-brick walls. To the right of the courtyard, in front of the **Temple of Hathor**, you can see two *mammisi* (birth houses), built in celebration of divine birth, both of the young gods and the pharaohs themselves.

The first one, next to the enclosure wall, was built during the Roman era, its interior decorated during Emperor Trajan's

PRACTICALITIES
- adult/student LE300/150; rooftop panorama LE100/50; crypts LE100/50
- 7am-5pm, last entry 4pm
- Scan to purchase tickets

reign (98–117 CE). The one nearest to the temple is older, built by the 30th-dynasty pharaoh Nectanebo I (380–362 BCE), while the decoration inside was added later by the Ptolemies. Between the *mammisi* are the remnants of a 5th-century Coptic basilica, adorned with carved crosses and scallop-shell niches.

Entering the Temple of Hathor

Stepping inside, the first enclosure you'll reach is the **outer hypostyle hall** built by Roman Emperor Tiberius. Note that the entrance's first six columns are capped with Hathor heads on all four sides (though some have been defaced by Christians). The surrounding walls are carved with scenes of Tiberius and his successors presenting offerings to the Egyptian gods: the message here is the continuity of tradition even under foreign rule.

Now look up. The reliefs covering the Hathor-head columns and the colours of the ceiling's intricate and highly detailed zodiac relief scenes, with their vibrant blue backgrounds, have been wonderfully restored. Right of the entrance, on the far-western aisle of the hall, crane your neck to see the sky goddess Nut swallowing the sun disc.

Inner Hypostyle Hall

Next you'll enter the older portion of the temple, built by the Ptolemies. Studded with six more Hathor columns, the **inner hypostyle hall** is covered with scenes of royal ceremonies. The many blank cartouches in the reliefs reveal much about the political instability of late Ptolemaic times – with such a rapid turnover of pharaohs, the stonemasons seem to have been reluctant to carve the names of those who might not be in the job for long.

Sanctuary

From the inner hypostyle hall, your ascent continues past a pair of vestibules to the **sanctuary** of Hathor, where the goddess's image and sacred barque were kept. Right of the first vestibule, a set of stairs leads to the roof, while right of the second is the elevated **Chapel of the New Year**, its ceiling covered with a vibrant painting of the sky goddess Nut.

Another set of stairs here descends to one of the temple's 12 small **crypts**, sacred storerooms. As of writing, three could be entered, unlocked by site guardians. Clambering inside, squeeze your way down the corridor to examine the well-preserved carvings. In celebration of the New Year, which fell in July (coinciding with the rising of the waters of the Nile), Hathor's image was brought from the temple's sanctuary to this chapel before being carried up the stairs to the roof.

To the Temple Roof

To trace the New Year ritual's path, climb the smooth steps of the western stairway, decorated with scenes from the procession. Emerging at the top, the open-air kiosk to the right (southwest) is where the gods awaited the first rays of the sun god Ra on New Year's Day. The statues were later taken down the eastern staircase (where you'll exit the roof), decorated with this scene.

THE GODDESS HATHOR

Hathor was ancient Egypt's goddess of fertility, beauty, music and love, and the centre of her worship was at Dendara. She was depicted either with a cow head (as in the Hathor-headed columns inside Dendara), or as a woman wearing a sun disc between cattle horns as a headdress.

REPATRIATING THE DENDARA ZODIAC?

In 2022, 100 years after the Dendara Zodiac's placement in Paris' Louvre, it was listed alongside the Rosetta Stone (in London's British Museum) and the famous bust of Nefertiti (Berlin's Neue Museum) in a petition for the return of Egypt's 'stolen' artefacts, launched by the eminent Egyptologist and former minister of tourism and antiquities Zahi Hawass.

TOP TIPS

- Tour buses begin shuttling in from Luxor at around 8am. If you can get here by opening time (7am) you, and the handful of other early risers, get to enjoy the huge temple at its eerie, quiet best.

- The extra tickets (for the panoramic roof-terrace and crypts) are worthwhile. If you didn't buy them but happen to change your mind, the guardians at the site will usually give you a pass in exchange for a tip.

- Bring plenty of water. The (overpriced) refreshments available on site are at the tourist bazaar, a five-minute walk from the temple entrance.

The roof's two suites of rooms are covered with scenes of the revival of Osiris by his sister-wife Isis. In the northeastern suite look up to see the plaster cast of the **Dendara Zodiac** on the ceiling. The original of this famous astronomical bas-relief was blasted from the ceiling and carted off by the French in the 18th century and now resides inside the Louvre.

Nearby steps lead to the temple's rooftop terrace, situated over the front of the temple and offering breathtaking views of the remnants of Dendara's perimeter of huge, mud-brick walls.

Around the Temple of Hathor

Exiting the temple, turn right to wrap around its eastern wall. Its upper reaches here are studded with lion-headed gargoyles, used to cope with the occasional rainfall. All the exterior walls are decked with reliefs of the pharaohs paying homage to the gods. The most famous relief of the bunch is around the corner to the right, at the end of the south wall and immediately opposite a small Temple of Isis built by Octavian (Emperor Augustus): the only surviving **relief of Cleopatra**, standing with Caesarion (her son by Julius Caesar). Right of the relief, at the wall's centre you'll note the depression in the wall that once housed a large, gold-plated head of Hathor, the focal point for lay devotion to the goddess, whose shrine lies just past the wall.

Completing the circle, wrap around the main temple's western side to glimpse the deep, empty, sacred lake – with date palms sprouting from its bed, which supplied the temple's water – and the mud-brick foundations of the sanatorium where the ill came to seek a cure from Hathor.

Interior walls

Places We Love to Stay

$ Budget $$ Midrange $$$ Top End

Al Fayoum
MAP p163

Khazfista $ Friendly, family-run guesthouse in Tunis with four tidy rooms in a garden of sunflowers and an on-site pottery workshop.

Zad Al Mosafer $ Long-running budget favourite with a range of good rooms and a nice pool in the centre of Tunis.

Barefoot in Tunis $$ A trio of self-catering 'tiny houses', packed with quirky boho style beside a shaded garden.

Queen Hotel $$ This is a spotless, central stalwart offering excellent value and relative quiet despite its central position in Medinat Al Fayoum.

Lazib Inn Resort & Spa $$$ High-class boutique frippery in Tunis with individually styled suites, three pools and manicured gardens. Popular for wedding parties; steer clear on weekends.

Tzila Lodge $$$ In Tunis, rustic-chic rooms in neutral tones utilising natural elements in its design. Plus there's a pool, an on-site bakery (for fresh *fiteer*) and lake glimpses.

Minya
MAP p168

C-Boat $ Minya's budget pick, with small, well-appointed rooms floating off the Corniche and breakfast on the deck's cafe.

Omar El-Khayam Hotel $$ On a quiet, leafy street around the corner from the Corniche, this immaculate hotel sets the standard in Minya, with all manner of mod cons and extremely helpful, English-speaking staff.

Savoy $$ A century ago, khedives (viceroys of Egypt under Ottoman suzerainty) stayed at this hotel facing the railway station. Lovingly restored and reopened in 2024 after decades of decrepitude, it offers spectacular value for money, with elegant, high-ceilinged rooms and a rooftop terrace restaurant.

Holy Family Hotel $$ Immediately opposite the ancient church atop Gebel At Teir, this hotel boasts fabulous views over the Nile from its rooms and the rooftop terrace complete with a pool.

Horus Resort $$ This resort has a pool, Nile-front restaurant terrace and retro time-warp decor. Noisy on weekends but otherwise peaceful.

Asyut
MAP p176

Agyad $ Budget-friendly option west of the tracks, with basic but adequate rooms and a laid-back rooftop terrace cafe with great city views.

Al Watania Palace Hotel $$ Asyut's one resort-style hotel, with bland, tired facilities but friendly staff and a decent location.

Assiutel $$$ Old-fashioned (and overpriced) but still among the most convenient options in Asyut; its 10th-storey bar is the only place in town to find yourself a cold Stella.

Sohag
MAP p179

Al Amir Palace Hotel $ Passable budget rooms in the narrow streets just west of the Corniche.

Diamond Azur Hotel $$ Excellent-value pick in Sohag, with rooms boasting balconies over the Nile. Quality breakfast buffet and friendly, English-speaking staff.

Grand Hotel Abo El-Wafa $$ Central, ageing high-rise hotel with well-kept rooms, helpful staff and a good ground-floor restaurant.

Abydos
p182

Flower of Life Guesthouse $$ Long-time, family-run lodgings in the village with spartan rooms, home-cooked meals (half-board) and a rooftop view over the adjacent ruins of the Temple of Ramses II.

House of Life $$$ Around 750m up the road from the temple entrance, this mid-rise may have gone too far with mock-Pharaonic decor but boasts a wellness centre, a pool and comfortable, well-maintained rooms.

Qena
p185

Grand Hotel Qena $ Solid budget pick for its clean, bland (but noisy) rooms within an easy walk of the train station. If full, try the nearby and nearly identical Dream.

Hathor Hotel $$ Recently renovated Nile-side resort with a restaurant, pool and, by a rather wide margin, the most comfortable rooms in town.

Researched by
Dr Jenny Walker

Luxor

WHERE THE LIVING HONOUR THE DEAD

Famed for its temples and tombs, Luxor since the time of Thebes has been less about death and more about life – and the hope of extending it.

The wonders of Luxor need little introduction. Clustered around the Nile, the splendid ancient temples of the east bank and the exquisite tombs of the west bank represent one of the most extensive concentrations of antiquities in the world and have justly been attracting visitors for centuries. So complex is the ancient narrative here that it could take a lifetime to fathom it – and for Egyptologists, many of whom can be seen at work digging and sifting through the grains of the past around ancient Thebes, the site represents a career spent searching while living with the possibility that there will be no reward for effort. In a sense, it was the same for the ancient Egyptians, who invested mightily in the afterlife with, of course, no promise of success.

Many of today's visitors follow punishing itineraries that press them around more monuments in two days than it's reasonable to absorb in a lifetime, and for them the focus similarly falls squarely both on the past and on the future, which is dominated by the next stop on the tour. Between the two, there's no space for the present.

There's an antidote in the underrated activity of sitting still. All along the banks of the Nile are sanctuaries of shade where you can enjoy a glass of mint tea and watch modern Luxor go about its business. How else to notice the snake charmer scooping their companion out of its bag and waving it menacingly at a boater? How else to notice the sun glancing off a temple facade, church dome or communications mast, or the wind filling the sails of a felucca between ferries lumbering upstream?

The Luxor day is a soundscape of activity: outboard motors, peeping cars, calls to prayer, wailing love songs and modern rap, and the tap-tapping of chisel on stone in a continuity of masonry skills that date back thousands of years. Sparrows and bulbuls join in the chatter of competing harmony and discord as two grey herons and a squadron of ibises flap along to check out the action and vendors shout, 'Welcome to Luxor!'

THE MAIN AREAS

EAST BANK
Luxor's beating heart, flanked by temples. **p198**

GEZIRA
Sleepy rim of west bank monuments. **p207**

THE VALLEY OF THE KINGS
Magnificent tombs buried in the mountains. **p211**

For places to stay in Luxor, see p229

THE GUIDE

LUXOR

From left: Artisans in Luxor (p227); Tomb of Ramses VI (p216), Valley of the Kings

THE VALLEY OF THE QUEENS
Tombs rivalling those of the kings. **p217**

WEST BANK TEMPLES
Assorted antiquities between desert and Nile. **p221**

THE WIDER NECROPOLIS
Where current digs unearth daily treasures. **p225**

Find Your Way

Luxor is defined by the Nile. Once separating the living from the dead, this great river still divides the modern city of the east bank from its more rural twin on the west bank. Shuttling between the two is a flotilla of boats, making it feasible to sample both in a day.

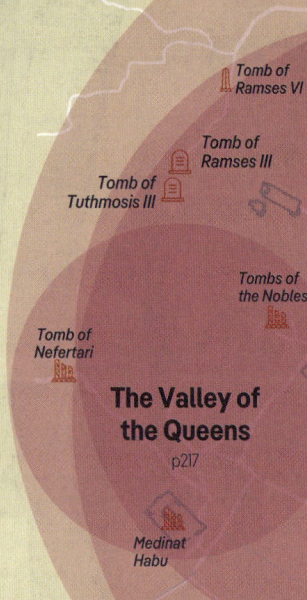

FROM THE AIRPORT

Taxis are readily available for the 20-minute, 10km journey from Luxor airport to the centre of town (LE200 to LE800; bargaining required).

TAXI & BAROUCHE

On the east bank, taxi drivers compete with the owners of horse-drawn *barouches* (carriages) to win fares. Both can be quite persistent in their efforts to get passengers on board. Fares are cheap (from LE50 depending on your haggling skills!) but are best agreed in advance.

FERRY & FELUCCA

There's a frequent public ferry (one way/return LE50/60) or it's easy to take one of the colourful, pennant-waving motorboats for the hop between riverbanks (LE100). You can charter these or take a felucca for a longer trip along the Nile (LE500 per hour).

TUK-TUK & BICYCLE

On the quieter west bank, three-wheeler tuk-tuks shuttle visitors around the antiquities (LE200 per half-day).

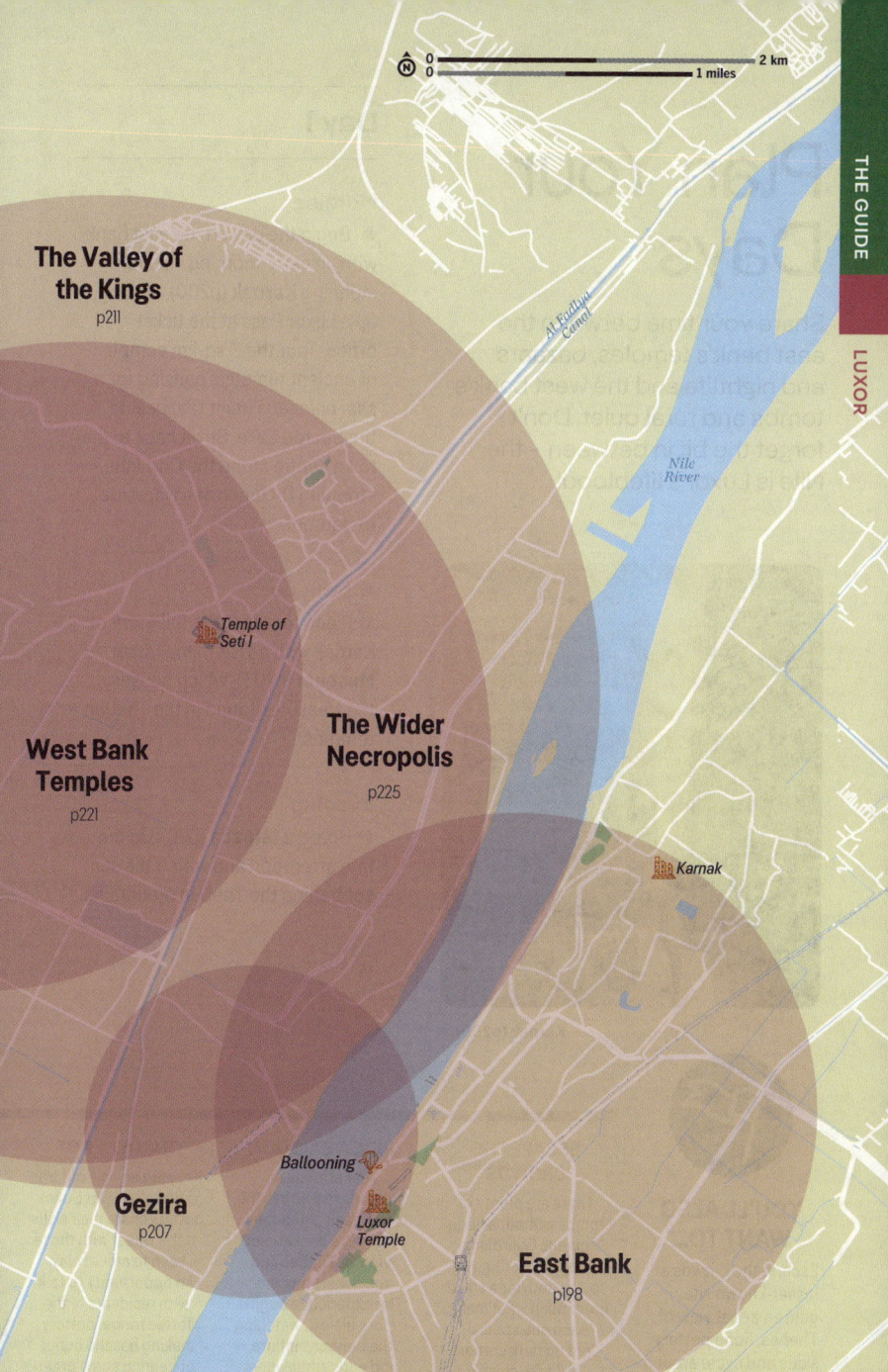

Plan Your Days

Share your time between the east bank's temples, bazaars and nightlife and the west bank's tombs and rural quiet. Don't forget the bit in between – the Nile is Luxor's lifeblood!

Karnak (p200)

Day 1

Morning

● Begin the day on the east bank with an early-morning visit to stunning **Karnak** (p200), picking up a Luxor Pass at the ticket office. Tour the 2-sq-km complex of ancient temples, pausing for *shai balnaana* (mint tea) beside the Sacred Lake. Stroll back to the town centre along the Corniche, stopping for lunch at a Nile-side restaurant.

Afternoon

● Piece together the full glory of Karnak with a visit to the **Luxor Museum** (p203), which houses the treasures found in the Theban temples.

Evening

● Board a **felucca** (p204) in the late afternoon and watch the sun set behind the Theban mountains.

YOU'LL ALSO WANT TO...

Escape the crowds at lesser-known sites, gain an aerial view of Thebes, hone pottery skills and cycle around the Nile's green fringe.

ESCAPE THE CROWDS

There are plenty of tombs without a huge queue. Guardians unlock lesser-known tombs and, for a small tip, explain what makes each one special, light up dark corners and take classic photographs.

RIDE A BALLOON

Just after dawn balloons rise above the west bank antiquities, offering a basket-side view of Thebes and the desert beyond. The experience begins before lift-off, watching the balloons inflate, and ends somewhere downwind.

THROW A POT

Keeping an age-old tradition alive, west-bank potters share their skills at the wheel with those keen to mould clay. An opportunity to talk with residents of the fertile fringe, pottery making has the bonus of hearing some great stories.

Day 2

Morning
- Spend the day on the west bank, greeted by the great seated **Colossi of Memnon** (p207). Enjoy the early-morning light tracing the hieroglyphics of the **Ramesseum** (p222) and contemplate the nature of mortality among the fallen masonry, as did poets of old.

Afternoon
- Enjoy a local lunch before calling in at **Howard Carter's House** (p214). Share the thrill of the archaeologist's find by visiting **The Valley of the Kings** (p211).

Evening
- Beat a retreat via the mortuary temple of **Medinat Habu** (p224), turned golden at sunset, and reflect on the day at a riverside restaurant.

Day 3

Morning
- With an eye now for detail, head to **The Valley of the Queens** (p217) and its exquisite tomb decorations. Pause at the **Workmen's Village** (p219) to see how royal tomb artisans were honoured in death and then admire the **Mortuary Temple of Hatshepsut** (p221), a monument to their skills.

Afternoon
- Sit and enjoy Theban tranquillity before heading back over the river. Pick mid-afternoon to explore graceful **Luxor Temple** (p202) before following in Pharaonic footsteps along the 3km **Avenue of Sphinxes** (p198).

Evening
- Shop for souvenirs while waiting for Karnak's **sound-and-light show** (p205) and end with a tour of modern Luxor by *barouche*.

THE GUIDE

LUXOR

ARRIVE BY TRAIN, LEAVE BY BOAT
Although you can fly in and out of Luxor, it's much more memorable to arrive on the overnight train from Cairo, with all its creaking eccentricities, and leave on a cruise ship for Aswan.

LEARN ABOUT MUMMIES
Describing preservation practices, the Mummification Museum offers a surprisingly touching experience. You'll see the remains of revered animals, including the small, leathery bodies of crocodiles, once frequent in the Nile.

WATCH ARCHAEOLOGISTS AT WORK
Archaeological work continues around the west bank, with a tomb just unearthed thought to belong to Tuthmosis II. Watching them work reveals the patience required to make history talk.

GO SHOPPING
Bartering for goods can be fun, whether it's a melon at the weekly vegetable market, paper from a papyrus workshop or hand-loomed cotton from a textile-weaving centre on the west bank or the east-bank bazaar.

HELP ME PICK:

Temples & Tombs

With more temples and tombs than can possibly be absorbed in the average three-day visit, it pays to do some planning to help prioritise the sights. Plan at least one day on each bank, and be sure to add a day to explore the Nile itself. Be prepared to be flexible, though, as not all tombs are open to the public every day and you may run out of energy, especially in the summer heat.

Which site to head for if you love...

Top Temples

Karnak Temple Complex (p200) This east-bank complex is the most impressive of all Luxor's sites, famous for superb hypostyle halls.

Luxor Temple (p202) Golden in the afternoon sun, this temple graces the east bank of the Nile and gave the town its name.

Tomb of Menna, Tombs of the Nobles

Mortuary Temple of Hatshepsut (p221) This elegant west-bank temple was built to face the Temple of Karnak across the Nile.

Medinat Habu (p224) The grand mortuary temple of Ramses III, this is one of the west bank's treasures.

Ramesseum (p195) Look for a pair of giant feet in this temple complex belonging to 'Ozymandias' (Ramses II) and trace around them remnants of the enormous trunk.

Must-visit Tombs

Tomb of Tuthmosis III (KV 34) This tomb, at the most southern reach of the Valley of the Kings, is ingenious in its design, reached via a steep staircase rising 20m above the valley floor.

Tomb of Seti I (KV 17) Cut 137m into the rock and lavishly decorated, this tomb's astronomical ceiling was the first of its kind.

Tomb of Tutankhamun (KV 62) This small tomb of a pharaoh who died young was overlooked by robbers and archaeologists until Howard Carter's epic discovery in 1922.

Tomb of Nefertari (p220) Walk into this celebrated Valley of the Queens tomb and you'll find yourself under a canopy of golden stars.

Tomb of Ramses VII (KV 1) (p213) and **Tomb of Ramses IV (KV 2)** (p213) Coptic crosses and inscriptions overlay the painting near the entrance of each tomb. KV 2 was even used as a hotel for early visitors.

Domestic Details

Tombs of the Nobles (p225) For an inkling of daily life 3500 years ago, head to the 6th-dynasty Tombs of the Nobles. More funerary chapel than tomb, they are boldly decorated with paintings (rather than reliefs).

Tomb of Nakht (p225) With its famous images of a blind harpist and three dancers, hunting scenes and rural life, the Tomb of Nakht is the best preserved of the Tombs of the Nobles.

Deir Al Medina (p219) The craftspeople and officials responsible for building Thebes lived next to the Valley of the Queens. Many were buried at Deir Al Medina in beautifully decorated tombs of their own.

Tomb of Seti I, Valley of the Kings

HOW TO

East and west bank Luxor's famous sites fall into three main categories: museums (on the east bank), temples (on both banks) and tombs (on the west bank).

Tickets Tickets for the Valley of the Kings, Valley of the Queens and Queen Hatshepsut's temple are bought on-site. All other tickets are bought on the day from the **Antiquities Inspectorate Ticket Office** (p207).

Tour agents Recommended local agents include **Jolleys Travel & Tours** (+20 100-997-7949) and **Far & Beyond** (farandbeyondtravel.com) near the Winter Palace Hotel, and **Go Luxor Tours** (goluxortours.com).

Hotel resources All hotels can arrange guided tours.

Deciphering the jargon

Bas relief Sculpture in 'low relief' protruding slightly from the background to appear in 3D.

Book of the Dead Ancient magic texts used to support the soul's anticipated onward journey.

Canopic jars Small vessels to store vital organs during mummification.

Hieroglyphics Ancient Egyptian writing system, composed of 1000 distinct characters.

Hypostyle hall A temple courtyard with ceiling set on massive pillars with decorated capitals.

Mortuary temple Part of the funerary complex of a pharaoh, standing between necropolis and Nile.

Mummification Process of embalming a body to preserve it after death.

Ostracon A piece of broken pottery used for writing. It functioned like a notepad does today.

Papyrus A parchment (early paper) made from papyrus stems that was used in ancient Egypt.

Pylon A monumental temple gateway made of two giant stone towers.

Sarcophagus A stone coffin used to encase a mummified corpse and then placed in a tomb.

Sphinx A sculpture featuring a human head and the body of a lion.

Theban necropolis Burial ground on the west bank of the Nile.

Thebes The ancient name for Luxor.

East Bank

LUXOR'S BEATING HEART, FLANKED BY TEMPLES

☑ TOP TIP

A premium Luxor Pass (visitor/student US$250/130) is valid for five days and covers all archaeological sites. A standard pass (US$130/70) excludes the Nefertari and Seti I tombs. The pass can only be purchased from Karnak and the Valley of the Kings (in US dollars; no credit cards) with a passport photograph.

GETTING AROUND

Most sights on Luxor's east bank are within easy walking distance. It's a short ferry trip to the west bank (one way/return LE50/60). It also connects Luxor Temple with Karnak.

Taxi drivers and horse-drawn *barouches* ply the Nile-side route between these two sights. It's important to haggle hard and agree on a price up front. You can walk between Luxor Temple and Karnak along the 3km Avenue of Sphinxes.

Stroll the Corniche of Luxor's east bank at sunset, when golden rays float across the Nile and settle on the lotus pillars of Luxor Temple, and it's obvious how the city earned its sobriquet as the greatest open-air museum in the world. Graced with ancient temples and two superb museums, the east bank is a treasure trove of remarkable sights.

Although the east bank has expanded away from the Nile, it has kept its small-town ambience. You'll feel it along the Avenue of Sphinxes, which connects the Temple of Luxor with Karnak. Pedestrianised, this newly restored ancient thoroughfare orients Luxor's two main sites of antiquity.

With so much from the past to explore, it's easy to overlook the present, but a tourist bazaar, shops, restaurants and cafes combine to make the east bank a vibrant traveller's destination. Sit beside the busy Nile at sunset and you'll find it's a hard place to leave.

Taking Shanks's Pony
Walking the Avenue of Sphinxes

There's bound to be a moment in your east bank experience when the unsolicited approaches of taxi driver, horse-carriage owner, felucca captain and ferry-boat pilot make you long for Shanks's pony. The good news for would-be walkers is that, thanks to the **Avenue of Sphinxes** *(6am-4pm)*, it's possible to stride along a 3km artery through the centre of town entirely free of vehicles.

Built and elaborated upon by four of Upper Egypt's great pharaohs, this broad esplanade was once flanked by ram's-headed sphinxes (a few of which remain) and was a processional way between Karnak and the Temple of Luxor. Signboards at the Luxor end of the avenue describe the splendour of the annual Opet celebrations that followed this route and document the thoroughfare's recently completed excavations.

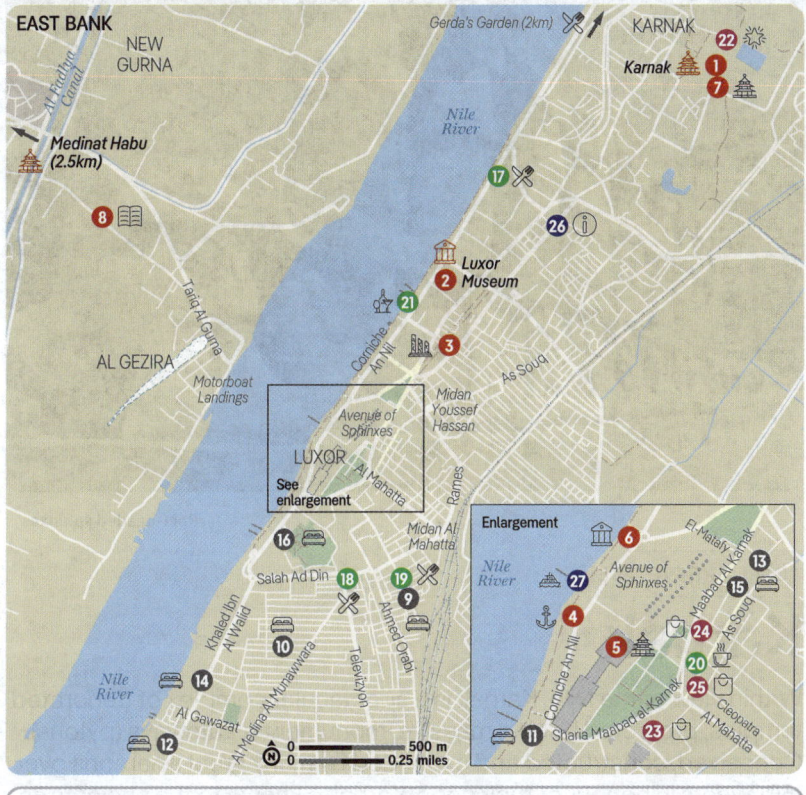

As many houses and a busy bazaar were demolished in the process of restoration, the project was not without its critics. For the visitor, though, it offers a tranquil stroll, some shaded seating, features such as wine presses, and (if walking north) arrival at the seldom-visited **Temple of Mut** by the 10th pylon at Karnak.

Tickets for the avenue are included in admission to the **Luxor Temple** *(visitor/student LE500/250, card only)*, but an additional ticket must be bought from outside the **Misr Public Library** to complete the walk into Karnak.

Ram-headed sphinxes

TOP EXPERIENCE

Karnak

Within view of the Nile, Karnak is a spectacular complex of decorated temples, protected behind massive, monumental gateways (pylons). Conceived, constructed and expanded by many great pharaohs over 1500 years in honour of their gods, Karnak – known to the ancients as Ipet-Sut (Most Esteemed of Places) – was Egypt's most significant site of worship. Today it's a Luxor highlight.

DON'T MISS

- View from the first pylon
- Great Hypostyle Hall
- Obelisk of Hatshepsut
- Sanctuary of Amun
- Sacred Lake
- Open-Air Museum
- Light show

Amun Temple Enclosure

Imagine owning 421,000 cattle, 65 cities, 83 ships and 276,400 hectares of agricultural land, worked by 81,000 people. This was **Amun Temple** at the height of its power, when the princes of Thebes ruled Egypt. They worshipped the local god Amun-Ra, and the temple, the biggest in Karnak, was built as his dwelling place on Earth, flanked by those of his wife Mut and their son Khonsu. Although sacked by Assyrians and Persians, this stunning edifice was considered a wonder even in ancient times.

PRACTICALITIES

- egymonuments.gov.eg/en/archaeological-sites/karnak
- visitor/student LE600/300
- 6am-8pm

First Pylon

Karnak is entered via a ramp above the quay where sacred barques, for transporting the triad of gods during Opet festivals, once moored. From here the first pylon looms majestically over a processional **avenue of ram-headed sphinxes**. Built like other such gateways to suggest a desert escarpment incised by a river, this unfinished masterpiece frames the sunrise and sunset and hints at the splendours spread along the east–west access beyond, each signalled by a pylon of its own.

Great Court

The first pylon leads into a large open court with three chapels for the sacred barques. Opposite lies the **Temple of Ramses III** – a miniature version of Medinat Habu. Three pharaohs contributed to the second pylon, including Ramses II, who is represented as giant red-granite statues flanking the gateway.

Great Hypostyle Hall

The second pylon opens into one of the wonders of Karnak: a forest of 134 columns that fill the enormous, 5500-sq-metre **Great Hypostyle Hall**. Each column resembles papyrus, which the ancients believed surrounded the primeval mound on which life was first created. Suggestive of a Nile swamp, they were designed to stand in water during the summer inundation.

Inner Temple

The third and fourth pylons lead to another hypostyle hall and the magnificent 30m-high **Obelisk of Hatshepsut**. One of a pair (the other, by the Sacred Lake, is truncated), it's the tallest in Egypt. Its tip was originally covered in electrum (a commonly used alloy of gold and silver).

Sanctuary of Amun

Beyond the ruined fifth pylon and small sixth pylon, with their columns of lotus and papyrus (symbols of Upper and Lower Egypt) and colossi of Amun and goddess Amunet, lies the sacred **Sanctuary of Amun**. Destroyed by Persians and rebuilt by Greeks, its Middle Kingdom Court is famous for the **Wall of Records**, a tally of tribute exacted from devotees of Amun. Of interest here too is the **Great Festival Hall of Tuthmosis III**, with columns imitating tent poles, referencing the military pharaoh's life under canvas, and the Botanical 'Gardens' – a vestibule depicting flora and fauna from Tuthmosis' campaigns abroad.

Secondary Axis

Not to be overlooked is Karnak's north–south access, punctuated by the seventh pylon (where thousands of discarded statues were discovered in 1903); the well-preserved eighth pylon, built by Queen Hatshepsut; the ninth pylon, giving access to the Temple of Khonsu; and the 10th pylon, near the Temple of Mut. Three beautiful chapels (white, red and alabaster) make the **Open-Air Museum** worth an extra fee.

SACRED LAKE

A highlight of Karnak is the **Sacred Lake**, where, according to Herodotus, the priests of Amun bathed nightly and twice daily for ritual purity. Flanking the lake is the Fallen Obelisk of Hatshepsut, only the top half of which remains, showing the queen's coronation. It's said that walking seven times clockwise around a **giant scarab** on a plinth here will bring you good luck.

TOP TIPS

● For the best photos, visit after 3pm, when the pylons turn to gold.

● Alternatively, go early: the site opens at 6am and tour groups arrive after breakfast.

● Wear comfortable shoes and a hat, and bring water, as refreshments are limited.

● Enjoy tea in the cafe by the Sacred Lake with its spectacular view.

● Visit Karnak more than once to absorb the details.

● Approach Karnak via the Avenue of Sphinxes from the Temple of Luxor.

● Visit the Temple of Mut, by Karnak's 10th pylon (extra admission fee).

● Join the crowds for the sound-and-light show, when Karnak is lit to perfection.

TOP EXPERIENCE

Luxor Temple

Luxor Temple is likely to be the first of the ancient Egyptian antiquities you'll encounter on a trip to the city. So intrinsic is it to the character of the place that it even gave the city its modern name, as a corruption of the Arabic 'Al Uqsur' (The Fortifications). Allow a couple of hours to examine this beautiful temple in detail.

TOP TIPS

● Visit Luxor Temple in the day, but save some time for a return at night when the temple grounds are at their most magical.

● Read the signboard at the start of the Avenue of Sphinxes, which gives a good account of the annual Opet festivities.

PRACTICALITIES

● egymonuments.gov.eg/en/monuments/luxor-temple
● adult/student LE500/250, card payment only
● 6am-8pm

Opet Celebrations

Stroll along the Corniche at sunset and your eye is drawn irresistibly towards a lotus-pillared apparition that appears so weightless in its grace and beauty it almost floats magically above the ground it occupies. Built by New Kingdom pharaohs Amenhotep III (1390–1352 BCE) and Ramses II (1279–1213 BCE), Luxor Temple came alive once a year during the inundation of the Nile. Stand at the foot of the **Avenue of Sphinxes**, by the temple's entrance, and you can picture the spectacle of the statues of Amun, Mut and Khonsu being brought in procession from Karnak to be reunited here as part of the Opet celebrations – festivities captured in relief in the magnificent **Colonnade of Amenhotep III** in the temple precinct.

Changing Purpose

The temple complex has had a complicated history, including as an *ipet* (harem) and private quarters of the god Amun; as a building project of Tutankhamun, Ramses II and Alexander the Great; and as a fort under the Romans. In the 14th century a mosque was built in an interior court for local sheikh (holy man) Abu Al Haggag; it's now all that remains of a village on this site.

Mona Lisa in Stone
Visiting Luxor Museum

Look up 'graywacke' and you'll find that this sandstone is seldom used for sculpture because it's hard to carve and fractures easily. It's remarkable, then, that it was chosen to fashion the most exquisite statue in Egyptian antiquity: the youthful image of Tuthmosis III. Found in the Temple of Karnak, this statue alone warrants a visit to **Luxor Museum** *(egymonuments.com/locations/details/LuxorMuseum; visitor/student LE400/200)*.

The sculpture (exhibited on a spot-lit dais near the entrance) depicts the young king shorn at the knees but confident of eternity, his false beard tipped towards the future. The miracle of the piece, though, is its profile. The high cheekbones, aquiline nose and kohl-rimmed eyes are as perfectly formed as those of any classical beauty, but there's a hint of a smile caught fleetingly when seen in the round.

In addition to this *Mona Lisa* of stone there's the alabaster statue of Amenhotep, embraced by a grinning crocodile god; finds from Tutankhamun's tomb; two royal mummies sensitively displayed; and hundreds of statuettes from the shabti find of 2019. But it's the details that leave the biggest impression: flies of valour cast in gold; heads of human, hawk, baboon and jackal peeping over a box of canopic jars; and the spare flesh of a leaning-over scribe (Amenhotep) rendered in grey granite.

Note too the architects' tools (a right angle carved from a single piece of wood and a cubit rod of schist). Recognisable by today's builders, they bridge the ages.

A Walk by the Nile
Strolling along Luxor's Corniche

If walking the Avenue of Sphinxes has given you a taste for city hikes, then consider making it a round trip by returning along the **Corniche**. The 3.5km-long stretch of broad pavement is almost like a park. Edged with bulrushes and partly tree-lined, it's scented with jasmine, pink oleander and flowering lantana attractive to butterflies.

Passing close to Luxor Museum and the Mummification Museum (p204), the Corniche offers plenty of places to stop, including restaurants on and beside the Nile. Popular with families in the evening, this elegant promenade allows a gentle return to the hustle and bustle of downtown.

FAIR TRADE

Shops clustered around Luxor Temple sell souvenirs, books and maps. The **Aboudi Bookshop & Coffeeshop** is one such establishment. Selling English-language books on the region for over a century, this family business almost doubles as a museum and is the place to read up about ancient gods and pharaohs.

Before spending all your money in the neighbouring **Tourist Souq** (the tourist bazaar, which sells everything you never knew you wanted, including bunches of dried herbs, copper plates and incense bottles), walk a few paces north to the **Fair Trade Centre**. Here, purchasing crafts (such as ceramics, textiles and basketry) from NGO-backed village projects ensures that money reaches the maker, helping to keep traditional skills alive.

 EATING ON THE EAST BANK: EGYPTIAN CLASSICS

Koshari Alzaeem: This local chain sells delicious *kushari* (noodles, rice, brown lentils and onion with tomato sauce), Egypt's fast food. *24hr* **$**

Sofra: Charming, with tiled floors and chandeliers, this local favourite serves tasty Egyptian classics. It's popular year-round, so it's best to reserve a table. *11am-midnight* **$$**

Gerda's Garden: The German–Egyptian couple at this popular bistro prepare Egyptian specials including grilled pigeon. *11am-9.30pm Tue-Thu, Sat & Sun, to midnight Fri* **$$**

Bab Sharq: On the Corniche, this attractive open-air restaurant serves grills and mezze so close to the Nile you can watch fish swimming in the shallows. *8am-2am* **$$**

BRIEF HISTORY OF THEBES

Struggling with 4000 years of history? Here's an A–Z crammer.
Amun: Local god whose cult centred on Thebes, the ancient city now called Luxor.
Luxor: 7th-century Arab rulers called Thebes 'Al Uqsur' meaning 'The Fortifications'.
Middle Kingdom (2055–1650 BCE): Thebes became capital of reunified Egypt.
New Kingdom (1550–1069 BCE): Heyday of Thebes, especially under Amenhotep III.
Solar god: Called Aten. Worshipped as a single deity by Amenhotep III's iconoclastic son, Akhenaten (1352–1336 BCE).
Tutankhamun: This famous young pharaoh (1336–1327 BCE) restored the priesthood after Akhenaten.
Valley of the Kings: Buried here, Ramses II (1279–1213 BCE) built superb tombs, the Ramesseum and Karnak's hypostyle hall.
Waset: Another ancient Egyptian name for Thebes.

Alas, Poor Yorick!
Visiting the Mummification Museum

Somewhere on Luxor's west bank, two visitors peer into a recess in the hillside and stare into the darkness. A tomb guardian senses their interest in the unopened spaces that honeycomb the hillside – a locked grille here, a blocked-up entryway there – and whispers conspiratorially, 'There are still mummies here, you know.' Perhaps the visitors had suspected as much, but suddenly their footsteps are prickled with a sense of trespass and they pick their way quietly and respectfully down the slope to the exit. It was an 'Alas, poor Yorick' moment – the imagined image of a wrapped body with no name, no fanfare and forgotten by history who yet reminded each witness of thier own mortality.

Perhaps it's moments like those that persuaded the ancients to reimagine their own fate, and the Egyptians, of course, were masters in extending their sense of self beyond the grave. When you visit the **Mummification Museum** (*egymonuments.gov.eg/museums/mummification-museum; visitor/student LE220/110*) on the east bank, the rituals involved in trying to cheat death are comprehensively described. It's only a small museum, but it charts each step of the process, including the sprinkling of water, the smearing of resins to preserve the skin, the removal of innards (brain, heart, liver and intestine) and the elaborate wrapping in bandages of the mummified corpse.

The tools used to scoop brain from skull or prise heart from chest cavity, and the brush used to remove lingering pieces of tissue before being dispatched to the relevant canopic jar, show a level of sophistication in anatomy and surgery that may come as a surprise. Perhaps more surprising still is how poignant it is to see the leathered feet of the wizened dead, whether of human being, cat or crocodile. It's a hard heart that can look at the tiny, wrapped mummy of a baby crocodile and not grieve just a little over its untimely death.

Sailing Upstream
Felucca ride on the Nile

Even more than temples or tombs, the most defining feature of Luxor is the Nile, that body of slow-moving water that cuts the city in two. Once this portion of Africa's longest river separated living from dead; today it divides urban from rural. But the river, with space and character all its own, is more than just a border between banks, and no visit to Luxor is

DRINKING ON LUXOR'S EAST BANK: SUNDOWNERS

Winter Palace Hotel: Just entering the grand foyer of this famous hotel is an experience, but sipping cocktails in the piano bar is going one better. *9am–midnight*

Sunset Cafe: Pausing for a coffee here has two advantages: the coffee is good and the restaurant (barge) is floating on the Nile. *24hr*

Nefertiti Hotel: For a grand view of Luxor Temple at sunset and a floodlit west bank, this is the perfect spot for sundowners. *11am–11pm*

Café Cubic: Sit in this tiny coffee shop at sunset to enjoy a sleepy souq returning to life. *7am–11pm*

Mummification Museum

complete without getting to know it. You can cross by bridge (6km south) or by ferry (*single/return LE50/60*), or charter a motorboat from the Corniche (*LE100*). To sense the soul of the river, though, you have to sail by **felucca**.

These graceful boats have made their way along the Nile for centuries. Similar to the barques illustrated on the walls of the Temple of Hatshepsut, but now sporting brightly coloured sheets rather than the linen sails of yore, feluccas are still used to transport goods along the river, and an afternoon's ride upstream has become one of the highlights of a Luxor visit.

Most boat owners offer a three-hour return ride *(from LE500)* from the Temple of Luxor jetty to Banana Island, but the dismal condition of the animals on view there means this is best avoided. It's better to opt instead for a sunset tour. With the afternoon wind bulging the sails and dragging the wooden boats across the water at speed, it's a thrilling experience.

Cutting from bank to bank on the return, these elegant vessels offer the perfect opportunity to spot birdlife – ibises flying in formation, kingfishers skimming the water and egrets that roost together in their hundreds. From the cushioned benches of your boat you can watch the age-old rhythms of the riverbank as donkeys graze on Nile islands and fishers in leaky boats stalk the Nile perch with their nets. As the sun sets, the water becomes an abstract canvas of light and colour, reflecting the sails of 100 feluccas, each vying to be first back to base.

Cue Lights, Sound & Action

Karnak's sound-and-light show

A palm tree is spotlit stage right, the ram-headed sphinxes are lit from below stage left and there's the hint of the massive Pharaonic pylon looming out of the darkness as backdrop. Tonight's 100 tourists wait in the wings for the show

BEST BOATING FROM LUXOR

Felucca Monaliza: Spend five days sailing upstream to Edfu with Captain Ali *(010-6248-0567)*, enjoying simple fare in lovely company.

Meroe: The *Meroe*, a perfect replica of a 19th-century, two-mast dahabiya (houseboat), combines antique charm with modern convenience.

SS Sudan: You can stay in the Agatha Christie suite of this Thomas Cook steamer, built in 1885 and used as a film set for the 2004 and 2022 films of *Death on the Nile*.

MS Sun Boat III: Egyptologists keep guests informed during cruises aboard this beautiful exclusive retreat run by Sanctuary.

MS Farah: A recommended Nile cruise ship that consciously tries to balance modern luxury against more affordable pricing.

to begin. They make impatient extras, stamping the ground in the winter chill for their walk-on part.

Suddenly, the music swells, the gateway is flooded in light and a theatrical voice intones the words of Seti I in an accent belonging to 1972, when the original soundtrack was recorded. Instead of the intended gasps of awe, the media-savvy crowd yawns, chats and glances at mobiles, perhaps wondering where to eat when the show is over.

Has the famous Karnak **sound-and-light show** *(LE1000)*, that so delighted its audiences 50 years ago outlived its power to amaze? The number of shows running in different languages each week suggests not, but it largely depends on the mindset of each visitor. For those interested in the history of the temple, the commentary communicates the key facts effectively. It's a must, too, for those who want to experience the majesty of the complex illuminated at night. But if you're willing to take the imaginative leap of faith into the world of the ancients, you'll swear you heard Ramses II whisper through the labyrinthine corridors and saw Queen Nefertiti reflected in the Sacred Lake.

The show runs in English at 7pm nightly.

Sleeper Class
Travelling by train to Luxor

There's no less likely label for the first few carriages of the night train from Cairo to Luxor than 'sleeping cars'. Shabby beside Bashtil Station's new platforms, **Service 86** is no *Orient Express;* all pretence of silver service departed decades ago. In fact, the wagons have barely changed since the first train left from Cairo's Misr Station in 1898. The hospitality of each wagon guard partly compensates for this, as they bring you hot food wrapped in foil, make the bed with spotless linen and promise a wake-up call an hour before arrival (don't rely on this last item too much, though).

The noise of the dilapidated track means it takes more than a feathered pillow to lull the imagination to sleep, but somehow sleep happens anyway and, just as dawn arrives, a knock on the door is perfectly timed for you to sprint along the corridor and disembark. The Art Deco wings of vulture goddess Nekhbet spread over the entrance of **Luxor Station**, a donkey cart trots by and, as so often happens in Egypt, you wonder why you ever doubted the happy dreams.

ANIMAL CARE IN EGYPT (ACE)

Riding in a horse-drawn carriage is widely considered to be a highlight of a Luxor trip. These east-bank *barouches* are dressed with colourful upholstery, adorned with various charms and feature pictures of loved ones tucked behind the hay that's spare fuel for a hard day's work. While some of the horses and donkeys that trot around Luxor's streets are in good condition, some are not and it can be harrowing to witness their maltreatment.

Opened in 2000 by a British-run charity, **ACE** provides free treatment for 200 working animals a day in a hospital and welfare centre. Crucially, ACE (which welcomes volunteers and donations) also provides education for local children, instilling a love for animals.

CRUISING THE NILE

Enjoyed an afternoon on a felucca? Fancy going further upstream? Dozens of cruisers line up along the jetty or at **Esra** (p241), an hour's drive south of Luxor. The most popular trips sell out in advance, but there's usually something with space available sailing to Aswan.

Gezira

SLEEPY RIM OF WEST BANK MONUMENTS

A short ferry ride from the modern east bank, the west bank could be a different city. From the jetty, fertile Nile floodplains stretch inland, farmed by the *fellaheen* (farmers) who compete to grow the most tomatoes, the tallest sugarcane and cabbages of epic proportions.

Beyond the plain rise the Theban mountains. Barren and austere, they mark the limit of Luxor, from where the desert rolls inexorably westward. It's at this junction between desert and sown that the ancient Egyptians built their city of the dead, with grand temples and tombs tunnelled into the hillsides. Site of royal burials since 2100 BCE, this vast necropolis continues to be a place of scholarly exploration and discovery.

Gateway to these antiquities is the town of Gezira. With friendly Nile-side hotels, restaurants overlooking temple masonry and quiet lanes perfect for cycling, Gezira makes a tranquil alternative base to the east bank.

Giants of Antiquity

A dawn visit to the Colossi of Memnon

The average weight of an adult African elephant is around 2 tonnes. Imagine, then, a stack of 500 elephants and you'll have some idea of the weight of each of the **Colossi of Memnon** *(free)* soaring above the plain on the west bank in Luxor.

These jaw-dropping monuments, cut from a single block of stone, appear to guard the gateway to the Theban necropolis (the burial site of the ancient Egyptians). In fact they were designed to sit at the entrance of the great funerary temple of Amenhotep III. Time has not been kind to what was once the largest such temple in all Egypt, though, with only a scattering of fallen or excavated masonry visible beyond these seated giants.

Many dawn visitors, for whom the faceless colossi are a first indication of the antiquities to come, take a quick photo and leave, but it's worth lingering at the feet of these 18m east-facing figures. As the sun comes up, they appear to stretch into the warmth of the day and, for those with a good imagination, they may just whistle!

☑ TOP TIP

Plan your itinerary before queuing at the tiny **Antiquities Inspectorate Ticket Office**. All tickets are bought here, except for Hatshepsut's temple, Assasif tombs, Valley of the Kings and Valley of the Queens, which have their own offices. Payment must be by card. Not all tombs open daily.

GETTING AROUND

Gezira is small, so it's feasible to get around on foot. The paved west-bank Corniche runs for 3km from the dahabiya mooring, past the west-bank ferry landing.

To explore rural lanes or reach the road to the Colossi, a bike (p209; *24hr hire LE300*) is the best bet. Visiting the Valley of the Kings by bike isn't recommended, though. Go by tuk-tuk *(half-day LE200)* or taxi, but haggle hard. Most drivers will move you from site to site for an agreed fee.

ACTIVITIES
1. Luxor Stables
2. Theban Community Library

SLEEPING
3. Al Fayrouz Hotel
4. Al Gezira Hotel
5. Cleopatra Hotel
6. El Mesala Hotel
7. Gold Ibis Hotel
8. Nile Valley Hotel

EATING
see 6 El Mesala Hotel
9. Freedom
10. Nile Panorama Restaurant
11. Rustic House Restaurant

TRANSPORT
12. Ferry Landing West Bank
13. Mohammed Setohe Bike Rental

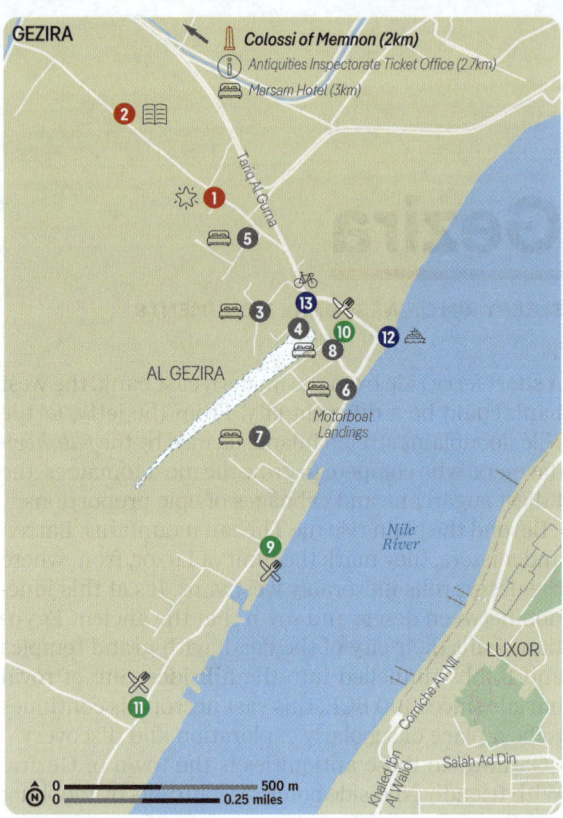

WHISTLING STATUE

Although we now know the colossi depict the pharaoh Amenhotep III, Graeco-Roman visitors attributed them to Memnon, the legendary African king slain by Achilles during the Trojan War. These early tourists came to listen to the northern statue whistling at sunrise, greeting his mother Eos, the goddess of the dawn, who grieved her son's death with tears of dew. More prosaically, the whistling is attributed to a crack that appeared after a 27 BCE earthquake. The damage was repaired in the 3rd century, silencing the statue, but if you use your imagination you may hear the whistling even now.

Precious Resource
Visiting the Theban Community Library

Fathoming antiquity in Luxor is rather like unbinding a mummy: the more history you unwrap, the more layers of complexity you discover. Thankfully, however, there's help at hand in the form of the **Theban Community Library**. This collection of more than 3500 books on Egyptology, together with topics useful to the local community, provides a key resource for archaeologists, a knowledge base for local guides and tomb guardians, and a pop-in centre for visitors. It also caters to youngsters, who explore their ancient heritage on local school trips.

The library was the inspiration of Professor Kent Weeks, founder of the ambitious **Theban Mapping Project** (TMP), the maps of which are kept at the library's rural premises in Gezira. With the library expanding with a laboratory and the addition of computers to aid those without access to the internet, the centre continues to require the support of donors, if only to allow for the continued free lending of books and services.

It's worth visiting the library if only to bump into the infectiously energetic Professor Weeks. Asked why he continues to visit Luxor each year even in semi-retirement, he says it's because Thebes is in his blood. If time doesn't allow, then look up the **TMP website** *(thebanmappingproject.com)* instead: if this superb resource doesn't help in solving your Egyptological problem, you may have stumbled on a PhD project!

Riding the West Bank
The complete package at Luxor Stables
One lovely way to engage with the west bank is to enjoy it on horseback. With a collection of beautiful, well-loved Arabian horses, **Luxor Stables** *(WhatsApp +20 10-0504-8558)* has been established for many years and the owner, Nobi, is proud of his certification of animal welfare.

With bread cooked by family members at the back of the family home in Gezira, and donkeys and camels also part of the menagerie, the stables offer more than just a trek around the paddock. As well as designing tours and camping trips, Nobi also organises five-day family holidays where kids can muck out the stables, groom the horses and ride every day while their folks have the use of an apartment.

Cycling the Green Fringe
Hiring a bike on the west bank
There's bound to come a point in a trip to Luxor's west bank when even the most dedicated lover of antiquities has seen one monument too many. That means it's time to hire a bike and go cycling instead.

Cycling is feasible all year round, but it's best to time a trip in the early morning or later afternoon in summer. Roads are generally well paved and quiet on the west bank, except in the centre of Gezira. The only thing to be wary of are the few territorial dogs lurking in the fields, especially further into the countryside.

A large range of bikes are available from **Mohammed Setohe Bike Rental**, where the owner will fit you up with the best bike for your build. You can also hire a bike from **Marsam Hotel** (p229), near the Ramesseum, which will mean you can avoid cycling through busy Gezira. If you'd rather have some company, **Go Luxor Tours** offers five-hour cycling trips of the west bank.

Gain your pedal legs away from the main road by skirting Luxor Stables and getting a feel for rural Gezira. If you're stopping at a temple or two, don't forget to purchase a ticket from the **Antiquities Inspectorate Ticket Office** (p207), near the colossi.

DISCOVERY OF KV 5

Commenced in 1978, the TMP (overseen by the American Research Center in Egypt, in partnership with the American University in Cairo's Egyptology Department and the Ministry of Tourism and Antiquities) set out to map and photograph every temple and tomb in the west bank necropolis. This has resulted in major archaeological finds, such as tomb KV 5 in 1998, and tangible conservation measures of the Theban sites. The TMP has even influenced agriculture, helping to reduce water-intensive sugar-cane crops, and was responsible for introducing ballooning as part of the project's surveying mandate.

Today, you'll notice canopies of canvas over earthworks. Excavation is ongoing and new finds are a daily occurrence.

 EATING ON LUXOR'S WEST BANK: NILE-VIEW DINING

Rustic House Restaurant: At the southern end of the Corniche, this small restaurant makes delicious home-prepared meals. *8am-midnight* €

El Mesala Hotel: The rooftop restaurant at this busy Nile-side hotel welcomes non-residents for tasty food, a beer and a view of Luxor Temple. *7-11pm* €€

Freedom: You can't get closer to the Nile (without getting your feet wet) than at this cosy favourite with seats under the oleandar bushes. *7am-midnight* €

Nile Panorama Restaurant: Part of the west-bank Corniche, this family restaurant does handsome portions of Egyptian rice dishes. *8am-1am Sat-Wed, to 1.30am Thu & Fri* €

TOP EXPERIENCE

Ballooning Over the West Bank

You may be a nervous flyer, or perhaps unsure a basket will hold the weight of a dozen fellow tourists, but if you take a leap of faith and go ballooning anyway, it's likely to be a memorable experience. Despite slightly chaotic appearances, Luxor ballooning is carefully regulated and involves licensed pilots, traveller manifests and approvals by the Civil Aviation Authority.

TOP TIPS

● Balloons fly in two shifts: at sunrise (the most popular time) and one hour later. The second shift may be less romantic, but the colours are more intense.

● The dawn flight costs around US$75, but the later flight is cheaper (around US$60).

PRACTICALITIES

● *Magic Horizon*, *Salam Balloons* and *Alaska Balloon* all offer reliable services and arrange hotel pick-up for the 40-minute flight (weather permitting).

The Launch

The excitement begins at the launch site as around 50 great hulks come alive from their listless piles on the ground, the air thick with the noise of generators, while dragon blasts of fire bring heat to a chilly morning. Then there's the command to board: the ground crew hold the beasts at bay while the wires that suspend the baskets are clamped in place and suddenly the balloons disperse.

Taking Flight

After the drama of departure, the flight is almost an afterthought. Slowly, as the balloon floats towards the heavens, the rising sun picks out the gems of antiquity – Colossi, Ramesseum, Temple of Hatshepsut – and sinks them back into the grander scale of the Nile, flanking fields of fertile green and the great Western Desert beyond.

Landing

With no steering, pilots must manoeuvre into a landing site downwind, as close to the ground crew as the wind allows, while missing villagers and their galloping donkeys. Feeling slightly drunk with the taste of heaven (or at least inner-ear sensitivity), passengers watch as the balloon deflates back into inanimate sheets of cloth before they return, unceremoniously by minibus, to the land of the living.

The Valley of the Kings

MAGNIFICENT TOMBS BURIED IN THE MOUNTAINS

The arid Valley of the Kings is isolated but seldom quiet. Perhaps it was ever thus as workers chiselled through rock to build 'The Place of Truth' for New Kingdom (1550–1069 BCE) pharaohs over 500 years. Despite theft, flood and mass tourism, the royal tombs honeycombing the cliffs are undeniable west-bank treasures.

Fair warning: a visit can be hot and tiring, compounded by fellow visitors elbowing their way through narrow corridors or holding up the queues behind them. Visitors are united, though, in a desire to engage with antiquity. But how, without a PhD in Egyptology or a knowledgeable guide, can visitors do so?

Heading for remote tombs for a sense of discovery, reading signboards for highlights and learning image basics (a king wears sandals, a god does not; one cartouche denotes a noble, two a king) helps. Each tomb is a 'book of the dead' for those who know the vocabulary.

Visitors Centre
Gateway to the Valley of the Kings

To start your visit, your taxi or tuk-tuk driver will drop you at the **Visitors Centre**, north of the entrance. This is where you'll purchase **tickets** *(visitor/student LE750/375; card only)*. Extra tickets apply to some tombs. The Premium Luxor Pass (payable in cash in US dollars or euros only) is also available from here and covers all tombs.

If you can wait before seeing the first tomb, then it's worth spending a few minutes watching the TV documentary featuring the newsreel of Howard Carter clearing treasures from the tomb of Tutankhamun. It sets the scene for the visit ahead.

Orienting the Valley
Numbering of tombs

Gain a sense of the whole valley by getting to grips with the ways the tombs are numbered. This is not, as you may expect, by age, significance or even discovery.

☑ TOP TIP

If you hire a bike (easy from Gezira; see p209), save your pedal power for pottering around the gorgeous rural reaches of the Nile rather than slogging it out to the Valley of the Kings. The approach to the tombs slopes uphill and tends to be hot and busy with coaches.

GETTING AROUND

Save your energy by taking the electric buggy from the ticket office at the head of the Valley of the Kings to the main tomb area.

Once in the tomb area, the only way of getting about is walking. That isn't easy unless you're reasonably fit: paths are unpaved and many of the tomb entrances lie up the slopes of the valley.

Descending into (and climbing back out) of the tombs requires considerable effort, walking through narrow corridors and negotiating many flights of steps.

THE VALLEY OF THE KINGS

★ HIGHLIGHTS
1. Luxor Museum
2. Tomb of Ramses VI (KV 9)
3. Tomb of Seti I (KV 17)

● SIGHTS
4. Howard Carter's House & the Replica Tomb of Tutankhamun
5. Tomb of Ay
6. Tomb of Ramses III (KV 11)
7. Tomb of Ramses IV (KV 2)
8. Tomb of Ramses VII (KV 1)
9. Tomb of Tutankhamun (KV 62)
10. Tomb of Tuthmosis III (KV 34)

● DRINKING & NIGHTLIFE
11. Cafe & Restaurant Maratonga

12. Marsam Hotel
13. Ramesseum Rest House
14. Valley of Kings Café

● INFORMATION
15. Valley of the Kings Visitors Centre & Ticket Booth

British Egyptologist Sir John Gardner Wilkinson was the first to number the tombs in 1821 and began by labelling the 21 tombs known at the time in sequence, starting from those closest to the entrance of the valley and working south. Named 'KV' (for Kings Valley) and 'WV' (for West Valley), the same nomenclature is used today, with newly discovered tombs simply added sequentially.

Each tomb is identified by a signboard that, invaluably, lists the highlights. Looking for the items on the list helps bring focus to your tomb visit.

Graffiti Hunting
KV 1 and KV 2 and their prior visitors

Forget having the Valley of the Kings to yourself and ignore suggestions about the quietest times of the day – as everyone is given the same advice, almost all times are equally busy. Instead, enjoy the sense of a shared experience. With the right mindset, the combined excitement of the site's multinational visitors may amplify your own. Besides, you're in good company. While the last pharaoh was buried here 3000 years ago, the site has attracted visitors for millennia, some welcome, others less so.

Robbers rifled most of the tombs even as new ones were being built, leading to ever more sophisticated methods of concealment or entry. The ancient Greeks and Romans graffitied their names on the walls, and medieval hermits made some of the tombs their home. Visit **KV 1** and **KV 2**, the tombs of Ramses VII (1136–1129 BCE) and Ramses IV (1176–1149 BCE) respectively, and you'll see Coptic crosses and inscriptions overlaying the tomb painting near the entrance. KV 2, with its beautiful goddess Nut ceiling, was even used as a hotel by 18th- and 19th-century visitors.

Monkey Business
Hiking to the Tomb of Ay

In peak periods the Valley of the Kings can feel intense. An excellent way to change the pace is by seeking out lesser-known tombs, and a visit to the **Tomb of Ay** may fit the bill.

The tomb is reached via West Valley, otherwise known as **Wadi Al Gurud** (Valley of the Monkeys), a 2km walk from the ticket office. So few visitors make it along the track that the tomb guardian may need to be summoned to open the gate. The walk, slightly uphill, is part of the charm, with cliffs opening into an amphitheatre of honey-coloured rock, in striking contrast with the blue sky above. Archaeologists have begun hopeful excavations here with some success, but the valley has mostly been reclaimed by nature – a vulture here, a beetle there and the odd lizard basking in the sun.

The tomb itself is modest, but its unadorned passage opens into a large burial chamber with an almost perfectly preserved sarcophagus. With a wall of 12 baboons (one for each hour of the night and giving the valley its Arabic name), it resembles Tutankhamun's burial chamber, but with the beautiful addition of Ay hunting hippopotamus and fishing in the marshes.

A TOMB MOST MODEST

Neither of the first two tombs in the Valley of the Kings is representative. And nor is KV 62, arguably the most famous in all Egypt, the **Tomb of Tutankhamun** (p196).

Aside from the superb treasures found inside, discovered by Howard Carter in 1922 and now dispersed to museums, KV 62 as a tomb is modest in every way. Most tombs have an entryway followed by three corridors, each punctuated with a gateway, at the bottom of which is the burial chamber, in which a stone sarcophagus would once have protected the owner's mummified body. Tutankhamun, like Ramses IV and Ramses VII, died young, though, and was hastily buried in a makeshift space adapted for the purpose.

 DRINKING ON LUXOR'S WEST BANK: COFFEE STOPS

Cafe & Restaurant Maratonga: Delightful cafe beside Medinat Habu with good coffee and delicious banana cake. *6am-8pm*

Marsam Hotel: This favourite coffee spot has a shady terrace and makes fresh lemon juice – perfect on a hot day. *11am-11pm*

Ramesseum Rest House: By the Ramesseum, this 'Castle of Beer' belongs to the family of one of the workers present at Carter's epic find. *6am-midnight Sat-Thu, 24hr Fri*

Valley of Kings Café: Under the shadow of Mt Qurn, this cafe is perfectly positioned to entice those gasping for a coffee after tomb touring. *6am-6pm*

EXPERT ADVICE

Aged eight, **Professor Kent Weeks** wanted to be an Egyptologist and, as instigator of the Theban Mapping Project (TMP), through which KV 5 was discovered, he's the most celebrated Egyptologist of today. He shares his top tomb tips.

Download the TMP website *(kv5.com)* to your mobile phone for free, comprehensive guides to individual Kings Valley tombs.

Spend any extra fee for KV 9, the lesser- visited tomb of Ramses V/VI, with beautiful decoration.

Bring guidebook and torch to fully appreciate the Tombs of the Nobles, showcasing domestic rather than religious scenes.

The tomb of Nefertari, although expensive, is the Queens Valley masterpiece.

Visit Howard Carter's House for a faithful facsimile, and cheaper experience, of Tutankhamun's tomb.

The comparison is a fair one, as Ay's reign (1327–1323 BCE) was similarly short and succeeded that of his more famous predecessor. There's even speculation that Ay's burial place was planned for Tutankhamun, whose untimely death led to a more hasty construction in the main valley. For now, Ay seems to have the better bargain – his spirit left in peace in the absolute silence of his tomb.

Much More Yet to Find
Discovery of the tomb of Tutmosis II

In 2025 there was considerable fanfare at the discovery of a new tomb. Belonging to Tutmosis II, it was discovered in the West Valley by the first British archaeological team since Howard Carter to have found a tomb. If you wander up towards the Tomb of Ay, consider that this valley is much bigger than the Valley of the Kings, but much less explored!

Wonderful Things
Visiting Howard Carter's house

Walk up to **Howard Carter's House** (scan the QR code to pay) late in the day when the crowds have left and you'll find it an intimate experience. Weary, dusty and with the sense you wanted to do more than time, energy or money allowed, you may sense something of what the British Egyptologist felt when six seasons of tireless digging had thrown up little more than a bone or a pottery shard.

Enter the house and you'll see the hook on the wall where Carter hung his hat; there's his bed with a mosquito net, where he probably slumped, disconcerted by the lack of progress. Here's the dining room of simple furniture where he regrouped his thoughts and the photographic studio where he nightly toiled to capture his findings. His spirit seems to linger in the two paintings on the wall, but mostly it bleeds out into the air of Thebes as the sun sets on the Valley of the Kings, rekindling hope for the next day.

Wander through the garden (a new addition since the centenary of Carter's monumental find in 2022) and you can visit a faithful **replica of King Tutankhamun's Tomb**. Feel Carter's heartbeat as you descend the ramp and glimpse the sarcophagus of the young king. Carter earned the right, with his patron Lord Carnarvon, to peer into the tomb after its discovery. Asked what he could see, he answered, 'Wonderful things!' Chances are, without the crush of visitors behind you, you'll feel the exaltation of discovery here, too.

Visiting the replica tomb (which is wheelchair accessible) instead of the real thing also represents doing your bit for sustainable tourism. Luxor is enjoying a new tourism boom, which begs the question: how much attention can the sites of Luxor withstand? Exhalation and perspiration have taken their toll in the tombs of the Valley of the Kings, so some tombs are opened only in rotation and visitors are restricted to three tombs per day. The solution may lie in building replicas, such as the Tomb of Tutankhamun here at Carter's House.

Tomb of Seti I (p216)

TOP EXPERIENCE

The Great Pharaonic Tombs

Along the Valley of the Kings, concrete bunkers are bored into the cliffs of Mt Qurn. These plain, modern structures give no inkling of the beauty hidden below. The anonymity of the tomb gateway mirrors the extraordinary lengths to which the pharaohs of the New Kingdom (1550–1069 BCE) went to conceal their burial sites. Unlocking their secrets is part of the magic.

DON'T MISS

Tomb of Seti I (KV 17)

Tomb of Ramses VI (KV 9)

Tomb of Ramses III (KV 11)

Tomb of Tuthmosis III (KV 34)

View of the valley from KV 34

Top Tombs

Why a Tomb, not a Pyramid?

If you're wondering why the 19th- and 20th-dynasty tombs in the Valley of the Kings were cut into rock, it had much to do with status. Tombs evolved from a desire to distinguish the 'elite' from the 'commoner'. Differentiated at first by a mound of sand heaped over a desert grave, the mound developed

PRACTICALITIES

- *kv5.com*
- *not all tombs are open every day*
- *visitors may be limited to three tombs per day (except with Luxor Pass)*

TREASURES OF TUTANKHAMUN

Four chambers containing masks, coffins and jewellery, carved furniture, canopic jars, musical instruments and chariots were found in the Tomb of Tutankhamun. Most are now displayed in Cairo's **Egyptian Museum** (p78), and a few pieces are in the **Luxor Museum** (p203). The entire collection is bound for **GEM** (p151), a purpose-built museum in Giza. A video in the visitors centre captures Carter's moment of discovery.

TOP TIPS

● Before heading into the valley, take a good look at the large model in the central hall of the Visitors Centre. It shows the depth of the tombs, giving you an idea of the effort involved in exploring them.

● If any of the tombs on your list are closed, chances are they'll be open the next day. If not, don't be disappointed: all the tombs have unique features, and it takes an expert to appreciate the shades of difference.

● Be ready with lots of small change to tip tomb guardians. They make ends meet by showing visitors their tomb's best features.

around 3100 BCE into a benchlike structure (a *mastaba*); this in turn evolved into a pyramid.

With their massive footprint, pyramids proved impractical in some locations; entombment in the cliffs provided a more secure option. Initially consisting of a single chamber, tombs developed into the complex structures seen in the Valley of the Kings under the direction of New Kingdom (1550–1069 BCE) pharaohs.

A Tomb Most Wondrous

Don't be put off by the extra charge; the **Tomb of Seti I (KV 17)** is worth it. Famed for his temple in Abydos and hypostyle hall at Karnak, Seti I (1291–1278 BCE) was a great patron of the arts and his tomb, cut 137m into the rock, is decorated from entrance to burial chamber. The tomb's astronomical ceiling, decorated with constellations, calendar and stars, was the first of its kind.

Discovered by Giovani Belzoni in 1817, the tomb suffered from Belzoni's copying technique but is still splendid, with images from ancient texts, including the Litany of Ra and the Book of the Dead.

Religious & Secular

To the casual eye, tomb paintings may appear unfathomable, but two key themes emerge. There's the king at prayer giving offerings to the gods, and there are descriptions of the underworld as explained in ancient texts such as the Book of the Dead.

The ancient Egyptians believed that Ra was the god of the living, who journeyed across the night sky to be reunited with Osiris, the god of the dead. The **Tomb of Ramses VI (KV 9)** shows this night journey conducted within the sky goddess Nut, who embodies the sky, swallowing the sun at dusk and giving birth to it each dawn.

Not all paintings were religious in nature, though: look for the blind harpists in the **Tomb of Ramses III (KV 11)**, last of the great warrior pharaohs (1184–1153 BCE), among secular scenes of pottery, weaponry and boats in the side chambers.

Hidden Depths

The **Tomb of Tuthmosis III (KV 34)**, at the most southerly reach of the Valley of the Kings, is extraordinary in the ingenuity of its design. Reached via a steep staircase rising 20m above the valley floor, the tomb was located in the most inaccessible place above a deep ravine, with nonaligned passages and fake doors designed to mislead robbers.

The tomb belonged to 'the Napoleon of ancient Egypt', Tuthmosis III (1479–1425 BCE), who was more warrior than art patron. Decorating the oval burial chamber of this early tomb, the linear drawings appear unsophisticated compared with later tomb decoration, but the sense of adventure in discovering the tomb's hidden depths and the view of the whole site that the entrance affords make it one of the valley's most popular tombs.

The Valley of the Queens

TOMBS RIVALLING THOSE OF THE KINGS

Pressed to visit just one site on the west bank, it would be hard to choose between the Valley of the Kings, at the northern end of the Theban mountains, and the Valley of the Queens to the south. While the former has the most famous tombs, the latter has arguably the most beautiful: that belonging to Nefertari, one of the five wives of Ramses II.

Only four of the 75 tombs are open for viewing, but the area has other attractions. About 1km towards the Valley of the Queens a road climbs to a small, beautifully proportioned Ptolemaic-era temple. Its name, Deir Al Medina, is often used to refer to the neighbouring Workmen's Village too. This complex of houses and burial sites belonged to the artisans of the royal tombs. Displaying those same skills, some of the tombs here, topped by mud-brick pyramids, rival those of royalty.

Princely Tombs

Tombs of Khaemwaset and Amunherkhepshef

As the name implies, the **Valley of the Queens** *(visitor/student LE220/110)* is the burial place of royal women…except that it isn't. Well, not exclusively.

Two of the main tombs on view, the **Tomb of Amunherkhepshef** and the **Tomb of Khaemwaset**, belong to two sons, dressed in kilt and sandals, of Ramses III. Look for sidelocks of hair signifying the youths as they are touchingly introduced by their father to the gods. Among the tombs currently open to the public in the valley, these are some of the most beautifully executed.

If you're wondering about the mummified five-month-old foetus on display in the Tomb of Amunherkhepshef, it's been the subject of speculation ever since it was found by Italian archaeologists. If you engage a guide, they'll no doubt share the suggestion that the foetus was aborted by Amunherkhepshef's mother, who was grieving over her son's untimely death. The truth is that no one knows.

☑ TOP TIP

It's easy to tell that there's something special about the tombs here. Studying the highlights illustrated outside each tomb offers some insight, but hiring an expert (at the ticket office) to guide you is a better bet.

GETTING AROUND

The Valley of the Queens lies 5km from the Nile's west bank, just 1.5km beyond the Antiquities Inspectorate Ticket Office, so it's feasible to cycle here from Gezira. To combine sites, though, it's better to hire a tuk-tuk or taxi for the 8km journey to the Valley of the Kings.

Inside the Valley of the Queens, the only way to visit the site is on foot. Not as expansive nor as crowded as the Valley of the Kings, it's similarly exposed and the tombs are just as deep, so comfortable shoes, a hat and water are essential in summer.

- ★ **HIGHLIGHTS**
- 1 Deir Al Medina
- 2 Tomb of Nefertari
- ● **SIGHTS**
- 3 Tomb of Amunherkhepshef
- 4 Tomb of Inherka
- 5 Tomb of Ipuy
- 6 Tomb of Khaemwaset
- 7 Tomb of Peshedu
- 8 Tomb of Sennedjem
- 9 Tomb of Titi
- 10 Valley of the Queens
- ● **EATING**
- 11 Marsam Restaurant
- ● **INFORMATION**
- 12 Antiquities Inspectorate Ticket Office

Female Rule

Tomb of Titi and Egypt's powerful women

Pause before the gods in the **Tomb of Titi** in the Valley of the Queens and you'll quickly get a sense of the importance of royal women in ancient Egypt. Protected by a jackal and a lion, two monkeys and a monkey with a bow, this queen is referred to as a royal wife, mother and daughter.

But women in ancient Egypt were also powerful rulers. It was common that they acted as regent on the death of a related pharaoh and were buried with full royal honours. In each dynasty a woman ruled as King's Mother, and some of the most famous women in history ruled after their husband's death.

Hatshepsut, for example, assumed the throne after husband and half-brother Tuthmosis II died. As pharaoh, her reign (1473–1458 BCE) was one of peace and growth. Some queens chose to be depicted cross-dressed as men, including Nefertari, wife of rebel pharaoh Akhenaten. Seti II's wife and self-proclaimed pharaoh Tawosret is even buried in the Valley of the Kings.

One thousand years after Tawosret, aged just 17, Cleopatra VII came to the throne in 51 BCE. Allying herself with Rome by her marriage to Julius Caesar, she valiantly tried to keep Egypt as independent as its famous female rulers.

Deir Al Medina

Visiting the Workmen's Village

Near the Valley of the Queens, a small **Ptolemaic-era temple** has a large history. Measuring just 10m by 15m, and built between 221 and 116 BCE, Set Maat (The Place of Truth) was dedicated to Hathor, the goddess of pleasure and love, and Maat, the goddess of truth.

Look closely and you'll see several Christian symbols overlaying the original hieroglyphics, signifying a change of purpose. Converted to a Coptic monastery, the structure acquired a new name, **Deir Al Medina** (Town Monastery), which is now also used for the adjacent village of workers and families who support the tomb-building industry.

Royal tombs represented highly ambitious engineering projects designed to resemble the underworld as well as works of aesthetic beauty. The architects, craftspeople and officials responsible for tomb execution worked for 10 days straight at Deir Al Medina and then took two days off to visit their family in other parts of Egypt. Throughout the 400 years the settlement was in use, many workers died and chose to be buried here. Some were laid to rest in beautifully decorated tombs of their own.

Visiting Deir Al Medina is generally an integral part of a guided visit to the Valley of the Queens, but if you're on your own you'll need to buy a ticket from the **Antiquities Inspectorate Ticket Office** *(p207); visitor/student LE220/110)*. Note that some of the entrance shafts are particularly steep here. Last admission during Ramadan is at 3pm.

Famous & Forgotten

Iconic images in workers' tombs

Their owners may have been forgotten, but the tombs at Deir Al Medina have become almost as famous as those of royalty, thanks to some celebrated images. At the one-room **Tomb of Inherka** look for a cat (sun god Ra) killing a snake (evil serpent Apophis) under a sacred tree.

The separately ticketed **Tomb of Peshedu** *(visitor/student LE120/60)* belongs to another 19th-dynasty artisan; his tomb famously depicts Peshedu praying under a palm tree beside a lake. Similarly iconic, in the nearby **Tomb of Ipuy**, a sculptor who worked in the time of Ramses II, are scenes of farming, hunting and a garden of flowers and fruit trees.

ANCIENT BACKLASH

Despite the prevalence of female rule in ancient Egypt, not everyone approved, it seems. Being depicted as a man was a queen's way of defusing some of the tension with the patriarchy. This tactic was used by Hatshepsut, a powerful rebel queen who was loved by some and loathed by others.

If 'loathe' seems too strong a word, consider that images of the queen throughout her mortuary temple complex have been systematically defaced. The act of Tuthmosis III, Hatshepsut's overshadowed co-regent (who also happened to be her stepson, son-in-law and nephew), the vandalism speaks volumes not just of family intrigue but also of prejudice against a woman occupying the throne of kings.

EATING ON LUXOR'S WEST BANK: OUR PICKS

Al Gezira Hotel: Popular with resident archaeologists, this cosy rooftop restaurant serves Egyptian fare including clay-pot dishes. *7-11pm* $$

Marsam Restaurant: The home-cooked food at this popular restaurant with its garden of palm trees is worth forgoing breakfast for. *11am-11pm* $

Paris Restaurant: Enjoy comforting fare such as soups and stews in a simple, two-storey house with a terrace view of the Colossi. *5am-11.30pm* $

Wannas Art Café: Using freshly picked ingredients cooked to order, this delightful cafe serves excellent vegetarian food. *11am-11pm Sat-Thu, from 2pm Fri* $

TOP EXPERIENCE
Tomb of Nefertari

As its name suggests, the Valley of the Queens houses around 75 tombs belonging to queens of the 19th and 20th dynasties. One of the most lavish is the Tomb of Nefertari. Described as a testament to love, every centimetre has been decorated with beautiful details that convey the instructions of a pharaoh for the treatment of his favourite queen.

TOP TIP
● At research time the tomb was closed due to a build-up of damaging humidity. If reopening is deemed safe, there'll likely be a large extra fee for admission.

● If the tomb is closed when you visit, you can still see its interior in detail at *nefertaritomb.com/history-tomb*.

PRACTICALITIES
● *egypt-museum.com/tomb-of-nefertari*
● *visits suspended until further notice*

A Loving Tribute

As you walk into the tomb, you'll find yourself under a stunning depiction of the night sky with a canopy of golden stars. Beside you the graceful figure of Nefertari, known as the 'Most Beautiful of Them', is hypnotic in a transparent white gown and golden headdress that trails a pair of vulture feathers.

Built for his favourite queen by the New Kingdom pharaoh Ramses II, this magnificent tomb is a tribute to Nefertari's beauty and, in its exquisite reliefs, decidedly a labour of love. Unfortunately, time has been unkind to the queen's mortal remains, with only the knees left of her mummified body beside a few fragments of a pink-granite sarcophagus, but the overwhelming impression of this tomb is of Nefertari's youth and beauty.

Replicating the Magic

So valuable is the ensemble of decorations here that there are plans to build a replica of Nefertari's tomb beside that of the Tomb of Tutankhamun at **Howard Carter's House** (p214). This is one of several constructive suggestions to preserve this ancient wonder from the effects of tourism, although it will be a challenge to recreate the wonder of the original.

West Bank Temples

ASSORTED ANTIQUITIES BETWEEN DESERT AND NILE

With the Valley of the Kings headlining the west bank, many visitors naturally rush towards the tombs to the exclusion of all else. That's a pity, because some of the most atmospheric sites in Luxor lie at the edge of the fields, where plain meets mountain. Tours often include the elaborate Mortuary Temple of Hatshepsut, stretched out elegantly along the foot of the mountains, and Ramses III's splendid mortuary temple of Medinat Habu, but few bother with the Ramesseum or the Temple of Seti I. Visit either and you're likely to have at least part of the complex to yourself.

Workshops dotted between temples promote traditional crafts. If the tranquillity of this area appeals to you, consider a night's stay or a meal in one of the nearby rural retreats, many of which have rooftop terraces. It's a great way to enjoy the Theban landscape after the crowds have left.

Fit for a Queen
Mortuary Temple of Hatshepsut

Amid the massive, heavy-structured monuments of ancient Egyptian kings, one building stands out for its lightness of touch: the **Mortuary Temple of Hatshepsut** *(visitor/student LE440/220)*. This stylish structure spreads across the bottom of the Theban cliffs like the outstretched wings of Nekhbet, the vulture goddess, and ascends the mountain in a series of three ramped terraces. Once graced with a fragrant garden, it was called *djeser-djeseru* (Most Holy of Holies) and befitted a woman considered 'beautiful and gifted' in her own time. Heavily restored over the years, it is nonetheless one of the loveliest buildings in Egypt.

Designed by Senenmut, a courtier and possible lover of Hatshepsut, to face the Temple of Karnak due east across the Nile, the temple broke with earlier architectural traditions. It also challenged religious iconography, as formerly only males were shown as the children of the sun god. In reliefs on the north

☑ TOP TIP

Timing is everything. At dawn the Ramesseum sits under a halo of balloons, on Tuesday morning the Temple of Seti I is enlivened by neighbouring Talaat Souq, at noon the parallel lines of Hatshepsut's temple are precision taut and at sunset Medinat Habu basks in honey-coloured light.

GETTING AROUND

Medinat Habu, the Ramesseum and the temple of Hatshepsut are within a short tuk-tuk ride of each other. On a cool day you could walk between Medinat Habu, the Ramesseum and the **Antiquities Inspectorate Ticket Office** (p207). Hatshepsut's temple has its own ticket office.

Cycling is a good way to explore; you can hire bikes at **Marsam Hotel** (p229).

HIGHLIGHTS
1 Medinat Habu

SIGHTS
2 Mortuary Temple of Hatshepsut
3 Ramesseum
4 Temple of Seti I

SLEEPING
5 Marsam Hotel

SHOPPING
6 Souq At Talaat

INFORMATION
7 Antiquities Inspectorate Ticket Office

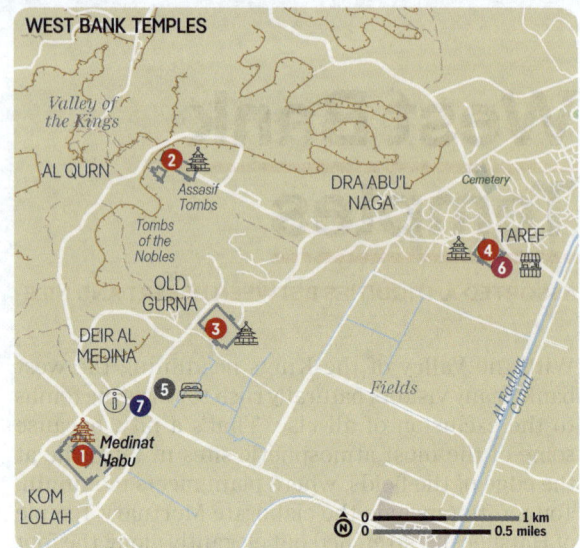

WEST BANK TEMPLES

colonnade of the middle terrace Hatshepsut is depicted as a boy at birth to avoid invoking the consternation of those who objected to a woman occupying the throne of kings, but her image was defaced regardless (see p219).

Allow at least two hours to explore, as the bas-relief details here are exceptional.

Decayed but Not Forgotten
Ozymandias and the Ramesseum

When you enter the **Ramesseum** (p195), the funerary temple of Ramses II, head past the three baboons (to the right of the entrance) to the bottom of the complex and look for a pair of feet. Shorn off at the ankles, they are so massive that by rights they should support the weight of a giant. In fact, they belong to the Colossus of Ramses II, who was known in antiquity by his Greek name, Ozymandias. The statue's forlornly crumpled form lies broken where it fell in three parts, a huge hulk of shoulder still visible in front of the 29 remaining columns of the hypostyle hall.

No one knows if it was the deliberate efforts of Persian king Cambyses, employing the elements of fire and water to crack the granite, or just the ravages of time that did for the statue. At any rate, in 1820 British poet Percy Bysshe Shelley was sufficiently moved by images of its ruin to write a sonnet on human hubris in trying to attain immortality. 'Round the decay/Of that colossal wreck', he wrote, 'The lone and level sands stretch far away': power and wealth inevitably crumble to nothing.

The irony of this is that it probably isn't true. The great granite carving may now lie prone, but it's still there, immortalising the memory of Ramses II and now also the Romantic

A COLOSSUS INDEED

Just how big was the Colossus of Ramses II (Ozymandias)? Carved from a single block of granite, it was once the biggest statue in all of Egypt. Here are its vital statistics:

Weight More than 1000 tonnes

Height 19m

Shoulder width 7m

Width of foot 1.25m

Index finger 1m

Identifying marks Pharaoh's name in hieroglyphics on both upper arms

poet who shares his limelight. Look up Ozymandias online and there he is again, somewhat disingenuously represented as a pair of boots and an upright head, and even shown with today's US president superimposed. Invoked in an episode of the TV series *Breaking Bad,* where the main character loses his empire, Ozymandias has been kept alive, it seems, by contemporary culture.

Salad Days
Shopping at Talaat Souq

Every Tuesday morning donkey carts and hay-laden lorries roll into the **Souq At Talaat**, piled high with the produce of local farms. If you think you've seen a big cabbage, think again, as some of the fattest brassicas in the Middle East are grown nearby, together with sweet onions and tomatoes, which flourish in the fields beside the Colossi.

Among the tables of leafy vegetables are baskets or sacks full of herbs. Some form of herb has apparently been grown in the area for millennia: the remains of *Thymbra spicata,* a species still used in *za'atar* (a mixture of crushed dried herbs, sesame seeds and sumac) were found in the tomb of Tutankhamun. Across the Middle East, preparations for making *za'atar* are a family tradition handed down from mothers to daughters.

If you're not averse to haggling, buy a reusable bag from one of the stalls along the lane connecting the market to the main road and shop for a salad and some fruit. Fresh dates in season make a great dessert. The market is open until 2pm.

Picnic among Ruins
The Temple of Seti I

If you've been overrun by eager shoppers at the Tuesday market in Talaat, pop across the road for a peaceful stroll under the palm trees at the **Temple of Seti I** *(visitor/student LE200/100)* opposite. Built for Seti I (responsible for the Temple of Abydos, Karnak's hypostyle hall and the famous tomb in the Valley of the Kings), it was finished after the pharaoh's death by his heavier-handed son.

Recently restored after flood damage in 1994, it is seldom visited, which is a pity because it has some beautiful reliefs. The walls of the columned portico on the west facade of the temple and the hypostyle court beyond have particularly fine decoration. If nothing else, it's a beautiful spot to have a picnic or simply sit and enjoy being in the presence of the ancients.

TELLING TALES

The less touristed sites of the Theban dead offer a great opportunity to chat with the living. Each site is protected by a guardian whose job includes unlocking a gate where necessary. Reportedly earning less than a petrol-pump attendant, guardians generally consider it their duty to educate visitors. That's partly in hopes of supplementing their meagre income, but also often with a genuine desire to share their knowledge.

With torch in *galabeya* (robe) pocket, many guardians illuminate temple and tomb both literally and metaphorically. Some archaeologists protest at the quality of their information, but that's hardly the point. They unlock the door to curiosity, after which you can navigate your own way through the labyrinths of history.

TOP EXPERIENCE

Medinat Habu

If you have time for only one temple visit on the west bank, choose Medinat Habu. For centuries the mortuary temple of Ramses III, last of the great pharaohs, formed the economic hub of Thebes. Today, the site is half buried in Kom Lolah village, where the management of market gardens is a world away from the glory days of high finance.

TOP TIPS

● Entering the two-storey Syrian Gate, modelled on a Syrian fortress, follow the wall to the left and climb the stairs to sense the scale of the complex.

● Let the sleeping dogs lie. They occupy the steps to the temple entrance and are happy if left alone.

PRACTICALITIES

● buy tickets at the Antiquities Inspectorate Ticket Office (p207)
● egymonuments.gov.eg/en/monuments/the-temple-of-medinet-habu
● visitor/student LE220/110
● 6am-5pm Apr-Sep, 6am-4pm Oct-Mar & Ramadan

Grand Design

At its height Medinat Habu encompassed temples, a royal palace, priest accommodation, offices, stores and workshops. The complex is remarkably well preserved, with excavation first carried out here in 1859 and ongoing since. It's a great place to sense the grand design of the ancients, especially at sunset, when the massive first pylon looms out of the golden light.

Temple Highlights

First pylon Reliefs of Ramses III's victory over the Libyans (seen wearing long robes and sporting sidelocks and beards).
First pylon relief Scribes counting enemies by severed hands and genitals.
Pharaoh's palace Three rooms designated as the royal harem.
Window of Appearances Where the pharaoh appeared to his subjects.
Second pylon relief Ramses III presents prisoners of war to Amun and his vulture-goddess wife, Mut.

Christian Centre

After the demise of the Ptolemies (the last Egyptian rulers before the Romans), Medinat Habu became an important Christian centre, inhabited until the 9th century, when a plague is thought to have decimated the town. The medieval town gave the site its Arabic name (*medina* means 'town' or 'city'), and mud-built houses still cling to the enclosure walls today.

The Wider Necropolis

WHERE CURRENT DIGS UNEARTH DAILY TREASURES

A necropolis may seem an unlikely place to call home, but for all the talk of death on the west bank, Thebes has mostly been about life – creative artisanal life, grasping at the immortality offered by the Pharaonic vision. Craftspeople and administrators lived around the perimeter of the Theban hillsides, leaving monuments to their own place in history, including beautiful tomb paintings that showcase mostly domestic lives.

Spend a day pottering around these 'Tombs of the Nobles' and you're likely to bump into the area's latest incumbents. 'I used to live here', sighs Abdullah, nodding at the picturesque houses of Old Gurna beside the tombs. These may have been partly demolished by the authorities in 2007 to preserve the antiquities, but the creative energy of the area thrives regardless. Shop for alabaster, textiles or pottery in the busy new workshops along the necropolis rim and you'll sense there's little appetite for looking back.

Daily Life of the Ancients

Tombs of the Nobles

While the royal tombs illustrate the complex belief systems of ancient Egypt, they betray little of the daily comings and goings of life 3500 years ago. For a window into this ancient domestic world, head to the 6th-dynasty **Tombs of the Nobles**.

More funerary chapel than tomb, each of these burial sites comprises an entry hall and a passageway with a niche for the owner's statue. The tombs are generally decorated with paintings that look dazzling against a chalky background.

There are dozens of these tombs (not all are open to the public) dotting the steep, exposed hillside and many have a delicate beauty. The **Tomb of Nakht**, for example, with its famous images of a blind harpist and three dancers, hunting scenes and rural life, is beautifully preserved. The **Tomb of Menna** (on the same ticket) is vividly colourful, while in the **Tomb of Amenemope** (not always open) the statues of the tomb incumbent and his wife and daughter are still in situ.

☑ TOP TIP

Rather than exhausting yourself by trying to visit all the tombs, try choosing one or two and studying them in detail. It's the decorative images' tiny gestures that speak volumes.

GETTING AROUND

The only way to visit the tombs is to walk steeply uphill and then down plunging steps to the underground chambers... and then haul yourself back to the surface. In summer it's punishing. Save your energy by hiring a tuk-tuk or taxi to shuttle you between sites, which has the benefit of free visits to craft workshops (drivers earn a small commission).

Buy tickets for the area (payable on day of use and by card only) from the **Antiquities Inspectorate Ticket Office** (p207). Tickets cover two neighbouring tombs. Choose which two before queuing up.

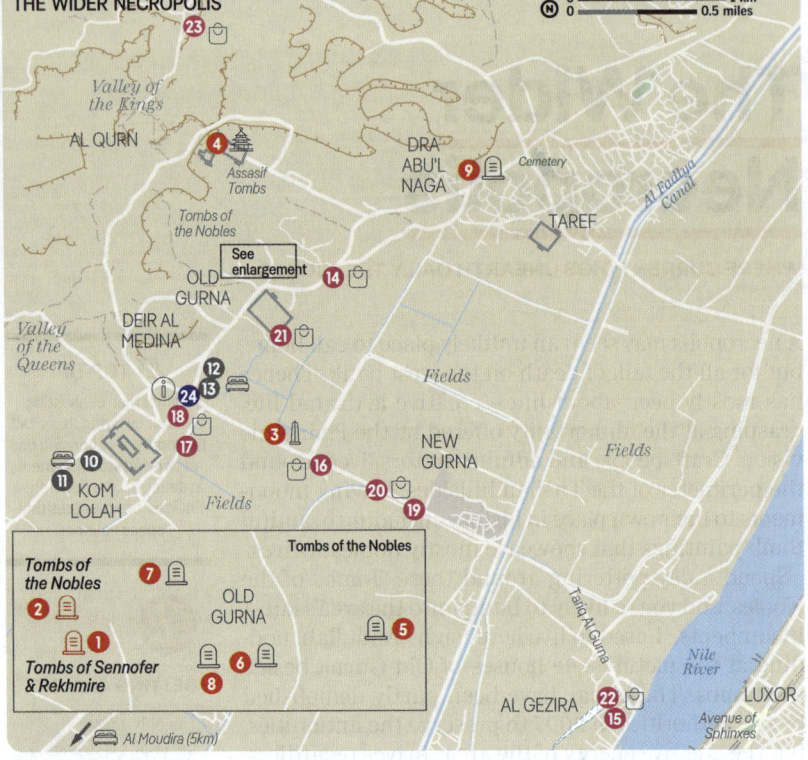

HIGHLIGHTS
1 Tombs of Sennofer & Rekhmire
2 Tombs of the Nobles

SIGHTS
3 Colossi of Memnon
4 Mortuary Temple of Hatshepsut
5 Tombs of Khonsu
6 Tombs of Menna, Nakht & Amenemope
7 Tombs of Neferronpet
8 Tombs of Ramose & Userhet
9 Tombs of Roy & Shuroy

SLEEPING
10 Beit Sabée
11 Malkata House Boutique Hotel
12 Marsam Hotel
13 Nour El Gourna

SHOPPING
14 Abo El Hassan Alabaster Factory
15 Abou Ali Crafts Collection
16 Cadeau
17 Caravanserai
18 Farouk Gallery
19 Habiba Hand Weaving
20 Nefertary Papyrus Institute
21 Ramesseum Pottery Workshop
22 Sandouk
23 Valley of the Kings Arcade

INFORMATION
24 Antiquities Inspectorate Ticket Office

Testimonials & Tonsorials

Tombs of Ramose and Userhet

The **Tomb of Ramose**, governor of Thebes under Amenhotep III and Akhenaten, is of great historical significance. It depicts rare images of worship of the sun disc, which the heretic king Akhenaten introduced in place of the polytheism of his predecessors.

Burial was big business in Thebes and attracted skills of all kinds, including professional mourners...and barbers. Both appear in the neighbouring **Tomb of Userhet**, together with gazelle hunting and wine making.

Recent Finds
Tombs of Roy and Shuroy

Beyond the Tombs of the Nobles, the necropolis stretches north, covering the tombs of rulers and officials dating largely from the 17th dynasty. It's a quiet area, albeit one of ongoing excavation: as recently as 2014 a royal tomb from the 11th dynasty was found here. Although most of the tombs have been plundered, the **Tomb of Roy**, with its wonderful ceiling, and the **Tomb of Shuroy**, which includes some fascinating early sketches rather than completed paintings, have survived.

Best of the Rest
Other TT Tombs

More than 400 tombs are catalogued under the generic term 'Tomb of the Nobles', identified by the label 'TT', which stands for 'Theban Tomb'. Not all are open all the time.

Favourites include the **Tomb of Sennofer**, which belongs to the overseer of the Garden of Amun. Reach up and you can almost pick the grapes depicted inside. The **Tomb of Rekhmire** offers the unusual sensation of walking up towards a false door in its long, narrow central chamber.

Look in the **Tomb of Neferronpet**, belonging to a treasury scribe, for a depiction of weighing gold. For a bit of birdwatching, check the ceiling of the **Tomb of Khonsu** (a priest who bore the title of First Prophet under the reign of Ramses II), where ducks are pictured flying around nests with eggs.

Learning a Trade
Workshop activities beside the necropolis

Suddenly industrious, youngsters beneath the Tombs of the Nobles start tapping rhythmically at rocks in front of them. On cue from the **alabaster workshop** supervisor, they hollow and chisel, file and polish, before exploding into a rendition of 'Happy Birthday to You'. With any luck the tourists filing into the showroom will buy something, but most do not.

It's kitsch for sure, but it's a practical demonstration of how the stone is made light and luminous, and these workshops provide essential support for apprentices. Even if you're not tempted to buy a piece, it's interesting to walk around the workshops, many of which line the road to the **Mortuary Temple of Hatshepsut** (p221), and see how stone can be made to sing.

There's a similarly fascinating experience to be had at the nearby **papyrus shops**. Visitors here learn how the fibrous stem of the papyrus plant is crushed and flattened, soaked and then arranged in right-angle strips to make paper.

Cotton Craft
Community project supporting women

The **handloom workshops** on the main road between Gezira and the Colossi of Memnon (p207) play a similar function for women as the alabaster, papyrus and pottery schools fulfil in supporting young men.

BEST CRAFT SHOPPING & DEMONSTRATIONS

Caravanserai: Family-run shop supporting women's earning potential.

Sandouk: A trove of gorgeous items, including rugs and ceramics. At research time the shop was moving to new premises. Check along the main road in Gezira.

Farouk Gallery: Antique shop selling 20th-century items.

Valley of the Kings Arcade: Covered souq en route to the ticket office. It's a bit intense but good for souvenirs.

Abou Ali Crafts Collection: Proudly displaying 'Made in Egypt' signs, this boutique sells interesting, quality crafts.

Habiba Hand Weaving: Watch handlooms in action at this fair-trade, fixed-price showroom.

Nefertary Papyrus Institute: See how papyrus is made at this workshop of fine paintings on the road to the ticket office.

Abo El Hassan Alabaster Factory: Listen to work in progress at this factory, one of many on the west bank. There's no pressure to buy.

An alabaster workshop (p227)

MASTER POTTER

Master potter **Komsan Abdo** owns **Ramesseum Pottery Workshop**; *facebook.com/komsan.abdo*

Pottery joins people together in special ways. It reaches across time and distance. When I put my hands on the wheel I work the clay in the same way our distant ancestors did. This makes me feel closer to the ancients buried in the hills opposite my workshop.

Making pots connects across countries. Recently a woman from the UK came to find me and now we are working on a project together. Visitors come here from many countries and we often don't speak the same language, but that doesn't matter because pottery speaks for us.

It feels good to be passing on this skill to our apprentices. It opens up a wider world for them.

Once better known for linen, Egypt is now world famous for cotton, and so fine is some of the yarn that it could almost be mistaken for silk or cashmere. The threads are generally dyed with natural, organic substances (derived from pomegranate, indigo, cochineal and henna, among others).

Cotton weaving and rug making are traditionally the work of women in Egypt, and those lucky enough to be given the opportunity to produce for a workshop earn more than just the sum of their labours: they earn a measure of economic independence too. Buying a handcrafted scarf or *galabeya* contributes too.

Made of Clay

Lessons at the pottery workshop

At digs around the Theban necropolis, shards of pot turn up so regularly that middens of baked clay have almost become a feature of the landscape. Look at these footnotes from the past and you'll see they vary in colour from burnt umber to terracotta. Only a trained eye is likely to detect whether they date from decades ago, when the village here was occupied, or are tomb contents from centuries earlier that have found their way to the surface. Either way, the shards illustrate a continuity in working with clay that links ancient and modern.

Reading about pottery making is one thing, but there's nothing quite like trying it in person, an experience offered at the **Pottery Workshop** beside the Ramesseum. The master potter operates the wheel and guides even the clumsiest of fingers through the elaborate techniques used to form different shapes. It's a sort of semaphore in clay, as complex as learning to play an instrument and requiring just as much sensitivity and expression.

The workshop supports apprentices and hopes to emulate the success of internationally renowned potters from Tunis in Fayoum. It's easy to see shared inspiration in the blue colours on a white background and the palm-plantation designs.

Places We Love to Stay

$ Budget $$ Midrange $$$ Top End

East Bank   MAP p199

Bob Marley Peace Hotel $ This travellers' favourite is run by helpful management and has a range of rooms and a cosy rooftop terrace.

Happy Land Hotel $ Popular with backpackers, this option continues to attract good reviews for its friendly atmosphere and good breakfasts.

Nefertiti Hotel $$ A wonderful family-run guesthouse, the Nefertiti has heaps of local character and an excellent Nile-view restaurant on the roof terrace. Tours are available through the on-site Aladin Tours Travel Agency.

Susanna Hotel $$ Offering simple, comfortable rooms, many with a Nile view, this centrally located hotel has a rooftop restaurant serving beers for sundowners.

Lotus Hotel $$ Wedged between bigger blocks, this small hotel is good value for money, with an attractive pool tucked under a giant dragon tree fronting the Nile.

Winter Palace Hotel (p204) **$$$** One of Egypt's most famous historic hotels, this grand establishment was built to attract Europe's aristocracy and continues to be something special, benefiting from a beautiful transformation of its garden and pools.

Iberotel $$$ With an interior vibe that's more business than resort, this competent hotel has the best Nile-side location of any central hotel on the east bank, a pool on a pontoon and beautiful gardens.

Sonesta St George Hotel $$$ A rather eccentric hotel that has somewhat overthought the cultural theme (complete with gilded lotus-decorated lift), this is nonetheless a central Nile-side choice.

Gezira   MAP p208

Al Gezira Hotel $ Sharing the facilities of the newer, more expensive Al Gezira Gardens, this popular option is excellent value, with bright rooms and a recommended restaurant on the terrace.

Cleopatra Hotel $ Sit on the terrace of this hotel, with its tranquil location and welcoming staff, and you'll soon get the measure of the rural west bank.

Al Fayrouz Hotel $ With a swimming pool in a sister hotel, this quaint guesthouse has a pretty garden and is appealingly decorated with local crafts.

El Mesala Hotel $$ Roll off a motorboat and onto the porch of this friendly, family-run hotel with Nile-view rooms and terrace. It has lots of experience in arranging tours.

Nile Valley Hotel $$ Cool off in the pool of this well-run hotel, owned by a Dutch-Egyptian couple. It's expanded over the years to be a tour de force in central Gezira.

Gold Ibis Hotel $$ The rooms of this family-run hotel have balconies that overlook Gezira towards the Nile, and the rooftop restaurant enjoys a 360-degree view.

Wider West Bank   MAP p222

Marsam Hotel $ Open your window onto green fields at this historic hotel from the 1920s, a favourite with archaeologists. Former guests include Howard Carter.

Nour El Gourna $ This traditional-style guesthouse, close to the ticket office, offers an equally traditional welcome. As one of the original hotels catering to archaeologists, it has earned its authentic ambience.

Beit Sabée $$ Enjoy home-cooked fare on the rooftop terrace of this friendly, family-run hotel. It has unsurpassed views of Medinat Habu and serves great food.

Malkata House Boutique Hotel $$$ One of the most aesthetically pleasing hotels in Luxor, this boutique hotel near Medinat Habu is chic in every detail, including in its luxury bathrooms.

Al Moudira $$$ Wake up to the sounds of rural Egypt in this gorgeous retreat with hammam (bathhouse), international head chef and palm-shaded pool.

For places to stay in the Southern Nile Valley, see p268

From left: Great Temple of Ramses II (p266); Nubian village in Aswan (p247)

Researched by
Mary Fitzpatrick

Southern Nile Valley

TEMPLES, TRADITIONS AND RIVER LIFE

A frontier land between two great kingdoms – Egypt and ancient Nubia – the southern Nile Valley straddles time, culture and history in dramatic desert surroundings.

Nowhere is the Nile more beautiful than at the ancient trading post of Aswan, which sits on the granite shelf of the river's First Cataract, where swift currents swirl around palm-studded islands and massive boulders. Impassable to boats, this barrier was for centuries the natural border between Egypt and Nubia, the powerful kingdom to the south that controlled trade from sub-Saharan Africa, from whence came gold, ivory, slaves, incense, dates and camels.

Such a dramatic backdrop naturally generates myth-making. Aswan and Elephantine Island are key elements of Egypt's origin story when Abu was capital of the first Upper Egyptian province in 3000 BCE. Hapi, the hermaphrodite river god responsible for the Nile's annual inundation, resided here, together with Anukis, Setis and Khnum, the ram-headed creator god of the cataract region.

Travelling here catapults you through the ages. In Esna, north of Aswan, Graeco-Roman ruins rub shoulders with Ottoman-era architecture. Nearby Al Kab, one of Egypt's oldest settlements, is home to some of the earliest-known hieroglyphs, while in the camel-trading hub of Daraw, herders haggle with buyers as they have done for centuries. South of Aswan, the modernistic High Dam rivals the engineering feat of the Giza Pyramids as it holds back the Nile's floodwaters, and at Abu Simbel, the magnificent temples of Ramses II rise dramatically from the desert on the edge of Lake Nasser.

THE MAIN AREAS

LUXOR TO ASWAN
Traditional villages and well-preserved temples. **p236**

ASWAN
Gateway to ancient Nubia. **p247**

LOWER NUBIA & LAKE NASSER
Ancient monuments and the High Dam. **p261**

ABU SIMBEL
Home to Egypt's most famous temples. **p265**

JON CHICA/SHUTTERSTOCK

Find Your Way

A combination of plane, train, bus and private taxi will get you around, but the best mode of transport is boat. Aswan is the terminus for southbound Nile cruises and the starting point for felucca (Egyptian sailing boat) trips northwards.

PRIVATE TAXI
Hiring a private taxi or car with driver is an efficient way to get around. Your driver will navigate police checks, arrange any necessary road permits and look after personal items while you visit the sights.

BUS & TRAIN
Daily trains connect Luxor (3½ to 4½ hours) and Cairo (12 to 15 hours) with Aswan, stopping also at Esna, Edfu and Kom Ombo. Frequent buses link Cairo and Luxor with Aswan and there are daily buses between Aswan and Abu Simbel.

AIR
Aswan International Airport is about 25km southwest of Aswan by road (allow 40 minutes). Daily flights link Aswan with Cairo. All flights between Cairo and Abu Simbel go via Aswan, often with lengthy layovers.

Abu Simbel, p265
This lively Nubian lakeside town is home to the magnificent Abu Simbel temples. It fills with visitors during the biannual solar alignment festival.

Abu Simbel

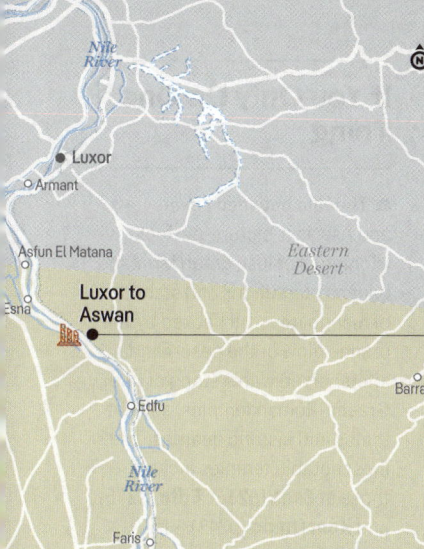

Luxor to Aswan, p236
Along this lovely stretch of the Nile, fringed by the Eastern Desert, the riverbanks are dotted with farms, traditional villages and Graeco-Roman temples.

Aswan, p247
In a beautiful setting overlooking the First Nile Cataract, Aswan – the old gateway to ancient Nubia – has been a strategic trading post for centuries.

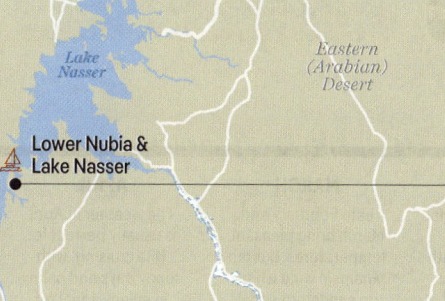

Lower Nubia & Lake Nasser, p261
Remote temples and lake cruises are the attractions of this area. Lower Nubia's villages are now mostly covered by the waters of Lake Nasser.

THE GUIDE

SOUTHERN NILE VALLEY

Plan Your Days

Don't miss Aswan and visits to Abu Simbel and the southern Nile Valley's other temples. But a highlight of your travels will undoubtedly be sailing on the Nile and immersing yourself in small-town Egyptian life.

Nubian decor

If You Only Do One Thing

● The Nile between Luxor and Aswan is picture-perfect: kilometres of lush green farmland, banana plantations and stands of mango trees, all backed by the orange glow of the desert and interspersed with a string of late Graeco-Roman temples, ancient tombs and historic quarries. The most notable temples include those at **Esna** (p236), **Edfu** (p245) and **Kom Ombo** (p243). Visit them by private vehicle or aboard a traditional boat, either on a luxurious dahabiya (houseboat) cruise from Esna to **Aswan** (p247) or sailing on a felucca between Aswan and Kom Ombo. Factor in several additional days at the beginning or end of the trip to enjoy Aswan's laid-back charms and to visit the not-to-be-missed **Abu Simbel temples** (p265).

SEASONAL HIGHLIGHTS

Summer days can top 45°C (113°F). April, October and November bring sunny days and balmy nights. Winter is pleasant, but nights can be cold on a boat.

FEBRUARY

The Aswan International Festival of Arts and Culture culminates with the Abu Simbel **solar alignment festival** on the 22nd (p267). It's celebrated with traditional music, dance performances and festive food stalls in the streets.

MARCH

Late February and March bring pleasant temperatures, but the *khamsin* wind whips up sandstorms that can disrupt flights and prevent Aswan's feluccas from sailing.

APRIL

The weather in April is usually perfect for Nile cruising, with sunny days and balmy evenings, ideal for relaxing on deck. In late April, Aswan hosts the **Aswan International Women Film Festival**.

A Week-Long Stay

● A few days in **Esna** (p236), getting acquainted with local life and customs, doing walking tours and seeing a side of Egypt far removed from the crowds, will likely be a highlight of your travels. From Esna, head south to **Aswan** (p247) for several nights in a Nubian guesthouse on charming **Elephantine Island** (p250), with days spent sailing and birdwatching on the river, learning about Nubian traditions and visiting the Graeco-Roman **Philae Temple** (p258). Finish with an excursion to Aswan's west bank to see the **Tombs of the Nobles** (p255), enjoy stunning views over the river and a camel ride to the ruins of the **Monastery of St Simeon** (p256), before sailing overnight on a felucca to **Kom Ombo** (p243).

If You Have More Time

● Sail on a **dahabiya** (p241) to experience Upper Egypt's timelessness from a riverine perspective. A dahabiya allows you to reach sites where large Nile cruisers don't go, including **Gebel Silsila** (p240). If the winds are good, also consider a few days on a **felucca** (p242), which is ideal for experiencing the bucolic Nile scenery as you drift along without the hum of a motor. In **Aswan** (p247), continue the riverine theme by hiring a small motorboat to explore the islands of the reservoir between the Low and High Dam. Finish up with a **Lake Nasser cruise** (p262), stopping en route at remote sites and watching flocks of pelicans framed by glowing sunsets before gliding up to the magnificent **Abu Simbel temples** (p265).

MAY
May is a good month for budget travellers. Temperatures start to rise, meaning fewer crowds, but the heat is still tolerable and prices are reasonable.

AUGUST
Sweltering. Aswan is one of the hottest places on earth in August, with summer temperatures regularly topping 45°C. If you're travelling, take refuge in cooler inner courtyards, sipping chilled hibiscus juice in the shade.

OCTOBER
October brings near-perfect temperatures and a lovely, soft light on the Nile. Aswan hosts another International Festival of Arts and Culture, ending with Abu Simbel's second **solar alignment festival** on the 22nd (p267).

DECEMBER
The December–January holiday season around Christmas and New Year is peak time for Nile cruising, so prices skyrocket and hotels fill up. Evenings can be cold, especially on the river.

Luxor to Aswan

TEMPLES | TRADITIONAL CUISINE | NILE CRUISING

☑ TOP TIP
Contact the **VISIT Esna** *(facebook.com/Discover .Esna; +20 10-2898-0167; okra@pr-ba.com)* cultural tourism initiative for walking tours, family visits and excursions, or stop in at the Pr. Ba Concept Store (p239).

GETTING AROUND

Trains between Luxor and Aswan stop in Esna, Edfu and Kom Ombo. Stations are connected with the temples and town centres by taxi and horse-drawn carriage. Recommended drivers: **Noby Alaam** *(+20 10-2213-5814)*, **Hamdy Allam** *(+20 10-1274-3378)*, **Elshafie** *(+20 10-2311-5581)* and **Muhammad Omar** *(+20 11-2522-2260)*.

Dahabiya trips from Luxor normally start at Esna. Felucca trips from Aswan terminate at either Kom Ombo or before Edfu, with road travel to cover the remainder.

The Nile between Luxor and Aswan is lined by a narrow belt of lush vegetation yielding abruptly to desert sands. This area was once thought to be the domain of the vulture and crocodile gods, yet many of its historical monuments date from the last period of ancient Egyptian history, when the country was ruled by the descendants of Alexander the Great's Macedonian general, Ptolemy I (323–283 BCE). The Ptolemies respected the country's traditions and religion and ensured peaceful rule in Upper Egypt by erecting temples in honour of the local gods. Those at Esna, Edfu, Kom Ombo and Philae are as notable for their strategic locations as they are for their artistic and architectural merit.

Another highlight is Esna town, the focal point of a cultural tourism initiative and a not-to-be-missed stop for travellers seeking to discover another side of Egypt, well off the beaten path.

Discovering Esna Past & Present
Experience local life and culture

About an hour's drive south of Luxor is the lively, riverside town of **Esna**, once an important stop on the centuries-old Darb Al Arba'een camel-caravan route linking Sudan with Egypt. Its hub was the atmospheric and still bustling **Al Qīsāriyya Market** where merchants congregated to barter and sell their wares. While subsequent decades of neglect eroded Esna's economic prosperity, they preserved much of its cultural heritage. And it is this that sustainable tourism initiative **VISIT Esna** has placed at the heart of its wonderful, community-led tourism project. Trained local guides such as **Rehab Mokhtar** *(+20 11-5660-8019)* lead walking tours that will take you deep into old Esna, as you listen to local stories, meet Esna residents and visit the town's many architectural highlights.

As you make your way around the compact central area, watch for the Fatimid-era **Al Amriyya minaret**, built in

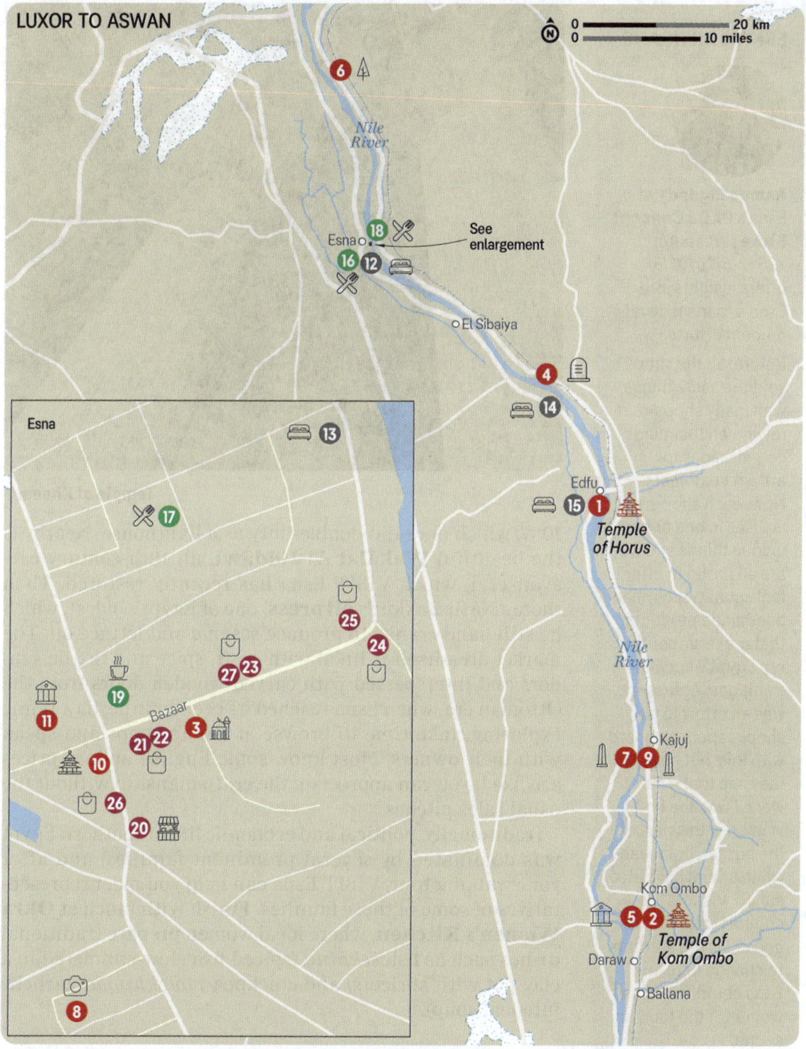

LUXOR TO ASWAN

Map: Southern Nile Valley — Luxor to Aswan

HIGHLIGHTS
1. Temple of Horus
2. Temple of Kom Ombo

SIGHTS
3. Al Amriyya Minaret
4. Al Kab Tombs
5. Crocodile Museum
6. Dababiya Natural Reserve
7. Gebel Silsila
8. Oil Press
9. Speos of Horemheb
10. Temple of Khnum
11. Wakālat Al Jiddāwī

SLEEPING
12. Al Haramain
13. El Salam Hotel
14. Funduk Al Shams
15. Horus Hotel

EATING
16. Okra Women's Kitchen
17. Taghmest Ramadan
18. Zalabia

DRINKING & NIGHTLIFE
19. Omar's Coffee Shop

SHOPPING
20. Al Qīsāriyya Market
21. Ali Baba
22. Iron Man
23. Khnum
24. King T-Shirts
25. Pottery Home
26. Pr.Ba Concept Store
27. Seba

ESNA'S ARTISANS

Asmaa Elgendy at Esna's **Pr.Ba Concept Store** *(WhatsApp: +20 12-8190-0215)* offers insights into Esna's tourism development efforts.

Before, all the shops sold the same things, with many shops relying on tour guide commissions to attract customers. Now, each shop specialises in one or two unique things and we are all proud to offer high-quality, Egyptian handmade products that preserve southern Egypt's special traditions. At first, it was an effort to get shopkeepers on board with this, but now, they see that it can work. I was the first woman in this part of the bazaar, but meanwhile others have also joined. Visitors are comfortable with us, and ideas are starting to change here in Esna about the role of women in the tourism sector.

Temple of Khnum

1087, which once did double-duty as a lighthouse. Nearby is the beautiful **Wakālat Al Jiddāwī**, an 18th-century caravanserai, which VISIT Esna has recently restored. Then there's Nāṣir Bakkūr's **oil press**, one of Egypt's oldest, which he still hand cranks to produce sesame and lettuce oil. The market area itself is lined with craft, spice and textile vendors and interspersed with carved wooden doors from the Ottoman era, when Esna reached its economic heyday. While exploring, take time to browse at Esna's shops and speak with their owners. Most know some English and, as prices are fixed, you can appreciate the craftsmanship without the usual sales pitches.

Traditionally, political and economic life in southern Egypt was dominated by several prominent families, and after your walking tour, VISIT Esna can help you meet representatives of some of these families. Finish with lunch at **Okra Women's Kitchen**, where local women prepare traditional dishes such as fish *sekhina* (spiced fish slow-simmered in a clay pot with apricots) and chickpea-*molokhiyya* (garlicky jute leaf soup).

Detail & Drama in Esna's Temple

Creation myths and cosmological scenes

It is Khnum – the ram-headed Lord of the First Nile Cataract and the creator god who moulded living creatures from the Nile's rich clay – who holds the place of honour at Esna's colourful **Temple of Khnum** *(adult/student LE200/100)*. The temple was begun by Ptolemy VI Philometor (180–145 BCE). Later, the Romans added its magnificent hypostyle hall, which is supported by 18 frescoed interior columns. For 15 centuries, the edifice lay buried by sand and silt until it was excavated in the 19th century by French archaeologist Auguste Mariette.

As you enter the dim interior from the bright sunlight, it takes a moment for the eyes to adjust before you can fully appreciate the columns' exuberant designs. Each one is unique. Some are topped with papyrus fans, others with lotus buds and some have a Roman addition – grapes. To the right of the entrance is the only original zodiac in Egypt's Graeco-Roman temples, over which arches the body of Nut, the sky goddess. The ceiling is covered with lavish cosmological scenes, while the walls are lined with a relief of temple patron Ptolemy VI Philometor with other Roman pharaohs, depicting them making respectful offerings to Esna's gods: Khnum, Neith (his consort) and Heka, their son. Khnum, meanwhile, is depicted inside the front facade sitting at his potter's wheel creating the first beings of the world. Flanking him are two hymns: the first a morning hymn of awakening and the second a hymn of creation.

To create the frescoes, limestone was covered with a gesso plaster (made of animal glue binder, chalk and white pigment) onto which natural pigments were applied. These pigments were sourced from minerals in the desert hills: red and yellow derived from ochre-containing iron oxides, with some reds from realgar (an arsenic sulfide). Blues and greens came from azurite and malachite, or hydrated copper chloride. Yellow was extracted from orpiment and black from carbon. As the frescoes at Esna are cleaned, the effect of the original colours is dazzling.

Ancient Clues to Global Warming
Geological treasures at Dababiya NR

We're not the only ones faced with climate change. Over 55 million years ago, during an era known as the Paleocene–Eocene Thermal Maximum (PETM), Earth's average surface temperature rose by over 5°C, accompanied by significant increases in atmospheric and oceanic carbon dioxide levels. Many species became extinct, although the period was also marked by advancements in mammalian evolution. Today, scientists study the PETM for clues to better understanding the effects of our current global warming.

About 30km north of Esna on the Nile's east bank, and an easy morning's excursion from town, is a quarry, now protected as **Dababiya Natural Reserve** *(beta.sis.gov.eg; adult/student LE100/50)*, that holds some of the most clearly visible evidence of the PETM. Your guide will point out the still intact and clearly visible layers of rock, which rock hounds read as

BEST PLACES TO SHOP IN ESNA

Iron Man: Quality *galabeyas* (men's robes) and traditional foot-ironing services.

Khnum: Textiles and scarves, and a loom where you can watch the weaver at work.

King T-Shirts: Save your souvenir T-shirt shopping for this place, which has designs reflecting Egyptian history and Esna life.

Pottery Home: Handcrafted ceramics and pottery, made from Nile clay.

Pr.Ba Concept Store: Esna's first woman-run shop, with beautiful locally produced bags, scarves and handicrafts.

Seba: Exquisite alabaster designs and locally carved woodwork.

Ali Baba: Well-made scarab charms, *ankh* carvings and more.

EATING IN ESNA: OUR PICKS

Okra Women's Kitchen: Traditional cuisine at a women's initiative opposite the Coptic church. *advance bookings essential (+20 10-2898-0167; okra@pr-ba.com)* $

Omar's Coffee Shop: Settle in for mint tea, chilled hibiscus juice and other refreshments at this cosy spot near Khnum temple. *8am-late* $

Taghmest Ramadan: Enjoy *fuul* (fava-bean stew) and other Egyptian breakfast favourites at this local-style place near El Salam Hotel. *5am-11am* $

Zalabia: This small street stand near Hasheem mosque serves up scrumptious *zalabiya* (Egyptian doughnuts) with your choice of toppings. *3pm-8pm* $

CULTURAL CONSERVATION IN SOUTHERN EGYPT

'Cities thrive with innovative solutions that have been researched, tested and implemented to meet the needs of communities and their built environments. In this way, inclusive urban spaces develop that will flourish for generations to come,' notes Sherine Zaghow of **Takween Integrated Community Development** *(takween-eg.com)*. Takween has been working with the local community in historical Esna (p236) for just under a decade. Yet, already, the partnership has transformed the tourist experience and put Esna on the map again. 'Esna stands out,' notes Zaghow, 'not only for its beautiful temple and multilayered history, but also for its range of authentic cultural experiences – something special in a country where tourism tends to be heavily site- and temple-focused.'

Gebel Silsila

documentation of the transition between the Paleocene and Eocene eras. Bookings (made through VISIT Esna) include a guide and lunch cooked by village women. Start early, before it gets too hot.

Explore the Tombs of Ancient Nekheb
One of Egypt's oldest settlements

About 40km southeast of Luxor lie the often overlooked ruins of **Al Kab** *(egymonuments.gov.eg; adult/student LE150/75)* – ancient Nekheb – one of southern Egypt's oldest settlements. Much of the area is closed to the public, but several New Kingdom tombs can be easily visited, including the well-preserved tomb of Ahmose, a naval captain under Pharaoh Ahmose I. The entrance is just off the Luxor–Esna–Aswan road, and an easy stop if you're travelling via private taxi. Across the road are the old walls of Nekheb, and stretching northeast of the main tombs area is **Wadi Hilal**, with several more sites, including a small shrine dedicated to Nekhbet (the vulture goddess) and Hathor and believed to have been built in part by Amenhotep III (1390–1352 BCE). Let the guard at the ticket office know if you'll be venturing to the shrine, which is over 3km from the entrance, so they can send someone to unlock the door. Also bring water and shade; it's a hot, bumpy drive.

Quarrying for Eternity
Sacred sites in a lunar landscape

If you're cruising between Esna and Aswan on a dahabiya, you'll likely stop at **Gebel Silsila** *(egymonuments.gov.eg; adult/student LE100/50),* where a dramatic gorge marks the narrowest point of the Nile and a change in the bedrock of Egypt from limestone to sandstone. Sandstone, although harder to work, has greater inherent strength that supported monumental temples. From the New Kingdom through to the Roman era, the surrounding hillsides were heavily quarried, as labourers hand-cut huge stone blocks and floated them downriver to Luxor to be used in building the temples of Karnak, Luxor, Dendara, Esna and Edfu.

Gebel Silsila was also a significant trading centre between Egypt and Nubia, and the area's many inscriptions attest to its long history as a crossroads. While Gebel Silsila spans both sides of the Nile, the most interesting monuments, and those open to tourists, are on the west bank, which is scattered with stelae and shrines. Watch for the **Speos of Horemheb**, a modest rock-cut temple dedicated to Pharaoh Horemheb (r 1319–1292 BCE) and seven deities. Smaller shrines to Seti I, Ramses II, Merenptah and other officials are nearby.

In the quarry itself, you can clearly see masons' marks sheering away the cliff face with extraordinary precision. Hieroglyphic and hieratic inscriptions give clues as to how the massive blocks were extracted, moved down ramps and onto boats so they could be floated away during the flood. At the southern end of the site is a massive pillar of rock known as the capstan, so-called because locals believe there was once a chain – *silsila* in Arabic – that ran from the east to the west bank. Note that if you approach Gebel Silsila by road from the east, you'll need to arrange a local motorboat to cross the river.

Cruising Between Luxor & Aswan

Travel in vintage style

While the big Nile cruisers offer some perks, the most atmospheric boat for vintage travel is the double-masted **dahabiya**, literally 'the golden one' for the gilding that once adorned the vessels of the rich and the royal. The boats had their heyday in the 19th and early 20th centuries, when they were the main way to cruise the Nile and served as the preferred mode of transport for everyone from aristocrats to archaeologists.

These days a handful of companies operate small fleets of dahabiyas, allowing you to glide along the Nile by day, towed by a tug when winds are unfavourable, and stopping en route at sites that are inaccessible to the large cruisers. Most mornings there's a tour of the temples – at Esna, Edfu and Kom Ombo, and often also visits to the tombs at Al Kab and the Gebel Silsila quarry. The pace is leisurely and the small scale of the Ptolemaic temples allows you to linger on the details. Back on board, gliding close to the water, the dahabiya cruise immerses you in the life of the river, with views of neatly tended farms, birds freewheeling off the water and buffaloes grazing docilely on grassy islands. At times, the riparian scene seems almost biblical, particularly when you disembark on uninhabited islands for stunning sunset walks. Nights are spent moored on the riverbank. Each dahabiya has between eight and 12 comfortable, en suite cabins with large windows that sit just above the level

THE BEST DAHABIYAS

Nour el Nil: A fleet of eight vintage-style dahabiyas with eight to 10 cabins furnished in varying styles, with an emphasis throughout on relaxed luxury.

Nile Dahabiya Boats: A fleet of four smaller dahabiyas with five to six cabins run by Luxor locals.

Dahabiya Nile Sailing: A fleet of five dahabiyas and a range of three- to five-night itineraries, with the chance to also kayak or fish.

La Flâneuse du Nil: A luxury dahabiya retrofitted with an ecofriendly electrical power system.

Sanctuary Zein Nile Chateau: A 50m luxury private charter with six cabins.

>
> **MORE ON NILE CRUISING**
> For more tips on planning a Nile cruise, including deciding when to go, what itinerary works best and what boat suits your style and needs, see p410.

of the water. Above is the shaded deck, which acts as an open-air drawing room and is furnished with divans, carpets and floor cushions. At the end of the journey, you'll glide into Aswan in the golden glow of sunset. You could, of course, make the journey faster by car or cruise ship, but you won't take with you such unforgettable memories of the Nile.

Downriver by Felucca
Experience the timelessness of the Nile

No trip to the southern Nile Valley would be complete without an adventure in a **felucca**. This ancient fishing boat with its large lateen sail has been in use by Nile fishers for centuries. Sailing in a felucca is an entirely different experience to being aboard a dahabiya or a cruise ship. Most trips start in Aswan and head northwards with the wind and the current, sometimes stopping en route at small villages. At night, the boat is moored, and calm returns as you drift to sleep under the stars after an evening bonfire on the riverbank.

Despite their romance, feluccas are working vessels and therefore frill- and cabin-free. Instead, passengers live, eat and sleep on a shaded deck. In winter it can get cold, so bring a sleeping bag or check there are blankets aboard. Feluccas also have no plumbing, with toilet breaks taken on the riverbank behind a screen. Check the supply of toilet paper or bring your own, and a torch. A more upmarket version of a felucca is a *sandal,* which does have an onboard toilet.

The most popular overnight felucca trip is from Aswan to Kom Ombo (one to two nights), with Edfu trips also possible (three nights, with most feluccas stopping short of Edfu). Guests are then picked up by car and driven on to either Edfu or Luxor. To test things out before committing to an overnight trip, try a sunset felucca sail in Aswan. Also, when planning, check with your captain about current wind conditions; if you're becalmed, your itinerary may need to be shortened. Recommended contacts include **Captain Safy** *(nubiansailing.com/NubianSailing.html),* who offers well-run cruises with tasty Nubian lunches; **Captain Ziggy** *(+20 12-0856-2850),* an individual operator with personalised service; **JJ Jamaica's Captain Nori** *(facebook .com/JJJamaicaFelucca),* who has a fleet of feluccas and a six-cabin *sandal;* and **Waleed** at Aswan Individual *(aswan-individual.com),* who offers an array of felucca trips with local captains. Note that sailing the full stretch from Aswan to Luxor isn't possible.

FELUCCA TIPS

- Felucca prices are reasonable. Consider splurging on a whole boat for your group.
- For a shared felucca, agree on the number of passengers and try to meet your fellow travellers beforehand.
- Confirm what the price includes, especially for food and water; 3L per person per day is a minimum.
- Make sure your felucca has sun shade and a mosquito net.
- Stay flexible. Confirm your drop-off point before departure, but be aware that this may change with the winds.
- Don't hand over your passport; a photocopy is sufficient to arrange permits.
- Bring a hat, sunscreen and insect repellent.
- Wherever you stop, burn all rubbish and bury bodily waste.
- Only swim in fast-moving water, as bilharzia is present in the Nile.

TOP EXPERIENCE

Temple of Kom Ombo

In ancient times, Kom Ombo was known as Pa-Sobek (Land of Sobek) in honour of the crocodile god, Sobek, who was believed to reside beside his fellow crocodiles on this bend of the Nile. One of the Nile Valley's most scenically sited temples, Kom Ombo is unique in being dedicated to two gods: Sobek and Haroeris, his brother, otherwise known as Horus the Elder.

DON'T MISS

Carvings of Sobek in the hypostyle hall

Crocodile Museum

Festival calendar

Early surgical instruments

Views of the Nile through ruins

Secret passage

Kom Ombo

Kom Ombo was an important military base and trading centre in the Ptolemaic Period (332 BCE–395 CE). It became capital of the first Upper Egyptian province during the reign of Ptolemy VI Philometor (180–145 BCE), father of the famous Cleopatra VII who built the temple. Gold, ivory and elephants were traded here between Nubia and Egypt and many Nubians still call Kom Ombo home, having relocated here when their towns were flooded during Aswan High Dam construction.

PRACTICALITIES
Scan the QR code for prices and opening hours.

EARLY SURGERY

On the outside (northern) wall of the passage surrounding Kom Ombo's temple is a scene depicting what appear to be early surgical instruments, including scalpels, saws, forceps, specula, scissors and medicine bottles. At the time, Egyptian medicine was likely the most advanced in the world. The oldest known medical document is the 'Edwin Smith surgical papyrus' dating from 1600 BCE (believed to be a copy of an older text), which lists 48 injury cases and effective treatments for them, without any mention of magic.

TOP TIPS

- The temple is about 4km from the train station (LE70 in a tuk-tuk).

- A private car from Luxor costs from LE1600, including a stop at Edfu.

- Between the temple and the Nile is a cafeteria with a large, pleasant garden.

- There are no recommendable hotels in Kom Ombo. It's best visited as a half-day excursion from Aswan, or as a stop en route between Luxor and Aswan.

The Twin Temple

An earlier New Kingdom temple once stood here, but the present structure dates from the Ptolemaic Period. Dedicated to two gods, it is unique in its design, with two perfectly symmetrical parallel temples along its main axis with twin entrances, hypostyle halls and separate sanctuaries. The eastern temple (on the right) is dedicated to the crocodile-god Sobek, the god of fertility, who resided here with Hathor (the goddess of fertility) and their son, the moon god Khonsu. The western temple was dedicated to Haroeris (Horus the Elder, so-called after his conquest of Seth), his companion Tasenetnefret (a form of Hathor) and their son Panebtawy, the 'Lord of the Two Lands' (Upper and Lower Egypt).

The Hypostyle Halls

The ruined outer and inner hypostyle halls sport 10 columns, each decorated with **carvings** of the temple gods and capitals of lotus leaves. Reliefs on the remaining walls show images glorifying the pharaoh. In the outer hall, on the right-hand side, Ptolemy XII is crowned by Nekhbet, the vulture goddess. In the inner hall, Haroeris presents Ptolemy VIII Euergetes with a curved weapon representing the sword of victory, while his sister-wife, Cleopatra II, looks on. More interesting are the smaller carvings, one depicting a woman giving birth and another showing an ancient Egyptian **festival calendar** with dates and rituals meticulously recorded.

The Inner Sanctuaries

From the inner hypostyle, three antechambers, each with double entrances, lead to the sanctuaries of Sobek and Haroeris. The now-ruined chambers on either side would have been used to store priests' vestments and liturgical papyri. The walls of the sanctuaries are now one or two courses high, exposing a **secret passage** in between. It is thought that this enabled the priests to listen to the petitions of pilgrims and answer them unseen – creating the impression of the cult statue miraculously answering the prayers of the devoted.

Crocodile Museum

Near the temple's exit is the **Crocodile Museum** (*egymonuments.gov.eg; entry included with Kom Ombo ticket*), well worth a visit for its collection of mummified crocodiles and sculptures associated with the Sobek cult. Live crocodiles were worshipped in Upper Egypt and the Kom Ombo priests cared for some in a pool near the temple. When a crocodile died, it was believed that the soul of the god transferred to another crocodile, and the dead crocodile was ritually mummified. The mummies in the museum – several over 4m long – come from the Middle Kingdom necropolis of El Shutb, about 2km south of Kom Ombo. A model tomb and some still carefully wrapped crocodile mummies demonstrate how the animals were buried in pottery coffins.

Falcon god Horus

TOP EXPERIENCE

Temple of Horus, Edfu

Edfu, midway between Luxor and Aswan, is home to the imposing Temple of Horus, which is considered to be one of the best-preserved temples of the ancient world. Built between 237 and 57 BCE by the Ptolemies, it is modelled on older Pharaonic designs. According to myth, the temple marks the spot where falcon god Horus defeated his murderous uncle, Seth, to avenge the death of his father, Osiris.

DON'T MISS

Pylon carvings of Ptolemy XII

Gateway with granite falcons

Perfume laboratory

Inner sanctuary and wooden barque

Great court reliefs

Hall of consecrations

Edfu's Temple Architecture

The Egyptian name for a temple, *het-netjer,* means 'mansion of the god', and Edfu's temple architecture is full of significance. Gold was considered to be the flesh of the gods, and the golden cult image of Horus once housed in the inner sanctum was the god's embodiment, while the surrounding temple was a model of the world. The wall decor showing plants and animals represented the earth, while the columns signified trees, and the ceiling – covered in stars – mirrored the cosmos.

PRACTICALITIES
Scan the QR code for prices and opening hours.

HORUS: THE FATHER OF PHARAOHS

Horus, son of Osiris, was the god of kingship, with pharaohs tracing their lineage to him. Protected by his magic-wielding mother, Isis, Horus defeated his rival Seth and restored cosmic order, leading to Osiris' resurrection. This myth was integral to ancient concepts of succession and gave rise to the people's duty to protect and respect the pharaoh – Horus' representative on earth – to maintain order in the universe.

TOP TIPS

● A car and driver from Luxor to Edfu will cost from about LE1300 one-way.

● The train station is on the east bank of the Nile. Tuk-tuks charge from LE70 to cover the approximately 4km to the temple.

● If you arrive by boat take a tuk-tuk or a horse-drawn carriage from the dock and ask the driver to wait. The round trip will cost from LE150 plus tip.

● As a stop for most large Nile cruisers, Edfu temple tends to get very crowded from around 8am. The best times to visit are early morning and late afternoon.

Court of Offerings

The public was not permitted into the temple, but rather gathered in the **great court** just inside the entrance. It is surrounded by 32 columns decorated with palms, lotus and papyrus and the walls are covered with reliefs. One, just inside the entrance, shows Horus greeting his consort Hathor, who resided at Dendara (p186). Her statue visited Edfu each year during the annual fertility celebrations.

The Hypostyle Halls

The outer hypostyle hall is decorated with reliefs of Pharaoh Euergetes. One shows him laying the foundation stone of the temple, while another depicts him and his wife Cleopatra bringing offerings to Horus, Hathor and their son, Harsomtus. On either side of these two columned halls are small chambers. One housed the temple library, while another was the **hall of consecrations** – a vestry for robes and ritual vases. The most interesting, in the inner hypostyle, was a **laboratory** decorated with reliefs depicting the recipes used to create temple perfumes and incense.

On either side of the inner hypostyle hall are doorways exiting into the **Passage of Victory**, with reliefs showing the reenactment of the battle between Horus and Seth, who is shown in the form of a hippopotamus.

Offering Chamber

Next is the chamber where the priest made offerings of food, flowers, wine, clothing and jewellery on behalf of the pharaoh to ensure their health, plentiful harvests and victory over enemies. On the temple's west side, 242 steps lead up to the roof (currently closed to visitors) and are lined with scenes from the New Year festival, when the priests carried the statue of Horus to the rooftop to be renewed by the sun.

Inner Sanctuary

The smallest room in the complex is the inner sanctuary. As you make your way back, watch how the halls narrow – decreasing in height and width – to create a sense of perspective and drama. It is here, upon the polished granite altar at the temple's heart, that the golden statue of Horus once stood. In front is a replica of the **wooden barque** that was used to carry a golden statue of Hathor on festival days.

Pylon (Gateway)

Following Theodosius I's edict in 391 CE banning non-Christian worship within the Roman Empire, Edfu's temple fell into disuse and was buried by layers of silt and rubbish. In 1798, when a French archaeological expedition arrived, only the tops of the two 36m-high pylon towers – flanked by **granite statues** of Horus and carved with images of the pharaoh smiting his enemies – were visible. Excavations started in 1860, gradually restoring the temple to its present grandeur.

Aswan

NUBIAN CULTURE | FELUCCA SAILING | NILE VIEWS

Aswan's history was always going to be different. However much Theban, Macedonian or Roman rulers in the north may have wanted to ignore the south, they dared not neglect this strategic border town. Settlement on Elephantine Island dates back to at least 3000 BCE. Named Abu (Ivory) after the trade that flourished here, it was a natural fortress positioned just below the First Nile Cataract, one of six sets of rapids between Aswan and Khartoum.

In subsequent eras, Aswan was a place of exile, a military hub for colonial troops and one of the earliest tourist destinations in the modern world thanks to Thomas Cook's Nile tours, which began in 1869. Today Aswan continues to thrive as a trading hub, university town and tourist favourite. There is a large Nubian community here, the pace is unhurried and the views of the Nile framed by the desert are enchanting. It's the perfect place to kick back and relax.

Colourful Spices & Abundant Fruits   MAP P252
A stroll through Aswan's souq

Midway along the riverside Corniche, head inland one block to **Sharia As Souq**, Aswan's bazaar street. It's wonderful to wander, full of merchants selling scarves, *galabeyas,* perfumes and spices. Vending only gets started after noon, with summer evenings the liveliest times to visit.

The further in you go, the less touristy it becomes. Items to seek out include sand-roasted *fuul sudani* (peanuts), top-quality henna powder, various teas, any spice you could imagine and the dried hibiscus flowers used to make *karkadai* (cold hibiscus tea).

Delving into Nubian History   MAP P252
Nubian art in an award-winning museum

The beautiful **Nubia Museum** *(egymonuments.gov.eg; adult/student LE300/150)* was created in response to UNESCO's

☑ TOP TIP

To minimise hassles and get the most from your visit to Aswan's sights, it's worth seeking out a quality guide. See our recommendations on p254. The **Aswan International Women Film Festival** *(aiwff.org/home/en)* attracted films from 30 countries in its most recent (2025) edition.

GETTING AROUND

There are three main areas: the east bank, Elephantine Island and the west bank. Public ferries run from just south of the KFC to Elephantine Island 'Siou side'; from just north of Fryal Gardens to Elephantine Island 'Koti side'; and from the Corniche near the train station for the west bank (Aswan Gharb), landing just below the Tombs of the Nobles. All cost LE10 one-way and run from 6am until late. Otherwise, use a mix of felucca, motorboat, taxis and tours.

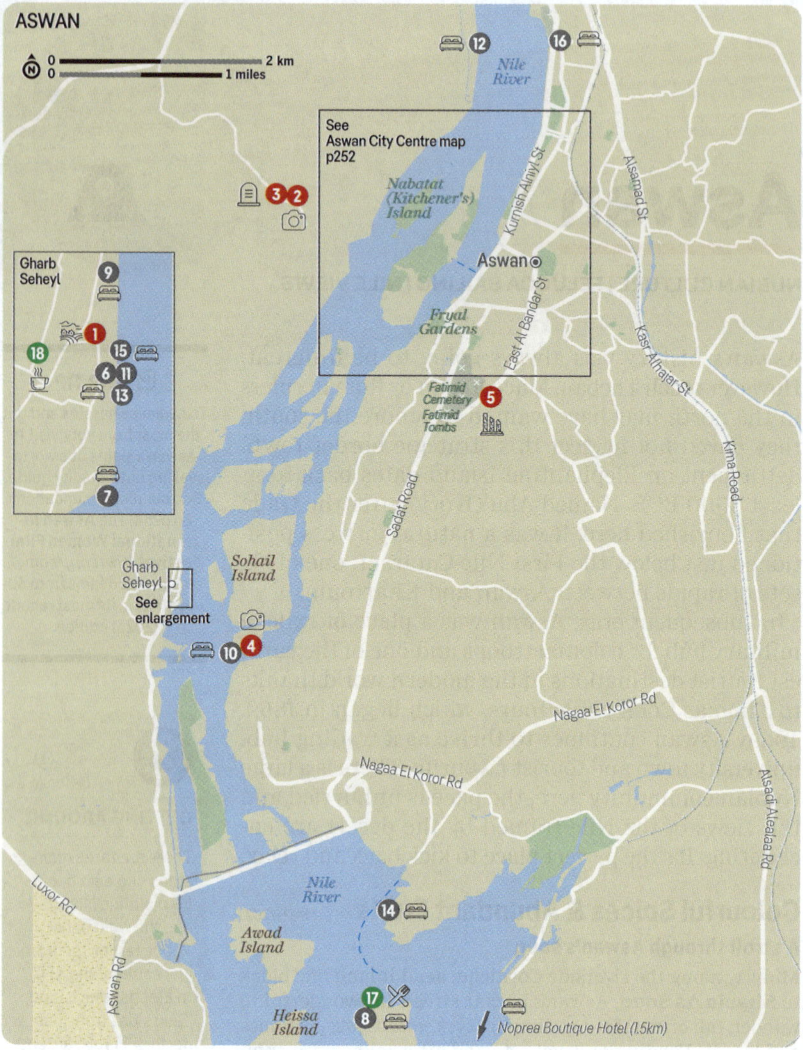

ASWAN

SIGHTS
1. Gharb Seheyl
2. Monastery of St Simeon
3. Qubbet Al Hawa
4. Seheyl Island
5. Unfinished Obelisk

SLEEPING
6. Anakato
7. Artika Wadi Kiki
8. Eco Nubia Lodge
9. Kato Dool Wellness Resort
10. Krouma Ecolodge
11. Lawanda
12. Maghrabi's Guesthouse
13. Nub Inn
14. Old Nubian Guesthouse
15. Onaty Ka
16. Tolip Hotel Aswan

EATING
see 7 Artika Wadi Kiki
see 9 Kato Dool
see 13 Nub Inn
see 15 Onaty Ka
17. Solaih Nubian Restaurant

DRINKING & NIGHTLIFE
18. Cafe Nasr

1960s salvage operation undertaken with the aim of preserving Nubian artefacts rescued from Lower Nubia before it was flooded. Designed by Mahmoud Al Hakim and housed in an attractive building fashioned out of Aswan's signature pink granite, it won the Aga Khan Award for Islamic architecture. Within are over 3000 artefacts (displayed on a rotating basis) spread over two dramatically lit floors. Among the highlights are early painted pottery bowls dating back 6000 years, which were found at Nabta Playa (about 100km west of Abu Simbel), where archaeologists also discovered the remains of houses, sculpted monoliths and one of the world's oldest calendars.

As you move through the museum, excellent explanations map the power struggle between Nubia and Egypt. The two cultures have been intertwined since at least 3500 BCE: when Egypt was strong, it dominated Nubia and exploited its natural resources; when Egypt was weak, the Nubians enjoyed periods of growth. These cross-cultural influences are clearly visible in the impressive statuary. Although wearing Egyptian attire, the high priest of Amun in Thebes has distinctive Nubian features, as does the granite head of Pharaoh Shabatka from the 25th dynasty, when the Nubians controlled Egypt for nearly a century (from 744 to 656 BCE).

Other treasures include a set of decorative silver livery and saddles mounted on two spot-lit horses. They date from the 5th to the 7th centuries BCE, just prior to the Christianisation of Nubia, and were discovered in one of 122 tombs at Ballana, near the Sudanese border and now underwater. Beside them, a row of silver crowns studded with carnelians glow in a glass cabinet. Subsequent rooms take you through the Coptic and Islamic eras, when Nubians were converted to Christianity and then to Islam.

The exhibit finally turns to modern times and efforts to control irrigation along the Nile. This is followed by documentation of the huge UNESCO effort to rescue Nubia's treasures and relocate 22 ancient temples before the High Dam's flooding in 1971. That event saw 100,000 people displaced from their homelands. Many moved to Abu Simbel, Aswan and Kom Ombo.

Before exiting, check out the dioramas showing scenes from traditional Nubian life – a traditional home, school and festival day. It all makes an ideal complement to experiencing the real thing for yourself when exploring Elephantine Island, Gharb Seheyl and other areas around Aswan, where Nubians continue to practise their ancient language, traditions and culture.

FINDING MAGIC IN ASWAN

Mena Zaki, an Egyptologist and local Aswan guide *(WhatsApp: +20 10-9611-4472; aswanluxor travel.com).*

Historically, Aswan is just as important as Luxor. It has ancient ruins and it also has a unique natural beauty with the cataract, the desert and the old historical settlement on Elephantine Island.

To get the real feel of Aswan you need time to sail in a felucca, explore the islands and visit the west bank's tombs and monastery. Don't miss the High Dam, symbolising Egypt's renaissance and challenges overcome. There's also Aswan's social tourism, focused around Nubian culture. And, there is beautiful Philae Temple which, guarded over by Isis, has survived as the last fortress of ancient Egyptian religion.

EATING IN ASWAN: FINE WINING & DINING

MAPS P248, P252

Oriental Kebabgy: Enjoy excellent Middle Eastern cuisine in a stylish interior in this classy place at the Old Cataract Hotel. *7pm-midnight* **$$$**

1902 Restaurant: The Moorish-inspired 1902 serves French nouvelle cuisine with serious wine pairings. Jacket and tie required. *6-10.30am & 7-11pm* **$$$**

Mezze: Beautifully prepared and presented Egyptian and Middle Eastern cuisine served with a backdrop of Nile views. *noon-10.30pm* **$$$**

Saraya: Dine on well-prepared Mediterranean cuisine inside or on the terrace, with its wonderful Nile views, in this restaurant at the Old Cataract Hotel. *7am-11pm* **$$$**

ANCIENT TRADITIONS ON ELEPHANTINE ISLAND

Fatma Sobhy *(WhatsApp +20 11-5360-6770)* is a Nubian guide and ornithologist with a special perspective.

Elephantine Island where I live is unique, because Nubians have been living here for thousands of years and were not relocated in the aftermath of the High Dam. That means people preserve their way of life and ancient traditions, like making offerings of seeds or pudding to the 'Angels of the Nile' during special festivals. Visitors are curious about these traditions when they visit my family home. I also lead walks around the village looking at the architecture and farms, or through the ruins of Abu. People are surprised by how quiet and green the island is.

Unfinished Obelisk

MAP P248

Clues about ancient stonecutting techniques

Aswan's Northern Quarries, off Sharia Al Haddadeen, were the source of some of Egypt's finest granite, used for statues, temples, pyramids and obelisks (*tekhenu,* or 'sky-piercer' to the ancient Egyptians). Today, they're notable as the site of an enormous **unfinished obelisk**, thought to have been ordered by Queen Hatshepsut (r 1479–1457 BCE). At 42m high and 1168 tonnes, it would have been the tallest and heaviest carving of its kind, but it was abandoned after cracks were discovered. You can still see marks from chiselling and other ancient tools, although questions remain about the exact methods of the ancient masons. It's best to visit with a guide, who can explain the ancient techniques.

Old-Fashioned Splendour at the Cataract Hotel

MAP P252

Hotel with history

The **Old Cataract Hotel** *(sofitel.accor.com),* perched on a small bluff, has magnificent views over the Nile and a long history. Built by Thomas Cook and opened in 1899 when Egypt was a sovereign state, it has hosted a long line of dignitaries and celebrities. One was Agatha Christie, who spent a year living here in 1937 writing her best-selling *Death on the Nile*. Even if you're not staying here, it's worth visiting to take in the the vistas, lush gardens and Victorian facade and to enjoy a meal served by waiters in vintage attire. Note that unless you have a room, you'll need to buy an LE1000 voucher to enter the grounds, redeemable inside at the restaurants.

Escapism on Elephantine Island

MAP P252

A rural Nubian retreat

Palm-shaded **Elephantine Island** is the oldest inhabited area of Aswan. In ancient times, its now-ruined city of **Abu** marked the limits of Egyptian power at the border of Nubia. The island's high granite outcrop provided a defensive site and natural cargo point for the thriving river trade in gold, slaves and ivory, from where the name *abw* (meaning 'ivory' or 'elephant') possibly originated.

continued on p254

 EATING IN ASWAN: THE WEST BANK — MAPS P248, P252

Cafe Nasr: Enjoy tea and freshly baked bread in the courtyard of a Nubian family home. It's on Bazaar St, one block back from the river. *11am-3pm* **$**

Onaty Ka: *Tagen* (clay-pot), grills and other Nubian favourites served on the breezy upper deck of this brightly painted guesthouse restaurant. *noon-7pm* **$**

Kato Dool: Settle beneath palm-leaf umbrellas and enjoy the views, plus Nubian and international cuisine prepared with locally grown ingredients. *7-11am & 2-11pm* **$$**

Artika Wadi Kiki: If you're in a group, try a Nubian evening here with traditional cuisine, music and dancing around a bonfire. *advance bookings only* **$$**

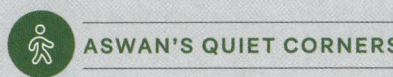

ASWAN'S QUIET CORNERS

Explore away from the tourist hubs and discover the appeal of Aswan's quieter side.

START	END	LENGTH
Corniche	Old Cataract Hotel	1.5km; 2–3 hours

Start early before the heat of the day and while the light is still soft and stroll along Aswan's ❶ **Corniche**. There's usually plenty of activity down on the water as captains ready their boats for the day. At the Corniche's southernmost end, just before the Old Cataract Hotel, are the public ❷ **Fryal Gardens** *(LE50)*. Except on holiday weekends, this small patch of green is a peaceful spot, and it's popular with Egyptian families. The main attractions are the Nile views, which are just as good as those from the neighbouring hotel.

From the gardens, it's a five-minute walk uphill to the imposing ❸ **Coptic Cathedral of the Archangel Michael**, one of Egypt's largest Coptic churches. The interior is open throughout the day from around 9am, depending on services, and there's often a volunteer around to explain some of the rich architectural symbolism. The two bell towers, for example, represent the Old and New Testaments. Inside, don't miss the iconostasis, with its detailed carvings and paintings.

From the church, continue 10 minutes uphill or take a taxi to the ❹ **Nubia Museum** (p247), which is well worth visiting. Afterwards, loop back down to the ❺ **Old Cataract Hotel** to enjoy tea or a meal at the Terrace (p255) restaurant overlooking the river.

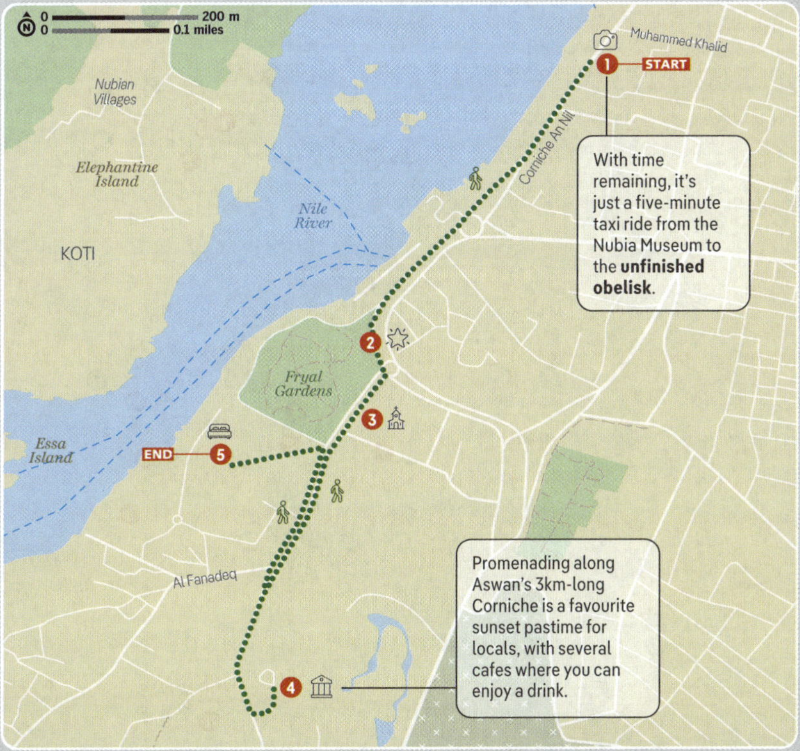

With time remaining, it's just a five-minute taxi ride from the Nubia Museum to the **unfinished obelisk**.

Promenading along Aswan's 3km-long Corniche is a favourite sunset pastime for locals, with several cafes where you can enjoy a drink.

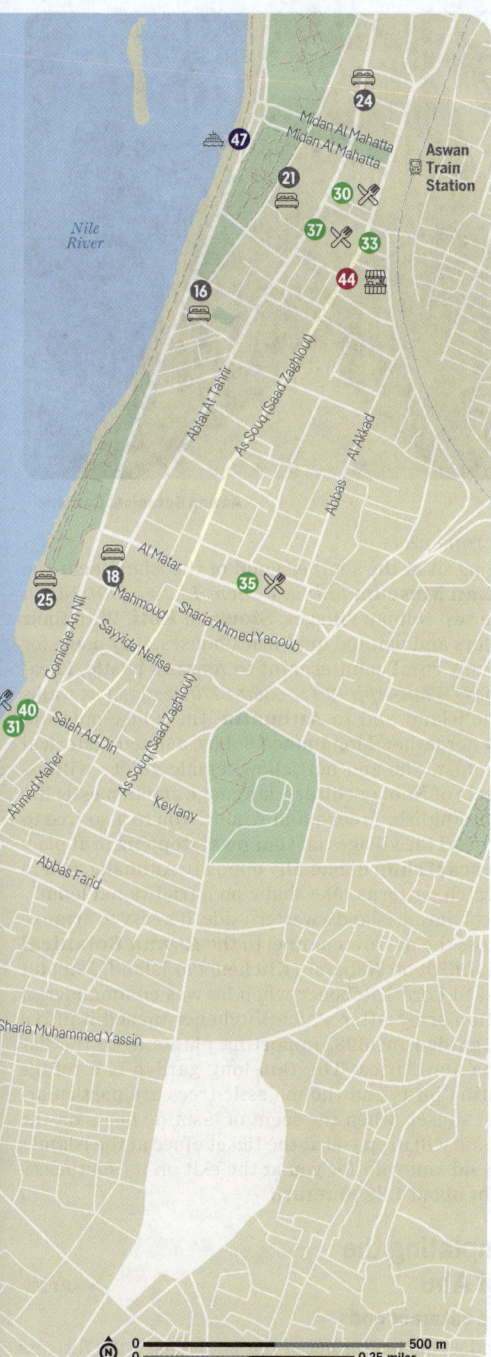

★ HIGHLIGHTS
1 Nubia Museum

● SIGHTS
2 Animalia
3 Aswan Botanical Gardens
4 Aswan Museum
5 Coptic Cathedral of the Archangel Michael
6 Corniche
7 Elephantine Island
8 Nilometer of Khnum
9 Ruins of Abu
10 Tombs of the Nobles

● ACTIVITIES
11 Fryal Gardens

● SLEEPING
12 Anakob
13 Baba Dool
14 Basma Hotel
15 Basmatic Nubian Guest House
16 Citymax Hotel Aswan
17 Go Inn Backpackers
18 Hotel Hapi
19 Kafana Guesthouse & Restaurant
20 Mango Guesthouse
21 Marhaba Palace Hotel
22 Mövenpick Resort Aswan
23 Nuba Dool
24 Nuba Nile Hotel
25 Obelisk Nile Hotel
26 Philae Hotel
27 Pyramisa Island Aswan
28 Sofitel Legend Old Cataract Hotel & Spa

● EATING
29 1902 Restaurant
30 Abeer
31 Aswan Moon
32 Bob Marley Guesthouse, Restaurant & Cafe
33 Chef Khalil
34 El Dokka
35 El Masry
see 19 Kafana
36 Makani
37 Makka Restaurant
see 22 Mezze
38 Nubian Dreams
39 Oriental Kebabgy
see 22 Panorama Restaurant
40 Salah Ad Din
41 Saraya
42 Terrace

● SHOPPING
43 Scarf Shop
44 Sharia As Souq

● TRANSPORT
45 Elephantine Island Ferry (Koti)
46 Elephantine Island Ferry (Siou)
47 Ferry to Aswan Gharb

BEST ASWAN TOUR AGENCIES & GUIDES

Aswan Individual: Waleed and his team offer great-value tours and/or private transport in and around Aswan.

Aswan Luxor Travel: Mena Zaki is an engaging guide who leads enriching tours to Aswan, Luxor and places in between.

Fatma Sobhy: Aswan local Fatma Sobhy *(WhatsApp +20 11-5360-6770)* offers birding and historical tours centred on Elephantine Island and the smaller islands.

Nour el Nil: The travel arm of this luxury dahabiya company can arrange tours around your cruise.

Osiris Tours: Bespoke tours with intriguing commentary on life in ancient and modern Egypt.

Aswan Botanical Gardens

continued from p250

Abu's ruins sit at the southern end of the island near the small **Aswan Museum** *(adult/student LE200/100)*. North of here are two Nubian villages, **Siou** and **Koti**. With their narrow alleys and painted mud-brick houses, they make for a surprisingly rural counterpoint to Aswan's bustle. Local Fatma Sobhy *(WhatsApp +20 11-5360-6770)* leads short walks around the island and to **Animalia**, the house-museum created by her father, Mohammed Sobhy, a noted historical preservationist. She and her fellow female guides will explain aspects of Nubian culture, language and domestic life in excellent English, French and Arabic. You're also free to wander around the villages on your own, stopping in at places like the **scarf shop** diagonally opposite Animalia, where you can watch patterns take shape on a traditional loom.

From Elephantine Island's western side, it's easy to arrange a boat across the narrow channel to the **Aswan Botanical Gardens** *(LE70)* on Nabatat (Kitchener's) Island. Nabatat was gifted to Lord Kitchener when he was commander of the Egyptian army, after which Kitchener turned it into a botanical garden in 1898, importing plants from the Far East, India and Africa. The 1km-long garden is a refuge for migrating birds and the majestic trees are particularly lovely at sunset, when the scent of jasmine floats on the breeze. Boats will drop you at the ticket office at the island's northern end and wait for you at the exit on its southeastern side for about LE200 return.

Contemplating the Ruins of Abu

MAP P252

Cult of the cataract gods

Established at the beginning of the 1st dynasty, the fortress city of Abu was a strategic customs point on the caravan route from central Africa. Trade delegations and military operations were mounted from here, particularly during the 6th dynasty (2345–2181 BCE), earning the governors of Abu the epithet of 'Keepers of the Southern Gateway'.

Now, their rich city lies in **ruins** at the southern tip of Elephantine Island. Numbered plaques and reconstructed buildings mark Abu's long history from 3000 BCE to the 14th century CE. The centrepiece is the partially reconstructed **Temple of Khnum** (signs 6, 12 and 13), the cult centre of the ram-headed creator god, who was believed to control the waters of the Nile from caves beneath the island.

Other stops include a small 4th-dynasty **step pyramid** thought to have been built by Sneferu (builder of the first pyramid, c 2600 BCE); a tiny **Ptolemaic chapel** (number 15) reconstructed from the Temple of Kalabsha (which is now just south of the High Dam); and a **cemetery for sacred rams** (number 11), where the German Archaeological Institute discovered the golden-headed mummified ram now displayed in the Nubia Museum (p247).

Below Khnum temple's southern balustrade is the **Nilometer** (sign 7), a small basin with markers for measuring the Nile's level, used to predict the likelihood of a bountiful harvest.

Off-Piste on the West Bank

MAP P252

Tombs, camels and monastery ruins

Hidden among the sandstone cliffs opposite Aswan are the **Tombs of the Nobles** *(adult/student LE100/50)*, where ancient governors of Elephantine Island were buried. The hillside makes a fine off-beat excursion from Aswan, with excellent views over the river. Many of the tombs date to the Old and Middle Kingdoms (2200–1750 BCE), although the most recent discovery, in 2022, is of a tomb from the Graeco-Roman Period containing 20 intact mummies.

Only a few of the tombs are open; the gatekeeper will unlock them (tipping appreciated). The best is the large **Tomb of**

ANGELS OF THE NILE

Nubians, says guide Fatma Sobhy, have a very close relationship with the Nile. 'We call the Nile *bahr* or "sea" and believe that the river and our lives, which are so intertwined with the river, are protected by the *malayket al bahr*, or angels of the Nile. Even today, many Nubians still seek the intercession of the angels of the Nile, for example, if a child is ill or to ask for fertility or to bless a wedding. Many traditions involve sprinkling sweets or other offerings on the water for the angels. And, there are sometimes lady mediators who have been able to speak with the angels.'

 EATING IN ASWAN: DINING WITH VIEWS ———— MAPS P248, P252

Nub Inn: The Nile views, good service and well-prepared Egyptian cuisine here make the trip over to Gharb Seheyl worth it. *8am-10pm* $

Kafana: Sit by the water on Elephantine Island and tuck into kofta and homemade camel *tagen* at this low-key budget restaurant. *8am-10pm* $

Salah Ad Din: This popular Nile-side restaurant serves Nubian, Egyptian and international food, plus refreshing fruit smoothies. *7am-2am* $$

Makani: This east-bank eatery serves flame-grilled shish kebab, burgers and wraps, fresh juices and peanut-based shakes. *10am-11pm* $$

Bob Marley Restaurant & Cafe: Rooftop over the Nile, with a mix of Egyptian and international dishes and Bob Marley in the background. *24hr* $$

Solaih Nubian Restaurant: Traditional Nubian dishes on Bigga Island overlooking Philae Temple. *advance bookings essential* $$

Terrace: Views of the Nile, vintage decor and excellent service at the Old Cataract Hotel. Famous for its English high tea. *8am-11pm* $$$

Panorama: The Mövenpick's tower restaurant is one of Aswan's best. High tea and North African cuisine with 360-degree views. *3.30-11pm* $$$

FINDING NUBIA

The area between the First and Second Nile Cataracts is known as Lower Nubia (ancient Egyptian Wawat), while further south between the Second and Sixth Nile Cataracts, in Sudan, is Upper Nubia (Kush). To the ancient Egyptians, Nubia was Ta-Sety, the Land of Bowmen, thanks to Nubian skills at archery. Nubia was the source of copper, ivory, ebony and gold, and some say the name Nubia comes from the ancient Egyptian *nbw*, meaning 'gold'.

Nubians have their own language, Nobiin, which is used by only 600,000 Nubians and is considered endangered. It's an oral language without any standardised orthography, although efforts to revive the Nubian alphabet are now underway.

Sarenput II (site 31), belonging to the governor of southern Egypt and overseer of the priesthood of Satet and Khnum in the 12th dynasty (1985–1795 BCE). Its entrance chamber sports statues of Sarenput II, with a further burial room decorated with paintings of him and his family.

Other tombs contain significant details about life and politics in Upper Egypt. The adjoining **Tombs of Mekhu and Sabni** (25 and 26) tell of Sabni's military campaign to Nubia to punish those responsible for murdering his father, Mekhu. The **Tomb of Governor Harkhuf** (site 34) contains a hieroglyphic text detailing trading expeditions into Africa, while the **Tomb of Governor Hekaib** (site 35) records missions to Nubia and Palestine to quash rebellions.

To get here, take the Aswan Gharb public ferry and climb the staircase from the landing. Perched on the ridge above the Tombs of the Nobles is **Qubbet Al Hawa**, the domed tomb of a Muslim sheikh. It's a stiff walk up the hillside, but worth it for the vistas.

Afterwards, make your way by camel or on foot (about 40 minutes through deep sand; bring water and a hat) across the barren hillside to the large ruins of the 7th-century **Monastery of St Simeon** *(adult/student LE100/50)*. The monastery was originally dedicated to local saint Anba Hedra, who renounced the world on his wedding day and became the bishop of Aswan in the late 4th century. In the 10th century, it was rebuilt and rededicated to St Simeon. The original rock-cut caves and church retain defaced frescoes of the Apostles, while the upper mud-brick fortress housed the monks' living quarters. The structure was partially destroyed by the troops of Saladin (Salah ad-Din) in 1173 and then abandoned. At sunset, the mud-brick walls glow red and offer fantastic views of the desert. From the monastery, make your way down to the river below the (closed) **Aga Khan Mausoleum**, where there are several small restaurants and boats back to Elephantine Island.

Sailing South Around Seheyl

MAP P248

Boulders, boats and village life

The Nile is full of character at Aswan. Explore it on a two- to three-hour dawn motorboat tour (arranged with the operators listed on p254 or through your hotel) around the islands south of Elephantine Island, including the large **Seheyl Island**, watching en route for herons and African swamp hens in the reeds.

EATING IN ASWAN: DINING LOCAL STYLE

MAPS P248, P252

Abeer: This bustling local institution is known for its kofta and kebabs served with bread, soup and tahini. *noon-1am* **$**

Makka Restaurant: A popular souq stop serving traditional Egyptian dishes, together with the usual sides and salads. *noon-1am* **$**

El Masry: Famous for stuffed pigeon and other traditional Egyptian dishes served in a nicely decorated restaurant. *10am-late* **$$**

Chef Khalil: This unassuming place is known for its fresh seafood from Lake Nasser and the Red Sea, served grilled, baked or fried. *10am-midnight* **$$**

Seheyl Island

Due to Seheyl's dramatic backdrop and swirling waters, the island was considered sacred to Anukis, goddess of the cataracts. As you motor by its southern tip, watch for a cliff with over 200 inscriptions dating to the 18th and 19th dynasties. The most famous is the so-called 'famine stele' from the 3rd dynasty, recounting a seven-year famine during the reign of Zoser (2667–2648 BCE). Opposite, on the west bank, is the colourful Nubian village of **Gharb Seheyl**. Although it has become a popular tourist attraction, spawning activities such as henna tattoos and visits to see baby crocodiles, it nevertheless offers genuine opportunities to get acquainted with Nubian life and culture.

DISCOVERING NUBIAN CULTURE

For an introduction to Nubian music and literature, start with the following:

Nights of Musk A collection of short stories documenting life and loss in old Nubia by award-winning writer Haggag Oddul.

Dongola This novel by Idris Ali examines the contrasts between Nubia's heyday in old Dongola, its medieval capital, and the grim realities of present-day Nubia.

Escaley: The Water Wheel This evocative recording is considered one of the finest of composer and oud player Hamza El Din.

Shababeek One of the best albums of legendary Nubian singer Mohammed Mounir, who also introduced jazz into Egyptian music.

A Room of Sabry's Own This is a heavy, searching story by contemporary female writer Samar Nour.

EATING AROUND ASWAN: ALSO WORTH A LOOK — MAPS P248, P252

El Dokka: This large, often crowded Nubian place on Essa Island has stuffed pigeon, grilled fish and other local favourites. Eat inside or out. *noon-midnight* $

Aswan Moon: The food – grills and pizza – isn't anything special, but the Nile views are soothing. *10am-late* $

Nubian Dreams: Sit among colourful cushions just above the Siou ferry dock and watch the river's bustle. The menu features standard fare and drinks. *8am-late* $

Lawanda: This guesthouse is also known for its tasty cuisine, with simple, Nubian-style dinners. Order in advance. *7pm-10pm* $

Beyond Aswan

Just south of Aswan are rocky islands between the Low and High Dams and picturesque Philae Temple. To the north is Daraw camel market.

Places
Between the Dams p258
Daraw p260

GETTING AROUND

Boats to Philae Temple leave from Philae Marina, about a 20-minute drive south of central Aswan. If you're travelling solo, you can trim costs by sharing a boat with other travellers. You can charter boats to other nearby islands here, or from the Heissa (Bitnyoon) marina, just to the north. If you're staying on one of the islands in the reservoir, check if your hotel offers free transfers.

At Aswan's southern edge is the 1950m-long and 36m-high granite curtain of the old (Low) Aswan Dam. Built between 1899 and 1902, its purpose was to support greater development and population growth in the Lower Nile Valley by controlling the Nile's annual floodwaters.

Running atop the dam is the main road to Aswan airport and Abu Simbel. To the south is a tranquil reservoir between the old dam and the newer High Dam, 6km beyond. It's dotted with quiet islands, including Agilika, where Philae Temple now stands, Bigga, site of an ecolodge and Nubian restaurant, and Heissa, with accommodation and restaurants.

North of Aswan in Daraw, experience a slice of local life at the camel-trading market.

Between the Dams

TIME FROM ASWAN: **30 MINS**

Time travel to Philae

Philae Temple (*egymonuments.gov.eg; adult/student LE550/275*), cult centre of Isis and Egypt's last classical-style temple, was revered by Nubians, Egyptians, Greeks and Romans, and its well-preserved monuments span centuries, from the pharaohs to the caesars. Originally located on Philae Island, Philae was flooded in 1902, when the old Aswan dam was completed. The island's lush vegetation was denuded and the vibrant colours of the reliefs were stripped by the silt that caked the sandstone. Early-20th-century travellers rowed out to see the romantic flooded temple but the government and UNESCO were concerned. Finally, when the High Dam was proposed, it was decided to relocate the Temple of Isis to nearby **Agilika Island**, a process that was completed in 1980.

A visit can be a charming excursion, especially if you go very early morning or late afternoon to avoid the crowds. To start out, take a taxi to **Philae Marina**, where you'll find dozens of small motorboats eagerly waiting to ferry you the short 10-minute stretch over to Agilika Island. You'll need to purchase your temple ticket before entering the marina to negotiate with the boat captains. Before starting discussions,

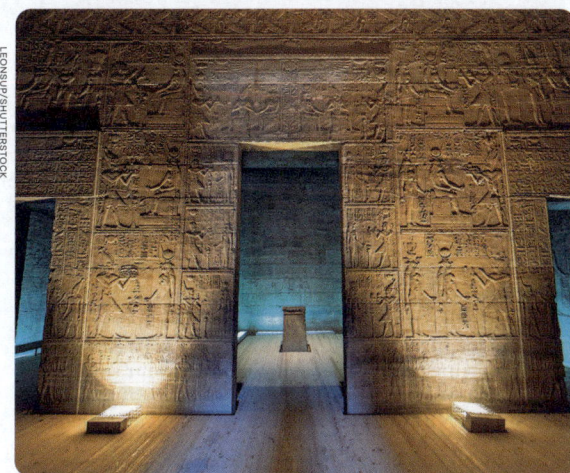

Philae Temple

check the sign near the entrance for the government price recommendation (currently LE340 per boat for up to nine passengers, including two hours waiting time) and use this as a reference when negotiating. Once you're in the boat, things get more enjoyable as you cruise past the western side of the golden-hued temple and duck between granite boulders towards Agilika, which is entirely covered by temple ruins, before docking on the island's southwestern edge.

Near the dock, you'll find the temple's oldest structure, the **Kiosk of Nectanebo II**. It dates to the 4th century BCE and was built during the reign of the last Egyptian-born king of Egypt. Beyond it stretches a long colonnaded courtyard with windows overlooking the water, while just beyond this is the **Temple of Isis**, built by the Ptolemies.

Ptolemy XII Neos Dionysos (282–145 BCE) looms large on the monumental pylon, beyond which is the principal courtyard.

Philae was also believed to be one of the burial sites of Osiris, Isis' brother-husband, whom she brought back to life with a single tear – which also caused the Nile's inundation – and there are many depictions of Isis with Horus (her son with Osiris). The **mammisi** (birth house), to your left when facing the temple, is dedicated to Horus and embellished with reliefs showing the birth of Ptolemy VI Philometor (180–145 BCE), emphasising his Pharaonic legitimacy as the descendant of Horus.

A guide can point out dozens of other interesting details, such as the *ankh* (key of life), converted to a Christian cross in the hypostyle hall, where you'll also find an altar. Pilgrim graffiti in Greek and Latin, dating to 116 BCE, is also in evidence, as are some of Egypt's last known hieroglyphs, which were carved on the **Gate of Hadrian** (left of the temple) in 394 CE.

CULT OF ISIS

Mother, magician, protectress and healer, Isis was one of the most important gods of the Egyptian pantheon. She was the sister-wife of Osiris, with whom she ruled until he was murdered by his brother Seth. Grief-stricken, Isis scoured the world to find his body, which she mummified, thereby facilitating his resurrection as the god of the afterlife. She also bore his son, Horus, and was considered the divine mother of the pharaoh. By the Roman era, Isis was the most popular Egyptian god worshipped across the empire as far as Britain and Afghanistan. To see her temple at Philae at its most romantic, attend the evening sound-and-light show. Buy tickets at the Philae ticket office, as shows with fewer than 13 people will be cancelled.

ASWAN'S HIGH DAM: REVITALISATION & LOSS

The 3830m-long, 111m-high Aswan High Dam, a marvel of modern engineering, was built to regulate the Nile's flooding and increase agricultural production and hydroelectric power. While the dam has undoubtedly benefited Egypt's economy, its massive capacity isn't immediately obvious. The turbine area is closed to the public and it is the tranquil views over Lake Nasser from the top that draw the crowds. Among many older Nubians, talk of the dam also calls forth a profound sadness. Human resettlement efforts were overshadowed by the millions spent on temple relocation, and many feel that nothing could ever really compensate for the loss of a way life that had been shaped for generations by the seasonal rhythms of the Nile.

On the island's eastern side is the **Temple of Hathor**, decorated with reliefs of musicians, and adjacent is the **Kiosk of Trajan**. The latter is Philae's most famous monument as it was the subject of many Victorian paintings made when the temple was originally flooded.

The complex's last additions – the ruined **Temple of Augustus** and **Gate of Diocletian** – were added in the 2nd century, when Christianity was already gaining a foothold in Egypt. Initially, Christianity coexisted with ancient Egyptian religion at Philae, but by the mid-6th century, the decline of the local priesthood and the increasingly strict monotheism of the Byzantines made survival of the cult untenable. The temple was finally closed during the rule of Emperor Justinian I (527–565 CE), thus ending the ancient Egyptian religion.

After viewing the temple, negotiate with your skipper for a lift to nearby **Bigga Island** for a Nubian meal at Eco Nubia's **Solaih Nubian Restaurant** (p255; advance booking essential).

Daraw

TIME FROM ASWAN: 1 HR

Centuries-old trading post

Daraw, one of Egypt's largest camel markets, has been a trading hub for centuries and was a major station on the Darb Al Arba'een (Forty Days Road), the old caravan route linking western Sudan with Egypt. Today, most of the camels come in caravans from Sudan to just north of Abu Simbel before being trucked to Daraw. The main Daraw market is held on Saturday mornings from 6am, and is fast and furious, sometimes with as many as 2000 camels. Most go on to the camel market in Birqash, about 35km northwest of Cairo, where they are sold, exported or slaughtered for their meat. It's fascinating to watch as the traders haggle over prices, although the treatment of the camels is disheartening. This is no tourist show and no place for the squeamish. While most traders are quite friendly towards curious visitors, be sure to wear conservative clothes and closed shoes. The market is about 45km north of Aswan. Expect to pay from about LE600 for a private return taxi.

Lower Nubia & Lake Nasser

ANCIENT NUBIA | TEMPLES | TRANQUIL CRUISING

For thousands of years, the First Nile Cataract marked the border between Egypt and Nubia, which stretched from just south of Aswan to the Sixth Nile Cataract near Khartoum. Although more desertified than Egypt, ancient Nubia was rich in raw materials such as gold, carnelian and copper. Nubians were also fearsome warriors and their territory was a crucial route for trade with sub-Saharan Africa.

Now, much of Nubia lies beneath the 5250 sq km of Lake Nasser (also known as Lake Nubia), the enormous artificial lake created by the building of the High Dam between 1958 and 1970. Its creation necessitated the relocation of about 100,000 Nubians, whose homes were submerged, along with numerous ancient monuments. With an extraordinary international effort, 22 temples, including those at Abu Simbel, were relocated to higher ground on the edge of lake, and can now be visited on a cruise through this austere desert landscape.

Alone at Kalabsha Temple
Sun gods and striking views

Fortress-like **Kalabsha Temple** *(egymonuments.gov.eg; adult/student LE200/100)* was the largest freestanding Egyptian temple in Nubia to be relocated to higher ground in 1970. The original monumental gate was gifted to the Germans, who funded the operation, and now resides in Berlin, but even without it, the long causeway from the mainland to the isolated, island-based temple is impressive. It is relatively seldom visited, so you may have it to yourself.

Built on older structures, Kalabsha dates to the reign of Roman Emperor Augustus (30 BCE–14 CE). It is dedicated to the Nubian sun god Merul (Mandulis in Greek) and reliefs within show Pharaonic predecessor Amenhotep II (r 1426–1400 BCE) offerings gifts to Merul. Other carvings show Augustus making offerings to Isis, Osiris and Horus, who in some myths is the father of Merul. There's also graffiti

☑ TOP TIP

When planning your Lake Nasser cruise, note that larger boats are limited to certain moorings. Smaller boats will be more rustic, but can dock almost anywhere and provide a more customised experience. If you don't have time for a multi-night cruise, consider a day visit by road from Aswan to Kalabsha Temple.

GETTING AROUND

The most direct way to reach Kalabsha Temple (including Beit Al Wali and Kertassi) from Aswan is by private taxi or on a tour. The other temples around Lake Nasser can only be reached via cruise from Aswan (four nights/five days) or from Abu Simbel (three nights/four days). These cruises, which all include a stop at Kalabsha, are a completely different experience to cruises between Luxor and Aswan, with many fewer visitors and much less boat traffic.

★ HIGHLIGHTS
1 Temples of Abu Simbel

● SIGHTS
2 Beit Al Wali
3 Kalabsha Temple
4 Kiosk of Kertassi
5 Temple of Amada
6 Temple of Dakka
7 Temple of Derr
8 Temple of Maharraqa
9 Temple of Ramses II
10 Tomb of Pennut

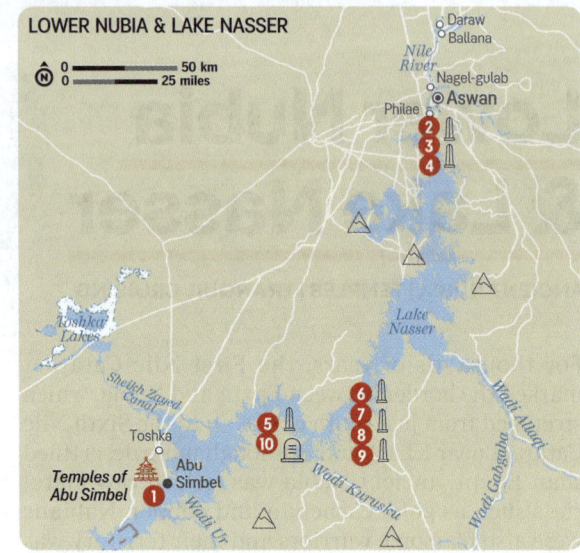

LOWER NUBIA & LAKE NASSER

FISH TALES

The main human presence on Lake Nasser is the 5000 or so fishers who spend up to six months at a time catching 50,000 tonnes of small fish each year. But Lake Nasser also harbours monsters in the deep, namely the Nile perch *(Lates niloticus)*. It is the most sought-after trophy of freshwater fishing and attracts anglers from around the world. Largely undisturbed, Nile perch reach record sizes here, as do the lake's tiger fish and catfish. The largest recorded Nile perch caught here weighed 104kg and measured over 1.8m in length.

from Roman soldiers and an inscription recording the 5th-century victory of the Nubian king Silko, who is dressed as a Roman soldier. Silko was a Christian and the temple was likely converted into a church in the 6th century.

Beyond the hypostyle hall is the sanctuary. Stairs lead up to the roof, from where there are fantastic views of Lake Nasser, the High Dam and the picturesque **Kiosk of Kertassi** (on the same island and a two-minute walk to the south). Also here (a few minutes' walk northwest) is the rock-cut temple of **Beit Al Wali**. It contains some coloured reliefs showing Ramses II smiting various enemies (Libyans, Syrians and Nubians) while also receiving generous tributes of animals and gold.

When the water level is low you can walk from the mainland to the site. Otherwise, you'll need to take a motor boat from the western side of the High Dam (LE200 return). Views from Kalabsha's ruins across the water towards the modernistic Egyptian-Soviet friendship memorial make a striking contrast.

Adventuring Around Lake Nasser
Remote temples and desert landscapes

Lake Nasser is one of the world's largest artificial lakes. To give an idea of its immense size, the flying distance from Cairo to London is 3524km, while the lake's shoreline measures 7844km. The lake was created as a result of the construction of the High Dam between 1958 and 1970, which aimed to control the Nile's epic annual inundation and support increasing cultivation in the lower Nile Valley.

Mövenpick MS *Prince Abbas* (p264), Lake Nasser

While it did this with great success, it also flooded all of Lower Nubia, its valleys, villages and ancient monuments.

Several cruise ships and a few small boats ply the waters of this great blue-green expanse, stopping at remote temples that were saved from submersion. Sitting aboard, you can contemplate the austere beauty of this surreal desert lake. The west bank is characterised by stretches of shallow shoreline favoured by feeding birds, while rugged mountains rise up to the east.

From Aswan, the first stop is **Wadi As Sabua** *(egy monuments.gov.eg; adult/student LE150/75)* – the Valley of the Lions – so called for the sphinxes that lead to the **Temple of Ramses II**. There are three Nubian temples here, including the **Temple of Dakka**, dedicated to Thoth, the god of wisdom. The **Temple of Maharraqa** is dedicated to Isis and Serapis, the Greek-Egyptian god of Alexandria.

The next temple group is at **Amada** *(egymonuments.gov. eg; adult/student LE150/75)* in an increasingly dramatic landscape. Here you'll find the colourful **Temple of Amada**, the oldest on Lake Nasser, built by Thutmose III and Amenhotep II in the 15th century BCE for the gods Amun-Ra and Ra-Horakhty. Some coloured reliefs also remain in the nearby **Temple of Derr**, while the **Tomb of Pennut**, just north, is a rare rock-cut tomb belonging to a viceroy of the Nubian Kingdom of Kush.

While large cruise ships sail down the middle of the lake (as they cannot navigate the shallows), smaller boats can dip in and out of the shoreline, which is rich in biodiversity. Look out for migrating birds (millions pass through here in spring and autumn), gazelles, foxes, jackals and crocodiles.

On boat-trekking cruises, you'll be dropped off in the morning to trek through the surreal landscape, where you may kick up millennia-old fossils in soft sand dunes or

GRAND ETHIOPIAN RENAISSANCE DAM

The Grand Ethiopian Renaissance Dam (GERD) is a hydropower project on one of the Nile's main tributaries. Billed as an existential economic necessity by Ethiopia, the dam has created a serious conflict with Egypt, which asserts it is a threat to Egypt's water supply and power security. Egypt has raised the matter in the UN and sought support from the Arab League, insisting that Ethiopia stop filling the dam until a legal agreement is reached. In contrast, Ethiopia insists Egypt is in breach of the 2015 Declaration of Agreement and must engage in negotiations within the African Union. As the climate crisis accelerates, these complex issues of identity, resource management and development become ever more critical.

THE TOSHKA PROJECT

Lake Nasser contains 135 billion cu metres of water. In 1996, its maximum capacity of 157 billion cu metres was reached, prompting the opening of the Toshka canal, 30km north of Abu Simbel. President Mubarak planned on using the canal to create a new Nile Valley, reclaiming several hundred thousand hectares of desert as farmland to support Egypt's exploding population. Although previously stalled, the Russian invasion of Ukraine prompted an energetic revival of the Toshka project to fill the gap left in Egypt's wheat supplies (Egypt imports 80% of its wheat), although critics question the wisdom of developing water-hungry agricultural production in one of the most water-scarce regions of the world.

spot Stone Age drawings and crude hieroglyphics carved by bored merchants on long trading missions. You'll also occasionally cross paths with Nubians tending their goats or fishers brewing cups of tea.

As evening draws in, your small cruiser will moor beside the shore for the night, with sundowners served on sandy beaches against a backdrop of extravagant pink, red and orange sunsets. This is followed by convivial meals on board beneath an inky black star-filled sky and a quiet night's sleep.

On your final day, you'll pass the Roman ruins of **Kasr Ibrim** (currently closed to the public) – the last Christian stronghold in Nubia until the 16th century – before the spectacular approach to **Abu Simbel**. It's a fitting journey's end, gliding slowly towards the immense, immutable colossi of Ramses II in the morning sunlight.

The beautifully crafted, 26m *Sai* (**Saï Safari**) offers small-boat intimacy and nature-focused activities en route. Other contacts include **Lake Nasser Adventures**, which offers cruises on the 18m *Dongolah,* and **Lake Nasser Experience**, which has small houseboats linked up with a larger 'mother ship' for meals and sleeping. Larger boats include the **Mövenpick MS *Prince Abbas*** – a retro, '70s luxury liner with 65 cabins, pool, sundeck, library and set departures – and the **Steigenberger MS *Omar el Khayam***, a luxury hotel on water with 80 balconied cabins, a spa, pool and hot tubs.

Temple of Hathor (p267)

TOP EXPERIENCE

Temples of Abu Simbel

Ramses II's magnificent monument to himself – set in a spectacular location overlooking Lake Nasser – is among Egypt's most imposing sights and a highlight of any itinerary. Make your visit even more memorable by timing it with the biannual solar alignment festival, when the sun's rays penetrate deep into the Great Temple's inner sanctuary.

TOP TIP

To avoid crowds, see the temples illuminated at night and appreciate sunrise and sunset views, it's highly recommended to spend at least one night in Abu Simbel. Many local hotels also offer sunrise boat trips on the lake.

Nubian Rescue Campaign

Near Abu Simbel village, in a stunning setting overlooking the southern part of Lake Nasser, are the Great Temple of Ramses II and the neighbouring Temple of Hathor. When plans were finalised for the Aswan High Dam in the 1950s, worldwide attention focused on the irreplaceable ancient monuments doomed by the rising waters of Lake Nasser. UNESCO launched the Nubian Rescue Campaign between 1960 and 1980, sending Egyptian and international

PRACTICALITIES
Scan the QR code for prices and opening hours.

TOP TIPS

- Watch the sound-and-light show to see the temples illuminated against the night sky.

- Enjoy a meal at **Al Modhish** *(9am-midnight)* in town, with delicious fresh fish, *makla* (fried) or *meshwi* (grilled), served with rice and salad.

- Many hotels offer sunrise boat cruises. Alternatively, visit the temples at dawn to experience them without the crowds.

- Time your visit to experience the solar alignment festival in February or October, but book ahead as hotels fill up.

- At the visitor centre, check out the scale model of the temple, where you can see the path of the sun's rays during solar alignment.

- Photos are free to take on your phone, but you'll need a ticket to use a camera.

- Timings vary for the sound-and-light show (US$18); enquire when purchasing your temple entry ticket.

- The Abu Simbel temples site is fully accessible.

archaeological teams to rescue ancient artefacts. Perhaps the greatest achievement of all was the preservation of the Abu Simbel temples. In a modern marvel of engineering, which matches Ramses II's original construction for sheer audacity, the temple complex was moved piece by piece to a location 65m above the original site at a cost of US$40 million. Today, in their new lakeside setting backed by the Western Desert, they are easily the most spectacularly situated and atmospheric temples in Egypt.

Great Temple of Ramses II

Carved out of the mountain on the west bank of the Nile between 1274 and 1244 BCE, the awesome **Great Temple of Ramses II** is dedicated as much to Ramses II as to the gods Ra-Horakhty, Amun-Ra and Ptah. From the ticket office, a winding path leads down to the water, the temple facade hidden from view until the last moment. Overlooking the intense blue of Lake Nasser, the first sight of it is breathtaking.

Facade

The facade's four famous **colossi**, each 20m high, depict Pharaoh Ramses II. He stares out enigmatically across the water with Ra-Horakhty, the falcon-headed sun god, in the centre. At 30m high, it's hard to fathom that the structure was once buried beneath the sand until, in 1813, Swiss explorer Jean-Louis Burchkardt caught sight of the smiling baboons on the top lintel. Smaller statues of some of Ramses' 160 children, his mother Queen Tuya and his wife Nefertari stand beside and between his legs. Nefertari reaches to his knee on the right side of the entrance.

The Great Hall

The Great Temple's interior is rich in detail. As you make your way through the massive door into the **Great Hall**, you'll find yourself dwarfed by eight giant statues of Ramses II supporting a ceiling adorned with vultures, symbolising the protective goddess Nekhbet. Fabulous, deeply carved battle scenes fill the walls, including – on the northern side – a depiction of the Battle of Kadesh (c 1274 BCE), in what is now Syria, where Ramses rallies his demoralised troops to defeat the Hittites. On the southern wall is an account of Ramses laying waste to Libyans and Nubians in his chariot.

Central Halls & Inner Sanctuary

As you continue inside, you'll enter a four-columned vestibule where Ramses and Nefertari are shown making offerings to the temple gods Amun-Ra and Ra-Horakhty. Deeper in, in the inner sanctuary, are (from left to right) the creator god Ptah, Amun-Ra, the crowned Ramses and Ra-Horakhty. During the solar alignment festivals, the rising sun first illuminates Ramses' face, spreading to Amun-Ra and Ra-Horakhty, with only Ptah remaining in the shadows to emphasise his links with the underworld.

Temple of Hathor

Immediately next to the Great Temple is the smaller **Temple of Hathor**, dedicated to Ramses' favoured wife, Nefertari, and to Hathor, the goddess of love, motherhood, fertility and music. In front are six 10m-high carvings of Ramses and Nefertari, who is dressed as Hathor. In a rare display of ancient equality, Nefertari is depicted at the same scale as Ramses, with her exalted place confirmed by an inscription stating that the pharaoh has cut this temple 'for his chief wife Nefertari...for whom the sun shines'.

The Interior

As you enter inside, the tale of spousal love and respect continues, with walls depicting scenes of Ramses II and Nefertari and Nefertari again shown as the equal of Ramses. The reliefs here are also softer in style and depict touching details, such as Nefertari playing the sistrum. Due to the relative shallowness of the temple, it glows in the sunlight while swallows swoop in and out. At the rear, look to either side of the vestibule for a pair of beautiful carvings of the goddess afloat in her sacred barque, surrounded by papyrus.

Abu Simbel Festivals

Abu Simbel's **solar alignment festivals** (22 February, 22 October) supposedly coincide with Ramses II's birth and coronation. But changes to the sun's approach angle over the millennia and the challenges of linking fixed dates with cyclical phenomena mean it's more likely the dates were tied to the annual planting and harvest seasons.

> **GETTING THERE**
>
> Most visitors to Abu Simbel come on an organised day tour by bus from Aswan (four hours one-way), leaving pre-dawn and returning by late afternoon. Prices start at about LE1200 per person. For a private vehicle with driver expect to pay from LE4000, including one overnight. There are also daily flights from Cairo via Aswan. The Abu Simbel airport is about 5km from the temples. Note that the Abu Simbel road is only open for tourist traffic between 5am and 5pm. Road trips require a police permit (arranged by the driver), and should be booked at least a day in advance.

Great Temple of Ramses II

Places We Love to Stay

$ Budget $$ Midrange $$$ Top End

Luxor to Aswan
MAP p237

El Salam Hotel $ It's worth overnighting in Esna just to stay at this spotless budget establishment, with its sun-filled rooms, Nile views and breakfast around the corner at Taghmest Ramadan.

Al Haramain $ This newly renovated place in Esna run by the welcoming Mr Osama has clean rooms sharing bathroom and comfortable common areas. It's about 250m southwest of the courthouse.

Horus Hotel $ If you need to stay in central Edfu, this no-frills establishment will do in a pinch. It has clean rooms and breakfast.

Funduk Al Shams $$ A welcoming country guesthouse about 15km north of Edfu (they'll help arrange a taxi). Its design incorporates principles of feng shui, making it the ideal antidote to Edfu's bustle.

Aswan – City Centre
MAP p252

Go Inn Backpackers $ A riverside terrace, helpful owner, kayaks for rent and dormitory-style accommodation; ideal for connecting with other travellers.

Nuba Nile Hotel $ This no-frills hotel is popular with Egyptian families and just a five-minute walk from the train station. Rooms vary, so check beforehand.

Philae Hotel $$ This multistorey place makes up for its lack of sparkle with helpful staff, pleasant rooms and a convenient central location.

Hotel Hapi $$ This centrally located choice is easy walking distance to Aswan's souq. Rooms are small but clean; day rates are available.

Citymax Hotel Aswan $$ A staid but reliable midrange choice in bustling central Aswan with a restaurant and a small rooftop pool.

Obelisk Nile Hotel $$ Consider the conveniently located Obelisk if you're after Nile-side views while being in the thick of things in the city centre.

Basma Hotel $$$ On a hilltop diagonally opposite the Nubia Museum, with quiet rooms (ask for one that's been renovated), a restaurant and a large pool.

Tolip Hotel Aswan $$$ About 3km north of town on the Corniche, this is a good choice for families, with its pool, tennis courts and bowling alley.

Sofitel Legend Old Cataract (p250) **$$$** An Aswan classic and the epitome of luxury, with excellent service and stunning Nile views.

Aswan – Elephantine Island
p250

Mango Guesthouse $ We can't say enough about this good-value place on Elephantine Island, with its small garden, helpful staff and spotless rooms.

Baba Dool $ This mud-brick house has a quiet, riverside location and rooms decorated in colourful Nubian style.

Kafana Guesthouse (p255) **$** Simple budget rooms by the water and good meals on the riverside terrace.

Bob Marley Guesthouse (p255) **$** A chill ambience, helpful staff and a range of rooms, some with bathroom.

Basmatic Nubian Guest House $ This low-key budget guesthouse on the western side of Elephantine Island has a rooftop restaurant and views.

Nuba Dool $ Travellers get a warm welcome at this popular place with its rooftop terrace and spacious, homey rooms, most with private bathroom.

Anakob $$ This fine riverboat moored on Elephantine Island's western side has modern interiors, air-con and views of the Tombs of the Nobles.

Pyramisa Island Aswan $$ Slightly faded facilities compensated for by a lovely island location (the hotel has its own ferry) in the middle of the First Nile Cataract, south of Elephantine.

Mövenpick Resort Aswan $$$ Set among expansive grounds, with two large pools, a raised restaurant with sublime views and its own boat to the mainland.

Aswan – West Bank
MAP p248

Maghrabi's Guesthouse $ This budget guesthouse near the Aswan Gharb ferry has affable hosts, views towards Aswan and its own boat.

Lawanda (p257) **$** Helpful owners, colourful, Nubian-style rooms and good meals are among the highlights at this Gharb Seheyl favourite.

Krouma Ecolodge $$ An offbeat place at the south end of Seheyl Island with Nubian-style rooms and meals. Kayaks can be arranged.

Anakato $$ One of the largest Nubian lodges in Gharb Seheyl, with a range of well-kept rooms and activities like kayaking and mud baths.

Onaty Ka (p250) **$$** In the centre of Gharb Seheyl village and deservedly popular, with bright, Nubian-style decor, clean rooms and meals.

Kato Dool Wellness Resort (p250) **$$$** This brightly painted, clifftop resort north of Gharb Seheyl has comfortable rooms, terrace views and a good restaurant.

Nub Inn (p255) **$$$** A boutique hotel in Gharb Seheyl with arched, Nubian-style ceilings and lovely views over the water.

Beyond Aswan p258

Noprea Boutique Hotel $$ On Heissa Island, with blue-and-white rooms, a restaurant overlooking the water and a shuttle boat to Philae Temple and the mainland.

Eco Nubia $$ This lodge on Bigga Island has rustic rooms and Solaih restaurant, with traditional Nubian cuisine and views. Advance bookings are essential for both rooms and meals.

Old Nubian Guesthouse $$ A quiet B&B near the Philae marina with small rooms, some with balconies. Advance bookings essential.

Abu Simbel p265

Tuya Hotel $$ Well-located near the temple, with comfortable rooms (request one facing the inner courtyard) and a restaurant. It also organises sunrise boat cruises.

Hllol Hotel $$ A reliable choice in the town centre, about 20 minutes on foot to the temples, with pleasant rooms, Nubian decor and a restaurant.

Eskaleh Nubian Ecolodge $$ Built by Nubian musician Fikry El Kashef, this good lakeside lodge is ideal for experiencing Nubian culture, with meals on an outdoor terrace, sunrise cruises and occasional music and dance performances.

Seti Abu Simbel Lake Resort $$$ Abu Simbel's most upmarket accommodation, with expansive lawns, a spacious pool, expansive bungalow-style rooms and sunrise cruises.

Kato Dool Wellness Resort

Researched by
Dr Jenny Walker

Siwa Oasis & the Western Desert

EGYPT'S DESERT HEART

Strike out from the Nile Valley to explore the wild landscapes that sweep across Egypt's west.

Fly over Egypt, or rise above the Nile Valley from Luxor in a balloon, and it becomes evident that the ribbon of green made possible by Nile waters is a fragile strip of fertility in an otherwise parched land. Beyond the river are limestone escarpments, vast seas of sand and arid gravel plains.

But what may at first appear to be intractable desert is in fact a more nuanced landscape scattered with oases, fed by aquifers and shaded by date palms. This region west of the Nile is known as the Western Desert and, though seldom visited by travellers today, it was of major importance during Pharaonic times as the route along which Nile goods were traded with other nations. With improved irrigation systems, it became productive in its own right under the Romans, growing grain and grapes for the empire.

Despite later flurries of activity, including President Nasser's New Valley plan to establish settlements in the desert in the 1950s, the Western Desert lapsed into a backwater in more recent centuries and remains sparsely populated.

Travelling here is an adventure in which it's easy to sense the fragility of life dependent on diminishing water resources. A trip to any of the oases is a lesson in survival in the face of extremes, offering a fascinating insight into the human capacity to endure against the odds.

THE MAIN AREAS

SIWA OASIS
An isolated place apart. **p278**

BAHARIYA OASIS
Easygoing desert-adventure hub. **p285**

FARAFRA OASIS
Home of the great White Desert. **p291**

DAKHLA OASIS
Traditional architecture and rural oasis life. **p295**

AL KHARGA OASIS
Ancient temples, tombs and forts. **p300**

For places to stay in Siwa Oasis & the Western Desert, see p303

THE GUIDE

SIWA OASIS & THE WESTERN DESERT

From left: Salt lake, Siwa Oasis (p278); Black Desert (p289)

SIWA OASIS & THE WESTERN DESERT   THE GUIDE

Find Your Way

Egypt's vast Western Desert stretches south from the Mediterranean coast to the border with Sudan and west from the Nile Valley to the border with Libya, encompassing about two-thirds of the country.

THE BAHARIYA–SIWA ROAD

Travelling along the road connecting Bahariya and Siwa was still forbidden for foreign travellers at research time. Until regulations change, if you want to travel between them you will need to backtrack through Cairo.

BUS & MICROBUS

Buses run (erratically) between Cairo and Siwa, a journey better undertaken by microbus in separate legs (Cairo, Alexandria, Marsa Matruh). Buses connect the oases of Bahariya, Farafra and Dakhla with Cairo and Al Kharga via Asyut.

PRIVATE DRIVER & TOUR

The easiest way to visit the Western Desert is on a tour or by hiring a vehicle and driver. At research time, visitors were only permitted to hire a microbus (not a car), which necessitated payment for empty seats. A 4WD and driver are essential for exploring off-road.

Bahariya Oasis, p285

The easiest oasis to reach from Cairo, Bahariya is the main gateway to adventures in and around the Black Desert.

Bahariya Oasis

Gebel Az Zuquq *Gebel Gala Siwa*

Siwa Oasis

Siwa Oasis, p278

Far-flung, home to a distinct Amazigh culture and with a mud-brick citadel at its heart, Siwa encapsulates oasis life.

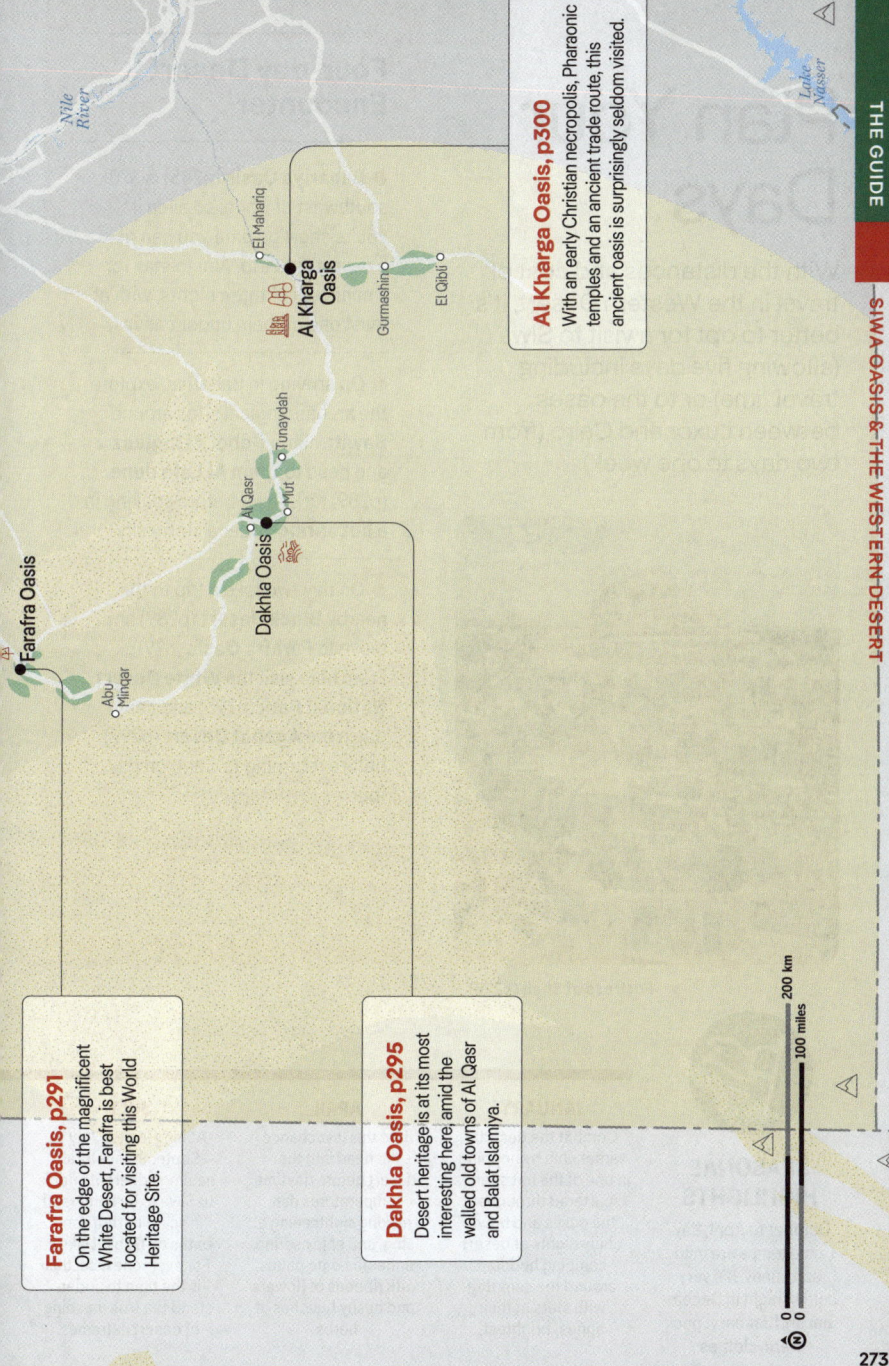

Plan Your Days

With the distances and cost of travel in the Western Desert, it's better to opt for a visit to Siwa (allowing five days including travel time) or to the oases between Luxor and Cairo (from two days to one week).

Fortress of Shali (p278)

Four-day Desert Encounter

● **Bahariya Oasis** (p285) is 370km southwest of Cairo, so even if you're short on time you can fit in a desert side trip. Aim to stay for a minimum of three nights, with at least one of them under canvas.

● On arriving in Bahariya, explore the archaeological sites around **Bawiti**, climb **Gebel Al Ingleez** and head to **Umm Al Lafa dune** (p289) for sunset before soaking in a **hot spring** under a starry sky.

● On day two take a trip to the nearby **Black Desert** (p289) and move to **Farafra Oasis** (p291). From here visit the **White Desert National Park** (p293) and camp out in the **Agabat Desert** (p292) before returning to Cairo on day four.

SEASONAL HIGHLIGHTS

October to April, daytime temps are mild and sunny. It's very cold at night in December and January; pack warm clothes.

JANUARY
Combat the desert's winter chill by hopping in one of the hot springs scattered throughout the oases and brave chilly nights of desert camping huddled around the campfire with stars at their annual brightest.

APRIL
Use this last chance to head into the desert before daytime temperatures rise, making sightseeing a slog, and enjoy spring under the date palms, with ribbons of flowers and bushy bunches of herbs.

JULY
Aching joints? July to September natural-healing adherents flock to Siwa to be immersed in scalding-hot sand baths on Gebel Dakrur. For everyone else, this is the time to understand the true meaning of desert extremes.

Three Days in Siwa

● **Siwa** (p278) sits way out west and takes a whole day to reach. Explore **Shali fortress** (p278), then hire a bike (or walk) around the sights of **Aghurmi** before heading to **Fatnas Spring** for sunset in the company of visitors from Masa Matrou.

● Prearrange a desert tour to **El Arag Oasis** (p283) for day two to experience one of the Western Desert's most dramatic landscapes or, if you're taking things easier, book a **Bir Wahed** (p283) tour for a soak, some sandboarding and sunset on a dune.

● On day three head out to the **salt pools** (p281), famous for photo-worthy floats in turquoise water, then hop on the overnight bus (if it's running) back to Cairo.

A Week's Desert Loop from Luxor

● Hire a driver for the six-hour trip along the badly potholed road from Luxor to **Al Kharga** (p300) and spend the rest of this day exploring ancient sites including the **Necropolis of Al Bagawat** (p302) and **Qasr Al Ghueita** (p301).

● On day two head to **Dakhla Oasis** (p295) to experience the slower pace of oasis life. Make sure to stroll through the shaded maze of alleys in both **Al Qasr** (p298) and **Balat Islamiya** (p295). Visit the painted tombs of **Qarat Al Muzawwaqa** (p297) and reserve some time to relax in a natural spring.

● Move north to **Farafra Oasis** (p291) on day four to organise a one-night **White Desert National Park** (p293) adventure, then move to traveller-friendly **Bahariya Oasis** (p285) for **Black Desert adventures** (p289).

AUGUST
This is the time to really want to understand what the desert's all about. It's too hot to walk on the sand, and the value of water takes on a whole different meaning.

SEPTEMBER
Peer under the canopy of palms to check on the date harvest. Around the end of the month the heat starts to give way, making for more bearable days and pleasant evenings – ideal for camping.

OCTOBER
Visit Siwa during the full moon to catch the three-day **Siyaha Festival** of the date harvest around Gebel Dakrur. Dates spill into the shops, are piled in crates and are served with every meal.

NOVEMBER
Plan a desert trip for November and you'll enjoy the perfect weather for exploring sites on foot, with soft light for photography. Expect balmy days and not-too-chilly nights for camping.

HELP ME PICK:

Western Desert Oases

High costs and long distances are involved in reaching any of the oases. You'll also need police permission and a police escort. Together these aspects mean a trip into the Western Desert won't be at the top of everyone's Egypt wish list. For those who do brave it, though, the desert is truly inspiring. The oases are barely visited by foreigners for much of the year. Choose any oasis to visit, and you'll receive a warm welcome.

Choosing your oasis

Siwa Oasis

Compact Siwa (p278), near the Libyan border, offers a unique experience. This isolated community has developed its own distinct culture and embraces the chance to share it with tourists.

One of the best Siwa tour operators, Aloush Abou Kasse, owner of **Nour Al Waha** (p280), is able to organise next-day trips with permits across the region, including to **El Arag Oasis** (p283).

Bahariya Oasis;

Bahariya Oasis

As the closest oasis to Cairo, Bahariya (p285) is the most visited of all the oases on the Cairo–Luxor loop. It sits beside the Black Desert and has lots of opportunities for hot spring bathing, hiking and dune camping.

Help with tours is available from two highly experienced Bedouin brothers who run **Eden Garden Tours** and from Peter Wirth (a German Western Desert expert), who has around 30 years of experience organising recommended trips through **White Desert Tours**.

Farafra Oasis

Farafra (p291) is home to the celebrated **White Desert National Park** (p293), the region's top destination.

White Desert expert Ahmed Abed Abouda organises camping trips from **Rahala Safari Hotel** (p303), while **Shahrazad Desert Camp**, right beside the White Desert, offers accommodation in a permanent tented camp for those who are less keen on roughing it. **Al Badawiya Safari & Hotel** also runs excellent tours.

Dakhla Oasis

If your interest lies more in history than in nature, Dakhla (p295) is the obvious choice. Accessible from Asyut as well as Luxor, the oasis hides the old towns of Al Qasr and Balat, and there are fine Graeco-Roman tombs and a Pharaonic temple here.

The owners of **Bedouin Camp** are Bedouin brothers and camel experts who can advise on nearby trips.

Al Kharga Oasis

Punctuating the ancient Darb Al Arba'een, an ancient north-south trade route that once stretched from Sudan's Darfur region up to Asyut, El Kharga (p300) is the most southerly and least visited of the oases. It encompasses a rich assortment of antiquities, including the significant Christian Necropolis of Bagawat.

Mohsen Abd Al Moneem *(WhatsApp +20 100-180-6127)* is head of **New Valley Tourist Office** (p302) in Al Kharga and a fount of knowledge about the southern oases.

Dakhla Oasis

HOW TO

When to go The Western Desert is prohibitively hot in summer and bitter in winter. March, April, October and November are the best months for desert activities.

Book ahead Some reports suggest you need to apply for permits three weeks in advance. This wasn't our experience during recent research, when permissions were gained one night ahead through transport and/or tour companies.

Getting there From Luxor, contact driver Bilal El Tayeb Omran Ali *(+20 101 0109546)* and transport operator Said Ahmed Badawi Hussein *(+20 100 3304329);* from Cairo to Siwa, contact Mohammad Saeed Ismail Salim *(+20 100 1938437).*

Budget To charter your own transport with a driver, factoring in off-road desert experiences and travel permits, allow US$250 per day (less if you can find fellow passengers to share costs).

DIY or guided tour?

For most visitors a DIY desert tour isn't feasible. The need to get police permits for travel within the Western Desert, and passing through multiple checkpoints, means it's difficult to go it alone. Hiring a car with a driver or taking a tour means this responsibility is taken off your hands. In our experience, booking one day ahead is sufficient time for transport or tour agencies to organise the paperwork, but check with your operator.

In addition to permits, there's the need to consider what's involved in a desert trip. While the oases are fascinating in their own right, for most travellers the highlight is getting into the surrounding desert. For this a 4WD and a driver with expert off-road driving skills are essential. Tours generally include not just the 4WD vehicle and driver but also bedding and catering for camping.

A compromise between DIY and a guided trip is to choose either Siwa or the Luxor to Cairo desert oasis loop, both of which can be reached by public transport (or hiring transport and a driver), and then booking a desert tour with the local experts at each oasis. This has the bonus of bringing much-needed revenue into the oases.

Siwa Oasis

DATE PLANTATIONS | AMAZIGH CULTURE | REMOTE DESERT

☑ TOP TIP
Unless you're visiting in summer, consider forgoing a tuk-tuk and walking instead. Siwa Town is the central hub, but a stroll along flat lanes brings you to Aghurmi, where the main archaeological sites are located. Gebel Dakrur can also be reached on foot by keen walkers.

GETTING AROUND

The daily bus at 10pm from Cairo (7.30pm from Siwa, arriving 6am in Cairo) doesn't always run. The alternative is to hire a taxi. At the time of writing, this meant (expensively) chartering a microbus. From Alexandria, a West & Mid Delta bus runs to Marsa Matruh, and microbuses and local taxis cover the 300km to Siwa (three hours).

Tuk-tuks and taxis are available for touring oasis sights. Bicycles can be rented from shops in front of Shali fortress, and 4WD tours into the desert are available.

Remote, rural and completely unique in Egypt, Siwa may be a bit of a slog to reach, but it more than repays the effort with stunning desert landscapes to explore and a rich heritage to appreciate.

Just 50km from the Libyan border and lying 25m below sea level, this fertile basin of date plantations, orchards and mud-brick hamlets is the epitome of slow-paced life in a desert oasis. Siwa's geographical isolation has helped to preserve Amazigh culture, defined by strong traditions and Siwi, the local dialect of the Tamazight language.

Although there are plenty of sights to see, Siwa's main attraction lies in its far-from-anywhere ambience. This is a place to slow down the pace, stroll through palm groves and soak in a natural spring before heading out to the edge of the Great Sand Sea, where the dunes stretch to the horizon.

Siwa's Medieval Town
A once-forbidding fortress

Sitting proud above Siwa's busy town square, a crumbling maze of walls and passages comprise the 13th-century **Fortress of Shali** *(free)*. It makes a wonderful place to explore, especially in the morning, when the light is at its softest.

A path leads from **Al Babinshal Heritage Hotel** past a bazaar selling local crafts to the entrance of the fort. Stairs continue up to the summit, winding their way around the fort's huddled buildings to a panoramic view across Siwa oasis. The fortress originally stood four or five storeys high and housed hundreds of people. In 1926 rain damaged the structure, and over the following decades inhabitants left for newer, more comfortable houses with electricity and running water.

Today the buildings are in ruins, but it's interesting to see the use of *kershef* (a local building material made of dried-out blocks of salt mixed with sand). Pop into the ethnographical museum in the **House of Siwa**, a restored house that helps in imagining fortress life in the glory days.

SIWA OASIS

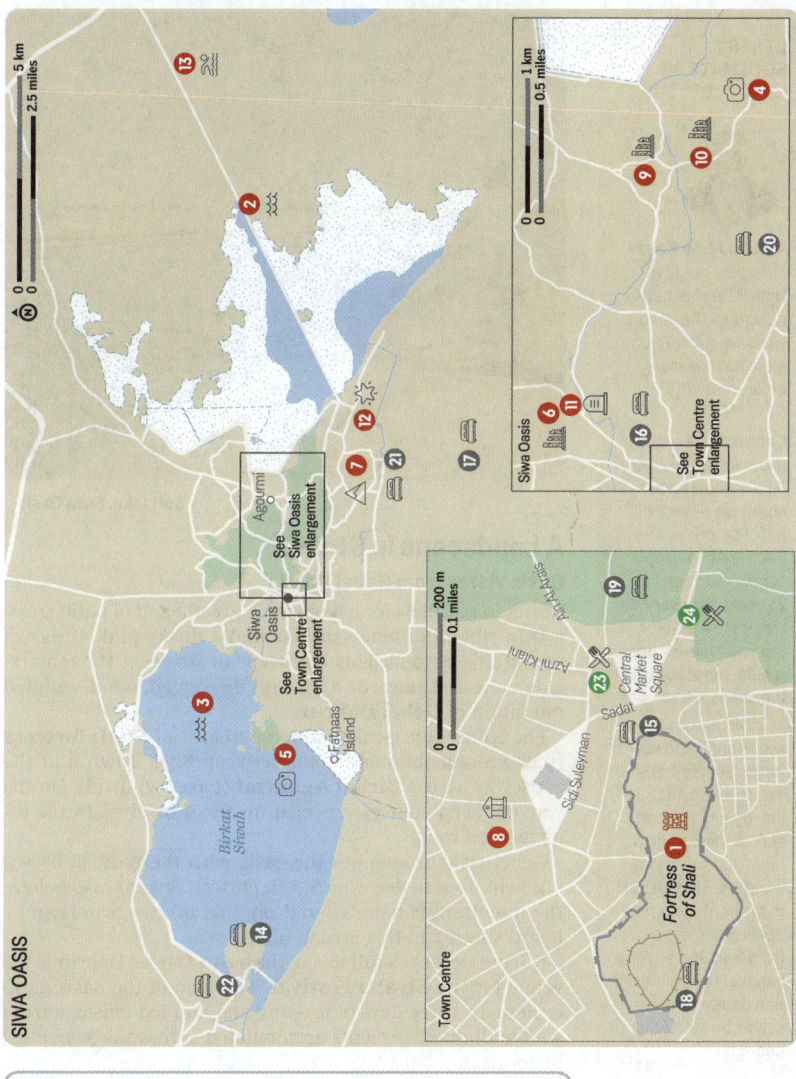

★ HIGHLIGHTS
1 Fortress of Shali

● SIGHTS
2 Birkat Aghurmi
3 Birkat Siwa
4 Cleopatra's Spring
5 Fatnas Spring
6 Gebel Al Mawta
7 Gebel Dakrur
8 House of Siwa Museum
9 Temple of the Oracle
10 Temple of Umm Ubayd
11 Tomb of Si Amun

● ACTIVITIES
12 Al Maaza Hot Spring
13 Salt Pools

● SLEEPING
14 Adrère Amellal
15 Al Babinshal Heritage Hotel
16 Forest Camp
17 Hayaat Siwa Hot Spring
18 Nanshaal Siwa
19 Nour Al Waha
20 Olive Garden House
21 Siwa Shali Resort
22 Taziry Eco Villages

● EATING
23 Abdu
see 15 Al Babinshal Restaurant
see 19 Nour El Waha
24 OLA

● INFORMATION
see 19 Nour Al Waha

DESERT SOULMATE

Aloush Abou Kasse, an expert guide at **Nour Al Waha** (p284), describes the sand sea's emotional pull. *aloushaboukasse@gmail.com; 0100 5435455.*

Can you believe these rocks were once trees? That's what I love about the desert: it's full of surprises. I've been leading people across the desert for 25 years and every day I return to it as if for the first time. My heart is here, particularly in the dunes.

Travel across the sea of sand and you'll forget yourself. It's like entering another life. By day you come across fossils and at night you see shooting stars. They're part of my heritage. The desert for me is a gift from God, but anyone can feel the connection if they let themselves be still for long enough.

Salt lake, Siwa Oasis

A Landscape in Stripes
Oasis vistas from Gebel Dakrur

Think in parallels for a moment: a green band of palm trees, a thin ribbon of blue salt lake and a dusky pink streak of mountains beyond. This landscape in stripes is the remarkable view that rewards a hike up the jagged, wind-sculpted mountain of **Gebel Dakrur**.

The 160m-high peak is 4km southeast of **Shali fortress** (p278) along the main road between Siwa Town and the causeway across **Birkat Aghurmi** (Lake Aghurmi). On the way up, keep your eyes peeled for fossil bivalves in the orange-hued rock.

Gebel Dakrur supplies the oasis with the reddish-brown pigment used to decorate Siwan pottery. Siwans also believe the mountain is haunted and say that *afrit* (spirits) can be heard singing in this area at night.

During October's full moon, the base of Gebel Dakrur is the venue for the **Siyaha Festival**. The men of the oasis gather here for three days of feasting and Sufi-led music, during which all disagreements accumulated across the year must be forgiven.

Sharing a Lakeside Sunset
Fatnas Island

Even in winter Fatnas Island, in the middle of **Birkat Siwa** (Lake Siwa), throngs with local tourists from the coast, especially at weekends. But there's a certain camaraderie in sharing sunset on this tiny island, accessible only across a narrow causeway 6km northwest of town.

Some swim in the natural pool of **Fatnas Spring**, a cool-water hollow in the middle of the island, and others take pedalos onto the lake. Most of the coachloads of visitors, though, just relax with a fruit juice from the lakeside cafe (which also sells tea and coffee) and watch the sun sink behind the lake.

Arrive before 4.30pm if you want to claim your spot for a sundowner or smoothie, and don't even think about sitting down without ordering something – the cushioned seats at the two pontoons and under the date palms are jealousy guarded by cafe staff. Return taxis from town cost around LE100.

Wallowing in Water

Siwa's natural springs

Siwa has an abundance of natural springs of varying temperatures, many of which have been diverted into pools for bathing. Everyone visits **Cleopatra's Spring**, and for good reason. This delightful spot is an oasis within an oasis, surrounded by date palms and cafes. Equally popular is **Bir Wahed** (p283), a surprising waterhole in the middle of the dunes. After dark many head for **Al Maaza Hot Spring** near the Lake Aghurmi causeway.

Hotels also get in on the act. **Siwa Shali Resort** channels the water through a pretty garden, while **Hayaat Siwa Hot Spring** and the gorgeous **Taziry Ecolodge**, 12km west of town, have also made the most of their bounty.

For rather more bizarre bathing, try the internet-sensation **salt pools** north of Lake Aghurmi. Confirm that your driver knows their location before you set out, and pack some old shoes as the bottoms of the pools are very sharp.

Exploring Siwa's Western Fringe

Hiking in the Maraqi area

The desert plain beside **Birkat Al Maraqi** is speckled with wind-whittled stone ridges and cone-shaped mountains. Situated 2½ hours' drive from Siwa, it's a great place for guided hiking (no permit required).

Walks begin near the Graeco-Roman **Dehiba Tombs** and head north for overnight trips or west for shorter day hikes skirting the lake. The desert floor is littered with fossilised shells, and there are grand vistas from the lakeside escarpment. Guides usually point out the ruins of **Bilad El Rum** on a cliff face, where small Roman-era tombs can be seen above the remnants of mud-brick buildings.

VIRAL STARFISH

Thanks to some widely shared drone footage of bathers floating in turquoise pools rimmed by white salt crystals, swimming in the **salt pools** along Lake Aghurmi's northern shoreline has become Siwa's most famous activity.

What the footage doesn't show is that the pools sit within a salt-extraction industrial zone complete with diggers scooping piles of rock and trucks trundling by.

The rectangular pools are part of the salt-extraction process and are a stunning colour. The ones where swimming is permitted look particularly bizarre, decked with bathers lounging on deckchairs. Four or so small and very deep (down to 45m) natural sinkholes within the zone are just large enough to fit one person floating in a starfish position.

EATING IN SIWA: OLD FAVOURITES

Abdu: Friendly, long-running village hub on the main square with simple Egyptian classics. *8am-1am* $

OLA: Traditional Siwan dishes, including camel, plus some European choices, served in a date-palm garden. *11am-11pm* $$

Nour El Waha: Garden restaurant with indoor-outdoor dining, Siwan and Egyptian classics and a particularly good breakfast. *8am-10pm* $$

Al Babinshal: Book for home-cooked dishes around a dining-room fire in winter and with a terrace view of the fortress in summer. *+20 109-963-8526; 8am-1pm* $$$

EXPLORING ANCIENT AGHURMI

Siwa's original main settlement at Aghurmi, 4km east of modern Siwa Town, is a perfect spot for hiking and cycling.

START	END	LENGTH
Shali fortress	Cleopatra's Spring	10km; 3-4 hours

Pack your swimmers and start at ❶ **Shali fortress** (p278), the key sight in Siwa Town. From here you can make out the main landmarks of the route rising above the plantation before you set off. Head north to ❷ **Gebel Al Mawta** (Mountain of the Dead), honeycombed with tombs that date from the 26th dynasty and the Ptolemaic and Roman eras. Look for the ❸ **Tomb of Si Amun**, which contains colourful reliefs of the tomb incumbent praying to Egyptian gods.

Skirt Gebel Al Mawta, follow a creek to the end of the lane and then zigzag along plantation roads to the crumbling mud-brick ruins of Aghurmi. The old settlement is crowned by the ❹ **Temple of the Oracle**. Dedicated to Amun, the temple dates from the 6th century BCE and once housed one of the most revered oracles of the ancient Mediterranean.

Follow the decorative lampposts from Aghurmi to the ❺ **Temple of Umm Ubayd**, only one wall of which remains. The wall is interesting, though, as it's covered in ancient inscriptions.

Continue through the plantation to ❻ **Cleopatra's Spring** (p281), the most famous spring in Siwa. The water gurgles up into a deep, circular stone pool that's rimmed with cafes, shaded seating and changing rooms. From here follow the street lamps to the main road back to town.

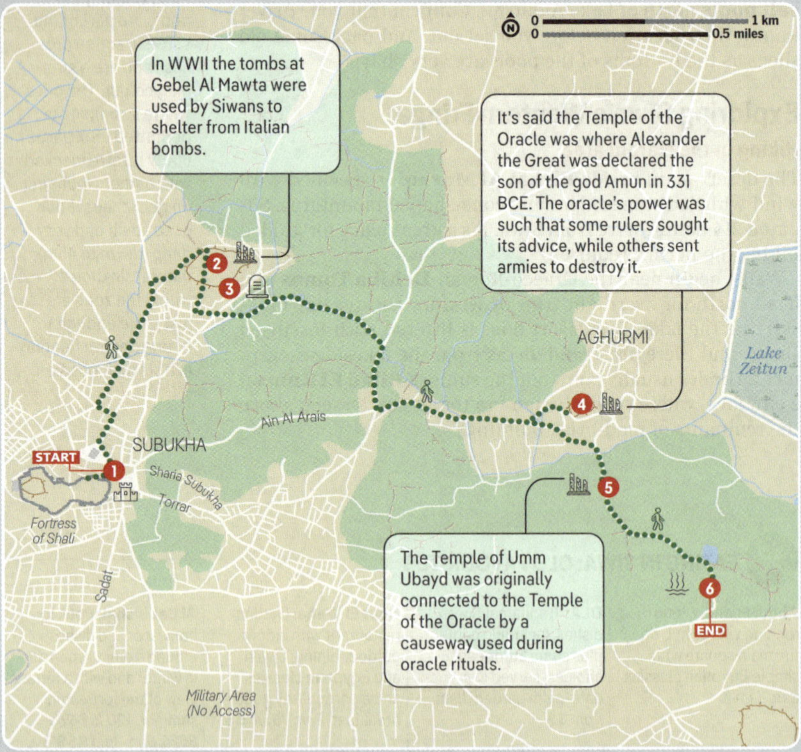

> In WWII the tombs at Gebel Al Mawta were used by Siwans to shelter from Italian bombs.

> It's said the Temple of the Oracle was where Alexander the Great was declared the son of the god Amun in 331 BCE. The oracle's power was such that some rulers sought its advice, while others sent armies to destroy it.

> The Temple of Umm Ubayd was originally connected to the Temple of the Oracle by a causeway used during oracle rituals.

Beyond Siwa Oasis

Tour the remote, rugged swath of desert that surrounds the oasis – the alter ego of Siwa's languid charms.

Outside Siwa it's all about the desert. Day trips to Bir Wahed and desert camping adventures provide a taster of the endless rolling dunes that sit on the doorstep of the oasis. These frame the Great Sand Sea that stretches all the way south to the Gilf Kabir (Great Barrier) at the toe-end of Egypt.

Security restrictions at the time of writing meant that most excursions penetrating deep into the Western Desert sadly remained out of bounds for foreign visitors. In a spot of good news, though, the area around El Arag Oasis (130km southeast of Siwa Town) is currently open, allowing travellers to access more of the Western Desert's striking beauty.

Places
Bir Wahed p283
El Arag Oasis p283

GETTING AROUND

The desert road between Siwa and Bahariya is off limits for foreigners beyond El Arag, so reaching Bahariya and the oases further south requires a lengthy detour via the coast and Cairo.

Desert excursions beyond Siwa require 4WD and permits issued by Siwa's police office (your operator will arrange these).

Bir Wahed
TIME FROM SIWA TOWN: **30 MINS** (4WD)
Sand-dune adventures

Siwa's most popular dune trip is an afternoon jaunt to **Bir Wahed**, starting around 2pm and stopping first at **Bir Wahed hot spring**. This blink-and-you-miss-it pool, about 12km south from town and open 24 hours, is shaded by date palms, and there are toilets and a cafe. While enjoying a soak, spare a thought for the Russian prospectors who were drilling for oil here in the 1960s when they struck hot water instead.

The tour continues to **Cold Water Lake**. It's still rimmed by reeds, but the water has very recently disappeared, a reminder of the precariousness of desert life. Next your driver will put his 4WD through its paces, skimming the dune ridge and descending near-vertical sand slopes to arrive at a high point for **sunset**. If you fancy **sandboarding** here, request this option when you book the tour.

Prices (around LE3000 for a three-hour trip) usually include the US$10 plus LE100 per person police permit and LE170 car permit. Have your passport handy for police inspection. As there are dozens of vehicles heading out this way, it's easy to find others to share the cost.

El Arag Oasis
TIME FROM SIWA: **90 MINS** (4WD)
Walking among pillars of stone

About 130km east of Siwa, accessed off the Siwa–Bahariya road, is one of Egypt's most astonishing desert landscapes.

BEST TOURS FROM SIWA

Hotels: Virtually all hotels in Siwa can arrange Bir Wahed tours, plus trips to Aghurmi's sights and the salt pools.

Abdu: A good place to ask about trips; has a solid reputation for fixing up travellers with experienced driver-guides.

Fathi Abdalla Benhgar: Highly recommended driver-guide (siwawi.com) with years of experience running Siwa tours and Western Desert expeditions.

Nour Al Waha: The owner of this hotel is a great advocate for the value of a desert encounter and has years of experience taking people to El Arag Oasis and, if it becomes permissible for foreigners to return, the Gilf Kabir.

Siwa Fahmi Tour: A recommended agency that organises 4WD, sandboarding and salt-pool tours and has its own tuk-tuk for local city excursions.

El Arag Oasis (p283)

El Arag Oasis is a vast depression where the desert floor is shaded cinnamon and tangerine or streaked white with fossils and sand dollars that crunch underfoot. The entire basin is rimmed with limestone escarpments and dotted with inselbergs that have been contoured over millennia by the wind. If you're very lucky you may spot a gazelle or one of El Arag's shy wild donkeys grazing here.

Until the Graeco-Roman era the oasis in the middle of this sublime desert basin was inhabited, and there are still some date palms watered by an ancient well. Tombs dotting the base of the escarpment also betray an ancient human presence, although thieves removed any contents long ago. There's one tomb treasure left, though, in the form of a red-pigment inscription dating from the Pharaonic era.

El Arag was closed to visitors in 2012 and reopened in 2022 for day visits, but few people journey out here, making this one of the most remote desert trips on offer. Many tour agencies are unaware that the area has reopened. Book through **Nour Al Waha** (p280), whose whole-day trip (from US$200 per vehicle, payable in dollars) includes all permits, 4WD and driver and most likely a police escort.

Bahariya Oasis

BLACK DESERT | GOLDEN MUMMIES | CAMPING TRIPS

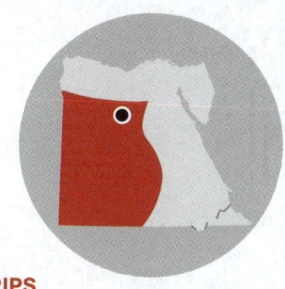

Only 365km from Cairo, Bahariya is the Western Desert's most accessible oasis. With its expanse of shady date palms enclosed by a mesa landscape that's punctuated by jagged cliffs and black peaks, it's a grand introduction to the Western Desert's barren beauty. The only settlement of any size is Bawiti, where narrow lanes run helter-skelter off the scruffy main road, leading to palm groves, gardens and natural springs.

Bahariya rose in prominence from ancient Egypt's Third Intermediate Period (1069–525 BCE) through to the Roman era, when it became a centre of agriculture. During Roman rule its grain and grapes were vital exports. Today it's mostly visited by travellers as a jumping-off point for further desert adventures, primarily to the nearby Black Desert and usually combined with a trip to White Desert National Park, next to Farafra Oasis. Linger an extra day to enjoy Bahariya's antiquities and nearby escarpment.

Bahariya's Natural Beauty
Rugged vistas and languid palm groves

At first glance Bahariya's main town of Bawiti may not look much, but it has some classic scenery on the doorstep.

For panoramic views, head up flat-topped **Gebel Al Ingleez**. The name is derived from the mountain's WWI lookout post, from where British officer Captain Williams monitored the movements of Libyan Senussi tribespeople. A dirt track and pathway leads to the plateau and the modest remnants of Williams' hut, and, of course, expansive views of the Bahariya Oasis.

Dinosaur bones were found at pyramid-shaped **Gebel Dist** in the early 20th century, and in 2001 researchers from the University of Pennsylvania found the remains of a giant new dinosaur species, *Paralititan stromeri*, here. The team's investigation indicated that it was standing beside a tidal

☑ TOP TIP

There's accommodation in Bawiti, at the heart of the oasis, and in the compact settlements and aquifer-fed gardens that surround it.

GETTING AROUND

Upper Egypt and EG run two buses daily between Bawiti and Cairo, and there are a couple of buses daily to Farafra Oasis and Dakhla Oasis. Buses leave from the Express El Wadi grocery store that doubles as a bus waiting room on the main road. Travellers are also allowed to use the microbuses that zip between Bawiti and Cairo.

Bahariya Oasis extends for many kilometres and lacks an obvious centre, so it doesn't lend itself to walking. Taxis ferry people around town, but to visit anywhere beyond (including the local hot springs and escarpment), a 4WD tour is required.

BAHARIYA OASIS SIWA OASIS & THE WESTERN DESERT

BAHARIYA OASIS

● **SIGHTS**
1. Birkat Maran
2. Gebel Al Ingleez
3. Gebel Dist
4. Golden Mummies Museum
5. Qarat Al Hilwa
6. Qarat Qasr Salim
7. Temple of Ain Al Muftella
8. Temple of Alexander
9. Tomb of Bannentiu

● **SLEEPING**
10. Aliyah Eco Lodge
11. Badry Sahara Camp
12. Eden Garden Camp
13. International Hot Spring Hotel
14. Old Oasis Hotel
15. Western Desert Hotel

● **EATING**
16. Bakar Oasis
17. Oasis Restaurant Bahariya
18. Twist Restaurant

channel when it died 94 million years ago, making it likely that the Bahariya area was once a swamp similar to the Florida Everglades.

At sunset, head to **Birkat Maran** (Lake Maran), a large salt lake with mirror-flat water that provides a perfect reflection of the plantation. The old lanes through the surrounding palm groves are a delight to explore; they're so narrow that the palm leaves create a canopy overhead.

Final Repose
Touring Bahariya's antiquities

Stop first at the **Golden Mummies Museum** (p274; *adult/student LE100/50*) in central Bawiti to buy your one-day ticket covering all five of the local archaeological sites. Ten of Bahariya's famous mummy cache are on display in the museum, preserved in a climate-controlled hall. It's fascinating to see the individuality of each of the painted faces, demonstrating a move away from Pharaonic decoration towards Fayoum portraiture.

Also in central Bawiti is the 26th-dynasty double tomb of **Qarat Qasr Salim**, which was discovered under local housing. The rock-cut tomb of high priest Zed-Amun-Ef-Ankh is covered in vibrant wall paintings, hinting at the wealth of its former occupant. Next door lies the **Tomb of Bannentiu**. It consists of a four-columned burial chamber with an inner sanctuary covered in fine reliefs depicting Bannentiu with the god Khonsu and goddesses Isis and Nephthys.

History buffs may like to head out to the western edge of Bawiti. The **Temple of Ain Al Muftella** here consists of four 26th-dynasty chapels now restored and roofed for protection. South of the temple are the ancient necropolis of **Qarat Al Hilwa** and the small and modest **Temple of Alexander**, one of the few places in Egypt where Alexander the Great's cartouche has been found.

THE GOLDEN MUMMIES

The vast Graeco-Roman necropolis known as the Valley of the Golden Mummies, at the southwestern edge of Bahariya Oasis, was discovered in the 1990s and has shed light on the wealth and importance of the oasis in ancient times. Some of the mummies found here have highly decorated gilded face masks and torsos, indicating that a section of oasis society during this period was rich enough to lavish its dead with extravagant funerary rites.

The necropolis stretches over 3 sq km, and while excavations have unearthed more than 250 mummies it has been estimated that there may be more than 10,000 still to be excavated. The site remains closed to the public, so Bawiti's museum offers the only opportunity to see any of the mummies.

 EATING IN BAWITI: LOCAL FAVOURITES

International Hot Spring Hotel: There's a good cook at this garden hotel, which has the Western Desert's only licensed bar. *+20 023-847-3014; 7-10pm* $$

Bakar Oasis: Note the pigeon turrets atop this main-road canteen with large garden; little wonder pigeon is on the menu. *+20 127-932-2905; 24hr* $

Oasis Restaurant Bahariya: A terrace of plasterwork genius marks this popular restaurant serving hearty rice dishes. *+20 105-007-3280; 8am-10pm* $

Twist Restaurant: The organic bean dishes are recommended in this tidy restaurant with cosy traditional seating. *+20 128-020-2321; 24hr* $

Beyond Bahariya Oasis

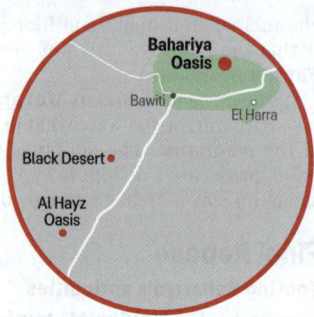

Explore the dramatic landscapes around Bahariya and discover why the Black Desert is black.

Places
Bahariya's Permanent Camps p288
Black Desert p289
Al Hayz Oasis p289

GETTING AROUND

Agents in Cairo can arrange desert trips, often undercutting the price of locally based tours. But before you rush to book one of these cut-price deals, take a moment to understand the impact this would have locally. Each oasis relies on tourism to some extent to help supplement its economy, but camping trips arranged in the capital often bypass the oases. If you'd prefer your visit to represent more sustainable tourism, arrange a Black Desert tour from Bahariya Oasis and reserve a visit to the White Desert National Park from neighbouring Farafra Oasis.

Bahariya's green belt of date palms extends across such an enormous expanse that when you're under their canopy you almost forget the surrounding desert. But make no mistake: the desert is there, ever eager to devour the tentative fertile strips at the oasis edge. This rocky habitat of vultures, scorpions and snakes is at its most menacing in the Black Desert on Bahariya's doorstep.

In the same vicinity, an excellent museum explains the relationship between desert and sown land in the small oasis of Al Hayz. The exhibits show how the oases would cease to exist without underground water. The levels of that precious resource are dropping alarmingly, but the museum's exhibits also offer helpful solutions.

Bahariya's Permanent Camps

TIME FROM BAWITI: **30 MINS**

Under the stars – well, almost

There are three ways to get a sense of life in the slow lane in and around Bahariya. You can book a desert trip from Cairo, you can wait until you reach the oasis and book a camping trip through your hotel or a tour agent, or (perhaps best of all) you can book into one of the permanent camps that are dotted in the farther reaches of the oasis, at the edge of the desert.

With huts or chalets rather than tents, they're more like budget resorts. Given the garden settings, natural pools and expert tour advice, they make the perfect place to acclimatise to the desert before heading out under canvas.

Two of the best camps include **Badry Sahara Camp** (p303), which has the prettiest pitch in the oasis, with simple *hoosha* (palm-thatch) huts with shared bathrooms. A more sophisticated option, **Eden Garden Camp** (p303) has the best facilities, is surrounded by an orchard and has its own hot and cold spring water. Both offer free pick-ups from the bus station and arrange excellent desert tours that observe rather than shortcut police security arrangements.

Black Desert

TIME FROM BAWITI: **45 MINS** (4WD)

A Jurassic landscape

Book a tour of the great *sahara suda* and an inevitable question occurs: why is the **Black Desert** black? The answer is simple, and the pyramidal mountains dotting the landscape some 50km from Bawiti provide a clue: in Jurassic times these were volcanoes. The reddish metamorphic rocks at the base of each mountain derive from hard iron quartzite, while the peaks are capped with layers of basalt. Even if geology isn't your thing, the view from the shoulder of one of these hulks is impressive, particularly when ribbons of heat thread across the rocky desert floor and the sun sparks against glittering traces of pyrite.

In the cooler months, particularly December to February, the Black Desert makes a great place for a guided hike, and you may spot a lizard, beetle or scorpion surviving against all odds in this harshest of environments. After rains there's even a tinge of green from opportunistic plants, the seeds of which can lie dormant for years.

The Black Desert isn't just about rock, though; it's also about sand. In fact, what makes the landscape so dramatic here is the contrast between the two. Some tours will take you to the **Al Muzeina dune**, a long line of tawny sand interrupting the rocky desert floor. Similarly, the **Umm Al Lafa dune**, at the edge of the Black Desert, slithers through a valley littered with black rock for around 1km and makes a popular sunset stop. Your guide may brew a herbal tea while you slide down the dunes on a sandboard (usually available from your hotel) and toil back up.

The Black Desert is often combined with a visit to the **White Desert National Park** (p293) from Bahariya or Farafra oases, but on a day trip it leaves little time to enjoy either fully. It's better to make the Black Desert a half-day trip from Bahariya or part of a two-night camping trip from either oasis.

Al Hayz Oasis

TIME FROM BAWITI: **45 MINS**

Going, going, gone...

The tiny oasis of Al Hayz lies 45km south of Bawiti along the main Bahariya–Farafra road. It's home to the **Al Hayz Water Education Center** (*adult/child LE45/10*), a small museum dedicated to water management. The project is the brainchild of Dr Tina Jaskolski, an expatriate geologist and expert in sustainable development who explains that water is becoming one of the most critical issues of our time.

With interactive displays, signboards in English and volunteers to guide you around the exhibits, the museum makes for a fascinating visit. It's not a wholly comfortable one, though, with some hard-hitting facts, such as that water levels in underground aquifers around Western Desert oases have dipped so low that water now has to be pumped to the surface. While 98% of the population lives on 7% of the land using Nile water, the rest rely on these aquifers for community

---

LESS PLEASURE, MORE LOVE

Talat Abdul Moulah and his brother **Mohammed** have been tour guides for 33 years. They remember travelling by camel through the desert with their mother as boys. *edengardentours.com*

Want to drive like a Bedouin? Stay with us at Eden Garden Camp (p303) and we'll teach you how.

Looking for less pleasure, more love? Book a camel trip – 10km before lunch and 10km after – and feel the magic.

Car kaput? We can fix it in our garage of recycled parts.

Want some advice from Bedouin brothers? What you give comes back, but don't forget that we come with nothing and leave with nothing. In the meantime, where you put yourself you'll find yourself.

Black Desert (p289)

BAHARIYA'S NATURAL SPRINGS

A local pleasure is a dip in therapeutic waters. This mostly involves turning up and getting in, but a bit of prep helps make the most of the experience.

Start by packing some old garb. All of Bahariya's springs have high mineral content, which can stain clothing, so avoid wearing your favourite swimmers. Women will feel more comfortable wearing shorts and T-shirts at public springs.

Next choose your preferred temperature. Some springs, such as those at **Bir Al Ramla**, are hot and sulphurous, while at **Bir Al Mattar** cold water makes for a super-refreshing summer dip.

At **El Jaffara**, inside Eden Garden Camp (p303), you can sample both if you stay for a meal at the camp.

survival. The water being drawn up today is from pockets captured by the Nubian sandstone that are thought to be one to two million years old. This resource isn't being replenished, so once it's used it's gone forever.

Look along the so-called New Valley in the Western Desert and you'll find it's characterised by huge agricultural projects that use around 85% of the available water. Sugar cane and rice (the planting of which is now illegal) were traditional cash crops, but less water-consuming farming is now being promoted.

Visitors can do their part too, explains Dr Jaskolski, through simple measures such as turning the tap off when brushing teeth, having a quick shower rather than filling a bathtub and generally making a conscious effort to avoid wasting water during their stay. It certainly gives you pause for thought while you're soaking in the pool at **Ain Gomma**. The natural spring's cold, crystal-clear water seems all the more remarkable when you know it's so ancient and could one day soon be gone.

Farafra Oasis

WHITE DESERT | SAND DUNES | CAMPING TRIPS

Known by the ancient Egyptians as 'land of cattle', the oasis of Farafra was once an important stop on the old caravan trading route and has been inhabited for millennia. Its name means 'fizzy water' and perhaps alludes to the quality of the spring water here, some of which has a high sulphur content. Its wealth attracted raids from Bedouins and Libyans, who eventually became assimilated into the local population. Today the walls of Qasr Al Farafra have been breached and much of the old mud-brick quarter has crumbled to dust, but the local community remains intact.

For the traveller, seldom-visited Farafra makes a welcome stopover on the Luxor–Cairo oasis route. As the nearest oasis to the splendours of the White Desert National Park, it's also an ideal base for camping trips.

Grandmother's House
Bayt Amana in the kasbah

Until 2021 Grandmother lived here. By Grandmother, we mean the beloved relative of at least 30 grandchildren. For one of those descendants, Maged Aziz, restoring **Bayt Amana** (*+20 1 02-125-1302; LE50*), Grandmother's home in the *kasbah,* became a year-long mission that was completed in 2025.

The incumbent of this mud-brick dwelling at the edge of the old fort in Farafra was 101 when she died, and saving her house from being sold or allowing it to retreat into rubble resonated with the whole family. When Amana was born here in 1920 there was a three-storey palace at the end of the covered alleyway. It was her responsibility to unlock the palace door each morning and close it at night. Ten families lived within the *kasbah* walls. But this was no closeted society. Many of those whom the palace was built to repel were at length welcomed in, and even the older grandchildren of Amana remember Saudis, Libyans and Moroccans living in close quarters in the 116 rooms of the palace.

The modest but beautifully restored Bayt Amana, with its ethnographical flavour, roof terrace and intriguing wooden key, is not just an interesting glimpse of times gone by but also a tribute to the values of an outward-looking oasis.

☑ TOP TIPS

From Farafra it's just half an hour to White Desert National Park (compared with the two-hour drive from Bahariya). It's possible to visit the main sights of the park as a half-day trip.

GETTING AROUND

Daily Egybus services leave Turgoman Bus Station in Cairo at 7am, arriving in Farafra at 3pm. A less favourable night service departs Cairo at 6pm. Return buses leave Farafra at 8am and noon. There are services from Bahariya and Dakhla too. Travelling by public bus to Farafra is permitted for foreigners, though this is subject to change.

A private car (chartered minibus) is the only way of reaching Luxor (~LE7000; seven hours via Asyut). To continue the journey through the oases by private car (from LE10,000), allow two days to reach Luxor, sightseeing en route.

- **SIGHTS**
1 Badr's Museum
2 Bayt Amana
- **SLEEPING**
3 Al Badawiya Safari & Hotel
4 Al Waha Hotel
5 Rahala Safari Hotel
- **EATING**
6 Al Chef Restaurant
7 Felafel Farafra Restaurant
8 Kalimary Sea Food
9 Kher Al Wadi Restaurant

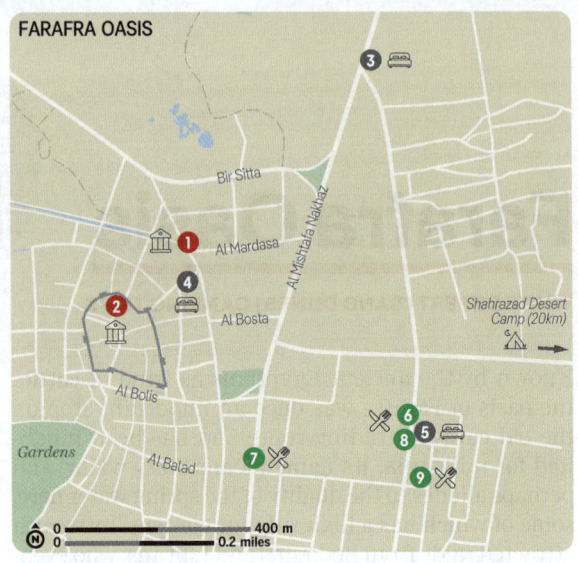

Outward looking is a phrase that may describe Farafra's other sight too. **Badr's Museum** is an extraordinary exhibition space for the late Badr Abdel Moghny, who recorded local life in painting and sculpture with a nod to a European tradition.

Riding the Dunes

The Agabat desert

Included in many itineraries for the White Desert National Park is a visit to the **Agabat dunes**. Meaning 'difficulty' or 'hurdle', Agabat earned its name from the camel caravans that used to avoid this area due to the effort of scaling the mountains of soft sand. It was easier to extend the journey in distance than to encourage camels up the steep inclines. Thanks to 4WD vehicles the area is no longer such an obstacle, although it takes some clever off-road skills to negotiate some of the longer slopes.

A trip here isn't just an exciting drive. It also offers some sublime landscapes. The dunes have drifted over time, crumpling against the escarpment and eroded pillars of sandstone. There's even a giant rock arch – a hole punched through the rock by sand particles grinding against the stone in the prevailing wind.

Some tour operators set up camp here. Outside the national park (where camping is forbidden), it makes a magnificent pitch for a night under canvas.

 EATING IN FARAFRA: OUR PICKS

Al Chef Restaurant: You can dine in or take away at this simple restaurant in the middle of Farafra. *24hr* $

Kher Al Wadi Restaurant: The kofta at this main-road grill is tasty, and there's an array of side dishes. *11am-2pm* $

Kalimary Sea Food: Perhaps this isn't the most obvious place to try seafood, but it makes a change from grilled chicken! *7am-10pm* $

Felafel Farafra Restaurant: Expect a warm welcome at this tiny palace of falafel with some tasty stuffed options. *6-11am & 6-11pm* $

Inselberg formations

TOP EXPERIENCE

White Desert National Park

The White Desert (Sahara Al Beida), with its surreal snow-coloured pinnacles, is protected by a national park and is the main highlight of the Western Desert. The park covers remarkable landscapes that are best experienced on an overnight tour from Farafra. It's not permitted to stay in the park, but local driver-guides find beautiful spots nearby to set up camp.

DON'T MISS

Desert 'mushroom' and 'chicken'

Inselbergs

Sea of white rock waves from site rim

White Desert from the dunes

Stargazing

Crystal Mountain

Central Inselberg Zone

Throughout the White Desert, clusters of extraordinary wind-eroded shapes dot the desert floor. Once under the Tethys Sea, the desert here is formed of the shells and bones of ancient marine animals that were deposited on the seabed over millennia. The softer layers of sediment were whittled away by the wind as the sea retreated, exposing harder rock that continues to be eroded into striking formations. Local guides take delight in spotting zoomorphic likenesses among

PRACTICALITIES
- US$5, cash only, pay at the 'mushroom and chicken' formation
- sunrise-sunset

> **A LIVING LANDSCAPE**
>
> Fennec and Rüppell's foxes are endemic in the park. It's unlikely you'll see one of these shy desert inhabitants, but their paw marks are readily spotted in the sands. The park protects several other mammals, including the endangered rhim gazelle and the vulnerable dorcas gazelle. Barbary sheep, jackals and sand cats are also reported as being present here.

> **TOP TIPS**
>
> ● For the best tours with experienced driver-guides who have the 4WD and catering skills to make the trip memorable, choose a Farafra operator.
>
> ● In winter the skies are blue (rather than white with heat), making for spectacular contrasts.
>
> ● Although you can spot many formations from the bus between Farafra and Bahariya, and even reach a few desert mushrooms by car, only a 4WD trip does the area justice.
>
> ● It's not permitted to enter the park on foot or without a guide.
>
> ● At sunset the white stone turns pink.
>
> ● Look for footprints in the morning to see who you shared the night with.

the scattered inselbergs (isolated rock formations), and no tour is complete without ticking off the horse, camel and rabbit. It's the giant **desert mushroom** and accompanying **chicken**, though, that attract the crowds at sunset and feature as the national park's logo.

Beyond, the desert stretches into waves of low chalk hummocks (highly eroded outcrops), like static waves in a strange, arid sea. Spiked knobs of black iron-pyrite, some shaped like flowers, others more like grenades, are scattered across parts of the desert floor. There are also twig-like pieces of fossilised wood, brittle sand dollars and other echinoid fossils here too.

Crystal Mountain

The White Desert National Park bestrides both sides of the Bahariya–Farafra Hwy, covering 300 sq km, but currently it is only permissible to visit the eastern side. If this changes, the western portion has less of the characteristic inselbergs typifying the White Desert but boasts instead some magnificent wind-eroded escarpments. These can be glimpsed along the left side of the road as you journey from Farafra to the northern entrance to the park, where they loom up like giant Pharaonic pylons – gateways to the deeper Sahara.

The northern entrance is by **Crystal Mountain**, a shelf composed nearly entirely of quartz and featuring a giant rock arch. The desert floor and the rock formations all around this area are littered with quartz crystals. Take a look at the signboard here; in the absence of a visitor centre, it provides a helpful map of the whole park.

Karawin Dunes Area

A set of low, undulating dunes, surrounded by a desert floor streaked with a white crust and studded by chalk formations, forms part of the White Desert landscape and makes for an interesting contrast to the gravel plains surrounding the main formations. On the rim of these dunes, farms rely on irrigation to water new date plantations, and large pockets of standing water near here appear magical in the desiccated terrain.

Overnight Camping

Local operators are experts at finding inspiring camp sites in designated zones beyond the park boundary, and driver-guides are masters of logistics. Within 30 minutes a windbreak will be up, tents will be erected with copious bedding, and the fire will be lit and the kettle hung over the flames. Dinner (soup, salad, grill) is likely to be one of the best of your trip.

Dakhla Oasis

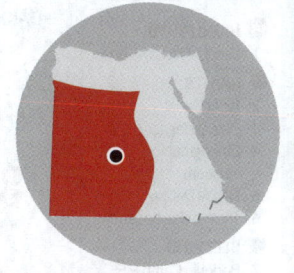

MUD-BRICK ARCHITECTURE | ROMAN MONUMENTS | PAINTED TOMBS

Sprawling Dakhla Oasis, sandwiched between grand escarpments, is a showcase for the Western Desert's best-preserved mud-brick architecture. In Neolithic times it was the site of a vast lake, and rock paintings show that elephants, zebras and ostriches wandered its shore. The oasis was an important producer of grapes, fruit and grain from the Pharaonic era and under Roman rule. With Al Kharga Oasis, Dakhla was known as Oasis Magna, and the area was prominent enough throughout the medieval age to be fortified for protection against Bedouin attacks. Rummaging around the assorted ruins from each of these eras is Dakhla's chief charm.

Apart from the main town of Mut (pronounced 'Moot'), Dakhla is largely a rural destination where palm-hatted *fellaheen* (farmers) drive their donkey carts past half-forgotten antiquities in slow time. You may well find yourself the only visitor in the oasis – together, that is, with your obligatory police escort.

Mud-brick Masterpieces
Balat and Mastaba of Khentika

The modern village of Balat does little to betray its ancient heritage, so stumbling on **Balat Islamiya**, a narrow-laned labyrinth dating to the Mamluk and Ottoman eras, feels like quite a find. With its roots in the Old Kingdom, this abandoned collection of mud-brick buildings has been partly restored and the site guardian will happily show you around (tip expected). It's fascinating to look behind the doors – unlocked with wooden sticks that act as keys – at ancient flour and olive-oil presses and to discover that the mosque, with its thatched roof resting on date-palm beams, is still in use today. The view from the roof puts the oasis nicely into its desert context.

☑ TOP TIP

Mut is the only town of any size in the oasis, but it's not feasible to explore on foot. Dakhla Oasis is huge. The mud-brick old quarter of Al Qasr (arguably the main sight of interest) is 30km west of town, while Balat lies 30km east.

GETTING AROUND

There are microbuses from Mut to Al Qasr from near Midan Al Tahrir (at the intersection of the highway and Sharia Al Wadi). Hiring a taxi in Mut is a viable means of getting around, albeit accompanied by police.

Al Wadi Bus Company operates from Mut bus station, on Sharia Al Wadi, with a service to Cairo. Upper Egypt and EG have a couple of daily buses to Asyut, Farafra and Bahariya. Microbus is the only way to reach Al Kharga from Dakhla without your own transport, but police permits aren't always forthcoming.

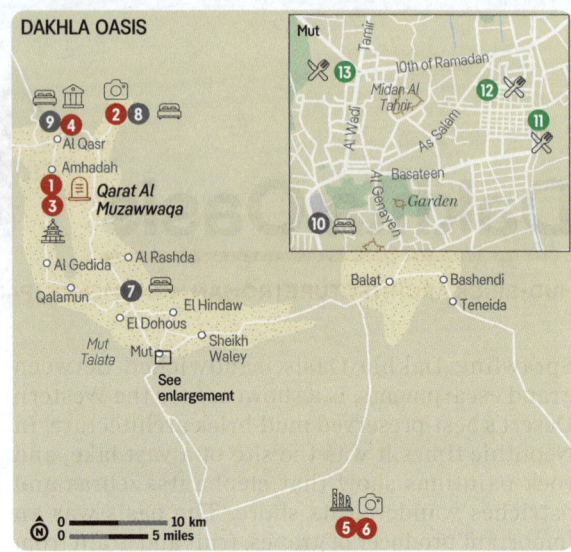

HIGHLIGHTS
1 Qarat Al Muzawwaqa

SIGHTS
2 Bir Al Gabal
3 Deir Al Haggar
4 Ethnographic Museum
5 Qila Al Dabba
6 Tomb of Pasha Hindi

SLEEPING
7 Bedouin Camp & El Dohous Village
8 Camp Bir Al Gabal
9 Desert Lodge
10 El Forsan Hotel

EATING
11 Abo Marwan Restaurant
12 Al Khayrat Restaurant
see 10 El Forsan Cafe
13 Shehab Restaurant

There are further mud-brick surprises at nearby **Qila Al Dabba** *(adult/student LE100/50)*, Balat's Old Kingdom necropolis. The five *mastabas* (early precursors of the pyramids) here date from the 6th dynasty and would once have been clad in fine limestone. You can descend shallow steps to excavated **Mastaba of Khentika**, which opens into a small tomb with wall paintings that portray farming and boating scenes.

Bewitched & Bewildering
Kharga's Oasis Magna sites

An elderly man, sporting a hat typical of the oasis, pauses with his donkey to stare at the three police cars and one microbus of two passengers that pull up beside him. Visitors are seldom seen in these parts and it takes a while for all concerned to process the moment. The sense of participating in a slightly bewitching experience continues on finding the temple of **Deir Al Haggar** *(adult/student LE100/50)* half-buried here. Dedicated to the Theban triad of Amun, Mut and Khonsu, as well as the falcon-headed god Horus, it was built between the reigns of Nero (54–68 CE)

EATING IN MUT: OUR PICKS

Al Khayrat Restaurant: Something for everyone, including pizzas, salads and mixed grills, is served at this popular restaurant. *10am-2am* $

El Forsan Cafe: Attractive garden cafe preparing grilled meats and all manner of *mahshi* (stuffed vegetables). *hours vary* $

Abo Marwan Restaurant: Serving copious mounds of barbecued meats, this restaurant has a small garden. *10am-11pm* $

Shehab Restaurant: In business since 1987, Said Shehab's meat-centric feasts and succulent shish kebab are a Mut institution. *10am-1am* $$

and Domitian (81–96 CE). Restored in much of its glorious sandstone beauty, it looks as if it's been picked up and spirited whole from the Nile.

Even more bewildering is seeing the names of the entire team of Gerhard Rohlfs, a 19th-century desert explorer, carved into the top section of a pillar near the **Porch of Titus**. Quite how they reached the top of the temple is a mystery until you factor in the shifting sand dunes nearby.

A few kilometres east there's another puzzle at the tombs of **Qarat Al Muzawwaqa** (*adult/student LE100/50*). From afar this 2nd-century necropolis appears to consist of tombs like those of Thebes that burrow into the sandstone outcrop. Inside the **Tomb of Oziri** (Petosiris) and the **Tomb of Badi Baset** (Petubastis) are familiar hieroglyphics and colourful paintings of Pharaonic gods – walls describing the measuring of souls and the journeys of the dead. But then there's the mystifying addition of a man in a toga, gardens of grapevines and fields of swaying barley with oasis ducks paddling under a zodiac spread across the tomb sky.

Both tombs from the Graeco-Roman era were discovered by Egyptian archaeologist Ahmed Fakri in 1971 and catch that relatively short moment in time when old gods prevailed in a new world order.

Taking the Plunge
Bir Al Gabal oasis springs

Dakhla's most famous natural spring is **Bir Al Gabal**, set amid soaring desert scenery. During winter and spring it can get busy with groups during the day. If blaring Egyptian pop music doesn't float your boat, come back after dark for a more peaceful experience and take a dip under the star-filled sky.

The Bir Al Gabal turn-off is signposted (just before the El Badawiya Hotel) on the main oasis road, around 20km north of Mut. The spring is another 5km from the turn-off and is part of Camp Bir Al Gabal, so there is a small entrance fee.

If the spring is chock-a-block when you arrive, there's another natural spring on the right about 500m before you get to Bir Al Gabal. It's concealed behind a brick pump house.

Off the Beaten Track
Exploring Dakhla villages

If you've hired a taxi in Mut, or have a private driver, consider visiting a handful of villages on the secondary road between Al Qasr and Mut on your way to or from Dakhla's northern sites.

The ruined village of **Amhadah** has several tombs nearby dating from the 2nd century. Further along towards Mut, the road passes through the villages of **Al Gedida** and **Qalamun**, both of which are good for a stroll as they're home to plenty of traditional mud-brick architecture.

YOUR ESCORT AWAITS (WHETHER YOU WANT IT OR NOT)

In the Western Desert oases, particularly between Baris and Farafra, you are obliged to be escorted by the police. Intended to keep you safe in remote areas, escorts vary in size and formality and could be two or three pick-up trucks with armed guards or a more discreet single officer riding a motorbike alongside your own vehicle or local taxi.

Rather than trying to dodge the escort (which is beyond your control anyway, as your whereabouts are legally required to be conveyed to the police by hotels and transport agencies), embrace it as part of the experience. Besides, it's not every day most of us get to be treated like a VIP.

Old Town, Al Qasr

TOP EXPERIENCE

Al Qasr

The fortified old town of Al Qasr sits at the foot of the limestone cliffs bordering the northern edge of Dakhla. This mud-brick maze was built over the foundations of a Roman city and is thought to be one of the oldest inhabited areas in the oases. A section of the village has been painstakingly restored, making for Dakhla's best excursion.

DON'T MISS

Mosque

Corn mill

Madrasa and court

Olive press

Large *bayt* (house)

Decorative brickwork

Miniature replicas of the old quarter

Touring the Old Town

Most of the buildings of Al Qasr date from the 16th- and 17th-century Ottoman era, although the covered lanes belong to the town's medieval origins. The narrow, winding alleyways trapped warmth in winter and kept out the sun in summer; they also protected the inhabitants from sandstorms. Note the huge doors that could seal off sections of the lanes from the rest of the town. These marked the boundaries between clusters of houses that were occupied by different family groups.

PRACTICALITIES
- *adult/student LE100/50*
- *8am-5pm*

Mosque & Craft School

The entrance to the old town is marked by the 12th-century, 21m-high minaret of the town mosque, housing the tomb of Sheikh Nasser El Din.

Immediately outside the mosque walls you may see some youngsters wielding chisels. They are some of the 300 apprentices working for artisanal carpenter Mr Kanooz Al Wahad. His workshop is nearby, and the elaborate miniature replicas of the old quarter he fashions from palm timber make great souvenirs. Asked how he knows which timbers are possible to carve, he said he has help from his friends – bees are attracted to nest in the old trunks of palm trees, and these are soft enough but still strong enough to carve.

Town Industry

Just around the corner from the mosque is a room containing a huge old corn mill that has been fully restored to function in a beautiful amalgam of stone and wood, powered by donkeys.

In a nearby workshop, intriguingly called 'The Succulents', there's a giant olive press and a secondary room where the olive pulp was squeezed into olive oil. Between the two mills, look for a shop selling local embroidery and assorted crafts that gives an inkling of what an ordinary house may have looked like.

Madrasa & Court

One of the most beautifully restored buildings in the old town is the madrasa (theological school), which was later used as the local courthouse and town hall. You can enter the soaring double-storey courtroom, with its red, white and black decorative brickwork framing the arches, and the small room that functioned as a prison beside it.

Large Bayt

This large family house is a little labyrinth within the wider maze. Guides lead you up the stairs and through the rooms to the roof terrace for quintessential views of the old town. You'll then go across the lane through a 2nd-storey corridor and back down to the other side of the lane.

The decorative brickwork in the main rooms here is beautifully executed. Note, too, the door of Abu Nafir nearby, incorporating massive blocks, carved with hieroglyphic reliefs, from an earlier structure – possibly a Ptolemaic temple – built into the mud-brick architecture.

Al Qasr Ethnographic Museum

Most tours end by passing by a small ethnographical **museum** (LE50) that occupies a house built in 1785.

Before you leave, take a look at some of the palm-frond crafts laid out on the ground nearby – you'll be a rarity if the enterprising women here let you leave without making a purchase!

LINTEL DECORATION

As you explore Al Qasr's narrow alleyways, don't forget to look up. Each house's entrance is marked by a carved acacia-beam lintel. There are 37 lintels in the old town, and the oldest dates to the early 16th century. The size of the houses in Al Qasr and the surviving fragments of decoration suggest the town's wealth and the importance the Ottomans afforded it.

TOP TIPS

● A guide is informally assigned to escort visitors through Al Qasr. Without them it's hard to fathom where to visit.

● Guides are the custodians of the area and they take their role seriously. As keeper of the keys they will unlock treasures you wouldn't be able to see otherwise.

● Although it may not look like it, there's a logic to the route the guides take, so it's best to just go with the flow.

● If you're keen to take photographs, the best time to visit is between 10.30am and 2.30pm, when the most light penetrates Al Qasr's walled alleys.

Al Kharga Oasis

CHRISTIAN NECROPOLIS | ANCIENT TEMPLES | TRADE ROUTE

☑ TOP TIP

If you want to detour to Baris – 80km south of Al Kharga town, beyond the turnoff to Luxor – notify your driver so they can organise the police paperwork.

GETTING AROUND

The only way to travel between Luxor and Al Kharga is to charter a microbus, booking at least a day ahead for the agency to obtain travel permits.

No public buses link Al Kharga with Dakhla, and permission to travel on microbuses between the two is not always forthcoming.

The sights of Al Kharga are widely dispersed, so use your Luxor transport to shuttle you around. The obligatory police escort only applies to the oasis belt, not the leg to Luxor. This lonesome road is badly potholed in parts and the going is slow (about six hours), but 4WD is not required.

Arriving at the T-junction at the end of the dilapidated road from Luxor, don't be surprised if armed guards rush your vehicle, checking and rechecking your passport and waving you into their station for a loo break. It may look dramatic, but you're the best entertainment they've had all day. So few visitors make it to Al Kharga that there's a sense it's pioneer county. In fact Al Kharga town is a bustling modern city and Saudi Arabia is investing heavily in a sophisticated new town nearby.

Al Kharga has always been a hub of sorts, located at the crossroads of vital trade routes, including the Darb Al Arba'een. This 'Forty Days Road' brought the oasis great prosperity, and a wealth of Pharaonic, Roman and Christian relics illustrate its former importance. In the 1890s the British built watchtowers to safeguard the 'back door' into Egypt, and their strategic value is recognised today.

Driving the 40-Day Road
New Valley artery

Drive the modern asphalt between Al Kharga Oasis and Baris and you're following the **Darb Al Arba'een**, a north–south trade route that stretched from Sudan's Darfur region to Asyut. Today, this '40-Day Road' runs through the New Valley Governate, an area of low depressions marked by oases. Once the surface of the desert sat atop the escarpment, but wind weathered away the rocky crust, leaving sunken basins. Closer to the water table, these depressions made for fertile farming. These days giant plantations are being laid out across the desert floor, bringing new prosperity to the villages that lie along the road.

Part Temple, Part Fort
Forts of the Darb Al Arba'een

Driving along the 40-Day Road you'll see some impressive reminders of the New Valley's ancient status as a busy trade

AL KHARGA OASIS

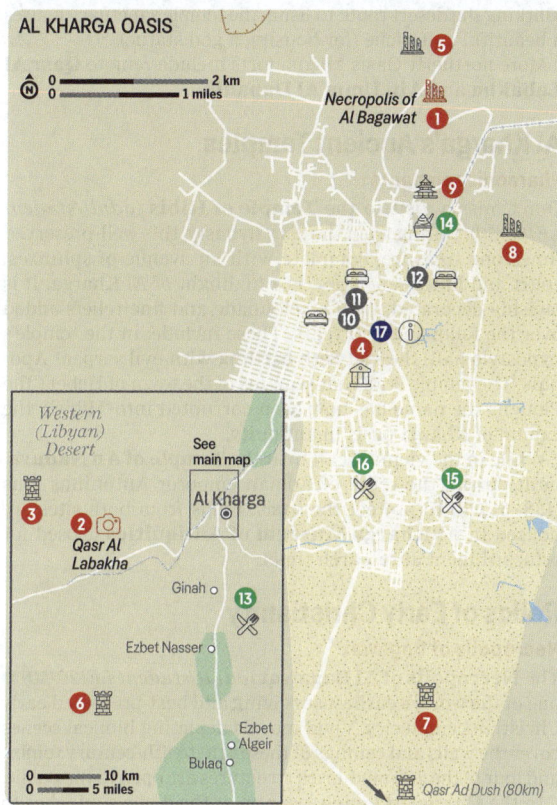

★ HIGHLIGHTS
1. Necropolis of Al Bagawat
2. Qasr Al Labakha

● SIGHTS
3. Ain Umm Al Dabadib
4. Al Kharga Museum of Antiquities
5. Monastery of Al Kashef
6. Qasr Al Ghueita
7. Qasr Al Zayyan
8. Temple of An Nadura
9. Temple of Hibis

● SLEEPING
10. Badr Hotel
11. King Hotel
12. Sol Y Mar Pioneers Hotel

● EATING
13. Bir Jinnah Hasrir
14. Dates Al Tahhan
15. Hawash Restaurant
16. Wimpy Albasateen

● INFORMATION
17. New Valley Tourist Office

A–Z OF DESERT FORMATIONS

Barchan Crescent dune made by the wind blowing in one direction; seen near Baris.

Erg Egypt and Libya share a vast erg (sea of sand) in the Gilf Kebir, south of Oasis Magna.

Escarpment Flat-topped cliffs with fertile depressions; abundant in Dakhla.

Inselberg Domes, pillars, rocks etc.; key formation of the White Desert.

Pedestal rock Giant rock mushrooms that emerge when soft sedimentary rock erodes.

Yardang Long protrusions of sedimentary rock, grooved by sand abrasion and wind.

---

route through fertile lands. Here, Pharaonic temples were refitted by the Romans as fortified garrisons to protect and control trade along the Oasis Magna (today's Dakhla and Al Kharga Oases).

Qasr Ad Dush *(LE100)*, near Baris, is one such amalgam. The Romans completed a fort here in 177 CE on the site of Kysis, and in 1986 a necklace and crown fashioned from 16g of gold were uncovered here. Arguably an even greater treasure is the 1st-century temple dedicated to Isis and Serapis that abuts the half-buried fortress. Its perfectly proportioned gateways frame the desert beyond and the intersection of five desert tracks marking the southern gateway into Egypt.

Some 60km north along the 40-Day Road brings you to **Qasr Al Ghueita** *(adult/student LE100/50)*. Close to Al Kharga Town, it's another example of a Roman fort enclosing an earlier Pharaonic structure. The temple here dates from the 25th dynasty and boasts some superb reliefs of Hapy, the pot-bellied Nile god, and a grand hypostyle hall. Qasr Al Ghueita means 'Fortress of the Small Garden' and alludes to the grapes that once grew in abundance here. Close by is another fortress-temple, **Qasr Al Zayyan** *(adult/student LE100/50)*.

TOURING AL KHARGA'S SITES

Al Kharga's **New Valley Tourist Office** on Midan Nasser is known for being very helpful to independent travellers, providing excellent information, arranging permits for desert trips and helping arrange transport in and around the oases and onward to Asyut and Luxor. **Mr Mohsen Abd Al Moneem** *(WhatsApp +20 100 180 6127)* heads New Valley tourism here and is a highly experienced guide. A mine of information on the oases, he recommends dune tours at sunset in Jenna, among other excursions, and explains how the dunes, moving at up to 6cm per year, impinge on the plantations.

Another Kharga-based desert operator is **Mazen Safari** *(ahmedosman9994@gmail.com; WhatsApp +20 100-673-2763)*.

Marking the desert route to Esna, the temple sanctuary houses a beautiful cult niche (for housing a god statue).

More northerly Oasis Magna forts include remote **Qasr Al Labakha** and **Ain Umm Al Dabadib**.

Al Kharga's Ancient Temples

Pharaonic remnants

Don't miss a visit to the **Temple of Hibis** (*adult/student LE180/50*). Dating from the 25th dynasty, this well-preserved limestone treasure, complete with an avenue of sphinxes, court and inner sanctuary, is a highlight of Al Kharga. It is lavishly decorated, with a colonnade and fine reliefs added over the following 300 years. These include, in the temple's hypostyle hall, the god Seth battling with evil serpent Apophis. The temple is all that remains of the town of Hebet ('the Plough'; the name has now been corrupted into 'Hibis'), the capital of Kharga oasis in antiquity.

While in the vicinity, call in at the **Temple of An Nadura**, built during the reign of Roman emperor Antoninus Pius (138–61 CE) to protect the oasis. Finds from both sites are housed in **Al Kharga Museum of Antiquities** (closed for refurbishment at research time).

Relics of Early Christianity

Necropolis of Bagawat

The **Necropolis of Al Bagawat** (*adult/student LE120/50*) is one of the world's earliest surviving and best-preserved early Christian cemeteries. Vivid murals depicting biblical scenes cover the walls and ceilings of these 4th- to 6th-century tombs, and four of the 263 mud-brick structures are open to the public.

In the **Chapel of Peace**, peer up at the dome squinches to see figures of the Apostles just visible through the 9th-century Greek graffiti. The best-preserved wall paintings are inside the **Chapel of the Exodus**, one of the oldest tombs, where Moses is depicted leading the Israelites out of Egypt. The interior of **Tomb 25** (a large family tomb) features a mural of Abraham sacrificing Isaac, while the **Chapel of the Grapes** is named after the images of grapevines that cover the walls.

The nearby **Monastery of Al Kashef** was strategically placed at the crossroads of the Darb Al Ghabari and the Darb Al Arba'een. The mud-brick monastery, which once stood five storeys high but is now in ruins, makes a grand vantage point across the desert beyond.

EATING IN AL KHARGA: OUR PICKS

Wimpy Albasateen: Delicious liver dishes and elaborate salads make this no-nonsense restaurant a local favourite. *8am-2.30am* $	**Hawash Restaurant:** Serves *fuul* (fava-bean paste) and falafel; there are also chicken meals from the extension next door. *24hr* $	**Dates Al Tahhan:** The coffee shop at this upmarket date shop serves snacks in delightful domed salons. *8am-midnight* $$	**Bir Jinnah Hasrir:** Delicious barbecues prepared underground are served at this rural hot-spring resort. *7am-10pm* $$

Places We Love to Stay

$ Budget $$ Midrange $$$ Top End

Siwa Oasis MAP p279

Forest Camp $ Simple, spick-and-span palm-thatch huts with shared bathrooms amid a date-palm garden with a tiny natural pool.

Olive Garden House $ Welcoming, simple guesthouse set amid a serene garden just at the southern edge of town.

Nanshaal Siwa $$ Tranquil *kershef*-brick guesthouse in Shali fortress with bags of traditional Siwan style and a roof terrace for lounging.

Al Babinshal Heritage Hotel $$ Labyrinthine *kershef*-brick hotel seamlessly grafted onto Shali fortress, with restaurant and rooftop terrace.

Nour El Waha $$ Friendly small hotel surrounded by date palms with a garden restaurant and expert help with visiting Siwa's sights.

Adrère Amellal $$$ Off-grid, candle-lit luxury resort; the ultimate in spartan-chic living, with stunning views across Lake Siwa.

Taziry Eco Villages $$$ Understated resort with attractive boutique touches beneath a prominent outcrop with good desert views; around 15km west of town.

Bahariya Oasis MAP p286

Badry Sahara Camp $ The prettiest pitch in the oasis, Badry's flowering garden, with simple *hoosha* (palm-thatch) huts with shared bathrooms, is part of a highly organised desert venture offering excellent tours.

Western Desert Hotel $ The clean, good-sized rooms may be run-down, but they're a solid, safe place to sleep in central Bawiti if you need to be near the bus stop.

International Hot Springs Hotel $$ More of a resort than a hotel, this gracious old lodge, run by knowledgeable expats, is set within a huge garden of mature trees.

Eden Garden Camp $$ Enjoy fruit trees, hammocks, lounging pavilions and a pool fed by a natural spring at this excellent resort run by desert experts.

Old Oasis Hotel $$ Domed rooms are arranged around various courtyards and pools here, and there's one of the best views of the plantation from the roof terrace.

Aliyah Eco Lodge $$ Stone-cut and brick-domed rooms amid a serene and shady date-palm garden on the main road running into Bawiti.

Farafra Oasis MAP p292

Al Waha Hotel $ Long-time favourite in central Farafra with basic rooms that do the job for the night.

Rahala Safari Hotel $$ This extremely well-run hotel has comfortable domed chalets amid a serene garden; it's a traveller's favourite for its friendly management and good-value desert tours.

Al Badawiya Safari & Hotel $$ This old faithful in the centre of town, with Bedouin decor, has been serving the travelling community for years while the town has grown around it. Excellent tours are run from here.

Shahrazad Desert Camp $$ In the middle of the desert, right beside the White Desert National Park, this lovely camp makes an excellent retreat.

Dakhla Oasis MAP p296

El Furson Hotel $ This simple hotel (the best budget hotel in Mut) has decent rooms and a restaurant and is just steps from the bus station.

Camp Bir Al Gabal $ Simple chalets here are set amid a garden on the edge of the desert, with the bonus of Bir Al Gabal hot spring on-site.

Bedouin Camp $$ An attractive lodge set in a desert garden with salmon-pink domed chalets, this well-kept camp is 9km north of Mut.

Desert Lodge $$$ This mud-brick lodge on a hill overlooking Al Qasr village has been in business for decades and offers comfortable, minimalist desert-style rooms.

Al Kharga Oasis MAP p301

King Hotel $ They've definitely seen better days, but the rooms inside this 1960s-built hotel still boast scraps of groovy mid-century architecture, and the manager is an archaeology buff.

Badr Hotel $$ One of the most comfortable places to stay in the oasis, this grand hotel sports classically styled rooms and a marble lobby.

Sol Y Mar Pioneers Hotel $$$ This huge resort, with pool and internal garden, is well run and comfortable, and there's a bar for a beer – something of a luxury in an oasis tour.

For places to stay in Alexandria & the Mediterranean Coast, see p335

From left: Fort Qaitbey (p310); Catacombs of Kom El Shoqafa (p317)

Researched by
Paula Hardy

Alexandria & the Mediterranean Coast

A COSMOPOLITAN COASTAL CITY

Lapped by aquamarine water, Egypt's Mediterranean coast stretches for 500km. At its centre stands atmospheric Alexandria, the country's largest port and second city.

Alexandria's fame and fortune are inextricably linked to its Mediterranean location beside a branch of the Nile, just 509 nautical miles from Athens. Alexander the Great spotted its potential and its deep harbour, and conceived his new Egyptian capital here, creating a bridge between the world of the pharaohs and his Hellenistic home. Foundations were laid in 331 BCE, although Alexander never got to see a single building raised before dying in Persia. His death gave rise to the last great Pharaonic dynasty – the Ptolemies – named for his Macedonian general Ptolemy, who brought Alexander's body home and buried it in the city, although it has never been found.

Since then, the city's fortunes have rested on its thriving port. Initially, it was an important stop on the trade route between Europe and Asia. It provided the entry into Egypt for the Romans, nurtured early Christianity and became a royal seat of power in the 19th century, when the city kickstarted a cosmopolitan makeover and became a muse for a long line of poets, writers and intellectuals. Even today, damaged as it has been by earthquakes, wars, and anti-colonial and contemporary rebellions, it remains one of Egypt's most atmospheric and little-touristed cities. Immerse yourself in its Mediterranean character and culture and explore the historic Ottoman-era towns, WWII cemeteries and miles of sandy beaches nearby.

THE MAIN AREAS

ALEXANDRIA
Mediterranean metropolis with a mythic history. **p310**

EL ALAMEIN
WWII cemeteries and new resort vibes. **p328**

MARSA MATRUH
Sandy beaches and stunning waters. **p332**

Find Your Way

The coast east of Cairo is well served by buses, and trains connect Alexandria with Cairo. A private taxi, or car and driver, gives you flexibility when exploring further afield. It makes no sense to fly.

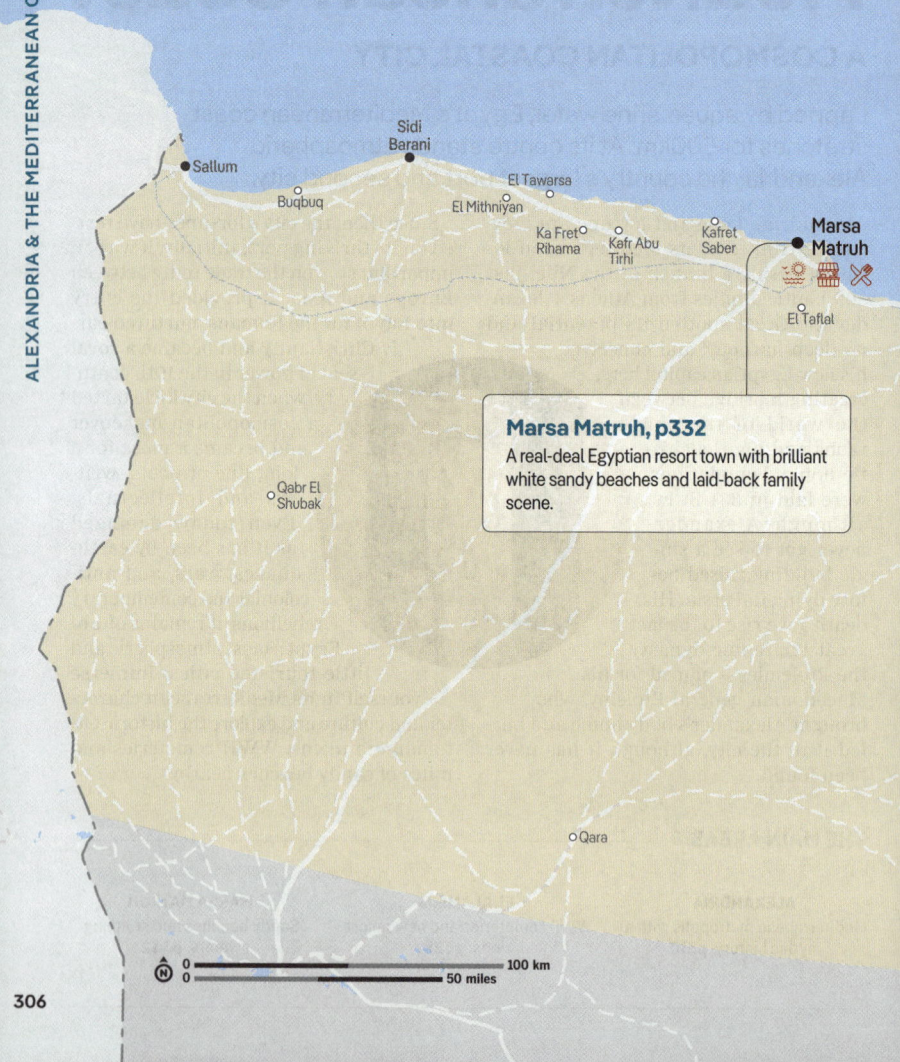

Marsa Matruh, p332
A real-deal Egyptian resort town with brilliant white sandy beaches and laid-back family scene.

CAR
For more flexibility, a private car and driver is best (LE1200 to Ar Rashid, LE1200 to LE1500 to El Alamein); hotels and guides can put you in touch with local drivers. Uber is another option.

BUS
Buses serve El Alamein and Marsa Matruh, but return services are limited. Cheap microbuses run regularly to Ar Rashid (Rosetta) and El Alamein from Alexandria, departing from the main Al Moaf Al Gedid bus station.

TAXIS
Taxis are plentiful in Alexandria and the easiest way to get around. Agree on a price before getting in (average LE50 for a short city trip) or use Uber. Taxis will also take you to Ar Rashid and El Alamein; agree on a round-trip price beforehand.

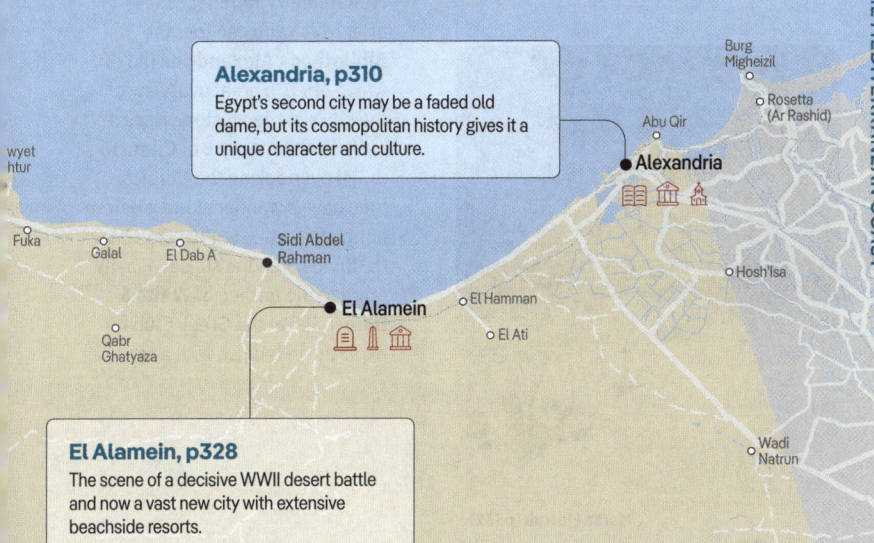

Alexandria, p310
Egypt's second city may be a faded old dame, but its cosmopolitan history gives it a unique character and culture.

El Alamein, p328
The scene of a decisive WWII desert battle and now a vast new city with extensive beachside resorts.

Plan Your Days

Alexandria is located three hours (220km) northwest of Cairo, and most tourists visit it as a day trip. But to really get under the skin of this city and the history-rich coastline, linger longer.

Marsa Matruh (p332)

If You Only Have One Day

● **Alexandria** (p310) is a big, bustling city that spreads 40km along the coastline, so you'll need to be strategic. Start the day in a historic cafe like **Trianon** (p319), then head to the newly opened **Graeco-Roman Museum** (p314), which will take all morning. Break for lunch in the atmospheric local restaurant of *fuul*-master **Mohammed Ahmed** (p313), after which you can tour the **Bibliotheca Alexandrina** (p325), which offers a great overview of the city's storied history. Have a coffee on the terrace of **Cilantro** (p314) overlooking the Corniche, then have a wander along it before hopping in a taxi to **Fort Qaitbey** (p310) to catch the sunset. Finally, retire to the terrace of **White & Blue** (p317) at the Greek Club for expertly grilled fish with a sea view.

SEASONAL HIGHLIGHTS

A popular holiday spot for Cairenes – many beach resorts only open in the summer months. Winter can be cold, breezy and wet.

FEBRUARY
The coldest month, with biting sea breezes and lots of rain; occasional storms can flood the city. Fog is also a feature and sometimes leads to the closure of the highway from Cairo.

APRIL
Coptic Christians celebrate Orthodox Holy Week with footwashing, church services and a feast of lamb on Easter Sunday. The following day, everyone celebrates the start of spring (Sham El Nessim) with picnics and kite-flying.

MAY
Perfect weather for strolling along the Corniche and exploring the city with daytime temperatures reaching a sunny 27°C and evenings a cool 16°C. Sea temperatures, meanwhile, remain a fresh 21°C.

A Long Weekend

● On your second day, take an alternative tour of **Alexandria** (p310), either a **food tour** (p313) in deepest Bahary and Anfushi or a tour of the city's surprising **churches and cemeteries** with Zahraa Adel Awad (p317). Lunch on local seafood at **Farag Fish** (p312) and stock up on delightful Alexandrian pastries at traditional **Talaat** (p321). The next day, dive into Egypt's only Roman catacombs of **Kom Ash Suqqafa** (p317) and visit the **Royal Jewellery Museum** (p321), housed in the gorgeous Liberty-style villa of Princess Fatma Al'Zahra. Then head to **Montazah Park** (p323) to admire the kitsch Khedival palaces and spend an afternoon swimming and sunbathing at the lido on Mamoura beach. Finally, retreat to the Four Seasons and dine in high style at **Byblos** (p317).

If You Have More Time

● Dig deeper into **Alexandria's** (p310) fascinating history with a visit to the **Eliyahu Hanavi Synagogue** (p319), the **Greek and Latin Cemeteries** (p318) with their monumental Art Nouveau and neoclassical tombs, and the **Mahmoud Said Museum** (p323), which showcases art from one of Egypt's great modernists. Then, head west to **El Alamein** (p328) and dig into fascinating war facts at the **Military Museum** (p330) before paying your respects at the poignant cemeteries of the Commonwealth, German and Italian troops who fell here in 1942. **Moneim Raouf** (p328) can put together more extensive explorations of more remote battle sites. Otherwise, during summer months, spend a few days relaxing at one of the swanky resorts in **Sidi Abdel Rahman** (p329), fringed by fabulous white sand beaches and aquamarine waters.

JULY
The 26 July is Alexandria's national day, marking the end of the monarchy and the establishment of the modern republic. There's also a carnival atmosphere on the beaches as Egypt's holiday season begins.

AUGUST
The International Summer Festival kicks off at the Bibliotheca with concerts, comedy and theatre in the plaza, Roman theatre and opera house. Outside the city is hot with humidity reaching 68%.

SEPTEMBER
Late in the month, crowds and hotel prices drop off and sea temperatures hover at a bath-like 28°C. Resorts remain open making this a perfect time to seek out the beaches of Sidi Abdel Rahman.

OCTOBER
Remembrance services are held on 23 October in Alexandria and El Alamein where they alternate between the Commonwealth and German cemeteries. Beach resorts close for the season at the end of the month.

Alexandria

GRAECO-ROMAN TREASURES|MULTICULTURAL HERITAGE|DINING

ORIENTATION

The main tram station at Midan Ramla is the centre of the city. Shopping streets Sharia Saad Zaghloul and Sharia Safiyya Zaghloul run off this square. Shops, restaurants and hotels cluster around Midan Ramla and Midan Saad Zaghloul.

GETTING AROUND

Taxis (negotiate price beforehand), Uber and microbuses are best for getting around; have small change to hand. Alexandria is well connected with Cairo by bus and train. There are two train stations in Alexandria – the main one is **Misr Train Station**, 1km from Midan Ramla. **Sidi Gaber** serves the eastern suburbs and trains from Cairo stop here first. Go Bus and Blue Bus operate the best intercity bus services; the main bus station is **Al Moaf Al Gedid**, several kilometres south of Midan Saad Zaghloul.

Founded in 331 BCE, Alexandria (Al Iskendariyya) is the stuff of legend. Its Pharos lighthouse was one of the Seven Wonders of the Ancient World and its Great Library was the archive of ancient knowledge. Alas, fate dealt the city some cruel blows. The Great Library was torched in 48 BCE and the lighthouse collapsed in 1375 CE; then, the ancient city disappeared partly beneath the waves and partly beneath the modern city.

Today, the original Alexandria lies buried beneath two millennia of urban evolution, its monuments shattered, its multicultural population scattered after the Revolution of 1952. But Alexandria remains a city of dreams for many, its university attracting aspiring undergraduates, its port booming, and its population of 5.6 million expanding rapidly. And, following the reopening of the Graeco-Roman Museum and the restoration of the lovely Montazah Palace Gardens, an air of renewal is blowing through this storied city.

Royal Heritage & Harbour Views MAP P311

Explore the Cape of Figs

Ras el-Tin, or the 'Cape of Figs', is the peninsula between the Eastern and Western harbours. At the tip of it is the crenellated **Fort Qaitbey** *(egymonuments.com; adult/student LE200/100)* built in 1477 by Sultan Qaitbey. It sits on the site of the legendary Lighthouse of Alexandria. Although the fort was damaged in the British bombardment of 1882, it has been beautifully restored. Its honey-coloured interior houses the oldest mosque in the city while its ramparts offer views of Alexandria and the Eastern bay.

Southwest of the fort are the shipyards and, beyond that, overlooking the Western Harbour, is the lavish – check out images online – Italianate **Ras El Tin Palace**, which is now enclosed within Admiralty headquarters and inaccessible to the public. However, if you're arriving on a cruise you'll spy it from the water. It was built in the early 1900s as a summer palace of Mohammed Ali (1805–48), the 'Father of Modern Egypt'.

ALEXANDRIA

★ **HIGHLIGHTS**
1 Bibliotheca Alexandrina
2 Graeco-Roman Museum

● **SIGHTS**
3 Abu Abbas Al Mursi Mosque
4 Alexandria National Museum
5 Coptic Cemetery
6 El Shorbagi Mosque
7 Fort Qaitbey
8 Greek Club Beach
9 Greek Orthodox Cemetery
10 Jewish Cemetery
11 Museum of Fine Arts
12 Terbana Mosque

● **EATING**
13 Abu Ashraf
14 Basilico
15 Cilantro
16 Croissant d'Alexia
17 El Nezamy
18 El Sheikh Wafik
19 Farag Fish
20 Gelati Fahmy
21 Hosny Grill
22 Kebdet Sami Masrawy
23 Koshary
24 Samakmak
see 8 Seaside
25 Sidi
26 Sidra By the Citadel
27 Talaat Patisserie
see 8 White & Blue

● **DRINKING & NIGHTLIFE**
28 El Qobesi
29 Farouk Café

● **SHOPPING**
30 Al Midan Fish Market
31 Zane't El-Settat

LIGHTHOUSE OF ALEXANDRIA

Considered one of the Seven Wonders of the Ancient World, the Pharos (lighthouse) of Alexandria was built in the 3rd century BCE. At over 100m tall, it was one of the tallest manmade structures in the world, topped with an oil-fed beacon reflected by sheets of polished bronze. Images of the Pharos still exist, most notably in a mosaic in St Mark's Basilica in Venice, and its three-tier design is thought to be the basis for many early Egyptian minarets. In use for 17 centuries, it was toppled by an earthquake in 1303. The ruins were reused by Mamluk sultan Qaitbey to fortify the harbour and underpin the fortress that now stands in its place.

Abu Abbas Al Mursi Mosque

Alexandria's Oldest Neighbourhoods   MAP P311
Ottoman alleys and Italian mosques

Sitting in the shadow of Fort Qaitbey, the **Anfushi** and **Bahary** warrens of tiny streets were once the hub of the Ottoman city (1517–1914). This is where Alexandrians once came to let loose, where Laurence Durrell sought out prostitutes, and where people still flock to the best fish restaurants in the city despite the neighbourhoods' rather rundown vibe.

It's still a fascinating district dotted with distinctive mosques. In the centre sits the **El-Shorbagi Mosque**, built in 1758, its gallery raised above the teeming souq. At the junction of Sharia Faransa and Wekalet Al Limon, the **Terbang Mosque**, was built in 1685 as a rest stop for pilgrims on their way to Mecca. It, too, is a 'hanging mosque', with the prayer hall above shops whose rent once supported it.

Most impressive is the **Abu Abbas Al Mursi Mosque**, dedicated to 13th-century Andalusian Sufi saint Abu Abbas – one of the four master saints in Egypt. It is the main congregational mosque in Alexandria and an important site of pilgrimage. Surprisingly, the current incarnation above the ancient mausoleum was built by an Italian – Mario Rossi – in 1945.

Rossi was invited to reconstruct the mosque's 18th-century predecessor as part of a new town plan envisioned by King

EATING IN ALEXANDRIA: WHERE TO EAT SEAFOOD   MAPS P311, P315

Samakmak: Cute checked tablecloths and delicious specials like spicy crayfish and crab *tagen* (stewed in a clay pot). *10am-2am* **$**

Sidi: A foodie find with views of the Abu Abbas mosque. Come here for fried shrimp and calamari, and crab and seafood tagine. *11am-10.30pm* **$$**

Seaside: Shaded rooftop seating and views of bobbing boats. The shrimp kofta and seafood *tagen* stand out. *12.30pm-1am* **$$**

Farag Fish: A local favourite serving seafood feasts including *samak singary*, oven-baked red snapper marinated in coriander, garlic and green chilli. *noon-2am* **$$**

Fouad I. While Rossi brought new techniques and materials, he also collaborated with Egyptian Chief Engineer Said Bey Mitwalli, and contractors Abd El Halim and Ibrahim Nossier. As a result, the structure blends renaissance and Islamic styles. The octagonal plan was an innovation in Egyptian architecture based on a Renaissance skeleton of a square and hemicycles. The two 73m-high minarets are Circassian in style and flank five elongated neo-Mamluk cupolas. It is an elegant and dynamic design that has inspired mosques around the world, most spectacularly the Sheikh Zayed Grand Mosque in Abu Dhabi.

Outside prayer time, you can visit the gorgeous interior where eight pink granite columns hold aloft the 24m-high cupola. Around the lantern, coloured windows illuminate the carved dome, while rich arabesque and carved plasterwork covers the walls and ceilings. On summer nights and during Ramadan, a carnival-like atmosphere surrounds the mosque.

Alexandrian Food Tours

MAP P311

Street life and local specialities

One of the best ways to experience Alexandrian life is on a food tour with **Karim Serrie** *(+20 10-0261-7885)* or **Rasha Aggag** *(+20 10-6208-8282)*. The tours take you deep into Anfushi as well as through the downtown souqs.

Fluent in French, English and German, Karim and Rasha are enthusiastic guides who introduce you to the city's most famous dishes in between wildly careening tuk-tuk and slow tram rides. Tours start at Alexandria's teeming fish market, **Al Midan**, where you browse the daily catch, watch locals haggle over the best crab, then buy some fish and have it cooked local style on the spot.

Afterwards, you dive deep into Anfushi for spicy *kebda Eskandarany*, beef-liver sandwiches sauteed with garlic and spices, and stuffed into a pale loaf of *aish fino* (similar to a hot dog bun); or, perhaps you'll head downtown to **Mohammed Ahmed's** tiny kitchen for a taste of his famous *ta'ameya* (fava-bean falafel) and stories of Queen Sofia of Spain dropping in.

Also unmissable is Alexandria's version of Egypt's national dish, *koshary*. Traditionally it's a mix of pasta, fried rice, vermicelli and lentils topped with tomato sauce, chickpeas and fried onions; Alexandrians like to add cumin and curry leaves – an adaptation from British soldiers stationed here in WWII. It is best sampled at places like **Koshary Masrawy** by the harbour.

The tour ends with coffee and traditional desserts like *om ali* (Egyptian bread pudding made with puff pastry, pistachios,

PASHA MOHAMMED ALI: FOUNDER OF MODERN EGYPT

Mohammed Ali – whose statue stands in Midan Tahrir – established Egypt as an independent state, ruled by his own hereditary dynasty. To achieve this, he built a modern military based on a strong navy whose headquarters were in Alexandria – his de-facto capital. He created a professional bureaucracy by establishing an education system that allowed for social mobility, and expanded the economy with new industries such as cotton and weapons manufacturing. While he failed to achieve formal independence for Egypt in his lifetime, he successfully laid the foundation for the modern Egyptian state, his dynasty lasting for nearly 150 years until the Revolution of 1952.

 EATING IN ALEXANDRIA: BEST ANFUSHI DINING — MAPS P311, P315

Kebdet Sami: Specialises in offal, particularly *kebda iskandaria* (liver prepared with bell pepper, garlic and cumin). *4pm-3am* $

Abu Ashraf: Fresh fish cooked in front of you. Stuffed sea bass and prawn *kishk* (casserole) are house specialities. *noon-2am* $$

El Sheikh Wafik: An Alexandrian institution serving typical desserts such as *om ali* (Egyptian bread pudding). *9am-2am* $

Hosny Grill: Plates up chargrilled, barbecue meat and kebabs with a mezze of tahini, salads and bread. *11am-midnight* $

> **KARIM SERRIE'S FAVOURITE MEALS**
>
>
>
> **Karim Serrie** *(+20 10-0261-7885)* is an Alexandrian tour guide. Here he shares his favourite Alexandrian meals.
>
> **Al Midan** (p313) Buy fish, squid or crab at the fish market and have it grilled nearby. The squid with tomato, onion, chilli and coriander is a highlight.
>
> **Kebda El Fallah** An Alexandrian institution serving the city's famous spicy beef liver sandwiches. It's always crowded in summer.
>
> **Koshary Masrawy** (p313) One of the best places to try the Alexandrian version of Egypt's national dish.
>
> **Fahmy** An unmissable Alexandrian treat is the lemon or chocolate ice cream from Fahmy's. Take it to the Corniche to enjoy it with sea views.

raisins and sweetened milk) and *Roz bi Laban* (Egyptian rice pudding spiced with cinnamon and cardamon) at retro **Patisserie Saber**. Either that or you can join the queue at **Fahmy's** ice-cream shop.

Graeco-Roman Masterpieces

MAP P311

Ancient art charting cultural changes

Alexandria's **Graeco-Roman Museum** *(egymonuments.com; adult/student LE400/200)* has always been the pride of the city, showcasing treasures that run the gamut from the 3rd century BCE to the 5th century CE. They are spread over 27 beautifully curated halls in a distinct Greek Revival building, modelled on the National Museum of Athens. Its columned entrance even bears the inscription ΜΟΥΣΕΙΟΝ (Mouseion) in Greek letters.

It was the brainchild of Italian archaeologist Giuseppe Botti, who arrived in Alexandria in 1884 and was incensed to learn that Alexandrian antiquities were being taken to Cairo and Europe because there was no museum to house them. Botti founded the Athenaeum Society and lobbied for a municipal museum, which Khedive Abbas Helmy II inaugurated in October 1895.

On opening, the museum showcased a collection of 4000 objects from wealthy Alexandrians such as Prince Omar Toussoun, who donated his entire collection, including the statue of Alexander the Great. And throughout the 20th century the museum's directors continued to add to it from excavations in Alexandria, the Delta and Fayoum.

Now the artefacts are on display in fully accessible, beautifully lit, state-of-the-art galleries that open with two fine stelae, detailing taxes on goods passing through the ports of Naukratis and Herakleion-Thonis. This is evidence of the important trading relationship that Egypt has had with Greece since the 8th century BCE, and upon which military alliances against Persia were brokered, which brought Alexander the Great and his army here in 332 BCE. From there, displays cover the Ptolemaic era that began with Ptolemy I, Alexander the Great's general and successor. Highlights include the fabulous floor mosaics (the one of Berenike II is one of the most intricate and best-preserved in the world), granite and marble statuary, intriguing *tanagra* terracotta figurines with their elaborate hairdos and luxuriously draped tunics, and the epic Apis bull – an embodiment of the syncretic god Serapis and formerly the symbol of Osiris-Hapi – that once stood in the Serapis Temple.

Most interesting are the recreated Roman villa and a hybrid Ptolemaic-Christian temple, as well as the numerous plans and

---

 DRINKING IN ALEXANDRIA: BEST TEA & COFFEE ──────── MAPS P311, P315

| **Farouk Café:** A historic, 1928 coffeehouse serving strong coffee and tea with shisha and games of dominoes. No food. *7am-1am* | **Baudrot Cafe:** Legendary downtown cafe serving rich confectionary with a side of people-watching on Sharia Saad Zaghloul. *8am-2am* | **Brazilian Coffee Stores:** Great espresso and Turkish coffee served at a long wooden bar. They also serve blueberry cheesecake. *7-10pm* | **Cilantro:** Very pleasant terrace at the edge of the Bibliotheca, serving excellent coffees and sandwiches with sea views. *8am-midnight* |

ALEXANDRIA CITY CENTRE

★ HIGHLIGHTS
- Cathedral of Evangelismos
- Eliyahu Hanavi Synagogue
- St Mark's Coptic Orthodox Cathedral

SIGHTS
1. Cathedral of Evangelismos
2. Eliyahu Hanavi Synagogue
3. St Mark's Coptic Orthodox Cathedral
4. Cavafy House
5. Kom Al Dikka
6. Monastery of St Savvas
7. Pasha Mohammed Ali statue
8. St Catherine's Cathedral
9. St Mark's Anglican Church

SLEEPING
10. Ithaka Hostel
11. Le Metropole Hotel
12. Steigenberger Cecil Hotel
13. Triomphe Hostel
14. Windsor Palace Hotel

EATING
15. Asteria
16. Chez Gaby Au Ritrovo
17. Genoise Le Cafe
18. Jeeda's
19. Kebda El Fallah Sokhn
20. Koshary'Ala
21. L'Apero Bistrot
22. Mohammed Ahmed
23. Preby Pastry
24. Santa Lucia Restaurant
25. Teatro Eskandariya
26. Trianon

● DRINKING & NIGHTLIFE
27. Baudrot Cafe
28. Brazilian Coffee Stores
29. Cap d'Or
30. Délices
31. Sky View Restaurant
32. Sofianopoulo
33. Spitfire Bar

■ ENTERTAINMENT
34. Alexandria Opera House
35. Amir Cinema
36. El Horreya Creativity Center

■ SHOPPING
37. Crystal Sweets
38. Souq Al Attarine

THE CANOPIC WAY

Interestingly, modern Alexandria is neatly overlaid on an ancient street grid. Sharia Al Horreya was the ancient Canopic Way, laid in 331 BCE to connect the two main gates of the Sun (east) and the Moon (west). It was lined with statues and columns, and it connected the Gymnasium, the Paneum, the Soma (now Sharia Al-Nabi Daniel), the Mouseion and the Temple of Serapis (now the Attarine Mosque). Following the 1882 British bombing of Alexandria, a new building boom revived the road as Rue Rosette, an elite residential neighbourhood that is home to consulates, the new Graeco-Roman Museum and the Zizinia Theatre (the Alexandria Opera house).

Cat effigies, Graeco-Roman Museum (p314)

images of what Alexandria looked like in different eras, giving you an idea of how Egyptian, Hellenic and Byzantine culture blended and merged, building on each other century after century. Midway round, you can take a coffee break in the lovely courtyard beneath the gaze of the monumental pink granite statue of Isis Faria. Upstairs galleries display new discoveries, including a rare collection of gold coins depicting miniature portraits of emperors and gods, and a huge hoard of ex-voto cat effigies symbolising the goddess Boubastis (the Egyptian god Bastet), worshipped by early Greek immigrants to Alexandria.

The Roman High Life

MAP P315

Revealing Roman ruins

Egypt's only remaining **Roman theatre** *(egymonuments. com; adult/student LE200/100)* sits in an area once known as the Park of Pan, a well-off residential area in Graeco-Roman times (4th to 7th centuries CE). The site was rediscovered in 1967, when foundations were being laid for an apartment building on a site known as **Kom Al Dikka** – 'Mound of Shards' – given the vast quantity of broken pottery in situ.

Compared with other Graeco-Roman sites around the world, the ruins, sunken below street level, aren't terribly impressive. But there are some fascinating details, such as 6th-century

EATING IN ALEXANDRIA: BEST PIZZA

MAPS P311, P315

Chez Gaby Au Ritrovo: Going strong since 1979, Gaby's has checkered tablecloths, great pizzas and an '80s French soundtrack. Alcohol served. *1pm-midnight* $$

Basilico: A very cute neighbourhood pizzeria in a leafy side street serving pizza from a wood-fired oven. Simplicity at its best. *noon-late* $$

Rubino's: On a mission to bring authentic pasta and pizza to Alexandria with all ingredients, including flour, imported from Italy. *noon-2am* $$

Asteria: A vintage pizzeria relaunched with an industrial-chic look and a cocktail bar in the back, attracting a hip crowd. *8am-1am* $$

graffiti supporting the Blue and Green teams (popular charioteers) on the white-marble terraces of the only Roman amphitheatre found in Egypt. Plus there are remains of a large imperial bath complex, and a series of auditoria used as 20 university lecture halls, which would have housed 500 to 600 students on any given day, making this a thriving civic centre.

In the southern corner of the site, there are also the remains of impressive early Roman villas dating between the 1st and 3rd century. The most interesting is the so-called **Villa of the Birds**, a dwelling from the time of Hadrian (117–138 CE). Despite being destroyed by fire in the 3rd century, its elaborate floor mosaic of peacocks, quails, parrots and water hens remains astonishingly well preserved.

Catacombs & Graveyards

Alexandria's multicultural legacy

Following Alexander the Great's sack of the great trade centre of Tyre (in modern-day Lebanon) in 332 BCE, Alexandria became the Mediterranean's most important city, sitting at a critical juncture between Egypt, Europe, the Red Sea and India. The Romans, who occupied the city in 30 BCE, were heavily dependent on Egyptian grain, trade in which made Alexandria fabulously rich. This wealth attracted merchants from around the Mediterranean, who settled in the city, forming the basis of Alexandria's cosmopolitan society.

Legacies of this cultural potpourri are evident in the city's cemeteries, the oldest of which are the **Catacombs of Kom El Shoqafa** *(egymonuments.com; adult/student LE200/100),* the largest known Roman burial site in Egypt and the last public works dedicated to the ancient Egyptian religion. They demonstrate Alexandria's unique fusion of Pharaonic and Hellenistic architectural styles, particularly in the principal tomb with its synthesis of ancient Egyptian, Greek and Roman funerary iconography. The doorway to the inner chamber is flanked by figures representing Anubis, the Egyptian god of the dead, but he is dressed as a Roman legionnaire and sports a serpent's tail representative of Agathos Daimon, a Greek divinity. From the antechamber, a couple of short passages lead to a large chamber lined with some 300 *loculi* (burial niches).

As well as Greeks and Christians, a significant Jewish population was resident in Alexandria during the Roman period, growing into a community of 400,000 in the 1940s. Their **Jewish cemetery** remains, although only family members with specific permission are currently allowed to visit. By the 18th

SIX UNDER-THE-RADAR SITES

Zahraa Adel Awad *(tourguide_egypt@ yahoo.com)* leads fascinating tours helping emigres rediscover their heritage, literary tours, and off-the-beaten track art and architecture tours.

Greek & Latin Cemetery (p318) A surprising cemetery where you'll find the tombs of Alexandria's most notable Greek and Roman Catholic families. It's an alfresco sculpture park.

St Mark's Coptic Orthodox Cathedral (p318) The original seat of the Coptic Patriarch founded by St Mark the Evangelist in 42 CE. He was buried here until the Venetians moved his body to St Mark's Basilica.

Eliyahu Hanavi Synagogue (p319) The city's most beautiful synagogue and one of the largest in the Middle East.

 EATING IN ALEXANDRIA: BEST FINE DINING — MAPS P311, P315

Byblos: Swanky Middle Eastern decor and sea views accompany the fine Syrian and Lebanese cuisine at this Four Seasons restaurant. *1pm-midnight* **$$$**

White & Blue: The Greek Club's restaurant has sweeping views of the bay. Grilled fish is the highlight. *noon-late* **$$$**

Sidra by the Citadel: This chic Lebanese harbour-view restaurant delivers Levantine favourites: *fattoush,* vine leaves and *kibbeh. 9am-midnight* **$$$**

Santa Lucia Restaurant: A vintage restaurant once popular with Italian actors and singers, still serving risottos and *vitello tonnato. 2pm-midnight* **$$**

ALEXANDRIA'S BEST CULTURAL NIGHTS OUT

Alexandria Opera House: Musical and theatrical performances from Egypt's top talent, national orchestra and international ensembles.

Jesuit Cultural Center: An active cultural centre offering contemporary theatre, film screenings, art exhibitions and music performances.

El Horreya Creativity Center: A beautiful vintage theatre hosting theatrical performances, music concerts, film screenings and literary talks.

Bibliotheca Alexandrina: Numerous concerts and cultural events are held at the library, particularly during the big summer festival.

Amir Cinema: Opened in 1952 with Bette Davis in *All About Eve*. Now part of the film festival circuit; often shows original-language, international blockbusters.

century, under the auspices of Pasha Mohammed Ali, new industrialisation swelled the city with Levantine and European immigration so the Pasha gifted the Christian communities a *feddan* of land in the Shabty area for the burial of their dead.

There you'll find the **Greek Orthodox Cemetery**, the **Coptic Cemetery**, the Cemeterium Latinorum Terra Sancta (Latin Cemetery of Alexandria for Roman Catholics), the Anglican Cemetery and the Armenian Cemetery, all next to each other. The most impressive of these is the Greek Orthodox Cemetery with its fine mausoleums and elaborate Gothic, Art Nouveau and neoclassical funeral sculpture commemorating the likes of Botty, the first director of the Greek Museum, Constantine Salvagos who helped to found the National Bank of Egypt, and poet Constantine Cavafy. Researcher **Zahraa Adel Awad** *(tourguide_egypt@yahoo.com)* leads knowledgeable tours of the cemeteries and assists many emigres in finding the graves of their relatives and exploring their Alexandrian heritage.

City of Churches

MAP P.315

Origins of Africa's Christianity

In one of the rooms of the Graeco-Roman Museum (p314) there's a naïve marble sculpture of a friendly-looking shepherd carrying a ram on his shoulders. It was unearthed in Marsa Matruh; it dates to the 4th century and is an image of Jesus. At the time, the patriarchate of Alexandria was in its most flourishing era, with the centre of Christianity on the African continent and its catechetical school playing key roles in the development of Christian theology. At its head, Patriarch Cyril I was ranked next to the Pope in Rome in terms of importance.

Cyril was already the 24th patriarch of Alexandria's **St Mark's Coptic Orthodox Cathedral**, founded by the Apostle and patron saint of Egypt, St Mark, in 42 CE. Although today's cathedral was built in 1952, it stands on the remains of St Mark's original house of worship, with a commemorative marble plaque, recording the names of all the patriarchs, by the stairs down to St Mark's desolate tomb. Here the saint's body lay until the Venetians stole it in 828 CE. By then the patriarchy was in crisis, the church split between the Coptic Orthodox and Eastern (or Greek) Orthodox patriarchates after the council of Chalcedon in 451 CE, while Egypt was part of the Islamic Abbasid Caliphate.

Still, through the centuries, Alexandria has maintained a multiplicity of churches, monasteries and religious establishments – a legacy of 40 churches established in the city by the Imperial permission of Constantine the Great. Aside from the Coptic cathedral, there is the dazzling neo-Byzantine Greek Orthodox **Cathedral of Evangelismos** (also known as the Cathedral of the Annunciation of Theotokos), inaugurated in 1856 and lavishly decorated with a gilded iconostasis, sporting icons made in Egypt and Constantinople, chandeliers from Russia, stained-glass windows from the Parisian workshop of Jean Gaudin and a clock on the facade made by Frederick Dent in London, who also made Big Ben. The patriarch is enthroned here and the church now has 300,000 followers in Egypt, the highest number since the Roman Empire. Meanwhile, at the

Monastery of St Savvas, the Academy of St Athanasios the Great still trains African priests in agronomy, nursing and theology as the Alexandrian Primate is also Patriarch of all of Africa.

Also of interest is the Moorish-style **St Mark's Anglican Church** on Midan Tahrir. It was the first Anglican church built in Egypt, in 1839 by the Church Mission Society, on land given to them by Pasha Mohammed Ali when Britain and Egypt had warm diplomatic relations.

Finally, make a visit to the Catholic **St Catherine's Cathedral**, a Baroque church designed by Franciscan architect Serafino da Baceno that looks like it has been teleported from Rome. It remains a Franciscan monastery, home to a community that has been here since the 17th century when the Franciscans served pilgrims on their way to the Holy Land. It is named after the world famous saint who was born here and whose body now lies in Sinai (see p392). Inside is the tomb of the exiled Italian king Victor Emanuel II, who died here in 1947 and whose body was only repatriated to Italy in 2017.

A Surprising Synagogue

MAP P315

Ancient Jewish place of worship

Jews have been part of the Alexandrian community since the city's founding. The Talmud mentions the Great Synagogue of Alexandria (now destroyed), while Alexandrian Jews such as Simeon the Just served as high priests in Jerusalem.

It was Mohammed Ali who saw to the reconstruction of **Eliyahu Hanavi Synagogue** (*10am-4.30pm Sun-Thu, 10am-2pm Fri*) in the 1830s after an older synagogue dating back to 1354 had been damaged during Napoleon's invasion. It sits on Sharia Al Naby Daniel, named after a Jewish prophet. It's a beautiful Italian Revival structure, held aloft by 28 pink marble columns and large enough to accommodate 700 congregants whose names are etched on brass plaques on the pews. It was the most important synagogue among the 20 that served a 40,000-strong community in the 1940s. Almost all of them emigrated to Israel following the Revolution of 1952, the 1956 Suez Crisis and the 1967 Six Day War. When the roof collapsed from rain damage in 2012, there were fewer than 20 Jews left in the city.

Now you can once again admire the restored elegant interior, bathed in rose-tinted light through the stained-glass windows. However, the real treasures here are 50 of the oldest copies of the Torah in the world, which are safely stored in the archives. The synagogue is closed on Friday afternoon and on Saturday, and you need to present your passport to obtain permission to enter.

BEST HISTORIC CAFES

Rasha Aggag (@rashaaa9434) leads city tours around her home town. Here are her go-to cafes:

Trianon: Established by Greeks Andrea Drikos and George Pericles in Ramleh Station in 1935. It is a pleasure to be in due to its beautiful interior and lovely location overlooking the Eastern Harbour. *8am-midnight*

Delices: A 1922 landmark, famous for its mango and strawberry syrup and traditional Greek sweets, breads and biscuits. They still make Easter eggs according to their original recipe. *8am-midnight*

Sofianopoulo: Established in 1908 on the site of the French post office on Sharia Saad Zaghloul. It specialises in Ethiopian, Yemeni, Brazilian and Colombian coffee. *2pm-midnight*

EATING IN ALEXANDRIA: BEST DOWNTOWN DINING

MAPS P311, P315

Mohammed Ahmed: A famous diner serving *fuul* (fava-bean paste) since 1957. The *fuul iskandarani* (mashed with lime juice) is delicious. *6am-midnight* $

L'Apero Bistrot: On pedestrianised Naby Daniel St, trendy L'Apero offers an international menu, a good breakfast and jazz soundtrack. *9am-1am* $$

Teatro Eskandariya: Popular with local artists and creatives, Teatro serves honest, simple food amid a lively atmosphere. *10am-1am* $$

Jeeda's: A smart modern Spanish restaurant with slick decor, authentic tapas and a great signature seafood paella. Alcohol served. *2pm-1am* $$$

ALEXANDRIA AT RISK

Boxed in between the Mediterranean and three lakes, habitable land in Alexandria is limited. Egyptian law states that newly built urban areas should house 100 to 150 people per *feddan* (equivalent to 1.038 acres), but parts of Alexandria house 900 to 1200 residents per *feddan*. By comparison, Manhattan has an average population density of 104 people per acre.

As a result, what land there is, is increasingly valuable and historic buildings are rapidly being replaced by hotels, high-rises and shopping malls. A more serious, silent threat is climate change. Alexandria is one of the lowest-lying cities in the world and one of the 10 most vulnerable to rising sea levels.

Alexandria National Museum

Egypt's National Story
An alternative narrative

MAP P311

The **Alexandria National Museum** (*egymonuments.com; adult/student LE220/110*), opened by President Hosni Mubarak in September 2003, was lauded as a model for national museums across the country. Even its location in the Italianate Bassili Palace was significant at the time. The repurposing of a villa in what used to be the Europeanised part of town as a museum dedicated to telling the story of Egypt spoke volumes.

Here the Hellenised city of the Ptolemic Dynasty is integrated into the broader national narrative. Starting with Pharaonic artefacts in the basement – including a beautifully lit mummy still snug in its sarcophagus – you ascend, in chronological order, through a small Graeco-Roman display, followed by Coptic (Byzantine) and Ottoman eras, finally reaching modern exhibits on the top floor. Here, Graeco-Roman Alexandria is seen as merely one stage in Egypt's national story rather than the high point of the city's history.

A Poetic Pilgrimage
Literary meanderings through Alexandria

MAP P315

Alexandria is one of those seemingly timeless cities – like Venice and Istanbul – that provide endless inspiration for writers. The celebrated English novelist EM Forster (1879–1970) arrived in 1916 and spent three years here working for the Red Cross. During that time he penned *Alexandria: A History & Guide*, which he explained as a guide to things that are not there, based on the premise that 'the sights of Alexandria are in themselves not interesting, but they fascinate when we approach them from the past'. The guide provided an introduction to the city for British novelist and poet Lawrence Durrell (1912–90), who arrived in Alexandria in 1941, having been evacuated from

Greece. He called Alexandria a 'smashed up, broken down, shabby Neapolitan town', but as visitors discover today, first impressions can be misleading, and his stay in the city led to him writing his most famous book, the *Alexandria Quartet*, a tale of four lovers told from their respective perspectives in multiethnic Alexandria.

A copy of Forster's guide is displayed in **Cavafy House** *(free; 10am-5pm Tue-Sun)*, the home of Constantine Cavafy (1863–1933), widely considered the most distinguished Greek poet of the 20th century. He was Forster's guide to the city, having been born there to one of Alexandria's wealthiest families. Due to a reversal of fortunes, Cavafy lived his later life in an apartment above a brothel on the former Rue Lepsius, which has been renovated by the Onassis Foundation. For those who love Cavafy's work, this is a place of pilgrimage where you can read his handwritten poems and manuscripts, and view a collection of photographs of early-20th-century Alexandria. The guardian, Said, speaks fluent Greek and is a wealth of information.

Another literary titan inspired by Alexandria is Nobel Literature Prize-winning Egyptian author, Naguib Mahfouz, who penned *Miramar*, the most famous Arabic-language novel set in the city and available in translation. It's the story of Egypt and its Revolution, which started here, as told by four very different men staying in an old-fashioned B&B. Meanwhile, Edwar al-Kharrat's novel *City of Saffron* is a good counterbalance to the *Alexandria Quartet*, offering a semi-autobiographical view of 1930s Alexandria from the perspective of a young Egyptian Coptic boy. To dig deeper into Alexandria's literary side, take a literary tour with **Zahraa Adel Awad** *(tourguide_egypt@yahoo.com)* who'll take you to places that loom large on the page and in the imagination.

A Dazzling Royal Jewellery Collection
Diamonds in a sumptuous setting

One of the best places to get a glimpse of the wealth of cosmopolitan Alexandria between the 1800s and the Revolution of 1952 is the **Royal Jewellery Museum** *(egymonuments.com; adult/student LE220/110)*. It is housed in an extravagant villa – the former home of the home of Princess Fatma al'Zahra, the granddaughter of Pasha Mohammed Ali – in the upmarket Zizinya district.

Built in the 1920s, the neoclassical beaux-arts building wouldn't look out of place on the French or Italian Riviera. It was built by Italian-Slovene Antonio Lasciac (1856–1946), who

BEST ALEXANDRIAN READS

Azazeel This novel by Youssef Ziedan – Arab Booker Prize winner – covers the schism in the Orthodox Church from the perspective of a Coptic monk.

Constantine Cavafy: A New Biography Gregory Jusdanis and Peter Jeffreys explore the complexities of Greek poet Cavafy's life and art.

No One Sleeps in Alexandria Ibrahim Abdel Meguid explores the impact of WWII through the friendship of a Muslim from northern Egypt and a southern Copt.

The Cleopatras Historian Lloyd Llewellyn Jones tells the intriguing story of Egypt's seven queens, all named Cleopatra.

The Prison of Life A memoir by Tawfiq al-Hakim set in the 1930s, offering an insight into Egyptian-Alexandrian family life and social relations.

 EATING IN ALEXANDRIA: BEST PASTRIES — MAPS P311, P315

Talaat Patisserie: So-called 'pioneers of delight', Talaat makes the best traditional sweets such as *basbousa*, *harissa* and *kunafa*. *8am-11.30pm* $

Preby Pastry: Ever-busy bakery known for its distinctive *fino* bread, which is baked in ovens across the road. *9am-1am* $

Genoise Le Cafe: A popular patisserie dishing out doughnuts, hazelnut frappes and all manner of cakes. Good coffee and Wi-Fi, too. *8am-midnight* $

Croissant d'Alexia: A cute cafe and patisserie serving sweet and savoury croissants stuffed with turkey, salmon and more. *7am-11pm* $

arrived in Alexandria to assist in the city's urban regeneration and became Egyptian court architect in 1907.

Lasciac is the most notable architect of Egypt's presidential palaces and spared no expense on the Art Deco interiors. The best oak and chestnut was imported from Türkiye to finish the fine Mamluk-inspired parquetry floors and wall panels; the ceilings were painted by Italian and French artists and depict Greek myths; the bathrooms are furnished with Sevres fittings and are covered in murals featuring the Fables of Fontainbleau; and the stained-glass windows contain scenes from romance tales, such as *Romeo and Juliet*.

This may strike visitors as strange in an Islamic country, but the villa speaks to the cultural fluidity of Alexandria. Obsessed with modernising his army and creating a political bureaucracy in line with European standards, Fatma's grandfather, Pasha Ali, invited French, English, Italian, Maltese, Turkish and Armenian emigres to live in Alexandria, his de facto capital. During his era, Alexandria, like Marseille, Trieste, Sarajevo, Beirut and Izmir, was a Mediterranean city – its fortunes inextricably tied to the web of relations around it. It's this heritage that the villa's Euro-Orientalist decor reflects.

For 147 years, Mohammed Ali's dynasty ruled Egypt, during which time they amassed extraordinary wealth and were assiduous collectors of art and jewellery. The villa's 10 halls are filled with a fraction of this, including a rare diamond- and emerald-inlaid collar that belonged to Mohammed Ali.

Other pieces attesting to the family's opulent tastes include King Farouk's gold- and diamond-studded chess board, Prince Youssef Kamal's diamond-inlaid gold desk, and even gold and sapphire cups. Dazzling diamond jewellery sets belonging to Princess Shuvekar, Queen Nazli and Queen Farida are also laid out in display cases, some designed by Boucheron and others by Van Cleef and Arpels. One of the most fabulous is a platinum crown, glittering with over 2000 diamonds.

Following the Revolution of 1952, the hoard was confiscated and the villa appropriated by the State. Princess al-Zahra was allowed to remain in the house until she moved to Cairo in 1964. It wasn't until 1986, after her death, that the villa was opened as a museum housing some of the 11,000-piece collection.

Alexandria's Art Trail

MAP P311

Egypt's contemporary art

Born to Alexandrian aristocracy – his father was a former prime minister and his niece became Queen Farida in 1938 – Mahmoud

ALEXANDRIA'S BEST BEACHES

Private beach clubs charge LE400 to LE500 per person. On public beaches, women should cover up when swimming.

Greek Club Beach: A tiny private beach beneath the White & Blue restaurant run by the Greek Club.

Mamoura Beach: A nice private beach near Montazah Gardens with a boardwalk and food stalls.

Four Seasons Beach: A luxe beachside experience. Day passes cost LE1850 to LE2400 per person.

Miami Beach: A public beach with a water slide and jungle gym in the sea.

Stanley Beach: A city-centre patch of sand on a tiny bay with the old Stanley Bridge above it.

EATING IN ALEXANDRIA: BEST LOCAL HAUNTS

MAPS P311, P315

El Qobesi: The so-called 'King of Mango' pulps the city's best mango smoothies 24 hours a day. Always busy, justifiably so. *24hr* $

Koshary 'Ala Sokhn: Crafts the perfect *koshary* (a mix of pasta, rice, chickpeas, lentils, fried onions) with signature lemon and chilli sauce. *9am-midnight* $

Kebda El Fallah: Serves beautifully arranged liver sandwich 'bouquets' in Viennese buns, seasoned with green peppers and tahini. *10am-1am* $

El Nezamy: An ice-cream hot spot specialising in a nutty croquant flavour with vanilla and caramelised nuts, plus a frozen berry yoghurt. *10am-5am* $

Said (1897–1964) was a pioneer of modern Egyptian art. A judge by profession, he moonlighted as a painter and became a key member of a group devoted to forging an Egyptian artistic identity in the 1920s and '30s. To date, he's the only Middle Eastern artist whose works have sold for over US$1 million.

Closed on Mondays, the **Mahmoud Said Museum** *(LE20)* is housed in his fine Italianate family villa on Sharia Mohammed Said Pasha and showcases his work among other important Egyptian modernists such as brothers Seif and Adham Wanly and El Hussein Fawzy. One of the rooms is dedicated to Said's paintings of Alexandrian women – most notably of his wife, draped in a green shawl. They are beautifully observed and are an attempt by Said to capture the essence of Egyptian beauty in which he believed the identity of place was rooted. Head out of the main house and right around the building to enter the ground-floor rooms to see some great works by Seif and Adham Wanly, among which is the fantastic *Abraham's Sacrifice*.

Other art can be found at the free **Museum of Fine Art**, closed on Mondays. It houses a collection of passable 16th- to 20th-century paintings, but it is the Egyptian modernists and temporary exhibitions that are of real interest. Look out for Mahmoud Moussa's and Jerman Shalboub's burnt clay busts of young women, Ezikel Baroukh's portrait of *Motherhood* and Mahmoud Mokhtar's sculptures. Bring your passport to enter.

A Green Retreat

Escaping the city's bustle

Alexandria's eastern edge once stretched no further than the El-Nasr tram stop near the **Four Seasons** (p335). Beyond this point lay sandy hillocks and bays lined with palm trees. It was such a picturesque headland that Khedive Abbas Helmy II (the last Ottoman viceroy of Egypt and Sudan who ruled between 1892 and 1914) bought the entire area on which to build his Salamlek hunting lodge, where he holidayed with his Austro-Hungarian mistress – Countess May Torok Von Szendro – who later became his wife. The larger Al Haramlek Palace was built by King Fouad in 1932 and designed in lavish Byzantine-Italianate style, modelled on Florence's Palazzo Vecchio. His son, Farouk, added a Roman-style Tea Pavilion and a greenhouse of exotic plants. The whole area, known as **Montazah Gardens**, was the royal family's summer residence until King Farouk was deposed in 1952.

Nowadays, the 370-acre garden and forest reserve is the largest green area in Alexandria. Following their opening to the public after independence, they have been enjoyed by Alexandrian families who've spent their summers swimming off the four gorgeous beaches – **Aida**, **Nefertiti**, **Cleopatra** and **Semiramis** – and picnicking in the shade of the forest reserve. The palaces were briefly open to the public, and the Haramlek was turned into a casino for a while, but eventually they were requisitioned by the state and turned into presidential palaces. Numerous foreign dignitaries were hosted there, including US President Jimmy Carter and, in 1964, the Royal Palestine Hotel was added to the grounds to host the Arab Summit.

ALEXANDRIA'S BEST TOUR GUIDES

Zahraa Adel Awad *(+20 10-0272-4324; tourguide_egypt@ yahoo.com)* A lecturer in modern history and a deeply knowledgeable guide specialising in cultural and historical tours, some with a focus on Jewish Alexandrian history.

Karim Serrie *(+20 10-0261-7885)* Fluent in French and English, Karim is an energetic guide who leads food and history tours, as well as trips to the cemeteries of El Alamein.

Rasha Aggag *(+20 10-6208-8282; @rashaaa9434)* Knowledgeable Rasha tailors tours to individual needs and covers both the historical and contemporary realities of Alexandria. Fluent in English, French and German.

ALEXANDRIA'S BEST SHOPPING

Souq Al Attarine: Vintage hunters will have a blast exploring this warren of an antiques market.

Zane't El-Settat: At the 'Ladies' Needs Market' you can find anything from clothes to perfume, jewellery and belly-dancing gear.

Melbalad for Egyptian Arts & Crafts: Handmade Egyptian heritage crafts, such as embroidered scarves, hand-painted pottery, jewellery and leather bags. *(@melbalad)*

Studio 104: Donia and Alaa's amazing macrame studio runs workshops and sells everything from macrame bags to wall-hangings. *(@studio.104)*

Crystal Sweets: A charming vintage sweet shop filled with treats, including the famous Manolidis chocolate-covered dates.

Montazah Gardens (p323)

Now the gardens are entering a new phase, managed by the Rixos Hotels Group that has invested millions in their transformation. This has included the controversial demolition of dozens of beachfront family cabins in order to build a five-star hotel and beach chalets in Cleopatra's Forest, and the conversion of the Salamlek Palace into an 18-room heritage hotel where you can stay in Khedive Abbas Helmy's royal suite. There's also a spa, a beach club and a sports club, and you can once again have a drink in King Farouk's **Tea Pavilion** *(incl cup of tea LE50),* perched on Nelson's island, or visit his hothouse greenhouse that has been replanted with exotic flora.

The gilded and frescoed **Al Haramlek Palace** remains closed to visitors, except for pre-booked tours for large groups. However, the public can access the **gardens** *(entry/parking LE200/100; 24hr)* that provide an idyllic escape from the thronging city. Golf carts are on hand to ferry you around the site for LE200 per 15 minutes. The better option is to hire a **bike** *(per hr LE100)* to go exploring before finding your way to one of the **beaches** *(LE150).* A variety of restaurants is due to open over the coming years; at research time, you could only get light lunches at beachside **Zanilli's**. The gardens are about 17km from downtown. You'll need to grab a taxi.

DRINKING IN ALEXANDRIA: BEST BARS

MAPS P311, P315

Cap d'Or: A time capsule and one of the only surviving typical Alexandrian bars. Beer flows freely among the bohemian crowd. *10am-3am*

Spitfire Bar: Probably the liveliest bar in town with a rough-and-ready feel, rocking soundtrack and very cheap beer. *5pm-2am*

Cigar Bar: The Hilton's bar serves Alexandria's most creative cocktails with sea views. Happy hour is 4pm to 6pm. *4pm-2am*

Sky View: The rooftop restaurant of the Metropole Hotel with spectacular views of the bay is a great spot for sundowners. *11am-2am*

TOP EXPERIENCE
Bibliotheca Alexandrina

Built in the 3rd century BCE, the original Library of Alexandria was one of antiquity's greatest intellectual centres. While replacing it will be a Herculean task, the 2002-built Bibliotheca Alexandrina is a serious attempt to rekindle the original's spirit of learning. Housed in an impressive modern edifice, it is one of Egypt's major cultural venues, home to several interesting museums.

DON'T MISS
- Exterior architecture and view of the sea
- Main reading hall
- The Manuscript Museum
- The Modern Art Galleries
- The Sadat Museum

Shrine of the Muses

The original Alexandrian library was known as the Mouseion (Shrine of the Muses; the source of today's word 'museum') and included lecture areas, laboratories, gardens, dining halls, a zoo and shrines. It acted more like a university and attracted renowned scholars from around the Mediterranean, such as the mathematician Euclid and the astronomer Eratosthenes, who first calculated the diameter of the Earth. Likewise, the new Biblioteca is deeply integrated with Alexandria's university,

PRACTICALITIES
- *bibalex.org/en/default*
- *adult/student LE150/20*
- *10am-7pm Sun-Thu, 10am-2pm Sat*

CULTURE HUB

The library is Alexandria's main cultural hub, hosting dozens of public lectures and events. These include concerts during the August **summer festival**; a well-attended **International Book Fair** in July; and the **Alexandria International Film Festival** in November, when the library hosts screenings and Q&As with directors.

TOP TIPS

- Allocate half a day for exploring the library.

- Although you have to check bags, you can take your camera inside.

- The entrance and ticket office are at the back of the building; some museums require extra tickets.

- Tours in English, French and Arabic are offered by library staff; check the website for the schedule.

- The library is closed on Friday and closes at 2pm on Saturday and during Ramadan.

- Don't miss the excellent BA Bookshop (open Monday to Thursday and Saturday).

- Children under six are not admitted to the reading room.

contains 13 research centres, and is now the main destination for students and researchers from all over Egypt, as well as sub-Saharan African countries.

The Architecture

Take one of the **free library tours** to admire the library's interesting architecture. The building is inspired by the Egyptian sun disc and takes the form of a gigantic angled discus rising out of the ground. The granite walls are carved with letters, pictograms, hieroglyphs and symbols from more than 120 different scripts, while sunlight pours in through shaded roof lights, bathing the vast tiered reading room in soft light. An open plaza and reflecting pool buffer the library from city noise, creating a genuine sense of tranquillity.

The Library

To create the great collection of knowledge in his 3rd century BCE library, Ptolemy I ordered manuscripts to be confiscated from docking ships and sent merchants to scour Mediterranean markets for scrolls in Babylonian, Persian, Assyrian, Hebrew and Indian. While not nearly as extensive, the new Biblioteca is trilingual, containing books in Classical Arabic, French and English. It is the main Francophone library in Africa and the 20,000-sq-metre reading room is the largest in the world, seating 2500 readers. The library currently holds around 500,000 books, although there is room for eight million.

While you're in the main reading room, take time to admire the golden *kiswah*, a velvet fabric once used to cover the holy Kaaba in Mecca, richly embroidered in gold and silver thread with verses from the Quran. Prior to 1962, many *kiswah* were woven in Egypt – specifically in Alexandria – and then transported by camel caravan to Saudi Arabia for the annual Hajj.

The Museums

The complex houses several small museums. The **Antiquities Museum** contains artefacts cherry-picked from across Egypt and spanning history from Pharaonic times through to Islamic eras. There's a fine collection of 2nd-century funerary masks, intricately decorated sarcophagi, faience blue shabti (funerary statues) and some Greek-era statuary.

The **Manuscript Museum** has a collection of ancient texts and antiquarian books, including a copy of the only surviving scroll from Alexandria's ancient library. Next door, the Impressions of Alexandria Exhibition documents the city's history through drawings, maps and early photographs.

Other exhibition halls showcase the work of contemporary Arab artists and are also home to a fascinating heritage collection of textiles, folk art and Arab science equipment from the medieval period. And, finally, there's a dedicated **Sadat Museum** that chronicles the life of President Anwar Sadat through touching personal memorabilia, including the bloodstained uniform he was wearing at the time of his assassination in 1981.

A DOWNTOWN WANDER

Discover Alexandria's belle-époque beauty in an architecture tour around its finest Art Deco and neoclassical landmarks.

START	END	LENGTH
Midan Tahrir	Midan Saad Zaghloul	4.5km; 2½ hours

Start beneath the bronze ❶ **statue of Pasha Mohammed Ali** (p313) in Midan Tahrir, surrounded by grand government buildings. Spy the crenellated crown of ❷ **St Mark's Anglican Church** (p319), built in a Byzantine-Moorish style. Walk southeast down Salah Salem. When you hit Sharia El Horreya you'll see the neo-Renaissance ❸ **El Horreya Creativity Center** (p318), a diplomats' club in 1887 and now a beautiful cultural venue.

Continue east along Sharia El Horreya to glimpse award-winning apartment blocks and, on your left, the ❹ **Graeco-Roman Museum** (p314) with its neoclassical facade. Grand villas line the road, most notably the one-time home of Lebanese timber magnate As'ad Bassili, now the ❺ **Alexandria National Museum** (p320).

Come back past the Graeco-Roman museum and turn right up Sharia San Savvas to check out the ❻ **Monastery of St Savvas** (p319), originally a temple to Mithras and Apollo and now Alexandria's principal monastic institution. Nearby is the ❼ **Alexandria Opera House** (p318), inspired by the Milan Opera House.

Finally, take Sharia Naby Daniel and head north to see the ❽ **Eliyahu Hanavi Synagogue** (p319), built on top of its 14th-century predecessor in Byzantine revival style. It's one of Egypt's largest synagogues. Finish in Midan Saad Zaghloul with coffee and cake at ornate, 1905-built ❾ **Trianon** (p319) beneath its Art Deco murals.

El Alamein

WWII CEMETERIES | DESERT BATTLEFIELDS | BEACHES

☑ TOP TIP

Forty kilometres west of Alamein, the beach-resort compounds and bikini-friendly beaches of Sidi Abdel Rahman are only open between June and September.

GETTING AROUND

The easiest option is to organise your own car and driver. A taxi will charge LE1200 to LE1500 to take you from Alexandria to the War Museum, ferry you between the cemeteries, make a stop at a beach and return to Alexandria.

Alternatively, catch any of the Marsa Matruh–bound buses (Go Bus is the best) or microbuses from Al Moaf Al Gedid Bus Station in Alexandria. You'll be dropped on the main road about 200m down the hill from the War Museum; organise a taxi in advance to take you to the cemeteries.

For a brief period in 1942, El Alamein commanded the attention of the entire world, because it was here that the Allies won control of North Africa in WWII. More than 80,000 soldiers were killed in the battles fought between Germany's Field Marshal Erwin Rommel and Bernard Montgomery, leader of the Allied forces. Alamein was the last defensible position before Cairo – and the critical Suez Canal – and the city's war cemeteries are a reminder of the price paid to hold that line.

These days, Alamein is looking to the future with the billion-dollar New Alamein City. One of Egypt's millennial cities, it aims to house three million new residents in 15 skyscrapers by 2030, alongside new educational, cultural and industrial facilities. There will also be a tourist district with a 14km-long promenade and seaside resort on reclaimed islands. Work is underway, with construction all along the coast as you approach.

El Alamein's Battlefields

Deep dive into military history

If you spend time in El Alamein, you may field offers of desert excursions to visit key battle sites such as Ruweisat Ridge. However, if you want to explore the WWII sites fully, you should consider opting for a tour with local guide **Moneim Raouf** *(+20 12-2351-3401)*. Moneim is the son of an Alamein Bedouin family whose grandfather helped build the **German War Memorial**; since then the family has been guardians of the memorial and have been involved in the ongoing burial of missing soldiers when their bodies are occasionally discovered in the desert (Allied forces chased hundreds of Axis troops into the wilderness after the 1942 rout). Many years after the war, Moneim's father invited Rommel's son back to El Alamein where the latter donated key memorabilia to the museum.

Moneim Raouf knows Alamein and its surrounding desert well and is a trusted guide to strategic battle grounds, such as Ruweisat Ridge, Tel El Eissa, Mitereiya Ridge, Point 29 and Alam el Halfa as well as the Egyptian Railway workers' building which served as a hospital where German and Australian doctors treated the wounded from both sides of the conflict.

Note that a guide with expert knowledge of the desert is essential for such explorations as there are still an unknown number of WWII landmines that remain concealed. Officially, you (or your guide) must also obtain approval from the Egyptian military to access the battlefields. It's a controlled area and if you're caught visiting without permission you risk getting into serious trouble.

A Seaside Rendezvous

Stunning beaches and top-notch resorts

The gorgeous white-sand beaches and glowing blue waters of **Sidi Abdel Rahman** await 30km north of El Alamein and are the raison d'etre for a US$1.74 billion, multi-season resort development, catering to international clientele and served by charter flights between Europe and El Alamein. Here you can indulge in parasailing, kayaking, tennis and cycling around gorgeous landscaped gardens and created lagoons. The luxurious facilities and fabulous beaches don't come cheap, though: you can expect to pay around US$250 per night for an overnight stay. The five-star **Al Alamein Hotel** (p335) is the area's standout hotel and is situated on one of Egypt's best beaches. The bus to Marsa Matruh will drop you at any given resort if you inform the driver of the name and location when boarding.

Commonwealth War Cemetery

TOP EXPERIENCE

El Alamein War Cemeteries

The haunting WWII cemeteries of El Alamein feature regimented rows of thousands of tombstones standing sentinel in a stark desert environment. The Commonwealth Cemetery is the largest, with 7240 graves – mostly of soldiers who died in the Battle of Alamein in October 1942. Also here are memorials to the Italian and German fallen, and a small military museum.

DID YOU KNOW?

The 1942 victory at El Alamein ensured control of North Africa, enabling Allied forces to launch the invasion of Sicily from its shores in 1943. On 10 July they launched 3000 ships from North Africa, liberating Sicily on 17 August.

El Alamein Military Museum

The **Military Museum** *(LE275)* of Alamein is a great place to get to grips with the Battle of El Alamein and the broader North African campaigns of WWII. As you enter, you'll find a garden full of tanks, military jeeps and planes. Inside, the museum has separate halls devoted to the four main countries involved in the battle: Great Britain, Italy, Germany and Egypt. It's a well-curated and informative display even

PRACTICALITIES

- cwgc.org/visit-us/find-cemeteries-memorials/cemetery-details/2019000/el-alamein-war-cemetery
- Military Museum LE275
- Military Museum 9am-4pm Sat-Thu, Commonwealth War Cemetery 9am-noon & 1-4pm Fri, 9am-2.30pm

if the mannequins in military uniform look slightly crazed. The turn-off to the museum is along the main highway; just look for the tank in the middle of the road.

Commonwealth War Cemetery

Like Dunkirk and Passchendaele, El Alamein was one of the most storied theatres of war, and this is one of the largest WWII cemeteries in the world. Designed by Herbert Worthington, the **Commonwealth War Cemetery** is an arresting sight: thousands of tombstones stretching as far as the eye can see in impeccable rows interspersed with cacti and bougainvillea. In the southeastern corner of the cemetery, a cremation memorial records the names of a further 11,866 forces whose bodies were never recovered. The Land Forces panel commemorates 8500 men who fell further afield in Tunisia and Libya, while an Air Force plaque honours 3000 men. The experience of wandering past the graves and reading the names and ages of the men is deeply moving. A Remembrance service is held here every year on 23 October, the start date of the bloody Second Battle of El Alamein, which continued until 11 November. The Commonwealth forces prevailed, but at a huge cost. Nevertheless the win gave the Allies a much-needed morale boost after losing Singapore and having to retreat from France. The cemetery is about 1km east of the Military Museum.

German War Memorial

Some 7km west of El Alamein, you'll see an octagonal sandstone fortress atop a promontory overlooking the sea. It is the **German War Memorial**, its blank facade embracing an octagonal interior around whose sides sit sarcophagi (symbolising Germany's regions) and panels listing the names of over 4000 German servicemen. At its centre there's a black granite obelisk guarded by eagles, reminiscent of the Egyptian falcon-god Horus. To reach the memorial, take the marked turn-off from the main highway; if the entrance is locked, wait for the keeper who will let you in.

Italian War Memorial

About 11km west of El Alamein, roughly at the location of the front line in WWII, you'll find the **Italian War Memorial**. Enter a one-room museum with scant memorabilia through the archway (closed during Friday prayers). Further down a wide path lined with oleander is a marble tower, almost as white as the surrounding sand. Designed as both a cemetery and a chapel, this sacraria is covered in square marble grave slabs, engraved with the names of 4800 soldiers, although an inscription in the chapel notes that 38,000 Italian soldiers remain missing. At the back of the memorial, a panoramic window looks out over the bright blue sea.

TOP TIPS

● El Alamein is 115km (70 miles) west of Alexandria.

● **Karim Serrie** (+20 10-0261-7885) runs guided tours to El Alamein.

● Go Bus has services to El Alamein from Alexandria. The station is a 10-minute walk from the War Museum.

● In summer there are food options at coastal resorts. In winter you need to head to old Alamein town.

TURNING POINT AT ALAMEIN

By 1942, Field Marshal Rommel had pushed the Allies back to the last defensible position before Cairo – El Alamein. Mussolini flew in for his triumphal entry into Cairo. Then, on 23 October, the Allies launched a counteroffensive. Intense fighting raged for 13 days until the Axis line finally crumbled. Rommel's routed legions retreated and he was recalled to Germany to avoid the shame of surrender.

Marsa Matruh

BEACHES | MARKET | CRYSTAL-CLEAR WATER

☑ TOP TIP

On public beaches, it's advised that women wear baggy clothing over their bathing suits. Resorts with private beaches are bikini-friendly. Beau Site offers a day-pass for nonguests. Accommodation in central Marsa Matruh is dated and overpriced; private resorts east of town are better.

GETTING AROUND

Taxis are required to reach the best beaches. During high season (June to September), bicycles can be hired along Sharia Alexandria (LE25 to LE50 per day), EgyptAir has flights between Cairo and Marsa Matruh, and there are sleeper trains between the two cities. The bus station and adjacent microbus lot are 3km southeast of town. Between them, Go Bus and West Delta offer the best services to Alexandria (4½ hours), Cairo (7½ hours) and Siwa (four to 4½ hours).

During summer, Marsa Matruh provides a real-deal Egyptian resort-town experience. From June to September it can seem as if half of the Nile Valley has decamped here for their holidays. Fringed by turquoise waters, the white-sand beaches are filled with sun worshippers, while the dusty streets and Corniche buzz with people well into the early hours of the morning. In the evening, the vibe is celebratory, when clusters of street stalls sell hot food and souvenirs and street musicians bang out rhythmic tunes.

For the rest of the year, however, Marsa Matruh presses the snooze button and returns to its usual soporific state. The city's turquoise bays lie empty and the only visitors are Bedouins and Siwans stocking up on essential goods. Whatever the time of year, few foreign tourists make the trip out here, except to break the journey to Siwa (310km to the south).

A Very Egyptian Beach Escape
Explore the local beach scene

Marsa Matruh is a genuine Egyptian holiday town that heaves with local holidaymakers during the summer months of July and August. The beaches here are truly spectacular, the limpid blue water framed by white chalk plateaus that collapse into wide strips of sand. Many have evocative names, such as Cleopatra's Beach, Shat' Agiba ('Wonder Beach') and Shat' El Gharam (Lovers Beach). **Agiba Beach**, 24km west of Marsa Matruh, is probably the best: a stunning cove with crystal clear waters, only accessible via a path leading down from the clifftop. However, the waves roll in forcefully so it's not ideal for swimmers.

From the city's main **Lido Beach** (very busy in summer) you can hop across to the tip of the breakwater opposite where you'll find **Shat Al'Gharam** (Lovers' Beach), made famous by singer Laila Mourad who sang of her love for

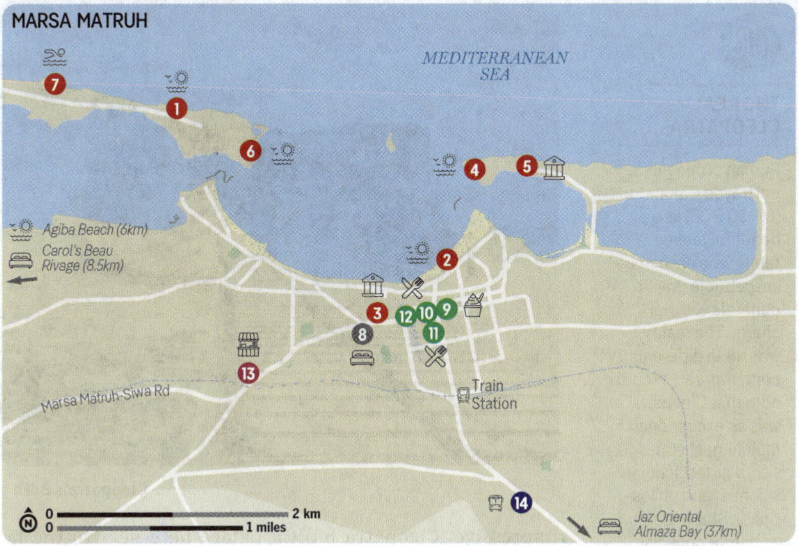

MARSA MATRUH

SIGHTS
1. Cleopatra's Beach
2. Lido Beach
3. Matrouh National Museum
4. Rommel's Beach
5. Rommel's Cave Museum
6. Shat Al'Gharam

ACTIVITIES
7. Cleopatra's Bath

SLEEPING
8. Adriatica Hotel

EATING
9. Azza Ice-Cream
10. Kamona Restaurant
11. Magdy Seafood
12. Sahar Restaurant

SHOPPING
13. Libya Souq

TRANSPORT
14. Bus Station

Matruh seated on a rock here. It's 17km from town so you'll need to get a taxi here.

Rommel's Beach is to the east of town and is so-called because German Commander Erwin Rommel laid out his battle plans in the cave system near the beach. Today, the caves house the very small **Rommel's Cave Museum** *(adult/concession LE100/50)*, a single room set among a network of tunnels that is host to some personal Rommel memorabilia – including his hand pistols – donated by his son. The beach here has calm shallow waters that are perfect for small children.

Cleopatra's Beach lies 14km northwest of Marsa Matruh, on the spindly breakwater that wraps around the bay. The sea here is an exquisite hue and the rock formations are

EATING IN MARSA MATRUH: OUR PICKS

Kamona: The most popular grill in town, famous for its lamb kebabs and chicken shish. *11am-3am* $

Sahar Restaurant: Don't mind the modest appearance, Sahar serves great grilled fillet, *molokheya* (jute mallow stew) and mezze. *9am-10pm Sat-Thu, 1-11pm Fri* $$

Magdy Seafood: Serves up huge platters of grilled langoustine and fish, fried prawns and chargrilled tilapia and squid. *6am-1am* $$

Azza Ice Cream: Join the crush outside Azza and order one of their signature rice pudding with nuts and raisins. *24hr* $

Cleopatra's Bath

THE REAL CLEOPATRA

Roman propaganda portrayed Cleopatra (69–30 BCE) as a beautiful femme fatale who ensnared susceptible Roman generals with her charm. The reality was quite different: contemporary records note that Cleopatra was an exceptional multilingual statesperson, a gifted scholar, scientist and philosopher. She was also an astute politician focused on protecting Egypt against Roman aggression. Cleopatra had a son with Julius Caesar and an affair with his protege Mark Anthony, who fought to protect her throne against Octavian (later Emperor Augustus), Caesar's adopted son. Finally defeated at the Battle of Actium in 30 BCE, she took her own life – allegedly dying from the bite of an Egyptian cobra – rather than be paraded around Rome as a prisoner.

impressive. Cleopatra built a palace here next to the famous **Cleopatra's Bath**, a natural pool where legend says the queen and Mark Antony enjoyed a dip. However, you can't actually swim in it because of the waves breaking on the rocks offshore.

When you're not at the beach, you'll probably just want to hang out on the Corniche watching the local scene. Or, you can pop into the **Matrouh National Museum** (*adult/concession LE180/90*), which has a small display of antiquities, coins and statues found in the surrounding area. It's also worth dropping into the **Libya Souq**, which you'll find back from the beach on Sharia Al'Galaa. Here you'll find the superior olive oil, dates, olives and Bedouin products made in the oasis of Siwa.

Places We Love to Stay

$ Budget $$ Midrange $$$ Top End

Alexandria   MAPS p311, p315

San Giovanni Stanly Hotel $ A old Italian hostelry that's had a colourful Egyptian makeover. Service is charming and there are views of the Stanley Bridge from the restaurant.

Ithaka Hostel $ A great hostel in a prime location with male and female dorms, a shared kitchen and living room, and super helpful staff.

Triomphe Hostel $ A vintage elevator leads to this top-floor hostel, where simple rooms with dark period furniture cling to shreds of former elegance.

Brass Bell $$ A great alternative to AirBnB, Brass Bell renovates run-down properties, furnishes them in chic modern style and rents them reasonably.

Steigenberger Cecil Hotel $$ Built in 1930, this is an Alexandrian institution and a memorial to the city's raffish 1940s heyday. It's also perfectly located overlooking the sea.

Le Metropole Hotel $$ Housed in a historic 19th-century structure and decorated in high French style, the Metropole is a nostalgia ride with a great rooftop restaurant.

Paradise Inn Beach Resort $$ A great summer option, Paradise Inn is next to Montazah gardens and has a private section of Marmoura Beach, a spa and pleasant pool- and garden-facing rooms.

Rixos Montaza Alexandria $$$ The swish new kid in Montazah Park offering 18 suites and a luxe spa in the historic Salamlek palace as well as 80 chic chalets with direct beach access.

Four Seasons San Stefano $$$ Opulent five-star accommodation, with a private beach, three pools, a fitness centre and four restaurants.

Hilton Alexandria Corniche $$$ It's true it isn't a beauty on the outside, but rooms are comfortable with great views, there's a pool and an excellent Greek restaurant and cigar bar.

Windsor Palace Hotel $$ A bejewelled Edwardian gem hosting travellers in a prime seafront location since 1906. Come from its gilt-edged decor and bygone atmosphere as well as comfortable rooms overlooking the sea.

El Alamein   MAP p329

Tolip North Coast Hotel & Resort $$ One of Alamein's expansive resorts with smart hotel and family-friendly chalet accommodation, a beautiful beach, multiple restaurants and two pools (one for kids).

Tolip Resort Paradise $$$ The other Tolip offering in New Alamein, this is a more slick and stylish development beside a beautiful sheltered beach, with 329 rooms, three pools (one adults-only) and evening entertainment.

Sidi Abd El Rahman   p329

Marassi Boutique Hotel-Marina 2 $$ A smaller, new hotel set back from the beach but offering the same high-gloss style and interior-designed rooms with balconies overlooking a pool.

Casa Cook North Coast $$$ Part of the Casa Cook lifestyle brand who brings their earthy style to bear on this high-style, adults-only resort, just 700m from Amwaj Beach.

Al Alamein Hotel $$$ The most luxurious resort on the coast favoured by wealthy Cairenes. Plush rooms overlook the stunning bay, there's a spa, and restaurants are top class.

Marsa Matruh   MAP p333

Adriatica Hotel $ An old-school downtown hotel where your hospitable hosts offer great advice, a good breakfast and the neat rooms have sea views.

Carol's Beau Rivage $$ Set around a lagoon-like pool beside a delightful bay 15km west of Marsa Matruh, this all-inclusive resort is a family-friendly favourite.

Jaz Oriental Almaza Bay $$$ A splashy hotel decked in acres of cool marble offering contemporary suite-style rooms, a huge pool and the most fabulous beach.

For places to stay on the Suez Canal, see p345

From left: Lake Timsah, Ismailia (p342); Suez Canal Authority (p342)

Researched by
Anthon Jackson

Suez Canal

EPIC CANAL, GARDEN CITIES & NATIONAL HERITAGE

Just a short hop from the Nile, the Suez Canal Zone remains off the tourist trail, despite being full of historic charm.

The Suez Canal Zone was a crossroads of continents for millennia before the earth-shaking launch of its canal – a mammoth feat of 19th-century ingenuity connecting the Mediterranean to the Red Sea. The three cities along the canal – Port Said, Ismailia and Suez – were neatly laid out by the canal's founders, each quickly swelling with populations of Egyptian, European and Levantine merchants, migrants, colonial officials and soldiers en route to 'the East', and prospering for almost a century. Then, in 1956, President Gamal Abdel Nasser's nationalisation of the canal led to the expulsion of the zone's Europeans. This precipitated the Suez Crisis, whereby British, French and Israeli forces jointly sought to reopen the Straits of Tiran and depose President Nasser, withdrawing months later after considerable political pressure from the United States and the USSR. More fighting with Israel followed between 1967 and 1973, shuttering the canal and virtually emptying its cities, each of them emerging badly scarred.

In reconstruction, these cities have been cemented as icons of Egyptian national pride, their cores now punctuated with patriotic murals, heroic statues and museums to showcase their distinctive roles in Egypt's story. Those keen on tracing the past will enjoy a meander here. For the rest, there's superlative seafood, ambles along canal-side corniches and the world's shortest transcontinental ferry – and not least, the chance to watch the supertankers rolling by.

THE MAIN AREAS

PORT SAID
Historic Mediterranean seafood hub. **p340**

ISMAILIA
Garden city with a star museum. **p342**

SUEZ
Gritty, characterful Red Sea port. **p344**

Find Your Way

From Port Said, at the canal's northern end, to Suez, at its southernmost point, the Suez Canal Zone stretches for 193km. Ismailia marks the halfway point, roughly an 80-minute journey from either city.

BUS & MICROBUS
East Delta Bus Company buses link the region's cities with Cairo and Alexandria, but scheduled departures are limited. Microbuses, leaving when full, are the fastest (and cheapest) way to travel along the Canal Zone.

TAXI & TRAIN
For short hops within cities, use taxis (blue and white in Port Said, orange in Ismailia and white in Suez); Uber is also available. Trains linking the Canal Zone's cities are worthwhile for the wonderful canal views.

Port Said, p340
The canal's Mediterranean portal, with wooden-porched streets, arcaded tenements and a spruced-up waterfront path.

Ismailia, p342
A garden city of colonial villas and parks along Lake Timsah, Ismailia boasts the zone's newest, best museum.

Suez, p344
The industrial port at the canal's southern terminus offers the best odds of glimpsing big boats in the canal.

Port Tawfik (p344)

Plan Your Time

A day trip from Cairo to one of the zone's three hubs is just about doable, but you're better off spending a night in Port Said or Ismailia.

Pressed for Time

● Choose between **Port Said** (p340) and **Ismailia** (p342) and get an early start. In Port Said, hit the side streets off Sharia Al Gomhoreya before boarding the ferry to the Asian side and feasting at **El Gendy** or **Aalim Al Behar**. In Ismailia, don't miss the **Canal Museum** (p342), set in the old Canal Company headquarters, and sample the seafood along Sharia Al Blajat.

Three Days to Travel

● Combine the two day trips with a night in **Port Said** (p340), where you can hit the beachfront **Corniche**; or **Ismailia** (p342), staying in the **historic home of Ferdinand De Lesseps** (p345). Better yet, book a night in both, then swing by **Suez** (p344) on the return to Cairo, strolling the canal at Port Tawfik and stopping by its **National Museum** (p344).

SEASONAL HIGHLIGHTS

SPRING
Green spaces fill with picnickers enjoying the year's best weather and celebrating the Sham An Nessim festival.

SUMMER
Mango season (August to October) brings visitors to scorching Ismailia. Suez is hotter and Port Said is muggy.

AUTUMN
A second stretch of warm, sunny weather. In October, Port Fouad welcomes large wintering flocks of flamingos.

WINTER
Weather remains mild, with some rain and chilly nights. Ismailia's Film Festival in February is a landmark event.

Port Said

MILITARY HISTORY | CANAL CROSSING | SEAFOOD

☑ TOP TIP

On arrival, pick up a free city map from the **tourist office** *(8am-3pm Sat-Thu)* inside the train station. While here, book a seat on the scenic train to Ismailia for the best canal views.

GETTING AROUND

Port Said's centre is compact and walkable. Short hops cost LE10 to LE15 in a taxi. The public ferry (*ma'adiya*) is free for pedestrians and departs every 10 to 15 minutes, taking five minutes to cross the canal. Port Said's train station is immediately south of the centre, with regular trains for Ismailia (1½ hours), Cairo (3¼ hours) and Alexandria (6½ hours). The bus station lies 5km west of the centre; a taxi costs roughly LE25.

A Mediterranean city at heart, Port Said was founded in 1859 as the gateway to the Suez Canal. Despite decades of demolitions and developments, more belle époque traces remain here than anywhere else along the canal, its arcaded tenements adorned with elegant verandas, some five storeys high. At the same time, Port Said's enduring vitality is entirely Egyptian, best felt in its bazaar, its beach-front corniche or crossing the canal on the Africa-to-Asia ferry. Here, you'll enjoy Bosporus vibes, with seagulls trailing as you admire the twin, dome-studded skylines, pierced by tankers and quay cranes in motion.

Echoes of War
Explore Port Said's military legacy

In the front yard of Port Said's **Military Museum** *(adult/student LE150/75)*, a quick taxi ride west of the old centre on Sharia 23 July, two captured Israeli tanks set the tone for what awaits: a memorable account of the Egypt–Israeli conflicts that rocked the locally-nicknamed 'Valiant City' and helped to shape nation.

Inside, head right to peruse the displays in chronological order, beginning with canal's construction and nationalisation by President Gamal Abdel Nasser. At the back, huge portraits of the president take pride of place amid displays on the Suez Crisis (known locally as the Tripartite Aggression) – a joint British, French and Israeli attempt to reclaim control over the canal. Left of the entrance, a further set of paintings, dioramas and weapons illustrate Egypt's efforts to defend against Israel's surprise attack in 1967, and to execute their own against Israel in the Yom Kippur War (October War) of 1973. In the latter, the Egyptians gained then lost ground, but the talks that followed were momentous: the 1978 Camp David Accords, which saw a full Israeli withdrawal from the Sinai in return for an unprecedented – and enduring – Egypt–Israel peace treaty.

PORT SAID ON FOOT

To soak up the historic vibes of 'The Valiant City', wander along – and over – the canal.

START	END	LENGTH
De Lesseps Plinth	Port Fouad	3.6km; 2 hours

Begin at the sizable ❶ **plinth** that once held a famous statue of Ferdinand De Lesseps, grantee of the canal concession, toppled in 1956. A statue of similar proportions, entitled ❷ **Umm Ad Dunya** (Mother of the World), Egypt's sobriquet, towers over a waterfront walkway and Midan Egypt. Outside the nearby ❸ **Italian House**, spot the fascist engraving invoking the 'animating power of Rome, once again imperial', inscribed with Il Duce's name.

Cut west to the spine of the old European quarter, Sharia Al Gomhoreya, to spot the surviving verandas in the side streets leading back to the canal. At ❹ **Salsabila**, sample the Sicilian *cassata* (cake) before diving into the lively ❺ **Bazar Abbas**, the city's souq since the 19th century. Head south to admire the frescoed interior of the Catholic ❻ **Church of Saint Eugénie**, the oldest in town.

Crossing Midan Al Manshiah (the former Place de Lesseps), walk the backstreets of the city's old red light district, then follow the crowds aboard the free ❼ **ferry** *(ma'adiya)* to Port Fouad, Port Said's sister city, looking back en route at the iconic, tri-domed ❽ **Suez Canal House**. Passing the soaring minarets of the city's ❾ **grand mosque**, you'll reach the French villas encircling Montazah Park, built in the 1920s for employees of the Suez Canal administration.

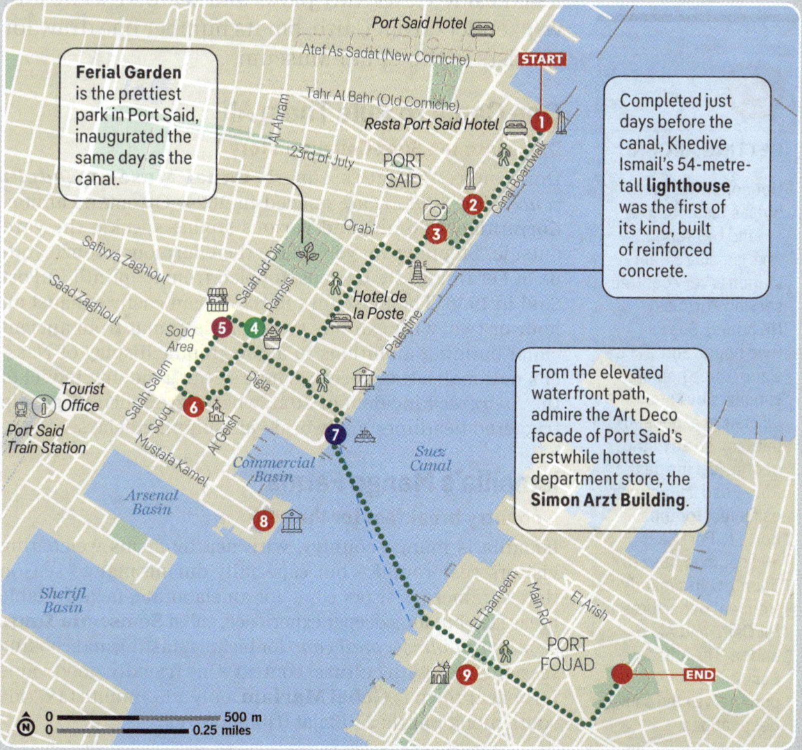

Ferial Garden is the prettiest park in Port Said, inaugurated the same day as the canal.

Completed just days before the canal, Khedive Ismail's 54-metre-tall **lighthouse** was the first of its kind, built of reinforced concrete.

From the elevated waterfront path, admire the Art Deco facade of Port Said's erstwhile hottest department store, the **Simon Arzt Building**.

Ismailia

HISTORIC CHARM | STAR MUSEUM | LAKESIDE VIEWS

☑ TOP TIP

Get under the skin of Ismailia by contacting **Semsemia Tours** *(semsemiatours@gmail.com)*, a group of local guides and storytellers specialising in slow travel. Taking the train to Port Said? Download the VesselFinder app to track passing tankers en route.

GETTING AROUND

Uber operates here but it's faster to get around by orange taxi. Ismailia's train station is very central, serving Port Said (1½ hours), Suez (two hours) and Cairo (three hours). Ismailia's bus station *(al maw'af al gedeed)* lies 3km north of the centre, just inside the Ring Road. Microbuses fill fast for trips north to Port Said and south to Suez (1¼ hours), with similarly frequent departures for Cairo and Alexandria. The adjacent East Delta Bus Company serves the same destinations.

The most laid-back of the Canal Zone's cities, Ismailia straddles the shores of Lake Timsah, the northernmost of the Bitter Lakes that widen the canal along its southerly course towards Suez. Founded in 1862 and named for the Khedive Ismail, it still serves as the headquarters of the Suez Canal Authority. Triumphant murals and statues sprinkle its core, celebrating the resilience of the city's *fedayeen* (resistance fighters) through decades of conflict. These days, its lakeside views, tidy parks and seafood scene lure weekenders from Cairo, but its number one draw for tourists is the Canal Museum.

One Canal to Rule Them All
Delve into the Suez Canal's history

Don't miss the city's superb **Canal Museum** *(adult/concession 300LE/150)*, opened in 2024. Ottoman cannon, Corinthian columns and various stellae speckle the yard outside. Stepping in, you'll face the enormous bronze statue of Ferdinand De Lesseps, toppled from its plinth in Port Said in 1956. The museum's 12 rooms can easily exhaust an hour or two, with exhibits running the gamut from ancient canal-building ambitions to a holographic display of Nasser's nationalisation speech. There's even a moving model of the *Evergreen* incident of 2021, when a grounded megaship triggered headlines and worldwide shipping delays.

Ismailia's Mango Farms
A country breakfast for the ages

Ismailia is mango country, with nearby farms welcoming visitors year-round – but especially during mango season (late summer). Visitors come for an elaborate, farm-to-table breakfast, but for a deeper experience, enlist **Semsemia Tours** *(semsemiatours@gmail.com)* for picking, tasting and cooking sessions, rich with cultural context. One friendly, good-value farm near town is **Gebel Mariam**, only a 15-minute taxi ride south along Sharia Al Blajat (Gomhoreya).

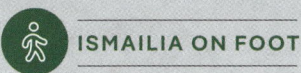

ISMAILIA ON FOOT

To scratch the surface of Ismailia's rich history, follow this route that roughly traces the Sweet Water Canal.

START	END	LENGTH
French villas	Abbasi Mosque	3.5km; 3 hours

Begin at the picturesque ❶ **Midan Al Sharq**, surrounded by the French villas of employees of the Canal Company. West of here, Pharaonic statues adorn the yard of the ❷ **Ismailia Museum**. Along Sharia Salah Salem you'll see banyan trees, planted during the city's founding, opposite a ❸ **statue of a resistance fighter**, built from the fragments of Israeli bombs dropped in 1967. Nearby, a statue of Anwar Sadat – celebrating his 1978 Peace Prize – marks the entrance to the ❹ **Muhammad Ali Gardens** to the north of the Sweetwater Canal, linking Lake Timsah to the Nile.

Shortly past Ismailia's old governorate building, across the street from the gardens' triumphant mural, veer right up Sharia Cleopatra, where the victorious ❺ **Steadfastness statue** commemorates the Battle of Ismailia, won by the city's defenders in 1973's October War.

Take your pick of cafes in the park of Midan Al Gomhoreya before ducking into Ismailia's fabulous ❻ **Canal Museum**. After glimpsing his giant statue, take a peek inside ❼ **De Lesseps' elegant home** (p345) next door, transformed in 2024 into a boutique hotel. At the edge of the Arab quarter, where scattered *mashrabiyya* (latticework) windows remain, visit the striking ❽ **Abbasi Mosque**, the city's oldest, completed in 1898.

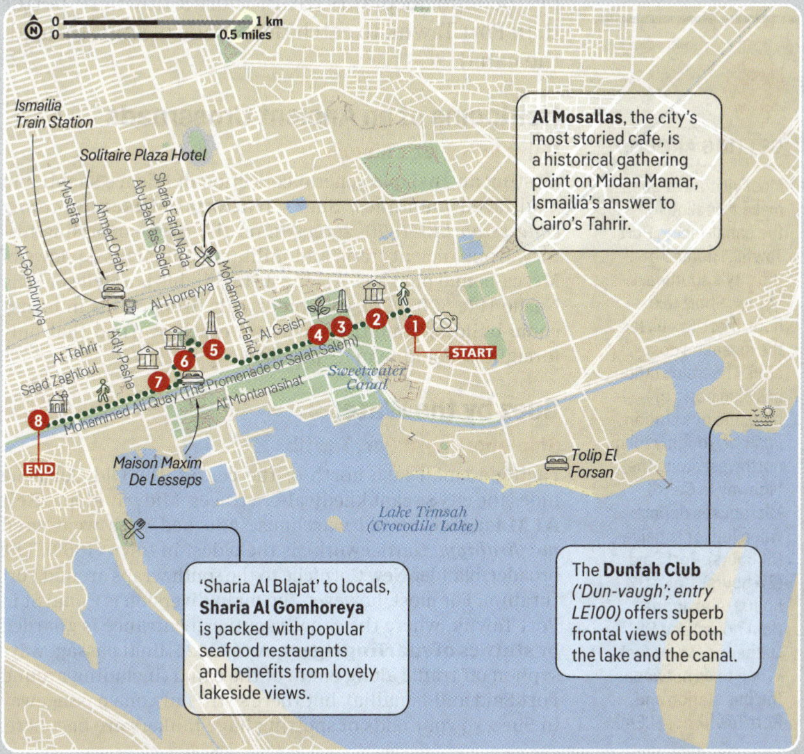

Al Mosallas, the city's most storied cafe, is a historical gathering point on Midan Mamar, Ismailia's answer to Cairo's Tahrir.

'Sharia Al Blajat' to locals, **Sharia Al Gomhoreya** is packed with popular seafood restaurants and benefits from lovely lakeside views.

The **Dunfah Club** ('Dun-vaugh'; entry LE100) offers superb frontal views of both the lake and the canal.

Suez

SHIP-SPOTTING | WATERFRONT WALKS | RED SEA

☑ TOP TIP

Track the location of tankers along the canal with the help of an app like VesselFinder. Be warned that the use of old-school cameras is strictly forbidden at Port Tawfik, a rule enforced by plain-clothes officers. But smartphone cameras are just fine!

GETTING AROUND

Most visitors to Suez make a beeline for the canal-facing Port Tawfik, situated at the city's southeast corner. Short taxi hops (Port Tawfik to the museum) cost LE15. The train station lies 6km north of here; the bus station (maw'af) roughly 10km northwest along the highway to Cairo. Microbuses depart when full for Ismailia (1¼ hours), Port Said (2¾ hours), Cairo (1¾ hours), Alexandria (four hours) and St Catherine (3¾ hours). White taxis between the bus station and Port Tawfik cost LE40.

Guarding the canal's southern terminus, Suez is the youngest of the Company cities (1867). As a key global junction, however, it's the oldest, linking the Gulf of Suez to the Nile (via Wadi Tumilat) since ancient times. Today, it serves as a crossroads for Cairo, Sinai and the Red Sea towns, yet few travellers stick around. Its older structures were largely lost in the conflicts of 1967–73, and its waterfront is dominated today by a bleak array of refineries and petrochemical plants. Still, there's nowhere better than Port Tawfik to catch the parade of ships through the canal.

Heirlooms of an Ancient Crossroads
Delve into Suez's history

Hosting an enviable general collection of faience shabti and gold-faced mummies, Suez's **National Museum** *(adult/concession LE180/90)* zeroes in on the city's surprising history, from ancient trade and military campaigns to flows of Mecca-bound pilgrims. Among its highlights is a stella of King Necho II (c 600 BCE), who reportedly dropped his immense canal-building ambitions after an oracle warned that only foreigners would reap its benefits.

Suez by the Water
Ship-spotting at Port Tawfik

Facing a small lake north of the centre, the Old Corniche hides the city's scant khedival-era traces. Midway along, **Beit Al Masagiri**, an old warehouse adorned with weathered *mashrabiyya* (latticework), is the oldest in town (1863). The broader, blander New Corniche to the south wraps around Port Ibrahim. For most, however, the main diversion is Canal St in Port Tawfik, where the canal's southern entrance is guarded by **statues of snarling tigers**. As of 2024, dual passageways syphon off traffic along 85km of the canal (including around Port Said and Ismailia), but there's still only one passageway in Suez, so your odds of spotting huge tankers are best here.

Places We Love to Stay

$ Budget $$ Midrange $$$ Top End

Port Said
MAP p340

Hotel De La Poste $ There's plenty of old-world charm at this two-star hotel at the heart of the old European quarter, some with balconies overlooking Sharia Al Gomhoreya.

Resta Port Said Hotel $$ As close as it gets to the entrance to the canal, this resort offers excellent value for Port Said, with well-kept rooms (some with waterfront views), a pool and a nostalgia-laced bar.

Port Said Hotel $$ Good deals at this ageing but nicely furnished hotel, conveniently within reach of both canal and coast and with an old-fashioned bar to boot.

Ismailia
MAP p342

Solitaire Plaza Hotel $ This good-value budget option lies immediately north of the tracks near the railway station. Its darkish rooms come with fridges, and some even have kitchenettes.

Maison Maxim De Lesseps $$$ Opened as an elegant, boutique hotel in 2024, this is Ismailia's historical ground zero, the city's first home and to none other than Ferdinand De Lesseps (credited as founder of the Suez Canal). Its grounds are now fitted with a pool and fitness centre.

Tolip El Forsan $$$ Centrally set between the Muhammad Ali Gardens and Lake Timsah with a pool, sandy beach and views of the canal, this popular resort can feel overrun on weekends, but is otherwise pleasantly calm.

Suez
p344

Red Sea $$ In a city of poor-value offerings, this high-rise in Port Tawfik's old French quarter stands out, with tidy grounds, well-kept rooms, a pool and canal views from its sixth-storey restaurant.

Tugboat, Port Tawfik

THE GUIDE

RED SEA COAST

Researched by
Lama Obeid

Red Sea Coast

UNDERWATER MAGIC BEYOND THE DESERT FRINGE

Famed for spectacular coral reefs, the Red Sea is renowned as a diver's destination, but the region's riches stretch inland as well as offshore.

The Red Sea coast has been inhabited for centuries. The ancients passed through the Eastern Desert to trading posts along the coast, the Romans mined the area for emeralds, and early Christians retreated into remote mountain hideouts.

Only in the past half-century has the emphasis changed from land to sea, with intensive tourist developments along the coastal strip from Safaga all the way south to Berenice. The coast became a popular getaway with all-inclusive resorts and international airports offering direct hops for sun-starved visitors.

The region attracts divers from all over the world, who come to explore its rich marine life and colourful coral reefs. With plenty of certified diving schools, mild water temperatures for the majority of the year and abundant dive sites and diving safaris to choose from, the Red Sea coast has become the second most popular diving destination in Egypt after Sharm El Sheikh.

One of Egypt's most modern cities, Hurghada was established in 1905 as a fishing village. In 1913 oil was discovered in the area and British companies began production and export. The village was developed into a resort with Egyptian and foreign investment in the 1980s, and more tourist attractions soon appeared. Among them were the vibrant Halaka fish market and the Hurghada Marina, built in 2008 to accommodate the city's growing number of local and international visitors.

STAS MOROZ/SHUTTERSTOCK

THE MAIN AREAS

HURGHADA
A fishing village turned into a vacation getaway.
p352

MARSA ALAM
Where desert meets sea. **p361**

For places to stay on the Red Sea Coast, see p367

THE GUIDE

RED SEA COAST

From left: Kitesurfing, Hamata (p365); butterflyfish

RED SEA COAST | THE GUIDE

Find Your Way

Most Red Sea visitors choose a single resort and organise day trips from there. For the pioneering few, however, it's possible to travel the coastal road by bus and taxi – if patience and time allow.

TAXI
Offering a characterful form of transport for those with the stomach for fast rides over potholed roads, taxis are readily available for travelling along the entire coastal strip and to visit the Coptic monasteries. Organise taxis from resorts and hotels to reduce white-knuckle moments.

Hurghada, p352
As the undeniable hub of the Red Sea, this modern city with all the amenities of a well-established tourist industry offers plenty of sun, sea and sand.

THE GUIDE

RED SEA COAST

BUS

Stand at a bus stop in summer and you may begin to panic that you'll be waiting there a long time. Thankfully, however, this isn't the case, as regular buses connect the main Red Sea destinations (as far as Berenice) with Egypt's major cities.

Marsa Alam, p361

Giving access to the Red Sea's 'Deep South', this small coastal town is a gateway to a more ecofriendly underwater adventure and an insight into the Bedouin way of life.

Plan Your Days

Fully inclusive diving or resort packages make it tempting to commit yourself to a single place. With a bit of planning, however, you can sample the full character of the region, both offshore and inland.

Hurghada Marina (p352)

If You Only Do One Thing

● Spend time choosing a **resort** (p357) that suits your underwater interests (there's everything from diving, snorkelling and glass-bottom-boating to parasailing and jet skiing on offer) and discover why people the world over flock to this destination. Learn how the **Red Sea** (p356) got its name and why its water is so crystal clear. Depending on your location, look for dugongs, the gentle giants of the seagrass, watch pods of **spinner dolphins** (p362) spiral out of the sea, and enjoy meeting sea turtles in their natural habitat. Swim next to vibrant corals and learn about preservation programs. Resorts with house reefs allow even non-swimmers to wade through the shallows and see spectacular marine life such as angelfish, bannerfish and butterflyfish.

SEASONAL HIGHLIGHTS

From beaches and water sports to deserts and celebrations, there's something wonderful to see and do all year long.

MARCH
With optimal water temperatures, March is a popular time for divers and those visiting to get their diving certification.

APRIL
Open-air bazaars start popping up and salted fish fills the markets for Egypt's Sham An Nessim spring holiday.

MAY
An ideal month to time your diving safari, with great weather and the chance to avoid the crowds before summer.

A Week in the North

● Base yourself at a resort in **Hurghada** (p352) and learn there's more to this mega-tourism destination than a beach holiday by taking a **city tour** (p352), visiting the excellent new **museum** (p352), admiring the architecture of the **Grand Mosque** (p354), visiting **Halaka Fish Market** (p354) for a seafood feast, then venturing to the **marina** (p352) to enjoy the nightlife. Slow the pace with a day or two at the residential and marina complex of **El Gouna** (p358) with its attractive cafe culture. Don't overdo the chill, though, because it would be a cultural crime to miss the monasteries of **St Paul** and **St Anthony** (p359), which make for an ideal day-long outing by tour or prebooked taxi from Hurghada.

A Few Days in the Deep South

● Here's fair warning: if you pitch up at the ecofriendly resort of **Marsa Shagra** (p361) with its pristine house reef and offshore access to magical Elphinstone Reef you won't want to go anywhere else! For those who do tear themselves away from the stunning dive sites, there's kitesurfing at **Hamata** (p365) and dolphin-spotting from **Marsa Wadi Lahami** (p365). Reserve a day, too, for an off-road excursion with the Bedouin to the Roman emerald mines of **Wadi Gimal** (p366). On the way back north, stop off at **Al Quseir** (p364). It was once an important port, and its old quarter is an interesting place for a stroll.

THE GUIDE

RED SEA COAST

AUGUST	**OCTOBER**	**NOVEMBER**	**DECEMBER**
A popular time for water sports, but Hurghada is humid, and this isn't the month for daytime desert safaris.	Actors and directors from all over the world come for the red-carpet Gouna Film Festival.	Desert safari season begins as desert temperatures become optimal both day and night.	Christmas and New Year celebrations are marked with fireworks and parties at resorts, restaurants and clubs. Low season for snorkelling and diving.

Hurghada

BEACHES | ISLANDS | EXCITING NIGHTLIFE

☑ TOP TIP

If you're travelling on a budget and not staying at a beachfront resort, you can enjoy the beach at beach clubs, resorts and private beaches for as little as LE100 for a day entry.

GETTING AROUND

Without a knowledge of Arabic, it's best to leave the bus to local residents and navigate Hurghada by taxi. Identifying an on-call taxi company from the outset avoids the need to use expensive hotel taxis for short trips and saves the struggle of trying to negotiate a reasonable price at the roadside.

Hurghada has a longstanding reputation as a place independent travellers love to loathe. With its back-to-back resorts, package-holiday emphasis and former preponderance of blandly globalised dining and shopping experiences, only the diving remained as a reason to visit. Even that suffered a dispiriting record of environmental catastrophe as ill-regulated developments brought illegal landfill offshore and overtourism detrimental to the reefs.

But this is not the Hurghada of today. While mass tourism continues to leave a chequered legacy, the income it has contributed over the years has allowed for new, more positive developments. These include an excellent museum, a lively marina area and attractive landscaping, combined with a genuine attempt to ensure more responsible underwater adventures. As a major transport hub, Hurghada is now the obvious first port of call when visiting the Red Sea and is also a sociable gathering point for less-travelled destinations further south.

Sun, Sea & City
An evening tour of Hurghada

With their all-inclusive packages, resorts can make it hard to venture beyond the foyer, but for those who do manage to stray outside, Hurghada has much to explore. Three-hour guided tours are offered by most hotels, but it's easy to take a taxi and make up your own itinerary (fixing the fare in advance). To avoid losing a day's sun and sea and to enjoy the city at its liveliest, leave it until late afternoon.

Start with a trip to **Hurghada Museum** in the city suburbs. Housing beautiful artefacts from recent Egyptian history, it also showcases some gems of antiquity. Next, head to **Ad Dahar Souq** in the most 'Egyptian' part of the city, and join the throngs of local shoppers haggling for textiles, readymade clothing and perfumes. In contrast to the cramped lanes of the bazaar, the pedestrianised **Hurghada Marina** in Sigala,

HURGHADA

⭐ HIGHLIGHTS
1 Hurghada Marina

● SIGHTS
2 Giftun Islands
3 Gota Abu Ramada
4 Grand Mosque
5 Hurghada Museum
6 Shedwan Island
7 Umm Qamar

● ACTIVITIES
8 Aquanaut Diving Club
9 Diving Star
10 Jasmin Diving Centre
11 Subex

● SLEEPING
12 Bedcoin Hostel
13 Oberoi Sahl Hasheesh
14 Steigenberger Al Dau Beach Hotel

● EATING
15 Abu Khadijah
16 El Dar Darak
17 El Halaka
18 Halaka Fish Market
19 Star Fish

● DRINKING & NIGHTLIFE
20 Caribbean Beach Bar
21 El Mashrabiya
22 Little Buddha
23 Tito's

● SHOPPING
24 Ad Dahar Souq

WHY I LOVE AD DAHAR SOUQ

Lama Obeid, Lonely Planet writer

A stroll along the streets of this seemingly never-ending souq among locals and more adventurous visitors stimulates all my senses. Sipping fresh sugar-cane juice, I follow the scent of freshly baked *fiteer* (sweet or savoury flaky pastry) into a local bakery. The market is buzzing with families and window shoppers. Proprietors call out 'Welcome!' to invite us into their stores and sell us their magic creams, which they promise will leave us with skin as clear as Cleopatra's. Tuk-tuks, cars and motorbikes whiz by, creating a charming chaos. With my treasures in my bags, I end my spree with a heart-filling bowl of *kushari* (a mix of noodles, rice, black lentils, fried onions and tomato sauce).

Hurghada's visitor hub, offers a breezy sunset stroll. With themed restaurants and cosy dockside bars, it's a perfect spot for sundowners.

From the marina it's a short hop to the **Grand Mosque**, which looks particularly striking at night, and end the tour with dinner at the famed **Star Fish**, a veritable Sigala institution. Here the catches of the day from the Red Sea and the Mediterranean are displayed on ice. A typical meal includes fish soup, grilled fillets priced by weight, salad and bread, and a glass of hot *karkade* (hibiscus tea) to finish. It's only a short hop from here to local Arab sweet shops. A few nuggets of nougat may help distract you from the apparently free-for-all driving as you head back to base.

A Seafood Feast at the Fish Market
Enjoy a local dining experience

Navigating the **Halaka Fish Market** (p351) as a visitor and having a meal there isn't too difficult, even if you don't speak Arabic. All you need are a few hand gestures and a calculator to confirm prices. Head inside and take a walk around (take it carefully, as the floors are often wet and slippery from the ice used to keep the fish fresh). After choosing your catch of the day, stand at the stall to place your order. Prices are per kilogram, and orders start at a quarter of a kilogram for seafood such as shrimp, calamari and oysters. If you're in the mood for fish, choose one and ask to have it weighed. Then, the fun part: you can have it cooked as you like. You can enjoy your meal as takeaway, but if you dine in you can order side plates of salad and rice that will be added to your tab. There's a small cost per person (LE15 to LE20) to dine in. You pay your bill, including the dine-in fee, after you finish your meal.

Hunting for Hare
Visiting Hurghada Museum

Picture this: a man carries a gazelle draped around his neck while a dog trots along at his feet. In his left hand he has a hare by the ears. Each game animal appears plump and well, even if it's destined for an early afterlife. The image is a touching one and crops up all over Egypt. When asked about the origin of the image, tomb guardians in Luxor each identify a different tomb – but minus the hare. Even a search engine dedicated to the identification of ancient Egyptian painting is elusive on the point of this third animal.

 EATING IN HURGHADA: OUR PICKS

El Dar Darak: Family restaurant playing songs of the Nubian artist Mohammed Mounir. One dish is enough per person, or order a few to share. *1pm-1am Sat-Fri* $$

Abu Khadijah: Typical local restaurant where your order is a full meal including salad, a vegetable side dish, soup and bread. *2-11pm Sat-Fri* $

Halaka Fish Market: Choose your fish or seafood, specify how you want it cooked and then order your side dishes. *9am-9pm Sat-Fri* $$

Al Halaka: Right in front of the fish market, this fish restaurant is a good family-friendly option. *noon-midnight Sat-Fri* $$

Hurghada Museum

Imagine the excitement, then, of finding a whole section of the new museum in Hurghada dedicated to artefacts depicting hunting and animal husbandry. And yes! There's the man with his gazelle, dog and hare on the information board, and here he is again, inscribed in stone on a piece of ancient carving...minus the hare.

Hunting for hares may not be your thing, but chances are you'll find something to be equally excited about in the perfectly formed **Hurghada Museum**. Small enough to enjoy in an hour but detailed enough in the areas of pottery, jewellery and the magnificent golden mummies of the Western Desert to warrant a return visit, this new museum is a joint venture between public and private parties, bringing a share of the country's heritage to Egypt's major cities. This explains the somewhat odd spectacle of a fixed-priced duty-free-style shopping arcade between the ticket office and the display rooms.

Still something of a work in progress, the museum (which includes beautiful Coptic artefacts and 19th-century jewellery) is open until late in the evening, and you'll likely be the only one visiting – together, that is, with one escaped long-eared herbivore.

COPTIC ART

Overshadowed by ancient art, the Coptic aesthetic tradition seldom receives the attention it deserves from visitors, despite its long pedigree. Originating in ancient Egypt and Greece, and largely practical in nature, it found rich expression in textiles, icons and wall paintings.

Striking Coptic art can be seen in museums and churches throughout Egypt, and especially in the monasteries of the Eastern Desert. Early Coptic Christians converted Egyptian temples into churches, covering Pharaonic reliefs with layers of plaster and overlaying pagan images with Christian ones. The mastery of dye mixing and gold stencilling led to a distinct Coptic style that is rich in symbolism. Some of the most resplendent examples of the style can be seen in the church at St Anthony's monastery.

DRINKING IN HURGHADA: OUR PICKS

Little Buddha: As the name suggests, this bar and club has a Buddha theme. Its DJ parties attract locals and international visitors. *3pm-4am Sat-Fri*

Carribean Beach Bar: Breezy beachside bar that's perfect for sundowners and often features live music. *7am-midnight Sat-Fri*

El Mashrabiya: Stretching along Sharia Sheraton, Sigala's main road, this local favourite serves juices, teas and shisha. *9am-midnight Sat-Fri*

Tito's: Enjoy the sunset and a shisha at this seafront open-air cafe-restaurant. There's a small entry fee. *9am-2am Sat-Fri*

BEST DIVE COMPANIES

Jasmin Diving Centre: The reef is protected partly thanks to this founding member of the Hurghada Environmental Protection & Conservation Association (HEPCA).

Aquanaut Diving Club: Longstanding Hurghada dive centre located off Sharia Sheraton.

Subex: Friendly, professional dive centre that only caters to small groups. It's ideal for independent travellers.

Hurghada Diving Centre: Diving school offering courses in various languages and expeditions with small groups.

Diving Star: School providing daily excursions and a seven-day diving safari across the Red Sea.

Bannerfish

Crystal Clear
Enjoying Red Sea water sports

Despite being renowned as one of the warmest (and saltiest) seas in the world, the Red Sea can still feel chilly in winter. Wading out, even in a wetsuit, takes determination at that time of year. But then there's that wonderful moment when the water washes over your mask and you come face-to-face with an extraordinary vision of light, colour and movement. With its exceptional clarity, the water alone is entertaining, with light shattering over the shallows in intricate designs. And then comes the marine life. The first sighting of lemon yellow on a butterfly fish or the pennant-waving fin of a bannerfish are thrilling experiences. Colour and shape seem extra sharp when suspended in the cut-glass water. All the excitement of the encounter is wrapped up in those first few moments of immersion – and that's before you even reach the reef.

The accessibility of some of the world's finest reefs is one of the reasons Egypt's Red Sea coast has become a world-class destination. Even if water sports aren't your thing, it's worth at least donning a mask and snorkel and wading in for a look.

For divers and snorkellers the opportunities here are legion. While the reefs immediately around Hurghada are damaged, there are still exceptional sites just offshore. The nearby **Giftun Islands**, for example, form part of a marine reserve with diving at depths up to 100m, or there's neighbouring **Gota Abu Ramada**, suitable for novice and night divers and popular with underwater photographers. Pilot whales and large pods of dolphins make **Shedwan Island** another popular option, while wreck divers will enjoy the explosion of life around the coral towers of **Umm Qamar**.

If there's one thing more crystal clear than the waters of the Red Sea it's that peering under the waves here shouldn't be missed, even if you just enjoy the sight from a glass-bottom boat.

Heaven or Hell?
Hurghada's resort experience

You can't write about Hurghada and not mention the resort experience, not least because it's a divisive issue that tends to make distinctions between travellers and tourists (though many would argue there are no such distinctions). It's hard to put your finger on what makes the resort experience heaven for some and hell for others. Everyone likes a sea view, and most resorts offer at least a glimpse of the Red Sea's famous multi-hued, crystal-clear waters. Most people enjoy a bit of beach, and with raked sand, sunshades and fresh towels, most resorts have this covered too. Many resorts offer a whole range of water sports in addition to diving and snorkelling, and there are even well-organised trips around town and out to nearby places of cultural interest. As a set, the resorts with their gardens of hollyhocks and vincas, wind-blown palms and scented frangipani have brought a garden habitat to the previously rocky shores of the Red Sea, attracting insects and birds where previously there were few.

With excellent deals on all-inclusive rates, patrolled pools for kids, often nightly entertainment and people from around the world to meet, one wonders what there is to dislike – and therein lies the problem. It's almost too pleasant, too easy and too organised: for the dogged few, travel perhaps relies on spontaneity and even punishing endeavour to be truly satisfying. For a day or two, though, there's much to be said for plumping up your pillow and enjoying Egypt's well-practised version of service with a smile.

COPTIC TREASURES

Mesmerised by the beauty of Coptic art in Hurghada Museum? Don't miss viewing it in situ at **St Anthony's monastery** (p359). With arguably the finest examples of *secco* (painting applied to dry plaster) in the Coptic tradition, the murals here have been restored to their 13th-century brilliance.

BEST SPAS SOUTH OF HURGHADA

Baron Palace Sahl Hasheesh: Romantics will enjoy the swim-up suites and private pools, while 2300 sq metres of spa delivers luxury treatments.

Jaz Makadi Star & Spa: After a traditional Egyptian treatment in the spa there's shopping and entertainment at nearby Souk Makadi.

Mövenpick Waterpark Resort & Spa Soma Bay: Kids keep busy in the extensive waterpark, leaving parents free to enjoy the sophisticated spa.

Cleopatra Luxury Resort Makadi Bay: Equipped with a full Turkish hammam.

Premier Le Reve Hotel & Spa: Adults-only resort that's heaven for holidaying couples. Ruma spa offers relaxing treatments.

Beyond Hurghada

Take a more relaxed approach to the resort experience at El Gouna or escape it all in the mountain monasteries.

Places
El Gouna p358
Monastery of St Paul p359
Monastery of St Anthony p359

GETTING AROUND

El Gouna is a 30-minute bus or taxi journey from Hurghada. Buses leave the main plaza every 20 minutes between 7am and midnight. The resort complex is 20km from Hurghada airport and is also connected (by Go Bus Co) to Cairo.

You can visit the monasteries on a long day tour from Hurghada (organised through most hotels) or by taxi. The distance between the monasteries is over 80km by road, so not all tours cover both.

Everyone knows that relaxation can be taxing, especially along Hurghada's resort strip, where each day, package guests arrive full of excitement for the holiday ahead. For those looking for respite from all that enthusiastic energy, a retreat to El Gouna, 30km north, may do the trick. The resort concept has long since spilt over from Hurghada, spreading south as well as north to Sahl Hasheesh, Makadi Bay and Soma Bay, each chasing an ever-decreasing sense of retreat.

For a true escape, follow Coptic monks inland on a tour of two monasteries. Founded 1600 years ago, these fascinating complexes developed around the hermitages of St Paul and St Anthony, and the appeal of asceticism remains alive to this day.

El Gouna

TIME FROM HURGHADA: **30 MINS**

City retreat

While Hurghada offers many cultural and nightlife opportunities, it can be hard to escape the constant din of a thriving city. There's the honking of car horns in downtown traffic, the call to prayer from the many mosques, the revving up of tour buses and outboard motors, and the construction noise of the latest resort or refurbishment activity after the COVID-19 pandemic. Even the humble lawnmower in the resort gardens makes it hard to enjoy a lie-in, as does the buzz of the sheer number of guests in the winter high season.

If it's peace you're after, you may be best heading 40km north to the low-rise, low-key tourist and residential complex of El Gouna. Here (other than during the film festival in October), the loudest noise is likely to be the chink of wine glasses over a late lunch or the flapping of halyards against the masts of chic boats. Electric buggies whisk visitors from the marina with its boutiques and Mediterranean-style restaurants to 'downtown', where rows of souvenir shops and cafes arranged around canals and lagoons make a perfect setting for an afternoon's stroll.

With 10km of sandy beachfront and excellent Red Sea activities on offer, El Gouna is an upmarket version of the friendly Sinai camps but marketed at a more independent clientele. As a result, individual travellers may feel more at home here than at the big city resorts that cater almost exclusively for all-inclusive tour groups. Best of all, there's no compulsory tagging by rubber bracelet to identify your meal plan!

Monastery of St Paul

TIME FROM HURGHADA: **2 HRS 30 MINS**

Community in the desert

Pilgrims come from all over the world to pay their respects at the **tomb of St Paul the Anchorite**. Although no longer reached at the end of an arduous journey across an unforgiving desert, the 5th-century monastery built around the saint's hermitage is still off the beaten track, hidden in the northern mountains of Egypt's Eastern Desert. The sense of isolation is absolute, with high walls looming above the desert floor, repelling Bedouin attack in the past and in modern times attempting to keep distractions at bay.

The common thread in a tradition that spans centuries (excepting a few interruptions) is the community of monastic life. There are currently 120 monks in residence, and the sense of brotherhood is felt in the greetings between members, in the tributes to a recently deceased monk who cared for the compound's cats and in the discipline required to ensure a harmonious existence in a cloistered space.

Several parts of the monastery, including the chapel with its beautiful wall paintings and the original refectory, are open to visitors. The miracle of water has made life here possible, and visitors are shown where it issues from the rock in unchanging volume. Some of the water is diverted into the garden at the heart of the monastery. This little oasis of date palms, fruit trees and vegetable plots still supplements the monks' table, showing that 'hope springs eternal' even in the harshest of environments – a fitting metaphor, explains one of the guiding fathers, of a life dedicated to prayer.

Check opening hours before journeying to the Coptic monasteries. Access is restricted during Advent and Lent, and the monastery is closed to visitors at Christmas and Easter.

Monastery of St Anthony

TIME FROM HURGHADA: **3 HRS**

Stairway to heaven

If after you've climbed half of the 1804 steps to the **cave of St Anthony** you feel the effort in your limbs, spare a thought

WHO WAS ST PAUL THE ANCHORITE?

History suggests that Christianity's first hermit was a wealthy 3rd-century Alexandrian who fled at a young age to the Eastern Desert to escape Roman persecution. Living alone in a mountain cave, sustained only by spring water and dates, St Paul was joined in solitude by a raven who, according to legend, brought him half a loaf of bread daily until he died, aged well over 100. It's said he was buried by his only other visitor, St Anthony (the founder of monasticism), with the help of two lions. St Paul is often represented by a palm tree, a raven and lions, symbols that remain important in the iconography of his last resting place.

EATING IN EL GOUNA: OUR PICKS

Le Garage: Fancy your burger served with truffles and edible gold leaf? This marina-side venue serves gourmet patties. *1pm-2am Sat-Fri* **$$**

Zia Amelia: Book early for El Gouna's cutest restaurant. The homestyle Italian dishes are extra enjoyable under the vines. *1.30-11.30pm* **$$**

Moods Restaurant & Beach Club El Gouna: Enjoy a meal on the patio or, better yet, order while you're at the private beachfront. *9am-2am Thu-Sat, to 1am Sun-Wed* **$$$**

Tandoor Restaurant: Welcoming outdoor seating area and a range of Indian and vegetarian dishes. Within the Ali Pasha hotel. *7.30-10.30am & noon-10.30pm Sat-Fri* **$$**

Monastery of St Anthony (p359)

LIVING LIKE A MONK

Postulants may no longer need to winch themselves into the fortified monastic compound on a rope through a trapdoor, but there's still nothing easy about being a monk in the modern world. Aside from the rules of obedience, chastity and poverty, the brothers must fulfil the cultural obligation of being a beacon of faith in a material world. Comfort is found, according to the monks, in the teaching of St Anthony; even he grew bored in the sequestered life and turned instead to a little work, a little food and a little rest, interspersed with prayer. Today's monks continue in this tradition, reaching out to local communities with their specialities in medicine, agriculture and technology while continuing their own spiritual journeys.

for the monks who every night make the same ascent for midnight Mass from the ancient Coptic monastery below. 'You get used to it', says one of the fathers assigned to guiding visitors. 'You focus on prayer and the walking just happens.' Clearly, that takes practice: a multitude of mundanities compete to crowd out the pieties for most mortals endeavouring to make the climb.

As you reach the summit of the stairway, though, the effort suddenly makes sense. A tiny cave, the ascetic home of St Anthony for 80 years, lies unguarded at the top. It's barely big enough to enter, and the walls of the narrow defile are polished smooth by the hands of countless pilgrims. Slowly the eye makes out a tiny chapel and an icon looms out of the darkness.

From the cave entrance the desert expands across the view, almost trackless and without human feature. Even the monastery – the oldest in the world with its 4th-century church of celebrated wall paintings and tiny monks' cells – shrinks back into nature. The height, the space and the breadth of nature combine to offer a different perspective from the onward rush of ordinary life. It's little wonder, then, that some of St Anthony's monks (nine at present) continue to seek solitude in the caves and crevices of a hermit's life lived in the privilege of prayer.

A MEETING OF MINDS

It's said that at the venerable age of 90, in 343 CE, St Anthony had a vision of neighbouring hermit St Paul and made the arduous trek over the mountains to meet him. They communed for a day and a night, and shared raven-delivered bread (p359).

Marsa Alam

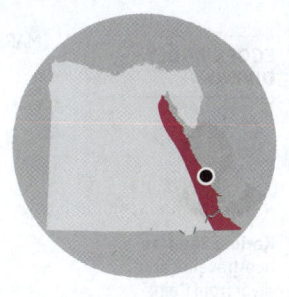

STARGAZING | MARINE LIFE | MOUNTAIN VIEWS

Blink and you might miss Marsa Alam. Lying 230km south of Safaga (at the Nile–Red Sea junction), this small fishing town acts as a resupply point for the Bedouin and a hub for independent travellers hoping to arrange a Deep South adventure.

At first sight, with its dusty bazaar and string of low-key tour agents, Marsa Alam makes an unlikely gateway for a Red Sea encounter. But it has hidden charm: it sits on the doorstep of Wadi Gimal National Park. Comprising 4770 sq km of mountainous desert terrain, this protected area also encompasses 2100 sq km of marine territory. With 450 species of coral supporting 1200 types of fish, this haven of aquatic life attracts divers from around the world.

The secret's getting out, though, and resorts now dot the coast on either side of Marsa Alam. Most keep a low profile, however, in pleasant contrast to the mega-resorts of the north.

Diving the Deep South

The dive centre experience

Dedicated to the underwater experience, **Marsa Shagra Village** offers inclusivity for all levels of seaworthiness, diving instruction, simple but good food, tranquil chalet or tented accommodation and opportunities to meet Bedouin people. Even a North Sea diver with 3000 dives under their belt is expected to spend day one on paperwork and a check dive, a precaution appreciated by most as part of the log-keeping discipline of the diving fraternity.

Marsa Shagra is one of many highly organised, well-run resorts along the Marsa Alam coastline. This outfit outperforms most in its dedication to preserving the underwater environment. If a lionfish has made its home under the jetty and squads of pipefish marshal in the shallows, that's partly due to this commitment to good practice. While this resort pioneered ecofriendly activity, other resorts have since

☑ TOP TIP

Although it's possible to arrive in Marsa Alam and organise accommodation and diving through the tour operators in town, it's worth doing some homework first to pick the resort that best suits your interests and budget. Most resorts can arrange transfers along the coast if you want to explore further south.

GETTING AROUND

In Marsa Alam airport pick-ups are available by taxi or you can arrange transport through your accommodation. Private company Egybus runs daily buses between Hurghada and Marsa Alam. Renting a car is a good option here, as traffic is very light in Marsa Alam and it's an easy place to drive around, especially if you want to venture into the city.

ECOFRIENDLY DIVING

Karima Saad, an eco-traveller and diver from Cairo, offers some tips for sustainable diving. @_karima

Red Sea Diving Safari *(redsea-divingsafari. com)* actively protects the reefs in front of their camps. It also protects the mangroves at its Wadi Lahami location. The team has worked for 30 years with HEPCA and the Red Sea Protectorate to build an environmentally friendly diving model.

At its three locations you will find a variety of room and tent types. The food is excellent, and the stay includes three meals per day. My favourite is the peaceful Wadi Lahami location. You can enjoy diving as well as windsurfing there thanks to the shallow lagoon. In the early mornings the mangroves attract a variety of birds.

followed suit with strict prohibitions on touching the reef and boats moored carefully. The most satisfying underwater experiences are enjoyed from resorts with a similar ethos.

Sataya Reef Dolphin House
Surreal underwater tour

Located 130km from Marsa Alam, **Sataya Reef** is home to abundant pods of spinner dolphins. You can book a trip to visit them from one of the local **tour operators** *(from per person US$65; marsaalamtours.com)* in the city centre, at your accommodation or online. Fluctuations in price tend to be tied to the length of time your guide will spend snorkelling with you. Trips take place just twice a week, so you'll need to plan in advance.

From Hamata harbour it's a 2½-hour boat ride to the reef. Head to the bow to watch the dolphins jump in and out of the pristine water along the way. As you near the reef, get your gear ready and then follow your guide into a speedboat, which will take you to the area where you'll be able to swim near the dolphins. As you swim, stay close to your guide, as they'll be the one pointing you in the direction of the dolphin pods. Keep a safe distance from the dolphins at all times so they don't feel threatened. You can snap some photos with your waterproof camera or pose for the underwater photographer to take your photo. The dolphins don't live near coral, but you'll still be able to spot some schools of fish swimming by.

There are coral reefs in Sataya, and most operators will give you the opportunity to explore the different fish and vibrant coral in a second snorkelling foray. In between snorkelling trips you can recharge on the boat and have lunch and refreshments.

Wild dolphins at Sataya Reef

The dolphins of Sataya Reef once lived undisturbed in their habitat, but that changed as bigger boats drove mass tourism to the area. Many marine-life professionals and enthusiasts began speaking to the authorities to have protective regulations put in place, as they did for other reefs in the country. Their efforts led the Hurghada Environmental Protection and Conservation Association (HEPCA) to come up with a plan to protect the reef. In 2013 Sataya was divided into different zones, with zones A1 and A2 closed to any activity other than scientific research. There are now zones for snorkelling, diving, small boats and larger tourist boats. A tourist tax funds the supervision of a park ranger, who has the authority to issue fines to anyone breaking the regulations.

A limited number of boats, snorkellers and divers are allowed into the reef, and tour operators must obtain a permit for each of their guests. Boats are only allowed in the reef at specific times: 10am to 2pm for boats with snorkellers and 9am to 3pm for boats with divers. Check the latest HEPCA regulations before you visit to avoid any disturbance to the reef's marine life.

BEST SOUTHERN DIVES

Elphinstone Reef: A diver's favourite for its steep walls of soft coral and gorgonian fans, Elphinstone Reef is frequented by seven species of shark.

Samadai Dolphin Sanctuary: A pod of spinner dolphins (numbering up to 480) regularly visits this lagoon.

Hamada: Keeled over in just 14m of water, the *Hamada* makes an easy and beautiful first wreck dive.

Rocky Island: A sandy (rather than stony) island east of Berenice, Rocky Island has a range of dive possibilities, including a 25m drop off the east side.

Sha'ab Sharm: Impressive topography and excellent marine life mark this large, kidney-shaped reef 30km northeast of Wadi Gimal.

KEEN TO DIVE RESPONSIBLY?

Diving is the principal activity of the Deep South. Environmentalist Hossam Hassan's highly reputable company, Red Sea Diving Safari, has the whole region covered, with camps at Marsa Nakari and Wadi Lahami (p365) in addition to **Marsa Shagra** (p361).

Beyond Marsa Alam

Dive into the Deep South for an ecofriendly adventure offshore or with the camel-owning Bedouin of the rocky desert interior.

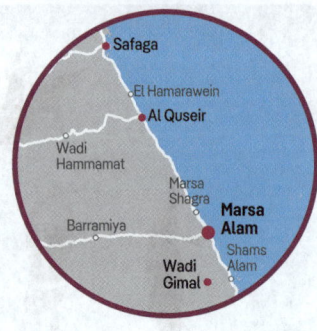

Places
Al Quseir p364
Safaga p365
Wadi Gimal p366

GETTING AROUND

Buses between Marsa Alam and Cairo stop at Al Quseir. Microbuses run around town, but to explore sites of interest it's more convenient to take a taxi from the bus station to the waterfront.

Most accommodation in Marsa Alam can arrange taxis to coastal resorts south of Marsa Alam; book a return to avoid getting stranded.

Eastern Desert tours require an official permit and can most easily be organised by **Marsa Shagra Village** (p361).

Few but the most determined divers and those looking for a more sustainable travel experience make it much beyond Marsa Alam, but if you're unfazed by potholed roads it's worth the effort. There's excellent diving around Wadi Lahami in the Deep South, and windy conditions attract kitesurfing enthusiasts to Hamata. Nearer to Marsa Alam lies inspiring Wadi Gimal, home to the nomadic Ababda people and boasting a rich history connected with gems.

Berenice with its new airport is currently the most southerly point open to visitors, and mass tourism may someday develop here and around the interesting town of Al Quseir. For now, though, this area offers the chance to get closer to nature in lower-impact, more ecofriendly lodges.

Al Quseir
TIME FROM MARSA ALAM: **1 HR 30 MINS**

Faded glory in the Old Quarter

The windswept, 5000-year-old city of Al Quseir, known as Tjau in ancient Egypt, knows a thing or two about life's fortunes. In ancient times it was a major port with, according to one Greek historian, a fleet of 120 ships delivering pottery, enslaved people and wine to the African kingdom of Punt in exchange for spices, silk and stone. These precious goods were transported by camel caravan across the Eastern Desert to Qift for dispersal along the Nile to Alexandria and the Mediterranean. In later years the port played a role in the Ottoman Empire and the British trade route with India. A final flourish in the early 20th century brought wealth through the phosphate industry, but with the Suez Canal established as the main artery of the region, the town slipped into decline. Even Al Quseir's long history as a point of departure for pilgrims bound for Mecca has been eclipsed by the port of Safaga further up the Red Sea coast.

So with its glory days behind it, who passes through town now? Very few, if truth be told. Intrepid tour groups venture out from nearby resorts after a day of kite-surfing and the occasional independent traveller holes up at the shorefront hotel, but otherwise the town has faded into quiet obscurity.

But that's exactly what makes Al Quseir so fascinating. It offers a rare chance to explore a town going about its daily business without any special attempt to be something else. Spending an afternoon strolling around this ancient village is like stepping into a rather derelict time warp. Seek out Al Quseir's 16th-century **Ottoman fortress**, which is especially evocative with its fortified walls, watchtower, cistern and courtyards. It houses a small, dusty exhibition of artefacts such as coffee cups from Yemen and pipes dating from the Ottoman Empire. Nearby is the port, backed by the old **granary**, which dates to the early 19th century, when it was used to store wheat bound for Mecca. Also near the port is the attractive **Faran mosque**, the town's oldest mosque, with its early-18th-century minaret, named after Sheikh Faran, a leader of an Arab tribe.

Continue your stroll with some enjoyable shopping in the small bazaar before heading to an excellent fish supper at **El Fardous**, where you can enjoy its famous lobster and shellfish on the shoreside.

Visitors to Al Quseir are also rewarded with old-fashioned hospitality. It might take the form of a herbal infusion from a shop owner, Arabic blessings bestowed by grandmothers or a nod from shisha-smoking *hajis* parked under the decaying *mashrabiyyas* (wooden shutters) of merchant houses that gesture to the town's long-ago wealth.

Safaga

TIME FROM MARSA ALAM: **2 HR 40 MINS**

Kitesurfing south of Marsa Alam

Step onto the shore anywhere south of Marsa Alam on an afternoon in March and you may find it difficult to stand upright. The wind keeps such a strong and steady pace that it helps define the very geology of the area, with eroded sandstone a feature of the rocky rim between shore and mountain. That's not good news for the sunbather, but it's excellent news for the kitesurfer who this is perfect weather for.

While El Gouna boasts year-round kitesurfing and wake boarding for all levels of skill, and Safaga (at the junction with the Nile road) is the key spot for windsurfing, kitesurfing aficionados head for the more rugged experience of the southern Red Sea. The **Kite Village** at Hamata offers the biggest station in all of Egypt for this activity, together with stand-up paddle boarding, and there's a centre at **Wadi Lahami** too. On a breezy day, 50 or more kites fill the sky, while boards skid along in an uninterrupted stretch of mangrove-rimmed water.

Intermediate-level kitesurfers can find shallow, flat waves at Al Quseir at Helioland and Shaab El Kenz.

GUARDIANS OF THE DESERT

For millennia the Eastern Desert has been home to the nomadic Ababda tribe, and until the 20th century the extent of their territory remained as described by their historical foes the Romans. Today a small number of these camel herders continue to live in their ancestral territory between Marsa Alam and Wadi Gimal.

Living in huts decorated with handwoven rugs, Ababda people have traditionally reared camels and livestock, but many now work alongside the tourist industry, typically as camp guards and guides. While sensitivity is required to avoid exploitative encounters, camel or 4WD safaris into their desert heartland offer a valuable chance to learn about Ababda culture, listen to their rhythmical music and sample *jibena* (sweetened coffee prepared from freshly roasted beans).

EATING AROUND AL QUSEIR: BEST SEAFOOD

El Fardous: With a cosy interior and shoreside tables, this local favourite prepares delicious lobster and shellfish. *10am-11pm* **$$**

Seagull's Restaurant: This fine-dining spot overlooking the Dead Sea offers a romantic atmosphere and a la carte dinner. *6.30am-10pm* **$$$**

Divers Club: In the sumptuous grounds of the Mövenpick, this alfresco venue serves fish with Swiss flair. *noon-6pm* **$$$**

Madeira Sea Food: This beachfront venue popular with locals and visitors prepares a rich, creamy seafood soup. *noon-midnight* **$**

ACTIVITIES ABOVE THE WATER

Lahami Bay Beach Resort & Gardens: With a protective reef and excellent wind patterns, this place has some of the Red Sea's finest windsurfing.

Kite-Village Hamata: Running basic, refresher and 'crash' courses (the latter not literally), this outfit caters for all levels of kitesurfing ability.

Marsa Alam Tours: Parasailing flights from Makadi take up to three people with no training required.

Bedouin Tent Marsa Alam: Offering serene desert excursions by horse and camel in Marsa Alam.

Marsa Alam Excursions: Join adrenaline-stimulating ATV quad tours in the desert of Marsa Alam.

Kite safaris have also become a sought-after adventure for advanced kitesurfers. You can spend a week at sea visiting the best kitesurfing spots in the area.

Wadi Gimal   TIME FROM MARSA ALAM: 1 HR 30 MINS (4WD)

Looking after dhub and crow

Undecided between a tomato scrap above and a cucumber slice below, a spiny-tailed dhub (a kind of lizard) lies prone on a slab of rock in between and changes colour. Suddenly the shadow of a crow floats above and the dhub darts into the nearest crevice, only its magnificent tail left protruding in the midday sun. Two empty tuna cans topped up with water – one for dhub and one for crow – await the settling of their dispute.

This is what makes a day in the desert in the company of the Bedouin so special. If you visit **Wadi Gimal National Park** on one of these excursions there are also the interesting ruins of a Roman temple to explore and the clearly visible remnants of workers' dwellings scattered across the arid valley floor. Nearby are the shafts of the ancient mines where these labourers would once have toiled, mining the desert escarpment for emeralds in support of the Roman Empire. Peer at the ground around these aged earthworks, the largest of their kind, and it seems to jump with glancing specks of light from mica-like deposits. These indicate the likely presence of beryl, the family to which emeralds belong. Mounds and middens show that caravan routes have passed this way for centuries, perhaps attracted by the possibility of hidden gems. All these relics of the past remain interesting to this day, but it's the living legacy of continued human occupation of the area, expressed through the Badawis' finely tuned interaction with their environment, that proves the most memorable.

The nomadic ability to make the most of very little is instructive. A loaf of flour and water is baked in the embers of a fire that has brewed tea. A *shimag* is used as headdress, scarf, rope, tray and tablecloth. Slices of cucumber never taste so good as when they're used as spoons for bean stew that has been cooked over a fire, the wood for which has been carefully culled from the brittle underside of an aged acacia.

It's this economy that takes little and still has something left to share with other members of the desert community – dhub and crow – that marks the Bedouin life. It also makes a day in their company well worth giving up a session of diving for. Tours can be organised through **Marsa Shagra Village** (p361).

Places We Love to Stay

$ Budget $$ Midrange $$ Top End

Hurghada
MAP p353

Bedcoin Hostel $ With modern design, this family-owned business is popular with backpackers and solo travellers. It's within walking distance of Hurghada Marina and most attractions in the city.

Steigenberger Al Dau Beach Hotel $$ Large, tastefully decorated rooms, a mind-boggling amount of activities on offer and an absolutely mammoth pool make the Steigenberger a long-running favourite for a family holiday.

Oberoi Sahl Hasheesh $$$ The Oberoi is an award-winning chain for good reason: stepping into this exquisite property, on an extensive private beach near Hurghada, is like walking into a tale from the Arabian Nights.

El Gouna
p358

Captain's Inn $$ More interested in camaraderie than cushions? This homely hotel off the main marina is the perfect home from home for water-sport enthusiasts.

La Maison Bleu $$$ This gorgeous adults-only villa and spa will delight the romantic at heart. Inspired by Minoan murals, Venetian marble and Catalan mosaic, it's borderline eccentric but, magically, it works.

Sheraton Miramar $$$ Not many hotels span several islands, but this is one of them. Fun for families, it's a retreat from reality as well as from mainland mayhem.

Marsa Alam
MAP p362

Deep South $ Palm-thatched huts, chalets painted with murals, and support for the local Ababda people make this a traveller's favourite.

Marsa Shagra Village $$ Well-organised, safety-conscious and sustainable, this is a top choice for underwater and desert encounters.

Wadi Lahami Village $$ A camp beside mangroves, Wadi Lahami offers kitesurfing and Fury Shoal dives, including Sataya Reef, which is famed for spinner dolphins.

Al Quseir
p364

Rocky Valley Beach Camp $$ Rocky Valley lures divers by offering a variety of affordable packages, which include Bedouin-style tents, beachside barbecues, late-night beach parties and some incredible reefs right off the shore.

Mövenpick Resort El Quseir $$$ Al Quseir's best hotel stretches around a coral bay 7km north of the centre, with the best rooms just above the shore.

Safaga
p365

Toubia Hotel $ Owner Hakim and his welcoming family create a homely atmosphere here, and there's a simple private beach just outside.

Menaville Resort $$ The hotel fronts a wonderful stretch of sand, and accommodation is in airy whitewashed bungalows surrounded by flowers and set around a large pool.

Nemo Dive Hotel $$ Nemo has attentive staff, neat modern decorative touches and a small, appealing beach with pool and bar. The rooftop sea-view restaurant serves simple international food and cold beers.

Steigenberger Al Dau Beach Hotel

From left: Blue Hole, Dahab (p389); sunrise at Mt Sinai (p399)

For places to stay in Sinai, see p403

Researched by
Jessica Buxbaum

Sinai

SUN, SAND AND A BEDOUIN SOUL

Spellbinding Sinai is a region of undeniable intrigue, where Egypt's loftiest mountains meet the creature-rich and coral-filled Red Sea.

Rugged and stark, the Sinai Peninsula has captured imaginations for centuries, with its deep religious significance and strategic position as a crossroads of empires.

Separated from the Egyptian mainland by the Suez Canal, Sinai is a tone shift from the rest of the country. A springboard to the Red Sea's underwater wonders, Sinai's seaside resorts offer sun-drenched holiday fun. Steer away from the coastal buzz, however, to discover Sinai's true heart, where its deep Bedouin roots show off the traditions and hospitality of the people who have long been stewards of this land.

Note that some countries have labelled parts of Sinai as 'do not travel' zones, so check with your local embassy before going.

The peninsula's sensitive location sandwiches it between a rock and a hard place, battered by a painful history of Israeli occupation, terrorist attacks and ongoing regional conflict that can quickly drive away tourists and much-needed income. But Sinai and its complex dualities soldier on. Hikers bag the peak of Egypt's highest mountain, and divers plunge into the depths of the sea. Basic palm-frond beach huts lie down the coast from internationally branded luxury resorts with sumptuous spas and infinity pools. Away from the coast's hubbub, hiking trails and star-studded nights in the mountains are enveloped in profound silence. No matter which side of Sinai you see, it casts a spell over all who visit.

KYLIE NICHOLSON/SHUTTERSTOCK

THE MAIN AREAS

SHARM EL SHEIKH
Reams of Red Sea resorts. **p374**

DAHAB
Laid-back coastal hub for free spirits. **p386**

Find Your Way

Sinai's main traveller hubs are dotted along the eastern coast, from Sharm El Sheikh at the southern tip to Taba at the border with Israel and the Palestinian Territories. The only commercial airport is in Sharm.

TOUR
Accommodation places of all sizes and stature offer guided tours and activities in and on the Red Sea and into Sinai's interior. Though tours are usually the easiest way to see the sights, they can be impersonal, and group sizes are often large.

TAXI
If you'd rather fly solo than join a big tour, you can negotiate with a driver to take you between Sinai's cities. Taxis are usually best organised through your accommodation or the activity operator, though hotels can upcharge significantly.

BUS
Taking the bus is the cheapest option for getting around Sinai, as well as to Cairo and elsewhere in Egypt, but there are only a few daily departures. East Delta and Go Bus services run along the coast from Sharm El Sheikh to Taba.

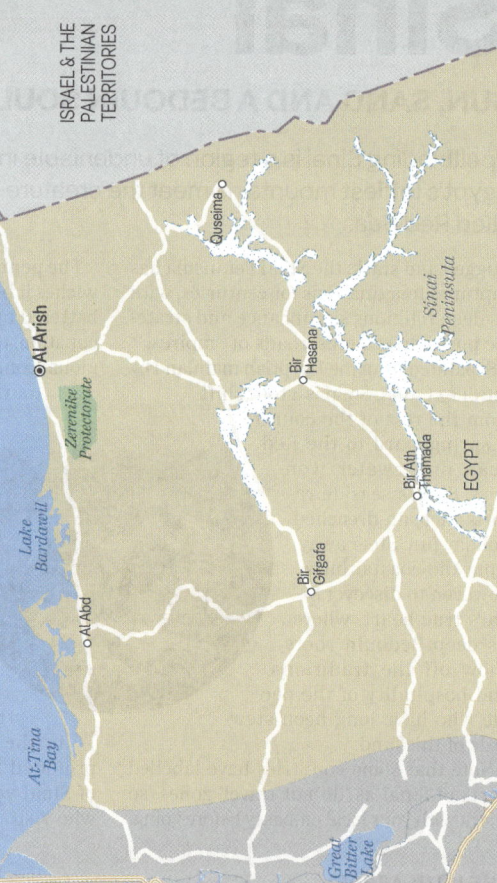

Plan Your Days

This region is no place to hustle. Sinai's coastal treasures are the most obvious draw, but leave enough time in your schedule to visit the majestic mountains of the interior.

Ras Ghozlani (p383)

Pressed for Time

● Many travellers pop over from Europe for a quick beach break. If you've arrived on a fly-and-flop flight to **Sharm El Sheikh** (p374), you'll want to make a beeline for the beach, either the private stretch at your resort or one of the public (but paid-for) spots at Na'ama Bay or El Fanar. Snorkelling and scuba diving are superb in these waters, and many **dive sites** (p376) are easily accessed from the shore.

● Depending on the atmosphere you're after and how long you have to spend, **Dahab** (p386) might make a better base if you prefer indie instead of international hotels.

SEASONAL HIGHLIGHTS

Balmy winters and blistering summers. Cooler months, can be chilly, while summer sees Red Sea marine life in abundance.

JANUARY
Coastal temperatures are mild, while inland is cold with a chance of snow.

APRIL
A colourful flurry of flowers carpets the sands after bursts of spring rain (which can also wash out roads).

MAY
The best time for hiking, with warmer temperatures and less rainfall.

A Week of Sun & Fun

● Book a diving or snorkelling trip to **Ras Mohammed National Park** (p382), an underwater wonderland of sea creatures and shipwrecks. Be sure to leave ample time to decompress and experience the park after hours at the Bedouin-operated camp of **Bedawi** (p384).

● Re-enter society with a flat white and wi-fi connection in **Dahab** (p386), an oasis for divers and digital nomads. Don a mask and peer into the depths of the **Blue Hole** (p389), one of the world's most infamous dive sites, and try not to get sucked into the laid-back lifestyle that frequently keeps travellers here much longer than they originally intended.

Explore More

● Even if you're only in Sinai for a short time, every itinerary should include a trip to the mountains. Watch a new day begin from the summit of **Mt Sinai** (Gebel Musa; p399) and then visit caramel-coloured **St Katherine's Monastery** (p393), the oldest continuously inhabited Christian monastery in the world, at its base.

● Marvel at blossoming orchards and turquoise pools in the desert on a longer **hike** (p401) through the wadis (valleys) surrounding St Katherine village (locally known as Katreen or Al-Milga, and often spelled St Catherine on maps and signs). Kick back at a **beach ecolodge** (p392) near Nuweiba.

THE GUIDE

SINAI

AUGUST	DECEMBER	RAMADAN	ORTHODOX FEAST DAYS
Air temperatures are scorching, but diving conditions and the chances of spotting sharks, rays and other sea life are at their peak.	The price of flights and hotels increases as Europeans leave the cold and migrate south to Sharm El Sheikh.	Life in the towns mostly carries on as usual, but many Bedouin guides press pause on trips into the mountains.	As a still-working religious compound, St Katherine's Monastery closes its doors on Orthodox holidays throughout the year.

Sharm El Sheikh

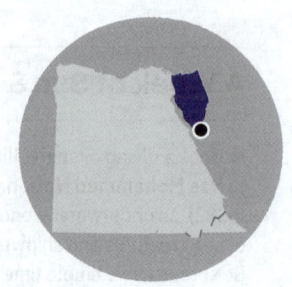

DIVING | BOAT JOURNEYS | MARINE LIFE

☑ TOP TIP
All-inclusive resorts mean a dearth of eating options outside the hotels. Check the menu when ordering or ask staff whether service tax and VAT are included.

GETTING AROUND
Not many people move around Sharm, instead staying cocooned at a resort. Most diving sites are visited on boat trips via one of the diving clubs lining the shores. But if you do want to get out and explore, you'll need a car. Renting isn't recommended as you can easily find taxis. Note, though, they drive a hard bargain – expect to be quoted a ridiculous price before negotiations begin. Hotels can also arrange taxis, albeit at inflated rates. Microbuses regularly ply the main roads and charge LE5. Arrange airport transfers through your accommodation.

Backed by jagged mountains and lapped by the sapphire waters of the Red Sea, the purpose-built resort town of Sharm El Sheikh stretches out like a lazy sunbather on a flat stretch of sand between crags and coast. Sharm's sprawling low-rise resorts cater to families and the fly-and-flop crowd, and it's a favourite winter sun warm-up spot for shivering Europeans.

What Sharm might be lacking in looks at sea level is summarily corrected when you don a mask and head underwater. Offshore are some of the world's best scuba diving and snorkelling sites, where colourful fish swim by the thousands and technicolour coral reefs have conquered rusted shipwrecks.

Nicknamed the 'City of Peace', Sharm often hosts high-profile conventions, including de-escalation negotiations between the Israelis and Palestinians and 2022's UN Climate Change Conference. But it remains subject to the start-and-stop whims – are those buildings half-constructed or half-abandoned? – of politics and economics.

A Night at the Museum
Explore Egyptian civilisation

Step back into ancient Egypt with a visit to **Sharm El Sheikh Museum** *(egymonuments.gov.eg/en/museums/sharm-al-sheikh-museum; adult/student/child under 6yr LE200/100/free),* the only antiquities museum in Sinai. With a maze of heritage compacted into three halls, an hour is all you need to be transported back to the past. The museum is only open in the mornings and evenings, so consider a nighttime visit after a day at the beach.

See a span of centuries, covering how Sinai's ancient Bedouin tribes lived and dressed to the ornate, 19th-century jewellery worn by the Mohammed Ali dynasty and the mosaic-floored Greek baths from Alexandria.

SHARM EL SHEIKH

● SIGHTS
1 Al Sahaba Mosque
2 Sharm El Sheikh Museum

● ACTIVITIES
3 Camel Dive Club
4 Gardens
5 Ras Ghamila
6 Ras Katy
7 Ras Nasrani
8 Ras Umm Sid
9 Reef Oasis
10 Temple
11 Tower

● SLEEPING
12 Camel Dive Centre Hotel
13 Cleopatra Luxury Resort
14 Four Seasons Sharm El Sheikh
15 Hilton Sharm El Sheikh Fayrouz Resort
16 Meraki Resort
17 Mövenpick Sharm El Sheikh
18 Novotel
19 Ras Katy Sunset Views
20 Rixos
21 Steigenberger Alcazar
22 Umbi Sharks Bay Diving Village

● EATING
23 Fairuz
24 Fares Seafood
25 Pomodoro
see 17 Rangoli

● DRINKING & NIGHTLIFE
see 12 Camel Bar & Rooftop
26 Farsha Mountain Lounge
27 Tavern Bar
28 View Bar & Terrace

● SHOPPING
29 Sharm Old Market
30 Soho Square

TOP EXPERIENCE

Under the Sea in Sharm

One of eight countries that border the Red Sea, Egypt has the most accessible stretch of coast and a well-developed network of scuba-diving centres. Sharm has about 15 dive sites right off its shore, plus a dozen more further-flung sites and shipwrecks around Tiran Island and in the Gulf of Aqaba between Egypt and Saudi Arabia.

DON'T MISS

- Ras Umm Sid
- Ras Ghamila
- Gardens
- Temple
- Ras Nasrani
- Ras Katy
- Tower

Southern Sharm

Tucked in a bay, the calm waters around **Ras Katy** make it a perfect spot for learning to dive. A large coral pinnacle, which drops from the surface to 18m, attracts schools of butterflyfish, pipefish, fusiliers and glassfish, while crocodilefish, blue-spotted stingrays and scorpionfish can be spotted in the sandy bottoms. When the tide rises, the current gets stronger, allowing for a drift dive to **Temple**, 400m away. Parrotfish, lionfish and butterflyfish flit among the colourful

PRACTICALITIES
- *padi.com/diving-in/sharm-el-sheikh*
- *one dive (half day) US$55-65*
- *two dives (one day) US$90-110*

coral that's punctuated with gorgonian fans. Located at El Fanar Beach, **Ras Umm Sid** is one of the area's best dive sites. It features a spectacular gorgonian forest along a dramatic drop-off that hosts a variety of reef fish, including barracuda, parrotfish and huge Napoleon wrasse. To the east, the sloping gardens of Paradise and Turtle Bays have shallow caves and a bounty of soft and hard coral. The pinnacles invite butterflyfish and giant moray eels. Amphoras, named after a 17th-century Ottoman shipwreck that spilt its cargo of mercury-filled jars, has similar topography but adds in archaeological fragments.

Tower has a 120m-deep canyon and coral-covered pinnacles where you'll spot plenty of nudibranchs and patrolling lionfish. Crevices and caves hide glassfish, squirrelfish, bigeyes and sometimes whitetip reef sharks. Divers might also see whale sharks and manta rays.

The Gardens

The perennially popular **Gardens** are actually several sites in one. Closest to Na'ama Bay, **Near Garden** has a lovely chain of pinnacles that are home to glassfish, triggerfish, shrimp and anemones. Larger critters such as moray eels, whitetip reef sharks, stingrays and hawksbill turtles might be spotted in the sloping coral garden. **Middle Garden** features a fringed ridge that gently descends to 20m-wide sandy 'roads' lined with hard corals. **Far Garden** has a wealth of coral formations and pinnacles frequented by clouds of orange anthias fish. Experienced divers can dip down to the roof of the 'Cathedral', a colourful overhang in deep water.

Sharks Bay & Northern Sharm

The calm waters of **Sharks Bay** make it a popular spot for training dives, and a large canyon on the southern flank attracts technical divers to its depths. To the north, well-sheltered White Knight has a series of crevices, canyons, tunnels and caves, as well as a group of garden eels near the boat mooring point at 10m. The current can be much stronger around **Ras Nasrani**. Look carefully in the large area of porites hard coral to spot the narrow squiggle openings of giant clams – this headland has the highest population density in the whole Red Sea.

Though not always labelled as such on maps, the southern part of Ras Nasrani is called Ras Bob, named after an underwater photographer who worked in the area. Weaker currents bring out beginner divers, and crocodilefish and blue-spotted stingrays rest on the sandy bottoms outside the small caves.

Ras Ghamila ('Beautiful Cape' in Arabic) lives up to its moniker, and is filled with diverse coral colonies, parrotfish and groupers. Marking the western edge of the **Straits of Tiran**, this spot is often visited in the afternoon after two morning dives around Tiran Island.

BEST DIVE CENTRES

Reef Oasis (p403): PADI five-star centre with a full schedule of daily dives and boat trips; its 'house reefs' are at the famous sites of Far Garden and Temple.

Camel Dive Club (p403): Long-standing spot with solid sustainability and inclusivity efforts, including specialised instructors for divers with disabilities.

Umbi Sharks Bay Diving Village (p403): Laid-back Bedouin-run centre with years of experience on a quieter bay.

SECURITY IN SINAI

Sinai's unique position straddling two continents and cultures means it's always struggled with security concerns. Travellers will come across an excessive number of roadside checkpoints and metal detectors at hotel entrances. Nearly every activity requires advance permission and a passport check. Foreign governments advise against travel to North Sinai, with some of these warnings trickling into the northern part of South Sinai. Advisories vary considerably: the US State Department warns against all travel to Sinai, while the UK's FCDO labels South Sinai green except for its northern area. The majority of travellers to South Sinai enjoy their visit without incident. Read your embassy's advice for updates.

Al Sahaba Mosque

The museum combines Egyptians' fascination with the afterlife with its fondness for wildlife, exhibiting a trove of mummified animals. Two massive cedar-wood boats belonging to Senusret III (r 1878–1839 BCE), which are thought to have carried the pharaoh's body down the Nile during his funeral, are also on display. Don't miss descending into the 'tomb' of Princess Maatkare to view her nested coffin set, painted with spells from the Book of the Dead.

Cultural Charms of Sharm
Enjoy a night out in Old Town Sharm

About 10km southwest of Sharm El Sheikh Museum, the fantastical **Al Sahaba Mosque** (also known as Al Mustafa Mosque; *free entry*) has welcomed worshippers only since 2017, but it fuses historic Fatimid, Mamluk and Ottoman architectural styles into a Disney-esque display of huge central domes, golden accents and swirling brickwork up the 70m-tall minarets. Entrance to the mosque's interior (which is, unfortunately, not as impressive as the exterior) is at the whim of the guardians. All visitors must dress modestly, covering their knees and shoulders. Women must cover their hair as well. On the right side of the mosque is a changing room filled with scarves and long dresses you can borrow to wear

 EATING IN SHARM EL SHEIKH: OUR PICKS

Fairuz: Named after the iconic Lebanese singer, this terrace restaurant offers a huge menu of Lebanese mezze and Middle Eastern favourites. *1pm-1am* $$

Rangoli: Head here for a romantic night out and perhaps the best Indian food outside of India; snag a balcony for sublime sunset views. *6.30-10.30pm* $$$

Fares Seafood: A Sharm institution for good-value seafood; pick your *poisson* from the selection on ice out front. *11am-1am* $$

Pomodoro: Beloved by locals and tourists alike, this Italian-inspired eatery serves homemade pizza and pasta with seating on Na'ama Bay's promenade. *6.30am-11.30pm* $$

inside. Scantily clad social media influencers are regularly shooed from the stairs.

The mosque is at the heart of **Sharm Old Market**, which, despite its name, is a modern complex built a few decades ago. Here, you can spend an evening perusing the shops and restaurants lining the square's streets. Stores line up cheek by jowl and sell standard tourist tat, plus luxury handbags, sunglasses and beach essentials. Smoking sticks of incense perfume linger in the plaza's alleys. Opening hours vary, but the bazaar is usually bustling by nightfall as tourists flock here after sightseeing along the sea. After sunset, the mosque lights up and touts offer camel rides to strolling families and tourists carrying shopping bags and ice-cream cones. On the eastern side of the market, a waterfall running down layers of rock provides an impressive backdrop to your shopping experience. Just next to it, a staircase cut into the mountain leads up to a cafe where you can dine hillside. Fish restaurants west of the mosque put the catch of the day on ice out front and charge by weight.

Light Up Your Night
Shop, dine, drink and play at Soho Square

Near the airport and nestled between the Savoy, Royal Savoy and Sierra Hotels, **Soho Square** is Sharm El Sheikh's modern shopping hub, with a Culturama centre that plays a film of Egyptian history, plus an ice-skating rink, tennis and squash courts, a bowling alley and fitness studio suitable for all ages. The square also houses a bar made entirely of ice – the first in the Middle East – where you can sample frosty vodka shooters and other frozen cocktails. Illuminated in champagne and glacial blue lights, the complex sparkles at night in starry bewilderment, while a dancing fountain glowing green, blue, red and purple adds to the luminescent ambience in a dazzling spectacle of water and colour.

An array of top-end restaurants dish up international cuisine to those abiding by the smart-casual dress code (no flip-flops), while more laid-back cafes and bars show football matches on TV and offer a spot to wind down with shisha (water pipes) and a few drinks.

DAY TRIPS TO CAIRO & JORDAN

Companies in Sharm El Sheikh offer a mind-boggling array of local tours, as well as day trips to Cairo and Petra by bus and plane. While it's tempting to squeeze in some of the region's most famous cities and archaeological sites, these whirlwind trips are not worth it. You'll spend most of your time in transit with only cursory visits to the places you signed up to see. Tours to Cairo can be particularly cumbersome. The road between Sharm and the capital has several security checkpoints, which can turn a theoretically six-hour one-way drive into 10 hours or more. Some operators offer flights instead, but consider their environmental impact.

DRINKING IN SHARM EL SHEIKH: OUR NIGHTLIFE PICKS

Camel Bar & Rooftop: Low-key place in the heart of Na'ama Bay. Start your evening here and swap stories with other divers about your adventures. *5pm-1am*

View Bar & Terrace: Bustling cliffside bar over Na'ama Bay with Latin dancing every Thursday, DJ and live music on Fridays, and karaoke singing Mondays. *1pm-midnight*

Tavern Bar: British pub serving English breakfasts and Sunday roasts. It's a vibrant place to grab a beer and watch the football. *3pm-3am*

Farsha Mountain Lounge: At Farsha, a jumble of knickknacks surrounds low seating. At night, lanterns glow orange and the air is filled with shisha smoke. *11am-1am*

Beyond Sharm El Sheikh

Explore Sinai's hypnotic national parks: float through a prismatic marine world, kayak in mangrove forests and ride over seaside dunes.

GETTING AROUND

Most visitors to Ras Mohammed National Park and Nabq Nature Reserve arrive on prearranged tours from Sharm El Sheikh or Dahab. All boats leave from the Wataneya Marina in southern Sharm for Ras Mohammed – boats do not travel all the way from Dahab. A tour bus will usually take you to Nabq on a one-day scheduled excursion. To camp, you can rent a car to get here or have your accommodation reserve a taxi.

Ras Mohammed National Park (RMNP), Egypt's first national park, preserves a barren coastline of extraordinary beauty, the crown jewel of the Red Sea. Deemed one of Egypt's sustainability success stories, RMNP is included on the International Union for the Conservation of Nature's Green List, where live coral cover in some areas is an impressive 80%, with an average of more than 65%, compared with 11% to 30% outside the reserve.

Located on the eastern side of the Sinai Peninsula, Nabq Nature Reserve covers approximately 600 sq km of vast, varied terrain and wildlife. It's home to several rare and endangered species, including one of the densest populations of gazelles in Egypt and the largest arak bushes in the Middle East.

Nabq Nature Reserve

TIME FROM SHARM EL SHEIKH: **30 MINS**

Immerse yourself in Bedouin culture

Explore what Sharm El Sheikh was like before the tourism boom. Established in 1992, **Nabq Nature Reserve** *(+20 69-366-0559; US$5/10 without/with vehicle)* is the Gulf of Aqaba's largest coastal park, located just 10 minutes from Sharm El Sheikh Airport and approximately 35km from the city itself. Spend a half-day or night exploring the protectorate's rich biodiversity, which includes 134 plant species, with six only found in Nabq.

Birdwatchers will be particularly entranced here by the diverse array of over 200 resident and migratory species such as herons, waders and eagles. Nabq is also noteworthy for its 5km stretch of mangrove trees – the largest in the Gulf of Aqaba and the most northerly stand in the world. Kayaking through this dense forest is a must: you'll comb through the mangroves' submerged roots along transparent waters the colour of liquid jade, and perhaps catch a glimpse of spoonbills and ospreys wading in the woodland.

Inland are the dunes of **Wadi Kid**, the most irrigated ravine in Sinai and therefore home to an abundance of vegetation, such as date palms, tamarisk trees and arak bushes (which

Quad biking, Nabq Nature Reserve

Bedouin traditionally use as toothbrushes). Hike, quad bike or ride a camel through the sand and you might spot Nubian ibexes and hyraxes.

Many visitors travel here on prearranged day trips from Sharm or Dahab, during which you often ride ATVs across the dunes before sitting down to an authentic Bedouin lunch prepared by the Mizena tribe residing on the reserve. Camping overnight in one of the beachfront huts can be a much-needed respite from the flashiness of Sharm El Sheikh, as you sip on aromatic Bedouin tea under a blanket of stars.

Rare coral can be found in the reefs of Nabq but visibility is often poor due to sediment filtering out from the mangrove swamp. From the shore, you can spot the wreck of *Maria Schroder,* a German cargo vessel that sank in 1956. Given the shallow depth of the water, you can walk to the shipwreck by foot, but it's best to wear water shoes if doing so.

While the area is a nature haven, rubbish, unfortunately, lines the beach due to an increase in tourism at the reserve and a lack of proper waste management.

THE BEDOUIN OF SINAI

Thanks to centuries of living in harsh desert conditions, Sinai's 12 Bedouin tribes have developed a sophisticated understanding of their environment. Despite their deep connection to the land, the indigenous people have often been left behind in the race to build up the 'Red Sea Riviera'. Nile Valley Egyptians are often hired over Bedouin in the tourism industry, while the sector's boom in Sinai led to the displacement of many Bedouin from their ancestral lands. Long excluded from mass-market tourism, Bedouin have been put front and centre by newer initiatives like **Wilderness Ventures Egypt** (p400) and **Desert Divers**, where Bedouin work as hiking guides and climbing and diving instructors – attracting adventure tourists looking for a more local connection when travelling.

Ras Mohammed

TOP EXPERIENCE

Reefs of Ras Mohammed

At the southernmost tip of the triangular Sinai Peninsula, Ras Mohammed National Park (RMNP) is a paradise for underwater explorers in search of shipwrecks, thousands of marine species and coral sitting on reefs that are up to two million years old. Established in 1983, the national park was named by local fishers after a cliff that resembles a man's profile ('ras' means head in Arabic).

DON'T MISS

Shark & Yolanda Reef

Ras Ghozlani

SS *Thistlegorm*

Million Hope

Ras Za'atar

Gordon Reef

Anemone City

Shark Observatory

Swimming Through Marine Gardens

The Red Sea is the equivalent of an immense underwater rainforest, home to more than 250 species of corals, 8% of which are found nowhere else in the world. Enticed by the prospect of marvelling at some of the world's most spectacular marine ecosystems, more than 150,000 visitors come to Ras Mohammed each year. Most, if not all, of the 1200 or so species of fish – with discoveries still being made – can be seen in the park's waters, including sought-after pelagics, such

PRACTICALITIES
- +20 69-366-0668
- US$5; 9am-5pm
- Scan this QR code for more information

Ras Ghozlani

RED SEA SAFARIS

If you're in Sharm simply to scuba dive, why stay on land? Independent companies, as well as some hotels and dive centres, offer liveaboard boats that head out on week-long sea voyages. They anchor offshore near Sinai's top dive sites, including Tiran Island, Ras Mohammed National Park and fascinating shipwrecks in the Gulf of Suez that either make very long day trips from Sharm or aren't visited at all.

as hammerheads, manta rays and whale sharks. Because of strong currents, some dive centres require beginners to go with personal guides.

RMNP has seven dive sites, some of which are also accessible for snorkellers. **Shark & Yolanda Reef** is the Red Sea's most famous dive, where you first descend down a massive wall of lavender coral at Shark Reef, as schools of goldfish swirl around you, before drifting towards Yolanda Reef, where broken pieces of porcelain litter the sea floor after the reef's namesake, a Cypriot merchant ship, sunk in 1980 while carrying British-made toilets and bathtubs.

While Shark & Yolanda Reef is, by far, the most popular diving destination at RMNP, the park does have a plethora of other sites to explore, including **Anemone City**, where hundreds of clownfish guard a jelly-like jungle of anemone from predatory fish. At the northern end of Marsa Bareika Bay is **Ras Ghozlani**, which is as beautiful as it is versatile. Beginner divers can feel at ease with the site's slow current, allowing you to float over a sandy plateau of golden brain coral. At the bay's southern tip lies **Ras Za'atar** ('head of thyme'), known for its stunning sunbeams streaming through the reef's caverns – a sublime photo stop.

Further south, **Jackfish Alley**, nicknamed for its sandy bottom where jackfish often congregate, has two caves pierced by streaks of sunlight and filled with shoaling glassfish. Larger marine life like whitetip reef sharks can also be found sleeping in the sand. **Eel Garden**, which is accessible by boat or land, is filled with endemic eels, which grow up to 80cm and can often be seen slithering through the sandy slope to catch plankton. **Shark Observatory** is named after its towering cliff used to spot sharks below, but the area isn't as shark-abundant as it once was. Here, you can drift along

EXPLORING THE LOCAL COAST

As recommended by **Fady Shawky**, diving instructor at **Camel Dive Club** (p377), Sharm El Sheikh.

For diving the local coast of Sharm El Sheikh, you have Ras Ghamila. You can also go to Ras Mohammed National Park from the land and camp there.

El Fanar at Ras Umm Sid in Sharm El Sheikh is a magnificent dive site where you can dive from the shore. On the cliff, beside El Fanar Restaurant, you can enjoy a sunset view.

TOP TIPS

- Don't forget your passport, as you'll need it to enter the park.

- You don't need to purchase an Egyptian visa if you plan to visit the park by boat. But if you plan to enter by land, then you'll need to get one.

- Make sure to carry motion-sickness medication with you in case you get seasick during the boat trip.

- If you're an avid scuba diver, then consider bringing your own equipment, as you may be able to negotiate a lower price for a dive package if you just need tanks and weights.

a coral wall and gaze into the blue to find hawksbill turtles and pelagic predators.

RMNP is visited almost exclusively by day-trippers, but camping overnight at **Bedawi** is a soul-soothing balm. This sustainable outfit has set up camp with canvas tents, a composting toilet and a communal Bedouin-style space on a prime slice of Ras Mohammed shore, meaning you can get first crack at early morning snorkelling in crystal-clear waters and linger long enough to stargaze and drink tea around the fire.

Tiran Island

Occupying part of the narrow 6km strait between **Tiran Island** and Sharm El Sheikh are a handful of brilliantly coloured reefs – four of which are named after the 19th-century English cartographers who made the first nautical map of the area. The geographical squeeze and Tiran Island's fairly shallow seabed give the waters a sparkling aquamarine appearance but also cause strong currents, meaning some dive centres don't allow beginners to go without a personal guide, increasing the cost of a visit, so check before you book. These reefs are popular, and you certainly won't have them to yourself, as dozens of boats disgorge divers here every day.

More than 1km long, **Woodhouse Reef** is a drift dive for those with experience. A 30m-deep wall reef and coral-lined canyon house giant morays, groupers and pufferfish, and this site is an excellent spot for seeing eagle rays, sea turtles and many species of shark. A dangerous whirling current that often churns at the northern end of the reef is nicknamed

RICH CAREY/SHUTTERSTOCK

SS *Thistlegorm*

'the washing machine' and should be crossed only in good conditions. **Thomas Reef** is another difficult but utterly spectacular drift dive. Colourful soft coral clings to the steeply plunging walls as schools of fish and sharks cruise by. With good air consumption and water conditions, you can circumnavigate the entire reef.

Sunken Ships

With an average depth of just 80m, the Gulf of Suez is surprisingly shallow, often spelling doom for cargo ships. The fate of many historic carriers has turned the Red Sea's floor into a freighter graveyard, with shipwrecks like the **SS *Thistlegorm***, a 126m-long British vessel that was bombed by German aircraft and sank during WWII. Experienced divers can explore the *Thistlegorm's* cargo of armaments and vehicles, including Bren gun carriers, motorbikes, Bedford trucks and jeeps. About 11km from RMNP, the **Dunraven**, a British steamer, ploughed into the reef, caught fire and sank in 1876 on its journey between India and England. Today, the upside-down cave-like wreck is encrusted in coral and home to groupers, goatfish and pipefish.

Located north of Tiran Island, **Million Hope** is the Red Sea's largest shipwreck, which sank in 1996 on its way from Jordan to Taiwan while carrying phosphates and potash after crashing into a reef near Nabq Bay.

Also on the northern side of Tiran, **Jackson Reef** is crowned with the remains of a Cypriot cargo ship, the *Lara,* which ran aground in the 1980s and has been partially demolished. Scalloped hammerhead sharks can sometimes be spotted nearby, especially between July and September. Dives usually start on the southern side, which is more protected from the currents, and then drift around either side of the reef past forests of fire coral and clownfish playing hide and seek in the anemones. Whitetip reef sharks, grey reef sharks and sea turtles are commonly sighted.

En route from Jordan in 1984, the phosphate-carrying *Kormoran* was wrecked on Laguna Reef at Tiran Island and now rests at a shallow 12m, making it the only wreck dive suitable for beginners. The anchor winch, propeller and engine are well preserved, but visiting requires a miracle of calm waters for slower currents and better visibility.

The southernmost dive site of Tiran, **Gordon Reef** has slightly calmer waters. The corroded Panamanian cargo ship *Loullia,* which was wrecked on the reef in 1981, is beached at its northern end, but divers are usually dropped on the southern section, which teems with cornetfish, bannerfish, goatfish and Napoleon wrasse. Manta rays, eagle rays, whitetip reef sharks and potato groupers often swim past.

TIRAN TAKEOVER

At the gateway to the Gulf of Aqaba, the two small uninhabited islands of Sanafir and Tiran hold immense strategic importance, overseeing maritime traffic to Jordan and Israel and the Palestinian Territories. Under Egyptian administration for decades, the islands were given by Egyptian President Abdel Fattah El Sisi to Saudi Arabia in 2016, a move deeply unpopular with Egyptians that set off public protests. Years later, the full transfer remains incomplete, said to be held up by Sisi in exchange for economic aid. Saudi Arabia wants to develop the islands for tourism, and for now, diving in the waters surrounding the islands remains unaffected. Going ashore is still not permitted.

Dahab

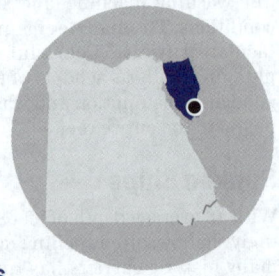

DIVING | ADVENTURE SPORTS | PRISTINE BEACHES

☑ TOP TIP

Dahab's beaches are rocky rather than sandy, so if your suitcase has space, pack water shoes for the spiky shoreline. Some accommodation options, such as **Dar Dahab** (p403), offer complimentary pairs for guests to borrow during their stay.

GETTING AROUND

The main area of Dahab is small enough to get around on foot, and a pedestrian promenade traces the shoreline. Driving here isn't ideal, with the narrow, one-way streets crammed with cars. As public transport isn't available, consider renting a bicycle or scooter for a faster mode of travel – just beware the traffic, as cars screech and honk in the town centre and dogs obliviously cross the roads. For places further afield, pickup-truck taxis idly queue on the main streets.

The antithesis of Sharm in nearly every way, low-key and laid-back Dahab is the Middle East's prime beach town for independent travellers. In just a few decades, it's undergone a startling transformation from dusty beach-hut outpost to spruced-up hipster village that now attracts more nomads of the digital sort than the Bedouin kind. This change has brought a great diversity to Dahab, with an impressive range of restaurants and coffee shops for such a tiny town, though it's come at the expense of local flavour. Reeled in by its mellow ambience, many travellers plan to spend a few nights and end up staying for weeks. Most are here to dive or simply do nothing. The pace here is slow and easy, giving way to blissed-out meditation circles and hammock hangs in the sunshine. Much of the town is delightfully walkable, and a cafe-lined pedestrian path traces the curve of the coastline for a few kilometres.

Surf Dahab's Coast

Riding the wind in Blue Lagoon

Guarded by a hook-like tongue of sand, Dahab's **Blue Lagoon** is the perfect spot for beginners to learn windsurfing and kitesurfing. The lagoon is shallow with a sandy bottom and sheltered from waves, yet the wind still blows consistently from the north, especially during the warmer months. A handful of schools line Dahab's shores with everything you need to start sailing. Blue Lagoon itself is a must-see, even if you don't plan on doing these activities. The cerulean crystal-clear waters set against hazy purple mountains make it feel like you've stepped into a postcard the moment your feet touch the sand. This isn't the best place for snorkelling or diving, however, due to a lack of coral and knee-deep waters. Rather, it's designed for wading in the waves while watching kiteboarders practise their tricks.

DAHAB

★ HIGHLIGHTS
1 Blue Hole

● SIGHTS
2 Bells
3 Blue Lagoon
4 Canyon
5 Eel Garden
6 Islands
7 Lighthouse Reef
8 Ras Abu Gallum Protectorate

● ACTIVITIES
9 Big Blue Dive Centre
10 Dive Urge
11 Nesima Dive Centre
12 Red Sea Relax Dive Centre

● SLEEPING
13 Acacia
14 Coral Coast
15 Daniela Diving Resort
16 Dar Dahab
17 Diamond Dahab House
18 Eldorado
19 Elite Residence Dahab
20 Jaz Dahabeya
21 Malakot Mountain Oasis
see 12 Red Sea Relax
22 Sindbad Camp
23 Swiss Inn Resort
24 Wind Farm

● EATING
25 Bayside Eatery
26 Ralph's German Bakery
27 Vegan Lab
28 Zanooba Slow Cooking

DIGITAL NOMADS IN DAHAB

Coastal Dahab has a boho allure unlike any other town in Egypt. The standard tourist hustle so pronounced elsewhere in the country fades significantly, and it's easy for travellers to take a deep breath and relax into the groove. Its beachy location and laid-back attitude have made Dahab a draw for digital nomads, who lug their laptops to the bayside cafes covered in colourful rugs and the glut of coffee shops serving European-style brews along the pedestrianised promenade.

While Bali it is not, Dahab ticks many of the boxes that characterise a remote-working hub. Year-round sunny skies, instant beach access, low prices, reasonable proximity to an international airport (in Sharm El Sheikh) and thrilling outdoor activities make the stock image of a remote worker on the beach a reality.

Kitesurfing, Blue Lagoon (p386)

The area outside the lagoon, known as the 'speedy' zone, is best suited for more advanced wind enthusiasts and freestylers. This 2km-long section is still shallow, but consistently strong winds interspersed with a few choppy waves equal a speedier ride. This section has a floating platform for safety or simply a nice break.

For the real experts, the waves just past **Napoleon Reef** in the open sea reach up to 4m high yet hardly break, giving the area the nickname the 'wave zone'. Here, you'll find kitesurfers and windsurfers alike jumping in between the surf.

 EATING IN DAHAB: OUR PICKS

Vegan Lab: Organic superfood dishes and drinks in a space to please vegans and non-vegans alike. Card payments have an additional 2% fee. *7am-9pm* $$$

Bayside Eatery: This cafe serves soul-nourishing breakfast dishes and soothing cups of coffee all day in a cosy, lime-green-walled space. *8am-5pm* $$

Ralph's German Bakery: Swift service and European-style coffee with a Middle Eastern vibe and hospitality. *7am-8pm* $$

Zanooba Slow Cooking: Creative vegetarian and meat dishes cooked for hours in a rich stew; order before noon via WhatsApp (+20 10-9699-2699). *11am-1pm* $$$

Blue Hole

TOP EXPERIENCE

Diving in Dahab

While diving in Dahab isn't as noteworthy as the underwater excursions in Sharm El Sheikh, the area still offers a number of photo-worthy dive sites, and emerging from below to sip *fakoush* (a blend of orange juice, ginger, honey, lemon, mint and cinnamon), while gazing at desert slopes dipping into a sapphire-blue sea, will certainly stay imprinted in your memory.

Into the Depths of Dahab

The most famous – or infamous – dive site in Dahab is the **Blue Hole**. This gaping sinkhole drops 130m and is linked to the open sea via a 26m-long tunnel with a ceiling depth of 52m. It's seen a number of fatal accidents, and a sobering wall of memorial plaques at the entrance to the site commemorates divers who have lost their lives here. Despite its reputation, the Blue Hole is safe for those who don't push their limits. It's a common training spot for technical divers

DON'T MISS

- Blue Hole
- Islands
- Canyon
- Gabr El Bint
- Three Pools
- Bells
- Lighthouse Reef

PRACTICALITIES
- *entry to Ras Abu Gallum Protectorate (location of some of Dahab's famous dives) US$10*
- *Scan this QR code for more information*

> ### BEST DIVE CENTRES
>
> **Dive Urge (p403):** A dive centre and ecohotel located on the shores of Eel Garden in Dahab. Commendable environmental credentials include no more than four divers per dive and daily dive litter clean-ups.
>
> **Nesima Dive Centre:** A reputable club and camp with welcoming instructors who teach a range of courses in a variety of languages. Offers boat trips in Dahab and Sharm El Sheikh.
>
> **Red Sea Relax Dive Centre:** Mere metres from the Lighthouse Reef in Dahab is this long-standing five-star PADI centre with an excellent reputation. Courses of all levels are taught by caring and careful instructors.
>
> **Big Blue Dive Centre:** One of Dahab's top-rated dive centres, this popular and friendly PADI shop has a good reputation and well-maintained equipment. Most visitors rave about the staff's professionalism and positive vibes.

and is popular with snorkellers, even though its sheer walls have few corals or fish. The biggest appeal for divers is entering at the **Bells**, a narrow breach in the reef table where you descend through a semi-enclosed chimney. Exit the hollow and drift by coral-covered walls, anemones and sponges before arriving at a saddle with a coral garden that leads to the Blue Hole.

Just south of Blue Hole is **Tiger House**, owing its name to the tiger sharks that once populated the reef. Today, you're more likely to find schools of parrotfish, triggerfish, bannerfish and damselfish circling the coral gardens here.

The Blue Hole is often combined with a dive at the **Canyon**, a gorgeous and popular site that contains a narrow, 30m-deep trench that runs perpendicular to the reef shelf. It's home to prolific hard and soft corals and schools of glassfish. The starkly beautiful **Ras Abu Gallum Protectorate**, which contains the Blue Hole, covers 500 sq km of coastline between Dahab and Nuweiba, mixing coastal mountains, narrow valleys, sand dunes and fine-gravel beaches with several diving and snorkelling sites. Scientists describe the area as a 'floristic frontier', where Mediterranean conditions are influenced by a tropical climate. With its 165 plant species (including 44 found nowhere else in Sinai) and a wealth of mammals and reptiles, this environmentally important area is a fascinating place to visit.

Named for its bounty of Napoleon wrasse, the **Napoleon Reef** is tucked within Laguna Beach. It's typically accessed by boat, with snorkellers and divers dropped off at the reef's tip, where a massive patch of madreporal coral lies. Floating through the reef, you may find a large diversity of fish, including parrotfish, clownfish and butterflyfish. Giant moray eels, blue-spotted stingrays and spotted eagle rays are also often seen here.

The shores of Dahab town also have several diving and snorkelling sites accessible simply by walking through the cafes that line the bay. On the northern end, **Eel Garden** takes its name from the countless garden eels that carpet the seafloor. Other highlights include huge coral boulders and dense congregations of barracudas. The sloping reef at **Lighthouse Reef**, the house reef of Red Sea Relax, is close to a number of other dive centres and is home to a bounty of parrotfish, lionfish, bream and sometimes octopus. A profusion of coral towers pokes skyward from the depths. Lighthouse Reef is Dahab's main night-diving site and is also used for beginners, with a buoyancy park and a few underwater statues.

The lesser-dived **Abu Helal** (Bay of the Crescent Moon) may be one of the prettiest in Dahab, but only if you reach 38m to 39m. Triggerfish, potato groupers and barracuda are prevalent here among the waving flanks of coral, but difficult entry and exit points coupled with the increased depth mean this is best for experienced divers.

Drifting Through Gardens & Pools

South of Dahab, the **Islands** is an underwater *Alice in Wonderland*-esque site with an outstanding labyrinthine topography of pools, coral alleyways and valleys. **Gabr El Bint**, 25km south of Dahab, features a dramatic seascape highlighted by a 60m wall cut by numerous chasms, faults and sandy ravines. If you access the site by land instead of by boat, the journey combines a 4WD trip and a Bedouin-led camel convoy, which takes a full day and includes multiple dives at this site, which is divided into northern and southern sections. Just before Gabr El Bint are the **Caves**. The name is misleading, however, as you're surrounded by large overhangs rather than what could be classified as a cave. The right is more favoured than the left for its abundance of black coral and sponges draping its wall. As you leave, take a look back and watch the sunrays burst through the Caves' opening in a brilliant dance of light and colour.

A 10-minute drive south of the main hub of Dahab is **Moray Garden**, a fairly easy dive given it's sheltered from the waves. The dive site is often combined as a drift dive with adjacent **Golden Blocks**, named for its large coral reef blocks the colour of gold, or **Three Pools**, a collection of sandy pools linked together by coral gates you'll see divers leap over. After exiting the last pool, you float into open water along hills of hard coral before finishing into a shallow sandy bottom where pockets of red coral wave you goodbye. While Moray Garden is named after the eel slinking through its waters, you'll find moray at most of this area's dives.

TOP TIPS

● Most dives in Dahab are from the shore instead of from boats, meaning they are often cheaper than boat trips in Sharm El Sheikh.

● That being said, don't go below around US$35 (per dive) when researching costs, as cheaper packages may mean your guide is skimping on safety.

● It's worth having an advanced diving qualification – or getting one while you're here – as the most interesting spots are below 18m.

● Diving in Dahab is best during late spring to early summer when water temperatures are warmer and you may spot larger marine life like sharks and dolphins.

Moray Garden

Beyond Dahab

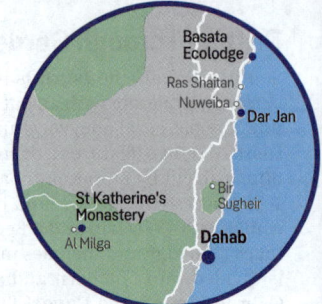

Hiking paths traverse barren mountains and wind-sculpted canyons, while blissed-out beach camps offer respite after time on the trail.

Places

Basata Ecolodge p392
St Katherine's Monastery p393
Dar Jan p394

GETTING AROUND

Sinai's northeastern coast and the interior mountains cover a large area. While a few buses operate along major roads, most travellers find it more convenient to organise transport through camps, trip operators or private taxis. Public buses don't travel to St Katherine and there isn't a reliable transit system in the cities of Nuweiba and Taba. Renting a car isn't recommended as roads can be quite windy, rarely lit and loaded with checkpoints that a local driver would be better able to navigate.

As the sun rises and falls over the soaring mountains outside of Dahab, the rocks and desert landscapes turn shades of pink, ochre and lilac. Bedouin wander through the wilderness, and travelling by camel or on foot is the best – or only – way to go, with much of the terrain too rocky even for a 4WD. Against this backdrop, some of the most sacred events in recorded human history are said to have taken place, immortalising Sinai in the annals of Christianity, Islam and Judaism. Where the peaks peter off near the Red Sea coast, low-key camps stake claims in the sand along the stretch of road around Nuweiba and up to the border with Israel and the Palestinian Territories.

Basata Ecolodge

TIME FROM DAHAB: **3 HRS**

Recharge, renew and relax at this beachy retreat

Opened in 1986, **Basata Ecolodge** *(basata.com)* means 'simplicity' and this encampment is the definition of simplicity. Rows of bamboo huts line its golden sands and mud-brick bungalows perch on its slopes. Discounted rates for solo female travellers are offered for all styles of accommodation – the only place we've come across this in the country. As one of Egypt's eco-pioneers, Basata has a strict sustainability ethos, meaning boats, scuba diving and fishing are not allowed in its waters and 80% of its waste is reused. To save energy, toiletries, towels and air conditioning aren't available, and water dispensers are located across the camp, encouraging guests to use their water bottles rather than purchase plastic. Additionally, single-use plastic and disposable tableware aren't offered.

Basata also doesn't have wi-fi, so while you might be beckoned to make the waves of glittering turquoise against the mountainous horizon of Saudi Arabia and Jordan the backdrop of your desktop, the logistics may not be on your side. Instead, the lodge favours community and restoration over remote working, where you can spend a few days recharging. Every night travellers gather around communal tables to meet fellow guests and tuck into meals heavy with organic produce and ethically sourced fish. It boasts a number of activities, from workshops to yoga and kickboxing retreats, provides kayaking and snorkelling equipment and can arrange day trips to the canyons and Petra.

Unlike other camps in Nuweiba whose beaches are often strewn with trash and tainted with revelling partygoers, Basata is placid and pristine, with a family-friendly atmosphere protected by hikeable hills.

St Katherine's Monastery

TIME FROM DAHAB: 1½ HRS

Walk in the footsteps of ancient pilgrims

Step inside the walled compound of the world's oldest continually functioning monastery and spend an hour perusing some of early Christianity's most ancient manuscripts and artefacts, including more than half of the world's surviving Byzantine icons. For centuries, pilgrims have flocked to **St Katherine's Monastery** *(sinaimonastery.com/index.php/en; free)*, built beside what's believed to be the burning bush where God spoke to Moses at the foot of Mt Sinai (Gebel Musa). Most visitors opt to go on a tour bus from Sharm El Sheikh or Dahab (departing at 10pm) in tandem with a sunrise hike to Mt Sinai before climbing down to visit the monastery in the morning, which is only open from 9am to 11.30am and closed on Fridays, Sundays and Greek Orthodox holidays.

Founded around 330 CE by Byzantine empress Helena, the Greek Orthodox monastery is named after St Katherine, believed to have been persecuted for her Christian faith and sentenced to death by Emperor Maxentius in Alexandria. The religious site and its surroundings are now a UNESCO World Heritage Site.

Inside the monastery's walls, the ornate 6th-century **Church of the Transfiguration** has a nave flanked by massive marble columns and walls covered in richly gilded icons and velvet tapestries. Giant golden chandeliers and censers suspended from chains line the church's ceiling. At the church's eastern end, a gilded 17th-century iconostasis separates the nave from the sanctuary and the apse, where St Katherine's remains are interred (off-limits for visitors). High in the apse above the altar is one of the monastery's most stunning artistic treasures, the 6th-century **mosaic of the Transfiguration**, although it can be difficult to see it past the chandeliers and the iconostasis. To the left of and below the altar is the monastery's holiest area, the **Chapel of the Burning Bush**, which is not accessible to the public.

continued on p396

RESPONSIBLE TOURISM?

A luxury ecohotel, mountainside resort and urban square are nearing completion in the heart of St Katherine. Dubbed the Great Transfiguration Project, the government-sponsored mega tourism endeavour promises closer links between the coast and the mountains and an increase in hospitality options. But despite being billed as a boost to the local economy, the project has been met with backlash from the area's Bedouin. Residents say the upgrade is defacing the ancient village and will push them out of the tourism market in favour of hiring Nile Valley Egyptians. Some fear that the ancient Jabaliya tribe, known as the guardians of St Katherine, will be expelled after homes and a cemetery were razed during development.

 EATING IN NUWEIBA: OUR PICKS

Castle Zaman: Slow-food restaurant dishing up roasted meats with sides of *molokhiyya* (jute leaf soup) and stunning Red Sea views. *noon-7pm* $$$

Beirut: Deservedly popular; here you can dine directly on Ras Shitan's sandy beach, one of the best in the area. *9am-8pm* $$$

Cleopatra Restaurant: Notable for its locally sourced seafood cuisine with a touch of Egyptian flavour. *10am-12.30am* $$$

Restaurant Dr Sheashkebab: Don't be fooled by the exterior: this classic Egypt eatery will satisfy your taste buds. Head here for some local flair. *10am-11.30pm* $

St Katherine's Monastery

❷ Fortifications
The formidable walls are 2m thick and 11m high, added by Emperor Justinian in a show of might. He also sent a Balkan garrison to watch over the newly fortified monastery, and today's local Jabaleya tribe is said to be their descendants.

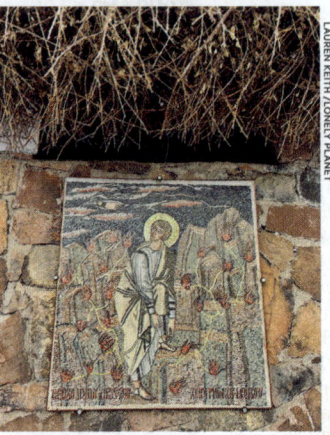

❶ The Burning Bush
This flourishing bramble (the endemic Sinai shrub Rubus sanctus) was transplanted in the 10th century to its present location. Tradition states that cuttings of the plant refuse to grow outside the monastery walls.

❹ Ahtiname
A monastery delegation sought the protection of Muhammad, and he signed this guarantee by handprint. When the Arab armies conquered Egypt in 641, the monastery was left untouched. The document on display is a copy; the original is in Istanbul.

❺ Ladder of Divine Ascent
This 12th-century icon is one of the monastery's most valuable. It depicts abbot St John Climacos leading a band of monks up the ladder of salvation to heaven.

❼ Codex Sinaiticus
One of the oldest and most complete manuscripts of the Bible. In 1859 German scholar Constantin von Tischendorf borrowed 347 pages of the Codex Sinaiticus from the monastery but failed to return his library books. Originally preserved at the monastery, some are still here, but the majority of the 'Sinai Bible' is in the British Library in London, with other leaves in Leipzig, Germany, and St Petersburg, Russia.

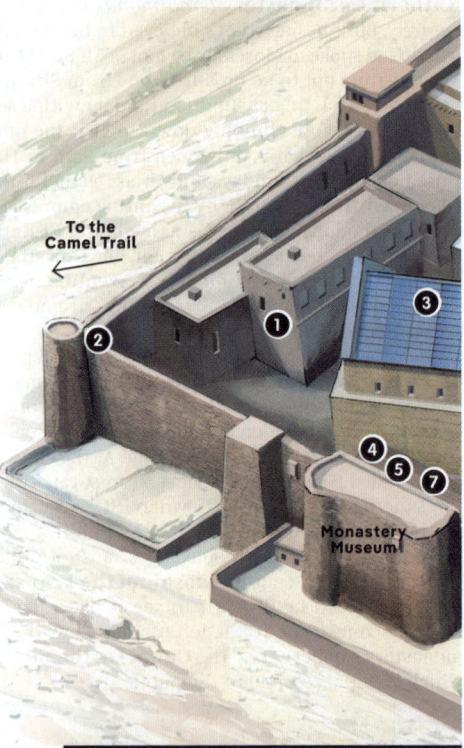

3 Mosaic of the Transfiguration

Justinian ordered the construction of the basilica, graced with Byzantine art. Lavishly made using thousands of pieces of glass, gold, silver and stone tesserae, the mosaic (completed in 551) recreates Christianity's gospel accounts of Jesus' miraculous revelation as the son of God.

8 Bell Tower

In 1871 Greek artisans travelled from the island of Tinos to help construct the bell tower. The nine bells inside were a present from Tsar Alexander II of Russia, which are rung for Sunday services. An older semantron (wooden percussion instrument) signals vespers and matins.

6 Ancient Gate

Frequent raids and attacks on the monastery led the monks to build the Ancient Gate to prevent the ransacking of church treasures and to keep the monastic community safe. Look up at the high walls and you'll see a ramshackle wooden structure. In times of strife, monks left via this primitive lift, lowered to the ground by a pulley.

ISRAEL–EGYPT RELATIONS

Israel's past occupation of Sinai has left a stain on relations between the two states and even caused a rift between the larger Egyptian public and Sinai's Bedouin, with the former suspecting the insistence by Bedouin to remain on their land despite Israeli rule meant they were collaborators. In reality, many Bedouin worked as guides assisting Egyptian soldiers to cross through Sinai's mountains without detection by Israel. While Egypt became the first Arab country to sign a peace treaty with Israel in 1979, this has been considered a cold peace, with the recent conflict intensifying hostilities. Israel often suggests Hamas' underground tunnels extend under the border into Sinai for weapons smuggling, despite Egypt saying it's dismantled this network, while Israeli officials' proposals to push Gaza's Palestinians into Sinai has further upset Egyptians.

continued from p393

Growing around the back of the church is thought to be a descendant of the original **burning bush** in the monastery compound. Up the stairs on the southern side of the walled area, the **Monastery Museum** *(US$2)* displays precious chalices, gold and silver crosses, and ancient manuscripts.

Dar Jan

TIME FROM DAHAB: **3 HRS**

Unleash your inner artist

Run by passionate couple Gihan Zakaria and Khaled Kamel, who decided to trade the Cairo metropolis for Sinai sands, **Dar Jan** *(+20 10-9212-5555)* is a 3.5-hectare organic farm and art space offering accommodation, yoga, desert hikes, and workshops on pottery, mosaic, painting, calligraphy, off-grid living, sustainable building and much more. Founded in 2016, it's the only artsy endeavour of its kind in Sinai and a perfect dose of entrepreneurship and creativity to counteract the large resort experiences elsewhere on the coast.

Courses are taught by artists and specialists in their fields and aim to encourage and channel participants' expression and free thinking. One of Dar Jan's signature activities is its one-day **art and gourmet experience** *(US$75)*. Start the day with a tour of their farm before immersing yourself in slow living. You'll choose between learning mosaic or pottery in a private class that ends in crafting your own creation to take home. After the workshop, enjoy a slow-cooked, fresh farm-to-table lunch or dinner with your hosts (accommodating your tastes and/or dietary restrictions). Throughout the day, you'll be offered endless refills of tea brewed with the farm's herbs and snacks to tide you over until you sit down to a colourful feast. The couple's hospitality is truly exceptional and their company so pleasantly delightful, you're bound to leave brimming with positivity. The spot is a true oasis in the desert and particularly beautiful at twilight, when you can sit among lush olive groves and date palms while watching the sun dip below the silhouette of Sinai's mountain range.

The farm also has a small shop where you can purchase herbal teas, leather goods made by local Bedouin women and other handicrafts. Their immune-boosting olive leaf tea and prized vegan hibiscus jam make perfect souvenirs or gifts.

Dar Jan also offers guided hikes led by a Bedouin guide (US$80) where you spend a half-day exploring **Nuweiba**'s treasured canyons – typically to Wadi Wishwashi. Dar Jan shuts down over the summer (mid-May to mid-September) given the area's scorching temperatures.

White Canyon

TOP EXPERIENCE

Nuweiba Canyons

Trade the sea for a daytime safari exploring the awe-inspiring canyons of Sinai. Spend the day scaling cavernous walls the colour of carnelian and take a dip in a mystical green pool. Note that this trip isn't suited for those fearing tight spaces and heights, as you'll be climbing, crawling and even jumping over rocks and slipping in between the shadows of boulders.

DON'T MISS
- Canyon Salama
- White Canyon
- Abu Hamata Canyon
- Wadi Wishwashi
- Closed Canyon
- Ain Khudra Oasis
- Malha Valley

Canyon Hopping

Just an hour's drive from Dahab, a hike through **White Canyon** features smooth, cream-coloured sands and narrowing limestone walls. Depending on where your guide has you start, you'll either begin or end at **Ain Khudra Oasis**, where a Bedouin camp sits among the lush ravine. The stroll through the canyon is relatively easy, but the entry and exit points are a bit of an obstacle course. Be prepared for shoddy ladders and a

PRACTICALITIES
- *tour per person (depending on operator) US$80-100*

> **COLOURED CANYON CLOSED**
>
> The Egyptian government has closed the route to the famous Coloured Canyon. While some Bedouin guides will offer to take you via a much longer route at a more expensive rate, this is illegal, meaning that if an accident occurs, emergency services may have trouble reaching hikers and jail time is possible for walking in an illegal area.
>
> As an alternative, Canyon Salama offers a similar experience with a rainbow of colours.

> **TOP TIPS**
>
> ● Your chosen tour operator will provide travel to and from your accommodation. Your lodging may also be able to arrange hikes.
>
> ● The ride may be a bit bumpy on the rough, mountainous terrain, and it's quite likely you'll be riding in the back of a pickup truck.
>
> ● All hikes into the canyons require a Bedouin guide, which will be set up by your tour operator.
>
> ● It's recommended to explore the canyons from March to May or September to November, when temperatures are mild and rainfall is minimal.
>
> ● Wadi Wishwashi is best visited in late spring, after winter rains fill the pools.

steep climb. Yet within the canyon – sheltered from movement and noise – you'll find a sense of peace and stillness.

Just after Ain Khudra Oasis and on the way to Wadi Ghazala is **Closed Canyon**, which gets its name from the narrow path that's often difficult to pass through. Named after the gazelles seen frolicking here, **Wadi Ghazala** is a valley filled with acacia groves, where you can rest your feet.

Hidden Treasure

A well-kept secret is **Abu Hamata Canyon**, located below Hadabat El Tih, a mountainous plateau running across Sinai. This remote canyon is nearly untouched by visitors so rubbish, graffiti and other traces of tourists are rare. Considered Sinai's longest canyon, you'll wind through tight passageways lined with layers of jagged red rock until eventually arriving at a panoramic view of Hadabat el Tih.

More well-known and on most travellers' bucket lists, **Wadi Wishwashi** is an hour-long, 2km hike close to Basata Ecolodge. This mostly flat walk winds along the valley floor of sand and loose gravel past soaring sandstone and basalt-streaked mountains, and ends at a stepped series of three pools surrounded by towering silver cliffs. While the hike to the pools isn't challenging, if you want to reach the upper watering holes, you'll need decent upper-body strength and scrambling skills to pull yourself up the rocks, ropes and makeshift ladders. Bring your bathing suit and water shoes. Though the wadi is in a protected area, litter and the scent of urine can be pervasive around the lowest pool. The uppermost pool, with opaque emerald-green waters, is the most photogenic, but is less visited because of the difficulty of the climb.

Continuing on an additional 4km, you'll reach the end of **Malha Valley**, where date palms and acacia trees bloom (fertilised by a small underground spring) in this serene oasis set against sandstone walls the size of skyscrapers. There's often a light breeze blowing, adding to the sense of calm this cliffside provides.

Just before the town of Nuweiba is **Canyon Salama**, a relatively easy, 800m hike whose hallmark is the supreme blend of colour that seems to have been done by swift brushstrokes rather than shaped and shaded by water and wind over thousands of years. The hike begins at the canyon's mouth – a wide and golden gorge that gradually narrows into a shoulder-width path tucked between salmon-coloured walls stacked like terraced fungi on a tree trunk. While the canyon is compact, its walls don't hover over you like other canyons, so you get to enjoy the sun's rays against the swirling rock formations.

St Katherine's Monastery

TOP EXPERIENCE

St Katherine Protectorate

Elevate your body and spirit to some of the tallest mountains in Egypt by hiking the hilltops of South Sinai. From the tallest mountain in Egypt to sacred summits teeming with ethereal energies, these majestic desert peaks above the Bedouin-majority village of St Katherine will shift your spiritual consciousness (and give your quads a good workout too).

DON'T MISS

- Gebel Abbas Pasha
- Gebel Katarina
- Mt Sinai
- Wadi Al Arbain Trail
- Gebel Abu Gasaba
- Gebel Serbal
- Gebel Um Shomer

Seeing Sunrise from Mt Sinai

Known locally as Gebel Musa (Mt Moses), **Mt Sinai** is revered by Christians, Muslims and Jews, all of whom believe that God delivered his 10 Commandments to Moses at its peak. The most popular way to visit is on a predawn hike to the summit, soaking in the scene and then returning to base for the opening of **St Katherine's Monastery** (p393) at 9.30 am.

The well-defined **Camel Trail** is the easiest route to the top, ascending gently over a series of long switchbacks. To save your

PRACTICALITIES
- *St Katherine Protectorate entry fee US$5*
- *Scan this QR code for prices and opening hours.*

Hike to Mt Sinai

ST KATHERINE HIKING

Although this is subject to change, at the time of research, hiking tourism in St Katherine was running illegally, as the Egyptian government had stopped issuing overnight permits. Hikers are only able to get a permit that allows one day of hiking but not overnight stays in the mountains. This is for all trails except the climb to Mt Sinai, which only takes half a day.

MONASTERY VISITS

For centuries, St Katherine's Monastery has been visited by pilgrims from around the world, many of whom braved extraordinarily difficult journeys to reach this remote and isolated site.

Today a paved access road has removed the hazards that used to accompany a trip here, and the monastery has become a popular day trip from Sharm El Sheikh and Dahab. The road from the coast and the path to the monastery have numerous security checkpoints and passport stops. As St Katherine's is still a functioning monastery, opening hours are restricted and modest dress is required (no shorts permitted, and women must cover their shoulders).

legs (or tire different muscles), hire a camel at the base from one of the many Bedouin men offering their services (for about LE650). Several kiosks on the route ensure you have enough fuel in the form of water, tea, coffee and sugary snacks to reach the finish line. The Camel Trail ends at a cafe near the plateau of **Elijah's Basin**, where the Prophet Elijah is said to have heard the voice of God, and then the real penitence begins. A series of 750 steep, rocky and uneven steps (lacking a sturdy railing) march to the top, where the congregation perches on the rocks to welcome the day. Take a deep breath and savour the sky's transformation from night to day – as flecks of soft gold and amber slowly creep above cider-coloured mountains. The journey to the top is a little under 5km and takes about three hours one way.

A small chapel and mosque take up some of the real estate at the summit – they are often locked but sometimes open to visitors. Peek through the chapel keyhole to see the frescoes. Under the mosque is a small cave where it's said that Moses spent 40 days and 40 nights. Wear sturdy shoes and bring plenty of water, a torch and warm layers – even in summer, it can be cold and windy at the top. Another option is to walk up for sunset when the peak rarely sees more than a handful of hikers.

The Camel Trail isn't the only way to the top, but security concerns and the whims of government officials can close other trails indefinitely and at short notice. Occasional alternatives include the taxing 3750 **Steps of Repentance**, laid by one monk as a form of penance, and the **Wadi Al Arbain Trail**, which threads up the neighbouring mountain of Gebel Safsafa (Willow Peak) and takes in more historical sites.

For the most memorable experience, arrange a trip with **Wilderness Ventures Egypt** (wilderness-ventures-egypt.

com; US$28-128), whose prices vary depending on the number of participants and whether you're taking a day or an overnight trip. One of its delightful Bedouin guides from the Jabaleya tribe takes you to Elijah's Basin and sets up camp, where you might be the only visitor enjoying delicious meals and tales around the fire before conquering the steps up to the summit the next morning.

Hiking the Valleys Around St Katherine

Mt Sinai might be the most famous peak around St Katherine's, but South Sinai's high mountain ranges put out a siren call for adventurous types. These mountains, once volcanic, are layered in colour – from glossy veins of black basalt to swirling waves of sandstone that blaze pink in the late afternoon sun. Paths wind through quiet valleys of tranquil pools, and hikers scramble above waterfalls past unexpectedly lush gardens growing almonds, pomegranates, olives, quinces, plums and figs. Aromatic herbs like sage, rosemary and thyme burst to life along the route, giving the sense that you're walking through a spice market. Caves built by hermits and ruins of storage posts from the Nabataeans, the ancient civilisation that had its HQ at the famous site of Petra in modern-day Jordan, hint at the centuries-long importance of the footsteps you're following.

A long but popular circuit travels through some of Sinai's mesmerising summit scenery, passing through red-rock valleys to the see-through aquamarine pool of **Galt El Azraq**, taking four to five days from the village. Shorter options include

SINAI TRAIL CLOSED

The Sinai Trail debuted in 2015 as Egypt's first long-distance hiking route. As part of the Bedouin Trail, a 1200km passage traversing Africa and Asia led by a collective of Bedouin tribes, the project helped spur the movement for grassroots, heritage-focused tourism in Sinai instead of commercialised, pre-packaged tours. Despite its success, the trail shut down in October 2024 as increasing government restrictions over wilderness access made the route too difficult to operate fully.

Galt El Azraq

TOP TIPS

- No buses go to St Katherine's (unless you're with a tour group for the day), so you'll need to book a taxi to take you here.

- The best time to travel here is March–May or September–November to avoid the area's extreme heat and winter rains.

- Consider taking a filtered water bottle or water-purification tablets, unless you trust drinking from springs.

- Tell your hike organiser before the trip if you have any dietary restrictions, as they'll be preparing your meals.

- Consider bringing a portable phone charger and flashlight.

- Most camps will have long-drop toilets and won't have toilet paper available, so best to bring your own.

mountain climbs that take in history and heights. Reaching the summit of **Gebel Katarina** (Mt Katherine), Egypt's highest peak at 2629m, requires about five hours along a straightforward but taxing trail. The views from the top are breathtaking, as you take in the scraggly series of sleek black and red stone amid a panorama that includes the mountains of Saudi Arabia and even the Red Sea on a clear day. A 120-year-old chapel sits at its summit, with adjoining cells where hikers can lodge for the night.

Crowning the top of **Gebel Abbas Basha** are the 18th-century ruins of an unfinished Swiss-style sanatorium that the namesake Ottoman ruler hoped would cure his tuberculosis. At its peak, you can see the edges of North Sinai and the plateau that divides the two regions.

Bedouin guides are required for all routes, and their knowledge of the flora, fauna and footpaths is unparalleled. **Wilderness Ventures Egypt** (p400) puts together wonderful bespoke itineraries based on your interests and abilities, or you can make arrangements at your accommodation in St Katherine's village. Some travellers like to combine all three mountain climbs into a route known as the Three Peaks Challenge, where you hike the three summits in 24 hours or less.

Other lesser-known and much more challenging peaks to climb include **Gebel Serbal**, lying far northwest of St Katherine's Monastery at the northern edge of South Sinai. Early Christians believed this mountain to be the real Mt Sinai, but that perspective changed once the monastery was built. Considered to be one of the Sinai's most beautiful summits, **Gebel Abu Gasaba** is a tough, scrambling climb but its views are well worth it. On a clear day, you can see Gebel Serbal, Gebel Katarina and Gebel Um Shomer. If conditions prove right, hikers may even be able to gaze over the Gulf of Suez to see the summits of mainland Egypt. Sinai's second-highest mountain after Gebel Katarina, **Gebel Um Shomer** is an impressive peak that feels more like it belongs in the European Alps than a Middle Eastern desert. Etched at the top are the names TE Yorke and TJ Prout – the first two Englishmen to have climbed the mountain in 1862. These peaks often take days to hike and are more suited for experienced trekkers.

Places We Love to Stay

$ Budget $$ Midrange $$$ Top End

Sharm El Sheikh MAP p375

Umbi Sharks Bay Diving Village $$ Bedouin-owned spot with basic rooms; feels delightfully local and laid-back.

Camel Dive Centre Hotel $$ Chilled-out Na'ama Bay hub for divers and budget travellers; quiet rooms surround a courtyard pool.

Ras Katy Sunset Views $$ A three-room self-catering villa high above the water on its namesake headland in the quiet Hadaba area.

Novotel $$ Choose the livelier Na'ama Bay side, or the 'Palm' wing with pools and colourfully blooming grounds.

Reef Oasis $$$ The elevated infinity pool and dive centre at Far Garden reef will lure you out of the room.

Four Seasons Sharm El Sheikh $$$ The height of secluded luxury. Huge rooms blend modern design with lattice woodwork and bronze fixtures.

Meraki Resort $$$ An adults-only hotel with an Ibiza-party ethos and sleek white and gold rooms made for Instagram.

Rixos $$$ This is an 'ultra all-inclusive' resort with seven pools, nine bars and a recommended sushi restaurant (plus eight other options).

Mövenpick Sharm El Sheikh $$$ A whitewashed hotel on a calm curve of Na'ama Bay, with private beaches, a spa, pool and on-site horse stables.

Hilton Sharm El Sheikh Fayrouz Resort $$$ This Na'ama Bay property is showing its age, but the bungalow-style rooms can't be found anywhere else.

Steigenberger Alcazar $$$ A grand lobby, huge pool and well-manicured grounds can be found here at the furthest reaches of Nabq's development.

Cleopatra Luxury Resort $$$ A firm family favourite, with a kids' club, two shallow pools for younger swimmers and an outdoor playground.

Dahab MAP p387

Sindbad Camp $ Chilled-out traditional Bedouin beach camp with a welcoming atmosphere in the heart of the Lighthouse Reef area.

Malakot Mountain Oasis $ Ecolodges in scenic Wadi Gnai, 15km from Dahab, with delicious Bedouin food and a healing sweat lodge.

Dive Urge $ Boutique ecohotel with bright garden rooms draped in bougainvillea and palm fronds and an on-site dive centre.

Wind Farm $ This place has the cleanliness of a five-star hotel but with chill and cosy beach-camp vibes.

Diamond Dahab House $ Modern, spacious rooms in close proximity to the Eel Garden dive site.

Elite Residence Dahab $$ Self-catering flats with fast internet and a rooftop terrace perfect for mingling.

Daniela Diving Resort $$ A charming arabesque-style hotel located just 50m from the sparkling sapphire shore.

Coral Coast $$ The rooms here get mixed reviews, but the well-being centre and yoga sessions get it all back in alignment.

Red Sea Relax $$ No-frills but spacious rooms wrapped around a central pool near the sea, plus an excellent dive centre.

Acacia $$ Great waterfront breakfasts; night owls will love the regular electronic dance sessions from Cosmic Nomads.

Eldorado $$ Oozes playful style; enjoy top-notch pizzas and a proper patch of sandy beach with loungers.

Dar Dahab $$$ A chic beachfront guesthouse with a gorgeous interior and furniture made from natural materials.

Swiss Inn Resort $$$ All the rooms here boast a private balcony or terrace overlooking the sea or gardens; guests particularly rave over the hotel's cuisine.

Jaz Dahabeya $$$ It's worth it to stay a bit outside of town at this hidden gem tucked near a quiet lagoon. Friendly, accommodating staff and an on-site dive centre.

St Katherine p393

Desert Fox Camp $ Basic rooms amid olive-tree groves; chill in the Bedouin tent or communal fireplace room after trekking. A swimming pool is coming.

Monastery Guesthouse $$ You can't get any closer to St Katherine's Monastery than these well-kept if slightly austere rooms.

TOOLKIT

Felucca on the Nile (p410)
ANTON_IVANOV/SHUTTERSTOCK

TOOLKIT

The chapters in this section cover the most important topics you'll need to know about in Egypt. They're full of nuts-and-bolts information and valuable insights to help you understand and navigate Egypt and get the most out of your trip.

Arriving
p406

Getting Around
p407

Bus & Train Travel
p408

Nile Cruising
p410

Money
p411

Accommodation
p412

Family Travel
p413

Health & Safe Travel
p414

Food, Drink & Nightlife
p416

Responsible Travel
p418

Accessible Travel
p420

Women Travellers
p421

Nuts & Bolts
p422

Visas, Embassies & Tour Operators
p423

Language
p424

Pharaonic Glossary
p426

Arriving

Cairo International Airport, about 20km northeast of central Cairo, is the main entry point. Many European budget airlines use Sphinx International Airport, about 45km west of the city centre near Giza. There are also direct flights from Europe to Hurghada, Luxor and Sharm El Sheikh airports.

ATMs & Exchange Kiosks

International terminals have ATMs (Visa or Mastercard) and exchange kiosks (major currencies). Rates are government-controlled and won't vary much between airport and town.

Transport Tips

Taxis wait at all terminals. Uber works well from Cairo International; from Sphinx International, it's better to arrange pick-up with your accommodation. Hotel shuttles are worth considering for middle-of-the-night arrivals.

SIM Cards

Prepaid SIM cards from Vodafone, Orange, Etisalat or We are the cheapest option and are sold at airport kiosks (passport required; queues likely). Buying in town offers no significant savings.

Wi-fi

Don't count on free wi-fi at any of Egypt's airports. If you manage to connect, the wi-fi generally only works inside terminal buildings and not near ride pick-up points.

Airport Taxis

From	To	Time	Fare
CAIRO INTL AIRPORT	City centre	20min–1hr	US$5–20
SPHINX INTL AIRPORT	Giza Pyramids	45min	US$20–25
SHARM EL SHEIKH INTL AIRPORT	Central Sharm	20min	US$5

ENTERING EGYPT OVERLAND

Land borders The only entry/exit point between Egypt and Israel and the Palestinian Territories is Sinai's Taba border crossing (open 24 hours), with unreliable ATMs on both sides. You can get a Sinai-only visa (p423) here, but if you plan to visit elsewhere in Egypt, arrange a full visa in advance, either online or through an embassy. The main crossing points between Egypt and Sudan are at Argeen (west bank) and Qustul (east bank; accessed by ferry from Abu Simbel); hours vary. There are no ATMs; arrange visas in advance.

Ferries Ferries link Duba (Saudi Arabia) with Safaga, south of Hurghada *(kcfmt.com)* and Aqaba (Jordan) with Nuweiba and Taba Heights in southern Sinai *(abmaritime.com.jo)*.

Getting Around

Transport in Egypt is fairly efficient and very reasonably priced. Flying is quickest, and among the cheapest options over long distances, but buses, trains and hired private cars (with driver) reach more places.

TRAVEL COSTS

Cairo–Aswan flight
US$50–100

Cairo–Luxor sleeper train
US$90/person

Luxor–Hurghada bus
US$6–8

1hr felucca sail
LE300

Air

EgyptAir (egyptair.com) is the main domestic carrier. There are also several smaller carriers, including **Nile Air** (nileair.com) and **Air Cairo** (aircairo.com), linking Cairo with major centres, although they have fewer flights and services. When booking online, switch your home country to Egypt to get the cheapest fares.

Boat

Many cruise ships and river boats ply the Nile, especially between Luxor and Aswan. These range from the simple felucca to large cruisers and dahabiyas (houseboats); see p410. The best place to organise overnight felucca trips is Aswan. Short sails can easily be arranged in Aswan, Luxor and Cairo. Smaller cruise boats (p262) run on Lake Nasser between Aswan and Abu Simbel.

TIP
Bolt, Careem and InDrive operate in Cairo, alongside Uber. You can also use these ride-hailing apps to book local taxis.

POLICE ESCORTS

In certain areas, especially in the Northern Nile Valley and Western Desert, tourists must be accompanied by a police escort. While this can sometimes cause delays, it's worth remembering that these possibly outdated measures are there for your safety. To minimise hassles, book excursions through an established local tour company.

ROAD-TRIP ESSENTIALS

Drive on the right.

In rural areas, prepare for frequent slowdowns due to livestock wandering into the road.

Have your passport handy for checkpoints.

Book long excursions at least a half day in advance so the driver can arrange permits.

Bus

Buses are a cheap option and go almost everywhere. Go Bus has a wide network and English-language website; it's worth splurging for Elite or Aero class. West & Mid Delta runs from Cairo's Torgoman station to the Western Desert, and Upper Egypt Bus Co runs Torgoman to Fayoum. See p408 for more.

Train

The sleeper train from Cairo to Luxor and Aswan is one of Egypt's classic journeys. Between Cairo and Alexandria, Port Said and Suez, train is the best option. Except for short runs, it's worth paying extra for express, where available. See p408 for more on train travel.

Car Hire, Taxi & Ride Sharing

Car rental is uncommon. To hire a car with driver, ask your hotel for recommendations. Rates start at LE1000 per half day, plus a tip of 10% or more. Regular taxis abound. Some have meters; otherwise, negotiate a price first. Uber operates in Cairo, Alexandria, Suez, Ismailia and Port Said.

LEFT TO RIGHT: FUSE/GETTY IMAGES, GOGLIK83/GETTY IMAGES

Bus & Train Travel

Transport in Egypt is fairly efficient and cheap. Train is the most comfortable option for travelling from Cairo to Alexandria, Luxor and Aswan if you're not in a hurry. Otherwise, frequent buses connect all major cities and towns. Delays are common later in the day, particularly when departing Cairo in traffic. Beyond the Nile Valley, buses are the best option. Note that due to security concerns some areas are or may become off-limits to foreign travellers.

Bus Tickets

Book tickets in advance, especially for Cairo–Sinai routes and infrequent Western Desert services. With the exception of Go Bus, this will need to be done in person. On board, retain your ticket to show inspectors and carry your passport to present at military checkpoints. This is commonly required on the road between Aswan and Abu Simbel and on all Sinai buses.

Bus Companies

Cairo's main long-distance station is Torgoman. Expect X-ray checks and metal detectors when entering the station. No buses serve St Katherine's Monastery, which is only accessible by taxi or tour, and the road between Siwa and Bahariya Oasis remains closed.

Go Bus (gobus-eg.com) Operates an expanding network of routes in northern Egypt, down the Red Sea coast and between Luxor and Hurghada. Ticket prices vary depending on bus class, but all have air-con and are non-smoking. Tickets can be booked and seats reserved on the English-language website.

East Delta Travel Co Operates between Cairo, the Suez Canal region and the Sinai Peninsula.

West & Mid Delta Bus Co Covers Alexandria, the Delta, the Mediterranean coast and Siwa. Services to Siwa are often cancelled in winter, so consider travelling via Alexandria and Marsa Matruh as part of a broader itinerary.

Upper Egypt Bus Co Services most Western Desert oases and the Nile Valley.

Egybus Public bus service operating throughout the Western Desert oases. Services depart from Torgoman to Farafra Oasis.

Bus Classes

Deluxe Air-con 'deluxe' buses connect major destinations. On Go Bus these are the Elite and Aero services. No-smoking policies are in place, and some buses on long-distance routes have toilets (though they may not be clean). On longer routes a 15- to 20-minute stop every three hours is the norm. Videos are usually shown – earplugs are useful if you want to sleep, as is an extra layer as overnight buses can get cold.

Standard The cheapest buses on all routes are overcrowded, noisy and markedly less comfortable, and they stop frequently. For trips under two hours, microbuses are usually preferable.

Microbuses

The microbus (pronounced *meekrobas*) is a van with seats for 14 passengers. Privately owned and usually unmarked, they run along the same routes as buses and are a bit cheaper. They also stop anywhere along the route on request

---

HOW TO RIDE A MICROBUS

- Microbuses run on no set schedule and only depart when full. They're usually cramped, but the upside is you can usually find one headed where you want to go no matter the time of day.
- Find microbuses outside bus and train stations or at designated depots – ask for the *maw'if meekrobas*. These parking lots are crowded with drivers shouting their destinations. Shout yours and eventually you'll find the right zone.
- Pay after boarding. This involves passing your money hand-to-hand up the rows; your change will be returned the same way.
- When it's time to get off, try saying *'All-uh gamb'*, a common way to request to get off in Arabic. The driver may not completely stop, so when you feel comfortable, jump off.
- Solo male travellers should avoid sitting next to women where possible.

ASWAN SLEEPER TRAINS

There are three Abela sleeper trains *(abelatrains.com)* per day between Cairo and Aswan, currently departing late afternoon/evening in both directions and taking 12 to 15 hours. Tickets, available online, should be booked at least a day ahead. Currently, the only Greater Cairo stop listed on the website is Giza.

Compartments are small but comfortable. Seats convert to a bed and an upper bunk folds down; linen, pillows and blankets are provided. There's also a small basin and shared toilets that usually have toilet paper. Middle compartments, away from doors, tend to be quieter. Bring a jacket or jumper as the air-con is cold at night.

Airline-style meals are served in the compartments. A steward serves drinks (sometimes including alcohol), and there's a club car.

and will pick up passengers along the way. In certain parts of the country, such as Siwa and the Western Oases, foreigners are not allowed to use microbuses. However, in some areas, such as from Cairo to Fayoum, Qena to Abydos and the Suez Canal Zone, they're often the faster option.

Train Tickets

Consult the Egyptian Railways website *(enr.gov.eg)* or the foreigners' window at major stations for schedules and tickets. Cairo's main train stations are Ramses and, for Upper Egypt destinations, Bashtil. Reaching Bashtil in traffic can take considerable time, so follow the advice and check in one hour before departure.

Train Classes

Express trains, including the older Spanish, the Special and the newer Talgo, have air-con, assigned seats and meal service.

1st class *(darga ula)* Preferable if you're going any distance. Air-con *(takyeef)*, padded seats, relatively clean toilets, tea and snack service.

2nd class *(darga tanya)* Seats are vinyl. Skip air-con if it's an option – it often doesn't work well. Toilets aren't well kept.

3rd class *(darga talta)* Bench seats, glacial pace and crowds, but lots of activity. Be prepared for attention – travellers are a rarity in this class.

Lower Egypt Services

The best trains on the Cairo–Alexandria route are speedy 'Spanish' *(esbani)* trains. Almost all go direct, or have just one stop, in 2½ hours. 'French' *(faransawi)* trains are less comfortable. Both count as 1st class with air-con, though, so specify Spanish when booking. Ordinary trains on this route are very basic and slow. Abela *(abelatrains.com)* runs a sleeper train from Cairo to Marsa Matruh three times a week.

Upper Egypt Services

Day trains At the time of writing tourists could ride all-day trains south of Cairo. The best is No 980, the express departing Cairo at 8am; it's an enjoyable 10½ hours to Luxor and 14 hours to Aswan. If you plan to get off at smaller stops such as Kom Ombo, verify that the train stops there. Aswan station has a separate ticket window for foreigner tickets. It's signposted in English and has English-language schedules.

Night trains (non-sleepers) If you don't mind missing the scenery, there are regular air-con night services between Cairo, Luxor and Aswan. Seats recline, are comfortable enough to get a decent sleep in and are cheaper than the sleeper train. Bring a jacket.

Nile Cruising

Cruising the world's longest river, admiring the beauty of the stunning Nile Valley set within an otherwise barren desert landscape and visiting Egypt's extraordinary ancient monuments adds up to a once-in-a-lifetime experience. Here are some tips on how to get the most out of this fabulous journey.

ITINERARIES & SIGHTS

Large cruisers stick to rigid itineraries on the Luxor–Aswan route. Days are spent visiting monuments and relaxing on deck. By night there's cocktails, dancing and fancy-dress parties. Feluccas (Egyptian sailing boats) and dahabiyas determine their own schedules and can stop at small islands or antiquities sites. Because they use sail power, a greater proportion of time is spent sailing (or being pulled by a tugboat). Nighttime entertainment involves leisurely dinners, socialising and impromptu music.

Luxor

Luxor (p190), the start or end of your journey, has some of Egypt's most famous ancient monuments from the New Kingdom. Most cruises only cover the bare minimum, so if you're interested in Luxor's sights, book an extra day or two here.

Luxor to Aswan

This most famous stretch of the river has stunning architecture and scenes of great natural beauty. All cruisers stop at the temples of **Edfu** (p245) and **Kom Ombo** (p243). Dahabiyas also stop at Esna, Al Kab and Gebel Silsila.

Aswan

Aswan is the picturesque end of the popular Luxor–Aswan cruise. Most itineraries include visits (by car) to the **Temple of Isis** (p259), the high dam and the **unfinished obelisk** (p250) at the end of the cruise. Some offer an optional excursion (by plane) to **Abu Simbel** (p265).

Lake Nasser

Because so few cruisers operate on Lake Nasser, moorings are never crowded and monuments – with the exception of the **Temple of Ramses II** (p266) at Abu Simbel – are not busy. Itineraries are three nights/four days from Aswan to Abu Simbel or four nights/five days from Abu Simbel to Aswan.

CRUISING TIPS

For information on the most sustainable Nile cruising options, turn to the Responsible Travel section (p418).

When to travel Summer (June to August) is the cheapest season due to the extreme heat at that time. Christmas and Easter are busy and expensive. Spring and autumn are ideal.

Where to start Most cruises starting from Luxor are a day longer than those starting from Aswan.

Cabin choice On cruisers avoid the lowest deck, as the banks of the Nile are high.

Sailing time Large cruisers cover distances quickly and cruise duration is often only four hours per day.

WHICH CRUISE IS BEST FOR YOU?

Best for adventure A felucca from Aswan to Kom Ombo or Edfu (p242).
Made for romantics Luxury dahabiyas evoke elegant 19th-century travel (p241).
Best cruisers SS *Sudan* paddle steamer for historic atmosphere; *Sanctuary Sun Boat III* and MS *Philae* for 1920s glamour and luxe trimmings; MS *Mayflower* and MS *Darakum* for well-priced itineraries.
Far from the crowds Lake Nasser cruises offer boat safaris to remote monuments in dramatic desert landscapes (p262).

Money

CURRENCY: EGYPTIAN POUND (LE, EGP); AMERICAN DOLLARS (USD)

Cash Versus Card

Cash is king, although Visa and Mastercard are accepted in many upmarket restaurants and hotels and at tourist-oriented places; always choose to be charged in local currency to avoid markups. When exchanging foreign currency for Egyptian pounds, only clean, untorn and unmarked bills are accepted.

ATMs

ATMs are common in main cities but can be unreliable in the oases, so stock up with cash before going somewhere remote. Many ATMs have a withdrawal limit of LE6000; some charge user fees. Banque Misr, Banque du Caire, National Bank of Egypt, CIB and HSBC are the most common.

Tipping

Baksheesh is expected everywhere, so keep small change handy and, if in doubt, tip. Many Egyptians depend on tips for their livelihoods, and generosity is appreciated.
Bathroom attendants LE5–10
Mosque attendants LE10
Restaurants 10% to 15%; more for great service.
Taxis Round up the fare or add 5% extra.

HOW MUCH FOR...

Abu Simbel entry
LE750

1hr camel ride at the Pyramids
LE500

Grand Egyptian Museum entry fee
LE600

Saqqara entry fee
LE1000

HOW TO... Save Some Egyptian Pounds

Student discounts (generally 50%) are available on museum and site entry fees with an International Student Identity Card (ISIC). Arrange this online in advance through **International Student Identity Card** *(isic.org)*. Watch out for counterfeit student ID card operations in Downtown Cairo. Many places will also accept a valid student ID card together with your passport.

LOCAL TIP

It's worth keeping small change handy for taxi fares, public toilets and purchases at markets and from street vendors. Shop owners are sometimes willing to break larger bills.

THE ART OF BARGAINING

Except at fixed-price shops, bargaining (p45) is expected, and negotiating with vendors is all part of the Egypt experience. Before starting, check fixed-price stores first, decide on a budget and then express a casual interest. You're never under any obligation to buy, but you shouldn't initiate bargaining on something you don't want and you shouldn't back out of an agreed-upon price. The 'best' price isn't necessarily the cheapest – it's one that you and the seller are happy with.

Accommodation

Camps & Ecolodges

Egypt's many rustic lodges, beach camps and desert camps offer a relaxed holiday. Marsa Alam, Marsa Nakari and Marsa Shagra on the Red Sea coast, the Nuweiba–Taba highway, where you'll find **Basata** (p392), and Dahab in Sinai feature some great camps with a laid-back vibe. Around Siwa and the oases, try **Badry** (p303) or **Eden** (p303).

Resorts

Egypt knows how to do resorts, with some of the best along the Red Sea coast. Many offer all-inclusive rates. Booking well in advance can yield major discounts, as can booking in low season (September to November and February to May). If you prefer independent resorts, head to Marsa Alam, Marsa Shagra, Al Quseir, El Gouna, Dahab or Nuweiba.

Floating Accommodation

Whether you're cruising on a dahabiya, sailing on a felucca, enjoying the perks of a large cruise ship or staying on a Nile houseboat in Cairo, the chance to sleep on the water is very special. Amenities range from very basic on a felucca to top-class facilities on some dahabiyas and cruise ships.

Desert Camping

Camping is the best way to experience the rich colours of the desert at dawn and dusk and to take in the clear, pitch-black night skies. Sleep amid sandstone formations and stark landscapes near White Desert National Park, surround yourself with rolling dunes near Siwa Oasis or camp in South Sinai's rugged terrain with Bedouin guides.

HOW MUCH FOR A NIGHT...

In a budget hotel
US$30 or less

On a dahabiya
From US$250

In a Red Sea resort
From US$60

Hotels

Good-value budget places are readily available in tourist centres, and there are many top-end hotels. Midrange options are surprisingly limited, particularly in Cairo and Alexandria. If you typically travel in this price bracket, consider budget options too; some can be dramatically more pleasant for half the price. Rates often rise during the feasts of Eid Al Fitr and Eid Al Adha.

HOME SHARING & ILLEGAL HOTELS

If you're considering home-sharing options, there are some real finds, especially in Cairo and Alexandria; check out *brassbell.net*. Remember that Egypt's home-sharing sector is unregulated and traveller complaints are rife. Illegal hotels are also an issue, especially in Giza and among some of the cheaper options in Aswan and Luxor, and a lack of insurance and basic safety standards may leave you at risk. Thoroughly inform yourself before booking. If possible, avoid paying for rooms in full upfront and seek out reliable recommendations from other travellers.

Family Travel

Egypt is a thrilling destination for children, full of fantastic ancient monuments, exciting experiences such as camel rides, felucca trips and tomb exploration, and an abundance of wonderful swimming pools. Egyptians' generally warm manner towards children and babies makes travel here special and helps smooth over any small practical hassles you may encounter.

Sights & Activities

Egypt suits kids old enough to engage with its epic history and activities. Before going, get them fired up with activities such as those at the **British Museum** *(britishmuseum.org/learn/schools/ages-7-11/ancient-egypt)* or with films set in Egypt, such as *Death on the Nile*. On the ground there are few family concessions, but student discounts and children's rates are widely available.

Attitudes

What Egypt lacks in child-friendly facilities, infrastructure and specialised activities it more than makes up for in its doting attitude to small children and families. Waiters are generally delighted to see kids and make every effort to accommodate their needs. By adolescence, separation of the sexes is more typical, so teens should abide by grown-up etiquette when meeting Egyptians of their age.

Eating Out

Hygiene in food preparation can be inconsistent and stomach problems may occur. Rehydration salts are readily available at all pharmacies. Check that juices, ice and salads are prepared with bottled water. High chairs are available in better restaurants.

Good to Know

Don't expect car seats or seatbelts in taxis.
Keep kids away from stray animals.
In cities and resort areas formula is available, as are disposable nappies.
With notice, most hotels are willing to add a cot to your room.

KID-FRIENDLY PICKS

Cairo
Cairo has the Pyramids, an atmospheric souq and fabulous museums for older kids (p56).

Luxor
World-famous temples and tombs, plus hot-air ballooning (p190).

Southern Nile Valley
Enjoy temples, camels and felucca sailing (p231).

Western Desert
Children will love the slow pace of oasis life, where they can roll down sand dunes, find fossils and sleep in a tent (p270).

Red Sea Coast
Beaches and swimming pools galore, with diving courses, snorkelling trips and kid-friendly resorts (p346).

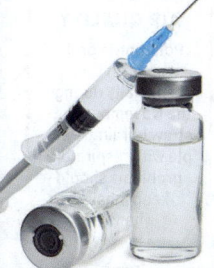

SAFETY TIPS

Make sure children are up to date with routine vaccinations.

Stock up your first-aid kit, pack good sunhats and don't skimp on the sunscreen or rehydration salts.

For infants you'll want a sling or back carrier rather than a stroller. Consider bringing your own child seat if travelling by car.

If you're travelling in the desert or on a boat between December and March, bring warm sweaters and hats to be prepared for chilly nights and early mornings.

It's nearly always worth paying a little extra for better standards of cleanliness and safety at hotels and restaurants.

Health & Safe Travel

Egypt is generally a safe and healthy destination, and most travellers visit without incident. However, certain precautions and preventative steps are worth taking to minimise risks.

DIVE INSURANCE

If you plan on diving while in Egypt, take out specific diving insurance, as many regular insurance policies exclude diving. Also confirm that your insurance covers the type of diving you will be doing. A helpful contact is the **Divers Alert Network** *(daneurope.org)*, which offers a variety of plans with worldwide validity for sport divers. At a minimum, check that the plan you choose covers evacuation to a recompression facility, hyperbaric chamber treatment and possibly also search and rescue.

Insurance

Travel insurance is highly recommended, particularly coverage of adventure activities and emergency evacuation. Also see your doctor and dentist before travelling. The best health care in Egypt is private. You'll need to show ability to pay prior to treatment and seek reimbursement from your insurance later.

Liveaboard Safety

There have been several recent tragedies on Red Sea liveaboard boats. If you are interested in a dive safari, do thorough advance research on the companies you are considering and seek out reliable information from other travellers and from independent operators. Also check out the recommendations of the UK government's **Marine Accident Investigation Branch** *(gov.uk/government/organisations/marine-accident-investigation-branch)*.

SAFE WATERS

- Bottled **drinking water** is cheap and readily available. Use containers such as Lifestraw to reduce plastic waste. Filtered water often isn't available for refills, but you can try iodine or a Steripen purifier.
- **Schistosomiasis** (bilharzia) is an infection of the bowel and bladder caused by a freshwater fluke and contracted through the skin. To avoid infection, it's best not to swim in slow-moving parts of the Nile.

AIR QUALITY

Pollution is problematic in Cairo, especially during the November rice-straw burning. People with respiratory problems should keep inhalers handy.

Vaccinations

No vaccines are required for Egypt, but it's recommended that you're up to date with vaccinations against hepatitis A and B and typhoid, which must be administered at least two weeks before travel, plus measles, tetanus and rabies (especially if travelling to remote locations). Government travel-health websites, including *cdc.gov/travel*, *gov.uk/foreign-travel-advice/egypt/health* and *smartraveller.gov.au/destinations/africa/egypt*, are useful sources of vaccine- and health-related information.

Medical Services

Private and university hospitals have good standards and quality doctors. For non-emergency care, Cairo and resort areas are well supplied with private clinics. You'll need to pay upfront for treatment, with a consultation averaging around US$50. For minor illnesses, consult a pharmacist first. They are well trained, speak English and can dispense all kinds of medication.

Heat Exhaustion

Heat exhaustion is common, with symptoms including headache, dizziness, tiredness and sometimes vomiting. Drink liquids (ideally sports drinks or water with rehydrating salts) before you're thirsty, and wear a hat. A more serious affliction is heatstroke, which occurs when the body's heat-regulating mechanism breaks down. Rapid cooling with ice and water, plus intravenous fluid replacement, is essential.

> **FOOD POISONING**
>
> Occasional bouts of food poisoning (bacterial diarrhoea) can be expected. The best cure is rest and fluids with oral rehydration salts. Stomach disinfectants such as Antinal (nifuroxazide) and Cipro (ciprofloxacin) are available and recommended above Immodium (loperamide), which only treats the symptoms rather than the cause. If symptoms persist for more than 72 hours or are accompanied by fever, consult a doctor.

Crime & Safety

Egypt depends heavily on tourism and the government goes to great lengths to ensure that nothing will happen to deter visitors. There is a heavy police presence at major sites and the country is generally very safe. Still, take normal street-smart precautions such as avoiding dark, empty streets at night and securing valuables in a hotel safe.

Terrorism

North Sinai has been off-limits to travellers for years because of the increased terrorism risk. These attacks are often aimed at Egyptian security forces, government targets and religious sites, but attacks against tourists have also occurred. When planning your trip, check your government's travel website for updates and advice.

LGBTIQ+ TRAVELLERS

Although homosexuality is technically not a crime in Egypt, homosexual acts in public are, and gay men have been prosecuted under morality laws. While there is an underground social scene in Cairo and Alexandria, accessing it as a foreigner is risky. Be discreet when (or refrain from) using LGBTIQ+ dating apps and avoid public displays of affection. Most upmarket accommodation will have no problem with a same-sex couple sharing a room. At smaller, local hotels, it's best to request separate beds.

Food, Drink & Nightlife

When to Eat

Fuul medames (fava-bean stew) is the Egyptian breakfast staple, usually eaten from about 8am onwards, with *a'aish baladi* (wholewheat flatbread). Lunch is the main meal, taken from 2pm, but more likely around 3pm or 4pm when everyone is home from work and school. At night, Egyptians often dine late, around 10pm, particularly in summer.

MENU DECODER

A'aish baladi Wholewheat flatbread, best eaten warm from the oven.

Fuul A hearty fava-bean stew.

Mezze Hot and cold small plates to start the meal.

Hummus Chickpeas smoothly mashed with lemon, garlic, tahini and cumin.

Tahini A fragrant paste of sesame seeds seasoned with garlic and lemon.

Ta'amiyya Egypt's version of a falafel, made with fava beans.

Tabbouleh Middle Eastern salad with bulgur wheat, parsley and chopped tomato.

Molokhiyya Classic soup of shredded green jute leaves, garlic and broth.

Hamam mahshi Roast pigeon stuffed with rice seasoned with cinnamon, cumin and other spices.

Kofta Spiced minced lamb or beef meatballs, skewered and grilled.

Kebab Flame-grilled meat, normally lamb; chicken equivalent is called *shish tawooq*.

Where to Eat & Drink

Restaurants Range from smart hotel dining, where booking ahead is essential, to home-style budget places dishing up Egyptian favourites (and normally not serving alcohol).

Cafes Usually open for most of the day and night, with drinks and shisha (water pipes), and only occasionally food. The classic Egyptian twist on the cafe is the *ahwa*.

Street food Street food is a huge part of the Egyptian food scene, with vendors selling fresh staples at local prices.

HOW TO... Enjoy Egyptian Seafood

When in Alexandria, in places along the Red Sea and in Sinai, you'll find a marvellous array of fresh seafood. Local favourites include *kalamaari* (squid), *balti* (fish that are about 15cm long, flattish and grey with a light belly) and the larger, tastier *bouri* (mullet). You'll also commonly find sea bass, sea bream, bluefish, sole and *gambari* (shrimp) on restaurant menus. The Red Sea is famous for its spiny lobsters, while the tilapia from Lake Nasser is a delight. The most popular ways to cook fish are grilling them over coals and frying them in olive oil.

Egyptian Copts are also very fond of *fesikh* (sun-dried, salted and fermented grey mullet), traditionally eaten during the springtime Sham An Nessim festival. Shops selling *fesikh* are recognisable by the smell; the flavour is an acquired taste.

HOW MUCH FOR A...

Cup of coffee
LE20–50

Fuul sandwich
LE30

Shawarma wrap
LE70–130

A'aish baladi
LE5

McDonald's burger
LE80

Midrange meal for two
LE150–300

Stella beer
LE60–80

Bottle of wine in a restaurant
From LE250

HOW TO... Hang in an Ahwa

The coffeehouse known as an *ahwa* is an Egyptian social institution: the Arabic word for coffee is now synonymous with the place in which it is drunk. Traditionally *ahwas* were all-male preserves, but it's now common to see young, mixed-sex groups of Egyptians in *ahwas*, especially in Cairo and Alexandria. The *ahwa* is a relaxed place where regulars go every day to sip a glass of tea, meet friends, talk about politics, play backgammon or wind down.

Egyptian *ahwa* (coffee) is a powerful Turkish-style brew served in small cups. You'll want to specify how much sugar you want: *ahwa mazboot* is a moderate amount, *ahwa saada* is without sugar, and *ahwa ziyada* (extra sweet) may make your teeth fall out. According to tradition, you can tell your future from the coffee mud left at the bottom of the cup.

Another popular feature is the shisha. Most people opt for traditional tobacco soaked in apple juice *(tuf-FAH)*, but in trendier places you'll find strawberry, melon, cherry or mixed-fruit flavours. A decorated glass pipe filled with water will be brought, hot coals will be placed in it and you will be given a disposable plastic mouthpiece to slip over the pipe's stem. To keep the coals hot, simply take a puff every now and then.

Shisha Sessions

Although there's less nicotine (0.05%) in shisha pipe tobacco than there is in cigarettes (0.95%), the amount smoked in a session is much higher. Thus, an hour of smoking shisha is equivalent to 10 cigarettes.

EGYPT'S NATIONAL DISH

There are few better ways to 'go local' than by joining Egyptians in eating a bowl of *kushari* (p83). There are many variations on this filling, carb-packed vegetarian meal whose appeal cuts across class and religious lines. However, they all share the basics in common: vermicelli, rice, brown lentils and chickpeas served with an array of toppings. These always include a hearty tomato sauce and seasoned, crispy fried onions for texture. To round things off, there's also a salsa-like hot sauce, vinegar or lemon and a light and aromatic garlic-cumin sauce. You can find *kushari* served at any time of day, but it's especially popular at lunch. It is almost always eaten either home-cooked, from a *kushari* vendor or at a *kushari* restaurant, where the only choices you'll need to make are small, medium or large and what toppings to include. The key to enjoying *kushari*, many Egyptians will tell you, is mixing things up just right while you eat so that each spoonful delivers the wonderful combination of flavours that makes *kushari* so special. Cairo is especially known for its *kushari*, as is Alexandria, where curry leaves and extra cumin are often added, and sometimes also eggs. Everyone has their favourite *kushari* spot, but some places to seek out include **Koshary Abou Tarek** (p83), the **Koshary Hend** (p142) branch on Sharia Abu Bakr Es Sidiq and **Koshary Goha** (p83), all in Cairo; **Koshari Alzaeem** (p203) in Luxor; and **Koshary Masrawy** (p313) and **Koshary 'Ala Sokhn** (p322), both in Alexandria.

Responsible Travel

Climate Change & Travel

It's impossible to ignore the impact we have when travelling; Lonely Planet urges all travellers to engage with their travel carbon footprint, which will mainly come from air travel. While there often isn't an alternative, travellers can look to minimise the number of flights they take, opt for newer aircrafts and use cleaner ground transport, such as trains. One proposed solution – purchasing carbon offsets – unfortunately does not cancel out the impact of individual flights. While most destinations will depend on air travel for the foreseeable future, for now, pursuing ground-based travel where possible is the best course of action.

The **UN Carbon Footprint Calculator** shows how flying impacts a household's emissions:

The **ICAO's Carbon Emissions Calculator** allows visitors to analyse the CO^2 generated by point-to-point journeys:

Go Local

Spend your money at locally owned guesthouses, eat and shop locally, engage local Egyptian guides and tour operators and, where possible, avoid all-inclusive deals where very little money is spent in-country.

Tread Carefully

Mass tourism threatens ancient monuments. Be aware and don't be tempted to tip guards to use your flash in tombs, clamber over pillars and statues or touch painted reliefs.

Egypt has a good network of flights between Cairo, Luxor, Aswan and Abu Simbel; most take less than 1½ hours. Consider the train or bus to lower your carbon footprint.

Join a **Bellies En-Route** (p83) food tour or take one of its cooking classes to learn how Cairenes cook and do their market shopping.

ANIMAL WELFARE

Sadly, you'll likely see many suffering animals in Egypt. Avoid activities where the animals appear skeletal or listless. To help, contact **Animal Care in Egypt** (ace-egypt.org.uk), **Brooke** (thebrooke.org) or **SPARE** (facebook.com/SPAREEGYPT).

TRADITIONAL CRAFTS

To support Egypt's weavers and tailors, try **Ramses Wissa Wassef Art Center** (p62) and the **Multicultural and Artistic Spaces at Qaitbey's** (p111; *@masq.hub*) in Cairo, Luxor's **Habiba Hand Weaving** (p227), Esna's **Pr.Ba Concept Store** (p239) and **Khnum** (p239) and Elephantine Island's **scarf shop** (p254).

VISIT Esna
This sustainable tourism initiative *(@discoveresna)* is invested in restoring historic sites and using local guides to get tourists better engaged in the culture and crafts of the Nile-side town of Esna (p236).

Protected Areas
Egypt currently has 30 Protected Areas preserving the country's incredible biodiversity, ranging from river islands and coral reefs to desert ecosystems. Go to *ecoegypt.org* for a listing.

Ras Mohammed National Park
Ras Mohammed National Park (ppage 382) is one of the best marine reserves in the world, encompassing an 850-sq-km fossilised coral headland that's home to more than 1000 species of fish.

Responsible Diving
For responsible Red Sea dive experiences, check out **Red Sea Diving Safari** *(redsea-divingsafari.com)*, which runs Dive Against Debris, a PADI clean-up program. **Green Fins** *(greenfins.net)* lists environmentally sound dive operators.

Cruise-ship Considerations
Cruise ships offer many comforts, but think twice before booking. Ask about the company's environmental commitment. For rooms near the stern, you may have to contend with engine vibrations and exhaust fumes.

Cruise-ship emissions can be up to four times greater per passenger-kilometre travelled than those of planes.

Fair Trade Egypt *(@fairtradeegypt)*, Egypt's first certified fair-trade shop, showcases hundreds of local crafts and products.

5th
In the 2024 Sustainable Development Report, Egypt ranked fifth out of 17 Middle East and North African countries and 83rd globally, with almost 40% of its sustainable development targets achieved or on track.

RESOURCES

redsea-project.com
Offers certified divers the opportunity to participate in projects such as sea turtle surveys.

preview.hepca.org
Red Sea reef conservation through public awareness and community action.

facebook.com/p/El-Heiz-Water-Education-Center-100063890179995
Promotes water conservation in the Western Desert.

Accessible Travel

There are an estimated 12 million Egyptians with disabilities, but the country is not well equipped for those with accessibility needs. That said, a number of tours offer accessible itineraries, and Egyptians are generally willing to assist.

Improving Wheelchair Access

While Egyptian cities, with their chaotic traffic and high kerbs, pose challenges to wheelchair users, some monuments and an increasing number of resort hotels offer accessible facilities.

Airport

The airports in Cairo, Luxor, Sharm El Sheikh, Hurghada and Aswan all offer assistance. Notify the airline or your tour operator at least 48 hours in advance and arrive at the airport three hours before departure.

Accommodation

Many international resorts and international chain hotels have accessible rooms and grounds. However, building standards vary; it's worth checking on details such as door width, shower/tub set-up and bed height before booking.

RESOURCES

AlHassan Foundation *(alhassan-fdn.org)* Focuses on the empowerment of wheelchair users throughout Egypt.

Arab Organisation of Persons with Disabilities *(internationaldisabilityalliance.org/AODP)* A Cairo nonprofit promoting the rights of people with disabilities.

Curb Free with Cory Lee *(curbfreewithcorylee.com)* Cairo-based accessible-travel blog.

Helm Egypt *(helmegypt.org)* Promotes the inclusion of people with disabilities.

Wheelchair Travel *(wheelchairtravel.org/cairo/attractions)* Accessible travel in Cairo.

TAXIS

Londoncabegypt.com, part of Sixt rental car, has a fleet of wheelchair-accessible cabs fitted with access ramps, and all drivers speak English. Book online or through its app.

Parking Permits

Cairo's **Grand Egyptian Museum** (p72), **Egyptian Museum** (p78) and **National Museum of Egyptian Civilization** (p119), Alexandria's **Graeco-Roman Museum** (p314), the main museums in **Luxor** (p190) and **Hurghada** (p352), and Aswan's **Nubia Museum** (p247) are all accessible.

Archaeological Sites

Many have pathways, although access can still be tricky. Sites with at least partial access include the **Pyramids of Giza** (p64) and the temples of **Karnak** (p200), **Hatshepsut** (p221), **Horus** (p245) and **Abu Simbel** (p265).

RED SEA RESORTS

Many resorts cater for travellers with mobility issues with ramps, handrails, wheelchair-friendly beaches and facilities for divers with disabilities. **Camel Dive Club** (p377) in Sharm El Sheikh is a standout.

Nile Cruising

For multiday wheelchair-accessible cruises, contact **Responsible Travel** *(responsibletravel.com)* or **Memphis Tours** *(memphistours.com)*. Both also offer land-based accessible itineraries taking in Cairo, Luxor, Aswan and Abu Simbel. The **Egypt Travel Gate** portal *(privatetoursinegypt.com)* is also useful.

Women Travellers

Many women travel solo in Egypt, and most have a great time. Unfortunately, however, some do encounter sexual harassment, which generally presents as cat-calling, leering and occasionally being followed or groped in crowded public spaces. Dressing conservatively, including covering shoulders and knees, helps considerably.

Changing Attitudes

Attitudes are slowly changing. In 2014 sexual harassment was made a criminal offence in Egypt, marking a leap forward in recognising a problem that has been brushed under the carpet for years. Over the past decade anti-sexual harassment units have been created at many Egyptian universities.

Women of Egypt

For a positive take on women's initiatives, check out the **Women of Egypt Network** (womenofegyptnetwork.com).

Travel Tips

- Pack a scarf. In addition to coming in handy as protection from sand and sun, it can be used to cover your head before entering mosques.
- Dress conservatively. Beach areas of the Red Sea resorts are more relaxed, but elsewhere, and when leaving the beaches, covering up beach-style attire helps minimise attention.
- Always sit in the rear seat in a taxi.
- Streets in central Cairo are generally full until shop closing time (usually around 10pm, sometimes later) and are safe to walk. However, avoid places that look dark and isolated.
- If getting around Cairo using the crowded Metro, take advantage of the women-only cars (although watch out for petty theft in whatever car you use). On Alexandria's blue trams the first car is generally reserved for women.
- Keep sunglasses handy for avoiding direct eye contact with men.
- While sanitary pads are readily available, they may not be what you're used to and tampons can be hard to find; it's best to bring what you'll need from home.
- If you find yourself feeling uncomfortable, don't hesitate to seek assistance from the tourist police.
- When going out for the evening, try to go in a group, although many areas, such as downtown Alexandria, are generally fine.
- Seek out women-run or women-owned places and experiences, such as the Women of Egypt food and shopping tour offered by Cairo-based Bellies En-Route, Pr.Ba Concept Store in Esna, the Nubian cultural and birdwatching tours of Fatma Sobhy and Walk Like An Egyptian (walklikeanegyptian.com).

WOMEN IN EGYPT: STATS

Literacy: 71%
Percentage of national parliamentary seats held by women: 27%
Managerial positions held by women: 14%
Female genital mutilation: 86% (of women between 15 and 49 years of age)
Gender-based violence by a recent partner: 15% (of women between 15 and 49 years of age)
UNDP Gender Inequality ranking: 0.389 (versus 0.023 for Sweden and 0.094 for the UK, with a lower number signifying greater equality)
Percentage of university students who are women: 49%

Nuts & Bolts

OPENING HOURS

The official weekend is Friday and Saturday. During Ramadan, many offices, museums and tourist sites keep shorter hours.

Banks 8.30am to 1.30pm Sunday to Thursday

Government offices 8am to 2pm Sunday to Thursday

Restaurants 7am or 8am to 11am, 2pm to 6pm and 7pm to 10m or later

Shops 9am to 1pm and 5pm to 7pm (until 10pm or later in summer)

Etiquette

Physical contact Couples should avoid public displays of affection.
Feet Don't show the soles of your feet; it's considered disrespectful.
Hands Eat and pass things with your right hand; the left hand is used for ablutions.
Ramadan Don't eat or drink in public during the fasting month of Ramadan.

GOOD TO KNOW

Time zone
GMT/UTC + 2hr

Calling code
20

Emergency no.
123 (ambulance),
126 (tourist police)

Population
107.1 million

PUBLIC HOLIDAYS

Businesses and government offices also close on major Islamic holidays.

New Year's Day 1 January

Coptic Christmas 7 January

Revolution Day 25 January

Sham An Nessim March/April

Sinai Liberation Day 25 April

Labour Day 1 May

Uprising Day 30 June

Revolution Day 23 July

Armed Forces Day 6 October

ISLAMIC CALENDAR

Moulid An Nabi Birthday of the Prophet Muhammad.

Eid Al Fitr (Feast of Fast-Breaking) The end of Ramadan; a three-day feast

Eid Al Adha (Feast of the Sacrifice) Commemorates Ibrahim's (Abraham's) sacrifice with the slaughter of a sheep; lasts four days

Ras As Sana (New Year) A national public holiday

Public Toilets
Rare, but you can use restaurant and hotel facilities.

Smoking
Common in restaurants and bars; few non-smoking facilities.

Alcohol
Drinking age is 21. Drinking in public spaces is prohibited.

Electricity

Type C
220V/50Hz

Type F
230V/50Hz

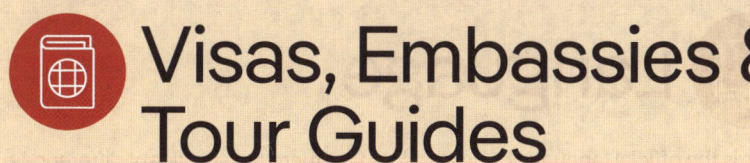

Visas, Embassies & Tour Guides

While regional conflicts in the Middle East cast shadows, entering into and travelling around Egypt is easy and straightforward. There's a heavy police presence and the government has imposed many regulations for visitor protection, but once you get going these tend to fade into the background. Taking an organised tour can minimise concerns in these areas and bring out Egypt's best.

Visas

Visas are required for most foreigners and can be purchased in advance online from the government's official site, *visa2egypt.gov.eg*, or on arrival (expect long queues) at approved bank kiosks at international airport arrivals halls. The current cost for a 30-day, single-entry visa on arrival is US$25, which must be paid in cash in US dollars, euros or British pounds only.

Embassies

There's a limit to how much embassies and consulates can do to help their nationals abroad, as all visitors are bound by the laws of the country in which they are travelling. In genuine emergencies, assistance may be available to help you arrange a new passport. Loans for onward travel will not be granted.

Government Advisories

Government travel advisories are a good source of information, especially for countries such as Egypt where the regional security situation can change fast. It's well worth having a look before setting your plans. Major sites include the following.

Australia *smartraveller.gov.au/destinations/africa/egypt*
UK *gov.uk/foreign-travel-advice/egypt*
USA *travel.state.gov/content/travel/en/international-travel/International-Travel-Country-Information-Pages/Egypt.html*

Tour Guides

Using the services of local tour guides can greatly enrich your Egypt travels. Many are trained Egyptologists and will be able to add depth to your visit with their insights and knowledge. Recommended local guides are listed throughout the regional chapters. An organised tour can also be a good way to visit Egypt's attractions in a time-efficient way. In addition to the guides mentioned in the regional sections of this book, other operators include the following.

Ancient World Tours *(ancient.co.uk)* Ancient Egypt specialists.
Dabuka *(dabuka.com)* Various tours, including Lake Nasser cruises and desert expeditions.
Intrepid Travel *(intrepidtravel.com)* A wide array of Egypt tours.
Memphis Tours *(memphistours.com)* Various Egypt itineraries, including some wheelchair-accessible tours.
Responsible Travel *(responsibletravel.com)* Resources and ideas for responsible travel.
Wild Guanabana *(wildguanabana.com)* Sinai hiking trips.

SINAI-ONLY VISAS

- If you are only visiting the resort towns on the Gulf of Aqaba coast and won't be going elsewhere in Egypt, you can apply for a 14-day Sinai-only visa. This will allow you to visit Sharm El Sheikh, Dahab, Nuweiba, Taba and St Katherine, but not Ras Mohammed National Park.
- Sinai-only visas are available at the Sharm El Sheikh airport, at the Taba border crossing and when arriving by ferry from Aqaba (Jordan).
- Note that if you enter at Taba and also plan to visit mainland Egypt, a full Egyptian visa must be arranged in advance online or through an embassy.

Language

Arabic is the official language of Egypt. Note that there are significant differences between the MSA (Modern Standard Arabic) – the official lingua franca of the Arab world – and the colloquial language, ie the everyday spoken variety of a particular region. The below is Egyptian Arabic.

Basics
Hello أهلاً *ah·lan*
Goodbye مع السلامة *ma'as·sa·la·ma*
Yes أيوة *ai·wa*
No لأ *la*
Please لو سماحت *law sa·maht* (m)
لو سمحتي *law sa·mah·tee* (f)
Thank you شكراً *shu·kran*
Excuse me عن إزنك *'an iz·nak* (m)
عن إزنك *'an iz·nik* (f)
Sorry متأسف *mu·ta·as·if* (m)
متأسفة *mu·ta·a·si·fa* (f)
What's your name?
إسمَك أيه؟ *is·mak ey* (m)
إسمِك أيه؟ *is·mik ey* (f)
My name is ... ...إسمي *is·mee ...*
Do you speak English?
بتتكلم/بتتكلمي *bi·tit·ka·lim/bi·tit·ka·lim·ee* (m/f)
إنجليزي؟ *in·gi·lee·zee*
I don't understand
مش فاهم *mish fa·him* (m)
مش فهمة *mish fah·ma* (f)

Signs
Entrance مدخل
Exit خروج
Open مفتوح
Closed مغلق
Information إستعلامات
Prohibited ممنوع
Toilets دورة المية
Men رجال
Women سيّدات

Directions
Where's (the market)?
فين (السوق)؟ *fayn is·sooq*

What's the address?
العنوان أيه؟ *il·'un·wan ey*
Could you please write it down?
ممكن تكتبه؟ *mum·kin tik·ti·boh* (m)
ممكن تكتبيه؟ *mum·kin tik·ti·beeh* (f)
Can you show me (on the map)?
ممكن توريني (على الخريطة)؟
mum·kin ti·wa·ree·nee ('al·kha·ree·ta)

Time
What time is it?
الساعة كم؟ *is·sa·'a kam*
It's (two) o'clock
الساعة (إثنين) *is·sa·'a (it·nayn)*
Half past (2) الساعة (إثنين) و نص
is·sa·'a (it·nayn) wi nus
morning الصبح *is·subh*
afternoon بعد الظهر *ba'd·duhr*
evening/night بالليل *bi·layl*
yesterday إمبارح *im·ba·rih*
tomorrow بكرة *buk·ra*

Emergencies
Help! إلحقني! *il.haq.nee*
Go away! إمشي! *im·shee*
I'm sick أنا عيّان *a·na ay·an* (m)
أنا عيّانة *a·na ay·an·a* (f)
Call ...! ...إتصل ب *i·tas·al bi ...*
a doctor دكتور *duk·toor*
the police البوليس *il·bu·lees*

Eating & Drinking
What would you recommend?
تقترح أيه؟ *tik·tar·ah ey*
What's the local speciality?
الأطباق المحلية أيه؟
il at.baaq il ma.ha.lee.ya ey

NUMBERS

1 ١	واحد	*wa·hid*
2 ٢	إثنين	*it·nayn*
3 ٣	ثلاثة	*ta·la·ta*
4 ٤	أربعة	*ar·ba·'a*
5 ٥	خمسة	*kham·sa*
6 ٦	ستة	*si·ta*
7 ٧	سبعة	*sa·ba·'a*
8 ٨	ثمانية	*ta·man·ya*
9 ٩	تسعة	*ti·sa·'a*
10 ١٠	عشرة	*'a·sha·ra*

DONATIONS TO ENGLISH

Many words originated from Arabic – **alchemy**, **alcove**, **caravan**, **ghoul**, **giraffe**, **jar**, **kohl**, **safari**, **zero**

ANCIENT ORIGINS

Ancient Egyptian, Arabic, Aramaic, Hebrew (biblical and modern), along with a smattering of living and extinct languages in East Africa and West Asia, all belong to the Afroasiatic language family. Coptic, the language of Christian Egyptians, was an amalgam of Greek and ancient Pharaonic languages. A few words survive from this earlier time, mostly in the form of place names and in the Coptic calendar, which is still used by farmers throughout the country. Coptic was largely supplanted by Arabic after the Muslim conquest of Egypt in 639, though there are still communities of Coptic speakers in Egypt.

Lingua Franca

With around 110 million people, Egypt has one of the largest single-country populations in the Arab world. Even so, Egypt's cultural and linguistic influence far outweighs its size. Because Cairo has been the centre of Arab broadcasting and film, the city has an unrivalled cultural domination in the Arab world, and also, more significantly, within Egypt. Cairo (often referred to by the same word in Arabic as Egypt, Masr) is a city synonymous with a country, a reflection of the effect the Cairene metropolis has had at both regional and local levels.

In the rest of the Arab world, rare is the community that has never heard Cairene (Egyptian) Arabic dialect in a soap opera or radio broadcast. Although there are regional variations within Egyptian Arabic, primarily between the north and the south, Cairene Arabic is spoken throughout the country.

WHO SPEAKS ARABIC?

Arabic is an official language of 23 countries in the Arab world, including Algeria, Bahrain, Egypt, Iraq, Lebanon, Oman and the United Arab Emirates.

313 million speak Arabic as a first language

109 million speak Arabic as a second language

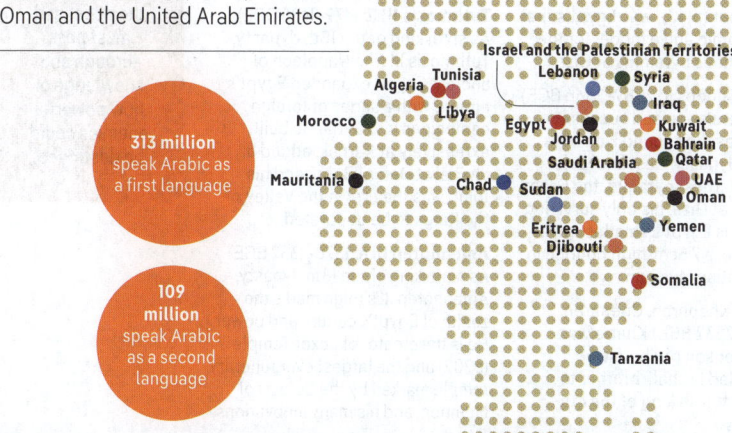

Pharaonic Glossary

WHO'S WHO

Egypt's Pharaonic history is based on the regnal years of each pharaoh, a word derived from *per-aa*, meaning palace. Among the many hundreds of pharaohs who ruled Egypt over a 3000-year period, the following are some of the names found most frequently around the ancient sites.

Narmer (Menes; c 3100 BCE) The first king to unite Lower and Upper Egypt. Narmer from south (Upper) Egypt is portrayed as victorious on the famous Narmer Palette in the Egyptian Museum (p78). He is perhaps to be identified with the semi-mythical King Menes, founder of Egypt's ancient capital city of Memphis.

Zoser (Djoser; c 2667–2648 BCE) As second king of the 3rd dynasty, Zoser was buried in Egypt's first pyramid, the world's oldest monumental stone building, designed by the architect Imhotep. Zoser's statue in the entrance hall galleries of the Egyptian Museum shows a long-haired king with a slight moustache.

Sneferu (c 2613–2589 BCE) The first king of the 4th dynasty, and held in the highest esteem by later generations, Sneferu was Egypt's greatest pyramid builder. He was responsible for four such structures, and his final resting place, the Red (Northern) Pyramid at Dahshur (p143), was Egypt's first true pyramid and a model for the more famous pyramids at Giza.

Khufu (Cheops; c 2589–2566 BCE) As Sneferu's son and successor, Khufu was the second king of the 4th dynasty. Best known for Egypt's largest pyramid, the Great Pyramid at Giza, his only surviving likeness is Egypt's smallest royal sculpture, a 7.5cm-high figurine in the Egyptian Museum.

Khafre (Khephren, Chephren; c 2558–2532 BCE) Khafre was a younger son of Khufu who succeeded his half-brother to become fourth king of the 4th dynasty. He built the second of Giza's famous pyramids and is best known as the model for the face of the Great Sphinx.

Menkaure (Mycerinus; c 2532–2503 BCE) As the son of Khafre and fifth king of the 4th dynasty, Menkaure built the smallest of Giza's three huge pyramids. He is also represented by a series of superb sculptures in the Egyptian Museum.

Amenhotep I (c 1525–1504 BCE) As second king of the 18th dynasty, Amenhotep I ruled for a time with his mother Ahmose-Nofretari. They founded the village of Deir Al Medina for the workers who built the tombs in the Valley of the Kings (p211), and Amenhotep I may have been the first king to be buried there.

Hatshepsut (c 1473–1458 BCE) As the most famous of Egypt's female pharaohs, Hatshepsut took power at the death of her brother-husband Tuthmosis II and initially ruled jointly with her nephew-stepson Tuthmosis III.

Tuthmosis III (c 1479–1425 BCE) As sixth king of the 18th dynasty, Tuthmosis III (the Napoleon of ancient Egypt) expanded Egypt's empire with a series of foreign campaigns into Syria. He built extensively at Karnak, added a chapel at Deir Al Bahri, and his tomb was the first in the Valley of the Kings to be decorated.

Amenhotep III (c 1390–1352 BCE) As ninth king of the 18th dynasty, Amenhotep III's reign marks the zenith of Egypt's culture and power. He is the creator of Luxor Temple (p202) and the largest ever funerary temple marked by the Colossi of Memnon, and his many innovations,

> **NAVIGATING THE AFTERLIFE**
>
> The funerary texts in the tombs gave the deceased all the knowledge that would be needed to reach the afterlife: knowledge of the power of those in the underworld, knowledge of the hidden forces, knowledge of each hour and each god, knowledge of the gates the deceased must pass through and knowledge of how powerful enemies could be destroyed.

including Aten worship, are usually credited to his son Amenhotep IV (later 'Akhenaten').

Akhenaten (Amenhotep IV; c 1352–1336 BCE) Changing his name from Amenhotep to distance himself from the state god Amun, Akhenaten relocated the royal capital to Amarna with his wife Nefertiti. While many still regard him as a monotheist and benign revolutionary, the evidence suggests he was a dictator whose reforms were political rather than religious.

Nefertiti (c 1338–1336 BCE) Famous for her painted bust in Berlin, Nefertiti ruled with her husband Akhenaten, and while the identity of his successor remains controversial, it may have been Nefertiti herself, using the throne name 'Smenkhkare'.

Tutankhamun (c 1336–1327 BCE) As the 11th king of the 18th dynasty, Tutankhamun's fame is based on the great quantities of treasure discovered in his tomb in 1922. The son of Akhenaten by one of Akhenaten's sisters, Tutankhamun reopened the traditional temples and restored Egypt's fortunes after the disastrous reign of his father.

Horemheb (c 1323–1295 BCE) As a military general, Horemheb restored Egypt's empire under Tutankhamun and after the brief reign of Ay, eventually became king himself, marrying Nefertiti's sister Mutnodjmet. His tomb at Saqqara was abandoned in favour of a royal burial in a superbly decorated tomb (p146) in the Valley of the Kings.

Seti I (c 1294–1279 BCE) The second king of the 19th dynasty, Seti I continued to consolidate Egypt's empire with foreign campaigns. Best known for building Karnak's Hypostyle Hall, a superb temple at Abydos (p183) and a huge tomb (p216) in the Valley of the Kings.

Ramses II (c 1279–1213 BCE) As son and successor of Seti I, Ramses II fought the Hittites at the Battle of Kadesh and built temples including Abu Simbel (p265) and the Ramesseum, once adorned with the statue that inspired the poet PB Shelley's 'Ozymandias'.

Ramses III (c 1184–1153 BCE) As second king of the 20th dynasty, Ramses III was the last of the warrior kings, repelling several attempted invasions, as portrayed in scenes at his funerary temple Medinat Habu (p224).

Taharka (690–664 BCE) As fourth king of the 25th dynasty, Taharka was one of Egypt's Nubian pharaohs and his daughter Amenirdis II was high priestess at Karnak, where Taharka undertook building work. A fine sculpted head of the king is in Aswan's Nubian Museum, and he was buried in a pyramid at Nuri in southern Nubia.

Alexander the Great (331–323 BCE) Alexander invaded Egypt in 331 BCE, founded Alexandria (p310), visited Amun's temple at Siwa Oasis to confirm his divinity, and after his untimely death in Babylon in 323 BCE, his mummy was eventually buried in Alexandria.

Ptolemy I (323–283 BCE) As Alexander's general and rumoured half-brother, Ptolemy seized Egypt at Alexander's death and established the Ptolemaic line of pharaohs. Ruling in traditional style for 300 years, they made Alexandria the greatest capital of the ancient world.

Cleopatra VII (51–30 BCE) As the 19th ruler of the Ptolemaic dynasty, Cleopatra VII ruled with her brothers Ptolemy XIII and then Ptolemy XIV before taking power herself. A brilliant politician who restored Egypt's former glories, she married Julius Caesar and then Mark Antony, whose defeat at Actium in 31 BCE led to the couple taking their own lives.

A LOST ART

Mummification began around 2600 BCE when Egyptians started to remove the internal organs where putrefaction begins. Lungs, liver, stomach and intestines were removed and placed in canopic jars, the brain was liquefied and drained, and the body covered in natron salt and left to dry for 40 days. Afterwards the body was washed and anointed with oils, spices and resins, then wrapped in linen with amulets to protect them on the journey to the afterlife.

JUDGEMENT DAY

The heart of the deceased (which contained a record of all their actions in life) was weighed against the feather of Maat, which symbolised truth and justice, in the presence of Osiris as judge. If their heart was light and free of sin the deceased was allowed to spend eternity as an *akh*, meaning 'transfigured soul', but if their heart was heavy with sin it was eaten by the Devourer, Ammut, and they were damned forever.

GODS & GODESSES

Initially representing aspects of the natural world, Egypt's gods and goddesses grew more complex through time. As they began to blend together and adopt each other's characteristics, they started to become difficult to identify, although their distinctive headgear and clothing can provide clues as to who they are. The following brief descriptions should help travellers spot at least a few of the many hundreds who appear on monuments and in museums.

> **ROYAL ERAS**
>
> Thirty royal dynasties ruled over a 3000-year period, now divided into the Old, Middle and New Kingdoms separated by intermittent periods of unrest (Intermediate periods) when the country split into north (Lower Egypt) and south (Upper Egypt).

> **EATING FOR ETERNITY**
>
> The vast quantities of food and drink offered in temples and tombs were duplicated on surrounding walls to ensure a constant supply for eternity. The offerings are shown piled up in layers, sometimes appearing to float in the air if the artist took this practice too far.

Amun The local god of Thebes (Luxor) who became the state god of the New Kingdom of Egypt. Originally he may have been associated with the power of the wind, and he was a creator god. Later he became closely associated with the fertility god Min and combined with the sun god to create Amun-Ra, king of the gods. He is generally portrayed seated on a throne with a double-plumed crown and sometimes the horns of his sacred ram to accentuate his procreative vigour.

Anubis The funerary god who deals with burial and afterlife, Anubis is the god of mummification, the patron of embalmers and guardian of cemeteries. He is generally depicted as a black jackal or jackal-headed man.

Apophis The huge snake embodying darkness and chaos was the enemy of the sun god Ra. It tried to destroy him every night during his journey through the underworld, to prevent him reaching the dawn. Seth speared the serpent, and the blood stain that was left explained the red sky at sunset and sunrise.

Aten The solar disc whose rays end in outstretched hands was worshipped as a god during the 18th dynasty, and became chief deity under the reign of Akhenaten.

Atum Creator god of Heliopolis who rose from the primeval waters and ejaculated (or sneezed, depending on the myth) to create gods and humans. He was also the god who would destroy everything at the end of times. Generally depicted as a man wearing the double crown, but sometimes also with the head of a ram or a scarab, Atum represented the setting sun.

Bastet Cat goddess whose cult centre was Bubastis; ferocious when defending her father Ra the sun god, she was often shown as a friendly deity and a symbol of motherhood, personified by the domestic cat.

Bes A household deity, Bes was a grotesque yet benign dwarf god fond of music and dancing; he kept evil from the home and protected women in childbirth by waving his knives and sticking out his tongue.

Geb God of the earth associated with vegetation and fertility, he is generally depicted as a green man lying beneath his sister-wife Nut, the sky goddess, supported by their father Shu, god of air. He is the father of Osiris, Isis, Seth and Nephtys.

Hapy God of the Nile flood and the plump embodiment of fertility, Hapy is shown as an androgynous figure with sagging breasts, a swollen belly and sometimes a clump of papyrus on his head.

Hathor Goddess of love, sexuality and pleasure represented as a cow or a woman with a crown of horns and a sun disc in her guise as the sun god's daughter. Patron of music and dancing whose principal cult centre was at Dendara, Hathor was known as 'she of the beautiful hair' and 'lady of drunkenness'. She was the wife of Horus.

Horus Falcon god of the sky and son of Isis and Osiris, he avenged his father to rule on earth and was personified by the ruling pharaoh. He can appear as a falcon or a man with a falcon's head, and his eye *(wedjat)* was a powerful amulet. Horus, the husband of Hathor, was closely associated with kingship and is often seen hovering as a falcon over the pharaoh's head.

Isis Goddess of magic and protector of her brother-husband Osiris and their son Horus. She represented the ideal wife, made the first mummy of Osiris' body and was a protector of the dead. As symbolic mother of the pharaoh, she appears as a woman with a throne-shaped crown, or sometimes has Hathor's cow horns. She is often seen suckling the infant Horus.

Khepri God of the rising sun represented by the scarab beetle, whose habit of rolling balls of dirt was likened to the sun's journey across the sky.

Khnum Ram-headed god who created life on a potter's wheel; he also controlled the waters of the Nile flood from his cave at Elephantine. His cult centre was Esna.

Khons Young god of the moon and son of Amun and Mut. He is generally depicted in human form wearing a crescent moon crown and the 'sidelock of youth' hairstyle.

Maat Goddess of cosmic order, truth and justice, depicted as a woman wearing an ostrich feather on her head, or sometimes by the feather alone.

Mut Amun's consort and one of the symbolic mothers of the king; her name means both 'mother' and 'vulture' and she is generally shown as a woman with a vulture headdress.

Nekhbet Vulture goddess of Upper Egypt worshipped at Al Kab; she often appears with her sister-goddess Wadjet the cobra, protecting the pharaoh.

Nut Sky goddess usually portrayed as a woman whose star-spangled body arches across tomb and temple ceilings. She swallows the sun each evening to give birth to it each morning.

Osiris God of death, fertility and resurrection whose main cult centre was at Abydos. As the first mummy created, he was magically revived by Isis to produce their son Horus, who took over the earthly kingship, while Osiris became ruler of the underworld and symbol of eternal life. He represented good, while his brother Seth represented evil.

Ptah Creator god of Memphis who brought the world into being by his thoughts and spoken words. He is patron of artisans, wears a tight-fitting robe and a skullcap, and usually clutches a tall sceptre (resembling a 1950s microphone).

Ra The supreme deity in the Egyptian pantheon, the sun god is generally shown as a man with a falcon's head topped by a sun disc, although he can take many forms (eg Aten, Khepri) and other gods merge with him to enhance their powers (eg Amun-Ra, Ra-Atum). In his underworld aspect he can be shown with a ram's head. Ra travelled through the skies in a boat, sinking down into the underworld each night before re-emerging at dawn to bring light.

Sekhmet Lioness goddess of Memphis whose name means 'the powerful one'. As a daughter of sun god Ra she was capable of great destruction and was the bringer of pestilence; her priests functioned as doctors, and her statues were erected to protect Egypt from the plague.

Seth God of chaos and confusion personified by a mythological composite animal. In pre-dynastic times the king was revered as the incarnation of both Horus and Seth. However, during the Old Kingdom, the myth arose that after murdering his brother Osiris he was defeated by Horus, and from then on he was regarded as evil, too dangerous to be depicted on temple walls, even as a hieroglyph.

Sobek Crocodile god representing Pharaonic might, he was worshipped at Kom Ombo and Fayyum. Both sites had sacred lakes with crocodiles.

Taweret Hippopotamus goddess who often appears upright to scare evil from the home and protect women in childbirth.

Thoth God of knowledge and writing, and patron of scribes. He is portrayed as an ibis or baboon, or most frequently as an ibis-headed man holding a scribe's palette, and his cult centre was at Hermopolis. He was closely identified with the moon and was considered the guardian of the deceased in the underworld.

THE EGYPT
STORYBOOK

Our writers delve deep into different aspects of Egyptian life

A History of Egypt in 15 Places
To limit Egypt to its ancient history is to do it an enormous disservice
Sanad Tabbaa
p432

Meet the Egyptians
The real Egypt can be found in the warm hearts of Egyptians
Shoroq Galal
p436

The Gastronomy of Egypt
According to an Egyptian proverb, one bite made with love is enough for a hundred people
Lama Obeid
p438

Understanding Egypt with Adel Emam
Dive into the Egyptian psyche through the works of this veteran comedian
Sanad Tabbaa
p440

The People of the Nile
Down the generations, the Nile has provided, defended and destroyed
Sanad Tabbaa
p442

Egypt's Environmental Challenges
A hot country that's mostly desert, Egypt has long grappled with environmental issues
Sanad Taaba
p446

Abydos (p182)
REDTEA/GETTY IMAGES

A HISTORY OF EGYPT IN
15 PLACES

From millennia of Pharaonic innovation to emerging as a hot spot first of Christianity and then of Islamic culture, Egypt has thrived. The country stood at the forefront of regional independence movements during both the colonial period and the Arab Spring. Well has Egypt earned its moniker Om el Donya (Mother of the World). By Sanad Tabbaa

EGYPT HAS BEEN inhabited since before the desertification of the Sahara, and its cities were likely begun shortly afterwards. To put that in perspective, Egypt had a postal service when most of the rest of humanity was still figuring out which berries were tasty and which were terminal. To limit Egypt to its ancient history, though, is to do it an enormous disservice. It was a cradle of Hellenistic civilisation before being conquered by the Roman Empire, it swiftly became the Romans' bread basket, and it was an intellectual powerhouse under various Islamic empires. It was the final stopping point of the Crusaders and the Mongols, the crown of Arabic literature in every era since Arabic became a language of significance, and the home of monastic orders and hermetic and gnostic thought. In the modern era Egypt has been home to the thinkers and politicians who spearheaded the concept of a modern industrialised Arab nation that demanded international recognition, even under colonialism. Since the mid-20th century, Egypt has been the cultural centre of the Arab world and the home of local anticolonial and postcolonial thought and action. To put it mildly, Egypt has a lot of history, and every stage of it is fascinating.

1. Great Pyramid of Khufu
ICONIC IMAGE OF DESERT MYSTERY

The Great Pyramid is often said to have been as old to the Romans as the Romans are to us. That isn't precisely true, but it will be in about 600 years. Pyramids housed mummified pharaohs who were interred throughout the era of the Old Kingdom (2700–2200 BCE). The Great Pyramid is the largest of these and was for most of human history the tallest built structure on the planet. Today the interior can be visited through a hole in the side that's thought to be the one used to inter the Pharaoh Khufu before it was sealed for thousands of years.

For more on the Great Pyramid of Khufu, see p64.

2. Karnak
WORSHIP THROUGH THE AGES

The Karnak Temple Complex in modern Luxor (ancient Thebes) is an oddity in that it continued to be constructed, added to and occasionally partially demolished for well over 1000 years. Erected in the era of the Middle Kingdom (around 2000–1700 BCE), it primarily served as a place of worship for the Theban triad of gods but was temporarily hijacked by the Pharaoh Amenhotep IV, commonly known as Akhenaten, for his abortive attempt at monotheism under the deity Aten. After the pharaoh's death his temples were dismantled and any references to him studiously erased.

For more on Karnak, see p200.

3. Temples of Abu Simbel
RELOCATED MONUMENTS OF THE NEW KINGDOM

Commissioned by the Pharaoh Ramses II (Ozymandias), often considered the greatest of the pharaohs, the temple complex of Abu Simbel was likely built to Egyptianise and impress the local Nubian population during the era of the New Kingdom (around 1500–1300 BCE). The complex's massive statues carved directly into the rock face remained in place for millennia until the building of the Aswan High Dam. Threatened by the creation of the reservoir that would become Lake Nasser, the entire site was moved to an artificial hill in 1968 through local and international cooperation.

For more on the Temples of Abu Simbel, see p265.

4. Temple of Hibis
TEMPLES OF THE INVADERS

The astute reader will notice that there are gaps of hundreds of years between the Old, Middle and New Kingdoms. Internecine and international struggles were common in ancient Egypt, with the country breaking apart and reuniting numerous times. The Late Period (700–300 BCE), when Egypt fell under foreign rule, represented one such interval. The Temple of Hibis was built by the Persian Pharaoh Achaemenid Darius I. Once surrounded by the city of Hibis, the temple today lies among struggling farmland in the Western Desert.

For more on the Temple of Hibis, see p302.

5. Temple of Hathor
THE START OF HELLENISTIC EGYPT

Welcomed into Egypt in 332 BCE as a liberator from Persian rule, Alexander the Great set about introducing progressive models of rule and taxation. When he departed he made one of his generals, Ptolemy, governor of Egypt. Rather unsurprisingly, Ptolemy declared himself pharaoh as soon as Alexander died. The Dendara Temple Complex is a typical example of Ptolemaic-era temples, showing a clear Greek influence. This fusion of cultures would continue as Alexandria ascended to become the intellectual centre of Hellenistic culture. The dynasty ended with the storied death of Cleopatra in 30 BCE and annexation by the Romans.

For more on Dendara's Temple of Hathor, see p186.

6. Monastery of St Anthony
BIRTHPLACE OF CHRISTIAN MONASTICISM

Egypt remained the richest and most populous of Roman provinces outside Italy throughout the entire period of the Roman Empire, with Alexandria the empire's second-largest city. As the Romans adopted Christianity, St Anthony of the Desert Fathers, who was one of the first to espouse shedding all material wealth and would become known as the Father of All Monks, was born in Upper Egypt. Soon after his death, around 300 CE, his followers built a monastery on the former

Karnak (p200), Luxor

site of his hermitage. The monastery still stands as a Coptic monument to humble, communal living.

For more on the Monastery of St Anthony, see p359.

7. St Katherine's Monastery
SINAI'S FABLED SITE OF THE BURNING BUSH

As the western provinces of the Roman Empire declined, the Eastern Roman Empire, popularly known as the Byzantine Empire, rose in importance, taking Egypt with it. Built around 550 CE during the reign of Justinian I, St Katherine's Monastery in Sinai is said to surround the burning bush seen by the Prophet Moses. The monastery would host Christians of all denominations throughout the next 1500 years and to the present day. It is the world's oldest continuously inhabited monastery. As the Byzantine Empire shrank, Egypt remained culturally and economically rich and began to be seen as a prize by the nascent Rashidun Caliphate.

For more on St Katherine's Monastery, see p393.

8. Mosque of Amr Ibn Al As
AFRICA'S FIRST MOSQUE

The Rashidun Caliphate, composed of the Companions of the Prophet Muhammad after his death, would wrest control of Egypt from the Byzantines in 642 CE. Amr Ibn Al As, a decorated general among the companions, would be its governor, introducing Islam to Egypt. He would almost immediately build its first mosque, which would bear his name, in the city of Fustat, a predecessor to Cairo, which he also had constructed. Islam would slowly supplant Christianity as the religion of the region over the following centuries, even as different caliphates traded the area between each other.

For more on the Mosque of Amr Ibn Al As, see p123.

9. Al Azhar University
ANCIENT HOME OF LEARNING

The Fatimids, hailing from Tunisia and taking their name from Fatima, the daughter of the Prophet Muhammad from whom they claimed descent, would conquer Egypt in 969. They would build the city of Cairo directly north of Fustat and proclaim it their capital. A few years later they would bestow upon the nascent city an unparalleled centre of Islamic learning that they called Al Azhar. It taught everything from Islamic jurisprudence to philosophy and astronomy. Over the millennia-long history of the institution it has undergone ideological changes, sectarian switches and renovations, but it continues to operate as a university to this very day.

For more on Al Azhar University, see p104.

10. Cairo Citadel
SALADIN'S CAIRENE LEGACY

The Fatimid Caliphate was in complete decline by 1171 and suffering from repeated onslaughts from regional hopefuls. Even Fustat, once so important, would be burned to the ground on the orders of its vizir to deny its riches to the Crusaders. The Kurdish general Salah ad-Din Al Ayyubi (Saladin) would construct a series of fortresses to aid him in driving away the Europeans, establishing the Ayyubid Sultanate in the process and making himself the leader of Egypt. Among the most opulent of these ostensibly military structures is the Cairo Citadel, which would remain in use as the ruler's palace until the 19th century.

For more on the Cairo Citadel, see p109.

11. Fort Qaitbey
CENTRAL AND EASTERN EUROPEAN STYLES IN ALEXANDRIA

Relative peace during the Ayyubid Sultanate would usher in an era of economic prosperity and intellectual blossoming, but strife between the ruling class and an enslaved caste of generals known as the Mamluks would result in the supremacy of the latter. The Mamluks would rule Egypt from 1250 to 1517, and they continued to exert much influence even after the Ottomans (who ruled in name only) conquered Egypt. With them the Mamluks brought new architectural styles associated with Central and Eastern Europe, mixing these with the local arabesque designs. Fort Qaitbey in Alexandria is a prime example of the unique result.

For more on Fort Qaitbey, see p310.

Fort Qaitbey (p310), Alexandria

12. Al Montazah Palaces
OPULENT ITALIAN-STYLE PALACES

Ottoman rule was not kind to Egypt, largely due to neglect. Following a disastrous defeat by Napoleon Bonaparte in 1801, the Ottomans sent an Albanian commander, Mohammed Ali, to rid the country of the corruption and poverty that had become commonplace. They were surprised when he seized power for himself. Mohammed Ali and his descendants tried to make Egypt a modern nation state, starting in 1805. The dynasty looked to Europe for inspiration, and the lavish Al Montazah Palaces in Alexandria, built in Italian Renaissance style, are characteristic of their vision.

For more on the Al Montazah Palaces, see p323.

13. Abdeen Palace
DISASTER IN THE SEAT OF POWER

In their efforts to modernise Egypt, the Mohammed Ali dynasty took massive loans from Britain and France, inadvertently placing themselves under British economic control. While the newly established Kingdom of Egypt had many of the trappings of modernity, including the gorgeous Abdeen Palace, which remains the presidential residence, the truth about who held the reins of power soon became evident. In 1942 the British surrounded Abdeen Palace with tanks to demand the immediate abdication of the king unless he chose a prime minister of whom they approved. The monarchy would not long survive the incident.

For more on Abdeen Palace, see p85.

14. Suez Canal
NATIONALISATION AND NATIONALISM

In 1952 a group known as the Free Officers, led by Colonel Gamal Abdel Nasser, conducted a bloodless coup d'etat and overthrew the monarchy. Nasser was the first native Egyptian ruler of a unified Egypt since the Late Period nearly 3000 years earlier. He championed socialism and Egyptian independence, and his greatest victory was the nationalisation of the Suez Canal in 1958. During his life he was a symbol of anticolonialism, though after his death he has been blamed for entrenching military rule in Egypt. His legacy is complex, but an Egyptian-owned and -operated Suez Canal is testament to his desire for a free Egypt.

For more on the Suez Canal, see p337.

15. Midan Tahrir
SITE OF ARAB SPRING PROTESTS

Since Nasser's death in 1970 Egypt has almost exclusively been ruled by military officers who stayed in power for life. In 2011 the region's Arab Spring protests gripped the Egyptian public (and the world). People congregated in and around Midan Tahrir – *tahrir* means 'liberation' – in Cairo to demand change. It came for a time, but after former minister of defence Abdel Fattah al Sisi became president in 2014 there was a quick return to business as usual. The 21st century has been a mixed bag for Egypt, but it will continue to do as it has always done: persevere and thrive.

For more on Midan Tahrir, see p77.

MEET THE EGYPTIANS

You might think Egypt is all about pyramids and history, but the real Egypt is in the warm hearts of the Egyptians. Shoroq Galal introduces her people.

YOU WON'T GET lost here, not because there's a map on your phone but because if you ask anyone for directions they'll help you without question, even if they have no idea where the place is (in which case they'll stop someone else and ask them). People visit Egypt for its tombs, pyramids and relics, but they stay for the kindness and warmth of the locals. You might be at the till and realise you're short on cash. 'Pay me back next time', the cashier will say. And they won't be joking. Feeling poorly? A passerby will stop to see if you're all right. Egyptians are passionate about helping, regardless of the reason.

In 2022 around 14 million Egyptians left to pursue opportunities in the West or the Gulf. But that didn't change their love for Egypt, the 'Mother of the World', as we call it in Arabic. Wherever they are, Egyptians will always be proud of being Egyptian.

Cairo remains the hub for opportunities in terms of education, entertainment, jobs and salaries. It has 20% of Egypt's population, a mix from all over the country. Egyptians can tell each other's origins by their accent – if we can't pinpoint the exact village then we can guess the region (especially when it comes to the distinctive dialects of Upper Egypt, the Delta and Port Said).

Ninety per cent of Egypt's 109 million people are Sunni Muslim and the other 10% are mostly (90%) Coptic Christians. Egyptian society tends to be conservative and traditional.

It's the same with football. There are 18 clubs in the Egyptian Premier League, but most Egyptians support only two: Al Ahly and Zamalek. Egyptians are united, however, in their love for Liverpool player and Egypt team captain Mohamed Salah, 'The Pride of the Arabs'.

We'll call out 'Mohamed' to catch someone's attention (because it's a common name) or say 'pssssst' (as if calling a cat). We're a curious bunch, so most people turn around for a chat. When we talk we believe we own the truth. It can be amusing to watch Egyptians having a long discussion in which each side is convinced by their own point, citing Facebook posts as sources. But what can sound like a full-blown argument will often enough end jovially. We take most things (not just food) with a pinch of salt.

Talking is how we kill time when we're queuing or stuck in traffic. Before we arrive at our destination we'll know the life story of the passengers around us. Lifelong friendships (and sometimes marriages) have been forged in queues or on public transport. When you travel in Egypt you'll come away with much more than memories.

Bread Means Life

'Bread' and 'life' are the same word in Arabic. The ancient Egyptians had more than 100 kinds of bread, and in modern Egypt every city has its own. In the 'cat ear' technique, bread is also used to scoop up food.

REDISCOVERING EGYPT AS A MOTHER

As the mother of a three-year-old girl, I often reflect on the importance of educating my daughter. I believe there's no better starting point than getting in touch with her roots. Since she is half-Egyptian and we currently live in Egypt, I thought this would be straightforward. (She is also half-English, and I plan to delve into tea, scones and rain once we visit the United Kingdom.) To my surprise, I discovered a stark contrast between the culture I grew up with in the Nile Delta and the language, customs and environment in South Sinai, where I live now. This led me to think about how Egypt embraces a rich tapestry of cultures and languages. Once again I began to appreciate the beauty of Egypt, a country steeped in history, heritage and diversity, and I realised that I needed to discover its treasures anew.

Pictured clockwise from top left: Man smoking a shisha, Luxor; Egypt fan at the Africa Cup of Nations; woman in a Nubian village, Aswan; Coptic priest giving a blessing

THE GASTRONOMY OF EGYPT

According to an Egyptian proverb, one bite made with love is enough for a hundred people. Essay by Lama Obeid

EGYPT SPANS OVER 1 million sq km, from coastal cities to oases and farms, and the gastronomy of the country is as vast as its topography. From quick-bite street foods such as *kushari* and liver sandwiches to full-blown meals including stuffed pigeon, *mahshi* and *molokhiyya,* Egypt has something to satisfy the taste buds of most visitors.

A Dish Fit for Kings

Molokhiyya, a green leafy plant cooked into a soup, is one of Egypt's most renowned dishes. There are many stories about how the dish came to be, but its first mention in history dates from the 15th dynasty (around 1638 BCE), when the Hyksos ruled the northern part of Egypt. Before the Hyksos' reign, locals stayed away from the plant known as *khiya* that grew on the banks of the Nile as they believed it to be poisonous. The Hyksos forced the locals to eat the plant as a form of torture, telling them *'kolo khiya'* (eat *khiya*). The locals were surprised by how good it tasted, and after they realised the plant wasn't poisonous it became a favourite food.

Other stories say the plant's health benefits were discovered under the Fatimid Caliphate. The Caliph Al Hakim bi Amr

Pictured clockwise from top left: *molokhiyya; fuul* and *baladi* bread; *Umm Ali; hammam mahshi*

Allah spread the false narrative among the working class that the plant was poisonous and banned them from eating it so that he could have it to himself. Another story goes that when the Caliph Al Mu'izz li Din Allah became ill with severe stomach pain a doctor suggested he eat the plant as a cure. After the caliph became aware of the plant's curative benefits he banned it for the masses and allowed it only for himself and his entourage. He called the plant *molokiyya,* which derives from the Arabic word for kings *(molok),* signalling that it was a dish for royals only.

The traditions of *tasha* and *shahqa* have grown up around *molokhiyya* in modern-day Egypt. *Tasha* (minced garlic, coriander and cumin pan-fried in vegetable oil) adds flavour to *molokhiyya.* When it's still searing hot, *tasha* is poured onto the *molokhiyya,* making a sizzling sound, hence its onomatopoeic name. As the *tasha* is poured, it's traditional to take a *shahqa* (a deep, quick gasp), which most Egyptians still do. Some people swear that *molokiyya* doesn't taste the same without the *shahqa* and others do it simply to keep the tradition alive.

Molokhia bil aranib is *molokiyya* cooked with rabbit, and the Nubian dish *kuskuti bil jakut* is *molokiyya* made with eggs scrambled into the soup. In Siwa Oasis the Bedouin make *molokiyya* using dried leaves, which gives it a distinctive taste. Despite the disputes about the dish's origin and how it should be prepared, most Egyptians agree that it's delicious.

Street Food

At the other end of the spectrum from food for royalty, Egypt's street-food culture is buzzing with cheap, flavourful eats. Many of these foods were originally sold in wooden push carts, and you can still find these carts scattered across local neighbourhoods. Some vendors have used the popularity of their cart to grow their business into small eateries and even restaurants.

Fuul wa ta'miyyah is a popular Egyptian equivalent to the hummus and falafel of the Levantine. *Fuul* is fava beans slow-cooked down to a soft paste. It's served on a plate to eat with Egyptian *baladi* bread or as a sandwich with *ta'miyyah,* which is also made from a fava-bean base and is deep-fried into a crispy treat.

On the coast of the Mediterranean, Alexandria is known for its *kebda iskandarani.* This spicy liver is served in soft *fino* bread with sliced Meyer lemons for squeezing over. It's a go-to meal that locals eat at any time of the day. In streets where these sandwiches are sold there are usually small convenience stalls selling potato chips. Alexandrians crush and scatter the chips into their sandwiches to give the soft textures some crunch.

Delicacies

In Egypt food is used as a means of hospitality and a way of warmly welcoming guests. Making sure that your guests are well fed (and sometimes overfed) with the best of foods is central to Egyptian culture. On special occasions that bring people together, dishes that take a lot of time to prepare, such as *mahshi* (stuffed foods), are served to show respect to guests.

Dining tables are adorned with several platters and an array of side dishes. Roast duck is typically served as the main course, and sometimes it's stuffed with seasoned short-grain rice as well. The head of the duck is a delicacy in itself, and if it is served the hosts will offer it to their guests as a gesture of hospitality. Another dish that is often served as a main course is *hammam mahshi* (roast pigeon stuffed with rice).

Stuffed vegetable dishes are also popular. The pulp or seeds of vegetables such as eggplants, zucchini and sweet peppers are removed and the vegetable cases are stuffed to the brim with a mixture of seasoned rice and dill. Other variations are *mahshi krumb* (rolled and stuffed cabbage leaves) and *mahshi wara innab* (rolled and stuffed grapevine leaves).

Sweets

Sweets are also an integral part of the cuisine in Egypt, with milk the base ingredient in many recipes. A few desserts are quite simple, such as *roz bi laban* (rice pudding). *Umm Ali* is a kind of bread pudding. It has a base of milk and cream on crumbled *fino* bread and it's topped with chopped nuts and raisins.

Adel Emam in 2014

UNDERSTANDING EGYPT WITH ADEL EMAM

Egyptians are regionally renowned for their comedic chops, so trying to understand them without first watching their comedies is like trying to understand bread without ever having eaten. Essay by Sanad Tabbaa

NOBODY DOES COMEDY quite like Egypt. This is neither an endorsement nor a condemnation; it's simply a fact that the comedies produced in Egypt are different in type, subject matter and basic feel from those produced anywhere else. At first glance these films may appear from their posters to be corny, garish and somewhat idiotic. Some of them are, but many more are not.

The Role of Comedy

In Egypt the primary way to demonstrate a grievance with culture, society, the government and pretty much anything else is by viciously mocking it. Comedies often centre on an unfortunate and basically normal though somewhat unhinged person who is placed in a completely insane situation, though never in a way that seems bleak. Unlike comedies that poke fun at misery or simply pretend that everything's great, Egyptian comedies have the mindset of 'everything's pretty messed up; isn't that hilarious?' This approach tends to make the films memorable. Egyptian films, especially the comedies, are quoted not only in Egypt but across the Arab world. This means that trying to limit even just the comedies to a few recommended titles doesn't do the field justice. That would be like trying to choose the top three Hollywood films of all time. A good place to start, though, is with the work of Adel Emam.

Adel Emam's Early Work

Every era of Egyptian cinema has its master. Ismail Yassin was dubbed the Arab Charlie Chaplin from the 1940s to the '60s, Mohammad Henedy was the main man of the early 2000s and Ahmad Helmy took the top spot in the 2010s. From the 1970s to the end of the '90s, though, Adel Emam reigned supreme, only retiring in 2024 after a 60-year career.

Emam skyrocketed to fame after his performance in *Madraset El Moshaghebeen* (The School of Mischief) in 1973 and quickly became one of the most sought-after comedians in Egypt. Part of a long history of filmed Egyptian theatre, *Madraset El Moshaghebeen* is a filmed play. A cultural touchstone that continues to be appreciated across the Arab world, it tells the story of a class of high schoolers who have been repeating their senior year for nearly a decade. They have driven successive sets of teachers to nervous breakdowns with their antics, but now a new female teacher has arrived. She comes in with a blend of tough love and low tolerance for silliness to reform the students and force them to graduate. The play is heavy on wordplay and exceedingly quotable characters whose words and behaviour are imitated even today. It has recently been released in colour and is also available subtitled on online streaming platforms.

Essential Films

The play highlighted a number of new actors who would go on to become celebrities in Egypt. In the 1980s Emam avoided becoming typecast by embracing versatility, acting in everything from light-hearted comedies to action to (very briefly) horror. That said, the peak of his career was in the 1990s. Already a very well-respected actor, Emam used the '90s to blend his quick wit and comedic timing with a degree of social critique. Two films in particular stand out: *Al Laib Ma El Kibar* (Playing with the Big Boys; 1991) and *Irhab Wa Kabab* (Terrorism and Kebab; 1992).

In *Al Laib Ma El Kibar* Emam plays Hassan, a chronically unemployed young man who, apparently in order to avoid paying his tab at a cafe, calls the Ministry of the Interior to report an impending arson at a plastic factory that very night at exactly 10.30pm. Hassan is immediately taken in for questioning and quizzed on the source of his knowledge. Initially reticent, he eventually admits that he saw it in a dream. Chaos ensues when the plastic factory is actually set on fire at exactly 10.30pm. The film is campy and fun to start with, but it tackles some serious issues including corruption, justice and police brutality. Its success inspired several crime comedies in Egypt.

Irhab Wal Kabab is on a whole other level, though. It's a Kafkian tale of bureaucracy, a condemnation of incompetence and an intricate study of the simple struggle for survival, all in one. Emam plays Ahmad, an everyman working two jobs to support his young children and a wife who evidently hates him. Attempting to traverse the complex bureaucratic nightmare known as El Mogamma in order to transfer his children to a school closer to home, Ahmad must confront laziness, corruption and false piety to get his paperwork signed, always searching for the probably fictitious Mr Methat. After losing his temper and being accosted by the guards, Ahmad accidentally comes into possession of a machine gun and finds himself inadvertently in charge of a hostage situation, having taken over the primary governmental office of the entire country. In this he is joined by a shoeshiner with a grudge, a much-abused young conscript, a hard-boiled hostess with a seemingly endless supply of props hidden in her bra and some poor guy who's simply trying to take his own life but keeps getting sidelined. The film is about posturing, social expectations, poverty and, of course, kebab.

The Tip of the Thread

These few films will not give you anything resembling a complete understanding of Egyptian media or the Egyptian people. That said, starting with Adel Emam's work will give you *taraf el kheit* (the tip of the thread), which you may use to unravel the deep, complex and highly entertaining world of Egyptian cinema. Happy viewing!

# THE PEOPLE OF THE NILE

Having relied on it for thousands of years, Egyptians have a deep, personal and beautiful relationship with the Nile. Essay by Sanad Tabbaa

CAIRENES CALL THE Nile 'El Bahr', which means 'The Sea'. Alexandrians make fun of them for it, but the Nile's width and glory do suggest it's something more than just a river. A vein of vibrant life that runs through a harsh and unforgiving desert, it's a fundamental marker of Egyptian national identity and a lifeline for millennia of successive civilisations. Down the generations the Nile has provided, defended and destroyed. The Greek historian Herodotus expressed it perfectly some 2400 years ago: 'Egypt is the gift of the Nile'.

The Nile Provides

Egypt depends on the Nile to this very day. More than 90% of the country's population presently lives near the river or utilises it directly. Like all large rivers, the Nile has long been used for fishing and agriculture and as a source of water for humans and livestock. The Nile is special, though, for its floods.

Before the Aswan High Dam was built, water burst across the banks of the Nile every summer after the monsoon season in Ethiopia, covering the nearby area with a layer of rich silt that allowed ancient Egypt to provide food for an estimated 2.5 to 12 million people. This alone gave Egypt self-sufficiency in the desert, and the country was later the breadbasket of the Roman Empire and successive Islamic empires.

The time of flooding was crucial to ancient Egyptians in particular, as it was only during the three months after the floods of August and September that crops for the entire year could be grown. It is unsurprising, then, that an extensive amount of belief and mythology grew up around the Nile and its effects on fertility. The river was considered to be an aspect of the god Hapi, and floods were believed to be the tears of the goddess Isis as she remembered her murdered husband, Osiris. The flooding was celebrated for two weeks from 15 August during the festival of Wafaa El Nil, and Coptic Christians still observe the festival by throwing an effigy into the waters.

As the centre of a rich ecosystem, the Nile was a vital resource for ancient Egyptians. The annual migration of birds in October provided a plentiful source of food, and the riverbanks' plant and animal life sustained the local people.

The river's sustenance was not just material and spiritual but also intellectual. The endemic papyrus plant that grows along the banks of the Nile allowed the Egyptians to be possibly the first people to create a precursor to paper, which in turn

STORYBOOK

Aswan High Dam

promoted the preservation and transmission of knowledge. The inks created by the ancient Egyptians were also products of the Nile, as were the reed pens they used. These resources allowed the sharing of knowledge in a cheap, easy and accessible fashion and were the basis of Egyptian innovations such as codified law and order, complex trade agreements and even a postal service.

The Nile was thus an inseparable part of the development of Egypt. It was central to its ability to cultivate a culture that venerated and respected knowledge, built the library of Alexandria, and recorded histories, philosophies and stories that continue to be studied today. In the modern era the Nile is still recognised and celebrated for its creative and intellectual value, appearing often and prominently in media as a fundamental marker of Egyptian cultural identity.

To understand the importance of the Nile in ancient Egyptian thought you need only consider the placement of the Pyramids in the Giza complex. The Pyramids overlooked a now-dry western branch of the Nile and were placed to the west of it. Their placement was partly born of convenience, so that workers could visit the complex by boat, but there was also a spiritual dimension to their positioning. The sun sets in the west and thus the ancient Egyptians believed the lands of the dead were there. From the perspective of the Pyramids, the demarcation point – the place where life and death separate from one another – was the Nile.

The Nile Defends

From providing a theatre for naval warfare to allowing the construction of defences in areas otherwise impossible to access, the Nile has been instrumental in repelling invaders since time immemorial.

The Crusaders attempted to invade Egypt during the decline of the Fatimid Empire in the 12th century. Following a complex set of broken agreements, a refusal to pay tribute and a desire to avoid being encircled by Islamic empires, the European Amalric, King of Jerusalem, launched an invasion of Fatimid Egypt. He came within 35km of the capital, besieging the fortress of Bilbais. In response, the Egyptians simply walled themselves inside and disengaged the floodgates, which forced a Crusader retreat. From then on Crusader invasions avoided the months of August and September.

Before the advent of aerial warfare the river's width made it impossible to cross except under very specific conditions. Egyptians understood these conditions far better than others, constructing labyrinthine canals in parts of the river where crossing was possible and fortifying multiple areas along the banks.

The Nile Destroys

The Nile was loved, but it was also respected and feared – far more so than it is today. The floods of the Nile had extreme destructive potential, with the ability to wipe out canals used for irrigation, homes and even entire villages. Inadequate floods could lead to famines. Control over the Nile was consistently attempted across history, notably by Islamic sultans and caliphs, though projects of this kind were often abandoned due to the sheer size and complexity of the task.

Floods were not the only danger the Nile posed. Especially around the Delta, the river was once thickly inhabited by Nile crocodiles. Also, the Nile, particularly its canals and tributaries, continues to be home to the parasitic worm that causes schistosomiasis, also known as bilharzia. In the early 20th century some 85% of the Egyptian population carried the parasite. In both ancient and early modern Egypt, bilharzia was so common that when men urinated blood it was considered to be part of a natural male menstrual cycle. One of the greatest Egyptian singers of all time, Abdel Halim Hafez, died from complications of the disease in 1977 at the age of 47.

Attempts to mitigate the negative aspects of the Nile include the eradication of crocodiles in the Delta, the introduction of novel irrigation systems in the Ottoman and Khedival eras to increase and stabilise agricultural yields, and reducing the incidence of bilharzia through modern medicine.

In the 1960s the Nile was finally tamed with the construction of the Aswan High Dam. The project, built from 1960 to 1970, has provided Egypt with hydroelectric power and a stable source of water, but it has also led to a set of unanticipated consequences, including potential desertification of the soil and an end to the distribution of the Nile's silt through the annual floods. That said, the positive features appear to outweigh the risks for many Egyptians, and the dam is a source of no small amount of national pride.

The Nile Beyond Egypt's Borders

The Aswan Dam recognises the symbiotic relationship Egypt has with the Nile, but the country's position downstream (the Nile flows from south to north) makes it vulnerable to the actions of the states that lie upstream. The Grand Ethiopian Renaissance Dam project led to an immediate rise in tensions between Egypt and Ethiopia, including threats of war and veiled suggestions of sabotage.

Many Egyptians felt threatened and personally offended that Ethiopia was planning to dam the Nile, both because of the very real possibility of water scarcity but also out of a sense that Egypt enjoys a unique relationship with the river. Similarly, many Ethiopians felt slighted that Egypt considers itself the primary arbiter of the use of the Nile, which negates the very real and deep connection other peoples have to the river. In a way this conflict is a very old one, reopening centuries-old wounds stretching back to ancient eras of Egyptian domination in the region.

The Nile's Future

Sadly, commercial activity means the Nile is now contaminated with factory pollution, plastic pollution and agricultural runoff. Climate change will almost certainly have a negative impact on the river, too.

In response to these threats, many governmental and small-scale projects aim to preserve the health of the river. In 2017 Egypt's environment ministry reported that directly polluting facilities had dropped from 102 to nine, with most pollution coming indirectly from wastewater treatment. A multitude of grassroots initiatives aim to reduce plastic pollution and maintain the aesthetic value of the river.

Down the centuries the Nile has taken care of Egypt, and in return Egypt continues to do its best to take care of the Nile.

EGYPT'S ENVIRONMENTAL CHALLENGES

A hot country that's mostly desert, Egypt grappled with the challenges of water availability and heat management even before the modern threats of climate change and overtourism added to the strain. Essay by Sanad Tabbaa

TWO HALLMARKS OF climate change are the global trend towards higher temperatures and the resultant rise in sea levels. Egypt is, unfortunately, no exception to this, and about 37% of its present population is threatened by water encroachment, particularly in the areas around the Mediterranean coast and Alexandria. This is not an issue for the distant future but a present reality. Already the village of Rosetta (Ar Rashid), of Rosetta Stone fame, is at extreme risk of being submerged.

In an ironic twist, just as Egypt's coastal areas are threatened by an excess of water, the rest of the country is suffering from water scarcity. About 95% of Egypt is functionally uninhabitable desert, but to make matters worse the habitable parts of the country are threatened by drought. Decreased rainfall and increased surface temperatures cause rain to evaporate so quickly that groundwater reserves cannot be replenished. Further, as Egypt's water needs grow, so the country's reliance on

Port Said (p340)

the Nile increases. Much of Egypt's freshwater is derived from its famous river, and the likely future impact of the growing strain on this precious resource remains unclear. Consider your water use carefully during your visit.

Between 1989 and 2018, Egypt's already sizable population doubled, and the country is now home to more than 100 million people. The population boom has had myriad knock-on effects, from extreme levels of noise pollution to an epidemic of littering to significant demands on the local infrastructure. The larger population has also led to increased traffic jams, rising electricity costs and major issues with the availability of public services and transport.

Be aware of these issues before you arrive and do your best to limit your impact on the country's overburdened infrastructure. Use electricity responsibly; don't litter, despite its prevalence; and if you're physically able to, make an effort to walk more within major urban centres such as Cairo, rather than travelling by car.

Plant on the Nile near Kom Ombo

Though Egypt contributes relatively little air pollution, especially given its size and population, its dusty climate and low rainfall, combined with vehicular emissions, mean that the country is suffering from severe air-quality challenges. This is especially pronounced in Cairo, where the air quality can vary from 10 to 100 times more polluted than worldwide acceptable standards. Travellers with breathing difficulties should limit their time in Cairo proper as much as they can.

The impact of this air pollution is not limited to humans. A black, sooty layer can often be seen on the upper exterior walls of many historic monuments in the capital. These are layers of pollutants that interact with the humidity in the air and progressively eat away at Egypt's architectural heritage. Limestone was a popular construction material for many medieval Islamic buildings in particular. Sadly, it interacts with these compound gases of pollutants and, as a result, the very integrity of the stone is compromised. Over time the damaged limestone sloughs off and falls to the ground, exponentially speeding up the erosion and degradation of historic buildings.

Scientists are working to develop methods to counteract the damage, but they're in a race against time so long as air pollution remains at current (or greater) levels.

Egypt isn't taking these challenges lying down. The government has committed to clean public transport through the Cairo Monorail project and has made a concerted effort to reduce urban congestion in Cairo by building neighbouring satellite cities, including a proposed new administrative capital.

The country has plans to derive nearly half of its energy from renewable sources by 2030. These practices are well underway, with reforms to the energy sector propelling positive change in an effort to kill two birds with one stone: revitalise the struggling economy by providing new jobs and divest from fossil fuels as a source of energy.

INDEX

A

Ababda people 365
Abu 254-5
Abu Simbel 265-7
  accommodation 269
Abu Simbel Temples 265-7
Abydos 182
  accommodation 189
accessible travel 420
accommodation 412, *see also* camping, dahabiyas, ecolodges, *individual locations*
activities 36-7, 46-7, 50-1, *see also individual activities*
adventure parks 116
Agilika Island 258-60
ahwa 417
  Cairo 96
air travel 407
airports 406
Akhenaten 174-5
Al Fayoum 162-7, **163**
  accommodation 189
  food 164
  travel within Al Fayoum 162
Al Hayz Oasis 289-90
Al Kharga Oasis 276, 300-2, **301**
  accommodation 303
  food 302
  tours 302
  travel within Al Kharga Oasis 300
Al Qasr 298-9
Al Quseir 364-5
  accommodation 367
alcohol 43, 422

Map Pages **000**

Alexandria 305-28, **306-7**, **311**, **315**
  accommodation 335
  activities 308-9
  climate 308-9
  drinking 314, 319, 324
  entertainment 318
  festivals & events 308-9
  food 312, 313, 314, 316, 317, 319, 321, 322
  itineraries 308-9
  navigation 306-7
  shopping 324
  tours 313, 317, 318, 319, 323
  travel seasons 308-9
  travel within Alexandria 306-7, 310
  walking tours 327, **327**
Ali, Mohammed 313, 322
al-Kharrat, Edwar 321
animal welfare 49, 418
  Luxor 206
Arabic language 39, 101, 424-5
  Cairo 101
archaeological sites 16-17, 19, 151, *see also* forts & fortresses, pyramids, temples, tombs & burial sites
  Abu 250
  Abydos 182
  Akhmim 181
  Al Fayoum pyramids 167
  Al Kharga Oasis 302
  Antinopolis 173
  Athribis 181
  Avenue of Sphinxes 198
  Colossi of Memnon 207
  Dahshur 143
  Dendara 186-8
  Dimeh El Sabaa 165
  Great Pyramid of Khufu 64-5, 432
  Hermopolis 172
  Karanis 153
  KV 5 209
  Medinat Madi 166-7
  Pyramid of Khafre 65-6
  Pyramid of Menkaure 66-7
  Pyramids of Giza 64-71, **68-9**

Roman sites (Cairo) 123
Roman theatre (Alexandria) 316-17
Saqqara 144-9
Speos Artemidos 171
Sphinx 67
Tell Al Amarna 174-5
Temple of Seti I at Abydos 183-4
Theban Mapping Project 208
Tihna Al Gebel 168-9
Tombs of Al Hawawish 181
Tuna Al Gebel 172-3
unfinished obelisk (Aswan) 250
Valley of the Golden Mummies 287
Villa of the Birds 317
Wadi Al Hitan 164-5
architecture 22, *see also* Islamic architecture
  Basuna Mosque 180
  conservation 116, 118
  Dakhla Oasis 295, 297
  House of Egyptian Architecture 113
  Ottoman architecture 106-7
  Royal Jewellery Museum (neoclassical beaux-arts villa) 321-2
art
  Coptic art 355
  Islamic art 93
  street art 116
art courses 393-4
art galleries, *see* museums & galleries
Aswan 236-42, 247-57, **237**, **248, 252-3**
  accommodation 268-9
  beyond Aswan 258-60
  food 249, 250, 255, 256, 257
  tours 249, 254
  travel within Aswan 247
  walking tours 251, **251**
Asyut 176-8, **177**
  accommodation 189
  food 178
  travel within Asyut 176
ATMs 406, 411

B

Bahariya Oasis 276, 285-7, **286**
  accommodation 303
  beyond Bahariya Oasis 288-90
  food 287
  tours 289
  travel within Bahariya Oasis 285
bathrooms 422
bazaars, *see* markets
beaches
  Alexandria 322, 323
  El Alamein 329
  Hurghada 357
  Marsa Matruh 332-3
  Sinai 392
Bedouin camps 288, 381
Bedouin people 366, 381, 392
Bibliotheca Alexandrina 325-6
bicycle travel 209
Bir Wahed 283
birdwatching 36, 380
Black Desert 289
boat travel 20-1, 407, 410
  Cairo 87, 133
  Luxor 205
  Luxor to Aswan 241-2
  Ras Mohammed National Park 383
  safety 414
bookbinding 101
books 39, 257, 321
border crossings 406
budget 411
burial sites, *see* tombs & burial sites
bus travel 407, 408-9
business hours 422

C

Cairo 56-155, **58-9, 102-3**
  accommodation 154-5
  activities 60-1
  beyond Cairo 143-53
  Coptic Cairo 119-24, **121**
  Dokki 125-33, **126-7**

448

Downtown Cairo 77-92, **82**, **88-9**
drinking 85, 86, 87, 96, 120, 131, 132, 138, 141
entertainment 131, 137
family travel 75, 114
food 62-3, 70-1, 83, 84, 85, 86, 90, 91, 95, 101, 115, 120, 122, 128, 129, 130, 131, 132, 133, 136, 137-8, 141, 142
Fustat 119-24, **121**
Garden City 134-8, **135**
Giza 62-76, **63**
Heliopolis 139-42, **140**
Islamic Cairo 93-118, **94**, **102-3**
itineraries 60-1
Maadi 119-24
navigation 58-9
New Cairo 139-42, **140**
nightlife 141
Roda Island 134-8, **135**
shopping 85, 87, 95, 108, 124, 125, 128, 136-7
tours 67, 83-4, 118
travel to Cairo 95
travel within Cairo 58-9, 62, 77, 93, 119, 125, 134, 139
walking tours 92, **92**
Zamalek 125-33, **126-7**
camel riding 49, 67, 70
camping 288, 412
car travel 407
caravanserai
  Wakālāt Al Jiddāwī 238
  Wikala of Al Ghouri 106
Carter, Howard 214
catacombs, see cemeteries & catacombs
Cavafy, Constantine 321
cemeteries & catacombs
  Al Qarafa 124
  Catacombs of Kom El Shoqafa 317-18
  Cemetery for sacred rams 255
  Commonwealth War Cemetery 331
  Coptic Cemetery (Alexandria) 318
  El Alamein War Cemeteries 330-1
  German War Memorial 331
  Greek & Latin Cemetery (Alexandria) 317
  Greek Orthodox Cemetery (Alexandria) 318
  Italian War Memorial 331
  Jewish cemetery (Alexandria) 317-18
  Northern Cemetery (Qarafa) 112, 113
ceramics
  Al Fayoum 162, 164
  Cairo 124
  Luxor 228
children, travel with, see family travel
churches 13, see also Coptic sites, monasteries & convents
  Basilique Notre Dame d'Heliopolis 140
  Cathedral of Evangelismos 318
  Cathedral of the Nativity of Christ 142
  Church of St Abahour 170
  Church of St Barbara 123
  Church of St Bishoi 173
  Church of St George 122
  Church of St John the Short 173
  Church of St Sergius & Bacchus 122
  Church of St Simon the Tanner 115
  Church of the Blessed Virgin (Minya) 169
  Church of the Martyrs of Faith & Homeland 170
  Church of the Transfiguration 392-3
  Church of the Virgin Mary (Asyut) 177
  Hanging Church 120-2
  St Catherine's Cathedral 319
  St Mark's Anglican Church 319
  St Mark's Coptic Orthodox Cathedral 317, 318
Citadel 109-10, 434
city culture 23
Cleopatra 334
climate 36-7, 418, see also individual regions
clothes 38
Colossi of Memnon 207
Colossus of Ramses II 222
cooking classes 84
Coptic art 355
Coptic sites 13
  Alexandria 318-19
  Coptic Cairo 122-3
  Coptic Museum 120
  Hanging Church 120-2
  Sohag 180
  St Mark's Coptic Orthodox Cathedral 317, 318
convents, see monasteries & convents
costs 411
  accommodation 412
  food & drinks 417
  travel 407
courses
  art courses 393-4
  cooking classes 84
  craft workshops 111
  pottery lessons 228
credit cards 411
crocodiles 167, 244
cruise ships 412, 419
cultural centres
  Darb 1718 123
  El Mastaba Center for Egyptian Folk Music 90
  El Sawy Culture Wheel 131
  Makan 136
  Multicultural & Artistic Spaces at Qaitbey's 111
cultural conservation 240
culture 436-7, 440-1, see also people
currency 411
currency exchange 406
cycling 209

D

Dahab 386-91, **387**
  accommodation 403
  beyond Dahab 392-4
  food 388
  travel within Dahab 386
dahabiyas 241, 241-2, 412
Dahshur 143
Dakhla Oasis 276, 295-7, **296**
  accommodation 303
  food 296
  travel within Dakhla Oasis 295
dams
  Aswan High Dam 260
  Grand Ethiopian Renaissance Dam (GERD) 263
dangers 415
Daraw 260
Darb Al Ahmar 117-18
Dendara 186-8
desert experiences 47, 280, 412
deserts 14-15
  Black Desert 289
  Western Desert 270-303, **272-3**
  White Desert National Park 293-4
digital nomads 388

disabilities, travellers with 420
diving 12, 46-7
  Dahab 389-91
  dive insurance 414
  Hurghada 356
  Marsa Alam 363
  Marsa Shagra Village 361-2
  Ras Mohammed National Park 382-5
  responsible diving 48, 362, 419
  Sharm El Sheikh 376-7
dolphins 362
drinking 416-17, see also individual locations
drinking water 414
dunes
  Agabat 292
  Black Desert 289
  White Desert National Park 294
Durrell, Lawrence 320-1

ecolodges 393, 392, 412
Edfu 245-6
  accommodation 268
Egyptian Museum 78-81, **80**
Eid Al Adha 37
El Alamein 328-31, **329**
  accommodation 335
  travel within El Alamein 328
El Alamein War Cemeteries 330-1
El Arag Oasis 283-4
El Gouna 358-9
  accommodation 367
electricity 422
Elephantine Island 250, 254
Emam, Adel 440-1
embassies 423
embroidery 96
emergencies 422
environmental issues 446-7
  Cairo's rubbish 115
  Nile, the 445
  responsible travel 418-19
Esna 236, 238-9, **237**
  accommodation 268
  food 239
  shopping 238, 239
  tours 236
etiquette 38, 422
  mosques 105, 106
events, see festivals & events

F

family travel 47, 413
  Cairo 75, 114
Farafra Oasis 276, 291-2, **292**
  accommodation 303
  food 292
  travel within Farafra Oasis 291
farms 342
Fatnas Island 280-1
feluccas 20-1, 242, 412
  Cairo 137
  Luxor 204-5, 205
  Luxor to Aswan 242
festivals & events 36-7
  Abu Simbel solar alignment festivals 37, 267
  Cairo International Film Festival 130
  Cairo Jazz Festival 85
  Citadel Festival for Music & Singing 116
  D-CAF 37, 91
  Eid Al Adha 37
  Forever is Now 67
  Qasr Qarun 37
  Ramadan 37
  Sham An Nessim 37
  Siyaha Festival 37, 280
  Tunis Village Festival 164
films 39, 440-1
fishing 262
food 42-4, 416-29, 438-9, see also individual foods, individual locations
food poisoning 415
food tours
  Alexandria 313-14
  Cairo 83-4
  Dar Jan 393-4
Forster, EM 320-1
forts & fortresses
  Bab Al Futuh 100
  Babylon Fortress 123
  Citadel 109-10, 434
  Fort Qaitbey 310, 434
  Fortress of Shali 278
  Ottoman fortress (Al Quseir) 365
  Wadi Natrun 151-2

G

galleries, see museums & galleries
gardens, see parks & gardens
gay travellers 415
Gebel Abbas Basha 402
Gebel Abu Gasaba 402
Gebel Al Ingleez 285
Gebel Asyut Al Gharbi 178
Gebel Dakrur 280
Gebel Dist 285
Gebel Katarina 402
Gebel Musa 399-401
Gebel Serbal 402
Gebel Silsila 240-1
Gebel Um Shomer 402
Giza 62-76, **63**
gods & goddesses 426-9
Grand Egyptian Museum 72-6

H

haggling 45
hammams 99
handcrafts 96
  alabaster workshops 227
  bookbinding 101
  ceramics 124, 162, 164, 228
  embroidery 96, 101
  handloom workshops 227-8
  metalwork 101
  papyrus workshops 227
  pottery 124, 162, 164, 228
  tarboosh (fez) making 101
  textiles 108
  Tunis 164
  weaving 62
Hathor 186-8
Hatshepsut 219
health 414-15
heat exhaustion 415
highlights 10-23
hiking 47
  Asyut 177
  Galt El Azraq 401-2
  Gebel Katarina 402
  Mt Sinai 399-401
  Nuweiba Canyons 397-8
  Siwa Oasis 281
  Wadi Al Hitan 165
history 432-5
  Abdeen Palace 435
  Al Azhar University 434
  Al Montazah Palaces 435
  Cairo 111
  Cairo Citadel 434
  El Alamein battlefields 328-31
  Fort Qaitbey 434

Great Pyramid of Khufu 432
  Islamic history 111
  Karnak 432-3
  Midan Tahrir 435
  Monastery of St Anthony 433-4
  Mosque of Amr Ibn Al As 434
  nomarchs 170
  Pharaonic 426-9
  Roman 123
  St Katherine's Monastery 434
  Suez Canal 435
  Temple of Hathor 433
  Temple of Hibis 433
  Temples of Abu Simbel 433
  Theban Mapping Project 208-9
  Thebes 204
  WWII 328-31
horse riding
  Abu Sir 151
  Giza 67, 70
  Luxor 209
Horus 246
hot-air ballooning 210
hotels 412
Hurghada 352-7, **353**
  accommodation 367
  beyond Hurghada 358-60
  drinking 355
  food 354
  travel within Hurghada 352

I

insurance 414
Isis (goddess) 259
Islamic architecture 22, 111
  Mosque of Qaitbey 108
  Nubia Museum 247, 249
  Sharia Al Muizz Li-Din Allah 97-100
Ismailia 342-3
  accommodation 345
  tours 342
  travel within Ismailia 342
  walking tours 343, **343**
Israel-Egypt relations 394
itineraries 26-35, **27**, **29**, **31**, **33**, **35**, see also individual regions

K

Karanis 153
Karnak 200-1, 205-6, 432-3
kayaking 133

kitesurfing
  Dahab 386, 388
  Safaga 365-6
Kom Ombo Temple 243-4
Kulthum, Umm 137
kushari 83, 417

L

Lake Nasser 261-4, **262**
lakes
  Birkat Maran 287
  Cold Water Lake 283
  Lake Nasser 261-4, **262**
  Lake Qarun 165
  Sacred Lake 201
  Wadi Rayyan Protected Area 165
language 39, 424-5
  Cairo 101
Lasciac, Antonio 321-2
LGBTIQ+ travellers 415
libraries
  Bibliotheca Alexandrina 325-6
  Theban Community Library 208
Lighthouse of Alexandria 312
Lower Nubia 256, 261-4, **262**
Luxor 190-229, **192-3**, see also Luxor to Aswan
  accommodation 229
  activities 194-5
  drinking 204, 213
  East Bank 198-206, **199**
  food 203, 209, 219
  Gezira 207-9, **208**
  itineraries 194-5
  navigation 192-3
  shopping 203
  tours 197, 223
  travel within Luxor 192, 198, 207, 211, 217, 221, 225
  Valley of the Kings 211-16, **212**
  Valley of the Queens 217-20, **218**
  West Bank Temples 221-4, **222**
  Wider Necropolis 225-8, **226**
Luxor Temple 202
Luxor to Aswan 236-42, **237**

M

madrasas & mausoleums
  Al Qasr 299
  Housh Al Basha 124
  Khanqah & Mausoleum of Farag Ibn Barquq 111-12

Madrasa & Mausoleum of Al Saleh Najm Al Din Ayyub 98
Madrasa & Mausoleum of Sultan Al Zahir Barquq 99
Mastaba of Al Faraun 149
Mausoleum & Madrasa of Qalawun 97-8
Mausoleum & Sabil-Kuttab of Al Ghouri 105
Mausoleum of Imam Al Shafi'i 124
Mosque & Madrasa of Al Nasir Muhammad Ibn Qalawun 99
Mosque & Madrasa of Sultan Al Ghuri 105
Mosque & Madrasa of Sultan Hassan 112-13
Mahfouz, Naguib 321
Mallawi 172-3
mangos 342
mansions, *see* palaces & mansions
markets 45
 Ad Dahar Souq 352
 Al Midan fish market 313
 Al Qīsāriyya Market 236
 Halaka Fish Market 354
 Khan El Khalili 95
 Libya Souq 334
 Sharia As Souq 247
 Sharm Old Market 379
 Souq At Talaat 223
 Tourist Souq 203
Marsa Alam 361-3, **362**
 accommodation 367
 beyond Marsa Alam 364-6
 travel within Marsa Alam 361
Marsa Matruh 332-4, **333**
 accommodation 335
 food 333
 tours 362
 travel within Marsa Matruh 332
mausoleums, *see* madrasas & mausoleums
medical services 415
Medinat Habu 224
Mediterranean coast 305-35, **306-7**
 activities 308-9
 Alexandria, *see individual location*
 climate 308-9
 El Alamein, *see individual location*
 festivals & events 308-9
 itineraries 308-9

Marsa Matruh, *see individual location*
navigation 306-7
travel seasons 308-9
travel within the Mediterranean Coast 306-7
Memphis 151
metalwork 101
Minya 168-71, **169**
 accommodation 189
 beyond Minya 172-3
 food 170
 travel within Minya 168
molokhiyya 438-9
monasteries & convents 13
 Deir Abu Makar 151-3
 Deir Al Adhra 169
 Deir Al Barsha 173
 Deir Al Muharraq 176-7
 Deir Anba Bishoy 152
 Deir Dirunka 177
 Deir El Sourian 152-3
 Monastery of Al Kashef 302
 Monastery of St Anthony 359-60, 433-4
 Monastery of St Paul 359
 Monastery of St Savvas 319
 Monastery of St Simeon 256
 Red Monastery 179
 St George's Convent 122
 St Katherine's Monastery 392-3, 434
 White Monastery 180
Monastery of St Anthony 359-60, 433-4
Monastery of St Paul 359
money 411
money exchange 406
mosques
 Abu Abbas Al Mursi Mosque 312
 Al Azhar Mosque 104-5
 Al Hakim Mosque 100
 Al Hussein Mosque 104
 Al Rifa'i Mosque 113
 Al Sahaba Mosque 378-9
 Al Tanbugha Al Maridani Mosque 118
 Aqsunqur Mosque 118
 Basuna Mosque 180, 181
 Cairo 104
 El-Shorbagi Mosque 312
 Faran mosque 365
 Grand Mosque (Hurghada) 354
 Manial Palace mosque 136
 Mausoleum & Sabil-Kuttab of Al Ghouri 105

Mosque & Madrasa of Sultan Al Ghuri 105
Mosque & Madrasa of Sultan Hassan 112-13
Mosque of Amr Ibn Al As 123-4, 434
Mosque of Ibn Tulun 114
Mosque of Qaitbey 108
Mosque of Sheikh Al Qenawi 185
Muhammad Ali Mosque 109-10
Suleiman Pasha Mosque 110
Sultan Al Nasir Muhammad Mosque 110
Terbang Mosque 312
Mt Sinai 399-401
mummification 204, 427
museums & galleries
 Access Art Space 91
 Aisha Fahmy Palace 129
 Al Hayz Water Education Center 289-90
 Al Kharga Museum of Antiquities 302
 Al Masar Gallery 130
 Al Qasr museum 299
 Alexandria National Museum 320
 Animalia 254
 Antiquities Museum 326
 Aswan Museum 254
 Badr's Museum 292
 Bayt Amana 291
 Cairopolitan 136-7
 Canal Museum 342
 Cavafy House 321
 Coptic Museum 120
 Crocodile Museum 244
 Egypt Capitals Museum 142
 Egyptian Museum 78-81, **80**
 Egyptian Postal Museum 91
 Egyptian Railway Museum 91
 El Alamein Military Museum 330-1
 Fossil & Climate Change Museum 165
 Gayer-Anderson Museum 114
 Gebel Qatrani Open-Air Museum 166
 Golden Mummies Museum 287
 Graeco-Roman Museum (Alexandria) 314
 Grand Egyptian Museum 72-6

Hermopolis museum 172
House of Siwa 278
Hurghada Museum 354-5
Imhotep Museum 149
Karnak Open-Air Museum 201
Kom Aushim Museum 153
Luxor Museum 203
Mahmoud Mukhtar Museum 129
Mahmoud Said Museum 323
Mallawi museum 172
Manuscript Museum 326
Matrouh National Museum 334
Military Museum (Port Said) 340
Mit Rahina 151
Mohamed Mahmoud Khalil Museum 129
Motion Art Gallery 130
Mummification Museum 204
Museum of Fine Art 323
Museum of Islamic Art 93
Museum of Islamic Ceramics 129
Museum of Modern Egyptian Art 129
National Military Museum 110
National Museum 344
National Museum of Egyptian Civilization 119-20
Nubia Museum 247, 249
Palace of Arts 129
Police Museum 110
Presidency Gifts Museum 86
Rawabet Art Space 91
Royal Carriages Museum 90
Royal Jewellery Museum 321-2
Sadat Museum 326
Safarkhan 130
Sharm El Sheikh Museum 374, 378
Sohag National Museum 180-1
St Katherine's Monastery Museum 393
Tintera 130
Ubuntu Art Gallery 131
Umm Kulthum Museum 137
Zamalek Art Gallery 130
music 39
 Cairo 131
 festivals 85, 116
 traditional 90, 131, 136

Nabatat (Kitchener's) Island 254
national parks & protected areas
 Dababiya Natural Reserve 239-40
 Nabq Nature Reserve 380-1
 Qarun Protected Area 165
 Ras Mohammed National Park 382-5
 Wadi Gimal National Park 366
 Wadi Rayyan Protected Area 164-5
 White Desert National Park 293-4
Nazla 164
New Administrative Capital 142
nightlife 416-17
Nile cruising 410
 Cairo 133, 137
 Luxor 204-5
 Luxor to Aswan 241-2
Nile river 442-5, see also northern Nile Valley, southern Nile Valley
 angels of the Nile 255
Zamalek 132
nomarchs 170
Northern Nile Valley 157-89, **158-9**
 activities 160-1
 Al Fayoum see individual location
 Asyut see individual location
 climate 160-1
 festivals & events 160-1
 itineraries 32-3, 160-1, **33**
 Minya see individual location
 navigation 158-9
 Qena see individual location
 Sohag see individual location
 travel seasons 160-1
 travel within Northern Nile Valley 158-9
 notable buildings

Map Pages **000**

Amir Khayrbak Funerary Complex 117
Bab Zuwayla 107-8
Cairo Tower 132
House of Egyptian Architecture 113
Iconic Tower 142
Mawlawiyya Takiyya 115
Nilometer 138
Old Cataract Hotel 250
Sabil-Kuttab of Abdel Rahman Katkhuda 99
Nubian people 256, 257
Nubian villages
 Gharb Seheyl 257
 Koti 254
 Siou 254
Nuweiba Canyons 397-8

oases
 Ain Khudra Oasis 395
 Al Hayz Oasis 289-90
 Al Kharga Oasis 276, 300-2, 301
 Bahariya Oasis 276, 285-7, 286
 Dakhla Oasis 276, 295-7, 296
 El Arag Oasis 283-4
 Farafra Oasis 276, 291-2, 292
 Siwa Oasis 270-82, 272-3, 279
 Western Desert oases 276-7
opening hours 422
Ozymandias 222

packing for Cairo 133
palaces & mansions
 Abdeen Palace 85-6, 435
 Aisha Fahmy Palace 129
 Al Haramlek Palace 324
 Bait Al Razzaz 118
 Baron Empain Palace 139-40, 141
 Bayt Al Suhaymi 104
 Beit Zeinab Al Khatoun 107
 Gezira Palace 131
 House of Al Harawy 107
 Manasterly Palace 138
 Manial Palace 134-6
 Maq'ad of Mamay Al Sayfi 95
 Museum of Islamic Ceramics 129
 Ras El Tin Palace 310

Wasila Historical House 106-7
paramotoring 70
parks & gardens
 Al Azhar Park 107
 Aswan Botanical Gardens 254
 Montazah Gardens 323-4
people 436-7
 Ababda people 365
 Bedouin people 366, 381, 394
 Nubian people 256, 257
Pharaonic history 19, 426-9
planning 38-9, see also etiquette
 camel riding 49
 clothes 38
 diving responsibly 48
 Egypt basics 38-9
 haggling 45
 packing for Cairo 133
 tickets for archaeological sites 151
police escorts 407, see also safe travel
 Minya 169
 Sinai 378
 Wadi Natrun 150
 Western Desert 297
population 320
Port Said 340-1
 accommodation 345
 travel within Port Said 340
 walking tours 341, **341**
pottery, see ceramics
protected areas, see national parks & protected areas
public holidays 422
public toilets 422
pyramids 19, see also archaeological sites, temples, tombs & burial sites
 Abu Sir Pyramids 151
 Al Fayoum 167
 Bent Pyramid 143, 150
 Black Pyramid 153
 Dahshur 143
 Great Pyramid of Khufu 64-5, 432
 Pyramid of Al Lahun 167
 Pyramid of Hawara 167
 Pyramid of Khafre 65-6
 Pyramid of Meidum 167
 Pyramid of Menkaure 66-7
 Pyramid of Pepi II 149
 Pyramid of Teti 149
 Pyramid of Unas 146

Pyramids of Giza 64-71, **68-9**
Red Pyramid 143
Saqqara 144-9
Step Pyramid of Djoser 144-5
Zawiyyet Al Amwat 170

Qena 185
 accommodation 189
quad biking
 Giza 70
 Marsa Alam 366
 Nabq Nature Reserve 381
quarries 171

Ramadan 37
Ras Mohammed National Park 382-5
Red Sea coast 346-67, **348-9**
 activities 350-1
 climate 350-1
 festivals & events 350-1
 Hurghada, see individual location
 itineraries 30-1, 350-1, **31**
 Marsa Alam, see individual location
 navigation 348-9
 travel seasons 350-1
 travel within the Red Sea coast 348-9
religion 40-1
resorts 357, 412
responsible diving 48, 419
 Marsa Alam 361
 Red Sea coast 362
responsible travel 48, 418-29
 St Katherine 393
ride sharing 406, 407
road trips 52-3
ruins, see archaeological sites
rural retreats 18

Safaga 365-6
 accommodation 367
safe travel 414-15, 421, see also police escorts
 Sinai 378
 Wadi Natrun 150
Said, Mahmoud 322-3
salt lakes 281
Saqqara 144-9

scuba diving, *see* diving
Seheyl Island 256-7
Sharia Al Muizz Li-Din Allah 97-100
Sharm El Sheikh 374-9, **375**
 accommodation 403
 beyond Sharm El Sheikh 380-1
 day trips from Sharm El Sheikh 379
 drinking 379
 food 378
 shopping 379
 travel within Sharm El Sheikh 374
Shelley, Percy Bysshe 222
shipwrecks 12, 385
 Hamada 363
 Nabq Nature Reserve 381
 Ras Mohammed National Park 385
 Thistlegorm 385
shisha 417
SIM cards 406
Sinai 369-403, **370-1**
 climate 372-3
 Dahab, *see individual location*
 festivals & events 372-3
 itineraries 34-5, 372-3, **35**
 navigation 370-1
 Sharm El Sheikh, *see individual location*
 tours 379
 travel seasons 372-3
 travel within Sinai 370-1
Siwa Oasis 270-82, **272-3**, **279**
 accommodation 303
 activities 274-5
 beyond Siwa Oasis 283-4
 climate 274-5
 festivals & events 274-5
 food 281
 itineraries 274-5
 navigation 272-3
 tours 284
 travel seasons 274-5
 travel within Siwa Oasis 272-3, 278
 walking tours 282, **282**
sleeper trains 409
slow travel 20-1
smoking 422
snorkelling 12
 Dahab 389-91
 Hurghada 356
 Marsa Alam 362-3
 Ras Mohammed National Park 382-5
 responsible snorkelling 48
 Sharm El Sheikh 376-7
Sobek 167

Sohag 179-81, **180**
 accommodation 189
 beyond Sohag 182
 food 181
 travel within Sohag 179
souqs, *see* markets
Southern Nile Valley 231-69, **232-3**
 activities 234-5
 Abu Simbel, *see individual location*
 Aswan, *see individual location*
 climate 234-5
 festivals & events 234-5
 itineraries 234-5
 Lake Nasser, *see individual location*
 Lower Nubia, *see individual location*
 Luxor to Aswan, *see individual location*
 navigation 232-3
 travel seasons 234-5
 travel within Southern Nile Valley 232-3
spas 357
Sphinx 67
springs
 Ain Gomma 290
 Al Maaza Hot Spring 281
 Bahariya Oasis 290
 Bir Al Gabal 297
 Bir Wahed 281, 283
 Cleopatra's Spring 281
 Fatnas Spring 280
 Hayaat Siwa Hot Spring 281
St Katherine Protectorate 399-402
 accommodation 403
St Paul the Anchorite 359
Straits of Tiran 384-5
street art 116
street food 43, 439
Suez 344
 accommodation 345
Suez Canal 337-45, 435, **338**
 activities 339
 climate 339
 festivals & events 339
 Ismailia, *see individual location*
 itineraries 339
 navigation 338
 Port Said, *see individual location*
 Suez, *see individual location*
 travel seasons 339
 travel within Suez Canal 338

Sufi dancing 107
synagogues
 Ben Ezra Synagogue 123
 Eliyahu Hanavi Synagogue 317, 319
 Shaar HaShamayim Synagogue 92

Tanis 153
tarbooshes 101
taxis 406, 407
Temple of Horus 245-6
Temple of Seti I at Abydos 183-4
Temples of Abu Simbel 265-7, 433
temples 16-17, *see also* archaeological sites, pyramids, tombs & burial sites
 Abydos 182
 Al Kharga Oasis 302
 Amun Temple 200-1
 Deir Al Haggar 296-7
 Deir Al Medina 219
 Dendara 186-8
 Great Temple of Aten 175
 Great Temple of Ramses II 266
 Karnak 200-1, 205-6, 432-3
 Kom Ombo Temple 243-4
 Luxor area 196-7
 Luxor Temple 202
 Medinat Habu 224
 Medinat Madi 166-7
 Mortuary Temple of Hatshepsut 221-2
 Philae Temple 258-60
 Qasr El Sagha 166
 Qasr Qarun 167
 Ramesseum 222
 Speos Artemidos 171
 Speos of Horemheb 241
 Temple of Ain Al Muftella 287
 Temple of Alexander 287
 Temple of Augustus 260
 Temple of Hathor 186-8, 260, 267, 433
 Temple of Horus 245-6
 Temple of Khnum 238-9, 255
 Temple of Ramses II 184
 Temple of Seti I at Abydos 183-4
 Temples of Abu Simbel 265-7, 433
terrorism 415
textiles 108
theatres
 Cairo Opera House 131

El Dammah Theatre 90
El Sakia Puppet Theatre 131
Roman theatre (Alexandria) 316-17
Thistlegorm 385
tipping 411
Tiran Island 384
toilets 422
Tomb of Nefertari 220
tombs & burial sites 10-11, *see also* archaeological sites, pyramids, temples
 Al Hammamiya 178
 Al Kab 240
 Al Kharga Oasis 302
 Baqet III (No 15) 171
 Beni Hasan 170-1
 Dakhla Oasis 297
 Fraser Tombs 168
 Great Pharaonic Tombs 215-16
 Luxor 196-7
 Mastaba of Khentika 296
 New Kingdom Tombs 146
 Qarat Al Hilwa 287
 Qarat Qasr Salim 287
 Royal Tomb of Akhenaten 175
 Saqqara 144-9
 Serapeum 147
 Tell Al Amarna 174-5
 Temple of Seti I 223
 Tomb of Akhethotep & Ptahhotep 147
 Tomb of Amenemhat (No 2) 171
 Tomb of Amenemope 225
 Tomb of Amunherkhepshef 217
 Tomb of Ay 213-14
 Tomb of Bannentiu 287
 Tomb of Horemheb 146
 Tomb of Inherka 219
 Tomb of Ipuy 219
 Tomb of Isadora 172-3
 Tomb of Kagemni 148
 Tomb of Khaemwaset 217
 Tomb of Khety (No 17) 171
 Tomb of Khnumhotep (No 3) 171
 Tomb of Khonsu 227
 Tomb of Maya 146
 Tomb of Mehu 146
 Tomb of Menna 225
 Tomb of Mereruka 148
 Tomb of Nakht 225
 Tomb of Neferronpet 227
 Tomb of Nefertari 220
 Tomb of Peshedu 219
 Tomb of Petosiris 172-3
 Tomb of Ramose 226
 Tomb of Ramses III 216
 Tomb of Ramses IV 213

tombs & burial sites *cont.*
 Tomb of Ramses VI 216
 Tomb of Ramses VII 213
 Tomb of Rekhmire 227
 Tomb of Roy 227
 Tomb of Sennofer 227
 Tomb of Seti I 216
 Tomb of Shuroy 227
 Tomb of Titi 218
 Tomb of Tutankhamun 216
 Tomb of Tuthmosis III 216
 Tomb of Tutmosis II 214
 Tomb of Ty 148
 Tomb of Userhet 226
 Tombs of Al Hawawish 181
 Tombs of Idut, Unasankh & Inerfert 146
 Tombs of Mir 176
 Tombs of the Nobles 255-6
 Valley of the Golden Mummies 287
 Wadi Hilal 240
 Zawiyyet Al Amwat 170
 Zawiyyet Al Mayyiteen 170
Toshka project 264
tours & tour guides 22, 423, *see also* food tours, walking tours
 Al Kharga 302
 Alexandria 313, 317, 318, 319, 323
 Aswan 249, 254
 Bahariya Oasis 289
 Cairo 83-4, 118
 Esna 236
 Giza 67
 Ismailia 342
 Luxor 197, 223
 Marsa Alam 362
 Sinai 379
 Siwa Oasis 284
 Western Desert 275-6
traffic 84
train travel 407, 408-9
 Luxor-Cairo 206
travel seasons 36-7, *see also individual locations*
travel to/from Egypt 406
travel within Egypt 407
travelling with kids 47, 413
 Cairo 75, 114
trekking, *see* hiking

Tuna Al Gebel 172-3
Tunis 162, 164
Tutankhamun 76, 216

vaccinations 413, 415
Valley of the Golden Mummies 287
Van Gogh, Vincent 129
vegetarian & vegan travellers 43
visas 423

Wadi Natrun 151-3
walking, *see* hiking
walking tours
 Alexandria 327, **327**
 Aswan 251, **251**
 Cairo 92, **92**
 Ismailia 343, **343**
 Port Said 341, **341**
 Siwa Oasis 282, **282**
waterwells 166
weather 36-7

weaving 62
Western Desert 270-303, **272-3**
 Al Kharga Oasis, *see individual location*
 activities 274-5
 Bahariya Oasis, *see individual location*
 climate 274-5
 Dakhla Oasis, *see individual location*
 Farafra Oasis, *see individual location*
 festivals & events 274-5
 itineraries 28-9, 274-5, **29**
 navigation 272-3
 oases (choosing) 276-7
 Siwa Oasis, *see individual location*
 tours 275-6
 travel seasons 274-5
 travel within Western Desert 272-3
White Desert National Park 293-4
wi-fi 406
women travellers 421

NOTES

'For tranquility and timelessness, nothing beats a sunset felucca sail, with the water lapping against the hull and the sun slowly disappearing behind Aswan's Tombs of the Nobles. (p255).'
MARY FITZPATRICK

'The first time I climbed Mount Sinai (p399), I was sick and exhausted, but my mood shifted when reaching the summit at dawn.'
JESSICA BUXBAUM

All rights reserved. No part of this publication may be copied, stored in a retrieval system, or transmitted in any form by any means, electronic, mechanical, recording or otherwise, except brief extracts for the purpose of review, and no part of this publication may be sold or hired, without the written permission of the publisher. Lonely Planet and the Lonely Planet logo are trademarks of Lonely Planet and are registered in the US Patent and Trademark Office and in other countries. Lonely Planet does not allow its name or logo to be appropriated by commercial establishments, such as retailers, restaurants or hotels. Please let us know of any misuses: lonelyplanet.com/legal/intellectual-property.

Mapping data sources:
© Lonely Planet; © OpenStreetMap http://openstreetmap.org/copyright

THIS BOOK

Destination Editor
Zara Sekhavati

Production Editor
Vicky Smith

Image Editor
Dermot Hegarty

Cartographer
Dorothy Davidson, Jennifer Johnston

Coordinating Editor
Sarah Bailey

Assisting Editors
Bridget Blair, Nigel Chin, Anna Cohen Kaminski, Helen Koehne, Anne Mulvaney, Charlotte Orr

Cover Researcher
Kat Marsh

Thanks Fergal Condon, Gwen Cotter, Jessica Lee, Ailbhe MacMahon, Kathryn Rowan, Akanksha Singh

FROM LEFT: CALIN STAN/GETTY IMAGES, ANTON PETRUS/GETTY IMAGES

Paper in this book is certified against the Forest Stewardship Council™ standards. FSC™ promotes environmentally responsible, socially beneficial and economically viable management of the world's forests.

Published by Lonely Planet Global Limited
CRN 554153
16th edition – Dec 2025
ISBN 978 1 83758 400 0
© Lonely Planet 2025 Photographs © as indicated 2025
10 9 8 7 6 5 4 3 2 1
Printed in Malaysia